AF861208

Introduction to Programming

ECE 1574

Virginia Tech

| PEARSON COLLECTIONS |

PEARSON

Cover Art: Courtesy of Photodisc/Getty Images

1 17

Attention bookstores: For permission to return any unsold stock, contact us at pe-uscustomreturns@pearson.com

Pearson Learning Solutions, 501 Boylston Street, Suite 900, Boston, MA 02116

A Pearson Education Company
www.pearsoned.com

PEARSON

ISBN 10: 1323713808

ISBN 13: 9781323713808

Printed in the USA

Table of Contents

Introduction to Computers and Programming

TOPICS

1 Why Program?

CONCEPT: Computers can do many different jobs because they are programmable.

Think about some of the different ways that people use computers. In school, students use computers for tasks such as writing papers, searching for articles, sending e-mail, and participating in online classes. At work, people use computers to conduct business transactions, communicate with customers and coworkers, analyze data, make presentations, control machines in manufacturing facilities, and many many other tasks. At home, people use computers for tasks such as paying bills, shopping online, social networking, and playing computer games. And don't forget that smartphones, MP3 players, DVRs, car navigation systems, and many other devices are computers as well. The uses of computers are almost limitless in our everyday lives.

Computers can do such a wide variety of things because they can be programmed. This means computers are not designed to do just one job, but any job that their programs tell them to do. A *program* is a set of instructions that a computer follows to perform a task. For example, Figure 1 shows screens using Microsoft Word and PowerPoint, two commonly used programs.

Programs are commonly referred to as *software*. Software is essential to a computer because without software, a computer can do nothing. All of the software we use to make our computers useful is created by individuals known as programmers or software developers. A *programmer*, or *software developer*, is a person with the training and skills necessary to design, create, and test computer programs. Computer programming is an exciting and rewarding career. Today, you will find programmers working in business, medicine, government, law enforcement, agriculture, academia, entertainment, and almost every other field.

From Chapter 1 of *Starting Out with C++: From Control Structures through Objects*, Ninth Edition. Tony Gaddis.

Figure 1 A word processing program and a presentation program

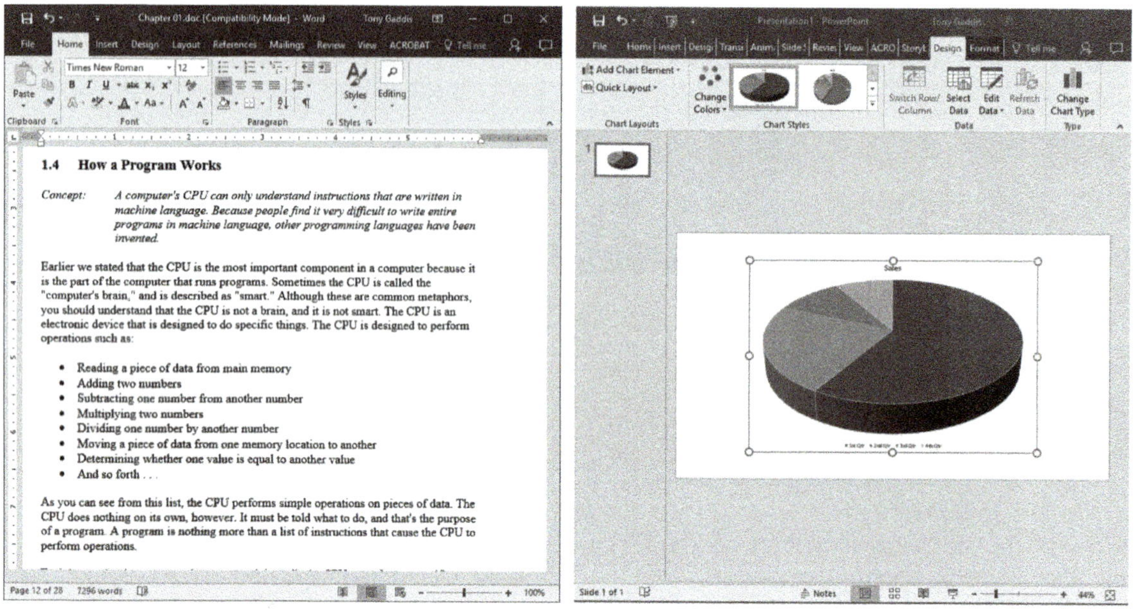

Computer programming is both an art and a science. It is an art because every aspect of a program should be carefully designed. Listed below are a few of the things that must be designed for any real-world computer program:

- The logical flow of the instructions
- The mathematical procedures
- The appearance of the screens
- The way information is presented to the user
- The program's "user-friendliness"
- Documentation, help files, tutorials, and so on

There is also a scientific, or engineering, side to programming. Because programs rarely work right the first time they are written, a lot of testing, correction, and redesigning is required. This demands patience and persistence from the programmer. Writing software demands discipline as well. Programmers must learn special languages like C++ because computers do not understand English or other human languages. Languages such as C++ have strict rules that must be carefully followed.

Both the artistic and scientific nature of programming make writing computer software like designing a car: Both cars and programs should be functional, efficient, powerful, easy to use, and pleasing to look at.

2 Computer Systems: Hardware and Software

CONCEPT: All computer systems consist of similar hardware devices and software components. This section provides an overview of standard computer hardware and software organization.

Hardware

Hardware refers to the physical components of which a computer is made. A computer, as we generally think of it, is not an individual device, but a system of devices. Like the instruments in a symphony orchestra, each device plays its own part. A typical computer system consists of the following major components:

- The central processing unit (CPU)
- Main memory
- Secondary storage devices
- Input devices
- Output devices

The organization of a computer system is depicted in Figure 2.

Figure 2 Typical devices in a computer system

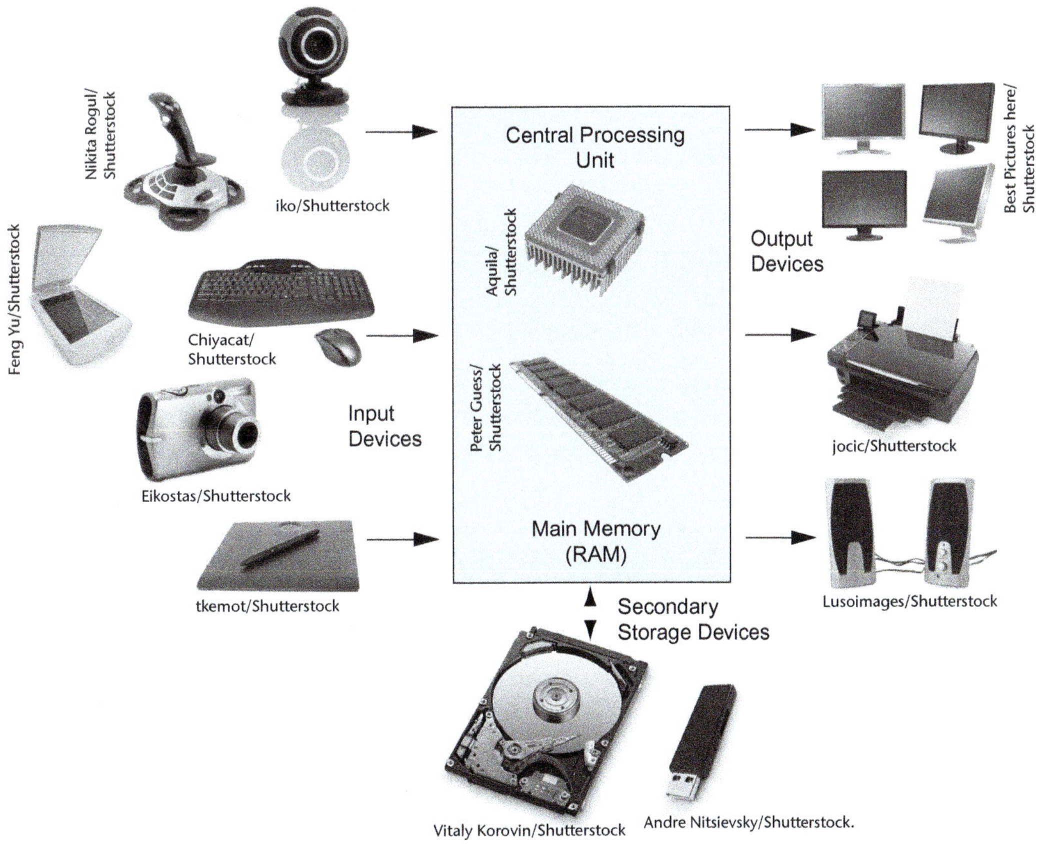

The CPU

When a computer is performing the tasks that a program tells it to do, we say that the computer is *running* or *executing* the program. The *central processing unit*, or *CPU*, is the part of a computer that actually runs programs. The CPU is the most important component in a computer because without it, the computer could not run software.

In the earliest computers, CPUs were huge devices made of electrical and mechanical components such as vacuum tubes and switches. Figure 3 shows such a device. The two women in

Figure 3 The ENIAC computer

U.S. Army Center of Military History

the photo are working with the historic ENIAC computer. The *ENIAC,* considered by many to be the world's first programmable electronic computer, was built in 1945 to calculate artillery ballistic tables for the U.S. Army. This machine, which was primarily one big CPU, was 8 feet tall, 100 feet long, and weighed 30 tons.

Today, CPUs are small chips known as *microprocessors*. Figure 4 shows a photo of a lab technician holding a modern-day microprocessor. In addition to being much smaller than the old electromechanical CPUs in early computers, microprocessors are also much more powerful.

Figure 4 A microprocessor

Creativa/Shutterstock

The CPU's job is to fetch instructions, follow the instructions, and produce some result. Internally, the central processing unit consists of two parts: the *control unit* and the *arithmetic and logic unit (ALU)*. The control unit coordinates all of the computer's operations. It is responsible for determining where to get the next instruction and regulating the other major components of the computer with control signals. The arithmetic and logic unit, as its name suggests, is designed to perform mathematical operations. The organization of the CPU is shown in Figure 5.

Figure 5 Organization of a CPU

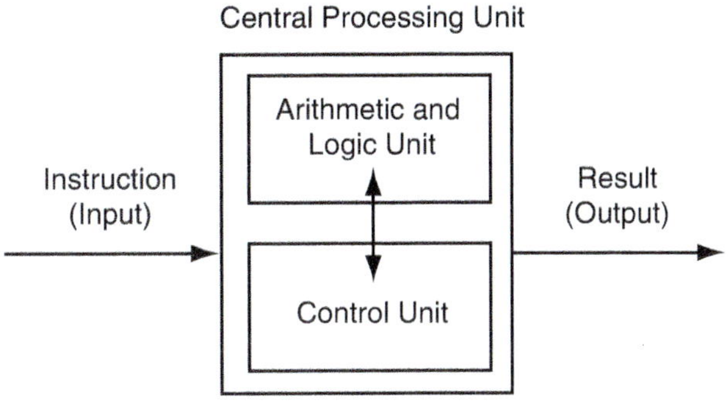

A program is a sequence of instructions stored in the computer's memory. When a computer is running a program, the CPU is engaged in a process known formally as the *fetch/decode/execute cycle*. The steps in the fetch/decode/execute cycle are as follows:

Fetch	The CPU's control unit fetches, from main memory, the next instruction in the sequence of program instructions.
Decode	The instruction is encoded in the form of a number. The control unit decodes the instruction and generates an electronic signal.
Execute	The signal is routed to the appropriate component of the computer (such as the ALU, a disk drive, or some other device). The signal causes the component to perform an operation.

These steps are repeated as long as there are instructions to perform.

Main Memory

You can think of main memory as the computer's work area. This is where the computer stores a program while the program is running, as well as the data with which the program is working. For example, suppose you are using a word processing program to write an essay for one of your classes. While you do this, both the word processing program and the essay are stored in main memory.

Main memory is commonly known as *random-access memory* or *RAM*. It is called this because the CPU is able to quickly access data stored at any random location in RAM. RAM is usually a *volatile* type of memory that is used only for temporary storage while a program is running. When the computer is turned off, the contents of RAM are erased. Inside your computer, RAM is stored in small chips.

A computer's memory is divided into tiny storage locations known as bytes. One *byte* is enough memory to store only a letter of the alphabet or a small number. In order to do anything meaningful, a computer must have lots of bytes. Most computers today have millions, or even billions, of bytes of memory.

Each byte is divided into eight smaller storage locations known as bits. The term *bit* stands for *binary digit*. Computer scientists usually think of bits as tiny switches that can be either on or off. Bits aren't actual "switches," however, at least not in the conventional sense. In most computer systems, bits are tiny electrical components that can hold either a positive or a negative charge. Computer scientists think of a positive charge as a switch in the *on* position, and a negative charge as a switch in the *off* position.

Each byte is assigned a unique number known as an *address*. The addresses are ordered from lowest to highest. A byte is identified by its address in much the same way a post office box is identified by an address. Figure 6 shows a group of memory cells with their addresses. In the illustration, sample data is stored in memory. The number 149 is stored in the cell with the address 16, and the number 72 is stored at address 23.

Figure 6 Memory

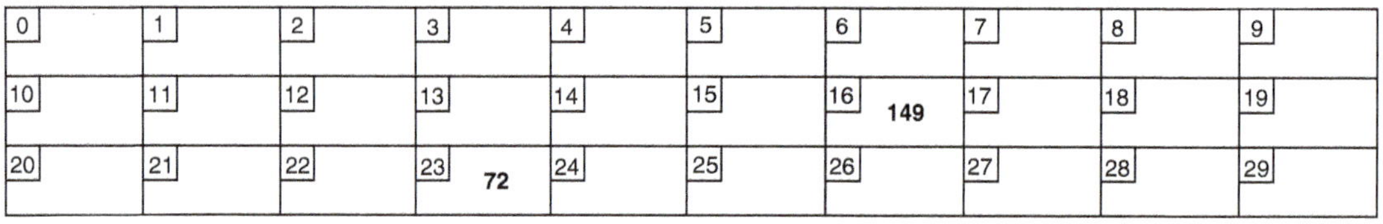

Secondary Storage

Secondary storage is a type of memory that can hold data for long periods of time, even when there is no power to the computer. Programs are normally stored in secondary memory and loaded into main memory as needed. Important data such as word processing documents, payroll data, and inventory records is saved to secondary storage as well.

The most common type of secondary storage device is the disk drive. A traditional *disk drive* stores data by magnetically encoding it onto a circular disk. *Solid-state drives*, which store data in solid-state memory, are increasingly becoming popular. A solid-state drive has no moving parts and operates faster than a traditional disk drive. Most computers have some sort of secondary storage device, either a traditional disk drive or a solid-state drive, mounted inside their case. External storage devices can be used to create backup copies of important data or to move data to another computer. For example, *USB (Universal Serial Bus) drives* and *SD (Secure Digital) memory cards* are small devices that appear in the system as disk drives. They are inexpensive, reliable, and small enough to be carried in your pocket.

Optical devices such as the *CD* (compact disc) and the *DVD* (digital versatile disc) are also used for data storage. Data is not recorded magnetically on an optical disc, but is encoded as a series of pits on the disc surface. CD and DVD drives use a laser to detect the pits and thus read the encoded data. Optical discs hold large amounts of data, and because recordable CD and DVD drives are now commonplace, they are good mediums for creating backup copies of data.

Input Devices

Input is any data the computer collects from the outside world. The device that collects the information and sends it to the computer is called an *input device*. Common input devices are the keyboard, mouse, touchscreen, scanner, digital camera, and microphone. Disk drives, CD/DVD drives, and USB drives can also be considered input devices because programs and information are retrieved from them and loaded into the computer's memory.

Output Devices

Output is any information the computer sends to the outside world. It might be a sales report, a list of names, or a graphic image. The information is sent to an *output device*, which formats and presents it. Common output devices are screens, printers, and speakers. Storage devices can also be considered output devices because the CPU sends them data to be saved.

Software

If a computer is to function, software is not optional. Everything a computer does, from the time you turn the power switch on until you shut the system down, is under the control of software. There are two general categories of software: system software and application software. Most computer programs clearly fit into one of these two categories. Let's take a closer look at each.

System Software

The programs that control and manage the basic operations of a computer are generally referred to as *system software*. System software typically includes the following types of programs:

- *Operating Systems*
  An *operating system* is the most fundamental set of programs on a computer. The operating system controls the internal operations of the computer's hardware, manages all the devices connected to the computer, allows data to be saved to and retrieved from storage devices, and allows other programs to run on the computer.
- *Utility Programs*
  A *utility program* performs a specialized task that enhances the computer's operation or safeguards data. Examples of utility programs are virus scanners, file-compression programs, and data-backup programs.
- *Software Development Tools*
  The software tools that programmers use to create, modify, and test software are referred to as *software development tools*. Compilers and integrated development environments, which we will discuss later in this chapter, are examples of programs that fall into this category.

Application Software

Programs that make a computer useful for everyday tasks are known as *application software*. These are the programs that people normally spend most of their time running on their computers. Figure 1, at the beginning of this chapter, shows screens from two commonly used applications—Microsoft Word, a word processing program, and Microsoft

PowerPoint, a presentation program. Some other examples of application software are spreadsheet programs, e-mail programs, web browsers, and game programs.

Checkpoint

1 Why is the computer used by so many different people, in so many different professions?

2 List the five major hardware components of a computer system.

3 Internally, the CPU consists of what two units?

4 Describe the steps in the fetch/decode/execute cycle.

5 What is a memory address? What is its purpose?

6 Explain why computers have both main memory and secondary storage.

7 What are the two general categories of software?

8 What fundamental set of programs control the internal operations of the computer's hardware?

9 What do you call a program that performs a specialized task, such as a virus scanner, a file-compression program, or a data-backup program?

10 Word processing programs, spreadsheet programs, e-mail programs, web browsers, and game programs belong to what category of software?

3 Programs and Programming Languages

CONCEPT: A program is a set of instructions a computer follows in order to perform a task. A programming language is a special language used to write computer programs.

What Is a Program?

Computers are designed to follow instructions. A computer program is a set of instructions that tells the computer how to solve a problem or perform a task. For example, suppose we want the computer to calculate someone's gross pay. Here is a list of things the computer should do:

1. Display a message on the screen asking "How many hours did you work?"
2. Wait for the user to enter the number of hours worked. Once the user enters a number, store it in memory.
3. Display a message on the screen asking "How much do you get paid per hour?"
4. Wait for the user to enter an hourly pay rate. Once the user enters a number, store it in memory.
5. Multiply the number of hours by the amount paid per hour, and store the result in memory.
6. Display a message on the screen that tells the amount of money earned. The message must include the result of the calculation performed in Step 5.

Collectively, these instructions are called an *algorithm*. An algorithm is a set of well-defined steps for performing a task or solving a problem. Notice these steps are sequentially ordered. Step 1 should be performed before Step 2, and so forth. It is important that these instructions be performed in their proper sequence.

Although you and I might easily understand the instructions in the pay-calculating algorithm, it is not ready to be executed on a computer. A computer's CPU can only process instructions that are written in *machine language*. If you were to look at a machine language program, you would see a stream of *binary numbers* (numbers consisting of only 1s and 0s). The binary numbers form machine language instructions, which the CPU interprets as commands. Here is an example of what a machine language instruction might look like:

```
1011010000000101
```

As you can imagine, the process of encoding an algorithm in machine language is very tedious and difficult. In addition, each different type of CPU has its own machine language. If you wrote a machine language program for computer *A* then wanted to run it on computer *B*, which has a different type of CPU, you would have to rewrite the program in computer B's machine language.

Programming languages, which use words instead of numbers, were invented to ease the task of programming. A program can be written in a programming language, such as C++, which is much easier to understand than machine language. Programmers save their programs in text files, then use special software to convert their programs to machine language.

Program 1 shows how the pay-calculating algorithm might be written in C++.

The "Program Output with Example Input" shows what the program will display on the screen when it is running. In the example, the user enters 10 for the number of hours worked and 15 for the hourly pay rate. The program displays the earnings, which are $150.

> **NOTE:** The line numbers that are shown in Program 1 are *not* part of the program. This text shows line numbers in all program listings to help point out specific parts of the program.

Program 1

```
// This program calculates the user's pay.
#include <iostream>
using namespace std;

int main()
{
    double hours, rate, pay;

    // Get the number of hours worked.
    cout << "How many hours did you work? ";
    cin >> hours;

    // Get the hourly pay rate.
    cout << "How much do you get paid per hour? ";
    cin >> rate;

    // Calculate the pay.
    pay = hours * rate;
```

(program continues)

Program 1 *(continued)*

```
    // Display the pay.
    cout << "You have earned $" << pay << endl;
    return 0;
}
```

Program Output with Example Input Shown in Bold

```
How many hours did you work? 10 [Enter]
How much do you get paid per hour? 15 [Enter]
You have earned $150
```

Programming Languages

In a broad sense, there are two categories of programming languages: low-level and high-level. A low-level language is close to the level of the computer, which means it resembles the numeric machine language of the computer more than the natural language of humans. The easiest languages for people to learn are *high-level languages*. They are called "high-level" because they are closer to the level of human readability than computer readability. Figure 7 illustrates the concept of language levels.

Figure 7 Low-level versus high-level languages

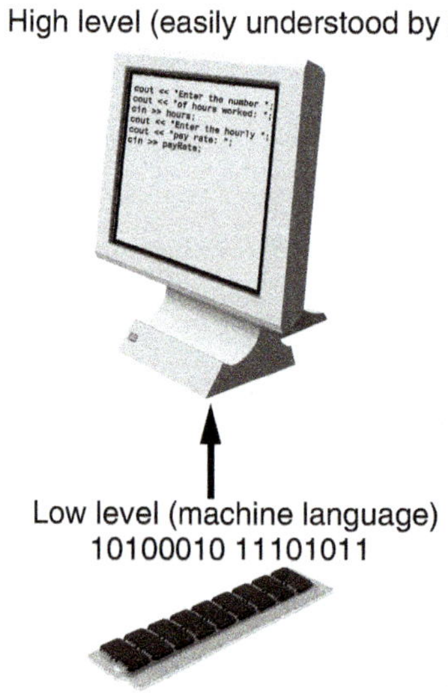

Many high-level languages have been created. Table 1 lists a few of the well-known ones.

In addition to the high-level features necessary for writing applications such as payroll systems and inventory programs, C++ also has many low-level features. C++ is based on the C language, which was invented for purposes such as writing operating systems and compilers. Since C++ evolved from C, it carries all of C's low-level capabilities with it.

Table 1 Programming Languages

Language	Description
BASIC	Beginners All-purpose Symbolic Instruction Code. A general programming language originally designed to be simple enough for beginners to learn.
FORTRAN	Formula Translator. A language designed for programming complex mathematical algorithms.
COBOL	Common Business-Oriented Language. A language designed for business applications.
Pascal	A structured, general-purpose language designed primarily for teaching programming.
C	A structured, general-purpose language developed at Bell Laboratories. C offers both high-level and low-level features.
C++	Based on the C language, C++ offers object-oriented features not found in C. Also invented at Bell Laboratories.
C#	Pronounced "C sharp." A language invented by Microsoft for developing applications based on the Microsoft .NET platform.
Java	An object-oriented language that may be used to develop programs that run on many different types of devices.
JavaScript	JavaScript can be used to write small programs that run in webpages. Despite its name, JavaScript is not related to Java.
Python	Python is a general-purpose language created in the early 1990s. It has become popular in both business and academic applications.
Ruby	Ruby is a general-purpose language that was created in the 1990s. It is increasingly becoming a popular language for programs that run on web servers.
Visual Basic	A Microsoft programming language and software development environment that allows programmers to quickly create Windows-based applications.

C++ is popular not only because of its mixture of low- and high-level features, but also because of its *portability*. This means that a C++ program can be written on one type of computer, then run on many other types of systems. This usually requires the program to be recompiled on each type of system, but the program itself may need little or no change.

NOTE: Programs written for specific graphical environments often require significant changes when moved to a different type of system. Examples of such graphical environments are Windows, the X-Window System, and the macOS operating system.

Source Code, Object Code, and Executable Code

When a C++ program is written, it must be typed into the computer and saved to a file. A *text editor*, which is similar to a word processing program, is used for this task. The statements written by the programmer are called *source code*, and the file they are saved in is called the *source file*.

After the source code is saved to a file, the process of translating it to machine language can begin. During the first phase of this process, a program called the *preprocessor* reads the source code. The preprocessor searches for special lines that begin with the # symbol. These lines contain commands that cause the preprocessor to modify the source code in some way.

During the next phase, the *compiler* steps through the preprocessed source code, translating each source code instruction into the appropriate machine language instruction. This process will uncover any *syntax errors* that may be in the program. Syntax errors are illegal uses of key words, operators, punctuation, and other language elements. If the program is free of syntax errors, the compiler stores the translated machine language instructions, which are called *object code*, in an *object file*.

Although an object file contains machine language instructions, it is not a complete program. Here is why: C++ is conveniently equipped with a library of prewritten code for performing common operations or sometimes-difficult tasks. For example, the library contains hardware-specific code for displaying messages on the screen and reading input from the keyboard. It also provides routines for mathematical functions, such as calculating the square root of a number. This collection of code, called the *runtime library*, is extensive. Programs almost always use some part of it. When the compiler generates an object file, however, it does not include machine code for any runtime library routines the programmer might have used. During the last phase of the translation process, another program called the *linker* combines the object file with the necessary library routines. Once the linker has finished with this step, an *executable file* is created. The executable file contains machine language instructions, or *executable code*, and is ready to run on the computer.

Figure 8 illustrates the process of translating a C++ source file into an executable file.

The entire process of invoking the preprocessor, compiler, and linker can be initiated with a single action. For example, on a Linux system, the following command causes the C++ program named `hello.cpp` to be preprocessed, compiled, and linked. The executable code is stored in a file named `hello`.

```
g++ -o hello hello.cpp
```

Figure 8 Translating a C++ source file to an executable file

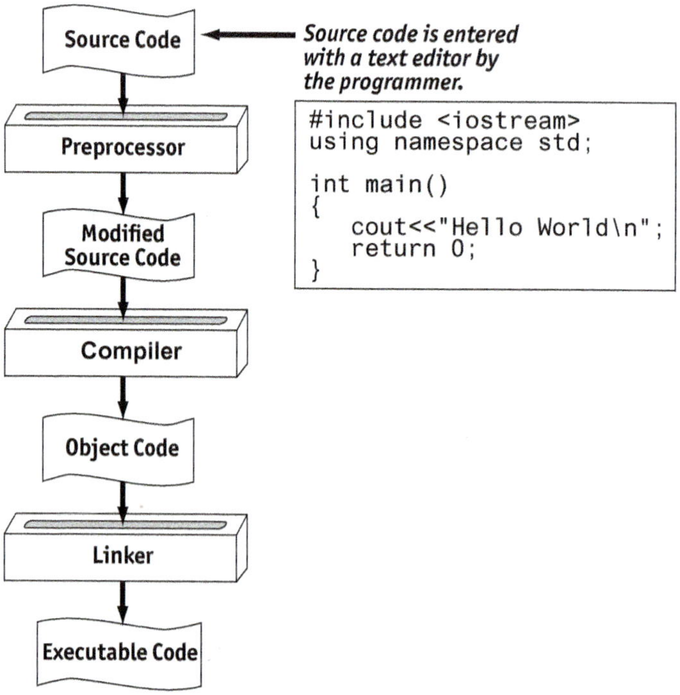

Appendix F explains how compiling works in .Net. You can download Appendix F from the Computer Science Portal at www.pearsonhighered.com/gaddis.

Many development systems, particularly those on personal computers, have *integrated development environments (IDEs)*. These environments consist of a text editor, compiler, debugger, and other utilities integrated into a package with a single set of menus. Preprocessing, compiling, linking, and even executing a program is done with a single click of a button, or by selecting a single item from a menu. Figure 9 shows a screen from the Microsoft Visual Studio IDE.

Figure 9 An integrated development environment (IDE)

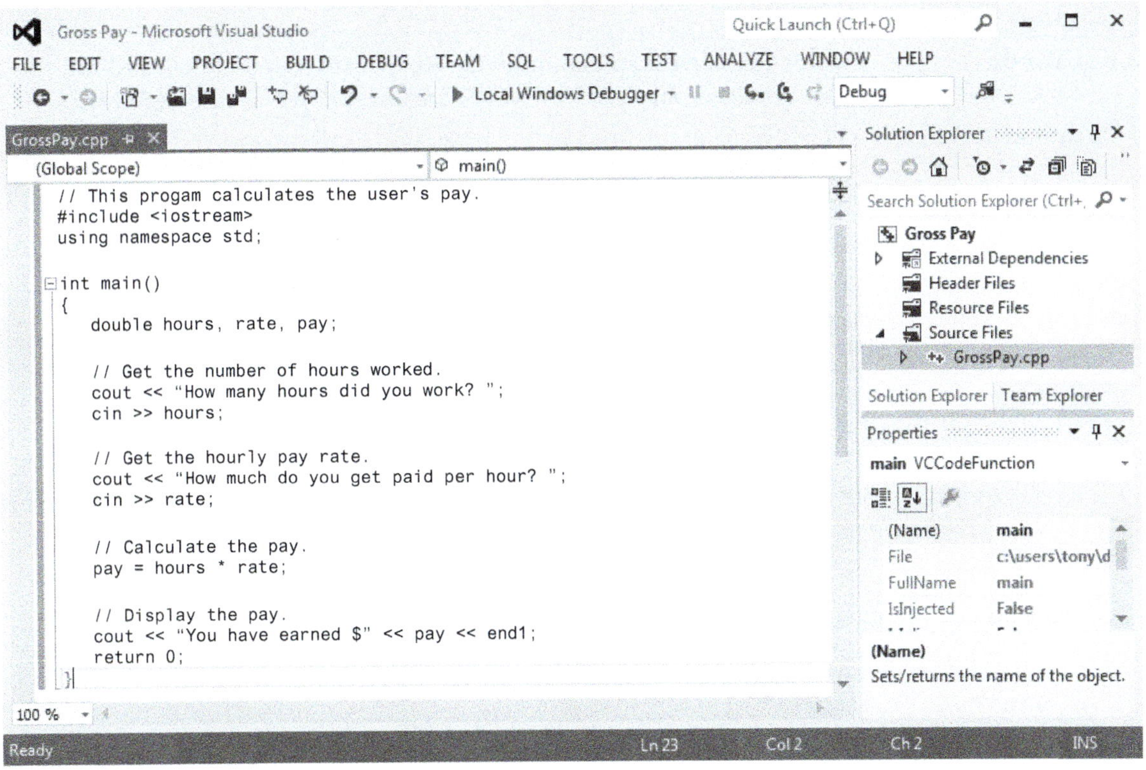

Checkpoint

11 What is an algorithm?

12 Why were computer programming languages invented?

13 What is the difference between a high-level language and a low-level language?

14 What does *portability* mean?

15 Explain the operations carried out by the preprocessor, compiler, and linker.

16 Explain what is stored in a source file, an object file, and an executable file.

17 What is an integrated development environment?

4 What Is a Program Made of?

CONCEPT: There are certain elements that are common to all programming languages.

Language Elements

All programming languages have a few things in common. Table 2 lists the common elements you will find in almost every language.

Table 2 Language Elements

Language Element	Description
Key Words	Words that have a special meaning. Key words may only be used for their intended purpose. Key words are also known as reserved words.
Programmer-Defined Identifiers	Words or names defined by the programmer. They are symbolic names that refer to variables or programming routines.
Operators	Operators perform operations on one or more operands. An operand is usually a piece of data, like a number.
Punctuation	Punctuation characters that mark the beginning or end of a statement, or separate items in a list.
Syntax	Rules that must be followed when constructing a program. Syntax dictates how key words and operators may be used, and where punctuation symbols must appear.

Let's look at some specific parts of Program 1 (the pay-calculating program) to see examples of each element listed in the table above. For your convenience, Program 1 is listed again.

Program 1

```
// This program calculates the user's pay.
#include <iostream>
using namespace std;

int main()
{
    double hours, rate, pay;

    // Get the number of hours worked.
    cout << "How many hours did you work? ";
    cin >> hours;

    // Get the hourly pay rate.
    cout << "How much do you get paid per hour? ";
    cin >> rate;

    // Calculate the pay.
    pay = hours * rate;
```

```
19
20       // Display the pay.
21       cout << "You have earned $" << pay << endl;
22       return 0;
23   }
```

Key Words (Reserved Words)

Three of C++'s key words appear on lines 3 and 5: using, namespace, and int. The word double, which appears on line 7, is also a C++ key word. These words, which are always written in lowercase, each have a special meaning in C++ and can only be used for their intended purposes. As you will see, the programmer is allowed to make up his or her own names for certain things in a program. Key words, however, are reserved and cannot be used for anything other than their designated purposes. Part of learning a programming language is learning what the key words are, what they mean, and how to use them.

> **NOTE:** The #include <iostream> statement in line 2 is a preprocessor directive.

> **NOTE:** In C++, key words are written in all lowercase.

Programmer-Defined Identifiers

The words hours, rate, and pay that appear in the program on lines 7, 11, 15, 18, and 21 are programmer-defined identifiers. They are not part of the C++ language, but rather are names made up by the programmer. In this particular program, these are the names of variables. As you will learn later in this chapter, variables are the names of memory locations that may hold data.

Operators

On line 18 the following code appears:

```
pay = hours * rate;
```

The = and * symbols are both operators. They perform operations on pieces of data known as operands. The * operator multiplies its two operands, which in this example are the variables hours and rate. The = symbol is called the assignment operator. It takes the value of the expression on the right and stores it in the variable whose name appears on the left. In this example, the = operator stores in the pay variable the result of the hours variable multiplied by the rate variable. In other words, the statement says, "Make the pay variable equal to hours times rate, or "pay is assigned the value of hours times rate."

Punctuation

Notice lines 3, 7, 10, 11, 14, 15, 18, 21, and 22 all end with a semicolon. A semicolon in C++ is similar to a period in English: It marks the end of a complete sentence (or statement, as it is called in programming jargon). Semicolons do not appear at the end of every line in a C++ program, however. There are rules that govern where semicolons are required and where they are not. Part of learning C++ is learning where to place semicolons and other punctuation symbols.

Lines and Statements

Often, the contents of a program are thought of in terms of lines and statements. A "line" is just that—a single line as it appears in the body of a program. Program 1 has 23 lines. Most of the lines contain something meaningful; however, some of the lines are empty. The blank lines are only there to make the program more readable.

A statement is a complete instruction that causes the computer to perform some action. Here is the statement that appears in line 10 of Program 1:

```
cout << "How many hours did you work? ";
```

This statement causes the computer to display the message "How many hours did you work?" on the screen. Statements can be a combination of key words, operators, and programmer-defined symbols. Statements often occupy only one line in a program, but sometimes they are spread out over more than one line.

Variables

A variable is a named storage location in the computer's memory for holding a piece of information. The information stored in variables may change while the program is running (hence the name "variable"). Notice in Program 1 the words `hours`, `rate`, and `pay` appear in several places. All three of these are the names of variables. The `hours` variable is used to store the number of hours the user has worked. The `rate` variable stores the user's hourly pay rate. The `pay` variable holds the result of `hours` multiplied by `rate`, which is the user's gross pay.

> **NOTE:** Notice the variables in Program 1 have names that reflect their purpose. In fact, it would be easy to guess what the variables were used for just by reading their names.

Variables are symbolic names that represent locations in the computer's random-access memory (RAM). When information is stored in a variable, it is actually stored in RAM. Assume a program has a variable named `length`. Figure 10 illustrates the way the variable name represents a memory location.

Figure 10 A variable name represents a memory location

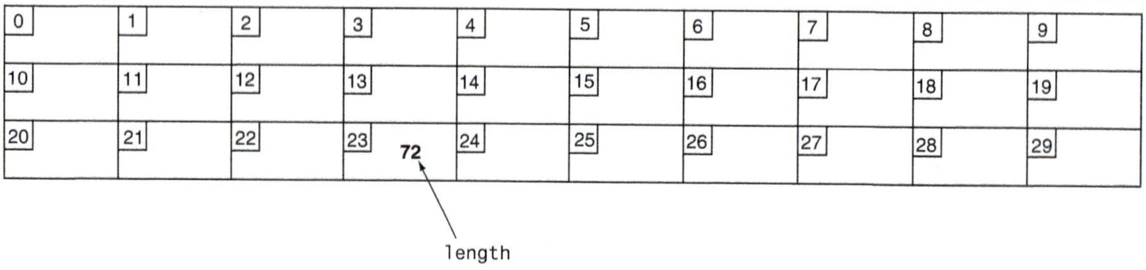

In Figure 10, the variable `length` is holding the value 72. The number 72 is actually stored in RAM at address 23, but the name `length` symbolically represents this storage location. If it helps, you can think of a variable as a box that holds information. In Figure 10, the number 72 is stored in the box named `length`. Only one item may be stored in the box at any given time. If the program stores another value in the box, it will take the place of the number 72.

Variable Definitions

In programming, there are two general types of data: numbers and characters. Numbers are used to perform mathematical operations, and characters are used to print data on the screen or on paper.

Numeric data can be categorized even further. For instance, the following are all whole numbers or integers:

```
5
7
-129
32154
```

The following are real or floating-point numbers:

```
3.14159
6.7
1.0002
```

When creating a variable in a C++ program, you must know what type of data the program will be storing in it. Look at line 7 of Program 1:

```
double hours, rate, pay;
```

The word `double` in this statement indicates that the variables `hours`, `rate`, and `pay` will be used to hold double precision floating-point numbers. This statement is called a *variable definition*. It is used to *define* one or more variables that will be used in the program and to indicate the type of data they will hold. The variable definition causes the variables to be created in memory, so all variables must be defined before they can be used. If you review the listing of Program 1, you will see that the variable definitions come before any other statements using those variables.

> **NOTE:** Programmers often use the term "variable declaration" to mean the same thing as "variable definition." Strictly speaking, there is a difference between the two terms. A definition statement always causes a variable to be created in memory. Some types of declaration statements, however, do not cause a variable to be created in memory.

5 Input, Processing, and Output

CONCEPT: The three primary activities of a program are input, processing, and output.

Computer programs typically perform a three-step process of gathering input, performing some process on the information gathered, then producing output. Input is information a program collects from the outside world. It can be sent to the program from the user, who is entering data at the keyboard or using the mouse. It can also be read from disk files or hardware devices connected to the computer. Program 1 allows the user to enter two pieces of information: the number of hours worked and the hourly pay rate. Lines 11 and 15 use the `cin` (pronounced "see in") object to perform these input operations:

```
cin >> hours;
cin >> rate;
```

Once information is gathered from the outside world, a program usually processes it in some manner. In Program 1, the hours worked and hourly pay rate are multiplied in line 18, and the result is assigned to the pay variable:

```
pay = hours * rate;
```

Output is information that a program sends to the outside world. It can be words or graphics displayed on a screen, a report sent to the printer, data stored in a file, or information sent to any device connected to the computer. Lines 10, 14, and 21 in Program 1 all perform output:

```
cout << "How many hours did you work? ";
cout << "How much do you get paid per hour? ";
cout << "You have earned $" << pay << endl;
```

These lines use the `cout` (pronounced "see out") object to display messages on the computer's screen.

Checkpoint

18 Describe the difference between a key word and a programmer-defined identifier.

19 Describe the difference between operators and punctuation symbols.

20 Describe the difference between a program line and a statement.

21 Why are variables called "variable"?

22 What happens to a variable's current contents when a new value is stored there?

23 What must take place in a program before a variable is used?

24 What are the three primary activities of a program?

6 The Programming Process

CONCEPT: The programming process consists of several steps, which include design, creation, testing, and debugging activities.

Designing and Creating a Program

Now that you have been introduced to what a program is, it's time to consider the process of creating a program. Quite often, when inexperienced students are given programming assignments, they have trouble getting started because they don't know what to do first. If you find yourself in this dilemma, the steps listed in Figure 11 may help. These are the steps recommended for the process of writing a program.

Figure 11 Steps for writing a program

1. Clearly define what the program is to do.
2. Visualize the program running on the computer.
3. Use design tools such as a hierarchy chart, flowcharts, or pseudocode to create a model of the program.
4. Check the model for logical errors.
5. Type the code, save it, and compile it.
6. Correct any errors found during compilation. Repeat Steps 5 and 6 as many times as necessary.
7. Run the program with test data for input.
8. Correct any errors found while running the program. Repeat Steps 5 through 8 as many times as necessary.
9. Validate the results of the program.

The steps listed in Figure 11 emphasize the importance of planning. Just as there are good ways and bad ways to paint a house, there are good ways and bad ways to create a program. A good program always begins with planning.

With the pay-calculating program as our example, let's look at each of the steps in more detail.

1. Clearly define what the program is to do.

This step requires that you identify the purpose of the program, the information that is to be input, the processing that is to take place, and the desired output. Let's examine each of these requirements for the example program:

Purpose	To calculate the user's gross pay.
Input	Number of hours worked, hourly pay rate.
Process	Multiply number of hours worked by hourly pay rate. The result is the user's gross pay.
Output	Display a message indicating the user's gross pay.

2. Visualize the program running on the computer.

Before you create a program on the computer, you should first create it in your mind. Step 2 is the visualization of the program. Try to imagine what the computer screen looks like while the program is running. If it helps, draw pictures of the screen, with sample input and output, at various points in the program. For instance, here is the screen produced by the pay-calculating program:

```
How many hours did you work? 10
How much do you get paid per hour? 15
You have earned $150
```

In this step, you must put yourself in the shoes of the user. What messages should the program display? What questions should it ask? By addressing these concerns, you will have already determined most of the program's output.

3. **Use design tools such as a hierarchy chart, flowcharts, or pseudocode to create a model of the program.**

While planning a program, the programmer uses one or more design tools to create a model of the program. Three common design tools are hierarchy charts, flowcharts, and pseudocode. A *hierarchy chart* is a diagram that graphically depicts the structure of a program. It has boxes that represent each step in the program. The boxes are connected in a way that illustrates their relationship to one another. Figure 12 shows a hierarchy chart for the pay-calculating program.

Figure 12 Hierarchy chart

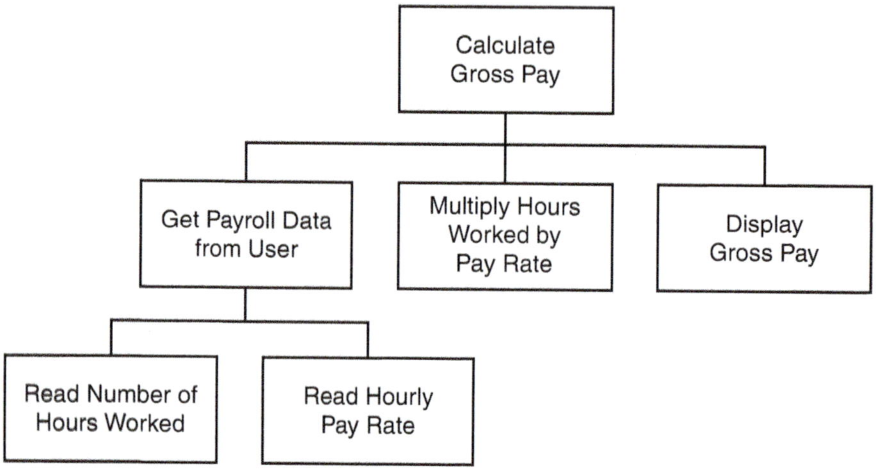

A hierarchy chart begins with the overall task then refines it into smaller subtasks. Each of the subtasks is then refined into even smaller sets of subtasks, until each is small enough to be easily performed. For instance, in Figure 12, the overall task "Calculate Gross Pay" is listed in the top-level box. That task is broken into three subtasks. The first subtask, "Get Payroll Data from User," is broken further into two subtasks. This process of "divide and conquer" is known as *top-down design*.

VideoNote **Introduction to Flowcharting**

A *flowchart* is a diagram that shows the logical flow of a program. It is a useful tool for planning each operation a program performs and the order in which the operations are to occur. For more information see Appendix C: Introduction to Flowcharting, available at www.pearsonhighered.com/gaddis.

Pseudocode is a cross between human language and a programming language. Although the computer can't understand pseudocode, programmers often find it helpful to write an algorithm in a language that's "almost" a programming language, but still very similar to natural language. For example, here is pseudocode that describes the pay-calculating program:

VideoNote **Designing a Program with Pseudocode**

Get payroll data.
Calculate gross pay.
Display gross pay.

Although the pseudocode above gives a broad view of the program, it doesn't reveal all the program's details. A more detailed version of the pseudocode follows:

Display "How many hours did you work?".
Input hours.
Display "How much do you get paid per hour?".
Input rate.
Store the value of hours times rate in the pay variable.
Display the value in the pay variable.

Notice the pseudocode contains statements that look more like commands than the English statements that describe the algorithm in Section 4 (What Is a Program Made of?). The pseudocode even names variables and describes mathematical operations.

4. **Check the model for logical errors.**

Logical errors are mistakes that cause the program to produce erroneous results. Once a hierarchy chart, flowchart, or pseudocode model of the program is assembled, it should be checked for these errors. The programmer should trace through the charts or pseudocode, checking the logic of each step. If an error is found, the model can be corrected before the next step is attempted.

5. **Type the code, save it, and compile it.**

Once a model of the program (hierarchy chart, flowchart, or pseudocode) has been created, checked, and corrected, the programmer is ready to write source code on the computer. The programmer saves the source code to a file and begins the process of translating it to machine language. During this step, the compiler will find any syntax errors that may exist in the program.

6. **Correct any errors found during compilation. Repeat Steps 5 and 6 as many times as necessary.**

If the compiler reports any errors, they must be corrected. Steps 5 and 6 must be repeated until the program is free of compile-time errors.

7. **Run the program with test data for input.**

Once an executable file is generated, the program is ready to be tested for runtime errors. A runtime error is an error that occurs while the program is running. These are usually logical errors, such as mathematical mistakes.

Testing for runtime errors requires that the program be executed with sample data or sample input. The sample data should be such that the correct output can be predicted. If the program does not produce the correct output, a logical error is present in the program.

8. **Correct any errors found while running the program. Repeat Steps 5 through 8 as many times as necessary.**

When runtime errors are found in a program, they must be corrected. You must identify the step where the error occurred and determine the cause. Desk-checking is a process that can help locate runtime errors. The term *desk-checking* means the programmer starts reading the program, or a portion of the program, and steps through each statement. A sheet of paper is often used in this process to jot down the current contents of all variables and sketch what the screen looks like after each output operation. When a variable's contents change, or information is displayed on the screen, this is noted. By stepping through each statement, many errors can be located and corrected. If an error is a result of incorrect logic (such as an improperly stated math formula), you must correct the statement or statements involved in the logic. If an error is due to an incomplete understanding of the program requirements, then you must restate the program purpose and modify the hierarchy and/or flowcharts, pseudocode, and source code. The program must then be saved, recompiled, and retested. This means Steps 5 through 8 must be repeated until the program reliably produces satisfactory results.

9. **Validate the results of the program.**

When you believe you have corrected all the runtime errors, enter test data and determine whether the program solves the original problem.

What Is Software Engineering?

The field of software engineering encompasses the whole process of crafting computer software. It includes designing, writing, testing, debugging, documenting, modifying, and maintaining complex software development projects. Like traditional engineers, software engineers use a number of tools in their craft. Here are a few examples:

- Program specifications
- Charts and diagrams of screen output
- Hierarchy charts and flowcharts
- Pseudocode
- Examples of expected input and desired output
- Special software designed for testing programs

Most commercial software applications are very large. In many instances, one or more teams of programmers, not a single individual, develop them. It is important that the program requirements be thoroughly analyzed and divided into subtasks that are handled by individual teams, or individuals within a team.

In Step 3 of the programming process, you were introduced to the hierarchy chart as a tool for top-down design. The subtasks identified in a top-down design can easily become modules, or separate components of a program. If the program is very large or complex, a team of software engineers can be assigned to work on the individual modules. As the project develops, the modules are coordinated to finally become a single software application.

7 Procedural and Object-Oriented Programming

CONCEPT: Procedural programming and object-oriented programming are two ways of thinking about software development and program design.

C++ is a language that can be used for two methods of writing computer programs: *procedural programming* and *object-oriented programming*.

In procedural programming, the programmer constructs procedures (or functions, as they are called in C++). The procedures are collections of programming statements that perform a specific task. The procedures each contain their own variables and commonly share variables with other procedures. This is illustrated in Figure 13.

Figure 13 Procedures in a program

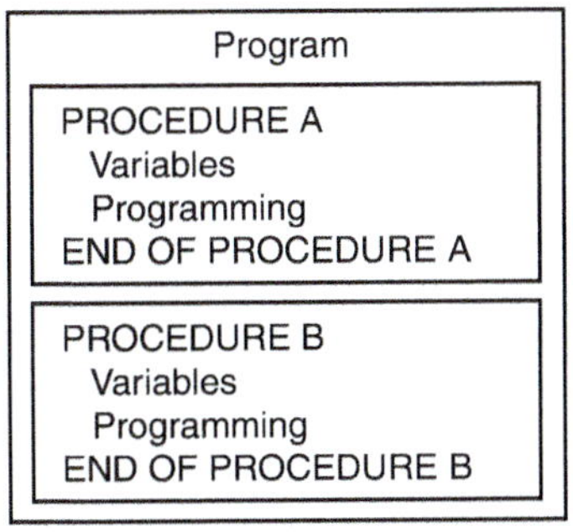

Procedural programming is centered on the procedure, or function. Object-oriented programming (OOP), on the other hand, is centered on the object. An object is a programming element that contains data and the procedures that operate on the data. It is a self-contained unit. This is illustrated in Figure 14.

Figure 14 Objects in a program

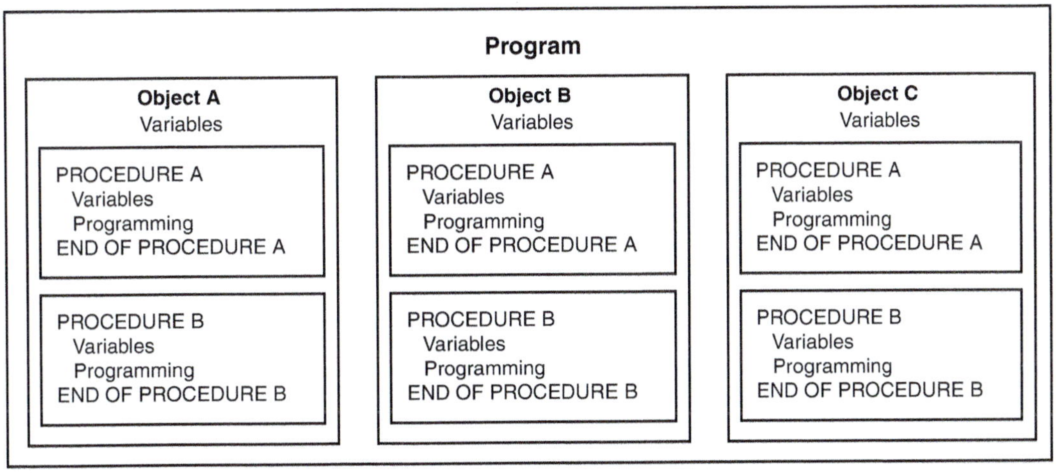

The objects contain, within themselves, both information and the ability to manipulate the information. Operations are carried out on the information in an object by sending the object a *message*. When an object receives a message instructing it to perform some operation, it carries out the instruction. As you study this text, you will encounter many other aspects of object-oriented programming.

Checkpoint

25 What four items should you identify when defining what a program is to do?

26 What does it mean to "visualize a program running"? What is the value of such an activity?

27 What is a hierarchy chart?

28 Describe the process of desk-checking.

29 Describe what a compiler does with a program's source code.

30 What is a runtime error?

31 Is a syntax error (such as misspelling a key word) found by the compiler or when the program is running?

32 What is the purpose of testing a program with sample data or input?

33 Briefly describe the difference between procedural and object-oriented programming.

Review Questions and Exercises

Short Answer

1. Both main memory and secondary storage are types of memory. Describe the difference between the two.
2. What is the difference between system software and application software?
3. What type of software controls the internal operations of the computer's hardware?
4. Why must programs written in a high-level language be translated into machine language before they can be run?
5. Why is it easier to write a program in a high-level language than in machine language?
6. Explain the difference between an object file and an executable file.
7. What is the difference between a syntax error and a logical error?

Fill-in-the-Blank

8. Computers can do many different jobs because they can be ________.
9. The job of the ________ is to fetch instructions, carry out the operations commanded by the instructions, and produce some outcome or resultant information.
10. Internally, the CPU consists of the ________ and the ________.
11. A(n) ________ is an example of a secondary storage device.
12. The two general categories of software are ________ and ________.
13. A program is a set of ________.
14. Since computers can't be programmed in natural human language, algorithms must be written in a(n) ________ language.
15. ________ is the only language computers really process.
16. ________ languages are close to the level of humans in terms of readability.
17. ________ languages are close to the level of the computer.
18. A program's ability to run on several different types of computer systems is called ________.
19. Words that have special meaning in a programming language are called ________.
20. Words or names defined by the programmer are called ________.
21. ________ are characters or symbols that perform operations on one or more operands.

22. __________ characters or symbols mark the beginning or end of programming statements, or separate items in a list.
23. The rules that must be followed when constructing a program are called __________.
24. A(n) __________ is a named storage location.
25. A variable must be __________ before it can be used in a program.
26. The three primary activities of a program are __________, __________, and __________.
27. __________ is information a program gathers from the outside world.
28. __________ is information a program sends to the outside world.
29. A(n) __________ is a diagram that graphically illustrates the structure of a program.

Algorithm Workbench

Draw hierarchy charts or flowcharts that depict the programs described below. (See Appendix C for instructions on creating flowcharts, available at www.pearsonhighered.com/gaddis).

30. Available Credit

    The following steps should be followed in a program that calculates a customer's available credit:

    1. Display the message "Enter the customer's maximum credit."
    2. Wait for the user to enter the customer's maximum credit.
    3. Display the message "Enter the amount of credit used by the customer."
    4. Wait for the user to enter the customer's credit used.
    5. Subtract the used credit from the maximum credit to get the customer's available credit.
    6. Display a message that shows the customer's available credit.

31. Sales Tax

    Design a hierarchy chart or flowchart for a program that calculates the total of a retail sale. The program should ask the user for:
    - The retail price of the item being purchased
    - The sales tax rate

    Once these items have been entered, the program should calculate and display:
    - The sales tax for the purchase
    - The total of the sale

32. Account Balance

    VideoNote **Designing the Account Balance Program**

    Design a hierarchy chart or flowchart for a program that calculates the current balance in a savings account. The program must ask the user for:
    - The starting balance
    - The total dollar amount of deposits made
    - The total dollar amount of withdrawals made
    - The monthly interest rate

Once the program calculates the current balance, it should be displayed on the screen.

Predict the Result

Questions 33–35 are programs expressed as English statements. What would each display on the screen if they were actual programs?

VideoNote
Predicting the Result of Problem 33

33. The variable x starts with the value 0.
    The variable y starts with the value 5.
    Add 1 to x.
    Add 1 to y.
    Add x and y, and store the result in y.
    Display the value in y on the screen.

34. The variable j starts with the value 10.
    The variable k starts with the value 2.
    The variable l starts with the value 4.
    Store the value of j times k in j.
    Store the value of k times l in l.
    Add j and l, and store the result in k.
    Display the value in k on the screen.

35. The variable a starts with the value 1.
    The variable b starts with the value 10.
    The variable c starts with the value 100.
    The variable x starts with the value 0.
    Store the value of c times 3 in x.
    Add the value of b times 6 to the value already in x.
    Add the value of a times 5 to the value already in x.
    Display the value in x on the screen.

Find the Error

36. The following *pseudocode algorithm* has an error. The program is supposed to ask the user for the length and width of a rectangular room, then display the room's area. The program must multiply the width by the length in order to determine the area. Find the error.

    area = width × length.
    Display "What is the room's width?".
    Input width.
    Display "What is the room's length?".
    Input length.
    Display area.

Answers to Checkpoints

1 Because the computer can be programmed to do so many different tasks

2 The Central Processing Unit (CPU), main memory, secondary storage devices, input devices, output devices

3 Arithmetic and Logic Unit (ALU), and Control Unit

4 Fetch: The CPU's control unit fetches the program's next instruction from main memory.

Decode: The control unit decodes the instruction, which is encoded in the form of a number. An electrical signal is generated.

Execute: The signal is routed to the appropriate component of the computer, which causes a device to perform an operation.

5 A unique number assigned to each section of memory

6 Program instructions and data are stored in main memory while the program is operating. Main memory is volatile, and loses its contents when power is removed from the computer. Secondary storage holds data for long periods of time—even when there is no power to the computer.

7 Operating Systems and Application Software

8 The operating system

9 A utility program

10 application software

11 A set of well-defined steps for performing a task or solving a problem

12 To ease the task of programming. Programs may be written in a programming language, and then converted to machine language.

13 A low-level language is close to the level of the computer, and resembles the system's numeric machine language. A high-level language is closer to the level of human readability, and resemble natural languages.

14 That a program may be written on one type of computer and run on another type

15 The preprocessor reads the source file searching for commands that begin with the # symbol. These are commands that cause the preprocessor to modify the source file in some way. The compiler translates each source code instruction into the appropriate machine language instruction, and creates an object file. The linker combines the object file with necessary library routines.

16 Source file: contains program statements written by the programmer.

Object file: contains machine language instructions, generated by the compiler translated from the source file.

Executable file: contains code ready to run on the computer. Includes the machine language from an object file, and the necessary code from library routines.

17 A programming environment that includes a text editor, compiler, debugger, and other utilities, integrated into one package

18 A key word has a special purpose, and is defined as part of a programming language. A programmer-defined identifier is a word or name defined by the programmer.

19 Operators perform operations on one or more operands. Punctuation symbols mark the beginning or ending of a statement, or separates items in a list.

20 A line is a single line as it appears in the body of a program. A statement is a complete instruction that causes the computer to perform an action.

21 Because their contents may be changed

22 The original value is overwritten.

23 The variable must be defined.

24 Input, processing, and output

25 The program's purpose, information to be input, the processing to take place, and the desired output

26 To imagine what the computer screen looks like while the program is running. This helps define input and output.

27 A chart that depicts each logical step of the program in a hierarchical fashion

28 The programmer steps through each statement in the program from beginning to end. The contents of variables are recorded, and screen output is sketched.

29 It translates each source code statement into the appropriate machine language statement.

30 A logical error that occurs while the program is running

31 By the compiler

32 To determine if a logical error is present in the program

33 Procedural programs are made of procedures, or functions. Object-oriented programs are centered on objects, which contain both data and the procedures that operate on the data.

Answers to Odd Numbered Review Questions

1. Main memory, or RAM, is volatile, which means its contents are erased when power is removed from the computer. Secondary memory, such as a disk, does not lose its contents when power is removed from the computer.
3. An operating system
5. Because high level languages are more like natural language.
7. A syntax error is the misuse of a key word, operator, punctuation, or other part of the programming language. A logical error is a mistake that causes the program to produce the wrong results.
9. CPU
11. disk
13. instructions
15. machine language
17. low-level

19. key words
21. operators
23. syntax
25. defined
27. input
29. hierarchy chart
31. Hierarchy chart:

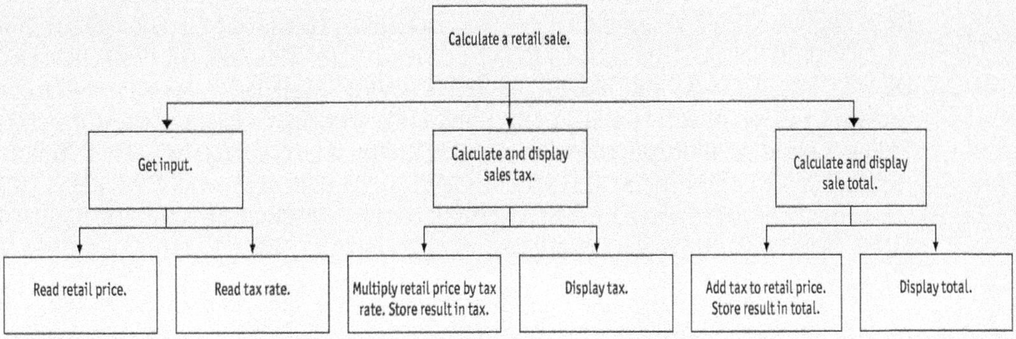

33. 7
35. 365

Credits

Credits are listed in order of appearance.

Figure 2a © iko/Shutterstock
Figure 2b © Nikita Rogul/Shutterstock
Figure 2c © Feng Yu/Shutterstock
Figure 2d © Chiyacat/Shutterstock
Figure 2e © Eikostas/Shutterstock
Figure 2f © tkemot/Shutterstock
Figure 2g © Vitaly Korovin/Shutterstock
Figure 2h © Lusoimages/Shutterstock
Figure 2i © jocic/Shutterstock
Figure 2j © Best Pictures here/Shutterstock
Figure 2k © Peter Guess/Shutterstock
Figure 2l © Aquila/Shutterstock
Figure 2m © Andre Nitsievsky/Shutterstock
Figure 3 © U.S. Army Center of Military History
Figure 4 © Creativa/Shutterstock

Introduction to C++

TOPICS

1 The Parts of a C++ Program

CONCEPT: **C++ programs have parts and components that serve specific purposes.**

Every C++ program has an anatomy. Unlike human anatomy, the parts of C++ programs are not always in the same place. Nevertheless, the parts are there, and your first step in learning C++ is to learn what they are. We will begin by looking at Program 1.

Let's examine the program line by line. Here's the first line:

```
// A simple C++ program
```

The `//` marks the beginning of a *comment*. The compiler ignores everything from the double slash to the end of the line. That means you can type anything you want on that line and the compiler will never complain! Although comments are not required, they are very important to programmers. Most programs are much more complicated than the example in Program 1, and comments help explain what's going on.

Program 1

```
1  // A simple C++ program
2  #include <iostream>
3  using namespace std;
4
5  int main()
6  {
7      cout << "Programming is great fun!";
8      return 0;
9  }
```

The output of the program is shown below. This is what appears on the screen when the program runs.

Program Output

```
Programming is great fun!
```

Line 2 looks like this:

```
#include <iostream>
```

Because this line starts with a #, it is called a *preprocessor directive*. The preprocessor reads your program before it is compiled and only executes those lines beginning with a # symbol. Think of the preprocessor as a program that "sets up" your source code for the compiler.

The `#include` directive causes the preprocessor to include the contents of another file, known as a *header file*, in the program. It is called a header file because it should be included at the head, or top, of a program. The word that is enclosed in brackets, `iostream`, is the name of the header file that is to be included. (The name of the file is `iostream`. The brackets <> indicate that it is a standard C++ header file.) The `<iostream>` header file contains code that allows a C++ program to display output on the screen and read input from the keyboard. Because this program uses `cout` to display screen output, the `<iostream>` header file must be included. The contents of the `<iostream>` file are included in the program at the point the `#include` statement appears.

Line 3 reads:

```
using namespace std;
```

Programs usually contain several items with unique names. In this chapter, you will learn to create variables. Variables, functions, and objects are examples of program entities that must have names. C++ uses *namespaces* to organize the names of program entities. The statement `using namespace std;` declares that the program will be accessing entities whose names are part of the namespace called `std`. (Yes, even namespaces have names.) The reason the program needs access to the `std` namespace is because every name created by the `iostream` file is part of that namespace. In order for a program to use the entities in `iostream`, it must have access to the `std` namespace.

Line 5 reads:

```
int main()
```

This marks the beginning of a function. A *function* can be thought of as a group of one or more programming statements that collectively has a name. The name of this function is main, and the set of parentheses that follows the name indicate that it is a function. The word int stands for "integer." It indicates that the function sends an integer value back to the operating system when it is finished executing.

Although most C++ programs have more than one function, every C++ program must have a function called main. It is the starting point of the program. If you are ever reading someone else's C++ program and want to find where it starts, just look for the function named main.

> **NOTE:** C++ is a case-sensitive language. That means it regards uppercase letters as being entirely different characters than their lowercase counterparts. In C++, the name of the function main must be written in all lowercase letters. C++ doesn't see "Main" the same as "main," or "INT" the same as "int." This is true for all the C++ key words.

Line 6 contains a single, solitary character:

```
{
```

This is called a left brace, or an opening brace, and it is associated with the beginning of the function main. All the statements that make up a function are enclosed in a set of braces. If you look at the third line down from the opening brace, you'll see the closing brace. Everything between the two braces is the content of the function main.

> **WARNING!** Make sure you have a closing brace for every opening brace in your program!

After the opening brace, you see the following statement in line 7:

```
cout << "Programming is great fun!";
```

To put it simply, this line displays a message on the screen. You will read more about cout and the << operator later in this chapter. The message "Programming is great fun!" is printed without the quotation marks. In programming terms, the group of characters inside the quotation marks is called a *string literal* or *string constant.*

> **NOTE:** This is the only line in the program that causes anything to be printed on the screen. The other lines, like #include <iostream> and int main(), are necessary for the framework of your program, but they do not cause any screen output. Remember, a program is a set of instructions for the computer. If something is to be displayed on the screen, you must use a programming statement for that purpose.

At the end of the line is a semicolon. Just as a period marks the end of a sentence, a semicolon marks the end of a complete statement in C++. Comments are ignored by the compiler, so the semicolon isn't required at the end of a comment. Preprocessor directives, like `#include` statements, simply end at the end of the line and never require semicolons. The beginning of a function, like `int main()`, is not a complete statement, so you don't place a semicolon there either.

It might seem that the rules for where to put a semicolon are not clear at all. Rather than worry about it now, just concentrate on learning the parts of a program. You'll soon get a feel for where you should and should not use semicolons.

Line 8 reads:

```
return 0;
```

This sends the integer value 0 back to the operating system upon the program's completion. The value 0 usually indicates that a program executed successfully.

Line 9 contains the closing brace:

```
}
```

This brace marks the end of the `main` function. Since `main` is the only function in this program, it also marks the end of the program.

In the sample program, you encountered several sets of special characters. Table 1 provides a short summary of how they were used.

Table 1 Special Characters

Character	Name	Description
//	Double slash	Marks the beginning of a comment.
#	Pound sign	Marks the beginning of a preprocessor directive.
< >	Opening and closing brackets	Enclose a filename when used with the `#include` directive.
( )	Opening and closing parentheses	Used in naming a function, as in `int main()`.
{ }	Opening and closing braces	Enclose a group of statements, such as the contents of a function.
" "	Opening and closing quotation marks	Enclose a string of characters, such as a message that is to be printed on the screen.
;	Semicolon	Marks the end of a complete programming statement.

Checkpoint

1 The following C++ program will not compile because the lines have been mixed up.

```
int main()
}
// A crazy mixed up program
return 0;
```

```
#include <iostream>
cout << "In 1492 Columbus sailed the ocean blue.";
{
using namespace std;
```

When the lines are properly arranged, the program should display the following on the screen:

```
In 1492 Columbus sailed the ocean blue.
```

Rearrange the lines in the correct order. Test the program by entering it on the computer, compiling it, and running it.

2 The cout Object

CONCEPT: Use the cout object to display information on the computer's screen.

In this section, you will learn to write programs that produce output on the screen. The simplest type of screen output that a program can display is *console output*, which is merely plain text. The word *console* is an old computer term. It comes from the days when a computer operator interacted with the system by typing on a terminal. The terminal, which consisted of a simple screen and keyboard, was known as the *console*.

On modern computers, running graphical operating systems such as Windows or Mac OS X, console output is usually displayed in a window such as the one shown in Figure 1. In C++, you use the `cout` object to produce console output. (You can think of the word `cout` as meaning console output.)

Figure 1 A console window

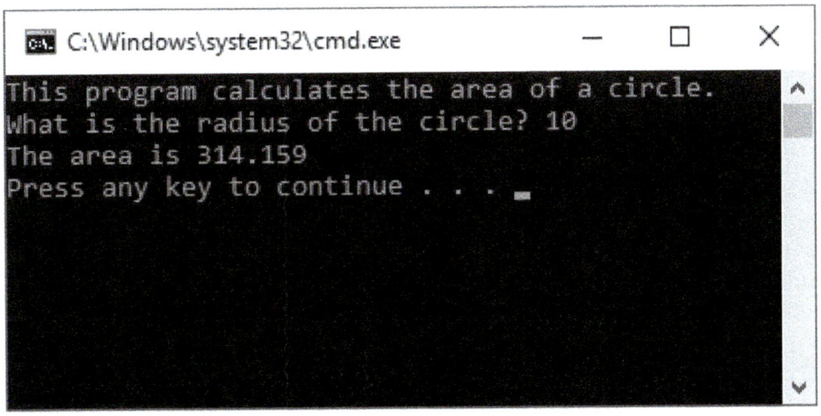

`cout` is classified as a *stream object*, which means it works with streams of data. To print a message on the screen, you send a stream of characters to `cout`. Let's look at line 7 from Program 1:

```
cout << "Programming is great fun!";
```

VideoNote
Using cout

Notice the << operator is used to send the string "Programming is great fun!" to `cout`. When the << symbol is used this way, it is called the *stream insertion operator.* The item immediately to the right of the operator is sent to `cout` then displayed on the screen.

The stream insertion operator is always written as two less-than signs with no space between them. Because you are using it to send a stream of data to the `cout` object, you can think of the stream insertion operator as an arrow that must point toward `cout`. This is illustrated in Figure 2.

Program 2 is another way to write the same program.

Figure 2 Think of << as an arrow pointing to cout

```
cout << "Programming is great fun!";
```

Think of the stream insertion operator as an arrow that points toward cout.

```
cout ←— "Programming is great fun!";
```

Program 2

```
// A simple C++ program
#include <iostream>
using namespace std;

int main()
{
    cout << "Programming is " << "great fun!";
    return 0;
}
```

Program Output

```
Programming is great fun!
```

As you can see, the stream insertion operator can be used to send more than one item to `cout`. The output of this program is identical to that of Program 1. Program 3 shows yet another way to accomplish the same thing.

Program 3

```
// A simple C++ program
#include <iostream>
using namespace std;

int main()
{
    cout << "Programming is ";
    cout << "great fun!";
    return 0;
}
```

Program Output

```
Programming is great fun!
```

An important concept to understand about Program 3 is that, although the output is broken up into two programming statements, this program will still display the message on one line. Unless you specify otherwise, the information you send to `cout` is displayed in a continuous stream. Sometimes this can produce less-than-desirable results. Program 4 is an example.

The layout of the actual output looks nothing like the arrangement of the strings in the source code. First, notice there is no space displayed between the words "sellers" and "during," or between "June:" and "Computer." `cout` displays messages exactly as they are sent. If spaces are to be displayed, they must appear in the strings.

Program 4

```
// An unruly printing program
#include <iostream>
using namespace std;

int main()
{
    cout << "The following items were top sellers";
    cout << "during the month of June:";
    cout << "Computer games";
    cout << "Coffee";
    cout << "Aspirin";
    return 0;
}
```

Program Output

```
The following items were top sellersduring the month of June:Computer
gamesCoffeeAspirin
```

Second, even though the output is broken into five lines in the source code, it comes out as one long line of output. Because the output is too long to fit on one line on the screen, it wraps around to a second line when displayed. The reason the output comes out as one long line is because `cout` does not start a new line unless told to do so. There are two ways to instruct `cout` to start a new line. The first is to send `cout` a *stream manipulator* called `endl` (which is pronounced "end-line" or "end-L"). Program 5 is an example.

Program 5

```
// A well-adjusted printing program
#include <iostream>
using namespace std;

int main()
{
    cout << "The following items were top sellers" << endl;
    cout << "during the month of June:" << endl;
```

(program continues)

Program 5 *(continued)*

```
    cout << "Computer games" << endl;
    cout << "Coffee" << endl;
    cout << "Aspirin" << endl;
    return 0;
}
```

Program Output

```
The following items were top sellers
during the month of June:
Computer games
Coffee
Aspirin
```

NOTE: The last character in `endl` is the lowercase letter L, *not* the number one.

Every time `cout` encounters an `endl` stream manipulator, it advances the output position to the beginning of the next line for subsequent printing. The manipulator can be inserted anywhere in the stream of characters sent to `cout`, outside the double quotes. The following statements show an example.

```
cout << "My pets are" << endl << "dog";
cout << endl << "cat" << endl << "bird" << endl;
```

Another way to cause `cout` to go to a new line is to insert an *escape sequence* in the string itself. An escape sequence starts with the backslash character (`\`) and is followed by one or more control characters. It allows you to control the way output is displayed by embedding commands within the string itself. Program 6 is an example.

Program 6

```
// Yet another well-adjusted printing program
#include <iostream>
using namespace std;

int main()
{
    cout << "The following items were top sellers\n";
    cout << "during the month of June:\n";
    cout << "Computer games\nCoffee";
    cout << "\nAspirin\n";
    return 0;
}
```

Program Output

```
The following items were top sellers
during the month of June:
Computer games
Coffee
Aspirin
```

The *newline escape sequence* is `\n`. When `cout` encounters `\n` in a string, it doesn't print it on the screen, but interprets it as a special command to advance the output cursor to the next line. You have probably noticed inserting the escape sequence requires less typing than inserting `endl`. That's why many programmers prefer it.

A common mistake made by beginning C++ students is to use a forward slash (`/`) instead of a backslash (`\`) when trying to write an escape sequence. This will not work. For example, look at the following code:

```
// Error!
cout << "Four Score/nAnd seven/nYears ago./n";
```

In this code, the programmer accidentally wrote `/n` when he or she meant to write `\n`. The `cout` object will simply display the `/n` characters on the screen. This code will display the following output:

```
Four Score/nAnd seven/nYears ago./n
```

Another common mistake is to forget to put the `\n` inside quotation marks. For example, the following code will not compile:

```
// Error! This code will not compile.

cout << "Good" << \n;
cout << "Morning" << \n;
```

This code will result in an error because the `\n` sequences are not inside quotation marks. We can correct the code by placing the `\n` sequences inside the string literals, as shown here:

```
// This will work.

cout << "Good\n";
cout << "Morning\n";
```

There are many escape sequences in C++. They give you the ability to exercise greater control over the way information is output by your program. Table 2 lists a few of them.

Table 2 Common Escape Sequences

Escape Sequence	Name	Description
`\n`	Newline	Causes the cursor to go to the next line for subsequent printing.
`\t`	Horizontal tab	Causes the cursor to skip over to the next tab stop.
`\a`	Alarm	Causes the computer to beep.
`\b`	Backspace	Causes the cursor to back up, or move left one position.
`\r`	Return	Causes the cursor to go to the beginning of the current line, not the next line.
`\\`	Backslash	Causes a backslash to be printed.
`\'`	Single quote	Causes a single quotation mark to be printed.
`\"`	Double quote	Causes a double quotation mark to be printed.

> **WARNING!** When using escape sequences, do not put a space between the backslash and the control character.

When you type an escape sequence in a string, you type two characters (a backslash followed by another character). However, an escape sequence is stored in memory as a single character. For example, consider the following string literal:

```
"One\nTwo\nThree\n"
```

The diagram in Figure 3 breaks this string into its individual characters. Notice how each of the `\n` escape sequences are considered one character.

Figure 3 Individual characters in a string

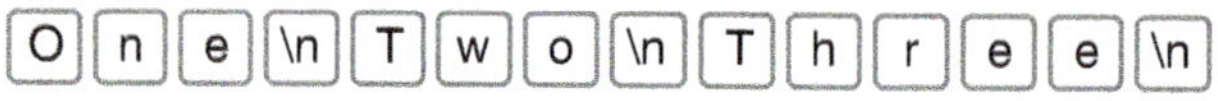

3 The `#include` Directive

CONCEPT: The `#include` directive causes the contents of another file to be inserted into the program.

Now is a good time to expand our discussion of the `#include` directive. The following line has appeared near the top of every example program.

```
#include <iostream>
```

The header file `iostream` must be included in any program that uses the `cout` object. This is because `cout` is not part of the "core" of the C++ language. Specifically, it is part of the *input–output stream library*. The header file, `iostream`, contains information describing `iostream` objects. Without it, the compiler will not know how to properly compile a program that uses `cout`.

Preprocessor directives are not C++ statements. They are commands to the preprocessor, which runs prior to the compiler (hence the name "preprocessor"). The preprocessor's job is to set programs up in a way that makes life easier for the programmer.

For example, any program that uses the `cout` object must contain the extensive setup information found in `iostream`. The programmer could type all this information into the program, but it would be too time consuming. An alternative would be to use an editor to "cut and paste" the information into the program, but that would quickly become tiring as well. The solution is to let the preprocessor insert the contents of `iostream` automatically.

> **WARNING!** Do not put semicolons at the end of processor directives. Because preprocessor directives are not C++ statements, they do not require semicolons. In many cases, an error will result from a preprocessor directive terminated with a semicolon.

An `#include` directive must always contain the name of a file. The preprocessor inserts the entire contents of the file into the program at the point it encounters the `#include` directive.

The compiler doesn't actually see the `#include` directive. Instead, it sees the code that was inserted by the preprocessor, just as if the programmer had typed it there.

The code contained in header files is C++ code. Typically, it describes complex objects like `cout`. Later, you will learn to create your own header files.

Checkpoint

2 The following C++ program will not compile because the lines have been mixed up.

```
cout << "Success\n";
cout << " Success\n\n";
int main()
cout << "Success";
}
using namespace std;
// It's a mad, mad program
#include <iostream>
cout << "Success\n";
{
return 0;
```

When the lines are properly arranged, the program should display the following on the screen:

```
Success
Success Success


Success
```

Rearrange the lines in the correct order. Test the program by entering it on the computer, compiling it, and running it.

3 Study the following program and show what it will print on the screen:

```
// The Works of Wolfgang
#include <iostream>
using namespace std;
int main()
{
   cout << "The works of Wolfgang\ninclude the following";
   cout << "\nThe Turkish March" << endl;
   cout << "and Symphony No. 40 ";
   cout << "in G minor." << endl;
   return 0;
}
```

4 Write a program that will display your name on the first line, your street address on the second line, your city, state, and ZIP code on the third line, and your telephone number on the fourth line. Place a comment with today's date at the top of the program. Test your program by compiling and running it.

4 Variables, Literals, and Assignment Statements

CONCEPT: Variables represent storage locations in the computer's memory. Literals are constant values that are assigned to variables.

Variables allow you to store and work with data in the computer's memory. They provide an "interface" to RAM. Part of the job of programming is to determine how many variables a program will need and what types of information they will hold. Program 7 is an example of a C++ program with a variable. Take a look at line 7:

```
int number;
```

VideoNote
Variable Definitions

This is called a *variable definition*. It tells the compiler the variable's name and the type of data it will hold. This line indicates the variable's name is `number`. The word `int` stands for integer, so `number` will only be used to hold integer numbers. Later in this chapter, you will learn all the types of data that C++ allows.

Program 7

```
1  // This program has a variable.
2  #include <iostream>
3  using namespace std;
4
5  int main()
6  {
7      int number;
8
9      number = 5;
10     cout << "The value in number is " << number << endl;
11     return 0;
12 }
```

Program Output

```
The value in number is 5
```

NOTE: You must have a definition for every variable you intend to use in a program. In C++, variable definitions can appear at any point in the program. Later in this chapter you will learn the best places to define variables.

Notice variable definitions end with a semicolon. Now look at line 9:

```
number = 5;
```

This is called an *assignment*. The equal sign is an operator that copies the value on its right (5) into the variable named on its left (`number`). After this line executes, `number` will be set to 5.

> **NOTE:** This line does not print anything on the computer's screen. It runs silently behind the scenes, storing a value in RAM.

Look at line 10:

```
cout << "The value in number is " << number << endl;
```

The second item sent to `cout` is the variable name `number`. When you send a variable name to `cout`, it prints the variable's contents. Notice there are no quotation marks around `number`. Look at what happens in Program 8.

Program 8

```
1  // This program has a variable.
2  #include <iostream>
3  using namespace std;
4
5  int main()
6  {
7      int number;
8
9      number = 5;
10     cout << "The value in number is " << "number" << endl;
11     return 0;
12 }
```

Program Output

```
The value in number is number
```

When double quotation marks are placed around the word `number`, it becomes a string literal and is no longer a variable name. When string literals are sent to `cout`, they are printed exactly as they appear inside the quotation marks. You've probably noticed by now that the `endl` stream manipulator has no quotation marks around it, for the same reason.

Sometimes a Number Isn't a Number

As shown in Program 8, just placing quotation marks around a variable name changes the program's results. In fact, placing double quotation marks around anything that is not intended to be a string literal will create an error of some type. For example, in Program 8, the number 5 was assigned to the variable `number`. It would have been incorrect to perform the assignment this way:

```
number = "5";
```

In this line, 5 is no longer an integer, but a string literal. Because `number` was defined as an integer variable, you can only store integers in it. The integer 5 and the string literal "5" are not the same thing.

The fact that numbers can be represented as strings frequently confuses students who are new to programming. Just remember that strings are intended for humans to read. They are to be printed on computer screens or paper. Numbers, however, are intended primarily for mathematical operations. You cannot perform math on strings. Before numbers can be displayed on the screen, they must first be converted to strings. (Fortunately, `cout` handles the conversion automatically when you send a number to it.)

Literals

A literal is a piece of data that is written directly into a program's code. One of the most common uses of literals is to assign a value to a variable. For example, in the following statement, assume `number` is an `int` variable. The statement assigns the literal value 100 to the variable `number`.

```
number = 100;
```

Another common use of literals is to display something on the screen. For example, the following statement displays the string literal "Welcome to my program."

```
cout << "Welcome to my program." << endl;
```

Program 9 shows an example that uses a variable and several literals.

Program 9

```
// This program has literals and a variable.
#include <iostream>
using namespace std;

int main()
{
    int apples;

    apples = 20;
    cout << "Today we sold " << apples << " bushels of apples.\n";
    return 0;
}
```

Program Output

```
Today we sold 20 bushels of apples.
```

Of course, the variable is `apples`. It is defined as an integer. Table 3 lists the literals found in the program.

Table 3 Literals and Their Types

Literal	Type of Literal
`20`	Integer literal
`"Today we sold"`	String literal
`"bushels of apples.\n"`	String literal
`0`	Integer literal

> **NOTE:** Literals are also called constants.

Checkpoint

5 Examine the following program:

```
// This program uses variables and literals.
#include <iostream>
using namespace std;
int main()
{
    int little;
    int big;
    little = 2;
    big = 2000;
    cout << "The little number is " << little << endl;
    cout << "The big number is " << big << endl;
    return 0;
}
```

List all the variables and literals that appear in the program.

6 What will the following program display on the screen?

```
#include <iostream>
using namespace std;
int main()
{
    int number;
    number = 712;
    cout << "The value is " << "number" << endl;
    return 0;
}
```

5 Identifiers

CONCEPT: **Choose variable names that indicate what the variables are used for.**

An *identifier* is a programmer-defined name that represents some element of a program. Variable names are examples of identifiers. You may choose your own variable names in C++, as long as you do not use any of the C++ *key words*. The key words make up the "core" of the language and have specific purposes. Table 4 shows a complete list of the C++ key words. Note they are all lowercase.

Table 4 The C++ Key Words

alignas	const	for	private	throw
alignof	constexpr	friend	protected	true
and	const_cast	goto	public	try
and_eq	continue	if	register	typedef
asm	decltype	inline	reinterpret_cast	typeid
auto	default	int	return	typename
bitand	delete	long	short	union
bitor	do	mutable	signed	unsigned
bool	double	namespace	sizeof	using
break	dynamic_cast	new	static	virtual
case	else	noexcept	static_assert	void
catch	enum	not	static_cast	volatile
char	explicit	not_eq	struct	wchar_t
char16_t	export	nullptr	switch	while
char32_t	extern	operator	template	xor
class	false	or	this	xor_eq
compl	float	or_eq	thread_local	

You should always choose names for your variables that give an indication of what the variables are used for. You may be tempted to define variables with names like this:

```
int x;
```

The rather nondescript name, x, gives no clue as to the variable's purpose. Here is a better example.

```
int itemsOrdered;
```

The name itemsOrdered gives anyone reading the program an idea of the variable's use. This way of coding helps produce self-documenting programs, which means you get an understanding of what the program is doing just by reading its code. Because real-world programs usually have thousands of lines, it is important that they be as self-documenting as possible.

You probably have noticed the mixture of uppercase and lowercase letters in the name `itemsOrdered`. Although all of C++'s key words must be written in lowercase, you may use uppercase letters in variable names.

The reason the `O` in `itemsOrdered` is capitalized is to improve readability. Normally "items ordered" is two words. Unfortunately, you cannot have spaces in a variable name, so the two words must be combined into one. When "items" and "ordered" are stuck together, you get a variable definition like this:

```
int itemsordered;
```

Capitalization of the first letter of the second word and succeeding words makes `itemsOrdered` easier to read. It should be mentioned that this style of coding is not required. You are free to use all lowercase letters, all uppercase letters, or any combination of both. In fact, some programmers use the underscore character to separate words in a variable name, as in the following.

```
int items_ordered;
```

Legal Identifiers

Regardless of which style you adopt, be consistent and make your variable names as sensible as possible. Here are some specific rules that must be followed with all identifiers.

- The first character must be one of the letters a through z, A through Z, or an underscore character (_).
- After the first character you may use the letters a through z or A through Z, the digits 0 through 9, or underscores.
- Uppercase and lowercase characters are distinct. This means `ItemsOrdered` is not the same as `itemsordered`.

Table 5 lists variable names and tells whether each is legal or illegal in C++.

Table 5 Some Variable Names

Variable Name	Legal or Illegal?
`dayOfWeek`	Legal.
`3dGraph`	Illegal. Variable names cannot begin with a digit.
`_employee_num`	Legal.
`June1997`	Legal.
`Mixture#3`	Illegal. Variable names may only use letters, digits, or underscores.

6 Integer Data Types

CONCEPT: There are many different types of data. Variables are classified according to their data type, which determines the kind of information that may be stored in them. Integer variables can only hold whole numbers.

Computer programs collect pieces of data from the real world and manipulate them in various ways. There are many different types of data. In the realm of numeric information, for example, there are whole numbers and fractional numbers. There are negative numbers and positive numbers. And there are numbers so large, and others so small, they don't even have a name. Then there is textual information. Names and addresses, for instance, are stored as groups of characters. When you write a program, you must determine what types of information it will be likely to encounter.

If you are writing a program to calculate the number of miles to a distant star, you'll need variables that can hold very large numbers. If you are designing software to record microscopic dimensions, you'll need to store very small and precise numbers. Additionally, if you are writing a program that must perform thousands of intensive calculations, you'll want variables that can be processed quickly. The data type of a variable determines all of these factors.

Although C++ offers many data types, in the very broadest sense there are only two: numeric and character. Numeric data types are broken into two additional categories: integer and floating point. Integers are whole numbers like 12, 157, −34, and 2. Floating-point numbers have a decimal point, like 23.7, 189.0231, and 0.987. Additionally, the integer and floating-point data types are broken into even more classifications. Before we discuss the character data type, let's carefully examine the variations of numeric data.

Your primary considerations for selecting a numeric data type are

- The largest and smallest numbers that may be stored in the variable
- How much memory the variable uses
- Whether the variable stores signed or unsigned numbers
- The number of decimal places of precision the variable has

The size of a variable is the number of bytes of memory it uses. Typically, the larger a variable is, the greater the range it can hold.

Table 6 shows the C++ integer data types with their typical sizes and ranges.

> **NOTE:** The data type sizes and ranges shown in Table 6 are typical on many systems. Depending on your operating system, the sizes and ranges may be different.

Table 6 Integer Data Types

Data Type	Typical Size	Typical Range
`short int`	2 bytes	−32,768 to +32,767
`unsigned short int`	2 bytes	0 to +65,535
`int`	4 bytes	−2,147,483,648 to +2,147,483,647
`unsigned int`	4 bytes	0 to 4,294,967,295
`long int`	4 bytes	−2,147,483,648 to +2,147,483,647
`unsigned long int`	4 bytes	0 to 4,294,967,295
`long long int`	8 bytes	−9,223,372,036,854,775,808 to 9,223,372,036,854,775,807
`unsigned long long int`	8 bytes	0 to 18,446,744,073,709,551,615

Here are some examples of variable definitions:

```
int days;
unsigned int speed;
short int month;
unsigned short int amount;
long int deficit;
unsigned long int insects;
```

Each of the data types in Table 6, except `int`, can be abbreviated as follows:

- `short int` can be abbreviated as `short`
- `unsigned short int` can be abbreviated as `unsigned short`
- `unsigned int` can be abbreviated as `unsigned`
- `long int` can be abbreviated as `long`
- `unsigned long int` can be abbreviated as `unsigned long`
- `long long int` can be abbreviated as `long long`
- `unsigned long long int` can be abbreviated as `unsigned long long`

Because they simplify definition statements, programmers commonly use the abbreviated data type names. Here are some examples:

```
unsigned speed;
short month;
unsigned short amount;
long deficit;
unsigned long insects;
long long grandTotal;
unsigned long long lightYearDistance;
```

Unsigned data types can only store nonnegative values. They can be used when you know your program will not encounter negative values. For example, variables that hold ages or weights would rarely hold numbers less than 0.

Notice in Table 6 the `int` and `long` data types have the same sizes and ranges, and that the `unsigned int` data type has the same size and range as the `unsigned long` data type. This is not always true because the size of integers is dependent on the type of system you are using. Here are the only guarantees:

- Integers are at least as big as short integers.
- Long integers are at least as big as integers.
- Unsigned short integers are the same size as short integers.
- Unsigned integers are the same size as integers.
- Unsigned long integers are the same size as long integers.
- The `long long int` and the `unsigned long long int` data types are guaranteed to be at least 8 bytes (64 bits) in size.

Later in this chapter, you will learn to use the `sizeof` operator to determine how large all the data types are on your computer.

11

NOTE: The `long long int` and the `unsigned long long int` data types were introduced in C++ 11.

As mentioned before, variables are defined by stating the data type key word followed by the name of the variable. In Program 10, an integer, an unsigned integer, and a long integer have been defined.

Program 10

```
// This program has variables of several of the integer types.
#include <iostream>
using namespace std;

int main()
{
    int checking;
    unsigned int miles;
    long days;

    checking = -20;
    miles = 4276;
    diameter = 100000;
    cout << "We have made a long journey of " << miles;
    cout << " miles.\n";
    cout << "Our checking account balance is " << checking;
    cout << "\nThe galaxy is about " << diameter;
    cout << " light years in diameter.\n";
    return 0;
}
```

Program Output

```
We have made a long journey of 4276 miles.
Our checking account balance is -20
The galaxy is about 100000 light years in diameter.
```

In most programs, you will need more than one variable of any given data type. If a program uses two integers, `length` and `width`, they could be defined separately, like this:

```
int length;
int width;
```

It is easier, however, to combine both variable definitions on one line:

```
int length, width;
```

You can define several variables of the same type like this, simply by separating their names with commas. Program 11 illustrates this.

Program 11

```
// This program shows three variables defined on the same line.
#include <iostream>
using namespace std;
```

```
4
5   int main()
6   {
7       int floors, rooms, suites;
8
9       floors = 15;
10      rooms = 300;
11      suites = 30;
12      cout << "The Grande Hotel has " << floors << " floors\n";
13      cout << "with " << rooms << " rooms and " << suites;
14      cout << " suites.\n";
15      return 0;
16  }
```

Program Output

```
The Grande Hotel has 15 floors
with 300 rooms and 30 suites.
```

Integer and Long Integer Literals

In C++, if a numeric literal is an integer (not written with a decimal point) and it fits within the range of an `int` (see Table 6 for the minimum and maximum values), then the numeric literal is treated as an `int`. A numeric literal that is treated as an `int` is called an *integer literal*. For example, look at lines 9, 10, and 11 in Program 11:

```
floors = 15;
rooms = 300;
suites = 30;
```

Each of these statements assigns an integer literal to a variable.

One of the pleasing characteristics of the C++ language is that it allows you to control almost every aspect of your program. If you need to change the way something is stored in memory, the tools are provided to do that. For example, what if you are in a situation where you have an integer literal, but you need it to be stored in memory as a long integer? (Rest assured, this is a situation that does arise.) C++ allows you to force an integer literal to be stored as a long integer by placing the letter L at the end of the number. Here is an example:

```
long amount;
amount = 32L;
```

The first statement defines a `long` variable named `amount`. The second statement assigns the literal value 32 to the `amount` variable. In the second statement, the literal is written as 32L, which makes it a *long integer literal*. This means the literal is treated as a `long`.

If you want an integer literal to be treated as a `long long int`, you can append LL at the end of the number. Here is an example:

```
long long amount;
amount = 32LL;
```

The first statement defines a `long long` variable named `amount`. The second statement assigns the literal value 32 to the `amount` variable. In the second statement, the literal is written as `32LL`, which makes it a *long long integer literal*. This means the literal is treated as a `long long int`.

> **TIP:** When writing long integer literals or long long integer literals, you can use either an uppercase or a lowercase L. Because the lowercase l looks like the number 1, you should always use the uppercase L.

If You Plan to Continue in Computer Science: Hexadecimal and Octal Literals

Programmers commonly express values in numbering systems other than decimal (or base 10). Hexadecimal (base 16) and octal (base 8) are popular because they make certain programming tasks more convenient than decimal numbers do.

By default, C++ assumes that all integer literals are expressed in decimal. You express hexadecimal numbers by placing 0x in front of them. (This is zero-x, not oh-x.) Here is how the hexadecimal number F4 would be expressed in C++:

```
0xF4
```

Octal numbers must be preceded by a 0 (zero, not oh). For example, the octal 31 would be written

```
031
```

> **NOTE:** You will not be writing programs for some time that require this type of manipulation. It is important, however, that you understand this material. Good programmers should develop the skills for reading other people's source code. You may find yourself reading programs that use items like long integer, hexadecimal, or octal literals.

Checkpoint

7 Which of the following are illegal variable names, and why?

```
x
99bottles
july97
theSalesFigureForFiscalYear98
r&d
grade_report
```

8 Is the variable name `Sales` the same as `sales`? Why or why not?

9 Refer to the data types listed in Table 6 for these questions.

A) If a variable needs to hold numbers in the range 32 to 6,000, what data type would be best?

B) If a variable needs to hold numbers in the range 240,000 to 140,000, what data type would be best?

C) Which of the following literals uses more memory? `20` or `20L`

10 On any computer, which data type uses more memory, an integer or an unsigned integer?

7 The `char` Data Type

The `char` data type is used to store individual characters. A variable of the `char` data type can hold only one character at a time. Here is an example of how you might declare a `char` variable:

```
char letter;
```

This statement declares a `char` variable named `letter`, which can store one character. In C++, *character literals* are enclosed in single quotation marks. Here is an example showing how we would assign a character to the `letter` variable:

```
letter = 'g';
```

This statement assigns the character `'g'` to the `letter` variable. Because `char` variables can hold only one character, they are not compatible with strings. For example, you cannot assign a string to a `char` variable, even if the string contains only one character. The following statement, for example, will not compile because it attempts to assign a string literal to a `char` variable.

```
letter = "g"; // ERROR! Cannot assign a string to a char
```

It is important that you do not confuse character literals, which are enclosed in single quotation marks, with string literals, which are enclosed in double quotation marks.

Program 12 shows an example program that works with characters.

Program 12

```
// This program works with characters.
#include <iostream>
using namespace std;

int main()
{
    char letter;

    letter = 'A';
    cout << letter << endl;
    letter = 'B';
    cout << letter << endl;
    return 0;
}
```

Program Output

```
A
B
```

Although the char data type is used for storing characters, it is actually an integer data type that typically uses 1 byte of memory. (The size is system dependent. On some systems, the char data type is larger than 1 byte.)

The reason an integer data type is used to store characters is because characters are internally represented by numbers. Each printable character, as well as many nonprintable characters, is assigned a unique number. The most commonly used method for encoding characters is ASCII, which stands for the American Standard Code for Information Interchange. (There are other codes, such as EBCDIC, which is used by many IBM mainframes.)

When a character is stored in memory, it is actually the numeric code that is stored. When the computer is instructed to print the value on the screen, it displays the character that corresponds with the numeric code.

You may want to refer to Appendix: The ASCII Character Set, which shows the ASCII character set. Notice the number 65 is the code for A, 66 is the code for B, and so on. Program 13 demonstrates that when you work with characters, you are actually working with numbers.

Program 13

```
// This program demonstrates the close relationship between
// characters and integers.
#include <iostream>
using namespace std;

int main()
{
    char letter;

    letter = 65;
    cout << letter << endl;
    letter = 66;
    cout << letter << endl;
    return 0;
}
```

Program Output

```
A
B
```

Figure 4 illustrates that when characters, such as A, B, and C, are stored in memory, it is really the numbers 65, 66, and 67 that are stored.

The Difference between String Literals and Character Literals

It is important that you do not confuse character literals with string literals. Strings, which are a series of characters stored in consecutive memory locations, can be virtually any

Figure 4 Characters and their ASCII codes

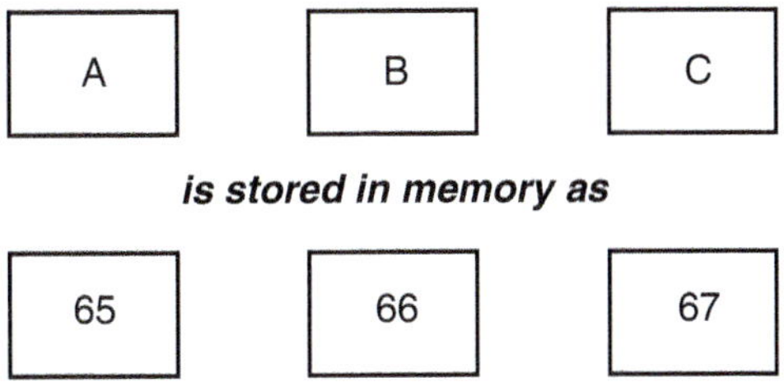

length. This means that there must be some way for the program to know how long a string is. In C++, an extra byte is appended to the end of string literals when they are stored in memory. In this last byte, the number 0 is stored. It is called the *null terminator* or *null character*, and it marks the end of the string.

Don't confuse the null terminator with the character `'0'`. If you look at Appendix: The ASCII Character Set, you will see that ASCII code 48 corresponds to the character `'0'`, whereas the null terminator is the same as the ASCII code 0. If you want to print the character 0 on the screen, you use ASCII code 48. If you want to mark the end of a string, however, you use ASCII code 0.

Let's look at an example of how a string literal is stored in memory. Figure 5 depicts the way the string literal `"Sebastian"` would be stored.

Figure 5 The string literal `"Sebastian"`

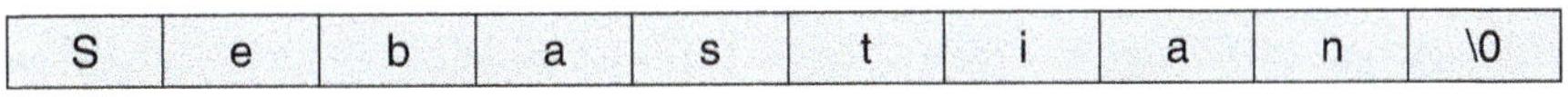

First, notice the quotation marks are not stored with the string. They are simply a way of marking the beginning and end of the string in your source code. Second, notice the very last byte of the string. It contains the null terminator, which is represented by the `\0` character. The addition of this last byte means that although the string `"Sebastian"` is 9 characters long, it occupies 10 bytes of memory.

The null terminator is another example of something that sits quietly in the background. It doesn't print on the screen when you display a string, but nevertheless, it is there silently doing its job.

NOTE: C++ automatically places the null terminator at the end of string literals.

Now let's compare the way a string and a `char` are stored. Suppose you have the literals `'A'` and `"A"` in a program. Figure 6 depicts their internal storage.

As you can see, `'A'` is a 1-byte element and `"A"` is a 2-byte element. Since characters are really stored as ASCII codes, Figure 7 shows what is actually being stored in memory.

Figure 6 'A' as a character and "A" as a string

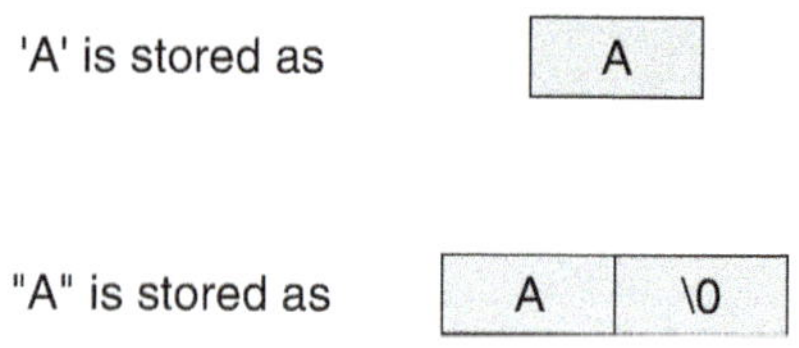

Figure 7 ASCII codes

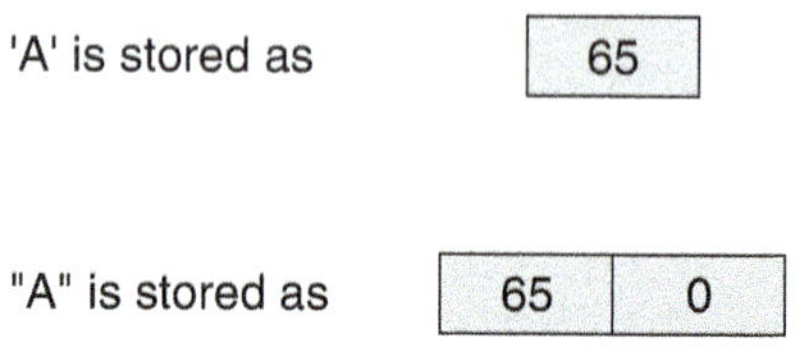

Because `char` variables are only large enough to hold one character, you cannot assign string literals to them. For example, the following code defines a `char` variable named `letter`. The character literal `'A'` can be assigned to the variable, but the string literal `"A"` cannot.

```
char letter;

letter = 'A';  // This will work.
letter = "A";  // This will not work!
```

One final topic about characters should be discussed. You have learned that some strings look like a single character but really aren't. It is also possible to have a character that looks like a string. A good example is the newline character, `\n`. Although it is represented by two characters, a slash and an `n`, it is internally represented as one character. In fact, all escape sequences, internally, are just 1 byte.

Program 14 shows the use of `\n` as a character literal, enclosed in single quotation marks. If you refer to the ASCII chart in Appendix: The ASCII Character Set, you will see that ASCII code 10 is the linefeed character. This is the code C++ uses for the newline character.

Program 14

```
// This program uses character literals.
#include <iostream>
using namespace std;

int main()
{
    char letter;

    letter = 'A';
    cout << letter << '\n';
    letter = 'B';
```

```
        cout << letter << '\n';
        return 0;
    }
```

Program Output

```
A
B
```

Let's review some important points regarding characters and strings:

- Printable characters are internally represented by numeric codes. Most computers use ASCII codes for this purpose.
- Characters normally occupy a single byte of memory.
- Strings are consecutive sequences of characters that occupy consecutive bytes of memory.
- String literals are always stored in memory with a null terminator at the end. This marks the end of the string.
- Character literals are enclosed in single quotation marks.
- String literals are enclosed in double quotation marks.
- Escape sequences such as '\n' are stored internally as a single character.

8 The C++ string Class

CONCEPT: Standard C++ provides a special data type for storing and working with strings.

Because a char variable can store only one character in its memory location, another data type is needed for a variable able to hold an entire string. Although C++ does not have a built-in data type able to do this, standard C++ provides something called the string class that allows the programmer to create a string type variable.

Using the string Class

The first step in using the string class is to #include the <string> header file. This is accomplished with the following preprocessor directive:

```
#include <string>
```

The next step is to define a string type variable, called a string object. Defining a string object is similar to defining a variable of a primitive type. For example, the following statement defines a string object named movieTitle.

```
string movieTitle;
```

You can assign a string literal to movieTitle with the assignment operator:

```
movieTitle = "Wheels of Fury";
```

You can use cout to display the value of the movieTitle object, as shown in the next statement:

```
cout << "My favorite movie is " << movieTitle << endl;
```

Program 15 is a complete program that demonstrates the preceding statements.

Program 15

```
// This program demonstrates the string class.
#include <iostream>
#include <string> // Required for the string class.
using namespace std;

int main()
{
    string movieTitle;

    movieTitle = "Wheels of Fury";
    cout << "My favorite movie is " << movieTitle << endl;
    return 0;
}
```

Program Output

```
My favorite movie is Wheels of Fury
```

As you can see, working with `string` objects is similar to working with variables of other types. Throughout this text, we will continue to discuss `string` class features and capabilities.

Checkpoint

11 What are the ASCII codes for the following characters? (Refer to Appendix: The ASCII Character Set.)

```
C
F
W
```

12 Which of the following is a character literal?

```
'B'
"B"
```

13 Assuming the `char` data type uses 1 byte of memory, how many bytes do the following literals use?

```
'Q'
"Q"
"Sales"
'\n'
```

14 Write a program that has the following character variables: `first`, `middle`, and `last`. Store your initials in these variables then display them on the screen.

15 What is wrong with the following program statement?

```
char letter = "Z";
```

16 What header file must you include in order to use `string` objects?

17 Write a program that stores your name, address, and phone number in three separate `string` objects. Display the contents of the `string` objects on the screen.

9 Floating-Point Data Types

CONCEPT: Floating-point data types are used to define variables that can hold real numbers.

Whole numbers are not adequate for many jobs. If you are writing a program that works with dollar amounts or precise measurements, you need a data type that allows fractional values. In programming terms, these are called *floating-point* numbers.

Internally, floating-point numbers are stored in a manner similar to *scientific notation.* Take the number 47,281.97. In scientific notation, this number is 4.728197×10^4. (10^4 is equal to 10,000, and $4.728197 \times 10{,}000$ is 47,281.97.) The first part of the number, 4.728197, is called the *mantissa.* The mantissa is multiplied by a power of 10.

Computers typically use *E notation* to represent floating-point values. In E notation, the number 47,281.97 would be 4.728197E4. The part of the number before the E is the mantissa, and the part after the E is the power of 10. When a floating-point number is stored in memory, it is stored as the mantissa and the power of 10.

Table 7 shows other numbers represented in scientific and E notation.

Table 7 Floating-Point Representations

Decimal Notation	Scientific Notation	E Notation
247.91	2.4791×10^2	`2.4791E2`
0.00072	7.2×10^{-4}	`7.2E-4`
2,900,000	2.9×10^6	`2.9E6`

In C++, there are three data types that can represent floating-point numbers. They are

```
float
double
long double
```

The `float` data type is considered *single precision.* The `double` data type is usually twice as big as `float`, so it is considered *double precision.* As you've probably guessed, the `long double` is intended to be larger than the `double`. Of course, the exact sizes of these data types are dependent on the computer you are using. The only guarantees are

- A `double` is at least as big as a `float`.
- A `long double` is at least as big as a `double`.

Table 8 shows the typical sizes and ranges of floating-point data types.

Table 8 Floating-Point Data Types on PCs

Data Type	Key Word	Description
Single precision	`float`	4 bytes. Numbers between ±3.4E–38 and ±3.4E38
Double precision	`double`	8 bytes. Numbers between ±1.7E–308 and ±1.7E308
Long double precision	`long double`	8 bytes*. Numbers between ±1.7E–308 and ±1.7E308

*Some compilers use 10 bytes for `long double`s. This allows a range of ±3.4E–4932 to ±1.1E4832.

You will notice there are no unsigned floating-point data types. On all machines, variables of the `float`, `double`, and `long double` data types can store positive or negative numbers.

Floating-Point Literals

Floating-point literals may be expressed in a variety of ways. As shown in Program 16, E notation is one method. When you are writing numbers that are extremely large or extremely small, this will probably be the easiest way. E notation numbers may be expressed with an uppercase E or a lowercase e. Notice in the source code, the literals were written as 1.495979E11 and 1.989E30, but the program printed them as 1.49598e+011 and 1.989e+30. The two sets of numbers are equivalent. (The plus sign in front of the exponent is also optional.)

Program 16

```
// This program uses floating-point data types.
#include <iostream>
using namespace std;

int main()
{
     float distance;
     double mass;

     distance = 1.495979E11;
     mass = 1.989E30;
     cout << "The Sun is " << distance << " meters away.\n";
     cout << "The Sun\'s mass is " << mass << " kilograms.\n";
     return 0;
}
```

Program Output

```
The Sun is 1.49598e+011 meters away.
The Sun's mass is 1.989e+030 kilograms.
```

You can also express floating-point literals in decimal notation. The literal 1.495979E11 could have been written as:

```
149597900000.00
```

Obviously the E notation is more convenient for lengthy numbers, but for numbers like 47.39, decimal notation is preferable to 4.739E1.

All of the following floating-point literals are equivalent:

```
1.4959E11
1.4959e11
1.4959E+11
1.4959e+11
149590000000.00
```

Floating-point literals are normally stored in memory as `doubles`. But remember, C++ provides tools for handling just about any situation. Just in case you need to force a literal to be stored as a `float`, you can append the letter F or f to the end of it. For example, the following literals would be stored as `floats`:

```
1.2F
45.907f
```

NOTE: Because floating-point literals are normally stored in memory as `doubles`, most compilers issue a warning message when you assign a floating-point literal to a `float` variable. For example, assuming `num` is a `float`, the following statement might cause the compiler to generate a warning message:

```
num = 14.725;
```

You can suppress the warning message by appending the f suffix to the floating-point literal, as shown below:

```
num = 14.725f;
```

If you want to force a value to be stored as a `long double`, append an `L` or `l` to it, as in the following examples:

```
1034.56L
89.2l
```

The compiler won't confuse these with long integers because they have decimal points. (Remember, the lowercase `L` looks so much like the number 1 that you should always use the uppercase `L` when suffixing literals.)

Assigning Floating-Point Values to Integer Variables

When a floating-point value is assigned to an integer variable, the fractional part of the value (the part after the decimal point) is discarded. For example, look at the following code:

```
int number;
number = 7.5;    // Assigns 7 to number
```

This code attempts to assign the floating-point value 7.5 to the integer variable `number`. As a result, the value 7 will be assigned to `number`, with the fractional part discarded. When part of a value is discarded, it is said to be *truncated.*

Assigning a floating-point variable to an integer variable has the same effect. For example, look at the following code:

```
int i;
float f;
f = 7.5;
i = f;             // Assigns 7 to i.
```

When the `float` variable `f` is assigned to the `int` variable `i`, the value being assigned (7.5) is truncated. After this code executes, `i` will hold the value 7 and `f` will hold the value 7.5.

NOTE: When a floating-point value is truncated, it is not rounded. Assigning the value 7.9 to an `int` variable will result in the value 7 being stored in the variable.

WARNING! Floating-point variables can hold a much larger range of values than integer variables can. If a floating-point value is being stored in an integer variable, and the whole part of the value (the part before the decimal point) is too large for the integer variable, an invalid value will be stored in the integer variable.

10 The `bool` Data Type

CONCEPT: Boolean variables are set to either `true` or `false`.

Expressions that have a `true` or `false` value are called *Boolean* expressions, named in honor of English mathematician George Boole (1815–1864).

The `bool` data type allows you to create small integer variables that are suitable for holding `true` or `false` values. Program 17 demonstrates the definition and assignment of a `bool` variable.

Program 17

```
// This program demonstrates boolean variables.
#include <iostream>
using namespace std;

int main()
{
    bool boolValue;

    boolValue = true;
    cout << boolValue << endl;
    boolValue = false;
    cout << boolValue << endl;
    return 0;
}
```

Program Output

```
1
0
```

As you can see from the program output, the value `true` is represented in memory by the number 1, and `false` is represented by 0. `Bool` variables are useful for evaluating conditions that are either true or false.

11 Determining the Size of a Data Type

CONCEPT: **The `sizeof` operator may be used to determine the size of a data type on any system.**

As you have seen in this chapter, one of the problems of portability is the lack of common sizes of data types on all machines. If you are not sure what the sizes of data types are on your computer, C++ provides a way to find out.

A special operator called `sizeof` will report the number of bytes of memory used by any data type or variable. Program 18 illustrates its use. The first line that uses the operator is line 10:

```
cout << "The size of an integer is " << sizeof(int);
```

The name of the data type or variable is placed inside the parentheses that follow the operator. The operator "returns" the number of bytes used by that item. This operator can be invoked anywhere you can use an unsigned integer, including in mathematical operations.

Program 18

```
1   // This program determines the size of integers, long
2   // integers, and long doubles.
3   #include <iostream>
4   using namespace std;
5
6   int main()
7   {
8       long double apple;
9
10      cout << "The size of an integer is " << sizeof(int);
11      cout << " bytes.\n";
12      cout << "The size of a long integer is " << sizeof(long);
13      cout << " bytes.\n";
14      cout << "An apple can be eaten in " << sizeof(apple);
15      cout << " bytes!\n";
16      return 0;
17  }
```

Program Output

```
The size of an integer is 4 bytes.
The size of a long integer is 4 bytes.
An apple can be eaten in 8 bytes!
```

Checkpoint

18 Yes or No: Is there an unsigned floating-point data type? If so, what is it?

19 How would the following number in scientific notation be represented in E notation?

$$6.31 \times 10^{17}$$

20 Write a program that defines an integer variable named `age` and a `float` variable named `weight`. Store your age and weight, as literals, in the variables. The program should display these values on the screen in a manner similar to the following:

```
My age is 26 and my weight is 180 pounds.
```

(Feel free to lie to the computer about your age and your weight—it'll never know!)

12 More about Variable Assignments and Initialization

CONCEPT: An assignment operation assigns, or copies, a value into a variable. When a value is assigned to a variable as part of the variable's definition, it is called an initialization.

As you have already seen in several examples, a value is stored in a variable with an *assignment statement*. For example, the following statement copies the value 12 into the variable `unitsSold`:

```
unitsSold = 12;
```

The = symbol is called the *assignment operator*. Operators perform operations on data. The data that operators work with are called *operands*. The assignment operator has two operands. In the previous statement, the operands are `unitsSold` and `12`.

In an assignment statement, C++ requires the name of the variable receiving the assignment to appear on the left side of the operator. The following statement is incorrect:

```
12 = unitsSold;     // Incorrect!
```

In C++ terminology, the operand on the left side of the = symbol must be an *lvalue*. It is called an lvalue because it is a value that may appear on the left side of an assignment operator. An lvalue is something that identifies a place in memory whose contents may be changed. Most of the time this will be a variable name. The operand on the right side of the = symbol must be an *rvalue*. An rvalue is any expression that has a value. The assignment statement takes the value of the rvalue and puts it in the memory location of the object identified by the lvalue.

You may also assign values to variables as part of the definition. This is called *initialization*. Program 19 shows how it is done.

Program 19

```
// This program shows variable initialization.
#include <iostream>
using namespace std;

int main()
{
    int month = 2, days = 28;

    cout << "Month " << month << " has " << days << " days.\n";
    return 0;
}
```

Program Output

```
Month 2 has 28 days.
```

As you can see, this simplifies the program and reduces the number of statements that must be typed by the programmer. Here are examples of other definition statements that perform initialization:

```
double interestRate = 12.9;
char stockCode = 'D';
long customerNum = 459L;
```

Of course, there are always variations on a theme. C++ allows you to define several variables and only initialize some of them. Here is an example of such a definition:

```
int flightNum = 89, travelTime, departure = 10, distance;
```

The variable `flightNum` is initialized to 89 and `departure` is initialized to 10. The variables `travelTime` and `distance` remain uninitialized.

11 Declaring Variables with the auto Key Word

C++ 11 introduces an alternative way to define variables, using the `auto` key word and an initialization value. Here is an example:

```
auto amount = 100;
```

Notice this statement uses the word `auto` instead of a data type. The `auto` key word tells the compiler to determine the variable's data type from the initialization value. In this example, the initialization value, 100, is an `int`, so `amount` will be an `int` variable. Here are other examples:

```
auto interestRate = 12.0;
auto stockCode = 'D';
auto customerNum = 459L;
```

In this code, the `interestRate` variable will be a `double` because the initialization value, 12.0, is a `double`. The `stockCode` variable will be a `char` because the initialization value,

'D', is a char. The customerNum variable will be a long because the initialization value, 459L, is a long.

These examples show how to use the auto key word, but they don't really show its usefulness. The auto key word is intended to simplify the syntax of declarations that are more complex than the ones shown here.

Alternative Forms of Variable Initialization

The most common way to initialize a variable is to use the assignment operator in the variable definition statement, as shown here:

```
int value = 5;
```

However, there are two alternative techniques for initializing variables. The first is to enclose the initialization value in a set of parentheses, just after the variable name. Here is how you would define the value variable and initialize it to 5 using this technique:

```
int value(5);
```

11 The second alternative, introduced in C++ 11, is to enclose the initialization value in a set of curly braces, just after the variable name. Here is how you would define the value variable and initialize it to 5 using the brace notation:

```
int value {5};        // This only works with C++ 11 or higher.
```

Most programmers continue to use the assignment operator to initialize regular variables. However, the brace notation offers an advantage. It checks to make sure the value you are initializing the variable with matches the data type of the variable. For example, assume that doubleVal is a double variable with 6.2 stored in it. Using the assignment operator, it is possible to write either of the following statements:

```
int value1 = 4.9;              // This will store 4 in value1
int value2 = doubleVal;        // This will store 6 in value2
```

In both cases, the fractional part of the value will be truncated before it is assigned to the variable being defined. This could cause problems, yet C++ compilers allow it. They do issue a warning, but they still build an executable file you can run. If the brace notation is used, however, the compiler indicates that these statements produce an error, and no executable is created. You will have to fix the errors and rebuild the project before you can run the program.

13 Scope

CONCEPT: A variable's scope is the part of the program that has access to the variable.

Every variable has a *scope*. The scope of a variable is the part of the program where the variable may be used. The rules that define a variable's scope are complex, and you will only be introduced to the concept here.

The first rule of scope you should learn is that a variable cannot be used in any part of the program before the definition. Program 20 illustrates this.

Program 20

```
1   // This program can't find its variable.
2   #include <iostream>
3   using namespace std;
4
5   int main()
6   {
7       cout << value; // ERROR! value not defined yet!
8
9       int value = 100;
10      return 0;
11  }
```

The program will not work because line 7 attempts to send the contents of the variable `value` to `cout` before the variable is defined. The compiler reads your program from top to bottom. If it encounters a statement that uses a variable before the variable is defined, an error will result. To correct the program, the variable definition must be put before any statement that uses it.

14 Arithmetic Operators

CONCEPT: There are many operators for manipulating numeric values and performing arithmetic operations.

C++ offers a multitude of operators for manipulating data. Generally, there are three types of operators: *unary*, *binary*, and *ternary*. These terms reflect the number of operands an operator requires.

VideoNote
Assignment Statements and Simple Math Expressions

Unary operators only require a single operand. For example, consider the following expression:

```
-5
```

Of course, we understand this represents the value negative five. The literal 5 is preceded by the minus sign. The minus sign, when used this way, is called the *negation operator*. Since it only requires one operand, it is a unary operator.

Binary operators work with two operands. The assignment operator is in this category. Ternary operators, as you may have guessed, require three operands. C++ has only one ternary operator.

Arithmetic operations are very common in programming. Table 9 shows the common arithmetic operators in C++.

Table 9 Fundamental Arithmetic Operators

Operator	Meaning	Type	Example
+	Addition	Binary	`total = cost + tax;`
−	Subtraction	Binary	`cost = total - tax;`
*	Multiplication	Binary	`tax = cost * rate;`
/	Division	Binary	`salePrice = original / 2;`
%	Modulus	Binary	`remainder = value % 3;`

Each of these operators works as you probably expect. The addition operator returns the sum of its two operands. In the following assignment statement, the variable `amount` will be assigned the value 12:

```
amount = 4 + 8;
```

The subtraction operator returns the value of its right operand subtracted from its left operand. This statement will assign the value 90 to `temperature`:

```
temperature = 120 - 30;
```

The multiplication operator returns the product of its two operands. In the following statement, `markUp` is assigned the value 3:

```
markUp = 12 * 0.25;
```

The division operator returns the quotient of its left operand divided by its right operand. In the next statement, `points` is assigned the value 5:

```
points = 100 / 20;
```

It is important to note that when both of the division operator's operands are integers, the result of the division will also be an integer. If the result has a fractional part, it will be thrown away. We will discuss this behavior, which is known as *integer division*, in greater detail later in this section.

The modulus operator, which only works with integer operands, returns the remainder of an integer division. The following statement assigns 2 to `leftOver`:

```
leftOver = 17 % 3;
```

In this chapter, you will not learn how to use these operators in more complex mathematical formulas. For now, we will concentrate on their basic usage. For example, suppose we need to write a program that calculates and displays an employee's total wages for the week. The regular hours for the work week are 40, and any hours worked over 40 are considered overtime. The employee earns $18.25 per hour for regular hours, and $27.78 per hour for overtime hours. The employee has worked 50 hours this week. The following pseudocode algorithm shows the program's logic:

Regular wages = base pay rate × regular hours
Overtime wages = overtime pay rate × overtime hours
Total wages = regular wages + overtime wages
Display the total wages

Program 21 shows the C++ code for the program.

Program 21

```
1  // This program calculates hourly wages, including overtime.
2  #include <iostream>
3  using namespace std;
4
5  int main()
6  {
7      double regularWages,              // To hold regular wages
8             basePayRate = 18.25,       // Base pay rate
9             regularHours = 40.0,       // Hours worked less overtime
10            overtimeWages,             // To hold overtime wages
11            overtimePayRate = 27.78,   // Overtime pay rate
12            overtimeHours = 10,        // Overtime hours worked
13            totalWages;                // To hold total wages
14
15     // Calculate the regular wages.
16     regularWages = basePayRate * regularHours;
17
18     // Calculate the overtime wages.
19     overtimeWages = overtimePayRate * overtimeHours;
20
21     // Calculate the total wages.
22     totalWages = regularWages + overtimeWages;
23
24     // Display the total wages.
25     cout << "Wages for this week are $" << totalWages << endl;
26     return 0;
27 }
```

Program Output

```
Wages for this week are $1007.8
```

Let's take a closer look at the program. As mentioned in the comments, there are variables for regular wages, base pay rate, regular hours worked, overtime wages, overtime pay rate, overtime hours worked, and total wages.

Here is line 16, which multiplies `basePayRate` by `regularHours` and stores the result in `regularWages`:

```
regularWages = basePayRate * regularHours;
```

Here is line 19, which multiplies `overtimePayRate` by `overtimeHours` and stores the result in `overtimeWages`:

```
overtimeWages = overtimePayRate * overtimeHours;
```

Line 22 adds the regular wages and the overtime wages and stores the result in `totalWages`:

```
totalWages = regularWages + overtimeWages;
```

Line 25 displays the message on the screen reporting the week's wages.

Integer Division

When both operands of a division statement are integers, the statement will result in *integer division*. This means the result of the division will be an integer as well. If there is a remainder, it will be discarded. For example, look at the following code:

```
double number;
number = 5 / 2;
```

This code divides 5 by 2 and assigns the result to the `number` variable. What will be stored in `number`? You would probably assume that 2.5 would be stored in `number` because that is the result your calculator shows when you divide 5 by 2. However, that is not what happens when the previous C++ code is executed. Because the numbers 5 and 2 are both integers, the fractional part of the result will be thrown away, or truncated. As a result, the value 2 will be assigned to the `number` variable.

In the previous code, it doesn't matter that the `number` variable is declared as a `double` because the fractional part of the result is discarded before the assignment takes place. In order for a division operation to return a floating-point value, one of the operands must be of a floating-point data type. For example, the previous code could be written as follows:

```
double number;
number = 5.0 / 2;
```

In this code, 5.0 is treated as a floating-point number, so the division operation will return a floating-point number. The result of the division is 2.5.

In the Spotlight:

Calculating Percentages and Discounts

Determining percentages is a common calculation in computer programming. Although the % symbol is used in general mathematics to indicate a percentage, most programming languages (including C++) do not use the % symbol for this purpose. In a program, you have to convert a percentage to a floating-point number, just as you would if you were using a calculator. For example, 50 percent would be written as 0.5, and 2 percent would be written as 0.02.

Let's look at an example. Suppose you earn $6,000 per month and you are allowed to contribute a portion of your gross monthly pay to a retirement plan. You want to determine the amount of your pay that will go into the plan if you contribute 5 percent, 7 percent, or 10 percent of your gross wages. To make this determination, you write the program shown in Program 22.

Program 22

```
// This program calculates the amount of pay that
// will be contributed to a retirement plan if 5%,
// 7%, or 10% of monthly pay is withheld.
#include <iostream>
```

```
5  using namespace std;
6
7  int main()
8  {
9      // Variables to hold the monthly pay and the
10     // amount of contribution.
11     double monthlyPay = 6000.0, contribution;
12
13     // Calculate and display a 5% contribution.
14     contribution = monthlyPay * 0.05;
15     cout << "5 percent is $" << contribution
16          << " per month.\n";
17
18     // Calculate and display a 7% contribution.
19     contribution = monthlyPay * 0.07;
20     cout << "7 percent is $" << contribution
21          << " per month.\n";
22
23     // Calculate and display a 10% contribution.
24     contribution = monthlyPay * 0.1;
25     cout << "10 percent is $" << contribution
26          << " per month.\n";
27
28     return 0;
29 }
```

Program Output

```
5  percent is $300 per month.
7  percent is $420 per month.
10 percent is $600 per month.
```

Line 11 defines two variables: `monthlyPay` and `contribution`. The `monthlyPay` variable, which is initialized with the value 6000.0, holds the amount of your monthly pay. The `contribution` variable will hold the amount of a contribution to the retirement plan.

The statements in lines 14 through 16 calculate and display 5 percent of the monthly pay. The calculation is done in line 14, where the `monthlyPay` variable is multiplied by 0.05. The result is assigned to the `contribution` variable, which is then displayed in line 15.

Similar steps are taken in lines 18 through 21, which calculate and display 7 percent of the monthly pay, and lines 24 through 26, which calculate and display 10 percent of the monthly pay.

Calculating a Percentage Discount

Another common calculation is determining a percentage discount. For example, suppose a retail business sells an item that is regularly priced at $59.95, and is planning to have a sale where the item's price will be reduced by 20 percent. You have been asked to write a program to calculate the sale price of the item.

To determine the sale price, you perform two calculations:

- First, you get the amount of the discount, which is 20 percent of the item's regular price.
- Second, you subtract the discount amount from the item's regular price. This gives you the sale price.

Program 23 shows how this is done in C++.

Program 23

```
1  // This program calculates the sale price of an item
2  // that is regularly priced at $59.95, with a 20 percent
3  // discount subtracted.
4  #include <iostream>
5  using namespace std;
6
7  int main()
8  {
9      // Variables to hold the regular price, the
10     // amount of a discount, and the sale price.
11     double regularPrice = 59.95, discount, salePrice;
12
13     // Calculate the amount of a 20% discount.
14     discount = regularPrice * 0.2;
15
16     // Calculate the sale price by subtracting the
17     // discount from the regular price.
18     salePrice = regularPrice - discount;
19
20     // Display the results.
21     cout << "Regular price: $" << regularPrice << endl;
22     cout << "Discount amount: $" << discount << endl;
23     cout << "Sale price: $" << salePrice << endl;
24     return 0;
25 }
```

Program Output

```
Regular price: $59.95
Discount amount: $11.99
Sale price: $47.96
```

Line 11 defines three variables. The `regularPrice` variable holds the item's regular price, and is initialized with the value 59.95. The `discount` variable will hold the amount of the discount once it is calculated. The `salePrice` variable will hold the item's sale price.

Line 14 calculates the amount of the 20 percent discount by multiplying `regularPrice` by 0.2. The result is stored in the `discount` variable. Line 18 calculates the sale price by subtracting `discount` from `regularPrice`. The result is stored in the `salePrice` variable. The cout statements in lines 21 through 23 display the item's regular price, the amount of the discount, and the sale price.

In the Spotlight:

Using the Modulus Operator and Integer Division

The modulus operator (%) is surprisingly useful. For example, suppose you need to extract the rightmost digit of a number. If you divide the number by 10, the remainder will be the rightmost digit. For instance, 123 ÷ 10 = 12 with a remainder of 3. In a computer program, you would use the modulus operator to perform this operation. Recall that the modulus operator divides an integer by another integer, and gives the remainder. This is demonstrated in Program 24. The program extracts the rightmost digit of the number 12345.

Program 24

```
// This program extracts the rightmost digit of a number.
#include <iostream>
using namespace std;

int main()
{
    int number = 12345;
    int rightMost = number % 10;

    cout << "The rightmost digit in "
         << number << " is "
         << rightMost << endl;

    return 0;
}
```

Program Output

```
The rightmost digit in 12345 is 5
```

Interestingly, the expression `number % 100` will give you the rightmost two digits in `number`, the expression `number % 1000` will give you the rightmost three digits in `number`, and so on.

The modulus operator (%) is useful in many other situations. For example, Program 25 converts 125 seconds to an equivalent number of minutes, and seconds.

Program 25

```
// This program converts seconds to minutes and seconds.
#include <iostream>
using namespace std;

int main()
{
    // The total seconds is 125.
```

(program continues)

Program 25 *(continued)*

```
 8      int totalSeconds = 125;
 9
10      // Variables for the minutes and seconds
11      int minutes, seconds;
12
13      // Get the number of minutes.
14      minutes = totalSeconds / 60;
15
16      // Get the remaining seconds.
17      seconds = totalSeconds % 60;
18
19      // Display the results.
20      cout << totalSeconds << " seconds is equivalent to:\n";
21      cout << "Minutes: " << minutes << endl;
22      cout << "Seconds: " << seconds << endl;
23      return 0;
24  }
```

Program Output

```
125 seconds is equivalent to:
Minutes: 2
Seconds: 5
```

Let's take a closer look at the code:

- Line 8 defines an `int` variable named `totalSeconds`, initialized with the value 125.
- Line 11 declares the `int` variables `minutes` and `seconds`.
- Line 14 calculates the number of minutes in the specified number of seconds. There are 60 seconds in a minute, so this statement divides `totalSeconds` by 60. Notice we are performing integer division in this statement. Both `totalSeconds` and the numeric literal 60 are integers, so the division operator will return an integer result. This is intentional because we want the number of minutes with no fractional part.
- Line 17 calculates the number of remaining seconds. There are 60 seconds in a minute, so this statement uses the `%` operator to divide the `totalSeconds` by 60, and get the remainder of the division. The result is the number of remaining seconds.
- Lines 20 through 22 display the number of minutes and seconds.

Checkpoint

21 Is the following assignment statement valid or invalid? If it is invalid, why?

```
72 = amount;
```

22 How would you consolidate the following definitions into one statement?

```
int x = 7;
int y = 16;
int z = 28;
```

23 What is wrong with the following program? How would you correct it?

```
#include <iostream>
using namespace std;

int main()
{
   number = 62.7;
   double number;
   cout << number << endl;
   return 0;
}
```

24 Is the following an example of integer division or floating-point division? What value will be stored in portion?

```
portion = 70 / 3;
```

15 Comments

CONCEPT: Comments are notes of explanation that document lines or sections of a program. Comments are part of the program, but the compiler ignores them. They are intended for people who may be reading the source code.

It may surprise you that one of the most important parts of a program has absolutely no impact on the way it runs. In fact, the compiler ignores this part of a program. Of course, I'm speaking of the comments.

As a beginning programmer, you might be resistant to the idea of liberally writing comments in your programs. After all, it can seem more productive to write code that actually does something! It is crucial, however, that you develop the habit of thoroughly annotating your code with descriptive comments. It might take extra time now, but it will almost certainly save time in the future.

Imagine writing a program of medium complexity with about 8,000 to 10,000 lines of C++ code. Once you have written the code and satisfactorily debugged it, you happily put it away and move on to the next project. Ten months later, you are asked to make a modification to the program (or worse, track down and fix an elusive bug). You open the file that contains your source code and stare at thousands of statements that now make no sense at all. If only you had left some notes to yourself explaining the program's code. Of course it's too late now. All that's left to do is decide what will take less time: figuring out the old program, or completely rewriting it!

This scenario might sound extreme, but it's one you don't want to happen to you. Real-world programs are big and complex. Thoroughly documented code will make your life easier, not to mention the other programmers who may have to read your code in the future.

Single-Line Comments

You have already seen one way to place comments in a C++ program. You simply place two forward slashes (//) where you want the comment to begin. The compiler ignores everything from that point to the end of the line. Program 26 shows that comments may be placed liberally throughout a program.

Program 26

```
// PROGRAM: PAYROLL.CPP
// Written by Herbert Dorfmann
// This program calculates company payroll
// Last modification: 8/20/2017
#include <iostream>
using namespace std;

int main()
{
   double payRate;     // Holds the hourly pay rate
   double hours;       // Holds the hours worked
   int employNumber;   // Holds the employee number
```

(The remainder of this program is left out.)

In addition to telling who wrote the program and describing the purpose of variables, comments can also be used to explain complex procedures in your code.

Multi-Line Comments

The second type of comment in C++ is the multi-line comment. *Multi-line comments* start with `/*` (a forward slash followed by an asterisk) and end with `*/` (an asterisk followed by a forward slash). Everything between these markers is ignored. Program 27 illustrates how multi-line comments may be used. Notice a multi-line comment starts in line 1 with the `/*` symbol, and it ends in line 6 with the `*/` symbol.

Program 27

```
1  /*
2       PROGRAM: PAYROLL.CPP
3       Written by Herbert Dorfmann
4       This program calculates company payroll
5       Last modification: 8/20/2017
6  */
7
8  #include <iostream>
9  using namespace std;
10
11 int main()
12 {
13      double payRate;        // Holds the hourly pay rate
14      double hours;          // Holds the hours worked
15      int employNumber;      // Holds the employee number
```

(The remainder of this program is left out.)

Unlike a comment started with //, a multi-line comment can span several lines. This makes it more convenient to write large blocks of comments because you do not have to mark every line. Consequently, the multi-line comment is inconvenient for writing single-line comments because you must type both a beginning and ending comment symbol.

> **NOTE:** Many programmers use a combination of single-line comments and multi-line comments in their programs. Convenience usually dictates which style to use.

Remember the following advice when using multi-line comments:

- Be careful not to reverse the beginning symbol with the ending symbol.
- Be sure not to forget the ending symbol.

Both of these mistakes can be difficult to track down and will prevent the program from compiling correctly.

16 Named Constants

CONCEPT: Literals may be given names that symbolically represent them in a program.

Assume the following statement appears in a banking program that calculates data pertaining to loans:

```
amount = balance * 0.069;
```

In such a program, two potential problems arise. First, it is not clear to anyone other than the original programmer what 0.069 is. It appears to be an interest rate, but in some situations there are fees associated with loan payments. How can the purpose of this statement be determined without painstakingly checking the rest of the program?

The second problem occurs if this number is used in other calculations throughout the program and must be changed periodically. Assuming the number is an interest rate, what if the rate changes from 6.9 percent to 7.2 percent? The programmer will have to search through the source code for every occurrence of the number.

Both of these problems can be addressed by using named constants. A *named constant* is like a variable, but its content is read-only and cannot be changed while the program is running. Here is a definition of a named constant:

```
const double INTEREST_RATE = 0.069;
```

It looks just like a regular variable definition except that the word `const` appears before the data type name, and the name of the variable is written in all uppercase characters. The key word `const` is a qualifier that tells the compiler to make the variable read-only. Its value will remain constant throughout the program's execution. It is not required that the variable name be written in all uppercase characters, but many programmers prefer to write them this way so that they are easily distinguishable from regular variable names.

An initialization value must be given when defining a constant with the `const` qualifier, or an error will result when the program is compiled. A compiler error will also result if there are any statements in the program that attempt to change the value of a named constant.

An advantage of using named constants is that they make programs more self-documenting. The statement

```
amount = balance * 0.069;
```

can be changed to read

```
amount = balance * INTEREST_RATE;
```

A new programmer can read the second statement and know what is happening. It is evident that `balance` is being multiplied by the interest rate. Another advantage to this approach is that widespread changes can easily be made to the program. Let's say the interest rate appears in a dozen different statements throughout the program. When the rate changes, the initialization value in the definition of the named constant is the only value that needs to be modified. If the rate increases to 7.2 percent, the definition is changed to the following:

```
const double INTEREST_RATE = 0.072;
```

The program is then ready to be recompiled. Every statement that uses `INTEREST_RATE` will then use the new value.

Named constants can also help prevent typographical errors in a program's code. For example, suppose you use the number 3.14159 as the value of *pi* in a program that performs various geometric calculations. Each time you type the number 3.14159 in the program's code, there is a chance that you will make a mistake with one or more of the digits. As a result, the program will not produce the correct results. To help prevent a mistake such as this, you can define a named constant for *pi*, initialized with the correct value, then use that constant in all of the formulas that require its value. Program 28 shows an example. It calculates the circumference of a circle that has a diameter of 10.

Program 28

```
// This program calculates the circumference of a circle.
#include <iostream>
using namespace std;

int main()
{
    // Constants
    const double PI = 3.14159;
    const double DIAMETER = 10.0;

    // Variable to hold the circumference
    double circumference;

    // Calculate the circumference.
    circumference = PI * DIAMETER;

    // Display the circumference.
    cout << "The circumference is: " << circumference << endl;
    return 0;
}
```

Program Output

```
The circumference is: 31.4159
```

Let's take a closer look at the program. Line 8 defines a constant `double` named `PI`, initialized with the value 3.14159. This constant will be used for the value of *pi* in the program's calculation. Line 9 defines a constant `double` named `DIAMETER`, initialized with the value 10. This will be used for the circle's diameter. Line 12 defines a `double` variable named `circumference`, which will be used to hold the circle's circumference. Line 15 calculates the circle's circumference by multiplying `PI` by `DIAMETER`. The result of the calculation is assigned to the `circumference` variable. Line 18 displays the circle's circumference.

Checkpoint

25 Write statements using the `const` qualifier to create named constants for the following literal values:

Literal Value	Description
2.71828	Euler's number (known in mathematics as *e*)
5.256E5	Number of minutes in a year
32.2	The gravitational acceleration constant (in ft/s^2)
9.8	The gravitational acceleration constant (in m/s^2)
1609	Number of meters in a mile

17 Programming Style

CONCEPT: Programming style refers to the way a programmer uses identifiers, spaces, tabs, blank lines, and punctuation characters to visually arrange a program's source code. These are some, but not all, of the elements of programming style.

Syntax rules govern the way a language may be used. The syntax rules of C++ dictate how and where to place key words, semicolons, commas, braces, and other components of the language. The compiler's job is to check for syntax errors and, if there are none, generate object code.

When the compiler reads a program, it processes it as one long stream of characters. The compiler doesn't care that each statement is on a separate line, or that spaces separate operators from operands. Humans, on the other hand, find it difficult to read programs that aren't written in a visually pleasing manner. Consider Program 29 for example.

Program 29

```
#include <iostream>
using namespace std;int main(){double shares=220.0;
double avgPrice=14.67;cout<<"There were "<<shares
<<" shares sold at $"<<avgPrice<<" per share.\n";
return 0;}
```

Program Output

```
There were 220 shares sold at $14.67 per share.
```

Although the program is syntactically correct (it doesn't violate any rules of C++), it is very difficult to read. The same program is shown in Program 30, written in a more reasonable style.

Program 30

```
// This example is much more readable than  Program 29.
#include <iostream>
using namespace std;

int main()
{
     double shares = 220.0;
     double avgPrice = 14.67;

     cout << "There were " << shares << " shares sold at $";
     cout << avgPrice << " per share.\n";
     return 0;
}
```

Program Output

```
There were 220 shares sold at $14.67 per share.
```

Programming style refers to the way source code is visually arranged. Ideally, it is a consistent method of putting spaces and indentions in a program so visual cues are created. These cues quickly tell a programmer important information about a program.

For example, notice in Program 30 that inside the function `main`'s braces each line is indented. It is a common C++ style to indent all the lines inside a set of braces. You will also notice the blank line between the variable definitions and the `cout` statements. This is intended to visually separate the definitions from the executable statements.

> **NOTE:** Although you are free to develop your own style, you should adhere to common programming practices. By doing so, you will write programs that visually make sense to other programmers.

Another aspect of programming style is how to handle statements that are too long to fit on one line. Because C++ is a free-flowing language, it is usually possible to spread a statement over several lines. For example, here is a `cout` statement that uses five lines:

```
cout << "The Fahrenheit temperature is "
     << fahrenheit
     << " and the Celsius temperature is "
     << celsius
     << endl;
```

This statement will work just as if it were typed on one line. Here is an example of variable definitions treated similarly:

```
int fahrenheit,
    celsius,
    kelvin;
```

There are many other issues related to programming style.

Review Questions and Exercises

Short Answer

1. How many operands does each of the following types of operators require?

   _______ Unary
   _______ Binary
   _______ Ternary

2. How may the `double` variables `temp`, `weight`, and `age` be defined in one statement?

3. How may the `int` variables `months`, `days`, and `years` be defined in one statement, with `months` initialized to 2 and `years` initialized to 3?

4. Write assignment statements that perform the following operations with the variables `a`, `b`, and `c`:

   A) Adds 2 to `a` and stores the result in `b`.

   B) Multiplies `b` by 4 and stores the result in `a`.

   C) Divides `a` by 3.14 and stores the result in `b`.

   D) Subtracts 8 from `b` and stores the result in `a`.

   E) Stores the value 27 in `a`.

   F) Stores the character 'K' in `c`.

   G) Stores the ASCII code for 'B' in `c`.

5. Is the following comment written using single-line or multi-line comment symbols?

```
/* This program was written by M. A. Codewriter*/
```

6. Is the following comment written using single-line or multi-line comment symbols?

```
// This program was written by M. A. Codewriter
```

7. Modify the following program so it prints two blank lines between each line of text.

```
#include <iostream>
using namespace std;
int main()
{
    cout << "Two mandolins like creatures in the";
    cout << "dark";
    cout << "Creating the agony of ecstasy.";
    cout << "                          - George Barker";
    return 0;
}
```

8. What will the following programs print on the screen?

   A)
```
#include <iostream>
using namespace std;
int main()
{
    int freeze = 32, boil = 212;
```

```
        freeze = 0;
        boil = 100;
        cout << freeze << endl << boil << endl;
        return 0;
    }
```

B)
```
#include <iostream>
using namespace std;

int main()
{
    int x = 0, y = 2;
    x = y * 4;
    cout << x << endl << y << endl;
    return 0;
}
```

C)
```
#include <iostream>
using namespace std;

int main()
{
    cout << "I am the incredible";
    cout << "computing\nmachine";
    cout << "\nand I will\namaze\n";
    cout << "you.";
    return 0;
}
```

D)
```
#include <iostream>
using namespace std;

int main()
{
    cout << "Be careful\n";
    cout << "This might/n be a trick ";
    cout << "question\n";
    return 0;
}
```

E)
```
#include <iostream>
using namespace std;

int main()
{
    int a, x = 23;
    a = x % 2;
    cout << x << endl << a << endl;
    return 0;
}
```

Multiple Choice

9. Every complete statement ends with a(n) ________.

   A) period
   B) # symbol
   C) semicolon
   D) ending brace

10. Which of the following statements is correct?

    A) #include (iostream)
    B) #include {iostream}
    C) #include <iostream>
    D) #include [iostream]
    E) All of the above

11. Every C++ program must have a ________.

    A) cout statement
    B) function main
    C) #include statement
    D) All of the above

12. Preprocessor directives begin with ________.

    A) #
    B) !
    C) <
    D) *
    E) None of the above

13. The following data

    72
    'A'
    "Hello World"
    2.8712

    are all examples of ________.

    A) variables
    B) literals or constants
    C) strings
    D) none of the above

14. A group of statements, such as the contents of a function, is enclosed in ________.

    A) braces { }
    B) parentheses ( )
    C) brackets <>
    D) all of the above will do

15. Which of the following are *not* valid assignment statements? (Select all that apply.)

    A) total = 9;
    B) 72 = amount;
    C) profit = 129
    D) letter = 'W';

16. Which of the following are *not* valid `cout` statements? (Select all that apply.)

    A) `cout << "Hello World";`
    B) `cout << "Have a nice day"\n;`
    C) `cout < value;`
    D) `cout << Programming is great fun;`

17. Assume `w = 5`, `x = 4`, `y = 8`, and `z = 2`. What value will be stored in `result` in each of the following statements?

    A) `result = x + y;`
    B) `result = z * 2;`
    C) `result = y / x;`
    D) `result = y - z;`
    E) `result = w % 2;`

18. How would each of the following numbers be represented in E notation?

    A) 3.287×10^{6}
    B) -978.65×10^{12}
    C) 7.65491×10^{-3}
    D) -58710.23×10^{-4}

19. The negation operator is ________.

    A) unary
    B) binary
    C) ternary
    D) none of the above

20. A(n) __________ is like a variable, but its value is read-only and cannot be changed during the program's execution.

    A) secure variable
    B) uninitialized variable
    C) named constant
    D) locked variable

21. When do preprocessor directives execute?

    A) Before the compiler compiles your program
    B) After the compiler compiles your program
    C) At the same time as the compiler compiles your program
    D) None of the above

True or False

22. T F A variable must be defined before it can be used.
23. T F Variable names may begin with a number.
24. T F Variable names may be up to 31 characters long.
25. T F A left brace in a C++ program should always be followed by a right brace later in the program.
26. T F You cannot initialize a named constant that is declared with the `const` modifier.

Algorithm Workbench

27. Convert the following *pseudocode* to C++ code. Be sure to define the appropriate variables.

    Store 20 in the *speed* variable.
    Store 10 in the *time* variable.
    Multiply *speed* by *time* and store the result in the *distance* variable.
    Display the contents of the *distance* variable.

28. Convert the following *pseudocode* to C++ code. Be sure to define the appropriate variables.

    Store 172.5 in the *force* variable.
    Store 27.5 in the *area* variable.
    Divide *area* by *force* and store the result in the *pressure* variable.
    Display the contents of the *pressure* variable.

Find the Error

29. There are a number of syntax errors in the following program. Locate as many as you can.

```
*/ What's wrong with this program? /*
#include iostream
using namespace std;
int main();
}
    int a, b, c \\ Three integers
    a = 3
    b = 4
    c = a + b
    Cout < "The value of c is %d" < C;
    return 0;
{
```

Programming Challenges

Visit www.myprogramminglab.com to complete many of these Programming Challenges online and get instant feedback.

1. Sum of Two Numbers

Write a program that stores the integers 50 and 100 in variables, and stores the sum of these two in a variable named `total`.

2. Sales Prediction

The East Coast sales division of a company generates 58 percent of total sales. Based on that percentage, write a program that will predict how much the East Coast division will generate if the company has $8.6 million in sales this year.

3. Sales Tax

Write a program that will compute the total sales tax on a $95 purchase. Assume the state sales tax is 4 percent, and the county sales tax is 2 percent.

VideoNote
Solving the Restaurant Bill Problem

4. Restaurant Bill

Write a program that computes the tax and tip on a restaurant bill for a patron with a $88.67 meal charge. The tax should be 6.75 percent of the meal cost. The tip should be 20 percent of the total after adding the tax. Display the meal cost, tax amount, tip amount, and total bill on the screen.

5. **Average of Values**

To get the average of a series of values, you add the values up then divide the sum by the number of values. Write a program that stores the following values in five different variables: 28, 32, 37, 24, and 33. The program should first calculate the sum of these five variables and store the result in a separate variable named `sum`. Then, the program should divide the `sum` variable by 5 to get the average. Display the average on the screen.

> **TIP:** Use the `double` data type for all variables in this program.

6. **Annual Pay**

Suppose an employee gets paid every two weeks and earns $2,200 each pay period. In a year, the employee gets paid 26 times. Write a program that defines the following variables:

`payAmount`	This variable will hold the amount of pay the employee earns each pay period. Initialize the variable with 2200.0.
`payPeriods`	This variable will hold the number of pay periods in a year. Initialize the variable with 26.
`annualPay`	This variable will hold the employee's total annual pay, which will be calculated.

The program should calculate the employee's total annual pay by multiplying the employee's pay amount by the number of pay periods in a year and store the result in the `annualPay` variable. Display the total annual pay on the screen.

7. **Ocean Levels**

Assuming the ocean's level is currently rising at about 1.5 millimeters per year, write a program that displays:

- The number of millimeters higher than the current level that the ocean's level will be in 5 years.
- The number of millimeters higher than the current level that the ocean's level will be in 7 years.
- The number of millimeters higher than the current level that the ocean's level will be in 10 years.

8. **Total Purchase**

A customer in a store is purchasing five items. The prices of the five items are as follows:

Price of item 1 = $15.95
Price of item 2 = $24.95
Price of item 3 = $6.95
Price of item 4 = $12.95
Price of item 5 = $3.95

Write a program that holds the prices of the five items in five variables. Display each item's price, the subtotal of the sale, the amount of sales tax, and the total. Assume the sales tax is 7 percent.

9. Cyborg Data Type Sizes

You have been given a job as a programmer on a Cyborg supercomputer. In order to accomplish some calculations, you need to know how many bytes the following data types use: `char`, `int`, `float`, and `double`. You do not have any technical documentation, so you can't look this information up. Write a C++ program that will determine the amount of memory used by these types and display the information on the screen.

10. Miles per Gallon

A car holds 15 gallons of gasoline and can travel 375 miles before refueling. Write a program that calculates the number of miles per gallon the car gets. Display the result on the screen.

Hint: Use the following formula to calculate miles per gallon (MPG):

MPG = Miles Driven/Gallons of Gas Used

11. Distance per Tank of Gas

A car with a 20-gallon gas tank averages 23.5 miles per gallon when driven in town, and 28.9 miles per gallon when driven on the highway. Write a program that calculates and displays the distance the car can travel on one tank of gas when driven in town and when driven on the highway.

Hint: The following formula can be used to calculate the distance:

Distance = Number of Gallons × Average Miles per Gallon

12. Land Calculation

One acre of land is equivalent to 43,560 square feet. Write a program that calculates the number of acres in a tract of land with 391,876 square feet.

13. Circuit Board Price

An electronics company sells circuit boards at a 35 percent profit. Write a program that will calculate the selling price of a circuit board that costs $14.95. Display the result on the screen.

14. Personal Information

Write a program that displays the following pieces of information, each on a separate line:

Your name
Your address, with city, state, and ZIP code
Your telephone number
Your college major

Use only a single `cout` statement to display all of this information.

15. Triangle Pattern

Write a program that displays the following pattern on the screen:

```
   *
  ***
 *****
*******
```

16. Diamond Pattern

Write a program that displays the following pattern:

```
   *
  ***
 *****
*******
 *****
  ***
   *
```

17. Stock Commission

Kathryn bought 750 shares of stock at a price of $35.00 per share. She must pay her stockbroker a 2 percent commission for the transaction. Write a program that calculates and displays the following:

- The amount paid for the stock alone (without the commission).
- The amount of the commission.
- The total amount paid (for the stock plus the commission).

18. Energy Drink Consumption

A soft drink company recently surveyed 16,500 of its customers and found that approximately 15 percent of those surveyed purchase one or more energy drinks per week. Of those customers who purchase energy drinks, approximately 58 percent of them prefer citrus-flavored energy drinks. Write a program that displays the following:

- The approximate number of customers in the survey who purchase one or more energy drinks per week.
- The approximate number of customers in the survey who prefer citrus-flavored energy drinks.

19. Annual High Temperatures

The average July high temperature is 85 degrees Fahrenheit in New York City, 88 degrees Fahrenheit in Denver, and 106 degrees Fahrenheit in Phoenix. Write a program that calculates and reports what the new average July high temperature would be for each of these cities if temperatures rise by 2 percent.

20. How Much Paint

A particular brand of paint covers 340 square feet per gallon. Write a program to determine and report approximately how many gallons of paint will be needed to paint two coats on a wooden fence that is 6 feet high and 100 feet long.

Answers to Checkpoints

1
```
// A crazy mixed up program
#include <iostream>
using namespace std;
```

```
int main()
{
    cout << "In 1492 Columbus sailed the ocean blue.";
    return 0;
}
```

2

```
// It's a mad, mad program
#include <iostream>
using namespace std;

int main()
{
    cout << "Success\n";
    cout << "Success";
    cout << " Success\n\n";
    cout << "Sucess\n";
    return 0;
}
```

3

```
The works of Wolfgang
include the following
The Turkish March
and Symphony No. 40 in G minor.
```

4

```
// Today's Date: September 3, 2012
#include <iostream>
using namespace std;

int main()
{
    cout << "Teresa Jones\n";
    cout << "127 West 423rd Street\n";
    cout << "San Antonio, TX 55555\n";
    cout << "555-555-1212\n";
    return 0;
}
```

5 Variables: `little` and `big`.

Constants: 2, 2000, "The little number is ", "The big number is "

6 The value is number.

7 `99bottles`: Variable names cannot begin with a number.

`r&d`: Variable names may only use alphabetic letters, digits, or underscores.

8 No. Variable names are case sensitive.

9 A) `short`, or `unsigned short`.
B) `int`
C) They both use the same amount of memory.

10 They both use the same amount of memory.

11 67, 70, 87

12 'B'

13 'Q' uses one byte

"Q" uses two bytes

"Sales" uses six bytes

'\n' uses one byte

14
```
#include <iostream>
using namespace std;

int main()
{
    char first, middle, last;
    first = 'T';
    middle = 'E';
    last = 'G';
    cout << first << " " << middle << " " << last << endl;
    return 0;
}
```

15 The string constant "Z" is being stored in the character variable `letter`.

16 The `string` header file

17
```
#include <iostream>
#include <string>
using namespace std;

int main()
{
    string name = "John Smith";
    string address = "224 Maple Street\nClyde, NC 28721";
    string phone = "555-5050";

    cout << name << endl;
    cout << address << endl;
    cout << phone << endl << endl;
    return 0;
}
```

18 No

19 6.31E17

20
```
#include <iostream>
using namespace std;
```

```
int main()
{
    int age;
    float weight;

    age = 26;
    weight = 180;
    cout << "My age is " << age << endl;
    cout << "My weight is " << weight << endl;
    return 0;
}
```

21 Invalid. The value on the left of the = operator must be an lvalue.

22 `int x = 7, y = 16, z = 28;`

23 The variable `number` is assigned a value before it is defined. Correct the program by moving the statement `number = 62.7;` to the point after the variable declaration. Here is the corrected program:

```
#include <iostream>
using namespace std;

int main()
{
    double number;
    number = 62.7;
    cout << number << endl;
    return 0;
}
```

24 Integer division. The value 23 will be stored in `portion`.

25
```
const float E = 2.71828;
const int MINUTES_IN_A_YEAR = 5.256E5;
const float G_FEET = 32.2;
const float G_METERS = 9.8;
const int METERS_IN_A_MILE = 1609
```

Answers to Odd Numbered Review Questions

1. 1, 2, 3
3. `int months = 2, days, years = 3;`
5. Multi-line comment

7.
```
#include <iostream>
int main()
{
    cout << "Two mandolins like creatures in the\n\n\n";
    cout << "dark\n\n\n";
    cout << "Creating the agony of ecstasy.\n\n\n";
    cout << " - George Barker\n\n\n";
    return 0;
}
```

9. C
11. B
13. B
15. B, C
17. A) 12
    B) 4
    C) 2
    D) 6
    E) 1
19. A
21. A
23. False
25. True
27.
```
int speed, time, distance;
speed = 20;
time = 10;
distance = speed * time;
cout << distance << endl;
```

29. The C-style comments symbols are backwards.
`iostream` should be enclosed in angle brackets.
There shouldn't be a semicolon after `int main`.
The opening and closing braces of function main are reversed.
There should be a semicolon after `int a, b, c`.
The comment `\\ Three integers` should read `// Three integers`.
There should be a semicolon at the end of the following lines:

```
a = 3
b = 4
c = a + b
```

`cout` begins with a capital letter.
The stream insertion operator (that appears twice in the `cout` statement) should read `<<` instead of `<`.
The `cout` statement uses the variable `C` instead of `c`.

Credits

Expressions and Interactivity

TOPICS

1 The cin Object

CONCEPT: The cin object can be used to read data typed at the keyboard.

So far you have written programs with built-in data. Without giving the user an opportunity to enter his or her own data, you have initialized the variables with the necessary starting values. These types of programs are limited to performing their task with only a single set of starting data. If you decide to change the initial value of any variable, the program must be modified and recompiled.

VideoNote
Reading Input with cin

In reality, most programs ask for values that will be assigned to variables. This means the program does not have to be modified if the user wants to run it several times with different sets of data. For example, a program that calculates payroll for a small business might ask the user to enter the name of the employee, the hours worked, and the hourly pay rate. When the paycheck for that employee has been printed, the program could start over again and ask for the name, hours worked, and hourly pay rate of the next employee.

Just as cout is C++'s standard output object, cin is the standard input object. It reads input from the console (or keyboard) as shown in Program 1.

From Chapter 3 of *Starting Out with C++: From Control Structures through Objects*, Ninth Edition. Tony Gaddis.

Program 1

```
1  // This program asks the user to enter the length and width of
2  // a rectangle. It calculates the rectangle's area and displays
3  // the value on the screen.
4  #include <iostream>
5  using namespace std;
6
7  int main()
8  {
9      int length, width, area;
10
11     cout << "This program calculates the area of a ";
12     cout << "rectangle.\n";
13     cout << "What is the length of the rectangle? ";
14     cin >> length;
15     cout << "What is the width of the rectangle? ";
16     cin >> width;
17     area = length * width;
18     cout << "The area of the rectangle is " << area << ".\n";
19     return 0;
20 }
```

Program Output with Example Input Shown in Bold

```
This program calculates the area of a rectangle.
What is the length of the rectangle? 10 [Enter]
What is the width of the rectangle? 20 [Enter]
The area of the rectangle is 200.
```

Instead of calculating the area of one rectangle, this program can be used to get the area of any rectangle. The values that are stored in the `length` and `width` variables are entered by the user when the program is running. Look at lines 13 and 14:

```
cout << "What is the length of the rectangle? ";
cin >> length;
```

In line 13, the `cout` object is used to display the question "What is the length of the rectangle?" This question is known as a *prompt*, and it tells the user what data he or she should enter. Your program should always display a prompt before it uses `cin` to read input. This way, the user will know that he or she must type a value at the keyboard.

Line 14 uses the `cin` object to read a value from the keyboard. The >> symbol is the *stream extraction operator*. It gets characters from the stream object on its left and stores them in the variable whose name appears on its right. In this line, characters are taken from the `cin` object (which gets them from the keyboard) and are stored in the `length` variable.

Gathering input from the user is normally a two-step process:

1. Use the `cout` object to display a prompt on the screen.
2. Use the `cin` object to read a value from the keyboard.

The prompt should ask the user a question, or tell the user to enter a specific value. For example, the code we just examined from Program 1 displays the following prompt:

```
What is the length of the rectangle?
```

When the user sees this prompt, he or she knows to enter the rectangle's length. After the prompt is displayed, the program uses the `cin` object to read a value from the keyboard and store the value in the `length` variable.

Notice the << and >> operators appear to point in the direction that data is flowing. In a statement that uses the `cout` object, the << operator always points toward `cout`. This indicates that data is flowing from a variable or a literal to the `cout` object. In a statement that uses the `cin` object, the >> operator always points toward the variable that is receiving the value. This indicates that data is flowing from `cin` to a variable. This is illustrated in Figure 1.

Figure 1 The << and >> operators

```
cout << "What is the length of the rectangle? ";
cin >> length;
```

Think of the << and >> operators as arrows that point in the direction that data is flowing.

```
cout ← "What is the length of the rectangle? ";
cin → length;
```

The `cin` object causes a program to wait until data is typed at the keyboard and the [Enter] key is pressed. No other lines in the program will be executed until `cin` gets its input.

`cin` automatically converts the data read from the keyboard to the data type of the variable used to store it. If the user types 10, it is read as the characters '1' and '0'. `cin` is smart enough to know this will have to be converted to an `int` value before it is stored in the `length` variable. `cin` is also smart enough to know a value like 10.7 cannot be stored in an integer variable. If the user enters a floating-point value for an integer variable, `cin` will not read the part of the number after the decimal point.

NOTE: You must include the `<iostream>` header file in any program that uses `cin`.

Entering Multiple Values

The `cin` object may be used to gather multiple values at once. Look at Program 2, which is a modified version of Program 1.

Line 15 waits for the user to enter two values. The first is assigned to `length` and the second to `width`.

```
cin >> length >> width;
```

Program 2

```
// This program asks the user to enter the length and width of
// a rectangle. It calculates the rectangle's area and displays
// the value on the screen.
#include <iostream>
using namespace std;

int main()
{
    int length, width, area;

    cout << "This program calculates the area of a ";
    cout << "rectangle.\n";
    cout << "Enter the length and width of the rectangle ";
    cout << "separated by a space.\n";
    cin >> length >> width;
    area = length * width;
    cout << "The area of the rectangle is " << area << endl;
    return 0;
}
```

Program Output with Example Input Shown in Bold

```
This program calculates the area of a rectangle.
Enter the length and width of the rectangle separated by a space.
10 20 [Enter]
The area of the rectangle is 200
```

In the example output, the user entered 10 and 20, so 10 is stored in `length` and 20 is stored in `width`.

Notice the user separates the numbers by spaces as they are entered. This is how `cin` knows where each number begins and ends. It doesn't matter how many spaces are entered between the individual numbers. For example, the user could have entered

```
10          20
```

NOTE: The [Enter] key is pressed after the last number is entered.

`cin` will also read multiple values of different data types. This is shown in Program 3.

Program 3

```
// This program demonstrates how cin can read multiple values
// of different data types.
#include <iostream>
using namespace std;

```

```
int main()
{
    int whole;
    double fractional;
    char letter;

    cout << "Enter an integer, a double, and a character: ";
    cin >> whole >> fractional >> letter;
    cout << "Whole: " << whole << endl;
    cout << "Fractional: " << fractional << endl;
    cout << "Letter: " << letter << endl;
    return 0;
}
```

Program Output with Example Input Shown in Bold

```
Enter an integer, a double, and a character: 4 5.7 b [Enter]
Whole: 4
Fractional: 5.7
Letter: b
```

As you can see in the example output, the values are stored in their respective variables. But what if the user had responded in the following way?

```
Enter an integer, a double, and a character: 5.7 4 b [Enter]
```

When the user types values at the keyboard, those values are first stored in an area of memory known as the *keyboard buffer*. So, when the user enters the values 5.7, 4, and b, they are stored in the keyboard buffer as shown in Figure 2.

Figure 2 The keyboard buffer

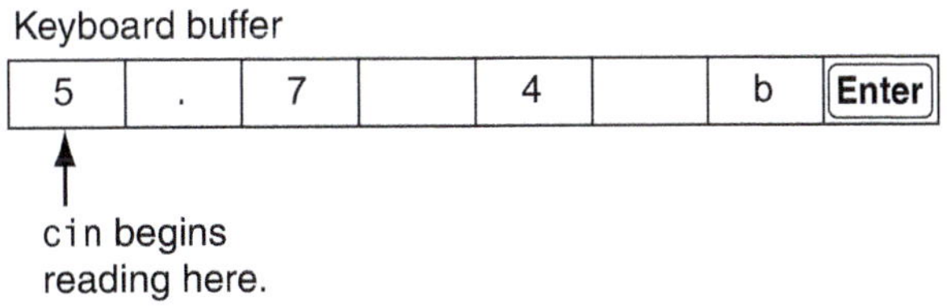

When the user presses the [Enter] key, `cin` reads the value 5 into the variable `whole`. It does not read the decimal point because `whole` is an integer variable. Next it reads .7 and stores that value in the `double` variable `fractional`. The space is skipped, and 4 is the next value read. It is stored as a character in the variable `letter`. Because this `cin` statement reads only three values, the b is left in the keyboard buffer. So, in this situation the program would have stored 5 in `whole`, 0.7 in `fractional`, and the character '4' in `letter`. It is important that the user enters values in the correct order.

Checkpoint

1 What header file must be included in programs using `cin`?

2 True or false: `cin` requires the user to press the [Enter] key when finished entering data.

3 Assume `value` is an integer variable. If the user enters 3.14 in response to the following programming statement, what will be stored in `value`?

```
cin >> value;
```

A) 3.14

B) 3

C) 0

D) Nothing. An error message is displayed.

4 A program has the following variable definitions.

```
long miles;
int feet;
float inches;
```

Write one `cin` statement that reads a value into each of these variables.

5 The following program will run, but the user will have difficulty understanding what to do. How would you improve the program?

```
// This program multiplies two numbers and displays the result.
#include <iostream>
using namespace std;

int main()
{
   double first, second, product;

   cin >> first >> second;
   product = first * second;
   cout << product;
   return 0;
}
```

6 Complete the following program skeleton so it asks for the user's weight (in pounds) and displays the equivalent weight in kilograms.

```
#include <iostream>
using namespace std;

int main()
{
   double pounds, kilograms;

   // Write code here that prompts the user
   // to enter his or her weight and reads
   // the input into the pounds variable.

   // The following line does the conversion.
   kilograms = pounds / 2.2;

   // Write code here that displays the user's weight
   // in kilograms.
   return 0;
}
```

2 Mathematical Expressions

CONCEPT: C++ allows you to construct complex mathematical expressions using multiple operators and grouping symbols.

An *expression* is a programming statement that has a value. Usually, an expression consists of an operator and its operands. Look at the following statement:

```
sum = 21 + 3;
```

Since 21 + 3 has a value, it is an expression. Its value, 24, is stored in the variable sum. Expressions do not have to be in the form of mathematical operations. In the following statement, 3 is an expression.

```
number = 3;
```

Here are some programming statements where the variable result is being assigned the value of an expression:

```
result = x;
result = 4;
result = 15 / 3;
result = 22 * number;
result = sizeof(int);
result = a + b + c;
```

In each of these statements, a number, variable name, or mathematical expression appears on the right side of the = symbol. A value is obtained from each of these and stored in the variable result. These are all examples of a variable being assigned the value of an expression.

Program 4 shows how mathematical expressions can be used with the cout object.

Program 4

```
// This program asks the user to enter the numerator
// and denominator of a fraction and it displays the
// decimal value.

#include <iostream>
using namespace std;

int main()
{
    double numerator, denominator;

    cout << "This program shows the decimal value of ";
    cout << "a fraction.\n";
```

(program continues)

Program 4 *(continued)*

```
    cout << "Enter the numerator: ";
    cin >> numerator;
    cout << "Enter the denominator: ";
    cin >> denominator;
    cout << "The decimal value is ";
    cout << (numerator / denominator) << endl;
    return 0;
}
```

Program Output with Example Input Shown in Bold

```
This program shows the decimal value of a fraction.
Enter the numerator: 3 [Enter]
Enter the denominator: 16 [Enter]
The decimal value is 0.1875
```

The `cout` object will display the value of any legal expression in C++. In Program 4, the value of the expression `numerator / denominator` is displayed.

> **NOTE:** The example input for Program 4 shows the user entering 3 and 16. Since these values are assigned to `double` variables, they are stored as the `double` values 3.0 and 16.0.

> **NOTE:** When sending an expression that consists of an operator to `cout`, it is always a good idea to put parentheses around the expression. Some advanced operators will yield unexpected results otherwise.

Operator Precedence

It is possible to build mathematical expressions with several operators. The following statement assigns the sum of 17, `x`, 21, and `y` to the variable `answer`.

```
answer = 17 + x + 21 + y;
```

Some expressions are not that straightforward, however. Consider the following statement:

```
outcome = 12 + 6 / 3;
```

What value will be stored in `outcome`? 6 is used as an operand for both the addition and division operators. `outcome` could be assigned either 6 or 14, depending on whether the addition operation or the division operation takes place first. The answer is 14 because the division operator has higher *precedence* than the addition operator.

Mathematical expressions are evaluated from left to right. When two operators share an operand, the operator with the highest precedence works first. Multiplication and division have higher precedence than addition and subtraction, so the statement above works like this:

A) 6 is divided by 3, yielding a result of 2
B) 12 is added to 2, yielding a result of 14

It could be diagrammed in the following way:

```
outcome = 12 + 6 / 3
                \ /
outcome = 12 +   2

outcome = 14
```

Table 1 shows the precedence of the arithmetic operators. The operators at the top of the table have higher precedence than the ones below them.

Table 1 Precedence of Arithmetic Operators (Highest to Lowest)

(unary negation) -
* / %
+ -

The multiplication, division, and modulus operators have the same precedence. This is also true of the addition and subtraction operators. Table 2 shows some expressions with their values.

Table 2 Some Simple Expressions and Their Values

Expression	Value
5 + 2 * 4	13
10 / 2 - 3	2
8 + 12 * 2 - 4	28
4 + 17 % 2 - 1	4
6 - 3 * 2 + 7 - 1	6

Associativity

An operator's *associativity* is either left to right, or right to left. If two operators sharing an operand have the same precedence, they work according to their associativity. Table 3 lists the associativity of the arithmetic operators. As an example, look at the following expression:

```
5 - 3 + 2
```

Both the - and + operators in this expression have the same precedence, and they have left to right associativity. So, the operators will work from left to right. This expression is the same as:

```
((5 - 3) + 2)
```

Here is another example:

```
12 / 6 * 4
```

Because the / and * operators have the same precedence, and they have left to right associativity, they will work from left to right. This expression is the same as:

```
((12 / 6) * 4)
```

Table 3 Associativity of Arithmetic Operators

Operator	Associativity
(unary negation) -	Right to left
`* / %`	Left to right
`+ -`	Left to right

Grouping with Parentheses

Parts of a mathematical expression may be grouped with parentheses to force some operations to be performed before others. In the following statement, the sum of a + b is divided by 4.

```
result = (a + b) / 4;
```

Without the parentheses, however, b would be divided by 4 and the result added to a. Table 4 shows more expressions and their values.

Table 4 More Simple Expressions and Their Values

Expression	Value
`(5 + 2) * 4`	28
`10 / (5 - 3)`	5
`8 + 12 * (6 - 2)`	56
`(4 + 17) % 2 - 1`	0
`(6 - 3) * (2 + 7) / 3`	9

Converting Algebraic Expressions to Programming Statements

In algebra, it is not always necessary to use an operator for multiplication. C++, however, requires an operator for any mathematical operation. Table 5 shows some algebraic expressions that perform multiplication and the equivalent C++ expressions.

Table 5 Algebraic and C++ Multiplication Expressions

Algebraic Expression	Operation	C++ Equivalent
$6B$	6 times B	`6 * B`
(3)(12)	3 times 12	`3 * 12`
$4xy$	4 times x times y	`4 * x * y`

When converting some algebraic expressions to C++, you may have to insert parentheses that do not appear in the algebraic expression. For example, look at the following expression:

$$x = \frac{a + b}{c}$$

To convert this to a C++ statement, $a + b$ will have to be enclosed in parentheses:

```
x = (a + b) / c;
```

Table 6 shows more algebraic expressions and their C++ equivalents.

Table 6 Algebraic and C++ Expressions

Algebraic Expression	C++ Expression
$y = 3\frac{x}{2}$	`y = x / 2 * 3;`
$z = 3bc + 4$	`z = 3 * b * c + 4;`
$a = \frac{3x + 2}{4a - 1}$	`a = (3 * x + 2) / (4 * a - 1)`

No Exponents Please!

Unlike many programming languages, C++ does not have an exponent operator. Raising a number to a power requires the use of a *library function*. The C++ library isn't a place where you check out books, but a collection of specialized functions. Think of a library function as a "routine" that performs a specific operation. One of the library functions is called `pow`, and its purpose is to raise a number to a power. Here is an example of how it's used:

```
area = pow(4.0, 2.0);
```

This statement contains a *call* to the `pow` function. The numbers inside the parentheses are *arguments*. Arguments are data being sent to the function. The `pow` function always raises the first argument to the power of the second argument. In this example, 4 is raised to the power of 2. The result is *returned* from the function and used in the statement where the function call appears. In this case, the value 16 is returned from `pow` and assigned to the variable `area`. This is illustrated in Figure 3.

Figure 3 The pow function

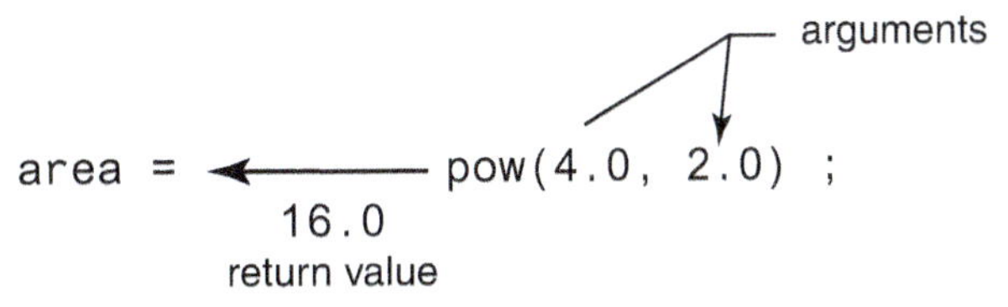

The statement `area = pow(4.0, 2.0)` is equivalent to the following algebraic statement:

$$area = 4^2$$

Here is another example of a statement using the `pow` function. It assigns 3 times 6^3 to `x`:

```
x = 3 * pow(6.0, 3.0);
```

And the following statement displays the value of 5 raised to the power of 4:

```
cout << pow(5.0, 4.0);
```

It might be helpful to think of `pow` as a "black box" that you plug two numbers into, and that then sends a third number out. The number that comes out has the value of the first number raised to the power of the second number, as illustrated in Figure 4:

Figure 4 The pow function as a "black box"

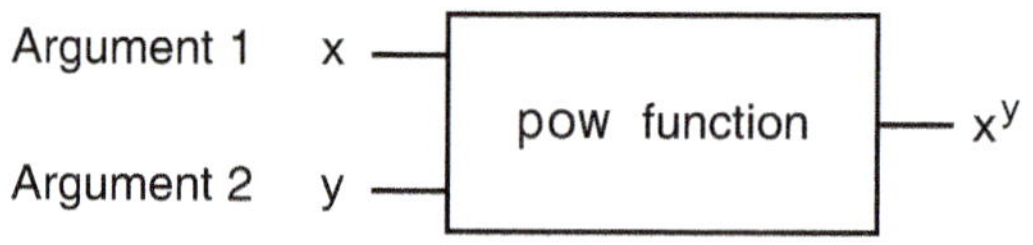

There are some guidelines that should be followed when the pow function is used. First, the program must include the <cmath> header file. Second, the arguments that you pass to the pow function should be doubles. Third, the variable used to store pow's return value should be defined as a double. For example, in the following statement the variable area should be a double:

```
area = pow(4.0, 2.0);
```

Program 5 solves a simple algebraic problem. It asks the user to enter the radius of a circle and then calculates the area of the circle. The formula is

$$\text{Area} = \pi r^2$$

which is expressed in the program as

```
area = PI * pow(radius, 2.0);
```

Program 5

```
// This program calculates the area of a circle.
// The formula for the area of a circle is Pi times
// the radius squared. Pi is 3.14159.
#include <iostream>
#include <cmath> // needed for pow function
using namespace std;

int main()
{
    const double PI = 3.14159;
    double area, radius;

    cout << "This program calculates the area of a circle.\n";
    cout << "What is the radius of the circle? ";
    cin >> radius;
    area = PI * pow(radius, 2.0);
    cout << "The area is " << area << endl;
    return 0;
}
```

Program Output with Example Input Shown in Bold

```
This program calculates the area of a circle.
What is the radius of the circle? 10 [Enter]
The area is 314.159
```

NOTE: Program 5 is presented as a demonstration of the pow function. In reality, there is no reason to use the pow function in such a simple operation. The math statement could just as easily be written as

```
area = PI * radius * radius;
```

The pow function is useful, however, in operations that involve larger exponents.

In the Spotlight:

Calculating an Average

Determining the average of a group of values is a simple calculation: You add all of the values, then divide the sum by the number of values. Although this is a straightforward calculation, it is easy to make a mistake when writing a program that calculates an average. For example, let's assume that a, b, and c are double variables. Each of the variables holds a value, and we want to calculate the average of those values. If we are careless, we might write a statement such as the following to perform the calculation:

```
average = a + b + c / 3.0;
```

Can you see the error in this statement? When it executes, the division will take place first. The value in c will be divided by 3.0, then the result will be added to the sum of a + b. That is not the correct way to calculate an average. To correct this error, we need to put parentheses around a + b + c, as shown here:

```
average = (a + b + c) / 3.0;
```

Let's step through the process of writing a program that calculates an average. Suppose you have taken three tests in your computer science class, and you want to write a program that will display the average of the test scores. Here is the algorithm in pseudocode:

Get the first test score.
Get the second test score.
Get the third test score.
Calculate the average by adding the three test scores and dividing the sum by 3.
Display the average.

In the first three steps, we prompt the user to enter three test scores. Let's say we store those test scores in the double variables test1, test2, and test3. Then in the fourth step, we calculate the average of the three test scores. We will use the following statement to perform the calculation and store the result in the average variable, which is a double:

```
average = (test1 + test2 + test3) / 3.0;
```

The last step is to display the average. Program 6 shows the program.

Program 6

```
// This program calculates the average
// of three test scores.
#include <iostream>
#include <cmath>
using namespace std;

int main()
{
    double test1, test2, test3;   // To hold the scores
    double average;               // To hold the average

    // Get the three test scores.
    cout << "Enter the first test score: ";
    cin >> test1;
    cout << "Enter the second test score: ";
    cin >> test2;
    cout << "Enter the third test score: ";
    cin >> test3;

    // Calculate the average of the scores.
    average = (test1 + test2 + test3) / 3.0;

    // Display the average.
    cout << "The average score is: " << average << endl;
    return 0;
}
```

Program Output with Example Input Shown in Bold

```
Enter the first test score: 90 [Enter]
Enter the second test score: 80 [Enter]
Enter the third test score: 100 [Enter]
The average score is 90
```

Checkpoint

7 Complete the table below by determining the value of each expression.

Expression	Value
`6 + 3 * 5`	
`12 / 2 - 4`	
`9 + 14 * 2 - 6`	
`5 + 19 % 3 - 1`	
`(6 + 2) * 3`	
`14 / (11 - 4)`	
`9 + 12 * (8 - 3)`	
`(6 + 17) % 2 - 1`	
`(9 - 3) * (6 + 9) / 3`	

8 Write C++ expressions for the following algebraic expressions:

$y = 6x$

$a = 2b + 4c$

$y = x^2$

$g = \dfrac{x + 2}{z^2}$

$y = \dfrac{x^2}{z^2}$

9 Study the following program and complete the table.

```
#include <iostream>
#include <cmath>
using namespace std;

int main()
{
    double value1, value2, value3;

    cout << "Enter a number: ";
    cin >> value1;
    value2 = 2 * pow(value1, 2.0);
    value3 = 3 + value2 / 2 - 1;
    cout << value3 << endl;
    return 0;
}
```

If the User Enters...	The Program Will Display What Number (Stored in `value3`)?
2	
5	
4.3	
6	

10 Complete the following program skeleton so it displays the volume of a cylindrical fuel tank. The formula for the volume of a cylinder is

Volume = $\pi r^2 h$

where

π is 3.14159,
r is the radius of the tank, and
h is the height of the tank.

```
#include <iostream>
#include <cmath>
using namespace std;
```

```
int main()
{
    double volume, radius, height;
    cout << "This program will tell you the volume of\n";
    cout << "a cylinder-shaped fuel tank.\n";
    cout << "How tall is the tank? ";
    cin >> height;
    cout << "What is the radius of the tank? ";
    cin >> radius;
    // You must complete the program.
}
```

3 When You Mix Apples and Oranges: Type Conversion

CONCEPT: When an operator's operands are of different data types, C++ will automatically convert them to the same data type. This can affect the results of mathematical expressions.

If an `int` is multiplied by a `float`, what data type will the result be? What if a `double` is divided by an `unsigned int`? Is there any way of predicting what will happen in these instances? The answer is yes. C++ follows a set of rules when performing mathematical operations on variables of different data types. It's helpful to understand these rules to prevent subtle errors from creeping into your programs.

Just like officers in the military, data types are ranked. One data type outranks another if it can hold a larger number. For example, a `float` outranks an `int`. Table 7 lists the data types in order of their rank, from highest to lowest.

Table 7 Data Type Ranking

`long double`
`double`
`float`
`unsigned long long int`
`long long int`
`unsigned long int`
`long int`
`unsigned int`
`int`

One exception to the ranking in Table 7 is when an `int` and a `long` are the same size. In that case, an `unsigned int` outranks `long` because it can hold a higher value.

When C++ is working with an operator, it strives to convert the operands to the same type. This automatic conversion is known as *type coercion*. When a value is converted to a higher data type, it is said to be *promoted*. To *demote* a value means to convert it to a lower data type. Let's look at the specific rules that govern the evaluation of mathematical expressions.

Rule 1: chars, shorts, and unsigned shorts are automatically promoted to int.

You will notice that char, short, and unsigned short do not appear in Table 7. That's because anytime they are used in a mathematical expression, they are automatically promoted to an int. The only exception to this rule is when an unsigned short holds a value larger than can be held by an int. This can happen on systems where shorts are the same size as ints. In this case, the unsigned short is promoted to unsigned int.

Rule 2: When an operator works with two values of different data types, the lower-ranking value is promoted to the type of the higher-ranking value.

In the following expression, assume that years is an int and interestRate is a float:

```
years * interestRate
```

Before the multiplication takes place, years will be promoted to a float.

Rule 3: When the final value of an expression is assigned to a variable, it will be converted to the data type of that variable.

In the following statement, assume that area is a long int, while length and width are both ints:

```
area = length * width;
```

Since length and width are both ints, they will not be converted to any other data type. The result of the multiplication, however, will be converted to long so that it can be stored in area.

Watch out for situations where an expression results in a fractional value being assigned to an integer variable. Here is an example:

```
int x, y = 4;
float z = 2.7;
x = y * z;
```

In the expression y * z, y will be promoted to float and 10.8 will result from the multiplication. Since x is an integer, however, 10.8 will be truncated and 10 will be stored in x.

Integer Division

When you divide an integer by another integer in C++, the result is always an integer. If there is a remainder, it will be discarded. For example, in the following code, parts is assigned the value 2.0:

```
double parts;
parts = 15 / 6;
```

Even though 15 divided by 6 is really 2.5, the .5 part of the result is discarded because we are dividing an integer by an integer. It doesn't matter that parts is declared as a double because the fractional part of the result is discarded *before* the assignment takes place. In order for a division operation to return a floating-point value, at least one of the operands must be of a floating-point data type. For example, the previous code could be written as:

```
double parts;
parts = 15.0 / 6;
```

In this code, the literal value 15.0 is interpreted as a floating-point number, so the division operation will return a floating-point number. The value 2.5 will be assigned to parts.

4 Overflow and Underflow

CONCEPT: When a variable is assigned a value that is too large or too small in range for that variable's data type, the variable overflows or underflows.

Trouble can arise when a variable is being assigned a value that is too large for its type. Here is a statement where `a`, `b`, and `c` are all short integers:

```
a = b * c;
```

If `b` and `c` are set to large enough values, the multiplication will produce a number too big to be stored in `a`. To prepare for this, `a` should have been defined as an `int`, or a `long int`.

When a variable is assigned a number that is too large for its data type, it *overflows*. Likewise, assigning a value that is too small for a variable causes it to *underflow*. Program 7 shows what happens when an integer overflows or underflows. (The output shown is from a system with two-byte short integers.)

Program 7

```
// This program demonstrates integer overflow and underflow.
#include <iostream>
using namespace std;

int main()
{
    // testVar is initialized with the maximum value for a short.
    short testVar = 32767;

    // Display testVar.
    cout << testVar << endl;

    // Add 1 to testVar to make it overflow.
    testVar = testVar + 1;
    cout << testVar << endl;

    // Subtract 1 from testVar to make it underflow.
    testVar = testVar - 1;
    cout << testVar << endl;
    return 0;
}
```

Program Output

```
32767
-32768
32767
```

Typically, when an integer overflows, its contents wrap around to that data type's lowest possible value. In Program 7, `testVar` wrapped around from 32,767 to −32,768 when 1 was added to it. When 1 was subtracted from `testVar`, it underflowed, which caused its contents to wrap back around to 32,767. No warning or error message is given, so be careful when working with numbers close to the maximum or minimum range of an integer. If an overflow or underflow occurs, the program will use the incorrect number, and therefore produce incorrect results.

When floating-point variables overflow or underflow, the results depend upon how the compiler is configured. Your system may produce programs that do any of the following:

- Produce an incorrect result and continue running.
- Print an error message and immediately stop when either floating-point overflow or underflow occurs.
- Print an error message and immediately stop when floating-point overflow occurs, but store a 0 in the variable when it underflows.
- Give you a choice of behaviors when overflow or underflow occurs.

You can find out how your system reacts by compiling and running Program 8.

Program 8

```
// This program can be used to see how your system handles
// floating-point overflow and underflow.
#include <iostream>
using namespace std;

int main()
{
    float test;

    test = 2.0e38 * 1000;     // Should overflow test.
    cout << test << endl;
    test = 2.0e-38 / 2.0e38;  // Should underflow test.
    cout << test << endl;
    return 0;
}
```

5 Type Casting

CONCEPT: Type casting allows you to perform manual data type conversion.

A *type cast expression* lets you manually promote or demote a value. The general format of a type cast expression is

```
static_cast<DataType>(Value)
```

where *Value* is a variable or literal value that you wish to convert, and *DataType* is the data type to which you wish to convert *Value*. Here is an example of code that uses a type cast expression:

```
double number = 3.7;
int val;
val = static_cast<int>(number);
```

This code defines two variables: `number`, a `double`, and `val`, an `int`. The type cast expression in the third statement returns a copy of the value in `number`, converted to an `int`. When a `double` is converted to an `int`, the fractional part is truncated, so this statement stores 3 in `val`. The original value in `number` is not changed, however.

Type cast expressions are useful in situations where C++ will not perform the desired conversion automatically. Program 9 shows an example where a type cast expression is used to prevent integer division from taking place. The statement that uses the type cast expression is

```
perMonth = static_cast<double>(books) / months;
```

Program 9

```
1  // This program uses a type cast to avoid integer division.
2  #include <iostream>
3  using namespace std;
4
5  int main()
6  {
7      int books;           // Number of books to read
8      int months;          // Number of months spent reading
9      double perMonth;     // Average number of books per month
10
11     cout << "How many books do you plan to read? ";
12     cin >> books;
13     cout << "How many months will it take you to read them? ";
14     cin >> months;
15     perMonth = static_cast<double>(books) / months;
16     cout << "That is " << perMonth << " books per month.\n";
17     return 0;
18 }
```

Program Output with Example Input Shown in Bold

How many books do you plan to read? **30** [Enter]

How many months will it take you to read them? **7** [Enter]

That is 4.28571 books per month.

The variable `books` is an integer, but its value is converted to a `double` before the division takes place. Without the type cast expression in line 15, integer division would have been performed, resulting in an incorrect answer.

WARNING! In Program 9, the following statement would still have resulted in integer division:

```
perMonth = static_cast<double>(books / months);
```

The result of the expression `books / months` is 4. When 4 is converted to a `double`, it is 4.0. To prevent the integer division from taking place, one of the operands should be converted to a `double` prior to the division operation. This forces C++ to automatically convert the value of the other operand to a `double`.

Program 10 further demonstrates the type cast expression.

Program 10

```
1   // This program uses a type cast expression to print a character
2   // from a number.
3   #include <iostream>
4   using namespace std;
5
6   int main()
7   {
8       int number = 65;
9
10      // Display the value of the number variable.
11      cout << number << endl;
12
13      // Display the value of number converted to
14      // the char data type.
15      cout << static_cast<char>(number) << endl;
16      return 0;
17  }
```

Program Output

```
65
A
```

Let's take a closer look at this program. In line 8, the `int` variable `number` is initialized with the value 65. In line 11, `number` is sent to `cout`, causing 65 to be displayed. In line 15, a type cast expression is used to convert the value in `number` to the `char` data type. Characters are stored in memory as integer ASCII codes. The number 65 is the ASCII code for the letter 'A', so this statement causes the letter 'A' to be displayed.

> **NOTE:** C++ provides several different type cast expressions. `static_cast` is the most commonly used type cast expression, so we will primarily use it in this chapter.

Checkpoint

11 Assume the following variable definitions:

```
int a = 5, b = 12;
double x = 3.4, z = 9.1;
```

What are the values of the following expressions?

A) `b / a`
B) `x * a`
C) `static_cast<double>(b / a)`
D) `static_cast<double>(b) / a`
E) `b / static_cast<double>(a)`
F) `static_cast<double>(b) / static_cast<double>(a)`
G) `b / static_cast<int>(x)`
H) `static_cast<int>(x) * static_cast<int>(z)`
I) `static_cast<int>(x * z)`
J) `static_cast<double>(static_cast<int>(x) * static_cast<int>(z))`

12 Complete the following program skeleton so it asks the user to enter a character. Store the character in the variable `letter`. Use a type cast expression with the variable in a `cout` statement to display the character's ASCII code on the screen.

```
#include <iostream>
using namespace std;
int main()
{
    char letter;

    // Finish this program
    // as specified above.
    return 0;
}
```

13 What will the following program display?

```
#include <iostream>
using namespace std;

int main()
{
    int integer1, integer2;
    double result;
    integer1 = 19;
    integer2 = 2;
    result = integer1 / integer2;
    cout << result << endl;
    result = static_cast<double>(integer1) / integer2;
    cout << result << endl;
    result = static_cast<double>(integer1 / integer2);
    cout << result << endl;
    return 0;
}
```

6 Multiple Assignment and Combined Assignment

CONCEPT: Multiple assignment means to assign the same value to several variables with one statement.

C++ allows you to assign a value to multiple variables at once. If a program has several variables, such as `a`, `b`, `c`, and `d`, and each variable needs to be assigned a value, such as 12, the following statement may be constructed:

```
a = b = c = d = 12;
```

The value 12 will be assigned to each variable listed in the statement.*

*The assignment operator works from right to left. 12 is first assigned to `d`, then to `c`, then to `b`, then to `a`.

Combined Assignment Operators

Quite often, programs have assignment statements of the following form:

```
number = number + 1;
```

The expression on the right side of the assignment operator gives the value of `number` plus 1. The result is then assigned to `number`, replacing the value that was previously stored there. Effectively, this statement adds 1 to `number`. In a similar fashion, the following statement subtracts 5 from `number`.

```
number = number - 5;
```

If you have never seen this type of statement before, it might cause some initial confusion because the same variable name appears on both sides of the assignment operator. Table 8 shows other examples of statements written this way.

Table 8 (Assume x = 6)

Statement	What It Does	Value of x After the Statement
`x = x + 4;`	Adds 4 to x	10
`x = x - 3;`	Subtracts 3 from x	3
`x = x * 10;`	Multiplies x by 10	60
`x = x / 2;`	Divides x by 2	3
`x = x % 4`	Makes x the remainder of x / 4	2

These types of operations are very common in programming. For convenience, C++ offers a special set of operators designed specifically for these jobs. Table 9 shows the *combined assignment operators*, also known as *compound operators*, and *arithmetic assignment operators*.

Table 9 Combined Assignment Operators

Operator	Example Usage	Equivalent to
`+=`	`x += 5;`	`x = x + 5;`
`-=`	`y -= 2;`	`y = y - 2;`
`*=`	`z *= 10;`	`z = z * 10;`
`/=`	`a /= b;`	`a = a / b;`
`%=`	`c %= 3;`	`c = c % 3;`

As you can see, the combined assignment operators do not require the programmer to type the variable name twice. Also, they give a clear indication of what is happening in the statement. Program 11 uses combined assignment operators.

Program 11

```
// This program tracks the inventory of three widget stores
// that opened at the same time. Each store started with the
// same number of widgets in inventory. By subtracting the
```

(program continues)

Program 11 *(continued)*

```
// number of widgets each store has sold from its inventory,
// the current inventory can be calculated.
#include <iostream>
using namespace std;

int main()
{
   int begInv,      // Beginning inventory for all stores
       sold,        // Number of widgets sold
       store1,      // Store 1's inventory
       store2,      // Store 2's inventory
       store3;      // Store 3's inventory

   // Get the beginning inventory for all the stores.
   cout << "One week ago, 3 new widget stores opened\n";
   cout << "at the same time with the same beginning\n";
   cout << "inventory. What was the beginning inventory? ";
   cin >> begInv;

   // Set each store's inventory.
   store1 = store2 = store3 = begInv;

   // Get the number of widgets sold at store 1.
   cout << "How many widgets has store 1 sold? ";
   cin >> sold;
   store1 -= sold; // Adjust store 1's inventory.

   // Get the number of widgets sold at store 2.
   cout << "How many widgets has store 2 sold? ";
   cin >> sold;
   store2 -= sold; // Adjust store 2's inventory.

   // Get the number of widgets sold at store 3.
   cout << "How many widgets has store 3 sold? ";
   cin >> sold;
   store3 -= sold; // Adjust store 3's inventory.

   // Display each store's current inventory.
   cout << "\nThe current inventory of each store:\n";
   cout << "Store 1: " << store1 << endl;
   cout << "Store 2: " << store2 << endl;
   cout << "Store 3: " << store3 << endl;
   return 0;
}
```

Program Output with Example Input Shown in Bold

One week ago, 3 new widget stores opened
at the same time with the same beginning
inventory. What was the beginning inventory? **100** [Enter]

```
How many widgets has store 1 sold? 25 [Enter]
How many widgets has store 2 sold? 15 [Enter]
How many widgets has store 3 sold? 45 [Enter]
The current inventory of each store:
Store 1: 75
Store 2: 85
Store 3: 55
```

More elaborate statements may be expressed with the combined assignment operators. Here is an example:

```
result *= a + 5;
```

In this statement, `result` is multiplied by the sum of `a + 5`. When constructing such statements, you must realize the precedence of the combined assignment operators is lower than that of the regular math operators. The statement above is equivalent to

```
result = result * (a + 5);
```

which is different from

```
result = result * a + 5;
```

Table 10 shows other examples of such statements and their assignment statement equivalencies.

Table 10 Example Usage of the Combined Assignment Operators

Example Usage	Equivalent to
`x += b + 5;`	`x = x + (b + 5);`
`y -= a * 2;`	`y = y - (a * 2);`
`z *= 10 - c;`	`z = z * (10 - c);`
`a /= b + c;`	`a = a / (b + c);`
`c %= d - 3;`	`c = c % (d - 3);`

Checkpoint

14 Write a multiple assignment statement that assigns 0 to the variables `total`, `subtotal`, `tax`, and `shipping`.

15 Write statements using combined assignment operators to perform the following:
- A) Add 6 to `x`.
- B) Subtract 4 from `amount`.
- C) Multiply `y` by 4.
- D) Divide `total` by 27.
- E) Store in `x` the remainder of `x` divided by 7.
- F) Add `y * 5` to `x`.
- G) Subtract `discount` times 4 from `total`.
- H) Multiply `increase` by `salesRep` times 5.
- I) Divide `profit` by `shares` minus 1000.

16 What will the following program display?

```
#include <iostream>
using namespace std;

int main()
{
    int unus, duo, tres;

    unus = duo = tres = 5;
    unus += 4;
    duo *= 2;
    tres -= 4;
    unus /= 3;
    duo += tres;
    cout << unus << endl;
    cout << duo << endl;
    cout << tres << endl;
    return 0;
}
```

7 Formatting Output

CONCEPT: The cout object provides ways to format data as it is being displayed. This affects the way data appears on the screen.

The same data can be printed or displayed in several different ways. For example, all of the following numbers have the same value, although they look different:

```
720
720.0
720.00000000
7.2e+2
+720.0
```

The way a value is printed is called its *formatting*. The cout object has a standard way of formatting variables of each data type. Sometimes, however, you need more control over the way data is displayed. Consider Program 12, for example, which displays three rows of numbers with a space between each one.

Program 12

```
// This program displays three rows of numbers.
#include <iostream>
using namespace std;

int main()
{
   int num1 = 2897, num2 = 5,    num3 = 837,
       num4 = 34,   num5 = 7,    num6 = 1623,
       num7 = 390,  num8 = 3456, num9 = 12;
```

```
    // Display the first row of numbers
    cout << num1 << " " << num2 << " " << num3 << endl;

    // Display the second row of numbers
    cout << num4 << " " << num5 << " " << num6 << endl;

    // Display the third row of numbers
    cout << num7 << " " << num8 << " " << num9 << endl;
    return 0;
}
```

Program Output

```
2897 5 837
34 7 1623
390 3456 12
```

Unfortunately, the numbers do not line up in columns. This is because some of the numbers, such as 5 and 7, occupy one position on the screen, while others occupy two or three positions. `cout` uses just the number of spaces needed to print each number.

To remedy this, `cout` offers a way of specifying the minimum number of spaces to use for each number. A stream manipulator, `setw`, can be used to establish print fields of a specified width. Here is an example of how it is used:

```
value = 23;
cout << setw(5) << value;
```

The number inside the parentheses after the word `setw` specifies the *field width* for the value immediately following it. The field width is the minimum number of character positions, or spaces, on the screen to print the value in. In the example above, the number 23 will be displayed in a field of 5 spaces. Since 23 only occupies 2 positions on the screen, 3 blank spaces will be printed before it. To further clarify how this works, look at the following statements:

```
value = 23;
cout << "(" << setw(5) << value << ")";
```

This will cause the following output:

```
(   23)
```

Notice the number occupies the last two positions in the field. Since the number did not use the entire field, `cout` filled the extra 3 positions with blank spaces. Because the number appears on the right side of the field with blank spaces "padding" it in front, it is said to be *right-justified*.

Program 13 shows how the numbers in Program 12 can be printed in columns that line up perfectly by using `setw`.

Program 13

```
// This program displays three rows of numbers.
#include <iostream>
#include <iomanip>      // Required for setw
using namespace std;

int main()
{
    int num1 = 2897, num2 = 5,    num3 = 837,
        num4 = 34,   num5 = 7,    num6 = 1623,
        num7 = 390,  num8 = 3456, num9 = 12;

    // Display the first row of numbers
    cout << setw(6) << num1 << setw(6)
         << num2 << setw(6) << num3 << endl;

    // Display the second row of numbers
    cout << setw(6) << num4 << setw(6)
         << num5 << setw(6) << num6 << endl;

    // Display the third row of numbers
    cout << setw(6) << num7 << setw(6)
         << num8 << setw(6) << num9 << endl;
    return 0;
}
```

Program Output

```
  2897     5   837
    34     7  1623
   390  3456    12
```

By printing each number in a field of 6 positions, they are displayed in perfect columns.

> **NOTE:** A new header file, `<iomanip>`, is included in Program 13. It must be used in any program that uses `setw`.

Notice how a `setw` manipulator is used with each value, because `setw` only establishes a field width for the value immediately following it. After that value is printed, `cout` goes back to its default method of printing.

You might wonder what will happen if the number is too large to fit in the field, as in the following statement:

```
value = 18397;
cout << setw(2) << value;
```

In cases like this, `cout` will print the entire number. `setw` only specifies the minimum number of positions in the print field. Any number larger than the minimum will cause `cout` to override the `setw` value.

You may specify the field width of any type of data. Program 14 shows `setw` being used with an integer, a floating-point number, and a `string` object.

Program 14

```
// This program demonstrates the setw manipulator being
// used with values of various data types.
#include <iostream>
#include <iomanip>
#include <string>
using namespace std;

int main()
{
    int intValue = 3928;
    double doubleValue = 91.5;
    string stringValue = "John J. Smith";

    cout << "(" << setw(5) << intValue << ")" << endl;
    cout << "(" << setw(8) << doubleValue << ")" << endl;
    cout << "(" << setw(16) << stringValue << ")" << endl;
    return 0;
}
```

Program Output

```
( 3928)
(    91.5)
(   John J. Smith)
```

Program 14 can be used to illustrate the following points:

- The field width of a floating-point number includes a position for the decimal point.
- The field width of a `string` object includes all characters in the string, including spaces.
- The values printed in the field are right-justified by default. This means they are aligned with the right side of the print field, and any blanks that must be used to pad it are inserted in front of the value.

The `setprecision` Manipulator

VideoNote
Formatting Numbers with `setprecision`

Floating-point values may be rounded to a number of *significant digits*, or *precision*, which is the total number of digits that appear before and after the decimal point. You can control the number of significant digits with which floating-point values are displayed by using the `setprecision` manipulator. Program 15 shows the results of a division operation displayed with different numbers of significant digits.

Program 15

```
1   // This program demonstrates how setprecision rounds a
2   // floating-point value.
3   #include <iostream>
4   #include <iomanip>
5   using namespace std;
6
7   int main()
8   {
9       double quotient, number1 = 132.364, number2 = 26.91;
10
11      quotient = number1 / number2;
12      cout << quotient << endl;
13      cout << setprecision(5) << quotient << endl;
14      cout << setprecision(4) << quotient << endl;
15      cout << setprecision(3) << quotient << endl;
16      cout << setprecision(2) << quotient << endl;
17      cout << setprecision(1) << quotient << endl;
18      return 0;
19  }
```

Program Output

```
4.91877
4.9188
4.919
4.92
4.9
5
```

The first value is displayed in line 12 without the `setprecision` manipulator. (By default, the system in the illustration displays floating-point values with 6 significant digits.) The subsequent `cout` statements print the same value, but rounded to 5, 4, 3, 2, and 1 significant digits.

If the value of a number is expressed in fewer digits of precision than specified by `setprecision`, the manipulator will have no effect. In the following statements, the value of `dollars` only has four digits of precision, so the number printed by both `cout` statements is 24.51.

```
double dollars = 24.51;
cout << dollars << endl;                     // Displays 24.51
cout << setprecision(5) << dollars << endl;  // Displays 24.51
```

Table 11 shows how `setprecision` affects the way various values are displayed.

Table 11 The `setprecision` Manipulator

Number	Manipulator	Value Displayed
28.92786	setprecision(3)	28.9
21	setprecision(5)	21
109.5	setprecision(4)	109.5
34.28596	setprecision(2)	34

Unlike field width, the precision setting remains in effect until it is changed to some other value. As with all formatting manipulators, you must include the header file <iomanip> to use setprecision.

Program 16 shows how the setw and setprecision manipulators may be combined to fully control the way floating-point numbers are displayed.

Program 16

```
// This program asks for sales amounts for 3 days. The total
// sales are calculated and displayed in a table.
#include <iostream>
#include <iomanip>
using namespace std;

int main()
{
    double day1, day2, day3, total;

    // Get the sales for each day.
    cout << "Enter the sales for day 1: ";
    cin >> day1;
    cout << "Enter the sales for day 2: ";
    cin >> day2;
    cout << "Enter the sales for day 3: ";
    cin >> day3;

    // Calculate the total sales.
    total = day1 + day2 + day3;

    // Display the sales amounts.
    cout << "\nSales Amounts\n";
    cout << "-------------\n";
    cout << setprecision(5);
    cout << "Day 1: " << setw(8) << day1 << endl;
    cout << "Day 2: " << setw(8) << day2 << endl;
    cout << "Day 3: " << setw(8) << day3 << endl;
    cout << "Total: " << setw(8) << total << endl;
    return 0;
}
```

Program Output with Example Input Shown in Bold

```
Enter the sales for day 1: 321.57 [Enter]
Enter the sales for day 2: 269.62 [Enter]
Enter the sales for day 3: 307.77 [Enter]

Sales Amounts
-------------
Day 1: 321.57
Day 2: 269.62
Day 3: 307.77
Total: 898.96
```

The `fixed` Manipulator

The `setprecision` manipulator can sometimes surprise you in an undesirable way. When the precision of a number is set to a lower value, numbers tend to be printed in scientific notation. For example, here is the output of Program 16 with larger numbers being input:

Program 16

Program Output with Example Input Shown in Bold

```
Enter the sales for day 1: 145678.99 [Enter]
Enter the sales for day 2: 205614.85 [Enter]
Enter the sales for day 3: 198645.22 [Enter]

Sales Amounts
-------------
Day 1: 1.4568e+005
Day 2: 2.0561e+005
Day 3: 1.9865e+005
Total: 5.4994e+005
```

Another stream manipulator, `fixed`, forces `cout` to print the digits in *fixed-point notation*, or decimal. Program 17 shows how the `fixed` manipulator is used.

Program 17

```
// This program asks for sales amounts for 3 days. The total
// sales are calculated and displayed in a table.
#include <iostream>
#include <iomanip>
using namespace std;

int main()
{
    double day1, day2, day3, total;

    // Get the sales for each day.
    cout << "Enter the sales for day 1: ";
    cin >> day1;
    cout << "Enter the sales for day 2: ";
    cin >> day2;
    cout << "Enter the sales for day 3: ";
    cin >> day3;

    // Calculate the total sales.
    total = day1 + day2 + day3;

```

```
22       // Display the sales amounts.
23       cout << "\nSales Amounts\n";
24       cout << "-------------\n";
25       cout << setprecision(2) << fixed;
26       cout << "Day 1:  " << setw(8) << day1 << endl;
27       cout << "Day 2:  " << setw(8) << day2 << endl;
28       cout << "Day 3:  " << setw(8) << day3 << endl;
29       cout << "Total:  " << setw(8) << total << endl;
30       return 0;
31   }
```

Program Output with Example Input Shown in Bold

```
Enter the sales for day 1: 1321.87 [Enter]
Enter the sales for day 2: 1869.26 [Enter]
Enter the sales for day 3: 1403.77 [Enter]

Sales Amounts
-------------
Day 1:     1321.87
Day 2:     1869.26
Day 3:     1403.77
Total:     4594.90
```

The statement in line 25 uses the `fixed` manipulator:

```
cout << setprecision(2) << fixed;
```

When the `fixed` manipulator is used, all floating-point numbers that are subsequently printed will be displayed in fixed-point notation, with the number of digits to the right of the decimal point specified by the `setprecision` manipulator.

When the `fixed` and `setprecision` manipulators are used together, the value specified by the `setprecision` manipulator will be the number of digits to appear after the decimal point, not the number of significant digits. For example, look at the following code:

```
double x = 123.4567;
cout << setprecision(2) << fixed << x << endl;
```

Because the `fixed` manipulator is used, the `setprecision` manipulator will cause the number to be displayed with two digits after the decimal point. The value will be displayed as 123.46.

The `showpoint` Manipulator

By default, floating-point numbers are not displayed with trailing zeros, and floating-point numbers that do not have a fractional part are not displayed with a decimal point. For example, look at the following code:

```
double x = 123.4, y = 456.0;
cout << setprecision(6) << x << endl;
cout << y << endl;
```

The `cout` statements will produce the following output:

```
123.4
456
```

Although six significant digits are specified for both numbers, neither number is displayed with trailing zeros. If we want the numbers padded with trailing zeros, we must use the `showpoint` manipulator as shown in the following code:

```
double x = 123.4, y = 456.0;
cout << setprecision(6) << showpoint << x << endl;
cout << y << endl;
```

These `cout` statements will produce the following output:

```
123.400
456.000
```

NOTE: With most compilers, trailing zeros are displayed when the `setprecision` and `fixed` manipulators are used together.

The `left` and `right` Manipulators

Normally output is right-justified. For example, look at the following code:

```
double x = 146.789, y = 24.2, z = 1.783;
cout << setw(10) << x << endl;
cout << setw(10) << y << endl;
cout << setw(10) << z << endl;
```

Each of the variables, `x`, `y`, and `z`, is displayed in a print field of 10 spaces. The output of the `cout` statements is

```
146.789
   24.2
  1.783
```

Notice each value is right-justified, or aligned to the right of its print field. You can cause the values to be left-justified by using the `left` manipulator, as shown in the following code.

```
double x = 146.789, y = 24.2, z = 1.783;
cout << left << setw(10) << x << endl;
cout << setw(10) << y << endl;
cout << setw(10) << z << endl;
```

The output of these `cout` statements is

```
146.789
24.2
1.783
```

In this case, the numbers are aligned to the left of their print fields. The `left` manipulator remains in effect until you use the `right` manipulator, which causes all subsequent output to be right-justified.

Table 12 summarizes the manipulators we have discussed.

Table 12 Stream Manipulators

Stream Manipulator	Description
`setw(`*n*`)`	Establishes a print field of *n* spaces.
`fixed`	Displays floating-point numbers in fixed-point notation.
`showpoint`	Causes a decimal point and trailing zeros to be displayed, even if there is no fractional part.
`setprecision(`*n*`)`	Sets the precision of floating-point numbers.
`left`	Causes subsequent output to be left-justified.
`right`	Causes subsequent output to be right-justified.

Checkpoint

17 Write `cout` statements with stream manipulators that perform the following:

A) Display the number 34.789 in a field of nine spaces with two decimal places of precision.

B) Display the number 7.0 in a field of five spaces with three decimal places of precision.
The decimal point and any trailing zeros should be displayed.

C) Display the number 5.789e+12 in fixed-point notation.

D) Display the number 67 left-justified in a field of seven spaces.

18 The following program will not compile because the lines have been mixed up:

```
#include <iomanip>
}
cout << person << endl;
string person = "Wolfgang Smith";
int main()
cout << person << endl;
{
#include <iostream>
return 0;
cout << left;
using namespace std;
cout << setw(20);
cout << right;
```

When the lines are properly arranged, the program should display the following:

```
    Wolfgang Smith
Wolfgang Smith
```

Rearrange the lines in the correct order. Test the program by entering it on the computer, compiling it, and running it.

19 The following program skeleton asks for an angle in degrees and converts it to radians. The formatting of the final output is left to you.

```
#include <iostream>
#include <iomanip>
using namespace std;

int main()
{
    const double PI = 3.14159;
    double degrees, radians;

    cout << "Enter an angle in degrees and I will convert it\n";
    cout << "to radians for you: ";
    cin >> degrees;
    radians = degrees * PI / 180;
    // Display the value in radians left-justified, in fixed
    // point notation, with 4 places of precision, in a field
    // 5 spaces wide, making sure the decimal point is always
    // displayed.
    return 0;
}
```

8 Working with Characters and `string` Objects

CONCEPT: Special functions exist for working with characters and `string` objects.

Although it is possible to use `cin` with the >> operator to input strings, it can cause problems of which you need to be aware. When `cin` reads input, it passes over and ignores any leading *whitespace* characters (spaces, tabs, or line breaks). Once it comes to the first nonblank character and starts reading, it stops reading when it gets to the next whitespace character. Program 18 illustrates this problem.

Program 18

```
// This program illustrates a problem that can occur if
// cin is used to read character data into a string object.
#include <iostream>
#include <string>
using namespace std;

int main()
{
    string name;
    string city;

    cout << "Please enter your name: ";
    cin >> name;
    cout << "Enter the city you live in: ";
    cin >> city;

```

```
    cout << "Hello, " << name << endl;
    cout << "You live in " << city << endl;
    return 0;
}
```

Program Output with Example Input Shown in Bold

Please enter your name: **Kate Smith** [Enter]
Enter the city you live in: Hello, Kate
You live in Smith

Notice the user was never given the opportunity to enter the city. In the first input statement, when `cin` came to the space between `Kate` and `Smith`, it stopped reading, storing just `Kate` as the value of `name`. In the second input statement, `cin` used the leftover characters it found in the keyboard buffer and stored `Smith` as the value of `city`.

To work around this problem, you can use a C++ function named `getline`. The `getline` function reads an entire line, including leading and embedded spaces, and stores it in a `string` object. The `getline` function looks like the following, where `cin` is the input stream we are reading from and `inputLine` is the name of the `string` object receiving the input:

```
getline(cin, inputLine);
```

Program 19 illustrates using the `getline` function.

Program 19

```
// This program demonstrates using the getline function
// to read character data into a string object.
#include <iostream>
#include <string>
using namespace std;

int main()
{
    string name;
    string city;

    cout << "Please enter your name: ";
    getline(cin, name);
    cout << "Enter the city you live in: ";
    getline(cin, city);

    cout << "Hello, " << name << endl;
    cout << "You live in " << city << endl;
    return 0;
}
```

Program Output with Example Input Shown in Bold

Please enter your name: **Kate Smith** [Enter]
Enter the city you live in: **Raleigh** [Enter]
Hello, Kate Smith
You live in Raleigh

Inputting a Character

Sometimes you want to read only a single character of input. For example, some programs display a menu of items for the user to choose from. Often the selections are denoted by the letters A, B, C, and so forth. The user chooses an item from the menu by typing a character. The simplest way to read a single character is with `cin` and the >> operator, as illustrated in Program 20.

Program 20

```
// This program reads a single character into a char variable.
#include <iostream>
using namespace std;

int main()
{
    char ch;

    cout << "Type a character and press Enter: ";
    cin >> ch;
    cout << "You entered " << ch << endl;
    return 0;
}
```

Program Output with Example Input Shown in Bold

```
Type a character and press Enter: A [Enter]
You entered A
```

Using `cin.get`

As with string input, however, there are times when using `cin` >> to read a character does not do what you want. For example, because it passes over all leading whitespace, it is impossible to input just a blank or [Enter] with `cin` >>. The program will not continue past the `cin` statement until some character other than the spacebar, tab key, or [Enter] key has been pressed. (Once such a character is entered, the [Enter] key must still be pressed before the program can continue to the next statement.) Thus, programs that ask the user to `"Press the Enter key to continue."` cannot use the >> operator to read only the pressing of the [Enter] key.

In those situations, the `cin` object has a built-in function named `get` that is helpful. Because the `get` function is built into the `cin` object, we say that it is a *member function* of `cin`. The `get` member function reads a single character, including any whitespace character. If the program needs to store the character being read, the `get` member function can be called in either of the following ways. In both examples, assume `ch` is the name of a `char` variable into which the character is being read.

```
cin.get(ch);
ch = cin.get();
```

If the program is using the `cin.get` function simply to pause the screen until the [Enter] key is pressed and does not need to store the character, the function can also be called like this:

```
cin.get();
```

Program 21 illustrates all three ways to use the `cin.get` function.

Program 21

```
// This program demonstrates three ways
// to use cin.get() to pause a program.
#include <iostream>
using namespace std;

int main()
{
    char ch;

    cout << "This program has paused. Press Enter to continue.";
    cin.get(ch);
    cout << "It has paused a second time. Please press Enter again.";
    ch = cin.get();
    cout << "It has paused a third time. Please press Enter again.";
    cin.get();
    cout << "Thank you!";
    return 0;
}
```

Program Output with Example Input Shown in Bold

```
This program has paused. Press Enter to continue. [Enter]
It has paused a second time. Please press Enter again. [Enter]
It has paused a third time. Please press Enter again. [Enter]
Thank you!
```

Mixing `cin >>` and `cin.get`

Mixing `cin >>` with `cin.get` can cause an annoying and hard-to-find problem. For example, look at Program 22.

Program 22

```
// This program demonstrates a problem that occurs
// when you mix cin >> with cin.get().
#include <iostream>
using namespace std;

int main()
{
    char ch;                         // Define a character variable
    int number;                      // Define an integer variable

```

(program continues)

Program 22 *(continued)*

```
11      cout << "Enter a number: ";
12      cin >> number;                   // Read an integer
13      cout << "Enter a character: ";
14      ch = cin.get();                  // Read a character
15      cout << "Thank You!\n";
16      return 0;
17  }
```

Program Output with Example Input Shown in Bold

Enter a number: **100** [Enter]
Enter a character: Thank You!

When this program runs, line 12 lets the user enter a number, but it appears as though the statement in line 14 is skipped. This happens because `cin >>` and `cin.get` use slightly different techniques for reading data.

In the example run of the program, when line 12 executed, the user entered 100 and pressed the [Enter] key. Pressing the [Enter] key causes a newline character (`'\n'`) to be stored in the keyboard buffer, as shown in Figure 5. The `cin >>` statement in line 12 begins reading the data that the user entered, and stops reading when it comes to the newline character. This is shown in Figure 6. The newline character is not read, but remains in the keyboard buffer.

Figure 5 Contents of the keyboard buffer

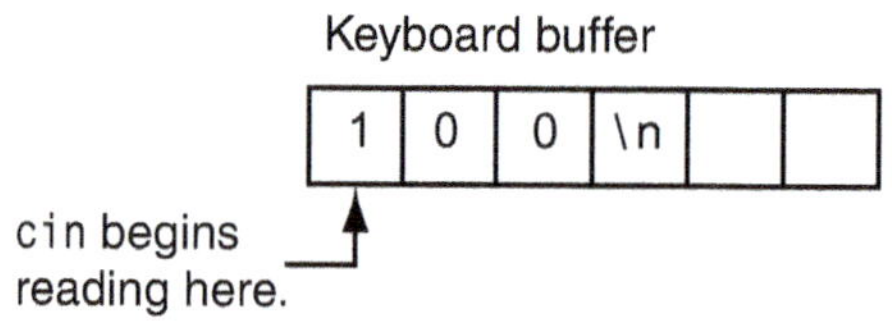

Figure 6 `cin` stops reading at the newline character

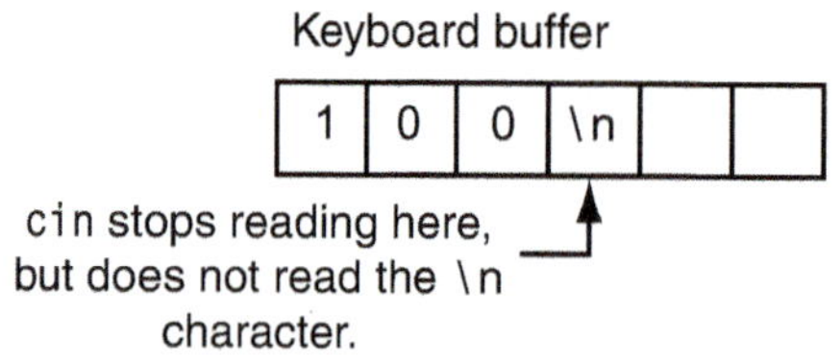

When the `cin.get` function in line 14 executes, it begins reading the keyboard buffer where the previous input operation stopped. That means `cin.get` reads the newline character, without giving the user a chance to enter any more input. You can remedy this situation by using the `cin.ignore` function, described in the following section.

Using `cin.ignore`

To solve the problem previously described, you can use another of the `cin` object's member functions named `ignore`. The `cin.ignore` function tells the `cin` object to skip one or more characters in the keyboard buffer. Here is its general form:

```
cin.ignore(n, c);
```

The arguments shown in the parentheses are optional. If used, *n* is an integer and *c* is a character. They tell `cin` to skip n number of characters, or until the character *c* is encountered. For example, the following statement causes `cin` to skip the next 20 characters or until a newline is encountered, whichever comes first:

```
cin.ignore(20,'\n');
```

If no arguments are used, `cin` will skip only the very next character. Here's an example:

```
cin.ignore();
```

Program 23, which is a modified version of Program 22, demonstrates the function. Notice a call to `cin.ignore` has been inserted in line 13, right after the `cin >>` statement.

Program 23

```
1  // This program successfully uses both
2  // cin >> and cin.get() for keyboard input.
3  #include <iostream>
4  using namespace std;
5
6  int main()
7  {
8      char ch;
9      int number;
10
11     cout << "Enter a number: ";
12     cin >> number;
13     cin.ignore();                // Skip the newline character
14     cout << "Enter a character: ";
15     ch = cin.get();
16     cout << "Thank You!\n";
17     return 0;
18 }
```

Program Output with Example Input Shown in Bold

Enter a number: **100** [Enter]
Enter a character: **Z** [Enter]
Thank You!

string Member Functions and Operators

C++ `string` objects also have a number of member functions. For example, if you want to know the length of the string that is stored in a `string` object, you can call the object's `length` member function. Here is an example of how to use it:

```
string state = "Texas";
int size = state.length();
```

The first statement creates a `string` object named `state` and initializes it with the string `"Texas"`. The second statement defines an `int` variable named `size` and initializes it with the length of the string in the `state` object. After this code executes, the `size` variable will hold the value 5.

Certain operators also work with `string` objects. One of them is the + operator. You have already encountered the + operator to add two numeric quantities. Because strings cannot be added, when this operator is used with string operands it *concatenates* them, or joins them together. Assume we have the following definitions and initializations in a program:

```
string greeting1 = "Hello ";
string greeting2;
string name1 = "World";
string name2 = "People";
```

The following statements illustrate how string concatenation works:

```
greeting2 = greeting1 + name1; // greeting2 now holds "Hello World"
greeting1 = greeting1 + name2; // greeting1 now holds "Hello People"
```

Notice the string stored in `greeting1` has a blank as its last character. If the blank were not there, `greeting2` would have been assigned the string `"HelloWorld"`.

The last statement in the previous example could also have been written using the += combined assignment operator, to achieve the same result:

```
greeting1 += name2;
```

9 More Mathematical Library Functions

CONCEPT: The C++ runtime library provides several functions for performing complex mathematical operations.

Earlier in this chapter, you learned to use the pow function to raise a number to a power. The C++ library has numerous other functions that perform specialized mathematical operations. These functions are useful in scientific and special-purpose programs. Table 13 shows several of these, each of which requires the `<cmath>` header file.

Table 13 <cmath> Library Functions

Function	Example	Description
`abs`	`y = abs(x);`	Returns the absolute value of the argument. The argument and the return value are integers.
`cos`	`y = cos(x);`	Returns the cosine of the argument. The argument should be an angle expressed in radians. The return type and the argument are `double`s.
`exp`	`y = exp(x);`	Computes the exponential function of the argument, which is `x`. The return type and the argument are `double`s.
`fmod`	`y = fmod(x, z);`	Returns, as a `double`, the remainder of the first argument divided by the second argument. Works like the modulus operator, but the arguments are `double`s. (The modulus operator only works with integers.) Take care not to pass zero as the second argument. Doing so would cause division by zero.
`log`	`y = log(x);`	Returns the natural logarithm of the argument. The return type and the argument are `double`s.
`log10`	`y = log10(x);`	Returns the base-10 logarithm of the argument. The return type and the argument are `double`s.
`round`	`y = round(x)`	The argument, `x`, can be a `double`, a `float`, or a `long double`. Returns the value of `x` rounded to the nearest whole number. For example, if `x` is 2.8, the function returns 3.0, or if `x` is 2.1, the function returns 2.0. The return type is the same as the type of the argument.
`sin`	`y = sin(x);`	Returns the sine of the argument. The argument should be an angle expressed in radians. The return type and the argument are `double`s.
`sqrt`	`y = sqrt(x);`	Returns the square root of the argument. The return type and argument are `double`s.
`tan`	`y = tan(x);`	Returns the tangent of the argument. The argument should be an angle expressed in radians. The return type and the argument are `double`s.

Each of these functions is as simple to use as the `pow` function. The following program segment demonstrates the `sqrt` function, which returns the square root of a number:

```
cout << "Enter a number: ";
cin >> num;
s = sqrt(num);
cout << "The square root of " << num << " is " << s << endl;
```

Here is the output of the program segment, with 25 as the number entered by the user:

```
Enter a number: 25
The square root of 25 is 5
```

Program 24 shows the `sqrt` function being used to find the hypotenuse of a right triangle. The program uses the following formula, taken from the Pythagorean theorem:

$$c = \sqrt{a^2 + b^2}$$

In the formula, c is the length of the hypotenuse, and a and b are the lengths of the other sides of the triangle.

Program 24

```
// This program asks for the lengths of the two sides of a
// right triangle. The length of the hypotenuse is then
// calculated and displayed.
#include <iostream>
#include <iomanip>     // For setprecision
#include <cmath>       // For the sqrt and pow functions
using namespace std;

int main()
{
    double a, b, c;

    cout << "Enter the length of side a: ";
    cin >> a;
    cout << "Enter the length of side b: ";
    cin >> b;
    c = sqrt(pow(a, 2.0) + pow(b, 2.0));
    cout << "The length of the hypotenuse is ";
    cout << setprecision(2) << c << endl;
    return 0;
}
```

Program Output with Example Input Shown in Bold

```
Enter the length of side a: 5.0 [Enter]
Enter the length of side b: 12.0 [Enter]
The length of the hypotenuse is 13
```

The following statement, taken from Program 24, calculates the square root of the sum of the squares of the triangle's two sides:

```
c = sqrt(pow(a, 2.0) + pow(b, 2.0));
```

Notice the following mathematical expression is used as the `sqrt` function's argument:

```
pow(a, 2.0) + pow(b, 2.0)
```

This expression calls the `pow` function twice: once to calculate the square of `a`, and again to calculate the square of `b`. These two squares are then added together, and the sum is sent to the `sqrt` function.

Random Numbers

Random numbers are useful for lots of different programming tasks. The following are just a few examples:

- Random numbers are commonly used in games. For example, computer games that let the player roll dice use random numbers to represent the values of the dice.

- Programs that show cards being drawn from a shuffled deck use random numbers to represent the face values of the cards.
- Random numbers are useful in simulation programs. In some simulations, the computer must randomly decide how a person, animal, insect, or other living being will behave. Formulas can be constructed in which a random number is used to determine various actions and events that take place in the program.
- Random numbers are useful in statistical programs that must randomly select data for analysis.
- Random numbers are commonly used in computer security to encrypt sensitive data.

The C++ library has a function, `rand()`, that you can use to generate random numbers. (The `rand()` function requires the `<cstdlib>` header file.) The number returned from the function is an `int`. Here is an example of its usage:

```
y = rand();
```

After this statement executes, the variable `y` will contain a random number. In actuality, the numbers produced by `rand()`are pseudorandom. The function uses an algorithm that produces the same sequence of numbers each time the program is repeated on the same system. For example, suppose the following statements are executed:

```
cout << rand() << endl;
cout << rand() << endl;
cout << rand() << endl;
```

The three numbers displayed will appear to be random, but each time the program runs, the same three values will be generated. In order to randomize the results of `rand()`, the `srand()` function must be used. `srand()` accepts an `unsigned int` argument, which acts as a seed value for the algorithm. By specifying different seed values, `rand()` will generate different sequences of random numbers.

A common practice for getting unique seed values is to call the `time` function, which is part of the standard library. The `time` function returns the number of seconds that have elapsed since midnight, January 1, 1970. The `time` function requires the `<ctime> header` file, and you pass 0 as an argument to the function. Program 25 demonstrates this. The program should generate three different random numbers each time it is executed.

Program 25

```
// This program demonstrates random numbers.
#include <iostream>
#include <cstdlib>    // For rand and srand
#include <ctime>      // For the time function
using namespace std;

int main()
{
    // Get the system time.
    unsigned seed = time(0);

    // Seed the random number generator.
    srand(seed);

```

(program continues)

Program 25 *(continued)*

```
    // Display three random numbers.
    cout << rand() << endl;
    cout << rand() << endl;
    cout << rand() << endl;
    return 0;
}
```

Program Output

```
23861
20884
21941
```

If you wish to limit the range of the random number, use the following formula:

```
y = (rand() % (maxValue - minValue + 1)) + minValue;
```

In the formula, `minValue` is the lowest number in the range, and `maxValue` is the highest number in the range. For example, the following code assigns a random number in the range of 1 through 100 to the variable y:

```
const int MIN_VALUE = 1;
const int MAX_VALUE = 100;
y = (rand() % (MAX_VALUE - MIN_VALUE + 1)) + MIN_VALUE;
```

As another example, the following code assigns a random number in the range of 100 through 200 to the variable y:

```
const int MIN_VALUE = 100;
const int MAX_VALUE = 200;
y = (rand() % (MAX_VALUE - MIN_VALUE + 1)) + MIN_VALUE;
```

The following *In the Spotlight* section demonstrates how to use random numbers to simulate rolling dice.

In the Spotlight:

Using Random Numbers

Dr. Kimura teaches an introductory statistics class and has asked you to write a program that he can use in class to simulate the rolling of dice. The program should randomly generate two numbers in the range of 1 through 6 and display them. Program 26 shows the program, with three examples of program output.

Program 26

```
// This program simulates rolling dice.
#include <iostream>
#include <cstdlib>   // For rand and srand
#include <ctime>     // For the time function
using namespace std;
```

```

int main()
{
    // Constants
    const int MIN_VALUE = 1;   // Minimum die value
    const int MAX_VALUE = 6;   // Maximum die value

    // Variables
    int die1;   // To hold the value of die #1
    int die2;   // To hold the value of die #2

    // Get the system time.
    unsigned seed = time(0);

    // Seed the random number generator.
    srand(seed);

    cout << "Rolling the dice...\n";
    die1 = (rand() % (MAX_VALUE - MIN_VALUE + 1)) + MIN_VALUE;
    die2 = (rand() % (MAX_VALUE - MIN_VALUE + 1)) + MIN_VALUE;
    cout << die1 << endl;
    cout << die2 << endl;
    return 0;
}
```

Program Output

```
Rolling the dice...
5
2
```

Program Output

```
Rolling the dice...
4
6
```

Program Output

```
Rolling the dice...
3
1
```

Checkpoint

20 Write a short description of each of the following functions:

```
cos     log     sin
exp     log10   sqrt
fmod    pow     tan
```

21 Assume the variables `angle1` and `angle2` hold angles stored in radians. Write a statement that adds the sine of `angle1` to the cosine of `angle2` and stores the result in the variable `x`.

22 To find the cube root (the third root) of a number, raise it to the power of ⅓. To find the fourth root of a number, raise it to the power of ¼. Write a statement that will find the fifth root of the variable `x` and store the result in the variable `y`.

23 The cosecant of the angle a is

$$\frac{1}{\sin a}$$

Write a statement that calculates the cosecant of the angle stored in the variable `a`, and stores it in the variable `y`.

10 Focus on Debugging: Hand Tracing a Program

Hand tracing is a debugging process where you pretend that you are the computer executing a program. You step through each of the program's statements one by one. As you look at a statement, you record the contents that each variable will have after the statement executes. This process is often helpful in finding mathematical mistakes and other logic errors.

To hand trace a program, you construct a chart with a column for each variable. The rows in the chart correspond to the lines in the program. For example, Program 27 is shown with a hand trace chart. The program uses the following four variables: `num1`, `num2`, `num3`, and `avg`. Notice the hand trace chart has a column for each variable, and a row for each line of code in function `main`.

Program 27

```
// This program asks for three numbers, then
// displays the average of the numbers.
#include <iostream>
using namespace std;

int main()
{
    double num1, num2, num3, avg;
    cout << "Enter the first number: ";
    cin >> num1;
    cout << "Enter the second number: ";
    cin >> num2;
    cout << "Enter the third number: ";
    cin >> num3;
    avg = num1 + num2 + num3 / 3;
    cout << "The average is " << avg << endl;
    return 0;
}
```

num1	num2	num3	avg

This program, which asks the user to enter three numbers and then displays the average of the numbers, has a bug. It does not display the correct average. The output of a sample session with the program follows.

Program Output with Example Input Shown in Bold

```
Enter the first number: 10 [Enter]
Enter the second number: 20 [Enter]
Enter the third number: 30 [Enter]
The average is 40
```

The correct average of 10, 20, and 30 is 20, not 40. To find the error, we will hand trace the program. To hand trace this program, you step through each statement, observing the operation that is taking place, then record the contents of the variables after the statement executes. After the hand trace is complete, the chart will appear as follows. We have written question marks in the chart where we do not know the contents of a variable.

Program 27 (with hand trace chart filled)

```
1  // This program asks for three numbers, then
2  // displays the average of the numbers.
3  #include <iostream>
4  using namespace std;

5  int main()

6  {
7      double num1, num2, num3, avg;
8      cout << "Enter the first number: ";
9      cin >> num1;
10     cout << "Enter the second number: ";
11     cin >> num2;
12     cout << "Enter the third number: ";
13     cin >> num3;
14     avg = num1 + num2 + num3 / 3;
15     cout << "The average is " << avg << endl;
16     return 0;
17 }
```

num1	num2	num3	avg
?	?	?	?
?	?	?	?
10	?	?	?
10	?	?	?
10	20	?	?
10	20	?	?
10	20	30	?
10	20	30	40
10	20	30	40

Do you see the error? By examining the statement that performs the math operation in line 14, we find a mistake. The division operation takes place before the addition operations, so we must rewrite that statement as

```
avg = (num1 + num2 + num3) / 3;
```

Hand tracing is a simple process that focuses your attention on each statement in a program. Often this helps you locate errors that are not obvious.

11 Focus on Problem Solving: A Case Study

General Crates, Inc. builds custom-designed wooden crates. With materials and labor, it costs GCI $0.23 per cubic foot to build a crate. In turn, they charge their customers $0.50 per cubic foot for the crate. You have been asked to write a program that calculates the volume (in cubic feet), cost, customer price, and profit of any crate GCI builds.

Variables

Table 14 shows the named constants and variables needed.

Table 14 Named Constants and Variables

Constant or Variable	Description
`COST_PER_CUBIC_FOOT`	A named constant, declared as a `double` and initialized with the value 0.23. This represents the cost to build a crate, per cubic foot.
`CHARGE_PER_CUBIC_FOOT`	A named constant, declared as a `double` and initialized with the value 0.5. This represents the amount charged for a crate, per cubic foot.
`length`	A `double` variable to hold the length of the crate, which is input by the user.
`width`	A `double` variable to hold the width of the crate, which is input by the user.
`height`	A `double` variable to hold the height of the crate, which is input by the user.
`volume`	A `double` variable to hold the volume of the crate. The value stored in this variable is calculated.
`cost`	A `double` variable to hold the cost of building the crate. The value stored in this variable is calculated.
`charge`	A `double` variable to hold the amount charged to the customer for the crate. The value stored in this variable is calculated.
`profit`	A `double` variable to hold the profit GCI makes from the crate. The value stored in this variable is calculated.

Program Design

The program must perform the following general steps:

1. Ask the user to enter the dimensions of the crate (the crate's length, width, and height).
2. Calculate the crate's volume, the cost of building the crate, the customer's charge, and the profit made.
3. Display the data calculated in Step 2.

A general hierarchy chart for this program is shown in Figure 7.

Figure 7 Hierarchy chart for the program

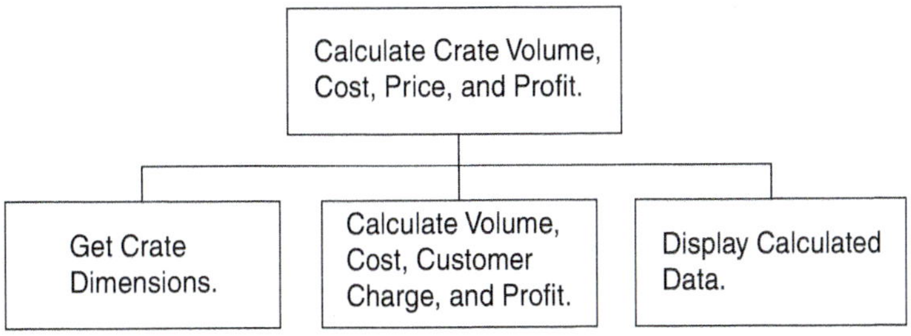

The "Get Crate Dimensions" step is shown in greater detail in Figure 8.

Figure 8 Hierarchy chart for the "Get Crate Dimensions" step

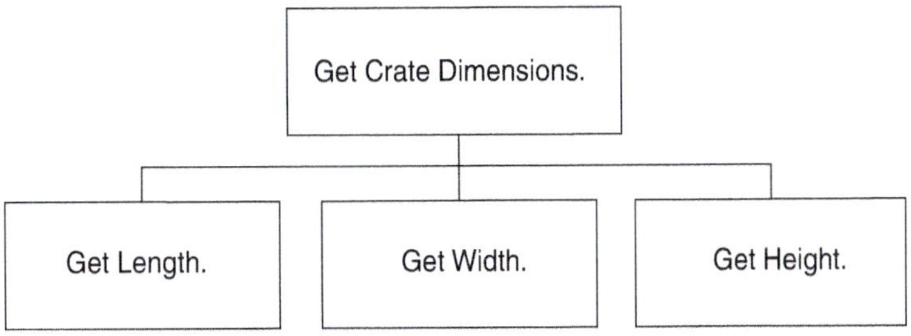

The "Calculate Volume, Cost, Customer Charge, and Profit" step is shown in greater detail in Figure 9.

Figure 9 Hierarchy chart for the "Calculate Volume, Cost, Customer Charge, and Profit" step

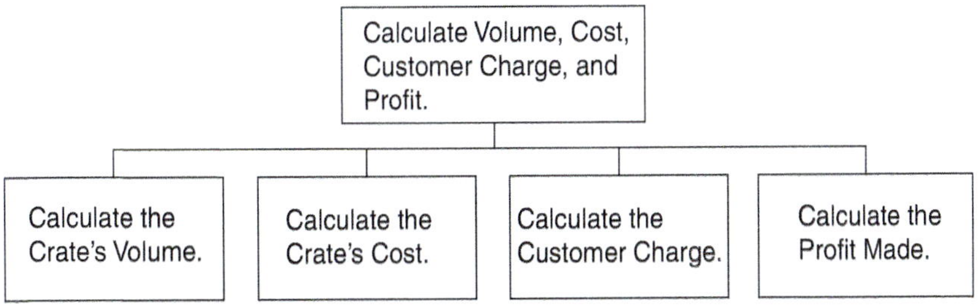

The "Display Calculated Data" step is shown in greater detail in Figure 10.

Figure 10 Hierarchy chart for the "Display Calculated Data" step

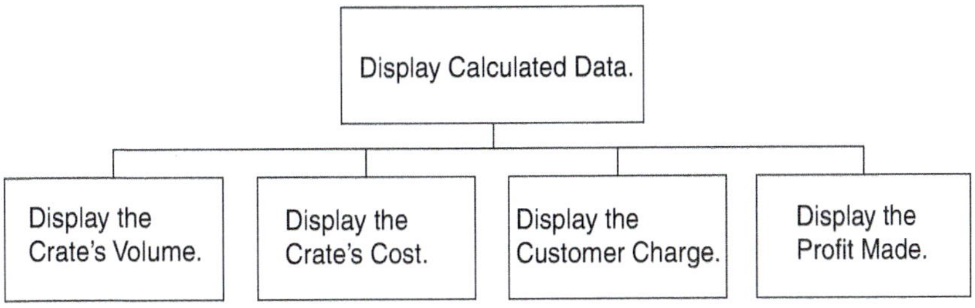

Pseudocode for the program is as follows:

```
Ask the user to input the crate's length.
Ask the user to input the crate's width.
Ask the user to input the crate's height.
Calculate the crate's volume.
Calculate the cost of building the crate.
Calculate the customer's charge for the crate.
Calculate the profit made from the crate.
Display the crate's volume.
Display the cost of building the crate.
Display the customer's charge for the crate.
Display the profit made from the crate.
```

Calculations

The following formulas will be used to calculate the crate's volume, cost, charge, and profit:

volume = length $\times$ width $\times$ height

cost = volume $\times$ 0.23

charge = volume $\times$ 0.5

profit = charge $-$ cost

The Program

The last step is to expand the pseudocode into the final program, which is shown in Program 28.

Program 28

```
// This program is used by General Crates, Inc. to calculate
// the volume, cost, customer charge, and profit of a crate
// of any size. It calculates this data from user input, which
// consists of the dimensions of the crate.
#include <iostream>
#include <iomanip>
using namespace std;

int main()
{
    // Constants for cost and amount charged
    const double COST_PER_CUBIC_FOOT = 0.23;
    const double CHARGE_PER_CUBIC_FOOT = 0.5;

    // Variables
    double length,  // The crate's length
           width,   // The crate's width
           height,  // The crate's height
           volume,  // The volume of the crate
           cost,    // The cost to build the crate
```

```
            charge,    // The customer charge for the crate
            profit;    // The profit made on the crate

    // Set the desired output formatting for numbers.
    cout << setprecision(2) << fixed << showpoint;

    // Prompt the user for the crate's length, width, and height.
    cout << "Enter the dimensions of the crate (in feet):\n";
    cout << "Length: ";
    cin >> length;
    cout << "Width: ";
    cin >> width;
    cout << "Height: ";
    cin >> height;

    // Calculate the crate's volume, the cost to produce it,
    // the charge to the customer, and the profit.
    volume = length * width * height;
    cost = volume * COST_PER_CUBIC_FOOT;
    charge = volume * CHARGE_PER_CUBIC_FOOT;
    profit = charge - cost;

    // Display the calculated data.
    cout << "The volume of the crate is ";
    cout << volume << " cubic feet.\n";
    cout << "Cost to build: $" << cost << endl;
    cout << "Charge to customer: $" << charge << endl;
    cout << "Profit: $" << profit << endl;
    return 0;
}
```

Program Output with Example Input Shown in Bold

Enter the dimensions of the crate (in feet):
Length: **10** [Enter]
Width: **8** [Enter]
Height: **4** [Enter]
The volume of the crate is 320.00 cubic feet.
Cost to build: $73.60
Charge to customer: $160.00
Profit: $86.40

Program Output with Different Example Input Shown in Bold

Enter the dimensions of the crate (in feet):
Length: **12.5** [Enter]
Width: **10.5** [Enter]
Height: **8** [Enter]
The volume of the crate is 1050.00 cubic feet.
Cost to build: $241.50
Charge to customer: $525.00
Profit: $283.50

Review Questions and Exercises

Short Answer

1. Assume the following variables are defined:

```
int age;
double pay;
char section;
```

Write a single `cin` statement that will read input into each of these variables.

2. Assume a `string` object has been defined as follows:

```
string description;
```

A) Write a `cin` statement that reads in a one-word string.

B) Write a statement that reads in a string that can contain multiple words separated by blanks.

3. What header files must be included in the following program?

```
int main()
{
    double amount = 89.7;
    cout << showpoint << fixed;
    cout << setw(8) << amount << endl;
    return 0;
}
```

4. Complete the following table by determining the value of each expression.

Expression	Value
`28 / 4 - 2`	
`6 + 12 * 2 - 8`	
`4 + 8 * 2`	
`6 + 17 % 3 - 2`	
`2 + 22 * (9 - 7)`	
`(8 + 7) * 2`	
`(16 + 7) % 2 - 1`	
`12 / (10 - 6)`	
`(19 - 3) * (2 + 2) / 4`	

5. Write C++ expressions for the following algebraic expressions:

$a = 12x$

$z = 5x + 14y + 6k$

$y = x^4$

$g = \dfrac{h + 12}{4k}$

$c = \dfrac{a^3}{b^2k^4}$

6. Assume a program has the following variable definitions:

```
int units;
float mass;
double weight;
```

and the following statement:

```
weight = mass * units;
```

Which automatic data type conversion will take place?

A) `mass` is demoted to an `int`, `units` remains an `int`, and the result of `mass * units` is an `int`.

B) `units` is promoted to a `float`, `mass` remains a `float`, and the result of `mass * units` is a `float`.

C) `units` is promoted to a `float`, `mass` remains a `float`, and the result of `mass * units` is a `double`.

7. Assume a program has the following variable definitions:

```
int a, b = 2;
float c = 4.2;
```

and the following statement:

```
a = b * c;
```

What value will be stored in `a`?

A) 8.4

B) 8

C) 0

D) None of the above

8. Assume `qty` and `salesReps` are both integers. Use a type cast expression to rewrite the following statement so it will no longer perform integer division.

```
unitsEach = qty / salesReps;
```

9. Rewrite the following variable definition so that the variable is a named constant.

```
int rate;
```

10. Complete the following table by providing statements with combined assignment operators for the right-hand column. The statements should be equivalent to the statements in the left-hand column.

Statements with Assignment Operator	Statements with Combined Assignment Operator
`x = x + 5;`	
`total = total + subtotal;`	
`dist = dist / rep;`	
`ppl = ppl * period;`	
`inv = inv - shrinkage;`	
`num = num % 2;`	

11. Write a multiple assignment statement that can be used instead of the following group of assignment statements:

```
east = 1;
west = 1;
north = 1;
south = 1;
```

12. Write a `cout` statement so the variable `divSales` is displayed in a field of 8 spaces, in fixed-point notation, with a precision of 2 decimal places. The decimal point should always be displayed.
13. Write a `cout` statement so the variable `totalAge` is displayed in a field of 12 spaces, in fixed-point notation, with a precision of 4 decimal places.
14. Write a `cout` statement so the variable `population` is displayed in a field of 12 spaces, left-justified, with a precision of 8 decimal places. The decimal point should always be displayed.

Fill-in-the-Blank

15. The ________ library function returns the cosine of an angle.
16. The ________ library function returns the sine of an angle.
17. The ________ library function returns the tangent of an angle.
18. The ________ library function returns the exponential function of a number.
19. The ________ library function returns the remainder of a floating-point division.
20. The ________ library function returns the natural logarithm of a number.
21. The ________ library function returns the base-10 logarithm of a number.
22. The ________ library function returns the value of a number raised to a power.
23. The ________ library function returns the square root of a number.
24. The ________ file must be included in a program that uses the mathematical functions.

Algorithm Workbench

25. A retail store grants its customers a maximum amount of credit. Each customer's available credit is his or her maximum amount of credit minus the amount of credit used. Write a pseudocode algorithm for a program that asks for a customer's maximum amount of credit and amount of credit used. The program should then display the customer's available credit.

    After you write the pseudocode algorithm, convert it to a complete C++ program.
26. Write a pseudocode algorithm for a program that calculates the total of a retail sale. The program should ask for the amount of the sale and the sales tax rate. The sales tax rate should be entered as a floating-point number. For example, if the sales tax rate is 6 percent, the user should enter 0.06. The program should display the amount of sales tax and the total of the sale.

    After you write the pseudocode algorithm, convert it to a complete C++ program.

27. Write a pseudocode algorithm for a program that asks the user to enter a golfer's score for three games of golf, and then displays the average of the three scores.

    After you write the pseudocode algorithm, convert it to a complete C++ program.

Find the Errors

Each of the following programs has some errors. Locate as many as you can.

28.
```
using namespace std;
int main ()
{
    double number1, number2, sum;

    Cout << "Enter a number: ";
    Cin << number1;
    Cout << "Enter another number: ";
    Cin << number2;
    number1 + number2 = sum;
    Cout "The sum of the two numbers is " << sum
    return 0;
}
```

29.
```
#include <iostream>
using namespace std;

int main()
{
    int number1, number2;
    float quotient;
    cout << "Enter two numbers and I will divide\n";
    cout << "the first by the second for you.\n";
    cin >> number1, number2;
    quotient = float<static_cast>(number1) / number2;
    cout << quotient
    return 0;
}
```

30.
```
#include <iostream>;
using namespace std;

int main()
{
    const int number1, number2, product;

    cout << "Enter two numbers and I will multiply\n";
    cout << "them for you.\n";
    cin >> number1 >> number2;
    product = number1 * number2;
    cout << product
    return 0;
}
```

31.
```
#include <iostream>;
using namespace std;

main
{
    int number1, number2;

    cout << "Enter two numbers and I will multiply\n"
    cout << "them by 50 for you.\n"
    cin >> number1 >> number2;
    number1 =* 50;
    number2 =* 50;
    cout << number1 << " " << number2;
    return 0;
}
```

32.
```
#include <iostream>;
using namespace std;

main
{
    double number, half;

    cout << "Enter a number and I will divide it\n"
    cout << "in half for you.\n"
    cin >> number1;
    half =/ 2;
    cout << fixedpoint << showpoint << half << endl;
    return 0;
}
```

33.
```
#include <iostream>;
using namespace std;

int main()
{
    char name, go;

    cout << "Enter your name: ";
    getline >> name;
    cout << "Hi " << name << endl;
    return 0;
}
```

Predict the Output

What will each of the following programs display? (Some should be hand traced and require a calculator.)

34. (*Assume the user enters 38700. Use a calculator.*)

```
#include <iostream>
using namespace std;
```

```
int main()
{
    double salary, monthly;
    cout << "What is your annual salary? ";
    cin >> salary;
    monthly = static_cast<int>(salary) / 12;
    cout << "Your monthly wages are " << monthly << endl;
    return 0;
}
```

35.
```
#include <iostream>
using namespace std;
int main()
{
    long x, y, z;

    x = y = z = 4;
    x += 2;
    y -= 1;
    z *= 3;
    cout << x << " " << y << " " << z << endl;
    return 0;
}
```

36. (*Assume the user enters George Washington.*)
```
#include <iostream>
#include <iomanip>
#include <string>
using namespace std;

int main()
{
    string userInput;
    cout << "What is your name? ";
    getline(cin, userInput);
    cout << "Hello " << userInput << endl;
    return 0;
}
```

37. (*Assume the user enters 36720152. Use a calculator.*)
```
#include <iostream>
#include <iomanip>
using namespace std;

int main()
{
    long seconds;
    double minutes, hours, days, months, years;

    cout << "Enter the number of seconds that have\n";
    cout << "elapsed since some time in the past and\n";
    cout << "I will tell you how many minutes, hours,\n";
    cout << "days, months, and years have passed: ";
    cin >> seconds;
```

```
    minutes = seconds / 60;
    hours = minutes / 60;
    days = hours / 24;
    years = days / 365;
    months = years * 12;
    cout << setprecision(4) << fixed << showpoint << right;
    cout << "Minutes: " << setw(6) << minutes << endl;
    cout << "Hours: " << setw(6) << hours << endl;
    cout << "Days: " << setw(6) << days << endl;
    cout << "Months: " << setw(6) << months << endl;
    cout << "Years: " << setw(6) << years << endl;
    return 0;
}
```

Programming Challenges

1. Miles per Gallon

Write a program that calculates a car's gas mileage. The program should ask the user to enter the number of gallons of gas the car can hold, and the number of miles it can be driven on a full tank. It should then display the number of miles that may be driven per gallon of gas.

2. Stadium Seating

VideoNote **Solving the Stadium Seating Problem**

There are three seating categories at a stadium. For a softball game, Class A seats cost $15, Class B seats cost $12, and Class C seats cost $9. Write a program that asks how many tickets for each class of seats were sold, then displays the amount of income generated from ticket sales. Format your dollar amount in fixed-point notation, with two decimal places of precision, and be sure the decimal point is always displayed.

3. Test Average

Write a program that asks for five test scores. The program should calculate the average test score and display it. The number displayed should be formatted in fixed-point notation, with one decimal point of precision.

4. Average Rainfall

Write a program that calculates the average rainfall for three months. The program should ask the user to enter the name of each month, such as June or July, and the amount of rain (in inches) that fell each month. The program should display a message similar to the following:

The average rainfall for June, July, and August is 6.72 inches.

5. Male and Female Percentages

Write a program that asks the user for the number of males and the number of females registered in a class. The program should display the percentage of males and females in the class.

Hint: Suppose there are 8 males and 12 females in a class. There are 20 students in the class. The percentage of males can be calculated as 8 ÷ 20 = 0.4, or 40 percent. The percentage of females can be calculated as 12 ÷ 20 = 0.6, or 60 percent.

6. Ingredient Adjuster

A cookie recipe calls for the following ingredients:

- 1.5 cups of sugar
- 1 cup of butter
- 2.75 cups of flour

The recipe produces 48 cookies with this amount of the ingredients. Write a program that asks the user how many cookies he or she wants to make, then displays the number of cups of each ingredient needed for the specified number of cookies.

7. Box Office

A movie theater only keeps a percentage of the revenue earned from ticket sales. The remainder goes to the movie distributor. Write a program that calculates a theater's gross and net box office profit for a night. The program should ask for the name of the movie, and how many adult and child tickets were sold. (The price of an adult ticket is $10.00 and a child's ticket is $6.00.) It should display a report similar to:

Movie Name:	"Wheels of Fury"
Adult Tickets Sold:	382
Child Tickets Sold:	127
Gross Box Office Profit:	$ 4,582.00
Net Box Office Profit:	$ 916.40
Amount Paid to Distributor:	$ 3,665.60

NOTE: Assume the theater keeps 20 percent of the gross box office profit.

8. How Many Widgets?

The Yukon Widget Company manufactures widgets that weigh 12.5 pounds each. Write a program that calculates how many widgets are stacked on a pallet, based on the total weight of the pallet. The program should ask the user how much the pallet weighs by itself and with the widgets stacked on it. It should then calculate and display the number of widgets stacked on the pallet.

9. How Many Calories?

A bag of cookies holds 30 cookies. The calorie information on the bag claims there are 10 "servings" in the bag and that a serving equals 300 calories. Write a program that asks the user to input how many cookies he or she actually ate, then reports how many total calories were consumed.

10. How Much Insurance?

Many financial experts advise that property owners should insure their homes or buildings for at least 80 percent of the amount it would cost to replace the structure. Write a program that asks the user to enter the replacement cost of a building, then displays the minimum amount of insurance he or she should buy for the property.

11. Automobile Costs

Write a program that asks the user to enter the monthly costs for the following expenses incurred from operating his or her automobile: loan payment, insurance, gas, oil, tires, and maintenance. The program should then display the total monthly cost of these expenses, and the total annual cost of these expenses.

12. Celsius to Fahrenheit

Write a program that converts Celsius temperatures to Fahrenheit temperatures. The formula is

$$F = \frac{9}{5}C + 32$$

F is the Fahrenheit temperature, and C is the Celsius temperature.

13. Currency

Write a program that will convert U.S. dollar amounts to Japanese yen and to euros, storing the conversion factors in the constants `YEN_PER_DOLLAR` and `EUROS_PER_DOLLAR`. To get the most up-to-date exchange rates, search the Internet using the term "currency exchange rate". If you cannot find the most recent exchange rates, use the following:

1 Dollar = 98.93 Yen
1 Dollar = 0.74 Euros

Format your currency amounts in fixed-point notation, with two decimal places of precision, and be sure the decimal point is always displayed.

14. Monthly Sales Tax

A retail company must file a monthly sales tax report listing the sales for the month and the amount of sales tax collected. Write a program that asks for the month, the year, and the total amount collected at the cash register (i.e. sales plus sales tax). Assume the state sales tax is 4 percent, and the county sales tax is 2 percent.

If the total amount collected is known and the total sales tax is 6 percent, the amount of product sales may be calculated as:

$$S = \frac{T}{1.06}$$

S is the product sales and T is the total income (product sales plus sales tax).

The program should display a report similar to:

```
Month: October
--------------------
Total Collected:      $ 26572.89
Sales:                $ 25068.76
County Sales Tax:     $   501.38
State Sales Tax:      $  1002.75
Total Sales Tax:      $  1504.13
```

15. Property Tax

A county collects property taxes on the assessment value of property, which is 60 percent of the property's actual value. If an acre of land is valued at $10,000, its assessment value is $6,000. The property tax is then 75¢ for each $100 of the assessment value. The tax for the acre assessed at $6,000 will be $45. Write a program that asks for the actual value of a piece of property, then displays the assessment value and property tax.

16. Senior Citizen Property Tax

Madison County provides a $5,000 homeowner exemption for its senior citizens. For example, if a senior's house is valued at $158,000, its assessed value would be $94,800, as explained above. However, he would only pay tax on $89,800. At last year's tax rate of $2.64 for each $100 of assessed value, the property tax would be $2,370.72. In addition to the tax break, senior citizens are allowed to pay their property tax in four equal payments. The quarterly payment due on this property would be $592.68. Write a program that asks the user to input the actual value of a piece of property and the current tax rate for each $100 of assessed value. The program should then calculate and report how much annual property tax a senior homeowner will be charged for this property, and what the quarterly tax bill will be.

17. Math Tutor

Write a program that can be used as a math tutor for a young student. The program should display two random numbers to be added, such as

```
 247
+129
----
```

The program should then pause while the student works on the problem. When the student is ready to check the answer, he or she can press a key and the program will display the correct solution:

```
 247
+129
----
 376
```

18. Interest Earned

Assuming there are no deposits other than the original investment, the balance in a savings account after one year may be calculated as

$$\texttt{Amount} = \texttt{Principal} \times \left(1 + \frac{\texttt{Rate}}{\texttt{T}}\right)^{\texttt{T}}$$

`Principal` is the balance in the savings account, `Rate` is the interest rate, and `T` is the number of times the interest is compounded during a year (`T` is 4 if the interest is compounded quarterly).

Write a program that asks for the principal, the interest rate, and the number of times the interest is compounded. It should display a report similar to:

```
Interest Rate:            4.25%
Times Compounded:            12
Principal:            $ 1000.00
Interest:             $   43.34
Amount in Savings:    $ 1043.34
```

19. Monthly Payments

The monthly payment on a loan may be calculated by the following formula:

$$\texttt{Payment} = \frac{\texttt{Rate} \times (1 + \texttt{Rate})^{\texttt{N}}}{((1 + \texttt{Rate})^{\texttt{N}} - 1)} \times \texttt{L}$$

`Rate` is the monthly interest rate, which is the annual interest rate divided by 12. (12 percent annual interest would be 1 percent monthly interest.) `N` is the number of payments, and `L` is the amount of the loan. Write a program that asks for these values then displays a report similar to:

```
Loan Amount:              $ 10000.00
Monthly Interest Rate:            1%
Number of Payments:               36
Monthly Payment:          $   332.14
Amount Paid Back:         $ 11957.15
Interest Paid:            $  1957.15
```

20. Pizza Pi

Joe's Pizza Palace needs a program to calculate the number of slices a pizza of any size can be divided into. The program should perform the following steps:

A) Ask the user for the diameter of the pizza in inches.
B) Calculate the number of slices that may be taken from a pizza of that size.
A) Display a message telling the number of slices.

To calculate the number of slices that may be taken from the pizza, you must know the following facts:

- Each slice should have an area of 14.125 inches.
- To calculate the number of slices, simply divide the area of the pizza by 14.125.
- The area of the pizza is calculated with this formula:

Area = πr^2

NOTE: π is the Greek letter pi. 3.14159 can be used as its value. The variable r is the radius of the pizza. Divide the diameter by 2 to get the radius.

Make sure the output of the program displays the number of slices in fixed-point notation, rounded to one decimal place of precision. Use a named constant for pi.

21. How Many Pizzas?

Modify the program you wrote in Programming Challenge 20 (Pizza Pi) so it reports the number of pizzas you need to buy for a party if each person attending is expected to eat an average of four slices. The program should ask the user for the number of people who will be at the party, and for the diameter of the pizzas to be ordered. It should then calculate and display the number of pizzas to purchase.

22. Angle Calculator

Write a program that asks the user for an angle, entered in radians. The program should then display the sine, cosine, and tangent of the angle. (Use the `sin`, `cos`, and `tan` library functions to determine these values.) The output should be displayed in fixed-point notation, rounded to four decimal places of precision.

23. Stock Transaction Program

Last month Joe purchased some stock in Acme Software, Inc. Here are the details of the purchase:

- The number of shares that Joe purchased was 1,000.
- When Joe purchased the stock, he paid $45.50 per share.

- Joe paid his stockbroker a commission that amounted to 2 percent of the amount he paid for the stock.

Two weeks later, Joe sold the stock. Here are the details of the sale:

- The number of shares that Joe sold was 1,000.
- He sold the stock for $56.90 per share.
- He paid his stockbroker another commission that amounted to 2 percent of the amount he received for the stock.

Write a program that displays the following information:

- The amount of money Joe paid for the stock.
- The amount of commission Joe paid his broker when he bought the stock.
- The amount that Joe sold the stock for.
- The amount of commission Joe paid his broker when he sold the stock.
- Display the amount of profit that Joe made after selling his stock and paying the two commissions to his broker. (If the amount of profit that your program displays is a negative number, then Joe lost money on the transaction.)

24. **Planting Grapevines**

A vineyard owner is planting several new rows of grapevines, and needs to know how many grapevines to plant in each row. She has determined that after measuring the length of a future row, she can use the following formula to calculate the number of vines that will fit in the row, along with the trellis end-post assemblies that will need to be constructed at each end of the row:

$$V = \frac{R-2E}{S}$$

The terms in the formula are:

V is the number of grapevines that will fit in the row.
R is the length of the row, in feet.
E is the amount of space, in feet, used by an end-post assembly.
S is the space between vines, in feet.

Write a program that makes the calculation for the vineyard owner. The program should ask the user to input the following:

- The length of the row, in feet
- The amount of space used by an end-post assembly, in feet
- The amount of space between the vines, in feet

Once the input data has been entered, the program should calculate and display the number of grapevines that will fit in the row.

25. **Word Game**

Write a program that plays a word game with the user. The program should ask the user to enter the following:

- His or her name
- His or her age
- The name of a city
- The name of a college
- A profession

- A type of animal
- A pet's name

After the user has entered these items, the program should display the following story, inserting the user's input into the appropriate locations:

There once was a person named ***NAME*** who lived in ***CITY***. At the age of ***AGE***, ***NAME*** went to college at ***COLLEGE***. ***NAME*** graduated and went to work as a ***PROFESSION***. Then, ***NAME*** adopted a(n) ***ANIMAL*** named ***PETNAME***. They both lived happily ever after!

Answers to Checkpoints

1 `iostream`

2 True

3 B

4 `cin >> miles >> feet >> inches;`

5 Include one or more `cout` statements explaining what values the user should enter.

6
```
#include <iostream>
using namespace std;

int main()
{
    double pounds, kilograms;

    cout << "Enter your weight in pounds: ";
    cin >> pounds;
    // The following line does the conversion.
    // One kilogram weighs 2.2 pounds.
    kilograms = pounds / 2.2;
    cout << "Your weight in kilograms is ";
    cout << kilograms << endl;
    return 0;
}
```

7 *Value*

21
2
31
5
24
2
69
0
30

8
```
y = 6 * x;
a = 2 * b + 4 * c;
y = x * x; or y = pow(x, 2.0);
g = (x + 2) / (z * z); or g = (x + 2.0) / pow(z, 2.0);
y = (x * x) / (z * z); or y = pow(x, 2.0) / pow (z, 2.0);
```

9

If the user enters…	*The program displays…*
2	6
5	27
4.3	20.49
6	38

10
```
#include <iostream>
#include <cmath>
using namespace std;

int main()
{
    double volume, radius, height;
    cout << "This program will tell you the volume of\n";
    cout << "a cylinder-shaped fuel tank.\n";
    cout << "How tall is the tank? ";
    cin >> height;
    cout << "What is the radius of the tank? ";
    cin >> radius;
    volume = 3.14159 * pow(radius, 2.0) * height;
    cout << "The volume of the tank is " << volume << endl;
    return 0;
}
```

11
A) 2
B) 17.0
C) 2.0
D) 2.4
E) 2.4
F) 2.4
G) 4
H) 27
I) 30
J) 27.0

12
```
#include <iostream>
using namespace std;

int main()
{
    char letter;

    cout << "Enter a character: ":
    cin >> letter;
```

```
    cout << "The ASCII code for " << letter;
    cout << " is " << static_cast<int>(letter) << endl;
    return 0;
}
```

13 9
9.5
9

14 `total = subtotal = tax = shipping = 0;`

15 A) `x += 6;`
B) `amount -= 4;`
C) `y *= 4;`
D) `total /= 27;`
E) `x %= 7;`
F) `x += (y * 5);`
G) `total -= (discount * 4);`
H) `increase *= (salesRep * 5);`
I) `profit /= (shares - 1000);`

16 3
11
1

17 A) `cout << setw(9) << fixed << setprecision(2) << 34.789;`
B) `cout << setw(5) << fixed << setprecision(3) << 7.0;`
C) `cout << fixed << 5.789e12;`
D) `cout << left << setw(7) << 67;`

18
```
#include <iostream>
#include <string>
using namespace std;

int main()
{
    string person = "Wolfgang Smith";
    cout << right;
    cout << setw(20);
    cout << person << endl;
    cout << left;
    cout << person << endl;
    return 0;
}
```

19
```
#include <iostream>
#include <iomanip>
using namespace std;

int main()
{
```

```
    const double PI = 3.14159;
    double degrees, radians;

    cout << "Enter an angle in degrees and I will convert it\n";
    cout << "to radians for you: ";
    cin >> degrees;
    radians = degrees * PI / 180;
    cout << degrees << " degrees is equal to ";
    cout << setw(5) << left << fixed << showpoint
         << setprecision(4) << radians << " radians.\n";
    return 0;
}
```

20 `cos:` Returns the cosine of the argument.

`exp:` Returns the exponential function of the argument.

`fmod:` Returns the remainder of the first argument divided by the second argument.

`log:` Returns the natural logarithm of the argument.

`log10:` Returns the base-10 logarithm of the argument.

`pow:` Returns the value of the first argument raised to the power of the second argument.

`sin:` Returns the sine of the argument.

`sqrt:` Returns the square root of the argument.

`tan:` Returns the tangent of the argument.

21 `x = sin(angle1) + cos(angle2);`

22 `y = pow(x, 0.2); // 0.2 is equal to 1/5`

23 `y = 1 / sin(a);`

Answers to Odd Numbered Review Questions

1. `cin >> age >> pay >> section;`

3. `iostream` and `iomanip`

5.
```
a = 12 * x;
z = 5 * x + 14 * y + 6 * k;
y = pow(x, 4);
g = (h + 12) / (4 * k);
c = pow(a, 3) / (pow(b, 2) * pow(k, 4));
```

7. B

9. `const int RATE = 12;`

11. `east = west = north = south = 1;`

13.
```
cout << setw(12) << fixed
     << setprecision(4) << totalAge;
```

15. `cos`

17. `tan`

19. `fmod`

21. `log10`

23. `sqrt`

25. *Display "Enter the customer's maximum amount of credit: ".*
Read maxCredit.
Display "Enter the amount of credit the customer has used: ".
Read creditUsed.
availableCredit = maxCredit – creditUsed.
Display "The customer's available credit is $".
Display availableCredit.

```
#include <iostream>
using namespace std;

int main()
{
    double maxCredit, creditUsed, availableCredit;

    cout << "Enter the customer's maximum amount of credit: ";
    cin >> maxCredit;
    cout << "Enter the amount of credit used by the customer: ";
    cin >> creditUsed;
    availableCredit = maxCredit - creditUsed;
    cout << "The customer's available credit is $";
    cout << availableCredit << endl;
    return 0;
}
```

27. *Display "Enter the score for the 1st game: ".*
Read score1.
Display "Enter the score for the 2nd game: ".
Read score2.
Display "Enter the score for the 3rd game: ".
Read score3.
averageScore = (score1 + score2 + score3) / 3.
Display "The average score is : ".
Display averageScore.

```
#include <iostream>
using namespace std;

int main()
{
```

```
    int score1, score2, score3, averageScore;

    cout << "Enter the score for the 1st game: ";
    cin >> score1;
    cout << "Enter the score for the 2nd game: ";
    cin >> score2;
    cout << "Enter the score for the 3rd game: ";
    cin >> score3;
    averageScore = (score1 + score2 + score3) / 3;
    cout << "The average score is :";
    cout << averageScore << endl;
    return 0;
}
```

29. The first `cin` statement should read:

```
cin >> number1 >> number2;
```

The assignment statement should read:

```
quotient = static_cast<float>(number1) / number2;
```

The last statement is missing a semicolon.

31. There shouldn't be a semicolon after the `#include` directive.
The function header for `main` should read:

```
int main()
```

The combined assignment operators improperly used.
Those statements should be:

```
number1 *= 50;
number2 *= 50;
```

33. There shouldn't be a semicolon after the `#include` directive.
`name` should be declared as a `string`, and the `#include <string>` directive should be used.
The following statement:

```
getline >> name;
```

should read:

```
getline(cin, name);
```

35. 6 3 12

37. Minutes: 612002.0000
Hours: 10200.0332
Days: 425.0014
Months: 13.9726
Years: 1.1644

Making Decisions

TOPICS

1 Relational Operators

CONCEPT: Relational operators allow you to compare numeric and `char` values and determine whether one is greater than, less than, equal to, or not equal to another.

So far, the programs you have written follow this simple scheme:

- Gather input from the user.
- Perform one or more calculations.
- Display the results on the screen.

Computers are good at performing calculations, but they are also quite adept at comparing values to determine whether one is greater than, less than, or equal to the other. These types of operations are valuable for tasks such as examining sales figures, determining profit and loss, checking a number to ensure it is within an acceptable range, and validating the input given by a user.

Numeric data is compared in C++ by using relational operators. Each relational operator determines whether a specific relationship exists between two values. For example, the greater-than operator (>) determines if a value is greater than another. The equality operator (==) determines if two values are equal. Table 1 lists all of C++'s relational operators.

Table 1 Relational Operators

Relational Operators	Meaning
>	Greater than
<	Less than
>=	Greater than or equal to
<=	Less than or equal to
==	Equal to
!=	Not equal to

All of the relational operators are binary, which means they use two operands. Here is an example of an expression using the greater-than operator:

```
x > y
```

This expression is called a *relational expression.* It is used to determine whether x is greater than y. The following expression determines whether x is less than y:

```
x < y
```

Table 2 shows examples of several relational expressions that compare the variables x and y.

Table 2 Relational Expressions

Expression	What the Expression Means
x > y	Is x greater than y?
x < y	Is x less than y?
x >= y	Is x greater than or equal to y?
x <= y	Is x less than or equal to y?
x == y	Is x equal to y?
x != y	Is x not equal to y?

> **NOTE:** All the relational operators have left-to-right associativity. Recall that associativity is the order in which an operator works with its operands.

The Value of a Relationship

So, how are relational expressions used in a program? Remember, all expressions have a value. Relational expressions are also known as *Boolean expressions*, which means their value can only be *true* or *false*. If x is greater than y, the expression x > y will be true, while the expression y == x will be false.

The == operator determines whether the operand on its left is equal to the operand on its right. If both operands have the same value, the expression is true. Assuming that a is 4, the following expression is true:

```
a == 4
```

But the following is false:

```
a == 2
```

WARNING! Notice the equality operator is two = symbols together. Don't confuse this operator with the assignment operator, which is one = symbol. The == operator determines whether a variable is equal to another value, but the = operator assigns the value on the operator's right to the variable on its left. There will be more about this later in the chapter.

A couple of the relational operators actually test for two relationships. The >= operator determines whether the operand on its left is greater than *or* equal to the operand on the right. Assuming a is 4, b is 6, and c is 4, both of the following expressions are true:

```
b >= a
a >= c
```

But the following is false:

```
a >= 5
```

The <= operator determines whether the operand on its left is less than *or* equal to the operand on its right. Once again, assuming a is 4, b is 6, and c is 4, both of the following expressions are true:

```
a <= c
b <= 10
```

But the following is false:

```
b <= a
```

The last relational operator is !=, which is the not-equal-to operator. It determines whether the operand on its left is not equal to the operand on its right, which is the opposite of the == operator. As before, assuming a is 4, b is 6, and c is 4, both of the following expressions are true:

```
a != b
b != c
```

These expressions are true because a is *not* equal to b and b is *not* equal to c. But the following expression is false because a *is* equal to c:

```
a != c
```

Table 3 shows other relational expressions and their true or false values.

Table 3 (Assume x is 10 and y is 7.)

Expression	Value
x < y	False, because x is not less than y.
x > y	True, because x is greater than y.
x >= y	True, because x is greater than or equal to y.
x <= y	False, because x is not less than or equal to y.
y != x	True, because y is not equal to x.

What Is Truth?

The question "what is truth?" is one you would expect to find in a philosophy book, not a C++ programming text. It's a good question for us to consider, though. If a relational expression can be either true or false, how are those values represented internally in a program? How does a computer store *true* in memory? How does it store *false*?

Those two abstract states are converted to numbers. In C++, relational expressions represent true states with the number 1, and false states with the number 0.

> **NOTE:** As you will see later in this chapter, 1 is not the only value regarded as true.

To illustrate this more fully, look at Program 1.

Program 1

```
// This program displays the values of true and false states.
#include <iostream>
using namespace std;

int main()
{
    bool trueValue, falseValue;
    int x = 5, y = 10;

    trueValue = x < y;
    falseValue = y == x;

    cout << "True is " << trueValue << endl;
    cout << "False is " << falseValue << endl;
    return 0;
}
```

Program Output

```
True is 1
False is 0
```

Let's examine the statements containing the relational expressions, in lines 10 and 11, a little closer:

```
trueValue = x < y;
falseValue = y == x;
```

These statements may seem odd because they are assigning the value of a comparison to a variable. In line 10, the variable `trueValue` is being assigned the result of `x < y`. Since `x` is less than `y`, the expression is true, and the variable `trueValue` is assigned the value 1. In line 11, the expression `y == x` is false, so the variable `falseValue` is set to 0. Table 4 shows examples of other statements using relational expressions and their outcomes.

> **NOTE:** Relational expressions have a higher precedence than the assignment operator. In the statement
>
> ```
> z = x < y;
> ```
>
> the expression `x < y` is evaluated first, then its value is assigned to `z`.

Table 4 (Assume `x` is 10, `y` is 7, and `z`, `a`, and `b` are `int`s or `bool`s.)

Statement	Outcome
`z = x < y`	`z` is assigned 0 because `x` is not less than `y`.
`cout << (x > y);`	Displays 1 because `x` is greater than `y`.
`a = x >= y;`	`a` is assigned 1 because `x` is greater than or equal to `y`.
`cout << (x <= y);`	Displays 0 because `x` is not less than or equal to `y`.
`b = y != x;`	`b` is assigned 1 because `y` is not equal to `x`.

When writing statements such as these, it sometimes helps to enclose the relational expression in parentheses, such as:

```
trueValue = (x < y);
falseValue = (y == x);
```

As interesting as relational expressions are, we've only scratched the surface of how to use them. In this chapter's remaining sections, you will see how to get the most from relational expressions by using them in statements that take action based on the results of the comparison.

Checkpoint

1 Assuming `x` is 5, `y` is 6, and `z` is 8, indicate whether each of the following relational expressions is true or false:

A) `x == 5`
B) `7 <= (x + 2)`
C) `z < 4`
D) `(2 + x) != y`
E) `z != 4`
F) `x >= 9`
G) `x <= (y * 2)`

2 Indicate whether the following statements about relational expressions are correct or incorrect:

A) `x <= y` is the same as `y > x`.
B) `x != y` is the same as `y >= x`.
C) `x >= y` is the same as `y <= x`.

3 Answer the following questions with a yes or no:

A) If it is true that `x > y` and it is also true that `x < z`, does that mean `y < z` is true?
B) If it is true that `x >= y` and it is also true that `z == x`, does that mean that `z == y` is true?
C) If it is true that `x != y` and it is also true that `x != z`, does that mean that `z != y` is true?

4 What will the following program display?

```
#include <iostream>
using namespace std;

int main ()
{
    int a = 0, b = 2, x = 4, y = 0;

    cout << (a == b) << endl;
    cout << (a != y) << endl;
    cout << (b <= x) << endl;
    cout << (y > a) << endl;
    return 0;
}
```

2 The `if` Statement

CONCEPT: The `if` statement can cause other statements to execute only under certain conditions.

VideoNote
The `if` Statement

You might think of the statements in a procedural program as individual steps taken as you are walking down a road. To reach the destination, you must start at the beginning and take each step, one after the other, until you reach the destination. The programs you have written so far are like a "path" of execution for the program to follow.

The type of code in Figure 1 is called a *sequence structure* because the statements are executed in sequence, without branching off in another direction. Programs often need more than one path of execution, however. Many algorithms require a program to execute some statements only under certain circumstances. This can be accomplished with a *decision structure.*

In a decision structure's simplest form, a specific action is taken only when a specific condition exists. If the condition does not exist, the action is not performed. The flowchart in Figure 2 shows the logic of a decision structure. The diamond symbol represents a yes/no

Figure 1 Sequence structure

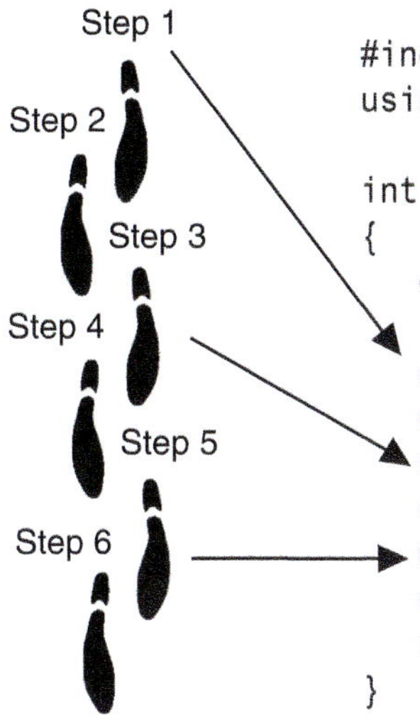


```
// A program to calculate the area of a rectangle

#include <iostream>
using namespace std;

int main()
{
   double length, width, area;

   cout << "Enter the length of the rectangle: ";
   cin >> length;
   cout << "Enter the width of the rectangle: ";
   cin >> width;
   area = length * width;
   cout << "The area is: " << area << endl
   return 0;
}
```

question or a true/false condition. If the answer to the question is yes (or if the condition is true), the program flow follows one path, which leads to an action being performed. If the answer to the question is no (or the condition is false), the program flow follows another path, which skips the action.

Figure 2 Decision structure

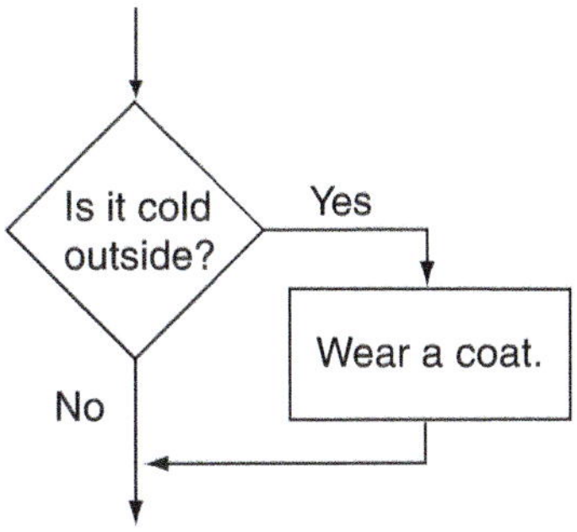

In the flowchart, the action "Wear a coat" is performed only when it is cold outside. If it is not cold outside, the action is skipped. The action is *conditionally executed* because it is performed only when a certain condition (cold outside) exists. Figure 3 shows a more elaborate flowchart, where three actions are taken only when it is cold outside.

We perform mental tests like these every day. Here are some other examples:

If the car is low on gas, stop at a service station and get gas.
If it's raining outside, go inside.
If you're hungry, get something to eat.

Figure 3 Decision structure

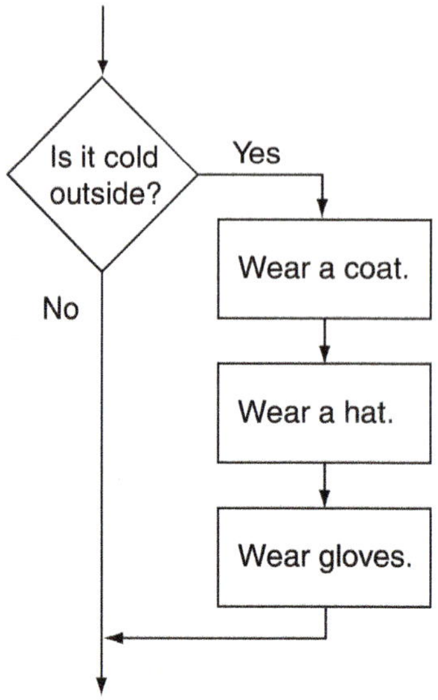

One way to code a decision structure in C++ is with the `if` statement. Here is the general format of the `if` statement:

```
if (expression)
    statement;
```

The `if` statement is simple in the way it works: If the value of the expression inside the parentheses is true, the very next ***statement*** is executed. Otherwise, it is skipped. The ***statement*** is *conditionally executed* because it only executes under the condition that the *expression* in the parentheses is true. Program 2 shows an example of an `if` statement. The user enters three test scores, and the program calculates their average. If the average is greater than 95, the program congratulates the user on obtaining a high score.

Program 2

```
// This program averages three test scores
#include <iostream>
#include <iomanip>
using namespace std;

int main()
{
   const int HIGH_SCORE = 95;  // A high score is 95 or greater
   int score1, score2, score3; // To hold three test scores
   double average;             // To hold the average score

```

```
12     // Get the three test scores.
13     cout << "Enter 3 test scores and I will average them: ";
14     cin >> score1 >> score2 >> score3;
15
16     // Calculate and display the average score.
17     average = (score1 + score2 + score3) / 3.0;
18     cout << fixed << showpoint << setprecision(1);
19     cout << "Your average is " << average << endl;
20
21     // If the average is a high score, congratulate the user.
22     if (average > HIGH_SCORE)
23        cout << "Congratulations! That's a high score!\n";
24     return 0;
25  }
```

Program Output with Example Input Shown in Bold

```
Enter 3 test scores and I will average them: 80 90 70 [Enter]
Your average is 80.0
```

Program Output with Different Example Input Shown in Bold

```
Enter 3 test scores and I will average them: 100 100 100 [Enter]
Your average is 100.0
Congratulations! That's a high score!
```

Lines 22 and 23 cause the congratulatory message to be printed:

```
if (average > HIGH_SCORE)
   cout << "Congratulations! That's a high score!\n";
```

The `cout` statement in line 23 is executed only if the average is greater than 95, the value of the `HIGH_SCORE` constant. If the average is not greater than 95, the `cout` statement is skipped. Figure 4 shows the logic of this `if` statement.

Figure 4 `if` statement logic

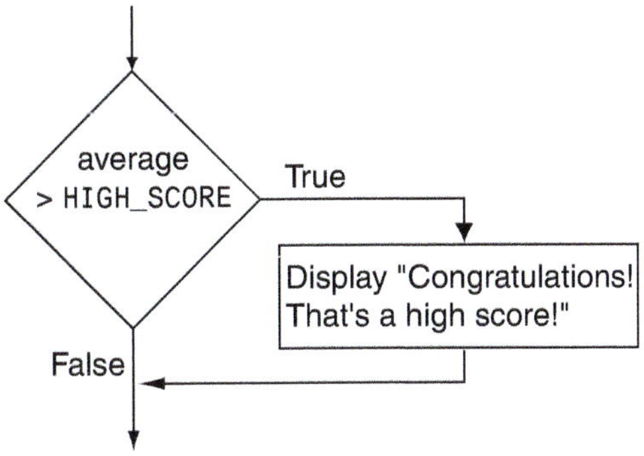

Table 5 shows other examples of `if` statements and their outcomes.

Table 5 `if` Statements and Their Outcomes

Statement	Outcome
`if (hours > 40)` `overTime = true;`	Assigns `true` to the `bool` variable `overTime` only if `hours` is greater than 40
`if (value > 32)` `cout << "Invalid number\n";`	Displays the message "Invalid number" only if `value` is greater than 32
`if (overTime == true)` `payRate *= 2;`	Multiplies `payRate` by 2 only if `overTime` is equal to `true`

Be Careful with Semicolons

Semicolons do not mark the end of a line, but the end of a complete C++ statement. The `if` statement isn't complete without the conditionally executed statement that comes after it. So, you must not put a semicolon after the `if (`*`expression`*`)` portion of an `if` statement.

No semicolon goes here.

```
if (expression)
   statement;
```

Semicolon goes here.

If you inadvertently put a semicolon after the `if` part, the compiler will assume you are placing a null statement there. The *null statement* is an empty statement that does nothing. This will prematurely terminate the `if` statement, which disconnects it from the statement that follows it. The statement following the `if` will always execute, as shown in Program 3.

Program 3

```
// This program demonstrates how a misplaced semicolon
// prematurely terminates an if statement.
#include <iostream>
using namespace std;

int main()
{
    int x = 0, y = 10;

    cout << "x is " << x << " and y is " << y << endl;
    if (x > y); // Error! Misplaced semicolon
       cout << "x is greater than y\n"; //This is always executed.
    return 0;
}
```

Program Output

```
x is 0 and y is 10
x is greater than y
```

Programming Style and the `if` Statement

Even though `if` statements usually span more than one line, they are technically one long statement. For instance, the following `if` statements are identical except in style:

```
if (a >= 100)
   cout << "The number is out of range.\n";
if (a >= 100) cout << "The number is out of range.\n";
```

In both the examples above, the compiler considers the `if` part and the `cout` statement as one unit, with a semicolon properly placed at the end. Indention and spacing are for the human readers of a program, not the compiler. Here are two important style rules you should adopt for writing `if` statements:

- The conditionally executed statement should appear on the line after the `if` statement.
- The conditionally executed statement should be indented one "level" from the `if` statement.

NOTE: In most editors, each time you press the tab key, you are indenting one level.

By indenting the conditionally executed statement, you are causing it to stand out visually. This is so that you can tell at a glance what part of the program the `if` statement executes. This is a standard way of writing `if` statements, and is the method you should use.

NOTE: Indentation and spacing are for the human readers of a program, not the compiler. Even though the `cout` statement following the `if` statement in Program 3 is indented, the semicolon still terminates the `if` statement.

Comparing Floating-Point Numbers

Because of the way floating-point numbers are stored in memory, rounding errors sometimes occur. This is because some fractional numbers cannot be exactly represented using binary. So, you should be careful when using the equality operator (`==`) to compare floating-point numbers. For example, Program 4 uses two `double` variables, `a` and `b`. Both variables are initialized to the value 1.5. Then, the value 0.0000000000000001 is added to `a`. This should make `a`'s contents different from `b`'s contents. Because of a round-off error, however, the two variables are still the same.

Program 4

```
// This program demonstrates how floating-point
// round-off errors can make equality operations unreliable.
#include <iostream>
using namespace std;

int main()
{
```

(program continues)

Program 4 *(continued)*

```
    double a = 1.5;                    // a is 1.5.
    double b = 1.5;                    // b is 1.5.

    a += 0.0000000000000001; // Add a little to a.
    if (a == b)
       cout << "Both a and b are the same.\n";
    else
       cout << "a and b are not the same.\n";

    return 0;
}
```

Program Output

```
Both a and b are the same.
```

To prevent round-off errors from causing this type of problem, you should stick with greater-than and less-than comparisons with floating-point numbers.

And Now Back to Truth

Now that you've gotten your feet wet with relational expressions and `if` statements, let's look at the subject of truth again. You have seen that a relational expression has the value 1 when it is true and 0 when false. In the world of the `if` statement, however, the concept of truth is expanded. 0 is still false, but all values other than 0 are considered true. This means that any value, even a negative number, represents as true as long as it is not 0.

Just as in real life, truth is a complicated thing. Here is a summary of the rules you have seen so far:

- When a relational expression is true, it has the value 1.
- When a relational expression is false, it has the value 0.
- Any expression that has the value 0 is considered false by the `if` statement. This includes the `bool` value `false`, which is equivalent to 0.
- Any expression that has any value other than 0 is considered true by the `if` statement. This includes the `bool` value `true`, which is equivalent to 1.

The fact that the `if` statement considers any nonzero value as true opens many possibilities. Relational expressions are not the only conditions that may be tested. For example, the following is a legal `if` statement in C++:

```
if (value)
    cout << "It is True!";
```

The `if` statement above does not test a relational expression, but rather the contents of a variable. If the variable, `value`, contains any number other than 0, the message "`It is True!`" will be displayed. If `value` is set to 0, however, the `cout` statement will be skipped. Here is another example:

```
if (x + y)
   cout << "It is True!";
```

In this statement, the sum of `x` and `y` is tested like any other value in an `if` statement: 0 is false and all other values are true. You may also use the return value of function calls as conditional expressions. Here is an example that uses the `pow` function:

```
if (pow(a, b))
   cout << "It is True!";
```

This `if` statement uses the `pow` function to raise `a` to the power of `b`. If the result is anything other than 0, the `cout` statement is executed. This is a powerful programming technique.

Don't Confuse == with =

Earlier you saw a warning not to confuse the equality operator (`==`) with the assignment operator (`=`), as in the following statement:

```
if (x = 2) //Caution here!
   cout << "It is True!";
```

The statement above does not determine whether `x` is equal to 2, it assigns `x` the value 2! Furthermore, the `cout` statement will *always* be executed because the expression `x = 2` is always true.

This occurs because the value of an assignment expression is the value being assigned to the variable on the left side of the = operator. That means the value of the expression `x = 2` is 2. Since 2 is a nonzero value, it is interpreted as a true condition by the `if` statement. Program 5 is a version of Program 2 that attempts to test for a perfect average of 100. The = operator, however, was mistakenly used in the `if` statement.

Program 5

```
// This program averages 3 test scores. The if statement
// uses the = operator, but the == operator was intended.
#include <iostream>
#include <iomanip>
using namespace std;

int main()
{
     int score1, score2, score3; // To hold three test scores
     double average;              // To hold the average score

     // Get the three test scores.
     cout << "Enter 3 test scores and I will average them: ";
     cin >> score1 >> score2 >> score3;

     // Calculate and display the average score.
     average = (score1 + score2 + score3) / 3.0;
     cout << fixed << showpoint << setprecision(1);
     cout << "Your average is " << average << endl;

```

(program continues)

Program 5 *(continued)*

```
      // Our intention is to congratulate the user
      // for having a perfect score. But, this doesn't work.
      if (average = 100) // WRONG! This is an assignment!
         cout << "Congratulations! That's a perfect score!\n";
      return 0;
}
```

Program Output with Example Input Shown in Bold

```
Enter three test scores and I will average them: 80 90 70[Enter]
Your average is 80.0
Congratulations! That's a perfect score!
```

Regardless of the average score, this program will print the message congratulating the user on a perfect score.

Checkpoint

5 Write an `if` statement that performs the following logic: if the variable `x` is equal to 20, then assign 0 to the variable `y`.

6 Write an `if` statement that performs the following logic: if the variable `price` is greater than 500, then assign 0.2 to the variable `discountRate`.

7 Write an `if` statement that multiplies `payRate` by 1.5 if `hours` is greater than 40.

8 True or False: Both of the following `if` statements perform the same operation.

```
if (sales > 10000)
   commissionRate = 0.15;

if (sales > 10000) commissionRate = 0.15;
```

9 True or false: Both of the following `if` statements perform the same operation.

```
if (calls == 20)
   rate *= 0.5;

if (calls = 20)
   rate *= 0.5;
```

3 Expanding the `if` Statement

CONCEPT: The `if` statement can conditionally execute a block of statements enclosed in braces.

What if you want an `if` statement to conditionally execute a group of statements, not just one line? For instance, what if the test-averaging program needed to use several `cout` statements when a high score was reached? The answer is to enclose all of the conditionally executed statements inside a set of braces. Here is the format:

```
if (expression)
{
   statement;
   statement;
   // Place as many statements here as necessary.
}
```

Program 6, another modification of the test-averaging program, demonstrates this type of `if` statement.

Program 6

```
// This program averages 3 test scores.
// It demonstrates an if statement executing
// a block of statements.
#include <iostream>
#include <iomanip>
using namespace std;

int main()
{
    const int HIGH_SCORE = 95;          // A high score is 95 or greater
    int score1, score2, score3;         // To hold three test scores
    double average;                     // To hold the average score

    // Get the three test scores.
    cout << "Enter 3 test scores and I will average them: ";
    cin >> score1 >> score2 >> score3;

    // Calculate and display the average score.
    average = (score1 + score2 + score3) / 3.0;
    cout << fixed << showpoint << setprecision(1);
    cout << "Your average is " << average << endl;

    // If the average is high, congratulate the user.
    if (average > HIGH_SCORE)
    {
       cout << "Congratulations!\n";
       cout << "That's a high score.\n";
       cout << "You deserve a pat on the back!\n";
    }
    return 0;
}
```

(program output continues)

Program 6 *(continued)*

Program Output with Example Input Shown in Bold

```
Enter 3 test scores and I will average them: 100 100 100 [Enter]
Your average is 100.0
Congratulations!
That's a high score.
You deserve a pat on the back!
```

Program Output with Different Example Input Shown in Bold

```
Enter 3 test scores and I will average them: 80 90 70 [Enter]
Your average is 80.0
```

Program 6 prints a more elaborate message when the average score is greater than 95. The `if` statement was expanded to execute three `cout` statements when `highScore` is set to `true`. Enclosing a group of statements inside a set of braces creates a *block* of code. The `if` statement will execute all the statements in the block, in the order they appear, only when `average` is greater than 95. Otherwise, the block will be skipped.

Notice all the statements inside the braces are indented. As before, this visually separates the statements from lines that are not indented, making it more obvious they are part of the `if` statement.

> **NOTE:** Anytime your program has a block of code, all the statements inside the braces should be indented.

Don't Forget the Braces!

If you intend to conditionally execute a block of statements with an `if` statement, don't forget the braces. Remember, without a set of braces, the `if` statement only executes the very next statement. Program 7 shows the test-averaging program with the braces inadvertently left out of the `if` statement's block.

Program 7

```
// This program averages 3 test scores. The braces
// were inadvertently left out of the if statement.
#include <iostream>
#include <iomanip>
using namespace std;

int main()
{
    const int HIGH_SCORE = 95;       // A high score is 95 or greater
    int score1, score2, score3;      // To hold three test scores
    double average;                  // To hold the average score

```

```
13        // Get the three test scores.
14        cout << "Enter 3 test scores and I will average them: ";
15        cin >> score1 >> score2 >> score3;
16
17        // Calculate and display the average score.
18        average = (score1 + score2 + score3) / 3.0;
19        cout << fixed << showpoint << setprecision(1);
20        cout << "Your average is " << average << endl;
21
22        // ERROR! This if statement is missing its braces!
23        if (average > HIGH_SCORE)
24           cout << "Congratulations!\n";
25           cout << "That's a high score.\n";
26           cout << "You deserve a pat on the back!\n";
27        return 0;
28    }
```

Program Output with Example Input Shown in Bold

```
Enter 3 test scores and I will average them: 80 90 70 [Enter]
Your average is 80
That's a high score.
You deserve a pat on the back!
```

The cout statements in lines 25 and 26 are always executed, even when `average` is not greater than 95. Because the braces have been removed, the `if` statement only controls execution of line 24. This is illustrated in Figure 5.

Figure 5 Conditionally executed statement

Only this statement is conditionally executed.

```
if (average > HIGH_SCORE)
  cout << "Congratulations!\n";
  cout << "That's a high score.\n";
  cout << "You deserve a pat on the back!\n";
```

These statements are *always* executed.

Checkpoint

10 Write an `if` statement that performs the following logic: if the variable `sales` is greater than 50,000, then assign 0.25 to the `commissionRate` variable, and assign 250 to the `bonus` variable.

11 The following code segment is syntactically correct, but it appears to contain a logic error. Can you find the error?

```
if (interestRate > .07)
   cout << "This account earns a $10 bonus.\n";
   balance += 10.0;
```

4 The `if/else` Statement

CONCEPT: **The `if/else` statement will execute one group of statements if the expression is true, or another group of statements if the expression is false.**

VideoNote
The `if/else` Statement

The `if/else` statement is an expansion of the `if` statement. Here is its format:

```
if (expression)
    statement or block
else
    statement or block
```

As with the `if` statement, an expression is evaluated. If the expression is true, a statement or block of statements is executed. If the expression is false, however, a separate group of statements is executed. Program 8 uses the `if/else` statement along with the modulus operator to determine if a number is odd or even.

Program 8

```
// This program uses the modulus operator to determine
// if a number is odd or even. If the number is evenly divisible
// by 2, it is an even number. A remainder indicates it is odd.
#include <iostream>
using namespace std;

int main()
{
     int number;

     cout << "Enter an integer and I will tell you if it\n";
     cout << "is odd or even. ";
     cin >> number;
     if (number % 2 == 0)
        cout << number << " is even.\n";
     else
        cout << number << " is odd.\n";
     return 0;
}
```

Program Output with Example Input Shown in Bold

```
Enter an integer and I will tell you if it
is odd or even. 17 [Enter]
17 is odd.
```

The `else` part at the end of the `if` statement specifies a statement that is to be executed when the expression is false. When `number % 2` does not equal 0, a message is printed indicating the number is odd. Note the program will only take one of the two paths in the `if/else` statement. If you think of the statements in a computer program as steps taken down a road, consider the `if/else` statement as a fork in the road. Instead of being a momentary detour, like an `if` statement, the `if/else` statement causes program execution to follow one of two exclusive paths. The flowchart in Figure 6 shows the logic of this `if/else` statement.

Figure 6 `if/else` statement logic

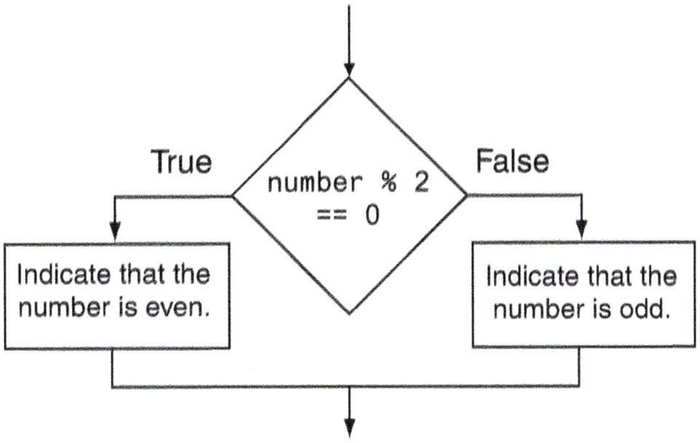

Notice the programming style used to construct the `if/else` statement. The word `else` is at the same level of indention as `if`. The statement whose execution is controlled by `else` is indented one level. This visually depicts the two paths of execution that may be followed.

Like the `if` part, the `else` part controls a single statement. If you wish to control more than one statement with the `else` part, create a block by writing the lines inside a set of braces. Program 9 shows this as a way of handling a classic programming problem: *division by zero*.

Division by zero is mathematically impossible to perform, and it normally causes a program to crash. This means the program will prematurely stop running, sometimes with an error message. Program 9 shows a way to test the value of a divisor before the division takes place.

Program 9

```
// This program asks the user for two numbers, num1 and num2.
// num1 is divided by num2 and the result is displayed.
// Before the division operation, however, num2 is tested
// for the value 0. If it contains 0, the division does not
// take place.
#include <iostream>
using namespace std;

int main()
{
    double num1, num2, quotient;

    // Get the first number.
    cout << "Enter a number: ";
    cin >> num1;

    // Get the second number.
    cout << "Enter another number: ";
    cin >> num2;
```

(program continues)

Program 9 *(continued)*

```
20
21       // If num2 is not zero, perform the division.
22       if (num2 == 0)
23       {
24          cout << "Division by zero is not possible.\n";
25          cout << "Please run the program again and enter\n";
26          cout << "a number other than zero.\n";
27       }
28       else
29       {
30          quotient = num1 / num2;
31          cout << "The quotient of " << num1 << " divided by ";
32          cout << num2 << " is " << quotient << ".\n";
33       }
34       return 0;
35    }
```

Program Output with Example Input Shown in Bold

```
Enter a number: 10 [Enter]
Enter another number: 0 [Enter]
Division by zero is not possible.
Please run the program again and enter
a number other than zero.
```

The value of num2 is tested in line 22 before the division is performed. If the user enters 0, the lines controlled by the `if` part execute, displaying a message that indicates that the program cannot perform a division by zero. Otherwise, the `else` part takes control, which divides num1 by num2 and displays the result.

Checkpoint

12 True or false: The following `if/else` statements cause the same output to display.

A)
```
if (x > y)
   cout << "x is the greater.\n";
else
   cout << "x is not the greater.\n";
```

B)
```
if (y <= x)
   cout << "x is not the greater.\n";
else
   cout << "x is the greater.\n";
```

13 Write an `if/else` statement that assigns 1 to x if y is equal to 100. Otherwise, it should assign 0 to x.

14 Write an `if/else` statement that assigns 0.10 to `commissionRate` unless `sales` is greater than or equal to 50000.00, in which case it assigns 0.20 to `commissionRate`.

5 Nested `if` Statements

CONCEPT: To test more than one condition, an `if` statement can be nested inside another `if` statement.

Sometimes an `if` statement must be nested inside another `if` statement. For example, consider a banking program that determines whether a bank customer qualifies for a special, low interest rate on a loan. To qualify, two conditions must exist: (1) the customer must be currently employed, and (2) the customer must have recently graduated from college (in the past 2 years). Figure 7 shows a flowchart for an algorithm that could be used in such a program.

Figure 7 Nested decision structures

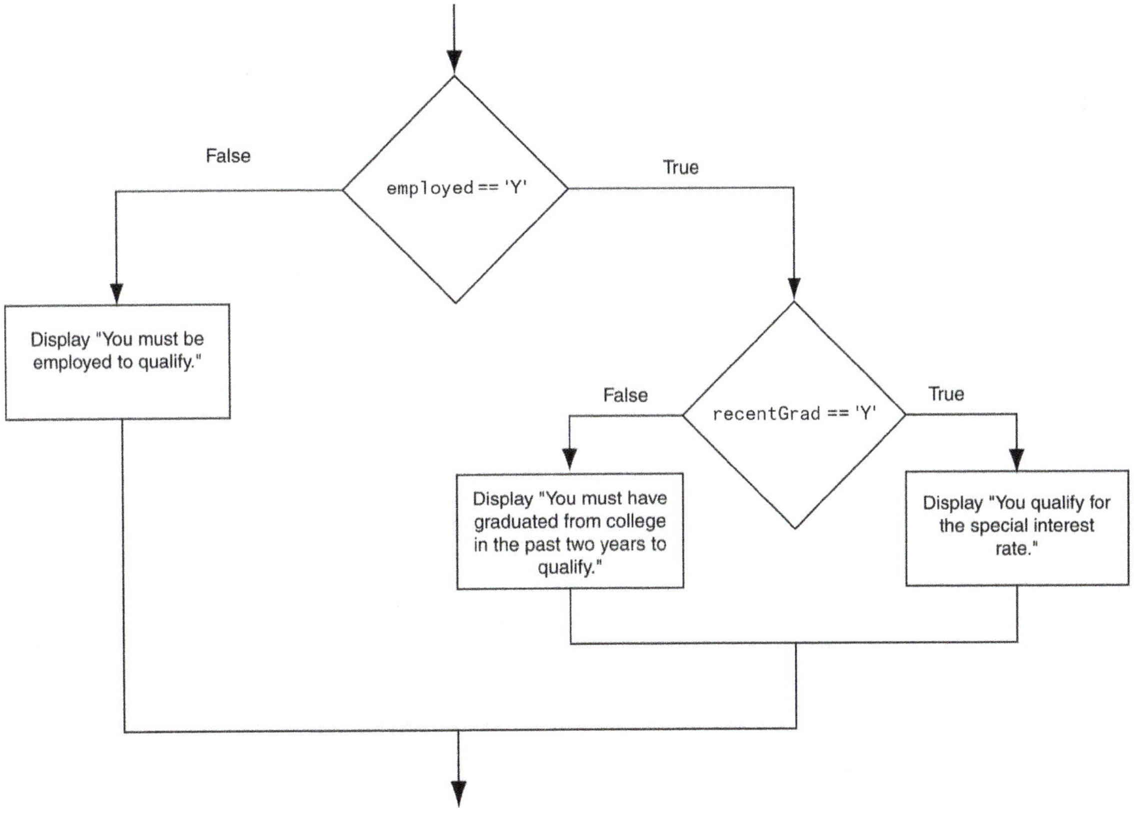

If we follow the flow of execution in the flowchart, we see that the expression `employed == 'Y'` is tested. If this expression is false, there is no need to perform further tests; we know that the customer does not qualify for the special interest rate. If the expression is true, however, we need to test the second condition. This is done with a nested decision structure that tests the expression `recentGrad == 'Y'`. If this expression is true, then the customer qualifies for the special interest rate. If this expression is false, then the customer does not qualify. Program 10 shows the code for the complete program.

Program 10

```
1  // This program demonstrates the nested if statement.
2  #include <iostream>
3  using namespace std;
4
5  int main()
6  {
7      char employed,     // Currently employed, Y or N
8           recentGrad;   // Recent graduate, Y or N
9
10     // Is the user employed and a recent graduate?
11     cout << "Answer the following questions\n";
12     cout << "with either Y for Yes or ";
13     cout << "N for No.\n";
14     cout << "Are you employed? ";
15     cin >> employed;
16     cout << "Have you graduated from college ";
17     cout << "in the past two years? ";
18     cin >> recentGrad;
19
20     // Determine the user's loan qualifications.
21     if (employed == 'Y')
22     {
23         if (recentGrad == 'Y') //Nested if
24         {
25             cout << "You qualify for the special ";
26             cout << "interest rate.\n";
27         }
28     }
29     return 0;
30 }
```

Program Output with Example Input Shown in Bold

```
Answer the following questions
with either Y for Yes or N for No.
Are you employed? Y [Enter]
Have you graduated from college in the past two years? Y [Enter]
You qualify for the special interest rate.
```

Program Output with Different Example Input Shown in Bold

```
Answer the following questions
with either Y for Yes or N for No.
Are you employed? Y [Enter]
Have you graduated from college in the past two years? N [Enter]
```

Look at the `if` statement that begins in line 21. It tests the expression `employed == 'Y'`. If this expression is true, the `if` statement that begins in line 23 is executed. Otherwise, the program jumps to the `return` statement in line 29 and the program ends.

Notice in the second sample execution of Program 10 that the program output does not inform the user whether he or she qualifies for the special interest rate. If the user enters an 'N' (or any character other than 'Y') for `employed` or `recentGrad`, the program does not print a message letting the user know that he or she does not qualify. An `else` statement should be able to remedy this, as illustrated by Program 11.

Program 11

```
// This program demonstrates the nested if statement.
#include <iostream>
using namespace std;

int main()
{
    char employed,    // Currently employed, Y or N
         recentGrad; // Recent graduate, Y or N

    // Is the user employed and a recent graduate?
    cout << "Answer the following questions\n";
    cout << "with either Y for Yes or ";
    cout << "N for No.\n";
    cout << "Are you employed? ";
    cin >> employed;
    cout << "Have you graduated from college ";
    cout << "in the past two years? ";
    cin >> recentGrad;

    // Determine the user's loan qualifications.
    if (employed == 'Y')
    {
        if (recentGrad == 'Y') // Nested if
        {
            cout << "You qualify for the special ";
            cout << "interest rate.\n";
        }
        else // Not a recent grad, but employed
        {
            cout << "You must have graduated from ";
            cout << "college in the past two\n";
            cout << "years to qualify.\n";
        }
    }
    else // Not employed
    {
        cout << "You must be employed to qualify.\n";
    }
    return 0;
}
```

Program Output with Example Input Shown in Bold

Answer the following questions
with either Y for Yes or N for No.
Are you employed? **N** [Enter]
Have you graduated from college in the past two years? **Y** [Enter]
You must be employed to qualify.

(program output continues)

Program 11 *(continued)*

Program Output with Different Example Input Shown in Bold

```
Answer the following questions
with either Y for Yes or N for No.
Are you employed? Y [Enter]
Have you graduated from college in the past two years? N [Enter]
You must have graduated from college in the past two years to qualify.
```

Program Output with Different Example Input Shown in Bold

```
Answer the following questions
with either Y for Yes or N for No.
Are you employed? Y [Enter]
Have you graduated from college in the past two years? Y [Enter]
You qualify for the special interest rate.
```

In this version of the program, both `if` statements have `else` clauses that inform the user why he or she does not qualify for the special interest rate.

Programming Style and Nested Decision Structures

For readability and easier debugging, it's important to use proper alignment and indentation in a set of nested `if` statements. This makes it easier to see which actions are performed by each part of the decision structure. For example, the following code is functionally equivalent to lines 21 through 38 in Program 11. Although this code is logically correct, it is very difficult to read, and would be very difficult to debug because it is not properly indented.

```
if (employed == 'Y')
{
if (recentGrad == 'Y') // Nested if
{
cout << "You qualify for the special ";
cout << "interest rate.\n";
}
else // Not a recent grad, but employed
{
cout << "You must have graduated from ";
cout << "college in the past two\n";
cout << "years to qualify.\n";
}
}
else // Not employed
{
cout << "You must be employed to qualify.\n";
}
```

Don't write code like this!

Proper indentation and alignment also makes it easier to see which `if` and `else` clauses belong together, as shown in Figure 8.

Figure 8 Proper indentation and alignment

```
if (employed == 'Y')
{
   if (recentGrad == 'Y') // Nested if
   {
      cout << "You qualify for the special ";
      cout << "interest rate.\n";
   }
   else // Not a recent grad, but employed
   {
      cout << "You must have graduated from ";
      cout << "college in the past two\n";
      cout << "years to qualify.\n";
   }
}
else  // Not employed
{
   cout << "You must be employed to qualify.\n";
}
```

This if and else go together.

This if and else go together.

Testing a Series of Conditions

In the previous example, you saw how a program can use nested decision structures to test more than one condition. It is not uncommon for a program to have a series of conditions to test then perform an action depending on which condition is true. One way to accomplish this is to have a decision structure with numerous other decision structures nested inside it. For example, consider the program presented in the following *In the Spotlight* section.

In the Spotlight:

Multiple Nested Decision Structures

Dr. Suarez teaches a literature class and uses the following 10-point grading scale for all of his exams:

Test Score	Grade
90 and above	A
80–89	B
70–79	C
60–69	D
Below 60	F

He has asked you to write a program that will allow a student to enter a test score and then display the grade for that score. Here is the algorithm that you will use:

Ask the user to enter a test score.
Determine the grade in the following manner:
If the score is greater than or equal to 90, then the grade is A.
  Otherwise, if the score is greater than or equal to 80, then the grade is B.
    Otherwise, if the score is greater than or equal to 70, then the grade is C.
      Otherwise, if the score is greater than or equal to 60, then the grade is D.
        Otherwise, the grade is F.

You decide that the process of determining the grade will require several nested decision structures, as shown in Figure 9. Program 12 shows the code for the complete program. The code for the nested decision structures is in lines 17 through 45.

Figure 9 Nested decision structure to determine a grade

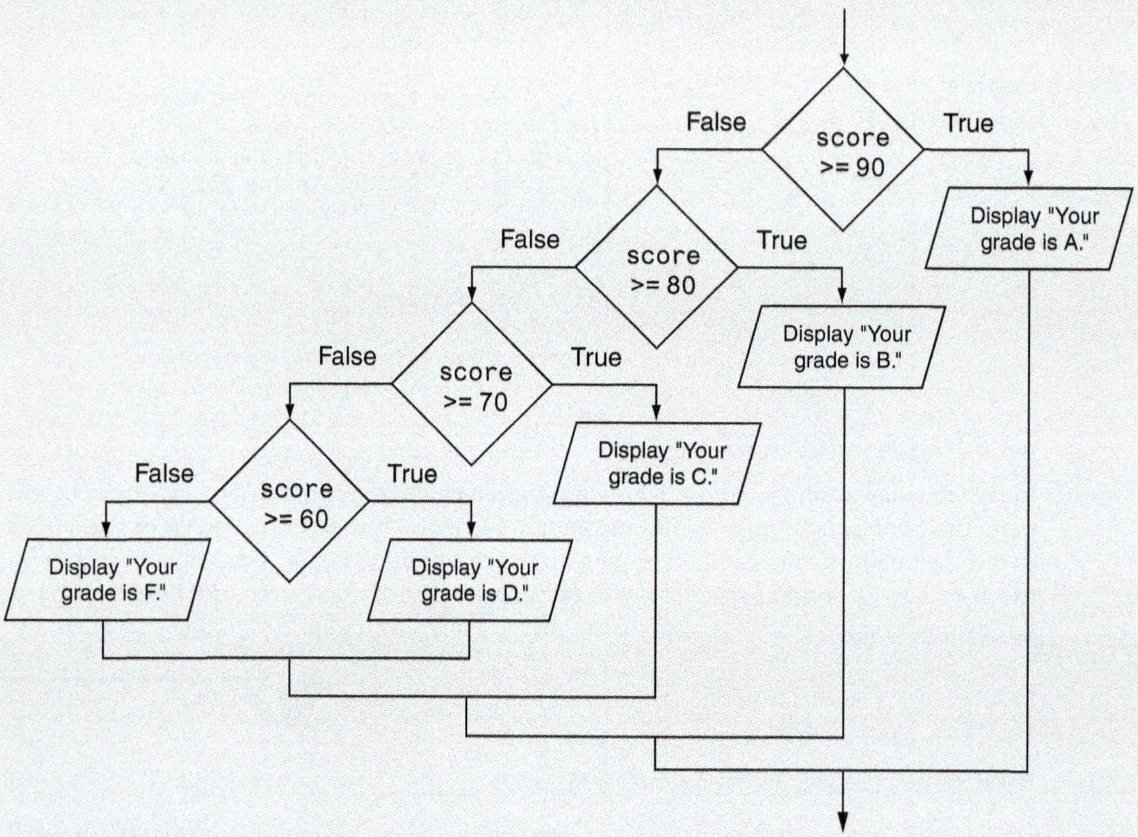

Program 12

```
1  // This program uses nested if/else statements to assign a
2  // letter grade (A, B, C, D, or F) to a numeric test score.
3  #include <iostream>
4  using namespace std;
5
6  int main()
7  {
8      // Constants for grade thresholds
9      const int A_SCORE = 90,
10               B_SCORE = 80,
11               C_SCORE = 70,
12               D_SCORE = 60;
13
14     int testScore; // To hold a numeric test score
15
16     // Get the numeric test score.
17     cout << "Enter your numeric test score and I will\n";
```

```
    cout << "tell you the letter grade you earned: ";
    cin >> testScore;

    // Determine the letter grade.
    if (testScore >= A_SCORE)
    {
       cout << "Your grade is A.\n";
    }
    else
    {
        if (testScore >= B_SCORE)
        {
            cout << "Your grade is B.\n";
        }
        else
        {
            if (testScore >= C_SCORE)
            {
                cout << "Your grade is C.\n";
            }
            else
            {
                if (testScore >= D_SCORE)
                {
                    cout << "Your grade is D.\n";
                }
                else
                {
                    cout << "Your grade is F.\n";
                }
            }
        }
    }

    return 0;
}
```

Program Output with Example Input Shown in Bold

```
Enter your numeric test score and I will
tell you the letter grade you earned: 78 [Enter]
Your grade is C.
```

Program Output with Different Example Input Shown in Bold

```
Enter your numeric test score and I will
tell you the letter grade you earned: 84 [Enter]
Your grade is B.
```

Checkpoint

15 If you executed the following code, what would it display if the user enters 5? What if the user enters 15? What if the user enters 30? What if the user enters –1?

```
int number;
cout << "Enter a number: ";
cin >> number;

if (number > 0)
{
   cout << "Zero\n";

   if (number > 10)
   {
      cout << "Ten\n";

      if (number > 20)
      {
         cout << "Twenty\n";
      }
   }
}
```

6 The `if/else if` Statement

CONCEPT: The `if/else if` statement tests a series of conditions. It is often simpler to test a series of conditions with the `if/else if` statement than with a set of nested `if/else` statements.

VideoNote
The `if/else if` Statement

Even though Program 12 is a simple example, the logic of the nested decision structure is fairly complex. In C++, and many other languages, you can alternatively test a series of conditions using the `if/else if` statement. The `if/else if` statement makes certain types of nested decision logic simpler to write. Here is the general format of the `if/else if` statement:

```
if (expression_1)
{
   statement      }   If expression_1 is true these statements
   statement      }   are executed, and the rest of the structure
   etc.           }   is ignored.
}
else if (expression_2)
{
   statement      }   Otherwise, if expression_2 is true these
   statement      }   statements are executed, and the rest of
   etc.           }   the structure is ignored.
}
Insert as many else if clauses as necessary
else
{
   statement      }   These statements are executed
   statement      }   if none of the expressions above
   etc.           }   are true.
}
```

When the statement executes, *`expression_1`* is tested. If *`expression_1`* is true, the block of statements that immediately follows is executed, and the rest of the structure is ignored. If *`expression_1`* is false, however, the program jumps to the very next `else if` clause and tests *`expression_2`*. If it is true, the block of statements that immediately follows is executed, and then the rest of the structure is ignored. This process continues, from the top of the structure to the bottom, until one of the expressions is found to be true. If none of the expressions are true, the last `else` clause takes over, and the block of statements immediately following it is executed.

The last `else` clause, which does not have an `if` statement following it, is referred to as the *trailing* `else`. The trailing `else` is optional, but in most cases you will use it.

> **NOTE:** The general format shows braces surrounding each block of conditionally executed statements. As with other forms of the `if` statement, the braces are required only when more than one statement is conditionally executed.

Program 13 shows an example of the `if/else if` statement. This program is a modification of Program 12, which appears in the previous *In the Spotlight* section.

Program 13

```
// This program uses an if/else if statement to assign a
// letter grade (A, B, C, D, or F) to a numeric test score.
#include <iostream>
using namespace std;

int main()
{
    // Constants for grade thresholds
    const int A_SCORE = 90,
              B_SCORE = 80,
              C_SCORE = 70,
              D_SCORE = 60;

    int testScore; // To hold a numeric test score

    // Get the numeric test score.
    cout << "Enter your numeric test score and I will\n"
         << "tell you the letter grade you earned: ";
    cin >> testScore;

    // Determine the letter grade.
    if (testScore >= A_SCORE)
       cout << "Your grade is A.\n";
    else if (testScore >= B_SCORE)
       cout << "Your grade is B.\n";
    else if (testScore >= C_SCORE)
       cout << "Your grade is C.\n";
    else if (testScore >= D_SCORE)
       cout << "Your grade is D.\n";
    else
       cout << "Your grade is F.\n";

```

(program continues)

Program 13 *(continued)*

```
33        return 0;
34    }
```

Program Output with Example Input Shown in Bold

```
Enter your numeric test score and I will
tell you the letter grade you earned: 78 [Enter]
Your grade is C.
```

Program Output with Different Example Input Shown in Bold

```
Enter your numeric test score and I will
tell you the letter grade you earned: 84 [Enter]
Your grade is B.
```

Let's analyze how the `if/else if` statement in lines 22 through 31 works. First, the expression `testScore >= A_SCORE` is tested in line 22:

```
→ if (testScore >= A_SCORE)
      cout << "Your grade is A.\n";
  else if (testScore >= B_SCORE)
      cout << "Your grade is B.\n";
  else if (testScore >= C_SCORE)
      cout << "Your grade is C.\n";
  else if (testScore >= D_SCORE)
      cout << "Your grade is D.\n";
  else
      cout << "Your grade is F.\n";
```

If `testScore` is greater than or equal to 90, the string `"Your grade is A.\n"` is displayed and the rest of the `if/else if` statement is skipped. If `testScore` is not greater than or equal to 90, the `else` clause in line 24 takes over and causes the next `if` statement to be executed:

```
  if (testScore >= A_SCORE)
       cout << "Your grade is A.\n";
→ else if (testScore >= B_SCORE)
      cout << "Your grade is B.\n";
  else if (testScore >= C_SCORE)
      cout << "Your grade is C.\n";
  else if (testScore >= D_SCORE)
      cout << "Your grade is D.\n";
  else
      cout << "Your grade is F.\n";
```

The first `if` statement handles all of the grades greater than or equal to 90, so when this `if` statement executes, `testScore` will have a value of 89 or less. If `testScore` is greater than or equal to 80, the string `"Your grade is B.\n"` is displayed and the rest of the `if/else if` statement is skipped. This chain of events continues until one of the expressions is found to be true, or the last `else` clause at the end of the statement is encountered.

Notice the alignment and indentation that is used with the `if/else if` statement: The starting `if` clause, the `else if` clauses, and the trailing `else` clause are all aligned, and the conditionally executed statements are indented.

Using the Trailing `else` to Catch Errors

The trailing `else` clause, which appears at the end of the `if/else if` statement, is optional, but in many situations you will use it to catch errors. For example, Program 13 will assign a grade to any number that is entered as the test score, including negative numbers. If a negative test score is entered, however, the user has probably made a mistake. We can modify the code as shown in Program 14 so the trailing `else` clause catches any test score that is less than 0 and displays an error message.

Program 14

```cpp
// This program uses an if/else if statement to assign a
// letter grade (A, B, C, D, or F) to a numeric test score.
#include <iostream>
using namespace std;

int main()
{
    // Constants for grade thresholds
    const int A_SCORE = 90,
              B_SCORE = 80,
              C_SCORE = 70,
              D_SCORE = 60;

    int testScore; // To hold a numeric test score

    // Get the numeric test score.
    cout << "Enter your numeric test score and I will\n"
         << "tell you the letter grade you earned: ";
    cin >> testScore;

    // Determine the letter grade.
    if (testScore >= A_SCORE)
       cout << "Your grade is A.\n";
    else if (testScore >= B_SCORE)
       cout << "Your grade is B.\n";
    else if (testScore >= C_SCORE)
       cout << "Your grade is C.\n";
    else if (testScore >= D_SCORE)
       cout << "Your grade is D.\n";
    else if (testScore >= 0)
       cout << "Your grade is F.\n";
    else
       cout << "Invalid test score.\n";

    return 0;
}
```

Program Output with Example Input Shown in Bold

```
Enter your numeric test score and I will
tell you the letter grade you earned: -1 [Enter]
Invalid test score.
```

The `if/else if` Statement Compared to a Nested Decision Structure

You never have to use the `if/else if` statement because its logic can be coded with nested `if/else` statements. However, a long series of nested `if/else` statements has two particular disadvantages when you are debugging code:

- The code can grow complex and become difficult to understand.
- Because indenting is important in nested statements, a long series of nested `if/else` statements can become too long to be displayed on the computer screen without horizontal scrolling. Also, long statements tend to "wrap around" when printed on paper, making the code even more difficult to read.

The logic of an `if/else if` statement is usually easier to follow than that of a long series of nested `if/else` statements. And, because all of the clauses are aligned in an `if/else if` statement, the lengths of the lines in the statement tend to be shorter.

Checkpoint

16 What will the following code display?

```
int funny = 7, serious = 15;
funny = serious % 2;

if (funny != 1)
{
   funny = 0;
   serious = 0;
}
else if (funny == 2)
{
   funny = 10;
   serious = 10;
}
else
{
   funny = 1;
   serious = 1;
}
cout << funny << "" << serious << endl;
```

17 The following code is used in a bookstore program to determine how many discount coupons a customer gets. Complete the table that appears after the program.

```
int numBooks, numCoupons;
cout << "How many books are being purchased? ";
cin >> numBooks;

if (numBooks < 1)
   numCoupons = 0;
else if (numBooks < 3)
   numCoupons = 1;
else if (numBooks < 5)
   numCoupons = 2;
```

```
else
   numCoupons = 3;
cout << "The number of coupons to give is "
     << numCoupons << endl;
```

If the customer purchases this many books	This many coupons are given.
1	
3	
4	
5	
10	

7 Flags

CONCEPT: A flag is a Boolean or integer variable that signals when a condition exists.

A *flag* is typically a `bool` variable that signals when some condition exists in the program. When the flag variable is set to `false`, it indicates that the condition does not exist. When the flag variable is set to `true`, it means the condition does exist.

For example, suppose a program that calculates sales commissions has a `bool` variable, defined and initialized as shown here:

```
bool salesQuotaMet = false;
```

In the program, the `salesQuotaMet` variable is used as a flag to indicate whether a salesperson has met the sales quota. When we define the variable, we initialize it with `false` because we do not yet know if the salesperson has met the sales quota. Assuming a variable named `sales` holds the amount of sales, code similar to the following might be used to set the value of the `salesQuotaMet` variable:

```
if (sales >= QUOTA_AMOUNT)
   salesQuotaMet = true;
else
   salesQuotaMet = false;
```

As a result of this code, the `salesQuotaMet` variable can be used as a flag to indicate whether the sales quota has been met. Later in the program, we might test the flag in the following way:

```
if (salesQuotaMet)
   cout << "You have met your sales quota!\n";
```

This code displays *You have met your sales quota!* if the `bool` variable `salesQuotaMet` is `true`. Notice we did not have to use the == operator to explicitly compare the `salesQuotaMet` variable with the value `true`. This code is equivalent to the following:

```
if (salesQuotaMet == true)
   cout << "You have met your sales quota!\n";
```

Integer Flags

Integer variables may also be used as flags. This is because in C++ the value 0 is considered false, and any nonzero value is considered true. In the sales commission program previously described, we could define the `salesQuotaMet` variable with the following statement:

```
int salesQuotaMet = 0;        // 0 means false.
```

As before, we initialize the variable with 0 because we do not yet know if the sales quota has been met. After the sales have been calculated, we can use code similar to the following to set the value of the `salesQuotaMet` variable:

```
if (sales >= QUOTA_AMOUNT)
    salesQuotaMet = 1;
else
    salesQuotaMet = 0;
```

Later in the program, we might test the flag in the following way:

```
if (salesQuotaMet)
    cout << "You have met your sales quota!\n";
```

8 Logical Operators

CONCEPT: Logical operators connect two or more relational expressions into one or reverse the logic of an expression.

In the previous section, you saw how a program tests two conditions with two `if` statements. In this section, you will see how to use logical operators to combine two or more relational expressions into one. Table 6 lists C++'s logical operators.

Table 6 Logical Operators

Operator	Meaning	Effect
&&	AND	Connects two expressions into one. Both expressions must be true for the overall expression to be true.
||	OR	Connects two expressions into one. One or both expressions must be true for the overall expression to be true. It is only necessary for one to be true, and it does not matter which.
!	NOT	The ! operator reverses the "truth" of an expression. It makes a true expression false, and a false expression true.

The && Operator

The && operator is known as the logical AND operator. It takes two expressions as operands and creates an expression that is true only when both subexpressions are true. Here is an example of an `if` statement that uses the && operator:

```
if (temperature < 20 && minutes > 12)
    cout << "The temperature is in the danger zone.";
```

In the statement above, the two relational expressions are combined into a single expression. The `cout` statement will only be executed if `temperature` is less than 20 AND `minutes` is greater than 12. If either relational test is false, the entire expression is false, and the `cout` statement is not executed.

TIP: You must provide complete expressions on both sides of the && operator. For example, the following statement is not correct because the condition on the right side of the && operator is not a complete expression:

```
temperature > 0 && < 100
```

The expression must be rewritten as

```
temperature > 0 && temperature < 100
```

Table 7 shows a truth table for the && operator. The truth table lists all the possible combinations of values that two expressions may have, and the resulting value returned by the && operator connecting the two expressions.

Table 7 Truth Table for the && Operator

Expression	Value of Expression
`true && false`	`false (0)`
`false && true`	`false (0)`
`false && false`	`false (0)`
`true && true`	`true (1)`

As the table shows, both subexpressions must be true for the && operator to return a true value.

NOTE: If the subexpression on the left side of an && operator is false, the expression on the right side will not be checked. Since the entire expression is false if only one of the subexpressions is false, it would waste CPU time to check the remaining expression. This is called *short-circuit evaluation.*

The && operator can be used to simplify programs that otherwise would use nested `if` statements. Program 15 performs a similar operation as Program 11, which qualifies a bank customer for a special interest rate. This program uses a logical operator.

Program 15

```
// This program demonstrates the && logical operator.
#include <iostream>
using namespace std;

int main()
{
    char employed,     // Currently employed, Y or N
         recentGrad;   // Recent graduate, Y or N

    // Is the user employed and a recent graduate?
    cout << "Answer the following questions\n";
    cout << "with either Y for Yes or N for No.\n";

```

(program continues)

Program 15 *(continued)*

```
    cout << "Are you employed? ";
    cin >> employed;

    cout << "Have you graduated from college "
         << "in the past two years? ";
    cin >> recentGrad;

    // Determine the user's loan qualifications.
    if (employed == 'Y' && recentGrad == 'Y')
    {
       cout << "You qualify for the special "
            << "interest rate.\n";
    }
    else
    {
       cout << "You must be employed and have\n"
            << "graduated from college in the\n"
            << "past two years to qualify.\n";
    }
    return 0;
}
```

Program Output with Example Input Shown in Bold

```
Answer the following questions
with either Y for Yes or N for No.
Are you employed? Y [Enter]
Have you graduated from college in the past two years? N [Enter]
You must be employed and have
graduated from college in the
past two years to qualify.
```

Program Output with Example Input Shown in Bold

```
Answer the following questions
with either Y for Yes or N for No.
Are you employed? N [Enter]
Have you graduated from college in the past two years? Y [Enter]
You must be employed and have
graduated from college in the
past two years to qualify.
```

Program Output with Example Input Shown in Bold

```
Answer the following questions
with either Y for Yes or N for No.
Are you employed? Y [Enter]
Have you graduated from college in the past two years? Y [Enter]
You qualify for the special interest rate.
```

The message `"You qualify for the special interest rate."` is displayed only when both the expressions `employed == 'Y'` and `recentGrad == 'Y'` are true. If either of these is false, the message `"You must be employed and have graduated from college in the past two years to qualify."` is printed.

NOTE: Although it is similar, Program 15 is not the logical equivalent of Program 11. For example, Program 15 doesn't display the message "You must be employed to qualify."

The || Operator

The || operator is known as the logical OR operator. It takes two expressions as operands and creates an expression that is true when either of the subexpressions are true. Here is an example of an if statement that uses the || operator:

```
if (temperature < 20 || temperature > 100)
   cout << "The temperature is in the danger zone.";
```

The cout statement will be executed if temperature is less than 20 OR temperature is greater than 100. If either relational test is true, the entire expression is true and the cout statement is executed.

TIP: You must provide complete expressions on both sides of the || operator. For example, the following code is not correct because the condition on the right side of the || operator is not a complete expression:

```
temperature < 0 || > 100
```

The expression must be rewritten as

```
temperature < 0 || temperature > 100
```

Table 8 shows a truth table for the || operator.

Table 8 Truth Table for the || Operator

Expression	Value of the Expression
true || false	true (1)
false || true	true (1)
false || false	false (0)
true || true	true (1)

All it takes for an OR expression to be true is for one of the subexpressions to be true. It doesn't matter if the other subexpression is false or true.

NOTE: The || operator also performs short-circuit evaluation. If the subexpression on the left side of an || operator is true, the expression on the right side will not be checked. Since it's only necessary for one of the subexpressions to be true, it would waste CPU time to check the remaining expression.

Program 16 performs different tests to qualify a person for a loan. This one determines if the customer earns at least $35,000 per year, or has been employed for more than 5 years.

Program 16

```
// This program demonstrates the logical || operator.
#include <iostream>
using namespace std;

int main()
{
    // Constants for minimum income and years
    const double MIN_INCOME = 35000.0;
    const int MIN_YEARS = 5;

    double income;  // Annual income
    int years;      // Years at the current job

    // Get the annual income
    cout << "What is your annual income? ";
    cin >> income;

    // Get the number of years at the current job.
    cout << "How many years have you worked at "
         << "your current job? ";
    cin >> years;

    // Determine the user's loan qualifications.
    if (income >= MIN_INCOME || years > MIN_YEARS)
        cout << "You qualify.\n";
    else
    {
        cout << "You must earn at least $"
             << MIN_INCOME << " or have been "
             << "employed more than " << MIN_YEARS
             << " years.\n";
    }
    return 0;
}
```

Program Output with Example Input Shown in Bold

What is your annual income? **40000** [Enter]
How many years have you worked at your current job? **2** [Enter]
You qualify.

Program Output with Example Input Shown in Bold

What is your annual income? **20000** [Enter]
How many years have you worked at your current job? **7** [Enter]
You qualify.

Program Output with Example Input Shown in Bold

What is your annual income? **30000** [Enter]
How many years have you worked at your current job? **3** [Enter]
You must earn at least $35000 or have been employed more than 5 years.

The string “You qualify\n.” is displayed when either or both the expressions `income >= 35000` or `years > 5` are true. If both of these are false, the disqualifying message is printed.

The ! Operator

The ! operator performs a logical NOT operation. It takes an operand and reverses its truth or falsehood. In other words, if the expression is true, the ! operator returns false, and if the expression is false, it returns true. Here is an `if` statement using the ! operator:

```
if (!(temperature > 100))
    cout << "You are below the maximum temperature.\n";
```

First, the expression `(temperature > 100)` is tested to be true or false. Then the ! operator is applied to that value. If the expression `(temperature > 100)` is true, the ! operator returns false. If it is false, the ! operator returns true. In the example, it is equivalent to asking “is the temperature not greater than 100?”

Table 9 shows a truth table for the ! operator.

Table 9 Truth Table for the ! Operator

Expression	Value of the Expression
`!true`	`false (0)`
`!false`	`true  (1)`

Program 17 performs the same task as Program 16. The `if` statement, however, uses the ! operator to determine if the user does *not* make at least $35,000, or has *not* been on the job more than 5 years.

Program 17

```
// This program demonstrates the logical ! operator.
#include <iostream>
using namespace std;

int main()
{
    // Constants for minimum income and years
    const double MIN_INCOME = 35000.0;
    const int MIN_YEARS = 5;

    double income; // Annual income
    int years;     // Years at the current job

    // Get the annual income
    cout << "What is your annual income? ";
    cin >> income;

    // Get the number of years at the current job.
    cout << "How many years have you worked at "
         << "your current job? ";
```

(program continues)

Program 17 *(continued)*

```
    cin >> years;

    // Determine the user's loan qualifications.
    if (!(income >= MIN_INCOME || years > MIN_YEARS))
    {
       cout << "You must earn at least $"
            << MIN_INCOME << " or have been "
            << "employed more than " << MIN_YEARS
            << " years.\n";
    }
    else
       cout << "You qualify.\n";
    return 0;
}
```

The output of Program 17 is the same as Program 16.

Precedence and Associativity of Logical Operators

Table 10 shows the precedence of C++'s logical operators, from highest to lowest.

Table 10 Precedence of Logical Operators

<table>
<tr><th>Logical Operators in Order of Precedence</th></tr>
<tr><td>!</td></tr>
<tr><td>&&</td></tr>
<tr><td>||</td></tr>
</table>

The ! operator has a higher precedence than many of the C++ operators. To avoid an error, you should always enclose its operand in parentheses unless you intend to apply it to a variable or a simple expression with no other operators. For example, consider the following expressions:

```
!(x > 2)
!x > 2
```

The first expression applies the ! operator to the expression x > 2. It is asking, "is x not greater than 2?" The second expression, however, applies the ! operator to x only. It is asking, "is the logical negation of x greater than 2?" Suppose x is set to 5. Since 5 is nonzero, it would be considered true, so the ! operator would reverse it to false, which is 0. The > operator would then determine if 0 is greater than 2. To avoid a catastrophe like this, always use parentheses!

The && and || operators rank lower in precedence than the relational operators, so precedence problems are less likely to occur. If you feel unsure, however, it doesn't hurt to use parentheses anyway.

```
(a > b) && (x < y)     is the same as   a > b && x < y
(x == y) || (b > a)    is the same as   x == y || b > a
```

The logical operators have left-to-right associativity. In the following expression, `a < b` is evaluated before `y == z`.

```
a < b || y == z
```

In the following expression, `y == z` is evaluated first, however, because the && operator has higher precedence than ||.

```
a < b || y == z && m > j
```

The expression is equivalent to

```
(a < b) || ((y == z) && (m > j))
```

9 Checking Numeric Ranges with Logical Operators

CONCEPT: Logical operators are effective for determining whether a number is in or out of a range.

When determining whether a number is inside a numeric range, it's best to use the && operator. For example, the following `if` statement checks the value in `x` to determine whether it is in the range of 20 through 40:

```
if (x >= 20 && x <= 40)
   cout << x << " is in the acceptable range.\n";
```

The expression in the `if` statement will be true only when `x` is both greater than or equal to 20 AND less than or equal to 40. `x` must be within the range of 20 through 40 for this expression to be true.

When determining whether a number is outside a range, the || operator is best to use. The following statement determines whether `x` is outside the range of 20 to 40:

```
if (x < 20 || x > 40)
   cout << x << " is outside the acceptable range.\n";
```

It's important not to get the logic of these logical operators confused. For example, the following `if` statement would never test true:

```
if (x < 20 && x > 40)
   cout << x << " is outside the acceptable range.\n";
```

Obviously, `x` cannot be less than 20 and at the same time greater than 40.

> **NOTE:** C++ does not allow you to check numeric ranges with expressions such as `5 < x < 20`. Instead, you must use a logical operator to connect two relational expressions, as previously discussed.

Checkpoint

18 The following truth table shows various combinations of the values `true` and `false` connected by a logical operator. Complete the table by indicating if the result of such a combination is True or False.

Logical Expression	Result (True or False)
`true && false`	
`true && true`	
`false && true`	
`false && false`	
`true || false`	
`true || true`	
`false || true`	
`false || false`	
`!true`	
`!false`	

19 Assume the variables `a = 2`, `b = 4`, and `c = 6`. Determine whether each of the following conditions is True or False:

A) `a == 4 || b > 2`
B) `6 <= c && a > 3`
C) `1 != b && c != 3`
D) `a >= -1 || a <= b`
E) `!(a > 2)`

20 Write an `if` statement that prints the message "The number is valid" if the variable `speed` is within the range 0 through 200.

21 Write an `if` statement that prints the message "The number is not valid" if the variable `speed` is outside the range 0 through 200.

10 Menus

CONCEPT: You can use nested `if/else` statements or the `if/else if` statement to create menu-driven programs. A *menu-driven* program allows the user to determine the course of action by selecting it from a list of actions.

A menu is a screen displaying a set of choices from which the user selects. For example, a program that manages a mailing list might give you the following menu:

1. Add a name to the list.
2. Remove a name from the list.
3. Change a name in the list.
4. Print the list.
5. Quit the program.

The user selects one of the operations by entering its number. Entering 4, for example, causes the mailing list to be printed, and entering 5 causes the program to end. Nested `if/else` statements or an `if/else if` structure can be used to set up such a menu. After the user enters a number, the program compares the number with the available selections and executes the statements that perform that operation.

Program 18 calculates the charges for membership in a health club. The club has three membership packages to choose from: standard adult membership, child membership, and senior citizen membership. The program presents a menu that allows the user to choose the desired package then calculates the cost of the membership.

Program 18

```
// This program displays a menu and asks the user to make a
// selection. An if/else if statement determines which item
// the user has chosen.
#include <iostream>
#include <iomanip>
using namespace std;

int main()
{
    int choice;      // To hold a menu choice
    int months;      // To hold the number of months
    double charges; // To hold the monthly charges

    // Constants for membership rates
    const double ADULT = 40.0,
                 SENIOR = 30.0,
                 CHILD = 20.0;

    // Constants for menu choices
    const int ADULT_CHOICE = 1,
              CHILD_CHOICE = 2,
              SENIOR_CHOICE = 3,
              QUIT_CHOICE = 4;

    // Display the menu and get a choice.
    cout << "\t\tHealth Club Membership Menu\n\n"
         << "1. Standard Adult Membership\n"
         << "2. Child Membership\n"
         << "3. Senior Citizen Membership\n"
         << "4. Quit the Program\n\n"
         << "Enter your choice: ";
    cin >> choice;

    // Set the numeric output formatting.
    cout << fixed << showpoint << setprecision(2);

    // Respond to the user's menu selection.
    if (choice == ADULT_CHOICE)
    {
       cout << "For how many months? ";
       cin >> months;
       charges = months * ADULT;
       cout << "The total charges are $" << charges << endl;
    }
    else if (choice == CHILD_CHOICE)
    {
       cout << "For how many months? ";
```

(program continues)

Program 18 *(continued)*

```
48          cin >> months;
49          charges = months * CHILD;
50          cout << "The total charges are $" << charges << endl;
51      }
52      else if (choice == SENIOR_CHOICE)
53      {
54          cout << "For how many months? ";
55          cin >> months;
56          charges = months * SENIOR;
57          cout << "The total charges are $" << charges << endl;
58      }
59      else if (choice == QUIT_CHOICE)
60      {
61          cout << "Program ending.\n";
62      }
63      else
64      {
65          cout << "The valid choices are 1 through 4. Run the\n"
66               << "program again and select one of those.\n";
67      }
68      return 0;
69  }
```

Program Output with Example Input Shown in Bold

```
        Health Club Membership Menu

1. Standard Adult Membership
2. Child Membership
3. Senior Citizen Membership
4. Quit the Program

Enter your choice: 3 [Enter]
For how many months? 6 [Enter]
The total charges are $180.00
```

Let's take a closer look at the program:

- Lines 10–12 define the following variables:
  - The `choice` variable will hold the user's menu choice.
  - The `months` variable will hold the number of months of health club membership.
  - The `charges` variable will hold the total charges.
- Lines 15–17 define named constants for the monthly membership rates for adult, senior citizen, and child memberships.
- Lines 20–23 define named constants for the menu choices.
- Lines 26–32 display the menu and get the user's choice.
- Line 35 sets the numeric output formatting for floating-point numbers.
- Lines 38–67 are an `if/else if` statement that determines the user's menu choice in the following manner:
  - If the user selected 1 from the menu (adult membership), the statements in lines 40–43 are executed.

- Otherwise, if the user selected 2 from the menu (child membership), the statements in lines 47–50 are executed.
- Otherwise, if the user selected 3 from the menu (senior citizen membership), the statements in lines 54–57 are executed.
- Otherwise, if the user selected 4 from the menu (quit the program), the statement in line 61 is executed.
- If the user entered any choice other than 1, 2, 3, or 4, the `else` clause in lines 63–67 executes, displaying an error message.

11 Focus on Software Engineering: Validating User Input

CONCEPT: As long as the user of a program enters bad input, the program will produce bad output. Programs should be written to filter out bad input.

Perhaps the most famous saying of the computer world is "Garbage in, garbage out." The integrity of a program's output is only as good as its input, so you should try to make sure garbage does not go into your programs. *Input validation* is the process of inspecting data given to a program by the user and determining if it is valid. A good program should give clear instructions about the kind of input that is acceptable, and not assume the user has followed those instructions. Here are just a few examples of input validations performed by programs:

- Numbers are checked to ensure they are within a range of possible values. For example, there are 168 hours in a week. It is not possible for a person to be at work longer than 168 hours in one week.
- Values are checked for their "reasonableness." Although it might be possible for a person to be at work for 168 hours per week, it is not probable.
- Items selected from a menu or other sets of choices are checked to ensure they are available options.
- Variables are checked for values that might cause problems, such as division by zero.

Program 19 is a test scoring program that rejects any test score less than 0 or greater than 100.

Program 19

```
// This test scoring program does not accept test scores
// that are less than 0 or greater than 100.
#include <iostream>
using namespace std;

int main()
{
    // Constants for grade thresholds
```

(program continues)

Program 19 *(continued)*

```
    const int A_SCORE = 90,
              B_SCORE = 80,
              C_SCORE = 70,
              D_SCORE = 60,
              MIN_SCORE = 0,     // Minimum valid score
              MAX_SCORE = 100;   // Maximum valid score

    int testScore; // To hold a numeric test score

    // Get the numeric test score.
    cout << "Enter your numeric test score and I will\n"
         << "tell you the letter grade you earned: ";
    cin >> testScore;

    // Validate the input and determine the grade.
    if (testScore >= MIN_SCORE && testScore <= MAX_SCORE)
    {
        // Determine the letter grade.
        if (testScore >= A_SCORE)
          cout << "Your grade is A.\n";
        else if (testScore >= B_SCORE)
          cout << "Your grade is B.\n";
        else if (testScore >= C_SCORE)
          cout << "Your grade is C.\n";
        else if (testScore >= D_SCORE)
          cout << "Your grade is D.\n";
        else
          cout << "Your grade is F.\n";
    }
    else
    {
        // An invalid score was entered.
        cout << "That is an invalid score. Run the program\n"
             << "again and enter a value in the range of\n"
             << MIN_SCORE << " through " << MAX_SCORE << ".\n";
    }

    return 0;
}
```

Program Output with Example Input Shown in Bold

Enter your numeric test score and I will
tell you the letter grade you earned: **-1** [Enter]
That is an invalid score. Run the program
again and enter a value in the range of
0 through 100.

Program Output with Example Input Shown in Bold

Enter your numeric test score and I will
tell you the letter grade you earned: **81** [Enter]
Your grade is B.

12 Comparing Characters and Strings

CONCEPT: **Relational operators can also be used to compare characters and `string` objects.**

Earlier in this chapter, you learned to use relational operators to compare numeric values. They can also be used to compare characters and `string` objects.

Comparing Characters

Characters are actually stored in memory as integers. On most systems, this integer is the ASCII value of the character. For example, the letter 'A' is represented by the number 65, the letter 'B' is represented by the number 66, and so on. Table 11 shows the ASCII numbers that correspond to some of the commonly used characters.

Table 11 ASCII Values of Commonly Used Characters

Character	ASCII Value
'0'–'9'	48–57
'A'–'Z'	65–90
'a'–'z'	97–122
Blank	32
Period	46

Notice every character, even the blank, has an ASCII code associated with it. Notice also that the ASCII code of a character representing a digit, such as `'1'` or `'2'`, is not the same as the value of the digit itself. A complete table showing the ASCII values for all characters can be found in Appendix: The ASCII Character Set.

When two characters are compared, it is actually their ASCII values that are being compared. `'A' < 'B'` because the ASCII value of `'A'` (65) is less than the ASCII value of `'B'` (66). Likewise `'1' < '2'` because the ASCII value of `'1'` (49) is less than the ASCII value of `'2'` (50). However, as shown in Table 11, lowercase letters have higher ASCII codes than uppercase letters, so `'a' > 'Z'`. Program 20 shows how characters can be compared with relational operators.

Program 20

```
// This program demonstrates how characters can be
// compared with the relational operators.
#include <iostream>
using namespace std;

int main()
{
    char ch;

```

(program continues)

Program 20 *(continued)*

```
    // Get a character from the user.
    cout << "Enter a digit or a letter: ";
    ch = cin.get();

    // Determine what the user entered.
    if (ch >= '0' && ch <= '9')
        cout << "You entered a digit.\n";
    else if (ch >= 'A' && ch <= 'Z')
        cout << "You entered an uppercase letter.\n";
    else if (ch >= 'a' && ch <= 'z')
        cout << "You entered a lowercase letter.\n";
    else
        cout << "That is not a digit or a letter.\n";

    return 0;
}
```

Program Output with Example Input Shown in Bold

`Enter a digit or a letter:` **t** [Enter]
`You entered a lowercase letter.`

Program Output with Example Input Shown in Bold

`Enter a digit or a letter:` **v** [Enter]
`You entered an uppercase letter.`

Program Output with Example Input Shown in Bold

`Enter a digit or a letter:` **5** [Enter]
`You entered a digit.`

Program Output with Example Input Shown in Bold

`Enter a digit or a letter:` **&** [Enter]
`That is not a digit or a letter.`

Comparing `string` Objects

`string` objects can also be compared with relational operators. As with individual characters, when two `string` objects are compared, it is actually the ASCII values of the characters making up the strings that are being compared. For example, assume the following definitions exist in a program:

```
string str1 = "ABC";
string str2 = "XYZ";
```

The `string` object `str1` is considered less than the `string` object `str2` because the characters `"ABC"` alphabetically precede (have lower ASCII values than) the characters `"XYZ"`. So, the following `if` statement will cause the message `"str1 is less than str2."` to be displayed on the screen.

```
if (str1 < str2)
    cout << "str1 is less than str2.";
```

One by one, each character in the first operand is compared with the character in the corresponding position in the second operand. If all the characters in both `string` objects match, the two strings are equal. Other relationships can be determined if two characters in corresponding positions do not match. The first operand is less than the second operand if the first mismatched character in the first operand is less than its counterpart in the second operand. Likewise, the first operand is greater than the second operand if the first mismatched character in the first operand is greater than its counterpart in the second operand.

For example, assume a program has the following definitions:

```
string name1 = "Mary";
string name2 = "Mark";
```

The value in `name1`, `"Mary"`, is greater than the value in `name2`, `"Mark"`. This is because the first three characters in `name1` have the same ASCII values as the first three characters in `name2`, but the `'y'` in the fourth position of `"Mary"` has a greater ASCII value than the `'k'` in the corresponding position of `"Mark"`.

Any of the relational operators can be used to compare two `string` objects. Here are some of the valid comparisons of `name1` and `name2`:

```
name1 > name2  // true
name1 <= name2 // false
name1 != name2 // true
```

`string` objects can also, of course, be compared to string literals:

```
name1 < "Mary Jane" // true
```

Program 21 further demonstrates how relational operators can be used with `string` objects.

Program 21

```
// This program uses relational operators to compare a string
// entered by the user with valid part numbers.
#include <iostream>
#include <iomanip>
#include <string>
using namespace std;

int main()
{
    const double PRICE_A = 249.0,    // Price for part A
                 PRICE_B = 199.0;    // Price for part B

    string partNum;                  // Holds a part number

    // Display available parts and get the user's selection
    cout << "The headphone part numbers are:\n"
         << "Noise canceling: part number S-29A \n"
         << "Wireless: part number S-29B \n"
         << "Enter the part number of the headphones you\n"
```

(program continues)

Program 21 *(continued)*

```
            << "wish to purchase: ";
        cin >> partNum;

        // Set the numeric output formatting
        cout << fixed << showpoint << setprecision(2);

        // Determine and display the correct price
        if (partNum == "S-29A")
            cout << "The price is $" << PRICE_A << endl;
        else if (partNum == "S-29B")
            cout << "The price is $" << PRICE_B << endl;
        else
            cout << partNum << " is not a valid part number.\n";
        return 0;
    }
```

Program Output with Example Input Shown in Bold

```
The headphone part numbers are:
Noise canceling: part number S-29A
Wireless: part number S-29B
Enter the part number of the headphones you
wish to purchase: S-29A [Enter]
The price is $249.00
```

Checkpoint

22 Indicate whether each of the following relational expressions is True or False. Refer to the ASCII table in Appendix: The ASCII Character Set if necessary.

A) `'a' < 'z'`

B) `'a' == 'A'`

C) `'5' < '7'`

D) `'a' < 'A'`

E) `'1' == 1`

F) `'1' == 49`

23 Indicate whether each of the following relational expressions is True or False. Refer to the ASCII table in Appendix: The ASCII Character Set if necessary.

A) `"Bill" == "BILL"`

B) `"Bill" < "BILL"`

C) `"Bill" < "Bob"`

D) `"189" > "23"`

E) `"189" > "Bill"`

F) `"Mary" < "MaryEllen"`

G) `"MaryEllen" < "Mary Ellen"`

13 The Conditional Operator

CONCEPT: You can use the conditional operator to create short expressions that work like `if/else` statements.

The conditional operator is powerful and unique. It provides a shorthand method of expressing a simple `if/else` statement. The operator consists of the question-mark (?) and the colon (:). Its format is:

```
expression ? expression : expression;
```

Here is an example of a statement using the conditional operator:

```
x < 0 ? y = 10 : z = 20;
```

The statement above is called a *conditional expression* and consists of three subexpressions separated by the ? and : symbols. The expressions are `x < 0`, `y = 10`, and `z = 20`, as illustrated here:

```
x < 0   ?   y = 10   :   z = 20;
```

> **NOTE:** Since it takes three operands, the conditional operator is considered a *ternary* operator.

The conditional expression above performs the same operation as the following `if/else` statement:

```
if (x < 0)
    y = 10;
else
    z = 20;
```

The part of the conditional expression that comes before the question mark is the expression to be tested. It's like the expression in the parentheses of an `if` statement. If the expression is true, the part of the statement between the ? and the : is executed. Otherwise, the part after the : is executed. Figure 10 illustrates the roles played by the three subexpressions.

Figure 10 Conditional expression

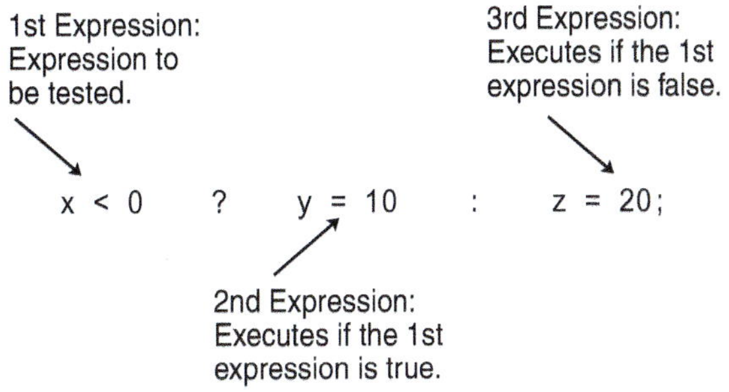

If it helps, you can put parentheses around the subexpressions, as in the following:

```
(x < 0) ? (y = 10) : (z = 20);
```

Using the Value of a Conditional Expression

Remember, in C++ all expressions have a value, and this includes the conditional expression. If the first subexpression is true, the value of the conditional expression is the value of the second subexpression. Otherwise, it is the value of the third subexpression. Here is an example of an assignment statement using the value of a conditional expression:

```
a = x > 100 ? 0 : 1;
```

The value assigned to a will be either 0 or 1, depending upon whether x is greater than 100. This statement could be expressed as the following if/else statement:

```
if (x > 100)
    a = 0;
else
    a = 1;
```

Program 22 can be used to help a consultant calculate her charges. Her rate is $50.00 per hour, but her minimum charge is for 5 hours. The conditional operator is used in a statement that ensures the number of hours does not go below five.

Program 22

```
// This program calculates a consultant's charges at $50
// per hour, for a minimum of 5 hours. The ?: operator
// adjusts hours to 5 if less than 5 hours were worked.
#include <iostream>
#include <iomanip>
using namespace std;

int main()
{
    const double PAY_RATE = 50.0; // Hourly pay rate
    const int MIN_HOURS = 5;      // Minimum billable hours
    double hours,                 // Hours worked
           charges;               // Total charges

    // Get the hours worked.
    cout << "How many hours were worked? ";
    cin >> hours;

    // Determine the hours to charge for.
    hours = hours < MIN_HOURS ? MIN_HOURS : hours;

    // Calculate and display the charges.
    charges = PAY_RATE * hours;
    cout << fixed << showpoint << setprecision(2)
         << "The charges are $" << charges << endl;
    return 0;
}
```

Program Output with Example Input Shown in Bold

```
How many hours were worked? 10 [Enter]
The charges are $500.00
```

Program Output with Example Input Shown in Bold

```
How many hours were worked? 2 [Enter]
The charges are $250.00
```

Notice in line 11 a constant named `MIN_HOURS` is defined to represent the minimum number of hours, which is 5. Here is the statement in line 20, with the conditional expression:

```
hours = hours < MIN_HOURS ? MIN_HOURS : hours;
```

If the value in `hours` is less than 5, then 5 is stored in `hours`. Otherwise, `hours` is assigned the value it already has. The `hours` variable will not have a value less than 5 when it is used in the next statement, which calculates the consultant's charges.

As you can see, the conditional operator gives you the ability to pack decision-making power into a concise line of code. With a little imagination, it can be applied to many other programming problems. For instance, consider the following statement:

```
cout << "Your grade is: " << (score < 60 ? "Fail." : "Pass.");
```

If you were to use an `if/else` statement, the statement above would be written as follows:

```
if (score < 60)
   cout << "Your grade is: Fail.";
else
   cout << "Your grade is: Pass.";
```

NOTE: The parentheses are placed around the conditional expression because the `<<` operator has higher precedence than the `?:` operator. Without the parentheses, just the value of the expression `score < 60` would be sent to `cout`.

Checkpoint

24 Rewrite the following `if/else` statements as conditional expressions:

A)
```
if (x > y)
   z = 1;
else
   z = 20;
```
B)
```
if (temp > 45)
   population = base * 10;
else
   population = base * 2;
```
C)
```
if (hours > 40)
   wages *= 1.5;
else
   wages *= 1;
```
D)
```
if (result >= 0)
   cout << "The result is positive\n";
else
   cout << "The result is negative.\n";
```

25 The following statements use conditional expressions. Rewrite each with an `if/else` statement.

A) `j = k > 90 ? 57 : 12;`
B) `factor = x >= 10 ? y * 22 : y * 35;`
C) `total += count == 1 ? sales : count * sales;`
D) `cout << (((num % 2) == 0) ? "Even\n" : "Odd\n");`

26 What will the following program display?

```
#include <iostream>
using namespace std;

int main()
{
   const int UPPER = 8, LOWER = 2;
   int num1, num2, num3 = 12, num4 = 3;

   num1 = num3 < num4 ? UPPER : LOWER;
   num2 = num4 > UPPER ? num3 : LOWER;
   cout << num1 << " " << num2 << endl;
   return 0;
}
```

14 The `switch` Statement

CONCEPT: The `switch` statement lets the value of a variable or an expression determine where the program will branch.

A branch occurs when one part of a program causes another part to execute. The `if/else if` statement allows your program to branch into one of several possible paths. It performs a series of tests (usually relational) and branches when one of these tests is true. The `switch` statement is a similar mechanism. However, it tests the value of an integer expression and then uses that value to determine to which set of statements to branch. Here is the format of the `switch` statement:

```
switch (IntegerExpression)
{
   case ConstantExpression:
        // place one or more
        // statements here

   case ConstantExpression:
        // place one or more
        // statements here

     // case statements may be repeated as many
     // times as necessary

   default:
        // place one or more
        // statements here
}
```

The first line of the statement starts with the word `switch`, followed by an integer expression inside parentheses. This can be either of the following:

- a variable of any of the integer data types (including `char`)
- an expression whose value is of any of the integer data types

On the next line is the beginning of a block containing several `case` statements. Each `case` statement is formatted in the following manner:

```
case ConstantExpression:
     // place one or more
     // statements here
```

After the word `case` is a constant expression (which must be of an integer type), followed by a colon. The constant expression may be an integer literal or an integer named constant. The `case` statement marks the beginning of a section of statements. The program branches to these statements if the value of the `switch` expression matches that of the `case` expression.

WARNING! The expression of each `case` statement in the block must be unique.

NOTE: The expression following the word `case` must be an integer literal or constant. It cannot be a variable, and it cannot be an expression such as `x < 22` or `n == 50`.

An optional `default` section comes after all the `case` statements. The program branches to this section if none of the `case` expressions match the `switch` expression. So, it functions like a trailing `else` in an `if/else if` statement.

Program 23 shows how a simple `switch` statement works.

Program 23

```
// The switch statement in this program tells the user something
// he or she already knows: the data just entered!
#include <iostream>
using namespace std;

int main()
{
    char choice;

    cout << "Enter A, B, or C: ";
    cin >> choice;
    switch (choice)
    {
        case 'A': cout << "You entered A.\n";
                  break;
        case 'B': cout << "You entered B.\n";
                  break;
        case 'C': cout << "You entered C.\n";
                  break;
        default:  cout << "You did not enter A, B, or C!\n";
    }
    return 0;
}
```

(program continues)

Program 23 *(continued)*

Program Output with Example Input Shown in Bold

```
Enter A, B, or C: B [Enter]
You entered B.
```

Program Output with Example Input Shown in Bold

```
Enter A, B, or C: F [Enter]
You did not enter A, B, or C!
```

The first `case` statement is `case 'A':`, the second is `case 'B':`, and the third is `case 'C':`. These statements mark where the program is to branch to if the variable `choice` contains the values `'A'`, `'B'`, or `'C'`. (Remember, character variables and literals are considered integers.) The `default` section is branched to if the user enters anything other than A, B, or C.

Notice the `break` statements in the `case 'A'`, `case 'B'`, and `case 'C'` sections.

```
switch (choice)
{
    case 'A':cout << "You entered A.\n";
             break;   <-------
    case 'B':cout << "You entered B.\n";
             break;   <-------
    case 'C':cout << "You entered C.\n";
             break;   <-------
    default: cout << "You did not enter A, B, or C!\n";
}
```

The `case` statements show the program where to start executing in the block, and the `break` statements show the program where to stop. Without the `break` statements, the program would execute all of the lines from the matching `case` statement to the end of the block.

> **NOTE:** The `default` section (or the last `case` section, if there is no `default`) does not need a `break` statement. Some programmers prefer to put one there anyway, for consistency.

Program 24 is a modification of Program 23, without the `break` statements.

Program 24

```
// The switch statement in this program tells the user something
// he or she already knows: the data just entered!
#include <iostream>
using namespace std;

int main()
{
    char choice;

```

```
    cout << "Enter A, B, or C: ";
    cin >> choice;
    // The following switch is
    // missing its break statements!
    switch (choice)
    {
        case 'A': cout << "You entered A.\n";
        case 'B': cout << "You entered B.\n";
        case 'C': cout << "You entered C.\n";
        default:  cout << "You did not enter A, B, or C!\n";
    }
    return 0;
}
```

Program Output with Example Input Shown in Bold

```
Enter A, B, or C: A [Enter]
You entered A.
You entered B.
You entered C.
You did not enter A, B, or C!
```

Program Output with Example Input Shown in Bold

```
Enter A, B, or C: C [Enter]
You entered C.
You did not enter A, B, or C!
```

Without the `break` statement, the program "falls through" all of the statements below the one with the matching `case` expression. Sometimes this is what you want. Program 25 lists the features of three TV models a customer may choose from. The Model 100 has remote control. The Model 200 has remote control and stereo sound. The Model 300 has remote control, stereo sound, and picture-in-a-picture capability. The program uses a `switch` statement with carefully omitted `breaks` to print the features of the selected model.

Program 25

```
// This program is carefully constructed to use the "fall through"
// feature of the switch statement.
#include <iostream>
using namespace std;

int main()
{
    int modelNum; // Model number

    // Get a model number from the user.
    cout << "Our TVs come in three models:\n";
    cout << "The 100, 200, and 300. Which do you want? ";
    cin >> modelNum;

```

(program continues)

Program 25 *(continued)*

```
    // Display the model's features.
    cout << "That model has the following features:\n";
    switch (modelNum)
    {
        case 300: cout << "\tPicture-in-a-picture.\n";
        case 200: cout << "\tStereo sound.\n";
        case 100: cout << "\tRemote control.\n";
                  break;
        default:  cout << "You can only choose the 100,";
                  cout << "200, or 300.\n";
    }
    return 0;
}
```

Program Output with Example Input Shown in Bold

```
Our TVs come in three models:
The 100, 200, and 300. Which do you want? 100 [Enter]
That model has the following features:
   Remote control.
```

Program Output with Example Input Shown in Bold

```
Our TVs come in three models:
The 100, 200, and 300. Which do you want? 200 [Enter]
That model has the following features:
   Stereo sound.
   Remote control.
```

Program Output with Example Input Shown in Bold

```
Our TVs come in three models:
The 100, 200, and 300. Which do you want? 300 [Enter]
That model has the following features:
   Picture-in-a-picture.
   Stereo sound.
   Remote control.
```

Program Output with Example Input Shown in Bold

```
Our TVs come in three models:
The 100, 200, and 300. Which do you want? 500 [Enter]
That model has the following features:
You can only choose the 100, 200, or 300.
```

Another example of how useful this "fall through" capability can be is when you want the program to branch to the same set of statements for multiple `case` expressions. For instance, Program 26 asks the user to select a grade of pet food. The available choices are A, B, and C. The `switch` statement will recognize either upper or lowercase letters.

Program 26

```
// The switch statement in this program uses the "fall through"
// feature to catch both uppercase and lowercase letters entered
// by the user.
#include <iostream>
```

```
using namespace std;

int main()
{
    char feedGrade;

    // Get the desired grade of feed.
    cout << "Our pet food is available in three grades:\n";
    cout << "A, B, and C. Which do you want pricing for? ";
    cin >> feedGrade;

    // Display the price.
    switch(feedGrade)
    {
        case 'a':
        case 'A': cout << "30 cents per pound.\n";
                  break;
        case 'b':
        case 'B': cout << "20 cents per pound.\n";
                  break;
        case 'c':
        case 'C': cout << "15 cents per pound.\n";
                  break;
        default:  cout << "That is an invalid choice.\n";
    }
    return 0;
}
```

Program Output with Example Input Shown in Bold

```
Our pet food is available in three grades:
A, B, and C. Which do you want pricing for? b [Enter]
20 cents per pound.
```

Program Output with Example Input Shown in Bold

```
Our pet food is available in three grades:
A, B, and C. Which do you want pricing for? B [Enter]
20 cents per pound.
```

When the user enters `'a'`, the corresponding `case` has no statements associated with it, so the program falls through to the next `case`, which corresponds with `'A'`.

```
case 'a':
case 'A': cout << "30 cents per pound.\n";
          break;
```

The same technique is used for `'b'` and `'c'`.

Using `switch` in Menu Systems

The `switch` statement is a natural mechanism for building menu systems. Recall that Program 18 gives a menu to select which health club package the user wishes to purchase. The program uses `if/else if` statements to determine which package the user has selected and displays the calculated charges. Program 27 is a modification of that program, using a `switch` statement instead of `if/else if`.

Program 27

```
// This program uses a switch statement to determine
// the item selected from a menu.
#include <iostream>
#include <iomanip>
using namespace std;

int main()
{
    int choice;      // To hold a menu choice
    int months;      // To hold the number of months
    double charges;  // To hold the monthly charges

    // Constants for membership rates
    const double ADULT = 40.0,
                 CHILD = 20.0,
                 SENIOR = 30.0;

    // Constants for menu choices
    const int ADULT_CHOICE = 1,
              CHILD_CHOICE = 2,
              SENIOR_CHOICE = 3,
              QUIT_CHOICE = 4;

    // Display the menu and get a choice.
    cout << "\t\tHealth Club Membership Menu\n\n"
         << "1. Standard Adult Membership\n"
         << "2. Child Membership\n"
         << "3. Senior Citizen Membership\n"
         << "4. Quit the Program\n\n"
         << "Enter your choice: ";
    cin >> choice;

    // Set the numeric output formatting.
    cout << fixed << showpoint << setprecision(2);

    // Respond to the user's menu selection.
    switch (choice)
    {
        case ADULT_CHOICE:
            cout << "For how many months? ";
            cin >> months;
            charges = months * ADULT;
            cout << "The total charges are $" << charges << endl;
            break;

        case CHILD_CHOICE:
            cout << "For how many months? ";
            cin >> months;
            charges = months * CHILD;
            cout << "The total charges are $" << charges << endl;
            break;

```

```
            case SENIOR_CHOICE:
                cout << "For how many months? ";
                cin >> months;
                charges = months * SENIOR;
                cout << "The total charges are $" << charges << endl;
                break;

            case QUIT_CHOICE:
                cout << "Program ending.\n";
                break;

            default:
                cout << "The valid choices are 1 through 4. Run the\n"
                     << "program again and select one of those.\n";
        }

        return 0;
}
```

Program Output with Example Input Shown in Bold

```
        Health Club Membership Menu

1. Standard Adult Membership
2. Child Membership
3. Senior Citizen Membership
4. Quit the Program

Enter your choice: 2 [Enter]
For how many months? 6 [Enter]
The total charges are $120.00
```

Checkpoint

27 Explain why you cannot convert the following `if/else if` statement into a `switch` statement.

```
if (temp == 100)
    x = 0;
else if (population > 1000)
    x = 1;
else if (rate < .1)
    x = -1;
```

28 What is wrong with the following `switch` statement?

```
switch (temp)
{
    case temp < 0 : cout << "Temp is negative.\n";
                    break;
    case temp == 0: cout << "Temp is zero.\n";
                    break;
    case temp > 0 : cout << "Temp is positive.\n";
                    break;
}
```

29 What will the following program display?

```
#include <iostream>
using namespace std;
int main()
{
    int funny = 7, serious = 15;

    funny = serious * 2;
    switch (funny)
    {     case 0 : cout << "That is funny.\n";
                   break;
          case 30: cout << "That is serious.\n";
                   break;
          case 32: cout << "That is seriously funny.\n";
                   break;
          default: cout << funny << endl;
    }
    return 0;
}
```

30 Complete the following program skeleton by writing a `switch` statement that displays "one" if the user has entered 1, "two" if the user has entered 2, and "three" if the user has entered 3. If a number other than 1, 2, or 3 is entered, the program should display an error message.

```
#include <iostream>
using namespace std;
int main()
{
    int userNum;
    cout << "Enter one of the numbers 1, 2, or 3: ";
    cin >> userNum;
    //
    // Write the switch statement here.
    //
    return 0;
}
```

31 Rewrite the following program. Use a `switch` statement instead of the `if/else if` statement.

```
#include <iostream>
using namespace std;
int main()
{
    int selection;
    cout << "Which formula do you want to see?\n\n";
    cout << "1. Area of a circle\n";
    cout << "2. Area of a rectangle\n";
    cout << "3. Area of a cylinder\n"
    cout << "4. None of them!\n";
    cin >> selection;
    if (selection == 1)
        cout << "Pi times radius squared\n";
```

```
      else if (selection == 2)
         cout << "Length times width\n";
      else if (selection == 3)
         cout << "Pi times radius squared times height\n";
      else if (selection == 4)
         cout << "Well okay then, good bye!\n";
      else
         cout << "Not good with numbers, eh?\n";
      return 0;
   }
```

15 More about Blocks and Variable Scope

CONCEPT: The scope of a variable is limited to the block in which it is defined.

C++ allows you to create variables almost anywhere in a program. Program 28 is a modification of Program 17, which determines if the user qualifies for a loan. The definitions of the variables `income` and `years` have been moved to later points in the program.

Program 28

```
// This program demonstrates late variable definition
#include <iostream>
using namespace std;

int main()
{
    // Constants for minimum income and years
    const double MIN_INCOME = 35000.0;
    const int MIN_YEARS = 5;

    // Get the annual income.
    cout << "What is your annual income? ";
    double income;  // Variable definition
    cin >> income;

    // Get the number of years at the current job.
    cout << "How many years have you worked at "
         << "your current job? ";
    int years;       // Variable definition
    cin >> years;

    // Determine the user's loan qualifications.
    if (income >= MIN_INCOME || years > MIN_YEARS)
       cout << "You qualify.\n";
    else
    {
        cout << "You must earn at least $"
             << MIN_INCOME << " or have been "
             << "employed more than " << MIN_YEARS
             << " years.\n";
    }
    return 0;
}
```

It is a common practice to define all of a function's variables at the top of the function. Sometimes, especially in longer programs, it's a good idea to define variables near the part of the program where they are used. This makes the purpose of the variable more evident.

The scope of a variable is defined as the part of the program where the variable may be used.

In Program 28, the scope of the `income` variable is the part of the program in lines 13 through 32. The scope of the `years` variable is the part of the program in lines 19 through 32.

The variables `income` and `years` are defined inside function `main`'s braces. Variables defined inside a set of braces have *local scope* or *block scope*. They may only be used in the part of the program between their definition and the block's closing brace.

You may define variables inside any block. For example, look at Program 29. This version of the loan program has the variable `years` defined inside the block of the `if` statement. The scope of `years` is the part of the program in lines 21 through 31.

Program 29

```
1   // This program demonstrates a variable defined in an inner block.
2   #include <iostream>
3   using namespace std;
4
5   int main()
6   {
7       // Constants for minimum income and years
8       const double MIN_INCOME = 35000.0;
9       const int MIN_YEARS = 5;
10
11      // Get the annual income.
12      cout << "What is your annual income? ";
13      double income;  // Variable definition
14      cin >> income;
15
16      if (income >= MIN_INCOME)
17      {
18          // Get the number of years at the current job.
19          cout << "How many years have you worked at "
20               << "your current job? ";
21          int years;  // Variable definition
22          cin >> years;
23
24          if (years > MIN_YEARS)
25              cout << "You qualify.\n";
26          else
27          {
28              cout << "You must have been employed for\n"
29                   << "more than " << MIN_YEARS
30                   << " years to qualify.\n";
31          }
32      }
33      else
```

```
    {
        cout << "You must earn at least $" << MIN_INCOME
             << " to qualify.\n";
    }
    return 0;
}
```

Notice the scope of years is only within the block where it is defined. The variable is not visible before its definition or after the closing brace of the block. This is true of any variable defined inside a set of braces.

> **NOTE:** When a program is running and it enters the section of code that constitutes a variable's scope, it is said that the variable *comes into scope*. This simply means the variable is now visible and the program may reference it. Likewise, when a variable *leaves scope*, or *goes out of scope*, it may no longer be used.

Variables with the Same Name

When a block is nested inside another block, a variable defined in the inner block may have the same name as a variable defined in the outer block. As long as the variable in the inner block is visible, however, the variable in the outer block will be hidden. This is illustrated by Program 30.

Program 30

```
// This program uses two variables with the name number.
#include <iostream>
using namespace std;

int main()
{
    // Define a variable named number.
    int number;

    cout << "Enter a number greater than 0: ";
    cin >> number;
    if (number > 0)
    {
        int number; // Another variable named number.
        cout << "Now enter another number: ";
        cin >> number;
        cout << "The second number you entered was "
             << number << endl;
    }
    cout << "Your first number was " << number << endl;
    return 0;
}
```

Program Output with Example Input Shown in Bold

```
Enter a number greater than 0: 2 [Enter]
Now enter another number: 7 [Enter]
The second number you entered was 7
Your first number was 2
```

Program 30 has two separate variables named `number`. The `cin` and `cout` statements in the inner block (belonging to the `if` statement) can only work with the `number` variable defined in that block. As soon as the program leaves that block, the inner `number` goes out of scope, revealing the outer `number` variable.

> **WARNING!** Although it's perfectly acceptable to define variables inside nested blocks, you should avoid giving them the same names as variables in the outer blocks. It's too easy to confuse one variable with another.

Case Study: See the Sales Commission Case Study on the computer science portal at www.pearsonhighered.com/gaddis.

Review Questions and Exercises

Short Answer

1. Describe the difference between the `if/else if` statement and a series of `if` statements.
2. In an `if/else if` statement, what is the purpose of a trailing `else`?
3. What is a flag and how does it work?
4. Can an `if` statement test expressions other than relational expressions? Explain.
5. Briefly describe how the && operator works.
6. Briefly describe how the || operator works.
7. Why are the relational operators called relational?
8. Why do most programmers indent the conditionally executed statements in a decision structure?

Fill-in-the-Blank

9. An expression using the greater-than, less-than, greater-than-or-equal-to, less-than-or-equal-to, equal-to, or not-equal-to operator is called a(n) __________ expression.
10. A relational expression is either __________ or __________.
11. The value of a relational expression is 0 if the expression is __________ or 1 if the expression is __________.
12. The `if` statement regards an expression with the value 0 as __________.
13. The `if` statement regards an expression with a nonzero value as __________.
14. For an `if` statement to conditionally execute a group of statements, the statements must be enclosed in a set of __________.
15. In an `if/else` statement, the `if` part executes its statement or block if the expression is __________, and the `else` part executes its statement or block if the expression is __________.
16. The trailing `else` in an `if/else if` statement has a similar purpose as the __________ section of a `switch` statement.

17. The `if/else if` statement is actually a form of the __________ `if` statement.
18. If the subexpression on the left of the __________ logical operator is false, the right subexpression is not checked.
19. If the subexpression on the left of the __________ logical operator is true, the right subexpression is not checked.
20. The __________ logical operator has higher precedence than the other logical operators.
21. The logical operators have __________ associativity.
22. The __________ logical operator works best when testing a number to determine if it is within a range.
23. The __________ logical operator works best when testing a number to determine if it is outside a range.
24. A variable with __________ scope is only visible when the program is executing in the block containing the variable's definition.
25. You use the __________ operator to determine whether one `string` object is greater than another `string` object.
26. An expression using the conditional operator is called a(n) __________ expression.
27. The expression that is tested by a `switch` statement must have a(n) __________ value.
28. The expression following a `case` statement must be a(n) __________ __________.
29. A program will "fall through" a `case` section if it is missing the __________ statement.
30. What value will be stored in the variable `t` after each of the following statements executes?

    A) `t = (12 > 1);` __________

    B) `t = (2 < 0);` __________

    C) `t = (5 == (3 * 2));` __________

    D) `t = (5 == 5);` __________

Algorithm Workbench

31. Write an `if` statement that assigns 100 to `x` when `y` is equal to 0.
32. Write an `if/else` statement that assigns 0 to `x` when `y` is equal to 10. Otherwise, it should assign 1 to `x`.
33. Using the following chart, write an `if/else if` statement that assigns .10, .15, or .20 to `commission`, depending on the value in `sales`.

Sales	Commission Rate
Up to \$10,000	10%
\$10,000 to \$15,000	15%
Over \$15,000	20%

34. Write an `if` statement that sets the variable `hours` to 10 when the flag variable `minimum` is set.
35. Write nested `if` statements that perform the following tests: If `amount1` is greater than 10 and `amount2` is less than 100, display the greater of the two.

36. Write an `if` statement that prints the message "The number is valid" if the variable `grade` is within the range 0 through 100.
37. Write an `if` statement that prints the message "The number is valid" if the variable `temperature` is within the range –50 through 150.
38. Write an `if` statement that prints the message "The number is not valid" if the variable `hours` is outside the range 0 through 80.
39. Assume `str1` and `str2` are `string` objects that have been initialized with different values. Write an `if/else` statement that compares the two objects and displays the one that is alphabetically greatest.
40. Convert the following `if/else if` statement into a `switch` statement:

```
if (choice == 1)
{
    cout << fixed << showpoint << setprecision(2);
}
else if (choice == 2 || choice == 3)
{
    cout << fixed << showpoint << setprecision(4);
}
else if (choice == 4)
{
    cout << fixed << showpoint << setprecision(6);
}
else
{
    cout << fixed << showpoint << setprecision(8);
}
```

41. Match the conditional expression with the `if/else` statement that performs the same operation.

A) `q = x < y ? a + b : x * 2;`

B) `q = x < y ? x * 2 : a + b;`

C) `x < y ? q = 0 : q = 1;`

```
____ if (x < y)
         q = 0;
     else
         q = 1;

____ if (x < y)
         q = a + b;
     else
         q = x * 2;

____ if (x < y)
         q = x * 2;
     else
         q = a + b;
```

True or False

42. T F The = operator and the == operator perform the same operation when used in a Boolean expression.

43. T F A variable defined in an inner block may not have the same name as a variable defined in the outer block.
44. T F A conditionally executed statement should be indented one level from the `if` statement.
45. T F All lines in a block should be indented one level.
46. T F It's safe to assume that all uninitialized variables automatically start with 0 as their value.
47. T F When an `if` statement is nested in the `if` part of another statement, the only time the inner `if` is executed is when the expression of the outer `if` is true.
48. T F When an `if` statement is nested in the `else` part of another statement, as in an `if/else if`, the only time the inner `if` is executed is when the expression of the outer `if` is true.
49. T F The scope of a variable is limited to the block in which it is defined.
50. T F You can use the relational operators to compare `string` objects.
51. T F `x != y` is the same as `(x > y || x < y)`
52. T F `y < x` is the same as `x >= y`
53. T F `x >= y` is the same as `(x > y && x = y)`

Assume the variables `x = 5`, `y = 6`, and `z = 8`. Indicate by circling the T or F whether each of the following conditions is True or False:

54. T F `x == 5 || y > 3`
55. T F `7 <= x && z > 4`
56. T F `2 != y && z != 4`
57. T F `x >= 0 || x <= y`

Find the Errors

Each of the following programs has errors. Find as many as you can.

58.
```
// This program averages 3 test scores.
// It uses the variable perfectScore as a flag.
include <iostream>
using namespace std;

int main()
{
    cout << "Enter your 3 test scores and I will ";
         << "average them:";
    int score1, score2, score3,
    cin >> score1 >> score2 >> score3;
    double average;
    average = (score1 + score2 + score3) / 3.0;
    if (average = 100);
        perfectScore = true; // Set the flag variable
    cout << "Your average is " << average << endl;
    bool perfectScore;
    if (perfectScore);
    {
        cout << "Congratulations!\n";
        cout << "That's a perfect score.\n";
        cout << "You deserve a pat on the back!\n";
        return 0;
}
```

59.
```
// This program divides a user-supplied number by another
// user-supplied number. It checks for division by zero.
#include <iostream>
using namespace std;

int main()
{
    double num1, num2, quotient;

    cout << "Enter a number: ";
    cin >> num1;
    cout << "Enter another number: ";
    cin >> num2;
    if (num2 == 0)
       cout << "Division by zero is not possible.\n";
       cout << "Please run the program again ";
       cout << "and enter a number besides zero.\n";
    else
       quotient = num1 / num2;
       cout << "The quotient of " << num1 <<
       cout << " divided by " << num2 << " is ";
       cout << quotient << endl;
    return 0;
}
```

60.
```
// This program uses an if/else if statement to assign a
// letter grade (A, B, C, D, or F) to a numeric test score.
#include <iostream>
using namespace std;

int main()
{
    int testScore;

    cout << "Enter your test score and I will tell you\n";
    cout << "the letter grade you earned: ";
    cin >> testScore;
    if (testScore < 60)
        cout << "Your grade is F.\n";
    else if (testScore < 70)
        cout << "Your grade is D.\n";
    else if (testScore < 80)
        cout << "Your grade is C.\n";
    else if (testScore < 90)
        cout << "Your grade is B.\n";
    else
        cout << "That is not a valid score.\n";
    else if (testScore <= 100)
        cout << "Your grade is A.\n";
    return 0;
}
```

61.
```
// This program uses a switch-case statement to assign a
// letter grade (A, B, C, D, or F) to a numeric test score.
#include <iostream>
using namespace std;

int main()
{
    double testScore;

    cout << "Enter your test score and I will tell you\n";
    cout << "the letter grade you earned: ";
    cin >> testScore;
    switch (testScore)
    {
        case (testScore < 60.0):
                  cout << "Your grade is F.\n";
                  break;
        case (testScore < 70.0):
                  cout << "Your grade is D.\n";
                  break;
        case (testScore < 80.0):
                  cout << "Your grade is C.\n";
                  break;
        case (testScore < 90.0):
                  cout << "Your grade is B.\n";
                  break;
        case (testScore <= 100.0):
                  cout << "Your grade is A.\n";
                  break;
        default:
                  cout << "That score isn't valid\n";
    return 0;
}
```

62. The following statement should determine if x is not greater than 20. What is wrong with it?

```
if (!x > 20)
```

63. The following statement should determine if count is within the range of 0 through 100. What is wrong with it?

```
if (count >= 0 || count <= 100)
```

64. The following statement should determine if count is outside the range of 0 through 100. What is wrong with it?

```
if (count < 0 && count > 100)
```

65. The following statement should assign 0 to z if a is less than 10, otherwise it should assign 7 to z. What is wrong with it?

```
z = (a < 10) : 0 ? 7;
```

Programming Challenges

1. **Minimum/Maximum**

   Write a program that asks the user to enter two numbers. The program should use the conditional operator to determine which number is the smaller and which is the larger.

2. **Roman Numeral Converter**

   Write a program that asks the user to enter a number within the range of 1 through 10. Use a `switch` statement to display the Roman numeral version of that number.

   Input Validation: Do not accept a number less than 1 or greater than 10.

3. **Magic Dates**

   The date June 10, 1960 is special because when we write it in the following format, the month times the day equals the year.

   6/10/60

   Write a program that asks the user to enter a month (in numeric form), a day, and a two-digit year. The program should then determine whether the month times the day is equal to the year. If so, it should display a message saying the date is magic. Otherwise, it should display a message saying the date is not magic.

4. **Areas of Rectangles**

   The area of a rectangle is the rectangle's length times its width. Write a program that asks for the length and width of two rectangles. The program should tell the user which rectangle has the greater area, or if the areas are the same.

5. **Body Mass Index**

   Write a program that calculates and displays a person's body mass index (BMI). The BMI is often used to determine whether a person is overweight or underweight for his or her height. A person's BMI is calculated with the following formula:

   $BMI = weight \times 703 / height^2$

   where *weight* is measured in pounds and *height* is measured in inches. The program should display a message indicating whether the person has optimal weight, is underweight, or is overweight. A person's weight is considered to be optimal if his or her BMI is between 18.5 and 25. If the BMI is less than 18.5, the person is considered to be underweight. If the BMI value is greater than 25, the person is considered to be overweight.

6. **Mass and Weight**

   Scientists measure an object's mass in kilograms and its weight in newtons. If you know the amount of mass that an object has, you can calculate its weight, in newtons, with the following formula:

   $Weight = mass \times 9.8$

   Write a program that asks the user to enter an object's mass, then calculates and displays its weight. If the object weighs more than 1,000 newtons, display a message indicating that it is too heavy. If the object weighs less than 10 newtons, display a message indicating that the object is too light.

7. Time Calculator

VideoNote
Solving the Time Calculator Problem

Write a program that asks the user to enter a number of seconds.

- There are 60 seconds in a minute. If the number of seconds entered by the user is greater than or equal to 60, the program should display the number of minutes in that many seconds.
- There are 3,600 seconds in an hour. If the number of seconds entered by the user is greater than or equal to 3,600, the program should display the number of hours in that many seconds.
- There are 86,400 seconds in a day. If the number of seconds entered by the user is greater than or equal to 86,400, the program should display the number of days in that many seconds.

8. Color Mixer

The colors red, blue, and yellow are known as primary colors because they cannot be made by mixing other colors. When you mix two primary colors, you get a secondary color, as shown here:

When you mix red and blue, you get purple.
When you mix red and yellow, you get orange.
When you mix blue and yellow, you get green.

Write a program that prompts the user to enter the names of two primary colors to mix. If the user enters anything other than "red," "blue," or "yellow," the program should display an error message. Otherwise, the program should display the name of the secondary color that results by mixing two primary colors.

9. Change for a Dollar Game

Create a change-counting game that gets the user to enter the number of coins required to make exactly one dollar. The program should ask the user to enter the number of pennies, nickels, dimes, and quarters. If the total value of the coins entered is equal to one dollar, the program should congratulate the user for winning the game. Otherwise, the program should display a message indicating whether the amount entered was more than or less than one dollar.

10. Days in a Month

Write a program that asks the user to enter the month (letting the user enter an integer in the range of 1 through 12) and the year. The program should then display the number of days in that month. Use the following criteria to identify leap years:

1. Determine whether the year is divisible by 100. If it is, then it is a leap year if and only if it is divisible by 400. For example, 2000 is a leap year but 2100 is not.
2. If the year is not divisible by 100, then it is a leap year if and only if it is divisible by 4. For example, 2008 is a leap year but 2009 is not.

Here is a sample run of the program:

```
Enter a month (1-12): 2 [Enter]
Enter a year: 2008 [Enter]
29 days
```

11. Math Tutor

This is a modification of Programming Challenge 17 from the chapter "Expressions and Interactivity". Write a program that can be used as a math tutor for a young student. The program should display two random numbers that are to be added, such as:

```
  247
+ 129
-----
```

The program should wait for the student to enter the answer. If the answer is correct, a message of congratulations should be printed. If the answer is incorrect, a message should be printed showing the correct answer.

12. Software Sales

A software company sells a package that retails for $99. Quantity discounts are given according to the following table.

Quantity	Discount
10–19	20%
20–49	30%
50–99	40%
100 or more	50%

Write a program that asks for the number of units sold and computes the total cost of the purchase.

Input Validation: Make sure the number of units is greater than 0.

13. Book Club Points

Serendipity Booksellers has a book club that awards points to its customers based on the number of books purchased each month. The points are awarded as follows:

- If a customer purchases 0 books, he or she earns 0 points.
- If a customer purchases 1 book, he or she earns 5 points.
- If a customer purchases 2 books, he or she earns 15 points.
- If a customer purchases 3 books, he or she earns 30 points.
- If a customer purchases 4 or more books, he or she earns 60 points.

Write a program that asks the user to enter the number of books he or she has purchased this month then displays the number of points awarded.

14. Bank Charges

A bank charges $10 per month plus the following check fees for a commercial checking account:

$.10 each for fewer than 20 checks
$.08 each for 20–39 checks
$.06 each for 40–59 checks
$.04 each for 60 or more checks

The bank also charges an extra $15 if the balance of the account falls below $400 (before any check fees are applied). Write a program that asks for the beginning balance and the number of checks written. Compute and display the bank's service fees for the month.

Input Validation: Do not accept a negative value for the number of checks written. If a negative value is given for the beginning balance, display an urgent message indicating the account is overdrawn.

15. Shipping Charges

The Fast Freight Shipping Company charges the following rates:

Weight of Package (in Kilograms)	Rate per 500 Miles Shipped
2 kg or less	$1.10
Over 2 kg but not more than 6 kg	$2.20
Over 6 kg but not more than 10 kg	$3.70
Over 10 kg but not more than 20 kg	$4.80

Write a program that asks for the weight of the package and the distance it is to be shipped, then displays the charges.

Input Validation: Do not accept values of 0 or less for the weight of the package. Do not accept weights of more than 20 kg (this is the maximum weight the company will ship). Do not accept distances of less than 10 miles or more than 3,000 miles. These are the company's minimum and maximum shipping distances.

16. Running the Race

Write a program that asks for the names of three runners and the time it took each of them to finish a race. The program should display who came in first, second, and third place.

Input Validation: Only accept positive numbers for the times.

17. Personal Best

Write a program that asks for the name of a pole vaulter and the dates and vault heights (in meters) of the athlete's three best vaults. It should then report, in order of height (best first), the date on which each vault was made and its height.

Input Validation: Only accept values between 2.0 and 5.0 for the heights.

18. Fat Gram Calculator

Write a program that asks for the number of calories and fat grams in a food. The program should display the percentage of calories that come from fat. If the calories from fat are less than 30 percent of the total calories of the food, it should also display a message indicating that the food is low in fat.

One gram of fat has 9 calories, so

Calories from fat = fat grams * 9

The percentage of calories from fat can be calculated as

Calories from fat ÷ total calories

Input Validation: Make sure the number of calories and fat grams are not less than 0. Also, the number of calories from fat cannot be greater than the total number of calories. If that happens, display an error message indicating that either the calories or fat grams were incorrectly entered.

19. Spectral Analysis

If a scientist knows the wavelength of an electromagnetic wave, he or she can determine what type of radiation it is. Write a program that asks for the wavelength of an electromagnetic wave in meters and then displays what that wave is according to the chart below. (For example, a wave with a wavelength of 1E−10 meters would be an X-ray.)

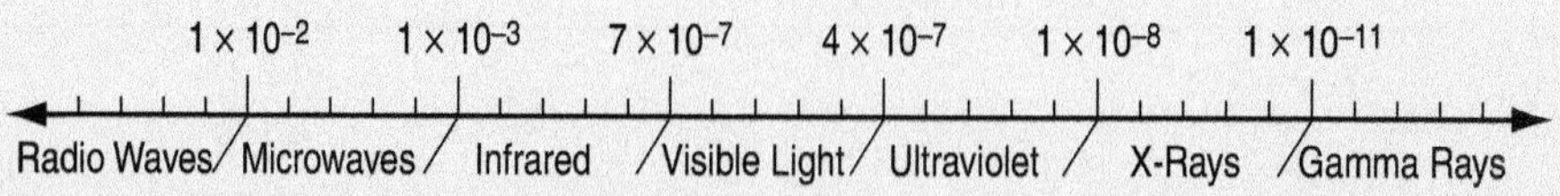

20. The Speed of Sound

The following table shows the approximate speed of sound in air, water, and steel.

Medium	Speed
Air	1,100 feet per second
Water	4,900 feet per second
Steel	16,400 feet per second

Write a program that displays a menu allowing the user to select air, water, or steel. After the user has made a selection, he or she should be asked to enter the distance a sound wave will travel in the selected medium. The program will then display the amount of time it will take. (Round the answer to four decimal places.)

Input Validation: Check that the user has selected one of the available choices from the menu. Do not accept distances less than 0.

21. The Speed of Sound in Gases

When sound travels through a gas, its speed depends primarily on the density of the medium. The less dense the medium, the faster the speed will be. The following table shows the approximate speed of sound at 0 degrees centigrade, measured in meters per second, when traveling through carbon dioxide, air, helium, and hydrogen.

Medium	Speed (Meters per Second)
Carbon dioxide	258.0
Air	331.5
Helium	972.0
Hydrogen	1,270.0

Write a program that displays a menu allowing the user to select one of these four gases. After a selection has been made, the user should enter the number of seconds it took for the sound to travel in this medium from its source to the location at which it was detected. The program should then report how far away (in meters) the source of the sound was from the detection location.

Input Validation: Check that the user has selected one of the available menu choices. Do not accept times less than 0 seconds or more than 30 seconds.

22. Freezing and Boiling Points

The following table lists the freezing and boiling points of several substances. Write a program that asks the user to enter a temperature then shows all the substances that will freeze at that temperature, and all that will boil at that temperature. For example, if the user enters −20, the program should report that water will freeze and oxygen will boil at that temperature.

Substance	Freezing Point (°F)	Boiling Point (°F)
Ethyl alcohol	-173	172
Mercury	-38	676
Oxygen	-362	-306
Water	32	212

23. Geometry Calculator

Write a program that displays the following menu:

```
Geometry Calculator

    1. Calculate the Area of a Circle
    2. Calculate the Area of a Rectangle
    3. Calculate the Area of a Triangle
    4. Quit

    Enter your choice (1-4):
```

If the user enters 1, the program should ask for the radius of the circle then display its area. Use the following formula:

area = πr^2

Use 3.14159 for π and the radius of the circle for r. If the user enters 2, the program should ask for the length and width of the rectangle, then display the rectangle's area. Use the following formula:

```
area = length * width
```

If the user enters 3, the program should ask for the length of the triangle's base and its height, then display its area. Use the following formula:

```
area = base * height * .5
```

If the user enters 4, the program should end.

Input Validation: Display an error message if the user enters a number outside the range of 1 through 4 when selecting an item from the menu. Do not accept negative values for the circle's radius, the rectangle's length or width, or the triangle's base or height.

24. Long-Distance Calls

A long-distance carrier charges the following rates for telephone calls:

Starting Time of Call	Rate per Minute
00:00–06:59	0.05
07:00–19:00	0.45
19:01–23:59	0.20

Write a program that asks for the starting time and the number of minutes of the call, and displays the charges. The program should ask for the time to be entered as a floating-point number in the form HH.MM. For example, 07:00 hours will be entered as 07.00, and 16:28 hours will be entered as 16.28.

Input Validation: The program should not accept times that are greater than 23:59. Also, no number whose last two digits are greater than 59 should be accepted. Hint: Assuming num is a floating-point variable, the following expression will give you its fractional part:

```
num - static_cast<int>(num)
```

25. Mobile Service Provider

A mobile phone service provider has three different data plans for its customers:

Package A: For $39.99 per month, 4 gigabytes are provided. Additional data costs $10 per gigabyte.

Package B: For $59.99 per month, 8 gigabytes are provided. Additional data costs $5 per gigabyte.

Package C: For $69.99 per month, unlimited data is provided.

Write a program that calculates a customer's monthly bill. It should ask which package the customer has purchased and how many gigabytes were used. It should then display the total amount due.

Input Validation: Be sure the user only selects package A, B, or C.

26. Mobile Service Provider, Part 2

Modify the Program in Programming Challenge 25 so it also displays how much money Package A customers would save if they purchased packages B or C, and how much money Package B customers would save if they purchased Package C. If there would be no savings, no message should be printed.

27. Wi-Fi Diagnostic Tree

Figure 11 shows a simplified flowchart for troubleshooting a bad Wi-Fi connection. Use the flowchart to create a program that leads a person through the steps of fixing a bad Wi-Fi connection. Here is an example of the program's output:

```
Reboot the computer and try to connect.
Did that fix the problem? no [Enter]
Reboot the router and try to connect.
Did that fix the problem? yes [Enter]
```

Notice the program ends as soon as a solution is found to the problem. Here is another example of the program's output:

```
Reboot the computer and try to connect.
Did that fix the problem? no [Enter]
Reboot the router and try to connect.
Did that fix the problem? no [Enter]
Make sure the cables between the router and modem are plugged in firmly.
Did that fix the problem? no [Enter]
Move the router to a new location.
Did that fix the problem? no [Enter]
Get a new router.
```

Figure 11 Troubleshooting a bad Wi-Fi connection

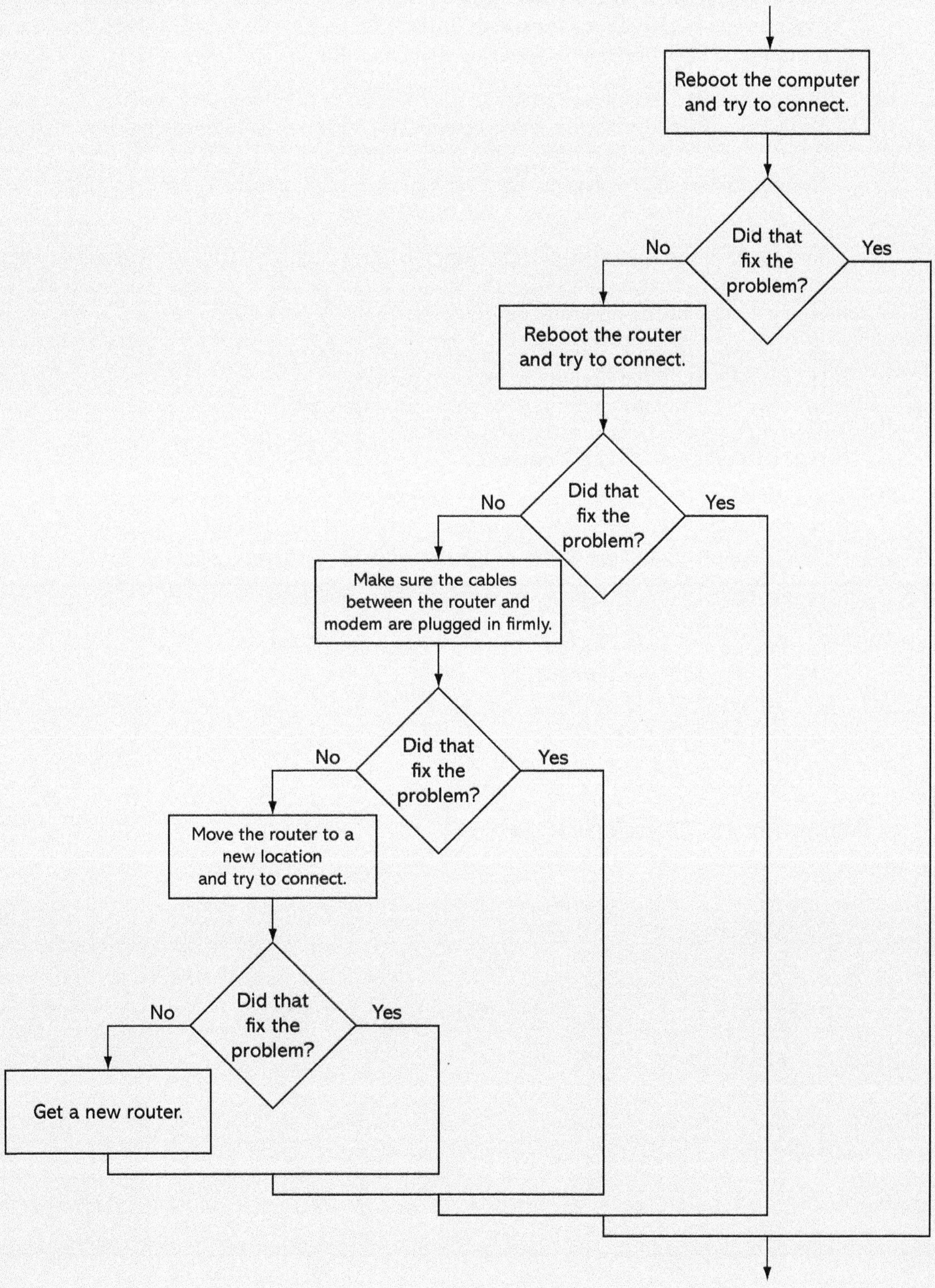

28. Restaurant Selector

You have a group of friends coming to visit for your high school reunion, and you want to take them out to eat at a local restaurant. You aren't sure if any of them have dietary restrictions, but your restaurant choices are as follows:

Joe's Gourmet Burgers—Vegetarian: *No*, Vegan: *No*, Gluten-Free: *No*
Main Street Pizza Company—Vegetarian: *Yes*, Vegan: *No*, Gluten-Free: *Yes*
Corner Café—Vegetarian: *Yes*, Vegan: *Yes*, Gluten-Free: *Yes*
Mama's Fine Italian—Vegetarian: *Yes*, Vegan: *No*, Gluten-Free: *No*
The Chef's Kitchen—Vegetarian: *Yes*, Vegan: *Yes*, Gluten-Free: *Yes*

Write a program that asks whether any members of your party are vegetarian, vegan, or gluten-free, then displays only the restaurants that you may take the group to. Here is an example of the program's output:

```
Is anyone in your party a vegetarian? yes [Enter]
Is anyone in your party a vegan? no [Enter]
Is anyone in your party gluten-free? yes [Enter]
Here are your restaurant choices:
   Main Street Pizza Company
   Corner Cafe
   The Chef's Kitchen
```

Here is another example of the program's output:

```
Is anyone in your party a vegetarian? yes [Enter]
Is anyone in your party a vegan? yes [Enter]
Is anyone in your party gluten-free? yes [Enter]
Here are your restaurant choices:
   Corner Cafe
   The Chef's Kitchen
```

Answers to Checkpoints

1 T, T, F, T, T, F, T

2 A) Incorrect
B) Incorrect
C) Correct

3 A) yes
B) no
C) no

4 0
0
1
0

5
```
if (x == 20)
    y = 0;
```

6
```
if (price > 500)
    discountRate = 0.2;
```

7
```
if (hours > 40)
    payRate *= 1.5;
```

8 True

9 False

10
```
if (sales > 50000)
{
    commissionRate = 0.25;
    bonus = 250;
}
```

11 Only the first statement after the `if` statement is conditionally executed. Both of the statements after the `if` statement should be enclosed in a set of braces.

12 False

13
```
if (y == 100)
    x = 1;
else
    x = 0;
```

14
```
if (sales >= 50000.00)
    commissionRate = 0.20;
else
    commissionRate = 0.10;
```

15 Zero
Zero Ten
Zero Ten Twenty
No Output

16 11

17

If the customer purchases this many books...	this many coupons are given.
1	1
2	1
3	2
4	2
5	3
10	3

18

Logical Expression	Result (True or False)
true && false	false
true && true	true
false && true	false
false && false	false
true || false	true
true || true	true
false || true	true
false || false	false
!true	false
!false	true

19 T, F, T, T, T

20
```
if (speed >= 0 && speed <= 200)
    cout << "The number is valid.";
```

21
```
if (speed < 0 || speed > 200)
    cout << "The number is not valid.";
```

22 A) True
B) False
C) True
D) False
E) False
F) True

23 A) False
B) False
C) False
D) True
E) False
F) False
G) False

24 A) `z = x > y ? 1 : 20;`
B) `population = temp > 45 ? base * 10 : base * 2;`
C) `wages *= hours > 40 ? 1.5 : 1;`
D)
```
cout << (result >= 0 ? "The result is positive\n" :
           "The result is negative.\n");
```

25 A)
```
if (k > 90)
    j = 57;
else
    j = 12;
```

B)
```
if (x >= 10)
     factor = y * 22;
else
     factor = y * 35;
```
C)
```
if (count == 1)
     total += sales;
else
     total += count * sales;
```
D)
```
if (num % 2)
     cout << "Odd\n";
else
     cout << "Even\n";
```

26 2 2

27 Because the `if /else if` statement tests several different conditions, consisting of different variables.

28 The case statements must be followed by an integer constant, not a relational expression.

29 That is serious.

30
```
switch (userNum)
{
    case 1 : cout << "One";
             break;
    case 2 : cout << "Two";
             break;
    case 3 : cout << "Three";
             break;
    default: cout << "Enter 1, 2, or 3 please.\n";
}
```

31
```
switch (selection)
{
    case 1 : cout << "Pi times radius squared\n";
             break;
    case 2 : cout << "Length times width\n";
             break;
    case 3 : cout << "Pi times radius squared times height\n";
             break;
    case 4 : cout << "Well okay then, good bye!\n";
             break;
    default : cout << "Not good with numbers, eh?\n";
}
```

Answers to Odd Numbered Review Questions

1. In an `if/else if` statement, the conditions are tested until one is found to be true. The conditionally executed statement(s) are executed and the program exits the `if/else if` statement. In a series of `if` statements, all of the `if` statements execute and test their conditions because they are not connected.

3. A flag is a Boolean variable signaling that some condition exists in the program. When the flag is set to `false`, it indicates the condition does not yet exist. When the flag is set to `true`, it indicates that the condition does exist.

5. It takes two expressions as operands and creates a single expression that is true only when both subexpressions are true.

7. Because they test for specific relationships between items. The relationships are greater-than, less-than, equal-to, greater-than or equal-to, less-than or equal-to, and not equal-to.

9. relational

11. False, True

13. True

15. True, False

17. nested

19. `||`

21. left-to-right

23. `||`

25. `>`

27. integer

29. break

31.
```
if (y == 0)
     x = 100;
```

33.
```
if (sales < 10000)
    commission = .10;
else if (sales <= 15000)
    commission = .15;
else
    commission = .20;
```

35.
```
if (amount1 > 10)
    if (amount2 < 100)
       cout << (amount1 > amount2 ? amount1 : amount2);
```

37.
```
if (temperature >= -50 && temperature <= 150)
    cout << "The number is valid.";
```

39.
```
if (str1 > str2)
    cout << str1;
else
    cout << str2;
```

41. C, A, B

43. False

45. True

47. True

49. True

51. True

53. False

55. False

57. True

59. The conditionally executed blocks in the `if/else` construct should be enclosed in braces.
The following statement:
```
cout << "The quotient of " << num1 <<
```
should read:
```
cout << "quotient of " << num1;
```

61. A `switch` statement cannot be used to test relational expressions. An `if/else if` statement should be used instead.

63. It should use && instead of `||`.

65. The : and ? are transposed. The statement should read:
```
z = (a < 10) ? 0 : 7;
```

Loops and Files

TOPICS

1 The Increment and Decrement Operators

CONCEPT: ++ and -- are operators that add and subtract 1 from their operands.

To *increment* a value means to increase it by one, and to *decrement* a value means to decrease it by one. Both of the following statements increment the variable `num`:

```
num = num + 1;
num += 1;
```

And `num` is decremented in both of the following statements:

```
num = num - 1;
num -= 1;
```

C++ provides a set of simple unary operators designed just for incrementing and decrementing variables. The increment operator is `++`, and the decrement operator is `--`. The following statement uses the `++` operator to increment `num`:

```
num++;
```

And the following statement decrements `num`:

```
num--;
```

From Chapter 5 of *Starting Out with C++: From Control Structures through Objects*, Ninth Edition. Tony Gaddis.

> **NOTE:** The expression num++ is pronounced "num plus plus," and num-- is pronounced "num minus minus."

Our examples so far show the increment and decrement operators used in *postfix mode*, which means the operator is placed after the variable. The operators also work in *prefix mode*, where the operator is placed before the variable name:

```
++num;
--num;
```

In both postfix and prefix modes, these operators add 1 to or subtract 1 from their operand. Program 1 shows how they work.

Program 1

```
// This program demonstrates the ++ and -- operators.
#include <iostream>
using namespace std;

int main()
{
    int num = 4;   // num starts out with 4.

    // Display the value in num.
    cout << "The variable num is " << num << endl;
    cout << "I will now increment num.\n\n";

    // Use postfix ++ to increment num.
    num++;
    cout << "Now the variable num is " << num << endl;
    cout << "I will increment num again.\n\n";

    // Use prefix ++ to increment num.
    ++num;
    cout << "Now the variable num is " << num << endl;
    cout << "I will now decrement num.\n\n";

    // Use postfix -- to decrement num.
    num--;
    cout << "Now the variable num is " << num << endl;
    cout << "I will decrement num again.\n\n";

    // Use prefix -- to increment num.
    --num;
    cout << "Now the variable num is " << num << endl;
    return 0;
}
```

Program Output

```
The variable num is 4
I will now increment num.
```

```
Now the variable num is 5
I will increment num again.

Now the variable num is 6
I will now decrement num.

Now the variable num is 5
I will decrement num again.

Now the variable num is 4
```

The Difference between Postfix and Prefix Modes

In the simple statements used in Program 1, it doesn't matter if the increment or decrement operator is used in postfix or prefix mode. The difference is important, however, when these operators are used in statements that do more than just incrementing or decrementing. For example, look at the following statements:

```
num = 4;
cout << num++;
```

This `cout` statement is doing two things: (1) displaying the value of `num`, and (2) incrementing `num`. But which happens first? `cout` will display a different value if `num` is incremented first than if `num` is incremented last. The answer depends on the mode of the increment operator.

Postfix mode causes the increment to happen after the value of the variable is used in the expression. In the example, `cout` will display 4, then `num` will be incremented to 5. Prefix mode, however, causes the increment to happen first. In the following statements, `num` will be incremented to 5, then `cout` will display 5:

```
num = 4;
cout << ++num;
```

Program 2 illustrates these dynamics further.

Program 2

```
// This program demonstrates the prefix and postfix
// modes of the increment and decrement operators.
#include <iostream>
using namespace std;

int main()
{
    int num = 4;

    cout << num << endl;     // Displays 4
    cout << num++ << endl;   // Displays 4, then adds 1 to num
    cout << num << endl;     // Displays 5
    cout << ++num << endl;   // Adds 1 to num, then displays 6
    cout << endl;            // Displays a blank line

```

(program continues)

Program 2 *(continued)*

```
16      cout << num << endl;    // Displays 6
17      cout << num-- << endl;  // Displays 6, then subtracts 1 from num
18      cout << num << endl;    // Displays 5
19      cout << --num << endl;  // Subtracts 1 from num, then displays 4
20
21      return 0;
22  }
```

Program Output

```
4
4
5
6

6
6
5
4
```

Let's analyze the statements in this program. In line 8, num is initialized with the value 4, so the cout statement in line 10 displays 4. Then, line 11 sends the expression num++ to cout. Because the ++ operator is used in postfix mode, the value 4 is first sent to cout, and then 1 is added to num, making its value 5.

When line 12 executes, num will hold the value 5, so 5 is displayed. Then, line 13 sends the expression ++num to cout. Because the ++ operator is used in prefix mode, 1 is first added to num (making it 6), and then the value 6 is sent to cout. This same sequence of events happens in lines 16 through 19, except the -- operator is used.

For another example, look at the following code:

```
int x = 1;
int y
y = x++;      // Postfix increment
```

The first statement defines the variable x (initialized with the value 1), and the second statement defines the variable y. The third statement does two things:

- It assigns the value of x to the variable y.
- The variable x is incremented.

The value that will be stored in y depends on when the increment takes place. Because the ++ operator is used in postfix mode, it acts *after* the assignment takes place. So, this code will store 1 in y. After the code has executed, x will contain 2. Let's look at the same code, but with the ++ operator used in prefix mode:

```
int x = 1;
int y;
y = ++x;      // Prefix increment
```

In the third statement, the ++ operator is used in prefix mode, so it acts on the variable x before the assignment takes place. So, this code will store 2 in y. After the code has executed, x will also contain 2.

Using ++ and -- in Mathematical Expressions

The increment and decrement operators can also be used on variables in mathematical expressions. Consider the following program segment:

```
a = 2;
b = 5;
c = a * b++;
cout << a << " " << b << " " << c;
```

In the statement c = a * b++, c is assigned the value of a times b, which is 10. The variable b is then incremented. The cout statement will display

```
2 6 10
```

If the statement were changed to read

```
c = a * ++b;
```

the variable b would be incremented before it was multiplied by a. In this case, c would be assigned the value of 2 times 6, so the cout statement would display

```
2 6 12
```

You can pack a lot of action into a single statement using the increment and decrement operators, but don't get too tricky with them. You might be tempted to try something like the following, thinking that c will be assigned 11:

```
a = 2;
b = 5;
c = ++(a * b);    // Error!
```

But this assignment statement simply will not work because the operand of the increment and decrement operators must be an lvalue. An lvalue identifies a place in memory whose contents may be changed. The increment and decrement operators usually have variables for their operands, but generally speaking, anything that can go on the left side of an = operator is legal.

Using ++ and -- in Relational Expressions

Sometimes you will see code where the ++ and -- operators are used in relational expressions. Just as in mathematical expressions, the difference between postfix and prefix modes is critical. Consider the following program segment:

```
x = 10;
if (x++ > 10)
    cout << "x is greater than 10.\n";
```

Two operations are happening in this if statement: (1) The value in x is tested to determine if it is greater than 10, and (2) x is incremented. Because the increment operator is used in postfix mode, the comparison happens first. Since 10 is not greater than 10, the cout statement won't execute. If the mode of the increment operator is changed, however, the `if` statement will compare 11 to 10, and the `cout` statement will execute:

```
x = 10;
if (++x > 10)
    cout << "x is greater than 10.\n";
```

Checkpoint

1 What will the following program segments display?

A)
```
x = 2;
y = x++;
cout << x << y;
```
B)
```
x = 2;
y = ++x;
cout << x << y;
```
C)
```
x = 2;
y = 4;
cout << x++ << --y;
```
D)
```
x = 2;
y = 2 * x++;
cout << x << y;
```
E)
```
x = 99;
if (x++ < 100)
    cout "It is true!\n";
else
    cout << "It is false!\n";
```
F)
```
x = 0;
if (++x)
    cout << "It is true!\n";
else
    cout << "It is false!\n";
```

2 Introduction to Loops: The `while` Loop

CONCEPT: A loop is part of a program that repeats.

VideoNote
The `while` Loop

Control structures direct the flow of a program. A *loop* is a control structure that causes a statement or group of statements to repeat. C++ has three looping control structures: the `while` loop, the `do-while` loop, and the `for` loop. The difference between these structures is how they control the repetition.

The `while` Loop

The `while` loop has two important parts: (1) an expression that is tested for a true or false value, and (2) a statement or block that is repeated as long as the expression is true. Figure 1 shows the logic of a `while` loop.

Figure 1 Logic of a `while` loop

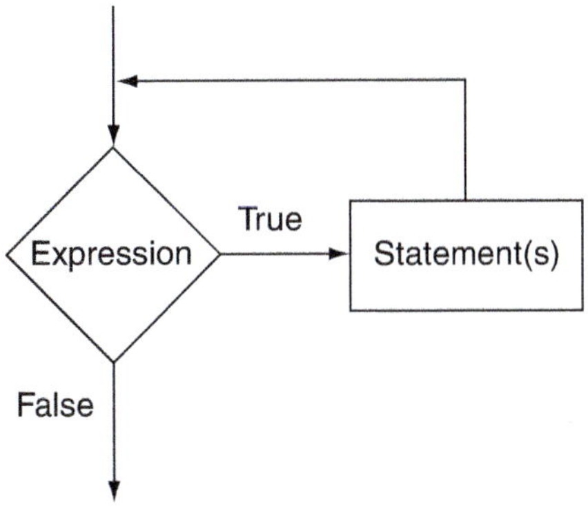

Here is the general format of the `while` loop:

```
while (expression)
    statement;
```

In the general format, ***expression*** is any expression that can be evaluated as true or false, and ***statement*** is any valid C++ statement. The first line shown in the format is sometimes called the *loop header*. It consists of the key word `while` followed by an ***expression*** enclosed in parentheses.

Here's how the loop works: the ***expression*** is tested, and if it is true, the ***statement*** is executed. Then, the ***expression*** is tested again. If it is true, the ***statement*** is executed. This cycle repeats until the ***expression*** is false.

The statement that is repeated is known as the *body* of the loop. It is also considered a conditionally executed statement, because it is executed only under the condition that the ***expression*** is true.

Notice there is no semicolon after the expression in parentheses. Like the `if` statement, the `while` loop is not complete without the statement that follows it.

If you wish the `while` loop to repeat a block of statements, its format is:

```
while (expression)
{
    statement;
    statement;
    // Place as many statements here
    // as necessary.
}
```

The `while` loop works like an `if` statement that executes over and over. As long as the expression inside the parentheses is true, the conditionally executed statement or block will repeat. Program 3 uses the `while` loop to print "Hello" five times.

Program 3

```
1   // This program demonstrates a simple while loop.
2   #include <iostream>
3   using namespace std;
4
5   int main()
6   {
7       int number = 0;
8
9       while (number < 5)
10      {
11          cout << "Hello\n";
12          number++;
13      }
14      cout << "That's all!\n";
15      return 0;
16  }
```

Program Output

```
Hello
Hello
Hello
Hello
Hello
That's all!
```

Let's take a closer look at this program. In line 7, an integer variable, `number`, is defined and initialized with the value 0. In line 9, the `while` loop begins with this statement:

```
while (number < 5)
```

This statement tests the variable `number` to determine whether it is less than 5. If it is, then the statements in the body of the loop (lines 11 and 12) are executed:

```
cout << "Hello\n";
number++;
```

The statement in line 11 prints the word "Hello." The statement in line 12 uses the increment operator to add one to `number`. This is the last statement in the body of the loop, so after it executes, the loop starts over. It tests the expression `number < 5` again, and if it is true, the statements in the body of the loop are executed again. This cycle repeats until the expression `number < 5` is false. This is illustrated in Figure 2.

Each repetition of a loop is known as an *iteration*. This loop will perform five iterations because the variable `number` is initialized with the value 0, and it is incremented each time the body of the loop is executed. When the expression `number < 5` is tested and found to be false, the loop will terminate and the program will resume execution at the statement that immediately follows the loop. Figure 3 shows the logic of this loop.

Figure 2 Actions of the `while` loop

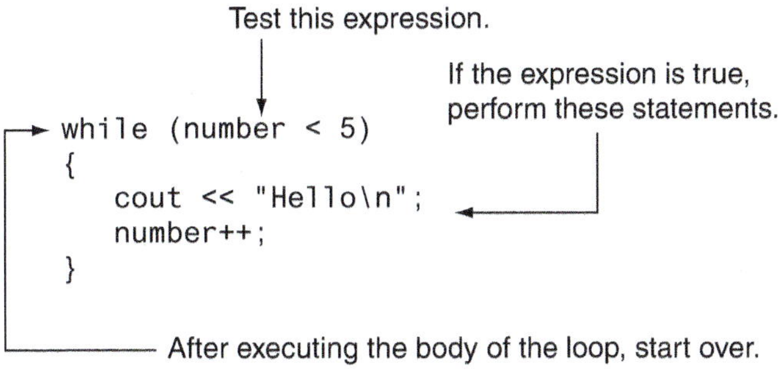

Figure 3 Flowchart for the `while` loop

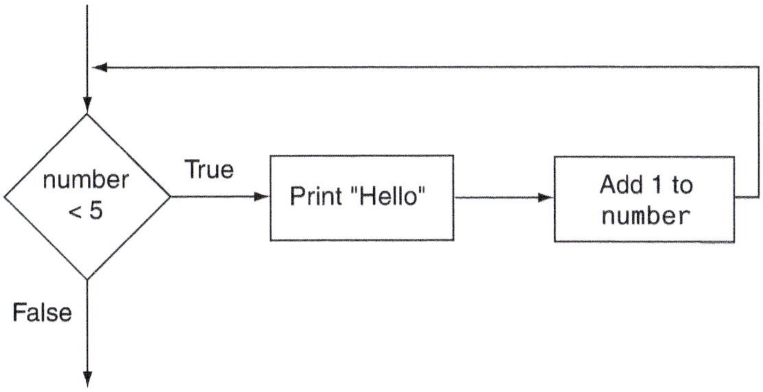

In this example, the `number` variable is referred to as the *loop control variable* because it controls the number of times that the loop iterates.

The `while` Loop Is a Pretest Loop

The `while` loop is known as a *pretest* loop, which means it tests its expression before each iteration. Notice the variable definition in line 7 of Program 3:

```
int number = 0;
```

The `number` variable is initialized with the value 0. If `number` had been initialized with the value 5 or greater, as shown in the following program segment, the loop would never execute:

```
int number = 6;
while (number < 5)
{
    cout << "Hello\n";
    number++;
}
```

An important characteristic of the `while` loop is that the loop will never iterate if the test expression is false to start with. If you want to be sure that a `while` loop executes the first time, you must initialize the relevant data in such a way that the test expression starts out as true.

Infinite Loops

In all but rare cases, loops must contain within themselves a way to terminate. This means that something inside the loop must eventually make the test expression false. The loop in Program 3 stops when the expression `number < 5` is false.

If a loop does not have a way of stopping, it is called an infinite loop. An *infinite loop* continues to repeat until the program is interrupted. Here is an example of an infinite loop:

```
int number = 0;
while (number < 5)
{
   cout << "Hello\n";
}
```

This is an infinite loop because it does not contain a statement that changes the value of the `number` variable. Each time the expression `number < 5` is tested, number will contain the value 0.

It's also possible to create an infinite loop by accidentally placing a semicolon after the first line of the `while` loop. Here is an example:

```
int number = 0;
while (number < 5); // This semicolon is an ERROR!
{
   cout << "Hello\n";
   number++;
}
```

The semicolon at the end of the first line is assumed to be a null statement and disconnects the `while` statement from the block that comes after it. To the compiler, this loop looks like:

```
while (number < 5);
```

This `while` loop will forever execute the null statement, which does nothing. The program will appear to have "gone into space" because there is nothing to display screen output or show activity.

Don't Forget the Braces with a Block of Statements

If you write a loop that conditionally executes a block of statements, don't forget to enclose all of the statements in a set of braces. If the braces are accidentally left out, the `while` statement conditionally executes only the very next statement. For example, look at the following code:

```
int number = 0;
// This loop is missing its braces!
while (number < 5)
   cout << "Hello\n";
   number++;
```

In this code, the `number++` statement is not in the body of the loop. Because the braces are missing, the `while` statement only executes the statement that immediately follows it. This loop will execute infinitely because there is no code in its body that changes the `number` variable.

Another common pitfall with loops is accidentally using the = operator when you intend to use the == operator. The following is an infinite loop because the test expression assigns 1 to `remainder` each time it is evaluated instead of testing whether `remainder` is equal to 1:

```
while (remainder = 1) // Error: Notice the assignment
{
    cout << "Enter a number: ";
    cin >> num;
    remainder = num % 2;
}
```

Remember, any nonzero value is evaluated as true.

Programming Style and the `while` Loop

It's possible to create loops that look like this:

```
while (number < 5) { cout << "Hello\n"; number++; }
```

Avoid this style of programming. The programming style you should use with the `while` loop is similar to that of the `if` statement:

- If there is only one statement repeated by the loop, it should appear on the line after the `while` statement and be indented one additional level.
- If the loop repeats a block, each line inside the braces should be indented.

This programming style should visually set the body of the loop apart from the surrounding code. In general, you'll find a similar style being used with the other types of loops presented in this chapter.

In the Spotlight:
Designing a Program with a `while` Loop

A project currently underway at Chemical Labs, Inc. requires that a substance be continually heated in a vat. A technician must check the substance's temperature every 15 minutes. If the substance's temperature does not exceed 102.5 degrees Celsius, then the technician does nothing. However, if the temperature is greater than 102.5 degrees Celsius, the technician must turn down the vat's thermostat, wait 5 minutes, and check the temperature again. The technician repeats these steps until the temperature does not exceed 102.5 degrees Celsius. The director of engineering has asked you to write a program that guides the technician through this process.

Here is the algorithm:

1. *Prompt the user to enter the substance's temperature.*
2. *Repeat the following steps as long as the temperature is greater than 102.5 degrees Celsius:*
   a. *Tell the technician to turn down the thermostat, wait 5 minutes, and check the temperature again.*
   b. *Prompt the user to enter the substance's temperature.*
3. *After the loop finishes, tell the technician that the temperature is acceptable and to check it again in 15 minutes.*

After reviewing this algorithm, you realize that steps 2a and 2b should not be performed if the test condition (temperature is greater than 102.5) is false to begin with. The `while` loop will work well in this situation, because it will not execute even once if its condition is false. Program 4 shows the code for the program.

Program 4

```
// This program assists a technician in the process
// of checking a substance's temperature.
#include <iostream>
using namespace std;

int main()
{
    const double MAX_TEMP = 102.5;  // Maximum temperature
    double temperature;             // To hold the temperature

    // Get the current temperature.
    cout << "Enter the substance's Celsius temperature: ";
    cin >> temperature;

    // As long as necessary, instruct the technician
    // to adjust the thermostat.
    while (temperature > MAX_TEMP)
    {
        cout << "The temperature is too high. Turn the\n";
        cout << "thermostat down and wait 5 minutes.\n";
        cout << "Then take the Celsius temperature again\n";
        cout << "and enter it here: ";
        cin >> temperature;
    }

    // Remind the technician to check the temperature
    // again in 15 minutes.
    cout << "The temperature is acceptable.\n";
    cout << "Check it again in 15 minutes.\n";

    return 0;
}
```

Program Output with Example Input Shown in Bold

```
Enter the substance's Celsius temperature: 104.7 [Enter]
The temperature is too high. Turn the
thermostat down and wait 5 minutes.
Then take the Celsius temperature again
and enter it here: 103.2 [Enter]
The temperature is too high. Turn the
thermostat down and wait 5 minutes.
Then take the Celsius temperature again
and enter it here: 102.1 [Enter]
The temperature is acceptable.
Check it again in 15 minutes.
```

3 Using the `while` Loop for Input Validation

CONCEPT: The `while` loop can be used to create input routines that repeat until acceptable data is entered.

Perhaps the most famous saying of the computer industry is "garbage in, garbage out." The integrity of a program's output is only as good as its input, so you should try to make sure garbage does not go into your programs. *Input validation* is the process of inspecting data given to a program by the user and determining if it is valid. A good program should give clear instructions about the kind of input that is acceptable, and not assume the user has followed those instructions.

The `while` loop is especially useful for validating input. If an invalid value is entered, a loop can require that the user reenter it as many times as necessary. For example, the following loop asks for a number in the range of 1 through 100:

```
cout << "Enter a number in the range 1-100: ";
cin >> number;
while (number < 1 || number > 100)
{
   cout << "ERROR: Enter a value in the range 1-100: ";
   cin >> number;
}
```

This code first allows the user to enter a number. This takes place just before the loop. If the input is valid, the loop will not execute. If the input is invalid, however, the loop will display an error message and require the user to enter another number. The loop will continue to execute until the user enters a valid number. The general logic of performing input validation is shown in Figure 4.

Figure 4 Flowchart for input validation

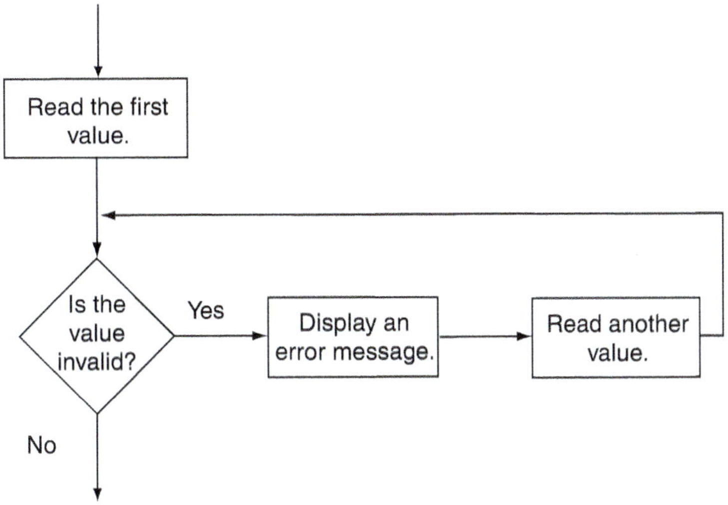

The read operation that takes place just before the loop is called a *priming read*. It provides the first value for the loop to test. Subsequent values are obtained by the loop.

Program 5 calculates the number of soccer teams a youth league may create, based on a given number of players and a maximum number of players per team. The program uses `while` loops (in lines 25 through 34 and lines 41 through 46) to validate the user's input.

Program 5

```
1  // This program calculates the number of soccer teams
2  // that a youth league may create from the number of
3  // available players. Input validation is demonstrated
4  // with while loops.
5  #include <iostream>
6  using namespace std;
7
8  int main()
9  {
10     // Constants for minimum and maximum players
11     const int MIN_PLAYERS = 9,
12               MAX_PLAYERS = 15;
13
14     // Variables
15     int players,        // Number of available players
16         teamPlayers,    // Number of desired players per team
17         numTeams,       // Number of teams
18         leftOver;       // Number of players left over
19
20     // Get the number of players per team.
21     cout << "How many players do you wish per team? ";
22     cin >> teamPlayers;
23
24     // Validate the input.
25     while (teamPlayers < MIN_PLAYERS || teamPlayers > MAX_PLAYERS)
26     {
27         // Explain the error.
28         cout << "You should have at least " << MIN_PLAYERS
29              << " but no more than " << MAX_PLAYERS << " per team.\n";
30
31         // Get the input again.
32         cout << "How many players do you wish per team? ";
33         cin >> teamPlayers;
34     }
35
36     // Get the number of players available.
37     cout << "How many players are available? ";
38     cin >> players;
39
40     // Validate the input.
41     while (players <= 0)
42     {
43         // Get the input again.
44         cout << "Please enter 0 or greater: ";
45         cin >> players;
46     }
47
```

```
    // Calculate the number of teams.
    numTeams = players / teamPlayers;

    // Calculate the number of leftover players.
    leftOver = players % teamPlayers;

    // Display the results.
    cout << "There will be " << numTeams << " teams with "
         << leftOver << " players left over.\n";
    return 0;
}
```

Program Output with Example Input Shown in Bold

```
How many players do you wish per team? 4 [Enter]
You should have at least 9 but no more than 15 per team.
How many players do you wish per team? 12 [Enter]
How many players are available? -142 [Enter]
Please enter 0 or greater: 142 [Enter]
There will be 11 teams with 10 players left over.
```

Checkpoint

2 Write an input validation loop that asks the user to enter a number in the range of 10 through 25.

3 Write an input validation loop that asks the user to enter 'Y', 'y', 'N', or 'n'.

4 Write an input validation loop that asks the user to enter "Yes" or "No".

4 Counters

CONCEPT: A counter is a variable that is regularly incremented or decremented each time a loop iterates.

Sometimes it's important for a program to control or keep track of the number of iterations a loop performs. For example, Program 6 displays a table consisting of the numbers 1 through 10 and their squares, so its loop must iterate 10 times.

Program 6

```
// This program displays a list of numbers and
// their squares.
#include <iostream>
using namespace std;

int main()
{
    const int MIN_NUMBER = 1,   // Starting number to square
              MAX_NUMBER = 10;  // Maximum number to square

```

(program continues)

Program 6 *(continued)*

```
    int num = MIN_NUMBER;     // Counter

    cout << "Number Number Squared\n";
    cout << "-------------------------\n";
    while (num <= MAX_NUMBER)
    {
        cout << num << "\t\t" << (num * num) << endl;
        num++; //Increment the counter.
    }
    return 0;
}
```

Program Output

```
Number Number Squared
-------------------------
1          1
2          4
3          9
4          16
5          25
6          36
7          49
8          64
9          81
10         100
```

In Program 6, the variable `num`, which starts at 1, is incremented each time through the loop. When `num` reaches 11, the loop stops. `num` is used as a *counter* variable, which means it is regularly incremented in each iteration of the loop. In essence, `num` keeps count of the number of iterations the loop has performed.

> **NOTE:** It's important that `num` be properly initialized. Remember, variables defined inside a function have no guaranteed starting value.

5 The `do-while` Loop

CONCEPT: The `do-while` loop is a posttest loop, which means its expression is tested after each iteration.

The `do-while` loop looks something like an inverted `while` loop. Here is the `do-while` loop's format when the body of the loop contains only a single statement:

```
do
   statement;
while (expression);
```

Here is the format of the do-while loop when the body of the loop contains multiple statements:

```
do
{
   statement;
   statement;
   // Place as many statements here
   // as necessary.
} while (expression);
```

NOTE: The do-while loop must be terminated with a semicolon.

The do-while loop is a *posttest* loop. This means it does not test its expression until it has completed an iteration. As a result, the do-while loop always performs at least one iteration, even if the expression is false to begin with. This differs from the behavior of a while loop, which you will recall is a pretest loop. For example, in the following while loop the cout statement will not execute at all:

```
int x = 1;
while (x < 0)
    cout << x << endl;
```

But the cout statement in the following do-while loop will execute once because the do-while loop does not evaluate the expression x < 0 until the end of the iteration.

```
int x = 1;
do
    cout << x << endl;
while (x < 0);
```

Figure 5 illustrates the logic of the do-while loop.

Figure 5 Flowchart for a do-while loop

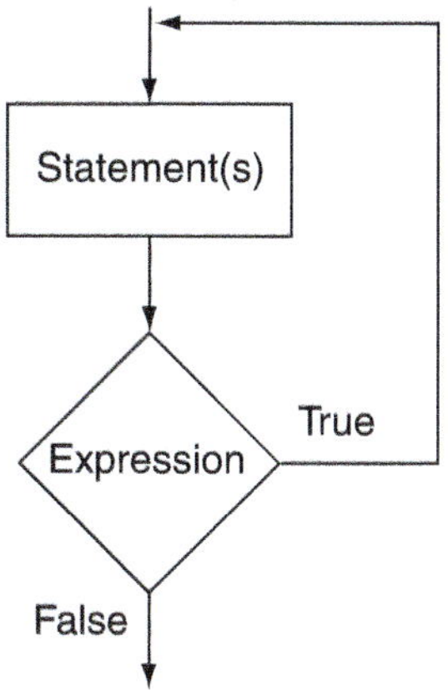

You should use the do-while loop when you want to make sure the loop executes at least once. For example, Program 7 averages a series of three test scores for a student.

After the average is displayed, it asks the user if he or she wants to average another set of test scores. The program repeats as long as the user enters Y for yes.

Program 7

```cpp
// This program averages 3 test scores. It repeats as
// many times as the user wishes.
#include <iostream>
using namespace std;

int main()
{
    int score1, score2, score3; // Three scores
    double average;             // Average score
    char again;                 // To hold Y or N input

    do
    {
        // Get three scores.
        cout << "Enter 3 scores and I will average them: ";
        cin >> score1 >> score2 >> score3;

        // Calculate and display the average.
        average = (score1 + score2 + score3) / 3.0;
        cout << "The average is " << average << ".\n";

        // Does the user want to average another set?
        cout << "Do you want to average another set? (Y/N) ";
        cin >> again;
    } while (again == 'Y' || again == 'y');
    return 0;
}
```

Program Output with Example Input Shown in Bold

```
Enter 3 scores and I will average them: 80 90 70 [Enter]
The average is 80.
Do you want to average another set? (Y/N) y [Enter]
Enter 3 scores and I will average them: 60 75 88 [Enter]
The average is 74.3333.
Do you want to average another set? (Y/N) n [Enter]
```

When this program was written, the programmer had no way of knowing the number of times the loop would iterate. This is because the loop asks the user if he or she wants to repeat the process. This type of loop is known as a *user-controlled loop*, because it allows the user to decide the number of iterations.

Using `do-while` with Menus

The `do-while` loop is a good choice for repeating a menu. See Program 27 of the chapter "Making Decisions", which displayed a menu of health club packages. Program 8 is a modification of that program, which uses a `do-while` loop to repeat the program until the user selects item 4 from the menu.

Program 8

```
// This program displays a menu and asks the user to make a
// selection. A do-while loop repeats the program until the
// user selects item 4 from the menu.
#include <iostream>
#include <iomanip>
using namespace std;

int main()
{
    // Constants for menu choices
    const int ADULT_CHOICE = 1,
              CHILD_CHOICE = 2,
              SENIOR_CHOICE = 3,
              QUIT_CHOICE = 4;

    // Constants for membership rates
    const double ADULT = 40.0,
                 CHILD = 20.0,
                 SENIOR = 30.0;

    // Variables
    int choice;        // Menu choice
    int months;        // Number of months
    double charges;    // Monthly charges

    // Set up numeric output formatting.
    cout << fixed << showpoint << setprecision(2);

    do
    {
        // Display the menu.
        cout << "\n\t\tHealth Club Membership Menu\n\n"
             << "1. Standard Adult Membership\n"
             << "2. Child Membership\n"
             << "3. Senior Citizen Membership\n"
             << "4. Quit the Program\n\n"
             << "Enter your choice: ";
        cin >> choice;

        // Validate the menu selection.
        while (choice < ADULT_CHOICE || choice > QUIT_CHOICE)
        {
            cout << "Please enter a valid menu choice: ";
            cin >> choice;
        }

        // Process the user's choice.
        if (choice != QUIT_CHOICE)
        {
            // Get the number of months.
            cout << "For how many months? ";
```

(program continues)

Program 8 *(continued)*

```
            cin >> months;

            // Respond to the user's menu selection.
            switch (choice)
            {
                case ADULT_CHOICE:
                     charges = months * ADULT;
                     break;
                case CHILD_CHOICE:
                     charges = months * CHILD;
                     break;
                case SENIOR_CHOICE:
                     charges = months * SENIOR;
            }

            // Display the monthly charges.
            cout << "The total charges are $"
                 << charges << endl;
        }
    } while (choice != QUIT_CHOICE);
    return 0;
}
```

Program Output with Example Input Shown in Bold

```
          Health Club Membership Menu

1. Standard Adult Membership
2. Child Membership
3. Senior Citizen Membership
4. Quit the Program

Enter your choice: 1 [Enter]
For how many months? 12 [Enter]
The total charges are $480.00

          Health Club Membership Menu

1. Standard Adult Membership
2. Child Membership
3. Senior Citizen Membership
4. Quit the Program

Enter your choice: 4 [Enter]
```

Checkpoint

5 What will the following program segments display?

A)
```
int count = 10;
do
{
   cout << "Hello World\n";
   count++;
} while (count < 1);
```

B)
```
int v = 10;
do
    cout << v << endl;
while (v < 5);
```

C)
```
int count = 0, number = 0, limit = 4;
do
{
    number += 2;
    count++;
} while (count < limit);
cout << number << " " << count << endl;
```

6 The `for` Loop

CONCEPT: The `for` loop is ideal for performing a known number of iterations.

In general, there are two categories of loops: conditional loops and count-controlled loops. A *conditional loop* executes as long as a particular condition exists. For example, an input validation loop executes as long as the input value is invalid. When you write a conditional loop, you have no way of knowing the number of times it will iterate.

VideoNote **The `for` Loop**

Sometimes you know the exact number of iterations that a loop must perform. A loop that repeats a specific number of times is known as a *count-controlled* loop. For example, if a loop asks the user to enter the sales amounts for each month in the year, it will iterate 12 times. In essence, the loop counts to 12 and asks the user to enter a sales amount each time it makes a count. A count-controlled loop must possess three elements:

1. It must initialize a counter variable to a starting value.
2. It must test the counter variable by comparing it to a maximum value. When the counter variable reaches its maximum value, the loop terminates.
3. It must update the counter variable during each iteration. This is usually done by incrementing the variable.

Count-controlled loops are so common that C++ provides a type of loop specifically for them. It is known as the `for` loop. The `for` loop is specifically designed to initialize, test, and update a counter variable. Here is the format of the `for` loop when it is used to repeat a single statement:

```
for (initialization; test; update)
   statement;
```

The format of the `for` loop when it is used to repeat a block is

```
for (initialization; test; update)
{
   statement;
   statement;
   // Place as many statements here
   // as necessary.
}
```

The first line of the `for` loop is the *loop header*. After the key word `for`, there are three expressions inside the parentheses, separated by semicolons. (Notice there is not a semicolon after the third expression.) The first expression is the *initialization expression*. It is normally used to initialize a counter variable to its starting value. This is the first action performed by the loop, and it is only done once. The second expression is the *test expression*. This is an expression that controls the execution of the loop. As long as this expression is true, the body of the `for` loop will repeat. The `for` loop is a pretest loop, so it evaluates the test expression before each iteration. The third expression is the *update expression*. It executes at the end of each iteration. Typically, this is a statement that increments the loop's counter variable.

Here is an example of a simple `for` loop that prints "Hello" five times:

```
for (count = 0; count < 5; count++)
   cout << "Hello" << endl;
```

In this loop, the initialization expression is `count = 0`, the test expression is `count < 5`, and the update expression is `count++`. The body of the loop has one statement, which is the `cout` statement. Figure 6 illustrates the sequence of events that takes place during the loop's execution. Notice Steps 2 through 4 are repeated as long as the test expression is `true`.

Figure 6 Sequence of events in a `for` loop

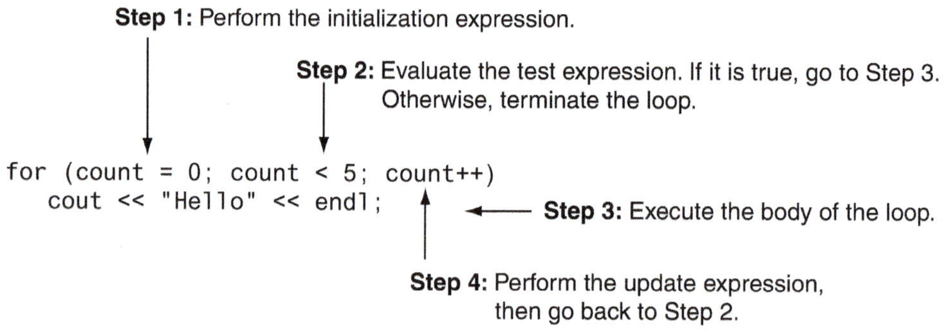

Figure 7 shows the loop's logic in the form of a flowchart.

Figure 7 `for` loop logic

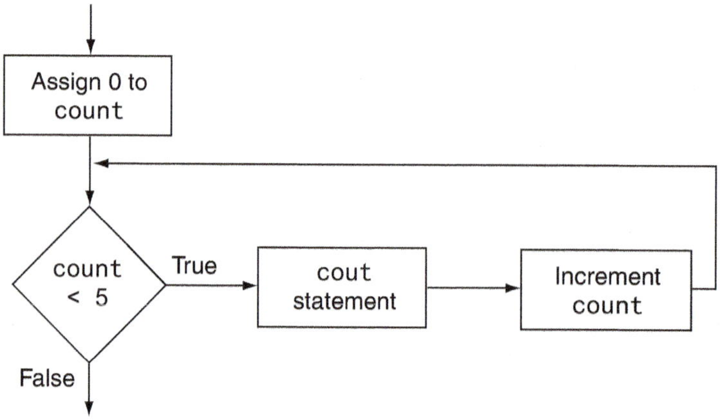

Notice how the counter variable, `count`, is used to control the number of times that the loop iterates. During the execution of the loop, this variable takes on the values 1 through 5, and when the test expression `count < 5` is false, the loop terminates. Also notice in this example the `count` variable is used only in the loop header, to control the number of loop iterations. It is not used for any other purpose. It is also possible to use the counter variable within the body of the loop. For example, look at the following code:

```
for (number = 1; number <= 10; number++)
    cout << number << " " << endl;
```

The counter variable in this loop is `number`. In addition to controlling the number of iterations, it is also used in the body of the loop. This loop will produce the following output:

```
1 2 3 4 5 6 7 8 9 10
```

As you can see, the loop displays the contents of the `number` variable during each iteration. Program 9 shows another example of a `for` loop that uses its counter variable within the body of the loop. This is yet another program that displays a table showing the numbers 1 through 10 and their squares.

Program 9

```
// This program displays the numbers 1 through 10 and
// their squares.
#include <iostream>
using namespace std;

int main()
{
     const int MIN_NUMBER = 1,    // Starting value
               MAX_NUMBER = 10;   // Ending value
     int num;

     cout << "Number Number Squared\n";
     cout << "-------------------------\n";

     for (num = MIN_NUMBER; num <= MAX_NUMBER; num++)
          cout << num << "\t\t" << (num * num) << endl;

     return 0;
}
```

Program Output

```
Number Number Squared
-------------------------
1             1
2             4
3             9
4             16
5             25
6             36
7             49
8             64
9             81
10            100
```

Figure 8 illustrates the sequence of events performed by this `for` loop, and Figure 9 shows the logic of the loop as a flowchart.

Figure 8 Sequence of events in the `for` loop

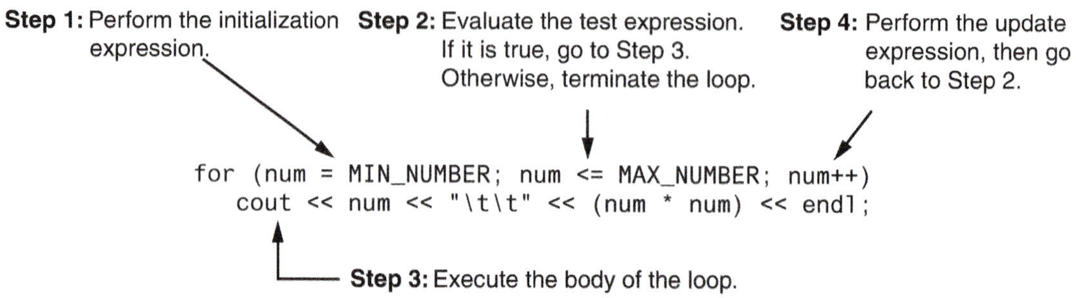

Figure 9 Flowchart for the `for` loop

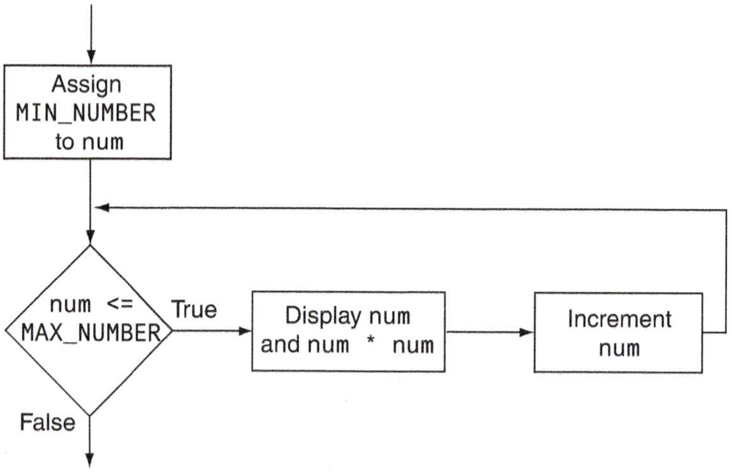

Using the `for` Loop instead of `while` or `do-while`

You should use the `for` loop instead of the `while` or `do-while` loop in any situation that clearly requires an initialization, uses a false condition to stop the loop, and requires an update to occur at the end of each loop iteration. Program 9 is a perfect example. It requires that the `num` variable be initialized to 1, it stops the loop when `num` is greater than 10, and it increments `num` at the end of each loop iteration.

When we first introduced the idea of a counter variable we examined Program 6, which uses a `while` loop to display the table of numbers and their squares. Because the loop in that program requires an initialization, uses a false test expression to stop, and performs an increment at the end of each iteration, it can easily be converted to a `for` loop. Figure 10 shows how the `while` loop in Program 6 and the `for` loop in Program 9 each have initialization, test, and update expressions.

Figure 10 Initialization, test, and update expressions

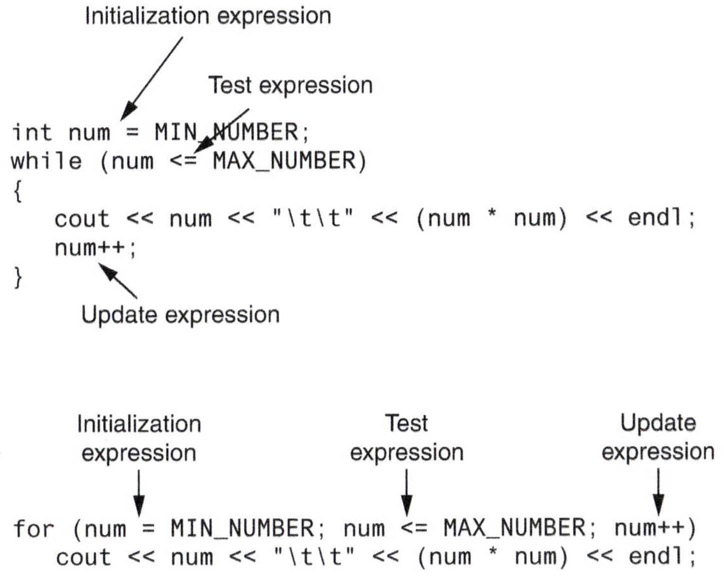

The for Loop Is a Pretest Loop

Because the `for` loop tests its test expression before it performs an iteration, it is a pretest loop. It is possible to write a `for` loop in such a way that it will never iterate. Here is an example:

```
for (count = 11; count <= 10; count++)
   cout << "Hello" << endl;
```

Because the variable `count` is initialized to a value that makes the test expression false from the beginning, this loop terminates as soon as it begins.

Avoid Modifying the Counter Variable in the Body of the for Loop

Be careful not to place a statement that modifies the counter variable in the body of the `for` loop. All modifications of the counter variable should take place in the update expression, which is automatically executed at the end of each iteration. If a statement in the body of the loop also modifies the counter variable, the loop will probably not terminate when you expect it to. The following loop, for example, increments `x` twice for each iteration:

```
for (x = 1; x <= 10; x++)
{
   cout << x << endl;
   x++;   // Wrong!
}
```

Other Forms of the Update Expression

You are not limited to using increment statements in the update expression. Here is a loop that displays all the even numbers from 2 through 100 by adding 2 to its counter:

```
for (num = 2; num <= 100; num += 2)
    cout << num << endl;
```

And here is a loop that counts backward from 10 down to 0:

```
for (num = 10; num >= 0; num--)
    cout << num << endl;
```

Defining a Variable in the `for` Loop's Initialization Expression

Not only may the counter variable be initialized in the initialization expression, it may be defined there as well. The following code shows an example. This is a modified version of the loop in Program 9.

```
for (int num = MIN_NUMBER; num <= MAX_NUMBER; num++)
    cout << num << "\t\t" << (num * num) << endl;
```

In this loop, the `num` variable is both defined and initialized in the initialization expression. If the counter variable is used only in the loop, it makes sense to define it in the loop header. This makes the variable's purpose more clear.

When a variable is defined in the initialization expression of a `for` loop, the scope of the variable is limited to the loop. This means you cannot access the variable in statements outside the loop. For example, the following program segment will not compile because the last `cout` statement cannot access the variable `count`.

```
for (int count = 1; count <= 10; count++)
    cout << count << endl;
cout << "count is now " << count << endl;    // ERROR!
```

Creating a User-Controlled `for` Loop

Sometimes you want the user to determine the maximum value of the counter variable in a `for` loop, and therefore determine the number of times the loop iterates. For example, look at Program 10. This is another program that displays a list of numbers and their squares. Instead of displaying the numbers 1 through 10, this program allows the user to enter the minimum and maximum values to display.

Program 10

```
// This program demonstrates a user-controlled for loop.
#include <iostream>
using namespace std;

int main()
{
    int minNumber,    // Starting number to square
        maxNumber;    // Maximum number to square
```

```
9
10        // Get the minimum and maximum values to display.
11        cout << "I will display a table of numbers and "
12             << "their squares.\n"
13             << "Enter the starting number: ";
14        cin >> minNumber;
15        cout << "Enter the ending number: ";
16        cin >> maxNumber;
17
18        // Display the table.
19        cout << "Number Number Squared\n"
20             << "-------------------------\n";
21
22        for (int num = minNumber; num <= maxNumber; num++)
23            cout << num << "\t\t" << (num * num) << endl;
24
25        return 0;
26    }
```

Program Output with Example Input Shown in Bold

```
I will display a table of numbers and their squares.
Enter the starting number: 6 [Enter]
Enter the ending number: 12 [Enter]
Number Number Squared
---------------------
6          36
7          49
8          64
9          81
10         100
11         121
12         144
```

Before the loop, the code in lines 11 through 16 asks the user to enter the starting and ending numbers. These values are stored in the `minNumber` and `maxNumber` variables. These values are used in the `for` loop's initialization and test expressions.

```
for (int num = minNumber; num <= maxNumber; num++)
```

In this loop, the `num` variable takes on the values from `maxNumber` through `maxValue`, and then the loop terminates.

Using Multiple Statements in the Initialization and Update Expressions

It is possible to execute more than one statement in the initialization expression and the update expression. When using multiple statements in either of these expressions, simply separate the statements with commas. For example, look at the loop in the following code, which has two statements in the initialization expression:

```
int x, y;
for (x = 1, y = 1; x <= 5; x++)
{
    cout << x << " plus " << y
         << " equals " << (x + y)
         << endl;
}
```

This loop's initialization expression is

```
x = 1, y = 1
```

This initializes two variables, x and y. The output produced by this loop is

```
1 plus 1 equals 2
2 plus 1 equals 3
3 plus 1 equals 4
4 plus 1 equals 5
5 plus 1 equals 6
```

We can further modify the loop to execute two statements in the update expression. Here is an example:

```
int x, y;
for (x = 1, y = 1; x <= 5; x++, y++)
{
    cout << x << " plus " << y
         << " equals " << (x + y)
         << endl;
}
```

The loop's update expression is

```
x++, y++
```

This update expression increments both the x and y variables. The output produced by this loop is

```
1 plus 1 equals 2
2 plus 2 equals 4
3 plus 3 equals 6
4 plus 4 equals 8
5 plus 5 equals 10
```

Connecting multiple statements with commas works well in the initialization and update expressions, but do *not* try to connect multiple expressions this way in the test expression. If you wish to combine multiple expressions in the test expression, you must use the && or || operators.

Omitting the `for` Loop's Expressions

The initialization expression may be omitted from inside the `for` loop's parentheses if it has already been performed or no initialization is needed. Here is an example of the loop in Program 10 with the initialization being performed prior to the loop:

```
int num = 1;
for ( ; num <= maxValue; num++)
    cout << num << "\t\t" << (num * num) << endl;
```

You may also omit the update expression if it is being performed elsewhere in the loop or if none is needed. Although this type of code is not recommended, the following `for` loop works just like a `while` loop:

```
int num = 1;
for ( ; num <= maxValue; )
{
    cout << num << "\t\t" << (num * num) << endl;
    num++;
}
```

You can even go so far as to omit all three expressions from the `for` loop's parentheses. Be warned, however, that if you leave out the test expression, the loop has no built-in way of terminating. Here is an example:

```
for ( ; ; )
    cout << "Hello World\n";
```

Because this loop has no way of stopping, it will display `"Hello World\n"` forever (or until something interrupts the program).

In the Spotlight:

Designing a Count-Controlled Loop with the `for` Statement

Your friend Amanda just inherited a European sports car from her uncle. Amanda lives in the United States, and she is afraid she will get a speeding ticket because the car's speedometer indicates kilometers per hour. She has asked you to write a program that displays a table of speeds in kilometers per hour with their values converted to miles per hour. The formula for converting kilometers per hour to miles per hour is:

$$MPH = KPH * 0.6214$$

In the formula, *MPH* is the speed in miles per hour and *KPH* is the speed in kilometers per hour.

The table your program displays should show speeds from 60 kilometers per hour through 130 kilometers per hour, in increments of 10, along with their values converted to miles per hour. The table should look something like this:

KPH	MPH
60	37.3
70	43.5
80	49.7
.	
.	
.	
130	80.8

After thinking about this table of values, you decide that you will write a `for` loop that uses a counter variable to hold the kilometer-per-hour speeds. The counter's starting value will be 60, its ending value will be 130, and you will add 10 to the counter variable after each iteration. Inside the loop, you will use the counter variable to calculate a speed in miles per hour. Program 11 shows the code.

Program 11

```
// This program converts the speeds 60 kph through
// 130 kph (in 10 kph increments) to mph.
#include <iostream>
#include <iomanip>
using namespace std;

int main()
{
    // Constants for the speeds
    const int START_KPH = 60, // Starting speed
              END_KPH = 130,  // Ending speed
              INCREMENT = 10; // Speed increment

    // Constant for the conversion factor
    const double CONVERSION_FACTOR = 0.6214;

    // Variables
    int kph;        // To hold speeds in kph
    double mph;     // To hold speeds in mph

    // Set the numeric output formatting.
    cout << fixed << showpoint << setprecision(1);

    // Display the table headings.
    cout << "KPH\tMPH\n";
    cout << "---------------\n";

    // Display the speeds.
    for (kph = START_KPH; kph <= END_KPH; kph += INCREMENT)
    {
        // Calculate mph
        mph = kph * CONVERSION_FACTOR;

        // Display the speeds in kph and mph.
        cout << kph << "\t" << mph << endl;

    }
    return 0;
}
```

Program Output

```
KPH     MPH
---------------
60      37.3
70      43.5
80      49.7
90      55.9
100     62.1
110     68.4
120     74.6
130     80.8
```

Checkpoint

6 Name the three expressions that appear inside the parentheses in the `for` loop's header.

7 You want to write a `for` loop that displays "I love to program" 50 times. Assume you will use a counter variable named `count`.

A) What initialization expression will you use?

B) What test expression will you use?

C) What update expression will you use?

D) Write the loop.

8 What will the following program segments display?

A)
```
for (int count = 0; count < 6; count++)
    cout << (count + count);
```

B)
```
for (int value = -5; value < 5; value++)
    cout << value;
```

C)
```
int x;
for (x = 5; x <= 14; x += 3)
    cout << x << endl;
cout << x << endl;
```

9 Write a `for` loop that displays your name 10 times.

10 Write a `for` loop that displays all of the odd numbers, 1 through 49.

11 Write a `for` loop that displays every fifth number, 0 through 100.

7 Keeping a Running Total

CONCEPT: A *running total* is a sum of numbers that accumulates with each iteration of a loop. The variable used to keep the running total is called an *accumulator*.

Many programming tasks require you to calculate the total of a series of numbers. For example, suppose you are writing a program that calculates a business's total sales for a week. The program would read the sales for each day as input and calculate the total of those numbers.

Programs that calculate the total of a series of numbers typically use two elements:

1. A loop that reads each number in the series.
2. A variable that accumulates the total of the numbers as they are read.

The variable that is used to accumulate the total of the numbers is called an *accumulator*. It is often said that the loop keeps a *running total* because it accumulates the total as it reads each number in the series. Figure 11 shows the general logic of a loop that calculates a running total.

Figure 11 Logic for calculating a running total

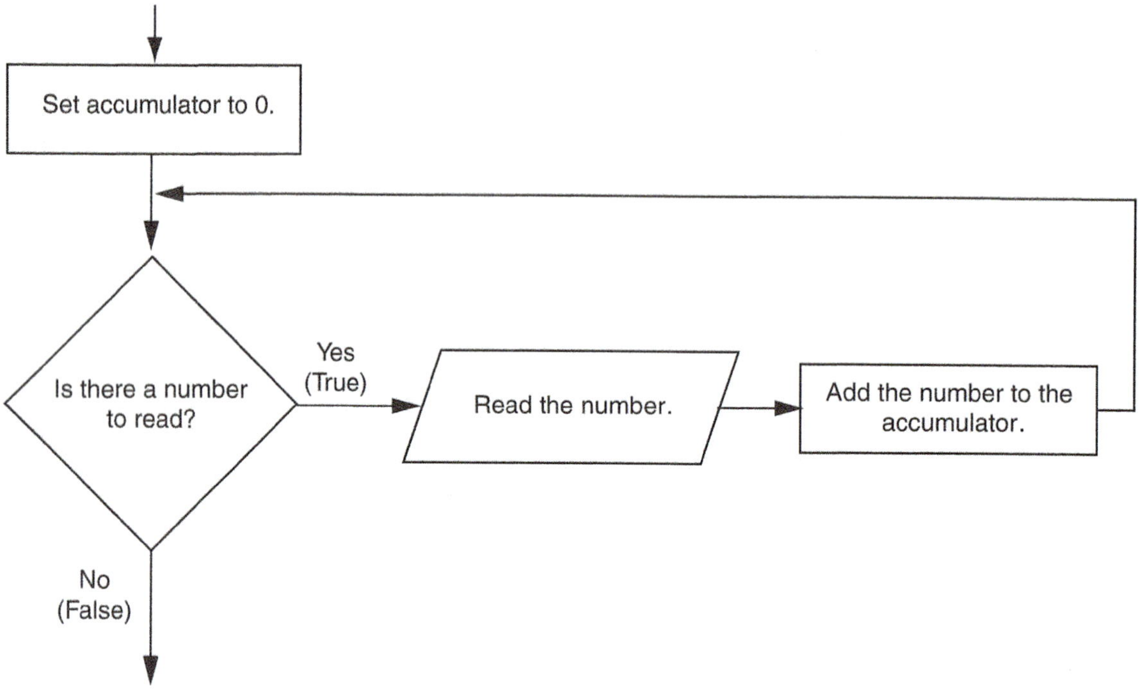

When the loop finishes, the accumulator will contain the total of the numbers that were read by the loop. Notice the first step in the flowchart is to set the accumulator variable to 0. This is a critical step. Each time the loop reads a number, it adds it to the accumulator. If the accumulator starts with any value other than 0, it will not contain the correct total when the loop finishes.

Let's look at a program that calculates a running total. Program 12 calculates a company's total sales over a period of time by taking daily sales figures as input and calculating a running total of them as they are gathered.

Program 12

```
// This program takes daily sales amounts over a period of time
// and calculates their total.
#include <iostream>
#include <iomanip>
using namespace std;

int main()
{
    int days;            // Number of days
    double total = 0.0;  // Accumulator, initialized with 0

    // Get the number of days.
    cout << "For how many days do you have sales amounts? ";
```

```
14        cin >> days;
15
16        // Get the sales for each day and accumulate a total.
17        for (int count = 1; count <= days; count++)
18        {
19            double sales;
20            cout << "Enter the sales for day " << count << ": ";
21            cin >> sales;
22            total += sales;   // Accumulate the running total.
23        }
24
25        // Display the total sales.
26        cout << fixed << showpoint << setprecision(2);
27        cout << "The total sales are $" << total << endl;
28        return 0;
29    }
```

Program Output with Example Input Shown in Bold

```
For how many days do you have sales amounts? 5 [Enter]
Enter the sales for day 1: 489.32 [Enter]
Enter the sales for day 2: 421.65 [Enter]
Enter the sales for day 3: 497.89 [Enter]
Enter the sales for day 4: 532.37 [Enter]
Enter the sales for day 5: 506.92 [Enter]
The total sales are $2448.15
```

Let's take a closer look at this program. Line 9 defines the `days` variable, which will hold the number of days for which we have sales figures. Line 10 defines the `total` variable, which will hold the total sales. Because `total` is an accumulator, it is initialized with 0.0.

In line 14, the user enters the number of days for which he or she has sales amounts. The number is assigned to the `days` variable. Next, the `for` loop in lines 17 through 23 executes. In the loop's initialization expression, in line 17, the variable `count` is defined and initialized with 1. The test expression specifies the loop will repeat as long as `count` is less than or equal to `days`. The update expression increments `count` by one at the end of each loop iteration.

Line 19 defines a variable named `sales`. Because the variable is defined in the body of the loop, its scope is limited to the loop. During each loop iteration, the user enters the amount of sales for a specific day, which is assigned to the `sales` variable. This is done in line 21. Then, in line 22, the value of `sales` is added to the existing value in the `total` variable. (Note line 22 does *not* assign `sales` to `total`, but *adds* `sales` to `total`. Put another way, this line increases `total` by the amount in `sales`.)

Because `total` was initially assigned 0.0, after the first iteration of the loop, `total` will be set to the same value as `sales`. After each subsequent iteration, `total` will be increased by the amount in `sales`. After the loop has finished, `total` will contain the total of all the daily sales figures entered. Now it should be clear why we assigned 0.0 to `total` before the loop executed. If `total` started at any other value, the total would be incorrect.

8 Sentinels

CONCEPT: **A *sentinel* is a special value that marks the end of a list of values.**

Program 12, in the previous section, requires the user to know in advance the number of days for which he or she wishes to enter sales figures. Sometimes, the user has a list that is very long and doesn't know how many items there are. In other cases, the user might be entering several lists, and it is impractical to require that every item in every list be counted.

A technique that can be used in these situations is to ask the user to enter a sentinel at the end of the list. A *sentinel* is a special value that cannot be mistaken as a member of the list and signals that there are no more values to be entered. When the user enters the sentinel, the loop terminates.

Program 13 calculates the total points earned by a soccer team over a series of games. It allows the user to enter the series of game points, then –1 to signal the end of the list.

Program 13

```
// This program calculates the total number of points a
// soccer team has earned over a series of games. The user
// enters a series of point values, then -1 when finished.
#include <iostream>
using namespace std;

int main()
{
    int game = 1,    // Game counter
        points,      // To hold a number of points
        total = 0;   // Accumulator

    cout << "Enter the number of points your team has earned\n";
    cout << "so far in the season, then enter -1 when finished.\n\n";
    cout << "Enter the points for game " << game << ": ";
    cin >> points;

    while (points != -1)
    {
        total += points;
        game++;
        cout << "Enter the points for game " << game << ": ";
        cin >> points;
    }
    cout << "\nThe total points are " << total << endl;
    return 0;
}
```

Program Output with Example Input Shown in Bold

```
Enter the number of points your team has earned
so far in the season, then enter -1 when finished.

Enter the points for game 1: 7 [Enter]
Enter the points for game 2: 9 [Enter]
Enter the points for game 3: 4 [Enter]
Enter the points for game 4: 6 [Enter]
Enter the points for game 5: 8 [Enter]
Enter the points for game 6: -1 [Enter]

The total points are 34
```

The value –1 was chosen for the sentinel in this program because it is not possible for a team to score negative points. Notice this program performs a priming read in line 18 to get the first value. This makes it possible for the loop to immediately terminate if the user enters –1 as the first value. Also note the sentinel value is not included in the running total.

Checkpoint

12 Write a for loop that repeats seven times, asking the user to enter a number. The loop should also calculate the sum of the numbers entered.

13 In the following program segment, which variable is the counter variable and which is the accumulator?

```
int a, x, y = 0;
for (x = 0; x < 10; x++)
{
    cout << "Enter a number: ";
    cin >> a;
    y += a;
}
cout << "The sum of those numbers is " << y << endl;
```

14 Why should you be careful when choosing a sentinel value?

15 How would you modify Program 13 so any negative value is a sentinel?

9 Focus on Software Engineering: Deciding Which Loop to Use

CONCEPT: Although most repetitive algorithms can be written with any of the three types of loops, each works best in different situations.

Each of the three C++ loops is ideal to use in different situations. Here's a short summary of when each loop should be used:

- **The `while` loop.** The `while` loop is a conditional loop, which means it repeats as long as a particular condition exists. It is also a pretest loop, so it is ideal in situations where you do not want the loop to iterate if the condition is false from the beginning.

For example, validating input that has been read and reading lists of data terminated by a sentinel value are good applications of the `while` loop.

- **The `do-while` loop.** The `do-while` loop is also a conditional loop. Unlike the `while` loop, however, `do-while` is a posttest loop. It is ideal in situations where you always want the loop to iterate at least once. The `do-while` loop is a good choice for repeating a menu.
- **The `for` loop.** The `for` loop is a pretest loop that has built-in expressions for initializing, testing, and updating. These expressions make it very convenient to use a counter variable to control the number of iterations that the loop performs. The initialization expression can initialize the counter variable to a starting value, the test expression can test the counter variable to determine whether it holds the maximum value, and the update expression can increment the counter variable. The `for` loop is ideal in situations where the exact number of iterations is known.

10 Nested Loops

CONCEPT: **A loop that is inside another loop is called a *nested loop*.**

A nested loop is a loop that appears inside another loop. A clock is a good example of something that works like a nested loop. The second hand, minute hand, and hour hand all spin around the face of the clock. Each time the hour hand increments, the minute hand increments 60 times. Each time the minute hand increments, the second hand increments 60 times.

Here is a program segment with a `for` loop that partially simulates a digital clock. It displays the seconds from 0 to 59.

```
cout << fixed << right;
cout.fill('0');
for (int seconds = 0; seconds < 60; seconds++)
    cout << setw(2) << seconds << endl;
```

> **NOTE:** The `fill` member function of `cout` changes the fill character, which is a space by default. In the program segment above, the `fill` function causes a zero to be printed in front of all single digit numbers.

We can add a `minutes` variable and nest the loop above inside another loop that cycles through 60 minutes.

```
cout << fixed << right;
cout.fill('0');
for (int minutes = 0; minutes < 60; minutes++)
{
    for (int seconds = 0; seconds < 60; seconds++)
    {
        cout << setw(2) << minutes << ":";
        cout << setw(2) << seconds << endl;
    }
}
```

To make the simulated clock complete, another variable and loop can be added to count the hours.

```
cout << fixed << right;
cout.fill('0');
for (int hours = 0; hours < 24; hours++)
{
     for (int minutes = 0; minutes < 60; minutes++)
     {
          for (int seconds = 0; seconds < 60; seconds++)
          {
               cout << setw(2) << hours << ":";
               cout << setw(2) << minutes << ":";
               cout << setw(2) << seconds << endl;
          }
     }
}
```

The output of the previous program segment follows:

```
00:00:00
00:00:01
00:00:02
    .
    .
    .
23:59:59
```

(The program will count through each second of 24 hours.)

The innermost loop will iterate 60 times for each iteration of the middle loop. The middle loop will iterate 60 times for each iteration of the outermost loop. When the outermost loop has iterated 24 times, the middle loop will have iterated 1,440 times and the innermost loop will have iterated 86,400 times!

The simulated clock example brings up a few points about nested loops:

- An inner loop goes through all of its iterations for each iteration of an outer loop.
- Inner loops complete their iterations faster than outer loops.
- To get the total number of iterations of a nested loop, multiply the number of iterations of all the loops.

Program 14 is another test-averaging program. It asks the user for the number of students and the number of test scores per student. A nested inner loop, in lines 26 through 33, asks for all the test scores for one student, iterating once for each test score. The outer loop in lines 23 through 37 iterates once for each student.

Program 14

```
1  // This program averages test scores. It asks the user for the
2  // number of students and the number of test scores per student.
3  #include <iostream>
4  #include <iomanip>
5  using namespace std;
6
```

(program continues)

Program 14 *(continued)*

```
int main()
{
    int numStudents,    // Number of students
        numTests;       // Number of tests per student
    double total,       // Accumulator for total scores
           average;     // Average test score

    // Set up numeric output formatting.
    cout << fixed << showpoint << setprecision(1);

    // Get the number of students.
    cout << "This program averages test scores.\n";
    cout << "For how many students do you have scores? ";
    cin >> numStudents;

    // Get the number of test scores per student.
    cout << "How many test scores does each student have? ";
    cin >> numTests;

    // Determine each student's average score.
    for (int student = 1; student <= numStudents; student++)
    {
        total = 0;      // Initialize the accumulator.
        for (int test = 1; test <= numTests; test++)
        {
            double score;
            cout << "Enter score " << test << " for ";
            cout << "student " << student << ": ";
            cin >> score;
            total += score;
        }
        average = total / numTests;
        cout << "The average score for student " << student;
        cout << " is " << average << ".\n\n";
    }
    return 0;
}
```

Program Output with Example Input Shown in Bold

```
This program averages test scores.
For how many students do you have scores? 2 [Enter]
How many test scores does each student have? 3 [Enter]
Enter score 1 for student 1: 84 [Enter]
Enter score 2 for student 1: 79 [Enter]
Enter score 3 for student 1: 97 [Enter]
The average score for student 1 is 86.7.

Enter score 1 for student 2: 92 [Enter]
Enter score 2 for student 2: 88 [Enter]
Enter score 3 for student 2: 94 [Enter]
The average score for student 2 is 91.3.
```

11 Using Files for Data Storage

CONCEPT: When a program needs to save data for later use, it writes the data in a file. The data can then be read from the file at a later time.

The programs you have written so far require the user to reenter data each time the program runs, because data kept in variables and control properties is stored in RAM and disappears once the program stops running. If a program is to retain data between the times it runs, it must have a way of saving it. Data is saved in a file, which is usually stored on a computer's disk. Once the data is saved in a file, it will remain there after the program stops running. Data stored in a file can be then retrieved and used at a later time.

Most of the commercial software that you use on a day-to-day basis store data in files. The following are a few examples:

- **Word processors:** Word processing programs are used to write letters, memos, reports, and other documents. The documents are then saved in files so they can later be edited and printed.
- **Image editors:** Image editing programs are used to draw graphics and edit images such as the ones that you take with a digital camera. The images that you create or edit with an image editor are saved in files.
- **Spreadsheets:** Spreadsheet programs are used to work with numerical data. Numbers and mathematical formulas can be inserted into the rows and columns of the spreadsheet. The spreadsheet can then be saved in a file for later use.
- **Games:** Many computer games keep data stored in files. For example, some games keep a list of players' names with their scores stored in a file. These games typically display the players' names in order of their scores, from highest to lowest. Some games also allow you to save your current game status in a file so you can quit the game then resume playing it later without having to start from the beginning.
- **Web browsers:** Sometimes when you visit a webpage, the browser stores a small file known as a *cookie* on your computer. Cookies typically contain information about the browsing session, such as the contents of a shopping cart.

Programs used in daily business operations rely extensively on files. Payroll programs keep employee data in files, inventory programs keep data about a company's products in files, accounting systems keep data about a company's financial operations in files, and so on.

Programmers usually refer to the process of saving data in a file as *writing data* to the file. When a piece of data is written to a file, it is copied from a variable in RAM to the file. This is illustrated in Figure 12. An *output file* is a file to which data is written. It is called an output file because the program stores output in it.

The process of retrieving data from a file is known as *reading data* from the file. When a piece of data is read from a file, it is copied from the file into a variable in RAM. Figure 13 illustrates this process. An *input file* is a file from which data is read. It is called an input file because the program gets input from the file.

Figure 12 Writing data to a file

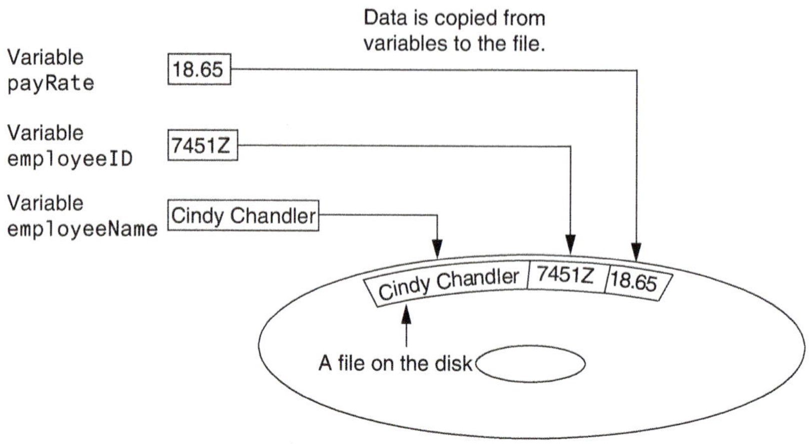

Figure 13 Reading data from a file

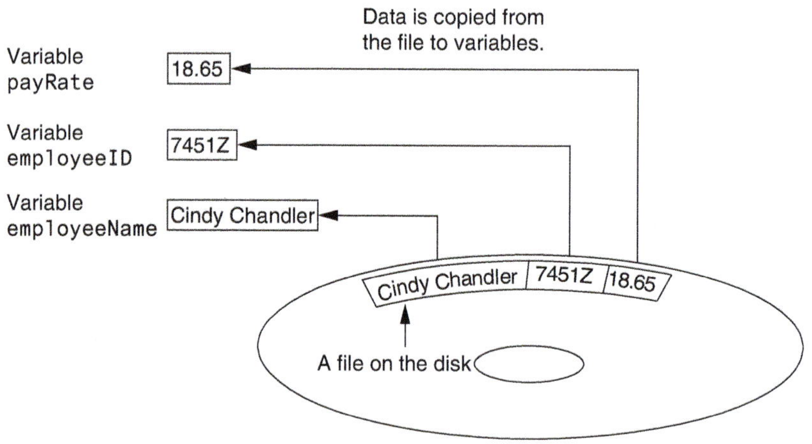

This section discusses ways to create programs that write data to files and read data from files. When a file is used by a program, three steps must be taken.

1. **Open the file**—Opening a file creates a connection between the file and the program. Opening an output file usually creates the file on the disk, and allows the program to write data to it. Opening an input file allows the program to read data from the file.
2. **Process the file**—Data is either written to the file (if it is an output file) or read from the file (if it is an input file).
3. **Close the file**—After the program is finished using the file, the file must be closed. Closing a file disconnects the file from the program.

Types of Files

In general, there are two types of files: text and binary. A *text file* contains data that has been encoded as text, using a scheme such as ASCII or Unicode. Even if the file contains numbers, those numbers are stored in the file as a series of characters. As a result, the file may be opened and viewed in a text editor such as Notepad. A *binary file* contains data that has not been converted to text. Thus, you cannot view the contents of a binary file with a text editor. In this chapter, we work only with text files.

File Access Methods

There are two general ways to access data stored in a file: sequential access and direct access. When you work with a *sequential-access file*, you access data from the beginning of the file to the end of the file. If you want to read a piece of data that is stored at the very end of the file, you have to read all of the data that comes before it—you cannot jump directly to the desired data. This is similar to the way that older cassette tape players work. If you want to listen to the last song on a cassette tape, you have to either fast-forward over all of the songs that come before it or listen to them. There is no way to jump directly to a specific song.

When you work with a *random-access file* (also known as a *direct access file*), you can jump directly to any piece of data in the file without reading the data that comes before it. This is similar to the way a CD player or an MP3 player works. You can jump directly to any song that you want to hear.

This chapter focuses on sequential-access files. Sequential-access files are easy to work with, and you can use them to gain an understanding of basic file operations.

Filenames and File Stream Objects

Files on a disk are identified by a *filename*. For example, when you create a document with a word processor then save the document in a file, you have to specify a filename. When you use a utility such as Windows Explorer to examine the contents of your disk, you see a list of filenames. Figure 14 shows how three files named cat.jpg, notes.txt, and resume.doc might be represented in Windows Explorer.

Figure 14 Three files

Each operating system has its own rules for naming files. Many systems, including Windows, support the use of *filename extensions*, which are short sequences of characters that appear at the end of a filename preceded by a period (known as a "dot"). For example, the files depicted in Figure 14 have the extensions .jpg, .txt, and .doc. The extension usually indicates the type of data stored in the file. For example, the .jpg extension usually indicates that the file contains a graphic image that is compressed according to the JPEG image standard. The .txt extension usually indicates that the file contains text. The .doc extension usually indicates that the file contains a Microsoft Word document.

In order for a program to work with a file on the computer's disk, the program must create a file stream object in memory. A *file stream object* is an object that is associated with a specific file and provides a way for the program to work with that file. It is called a "stream" object because a file can be thought of as a stream of data.

File stream objects work very much like the cin and cout objects. A stream of data may be sent to cout, which causes values to be displayed on the screen. A stream of data may be read from the keyboard by cin, and stored in variables. Likewise, streams of data may be sent to a file stream object, which writes the data to a file. When data is read from a file, the data flows from the file stream object that is associated with the file into variables.

Setting Up a Program for File Input/Output

Just as cin and cout require the iostream file to be included in the program, C++ file access requires another header file. The file <fstream> contains all the declarations necessary for file operations. It is included with the following statement:

```
#include <fstream>
```

The <fstream> header file defines the data types ofstream, ifstream, and fstream. Before a C++ program can work with a file, it must define an object of one of these data types. The object will be "linked" with an actual file on the computer's disk, and the operations that may be performed on the file depend on which of these three data types you pick for the file stream object. Table 1 lists and describes the file stream data types.

Table 1 File Stream Objects

File Stream Data Type	Description
ofstream	Output file stream. You create an object of this data type when you want to create a file and write data to it.
ifstream	Input file stream. You create an object of this data type when you want to open an existing file and read data from it.
fstream	File stream. Objects of this data type can be used to open files for reading, writing, or both.

NOTE: In this chapter, we discuss only the ofstream and ifstream types.

Creating a File Object and Opening a File

Before data can be written to or read from a file, the following things must happen:

- A file stream object must be created.
- The file must be opened and linked to the file stream object.

The following code shows an example of opening a file for input (reading).

```
ifstream inputFile;
inputFile.open("Customers.txt");
```

The first statement defines an ifstream object named inputFile. The second statement calls the object's open member function, passing the string "Customers.txt" as an argument. In this statement, the open member function opens the Customers.txt file and links it with the inputFile object. After this code executes, you will be able to use the inputFile object to read data from the Customers.txt file.

The following code shows an example of opening a file for output (writing).

```
ofstream outputFile;
outputFile.open("Employees.txt");
```

The first statement defines an `ofstream` object named `outputFile`. The second statement calls the object's `open` member function, passing the string `"Employees.txt"` as an argument. In this statement, the `open` member function creates the Employees.txt file and links it with the `outputFile` object. After this code executes, you will be able to use the `outputFile` object to write data to the Employees.txt file. It's important to remember that when you call an `ofstream` object's `open` member function, the specified file will be created. If the specified file already exists, it will be deleted, and a new file with the same name will be created.

Often, when opening a file, you will need to specify its path as well as its name. For example, on a Windows system the following statement opens the file `C:\data\inventory.txt`:

```
inputFile.open("C:\\data\\inventory.txt")
```

In this statement, the file `C:\data\inventory.txt` is opened and linked with `inputFile`.

> **NOTE:** Notice the use of two backslashes in the file's path. Two backslashes are needed to represent one backslash in a string literal.

It is possible to define a file stream object and open a file in one statement. Here is an example:

```
ifstream inputFile("Customers.txt");
```

This statement defines an `ifstream` object named `inputFile` and opens the Customer.txt file. Here is an example that defines an `ofstream` object named `outputFile` and opens the Employees.txt file:

```
ofstream outputFile("Employees.txt");
```

Closing a File

The opposite of opening a file is closing it. Although a program's files are automatically closed when the program shuts down, it is a good programming practice to write statements that close them. Here are two reasons a program should close files when it is finished using them:

1. Most operating systems temporarily store data in a *file buffer* before it is written to a file. A file buffer is a small "holding section" of memory to which file-bound data is first written. When the buffer is filled, all the data stored there is written to the file. This technique improves the system's performance. Closing a file causes any unsaved data that may still be held in a buffer to be saved to its file. This means the data will be in the file if you need to read it later in the same program.
2. Some operating systems limit the number of files that may be open at one time. When a program closes files that are no longer being used, it will not deplete more of the operating system's resources than necessary.

Calling the file stream object's `close` member function closes a file. Here is an example:

```
inputFile.close();
```

Writing Data to a File

You already know how to use the stream insertion operator (<<) with the `cout` object to write data to the screen. It can also be used with `ofstream` objects to write data to a file. Assuming `outputFile` is an `ofstream` object, the following statement demonstrates using the << operator to write a string literal to a file:

```
outputFile << "I love C++ programming\n";
```

This statement writes the string literal `"I love C++ programming\n"` to the file associated with `outputFile`. As you can see, the statement looks like a `cout` statement, except the name of the `ofstream` object name replaces `cout`. Here is a statement that writes both a string literal and the contents of a variable to a file:

```
outputFile << "Price: " << price << endl;
```

The statement above writes the stream of data to `outputFile` exactly as `cout` would write it to the screen: It writes the string `"Price: "`, followed by the value of the `price` variable, followed by a newline character.

Program 15 demonstrates opening a file, writing data to the file, and closing the file. After this code has executed, we can open the demofile.txt file using a text editor and look at its contents. Figure 15 shows how the file's contents will appear in Notepad.

Program 15

```
// This program writes data to a file.
#include <iostream>
#include <fstream>
using namespace std;

int main()
{
    ofstream outputFile;
    outputFile.open("demofile.txt");

    cout << "Now writing data to the file.\n";

    // Write four names to the file.
    outputFile << "Bach\n";
    outputFile << "Beethoven\n";
    outputFile << "Mozart\n";
    outputFile << "Schubert\n";

    // Close the file
    outputFile.close();
    cout << "Done.\n";
    return 0;
}
```

Program Screen Output

```
Now writing data to the file.
Done.
```

Figure 15 Contents of demofile.txt

Notice in lines 14 through 17 of Program 15, each string that was written to the file ends with a newline escape sequence (`\n`). The newline specifies the end of a line of text. Because a newline is written at the end of each string, the strings appear on separate lines when viewed in a text editor, as shown in Figure 15.

Program 16 shows what happens if we write the same four names without the `\n` escape sequence. Figure 16 shows the contents of the file that Program 16 creates. As you can see, all of the names appear on the same line in the file.

Program 16

```
// This program writes data to a single line in a file.
#include <iostream>
#include <fstream>
using namespace std;

int main()
{
    ofstream outputFile;
    outputFile.open("demofile.txt");

    cout << "Now writing data to the file.\n";

    // Write four names to the file.
    outputFile << "Bach";
    outputFile << "Beethoven";
    outputFile << "Mozart";
    outputFile << "Schubert";

    // Close the file
    outputFile.close();
    cout << "Done.\n";
    return 0;
}
```

Program Screen Output

```
Now writing data to the file.
Done.
```

Figure 16 Output written as one line

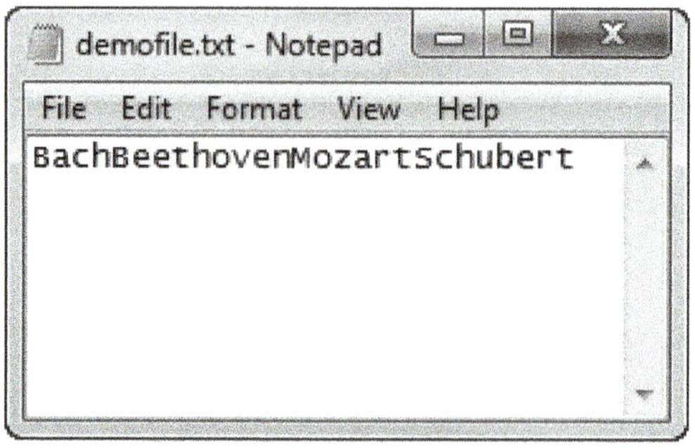

Program 17 shows another example. This program reads three numbers from the keyboard as input then saves those numbers in a file named Numbers.txt.

Program 17

```
// This program writes user input to a file.
#include <iostream>
#include <fstream>
using namespace std;

int main()
{
    ofstream outputFile;
    int number1, number2, number3;

    // Open an output file.
    outputFile.open("Numbers.txt");

    // Get three numbers from the user.
    cout << "Enter a number: ";
    cin >> number1;
    cout << "Enter another number: ";
    cin >> number2;
    cout << "One more time. Enter a number: ";
    cin >> number3;

    // Write the numbers to the file.
    outputFile << number1 << endl;
    outputFile << number2 << endl;
    outputFile << number3 << endl;
    cout << "The numbers were saved to a file.\n";

    // Close the file
    outputFile.close();
    cout << "Done.\n";
    return 0;
}
```

Program Screen Output with Example Input Shown in Bold

```
Enter a number: 100 [Enter]
Enter another number: 200 [Enter]
One more time. Enter a number: 300 [Enter]
The numbers were saved to a file.
Done.
```

In Program 17, lines 23 through 25 write the contents of the `number1`, `number2`, and `number3` variables to the file. Notice the `endl` manipulator is sent to the `outputFile` object immediately after each item. Sending the `endl` manipulator causes a newline to be written to the file. Figure 17 shows the file's contents displayed in Notepad, using the example input values 100, 200, and 300. As you can see, each item appears on a separate line in the file because of the `endl` manipulators.

Figure 17 Contents of Numbers.txt

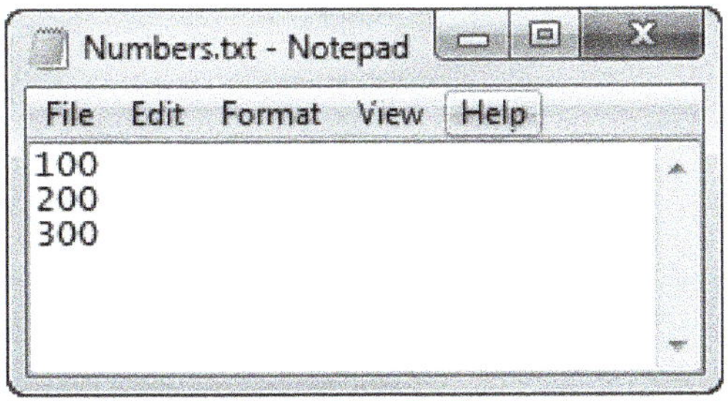

Program 18 shows an example that reads strings as input from the keyboard then writes those strings to a file. The program asks the user to enter the first names of three friends, then it writes those names to a file named Friends.txt. Figure 18 shows an example of the Friends.txt file opened in Notepad.

Program 18

```
// This program writes user input to a file.
#include <iostream>
#include <fstream>
#include <string>
using namespace std;

int main()
{
    ofstream outputFile;
    string name1, name2, name3;

    // Open an output file.
    outputFile.open("Friends.txt");

```

(program continues)

Program 18 *(continued)*

```
    // Get the names of three friends.
    cout << "Enter the names of three friends.\n";
    cout << "Friend #1: ";
    cin >> name1;
    cout << "Friend #2: ";
    cin >> name2;
    cout << "Friend #3: ";
    cin >> name3;

    // Write the names to the file.
    outputFile << name1 << endl;
    outputFile << name2 << endl;
    outputFile << name3 << endl;
    cout << "The names were saved to a file.\n";

    // Close the file
    outputFile.close();
    return 0;
}
```

Program Screen Output with Example Input Shown in Bold

```
Enter the names of three friends.
Friend #1: Joe [Enter]
Friend #2: Chris [Enter]
Friend #3: Geri [Enter]
The names were saved to a file.
```

Figure 18 Contents of Friends.txt

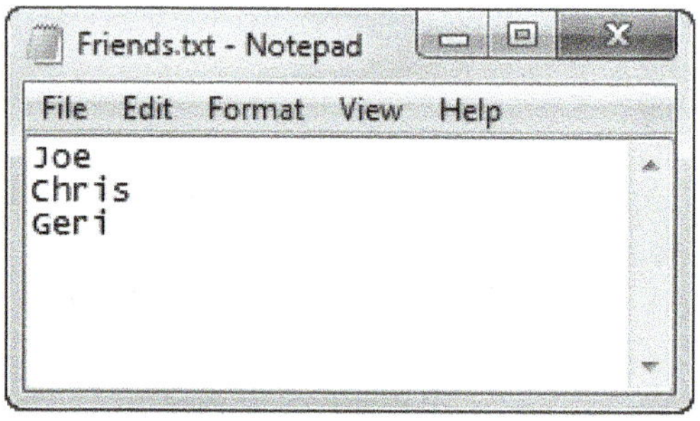

Reading Data from a File

VideoNote
Reading Data from a File

The >> operator reads not only user input from the `cin` object, but also data from a file. Assuming `inputFile` is an `ifstream` object, the following statement shows the >> operator reading data from the file into the variable name:

```
inputFile >> name;
```

Let's look at an example. Assume the file Friends.txt exists, and it contains the names shown in Figure 18. Program 19 opens the file, reads the names and displays them on the screen, then closes the file.

Program 19

```
1  // This program reads data from a file.
2  #include <iostream>
3  #include <fstream>
4  #include <string>
5  using namespace std;
6
7  int main()
8  {
9      ifstream inputFile;
10     string name;
11
12     inputFile.open("Friends.txt");
13     cout << "Reading data from the file.\n";
14
15     inputFile >> name;        // Read name 1 from the file
16     cout << name << endl;     // Display name 1
17
18     inputFile >> name;        // Read name 2 from the file
19     cout << name << endl;     // Display name 2
20
21     inputFile >> name;        // Read name 3 from the file
22     cout << name << endl;     // Display name 3
23
24     inputFile.close();        // Close the file
25     return 0;
26 }
```

Program Output

```
Reading data from the file.
Joe
Chris
Geri
```

The Read Position

When a file has been opened for input, the file stream object internally maintains a special value known as a *read position*. A file's read position marks the location of the next byte that will be read from the file. When an input file is opened, its read position is initially set to the first byte in the file. So, the first read operation extracts data starting at the first byte. As data is read from the file, the read position moves forward, toward the end of the file.

Let's see how this works with the example shown in Program 19. When the Friends.txt file is opened by the statement in line 12, the read position for the file will be positioned as shown in Figure 19.

Figure 19 Initial read position

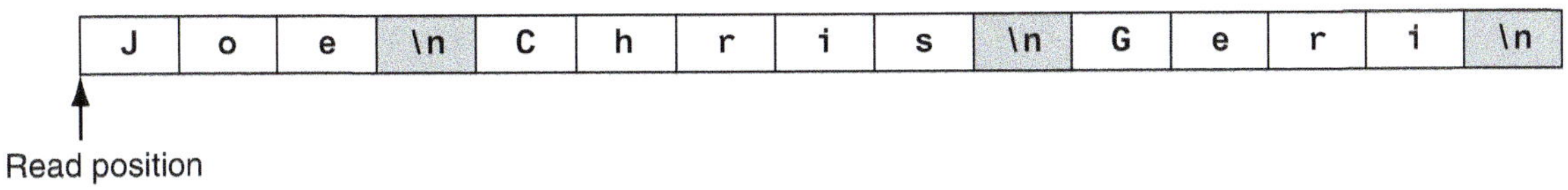

Keep in mind when the >> operator extracts data from a file, it expects to read pieces of data that are separated by whitespace characters (spaces, tabs, or newlines). When the statement in line 15 executes, the >> operator reads data from the file's current read position, up to the `\n` character. The data read from the file is assigned to the `name` object. The `\n` character is also read from the file, but is not included as part of the data. So, the `name` object will hold the value `"Joe"` after this statement executes. The file's read position will then be at the location shown in Figure 20.

Figure 20 The next read position

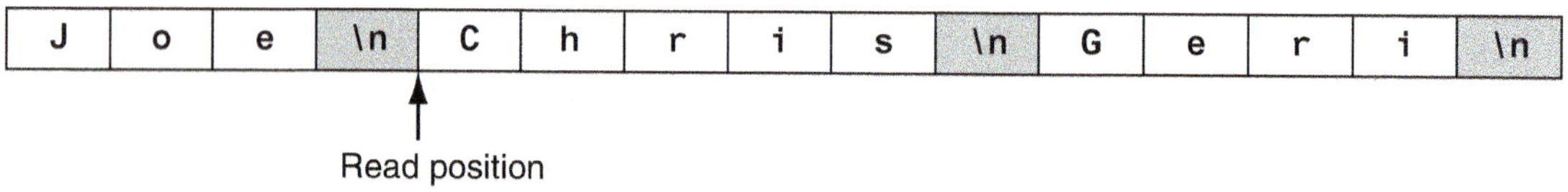

When the statement in line 18 executes, it reads the next item from the file, which is `"Chris"`, and assigns that value to the `name` object. After this statement executes, the file's read position will be advanced to the next item, as shown in Figure 21.

Figure 21 The next read position

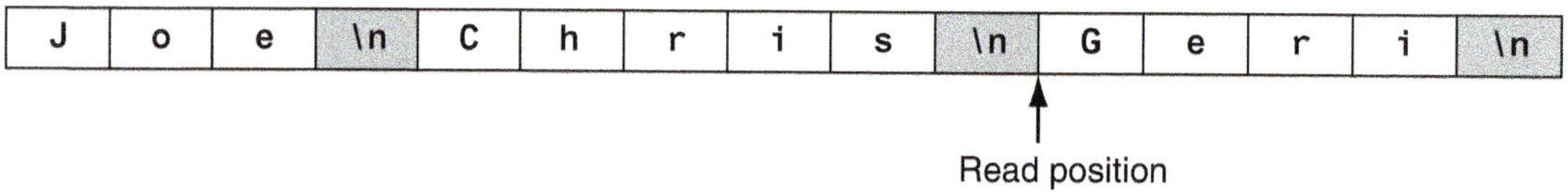

When the statement in line 21 executes, it reads the next item from the file, which is `"Geri"`, and assigns that value to the `name` object. After this statement executes, the file's read position will be advanced to the end of the file, as shown in Figure 22.

Figure 22 The read position at the end of the file

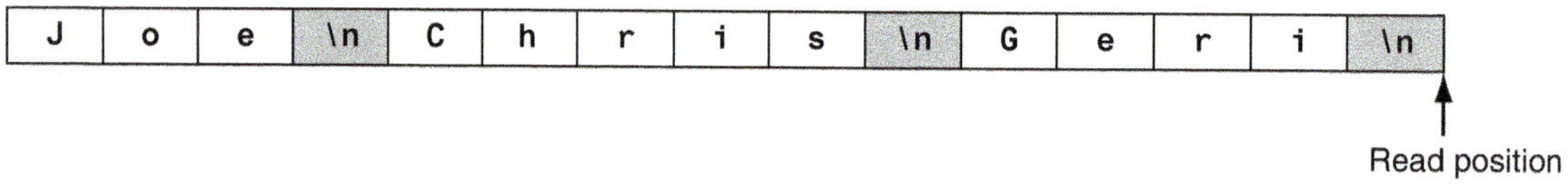

Reading Numeric Data from a Text File

Remember when data is stored in a text file, it is encoded as text, using a scheme such as ASCII or Unicode. Even if the file contains numbers, those numbers are stored in the file as a series of characters. For example, suppose a text file contains numeric data, such as that shown in Figure 17. The numbers that you see displayed in the figure are stored in the file as the strings `"10"`, `"20"`, and `"30"`. Fortunately, you can use the >> operator to read data such as this from a text file into a numeric variable, and the >> operator will automatically convert the data to a numeric data type. Program 20 shows an example. It opens the file shown in Figure 23, reads the three numbers from the file into `int` variables, and calculates their sum.

Figure 23 Contents of NumericData.txt

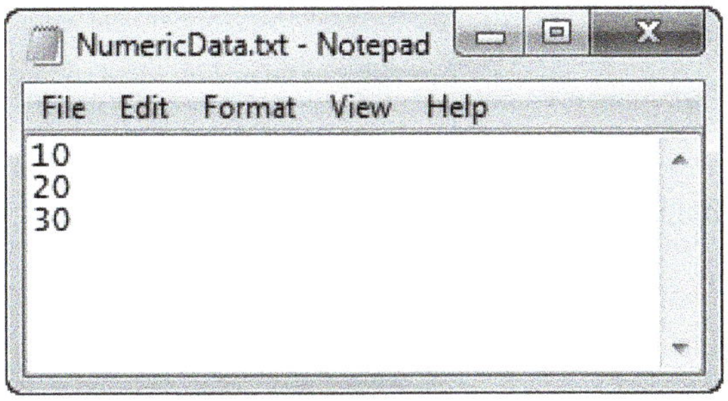

Program 20

```
// This program reads numbers from a file.
#include <iostream>
#include <fstream>
using namespace std;

int main()
{
    ifstream inFile;
    int value1, value2, value3, sum;

    // Open the file.
    inFile.open("NumericData.txt");

    // Read the three numbers from the file.
    inFile >> value1;
    inFile >> value2;
    inFile >> value3;

    // Close the file.
    inFile.close();

    // Calculate the sum of the numbers.
    sum = value1 + value2 + value3;

    // Display the three numbers.
    cout << "Here are the numbers:\n"
         << value1 << " " << value2
         << " " << value3 << endl;

    // Display the sum of the numbers.
    cout << "Their sum is: " << sum << endl;
    return 0;
}
```

Program Output

```
Here are the numbers:
10 20 30
Their sum is: 60
```

Using Loops to Process Files

Although some programs use files to store only small amounts of data, files are typically used to hold large collections of data. When a program uses a file to write or read a large amount of data, a loop is typically involved. For example, look at the code in Program 21. This program gets sales amounts for a series of days from the user and writes those amounts to a file named Sales.txt. The user specifies the number of days of sales data he or she needs to enter. In the sample run of the program, the user enters sales amounts for 5 days. Figure 24 shows the contents of the Sales.txt file containing the data entered by the user in the sample run.

Program 21

```
// This program reads data from a file.
#include <iostream>
#include <fstream>
using namespace std;

int main()
{
    ofstream outputFile;  // File stream object
    int numberOfDays;     // Number of days of sales
    double sales;         // Sales amount for a day

    // Get the number of days.
    cout << "For how many days do you have sales? ";
    cin >> numberOfDays;

    // Open a file named Sales.txt.
    outputFile.open("Sales.txt");

    // Get the sales for each day and write it
    // to the file.
    for (int count = 1; count <= numberOfDays; count++)
    {
        // Get the sales for a day.
        cout << "Enter the sales for day "
             << count << ": ";
        cin >> sales;

        // Write the sales to the file.
        outputFile << sales << endl;
    }

    // Close the file.
    outputFile.close();
    cout << "Data written to Sales.txt\n";
    return 0;
}
```

Program Output (with Input Shown in Bold)

```
For how many days do you have sales? 5 [Enter]
Enter the sales for day 1: 1000.00 [Enter]
Enter the sales for day 2: 2000.00 [Enter]
Enter the sales for day 3: 3000.00 [Enter]
Enter the sales for day 4: 4000.00 [Enter]
Enter the sales for day 5: 5000.00 [Enter]
Data written to sales.txt.
```

Figure 24 Contents of Sales.txt

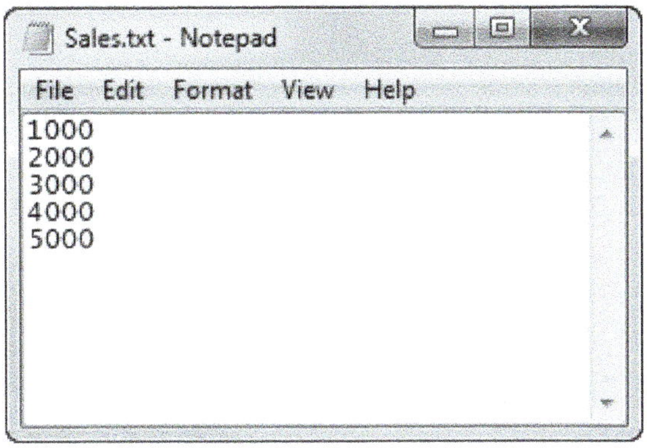

Detecting the End of the File

Quite often a program must read the contents of a file without knowing the number of items that are stored in the file. For example, suppose you need to write a program that displays all of the items in a file, but you do not know how many items the file contains. You can open the file then use a loop to repeatedly read an item from the file and display it. However, an error will occur if the program attempts to read beyond the end of the file. The program needs some way of knowing when the end of the file has been reached so it will not try to read beyond it.

Fortunately, the >> operator not only reads data from a file, but also returns a true or false value indicating whether the data was successfully read or not. If the operator returns true, then a value was successfully read. If the operator returns false, it means that no value was read from the file.

Let's look at an example. A file named ListOfNumbers.txt, which is shown in Figure 25, contains a list of numbers. Without knowing how many numbers the file contains, Program 22 opens the file, reads all of the values it contains, and displays them.

Figure 25 Contents of ListOfNumbers.txt

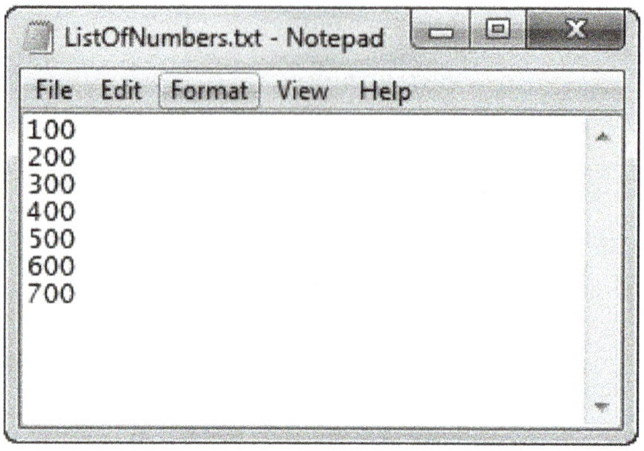

Program 22

```
// This program reads data from a file.
#include <iostream>
#include <fstream>
using namespace std;

int main()
{
    ifstream inputFile;
    int number;

    // Open the file.
    inputFile.open("ListOfNumbers.txt");

    // Read the numbers from the file and
    // display them.
    while (inputFile >> number)
    {
        cout << number << endl;
    }

    // Close the file.
    inputFile.close();
    return 0;
}
```

Program Output

```
100
200
300
400
500
600
700
```

Take a closer look at line 16:

```
while (inputFile >> number)
```

Notice the statement that extracts data from the file is used as the Boolean expression in the `while` loop. It works like this:

- The expression `inputFile >> number` executes.
- If an item is successfully read from the file, the item is stored in the `number` variable, and the expression returns true to indicate that it succeeded. In that case, the statement in line 18 executes and the loop repeats.
- If there are no more items to read from the file, the expression `inputFile >> number` returns false, indicating that it did not read a value. In that case, the loop terminates.

Because the value returned from the `>>` operator controls the loop, it will read items from the file until the end of the file has been reached.

Testing for File Open Errors

Under certain circumstances, the `open` member function will not work. For example, the following code will fail if the file info.txt does not exist:

```
ifstream inputFile;
inputFile.open("info.txt");
```

There is a way to determine whether the `open` member function successfully opened the file. After you call the `open` member function, you can test the file stream object as if it were a Boolean expression. Program 23 shows an example.

Program 23

```
// This program tests for file open errors.
#include <iostream>
#include <fstream>
using namespace std;

int main()
{
    ifstream inputFile;
    int number;

    // Open the file.
    inputFile.open("BadListOfNumbers.txt");

    // If the file successfully opened, process it.
    if (inputFile)
    {
        // Read the numbers from the file and
        // display them.
        while (inputFile >> number)
        {
            cout << number << endl;
        }

```

(program continues)

Program 23 *(continued)*

```
24          // Close the file.
25          inputFile.close();
26       }
27       else
28       {
29          // Display an error message.
30          cout << "Error opening the file.\n";
31       }
32       return 0;
33   }
```

Program Output (Assume BadListOfNumbers.txt does not exist)

```
Error opening the file.
```

Let's take a closer look at certain parts of the code. Line 12 calls the `inputFile` object's `open` member function to open the file ListOfNumbers.txt. Then, the `if` statement in line 15 tests the value of the `inputFile` object as if it were a Boolean expression. When tested this way, the `inputFile` object will give a true value if the file was successfully opened. Otherwise, it will give a false value. The example output shows this program will display an error message if it could not open the file.

Another way to detect a failed attempt to open a file is with the `fail` member function, as shown in the following code:

```
ifstream inputFile;
inputFile.open("customers.txt");
if (inputFile.fail())
{
    cout << "Error opening file.\n";
}
else
{
    // Process the file.
}
```

The `fail` member function returns true when an attempted file operation is unsuccessful. When using file I/O, you should always test the file stream object to make sure the file was opened successfully. If the file could not be opened, the user should be informed and appropriate action taken by the program.

Letting the User Specify a Filename

In each of the previous examples, the name of the file that is opened is hard-coded as a string literal into the program. In many cases, you will want the user to specify the name of a file for the program to open. In C++ 11, you can pass a `string` object as an argument to a file stream object's `open` member function. Program 24 shows an example. This is a modified version of Program 23. This version prompts the user to enter the name of the file. In line 15, the name the user enters is stored in a `string` object named `filename`. In line 18, the `filename` object is passed as an argument to the `open` function.

Program 24

```cpp
// This program lets the user enter a filename.
#include <iostream>
#include <string>
#include <fstream>
using namespace std;

int main()
{
    ifstream inputFile;
    string filename;
    int number;

    // Get the filename from the user.
    cout << "Enter the filename: ";
    cin >> filename;

    // Open the file.
    inputFile.open(filename);

    // If the file successfully opened, process it.
    if (inputFile)
    {
        // Read the numbers from the file and
        // display them.
        while (inputFile >> number)
        {
            cout << number << endl;
        }

        // Close the file.
        inputFile.close();
    }
    else
    {
        // Display an error message.
        cout << "Error opening the file.\n";
    }
    return 0;
}
```

Program Output with Example Input Shown in Bold

```
Enter the filename: ListOfNumbers.txt [Enter]
100
200
300
400
500
600
700
```

Using the `c_str` Member Function in Older Versions of C++

In older versions of the C++ language (prior to C++ 11), a file stream object's `open` member function will not accept a `string` object as an argument. The `open` member function requires you pass the name of the file as a null-terminated string, which is also known as a *C-string*. String literals are stored in memory as null-terminated C-strings, but `string` objects are not.

Fortunately, `string` objects have a member function named `c_str` that returns the contents of the object formatted as a null-terminated C-string. Here is the general format of how you call the function:

```
stringObject.c_str()
```

In the general format, *`stringObject`* is the name of a `string` object. The `c_str` function returns the string that is stored in *`stringObject`* as a null-terminated C-string.

For example, line 18 in Program 24 could be rewritten in the following manner to make the program compatible with an older version of C++:

```
inputFile.open(filename.c_str());
```

In this version of the statement, the value that is returned from `filename.c_str()` is passed as an argument to the `open` function.

Checkpoint

16 What is an output file? What is an input file?

17 What three steps must be taken when a file is used by a program?

18 What is the difference between a text file and a binary file?

19 What is the difference between sequential access and random access?

20 What type of file stream object do you create if you want to write data to a file?

21 What type of file stream object do you create if you want to read data from a file?

22 Write a short program that uses a `for` loop to write the numbers 1 through 10 to a file.

23 Write a short program that opens the file created by the program you wrote for Checkpoint 22, reads all of the numbers from the file, and displays them.

12 Optional Topics: Breaking and Continuing a Loop

CONCEPT: The `break` statement causes a loop to terminate early. The `continue` statement causes a loop to stop its current iteration and begin the next one.

> **WARNING!** Use the `break` and `continue` statements with great caution. Because they bypass the normal condition that controls the loop's iterations, these statements make code difficult to understand and debug. For this reason, you should avoid using `break` and `continue` whenever possible. However, because they are part of the C++ language, we discuss them briefly in this section.

Sometimes it's necessary to stop a loop before it goes through all its iterations. The `break` statement can also be placed inside a loop. When it is encountered, the loop stops, and the program jumps to the statement immediately following the loop.

The `while` loop in the following program segment appears to execute 10 times, but the `break` statement causes it to stop after the fifth iteration.

```
int count = 0;
while (count++ < 10)
{
    cout << count << endl;
    if (count == 5)
        break;
}
```

Program 25 uses the `break` statement to interrupt a `for` loop. The program asks the user for a number, then displays the value of that number raised to the powers of 0 through 10. The user can stop the loop at any time by entering Q.

Program 25

```
// This program raises the user's number to the powers
// of 0 through 10.
#include <iostream>
#include <cmath>
using namespace std;

int main()
{
    double value;
    char choice;

    cout << "Enter a number: ";
    cin >> value;
    cout << "This program will raise " << value;
    cout << " to the powers of 0 through 10.\n";
    for (int count = 0; count <= 10; count++)
    {
        cout << value << " raised to the power of ";
        cout << count << " is " << pow(value, count);
        cout << "\nEnter Q to quit or any other key ";
        cout << "to continue. ";
        cin >> choice;
        if (choice == 'Q' || choice == 'q')
            break;
    }
    return 0;
}
```

(program output continues)

Program 25 *(continued)*

Program Output with Example Input Shown in Bold

```
Enter a number: 2 [Enter]
This program will raise 2 to the powers of 0 through 10.
2 raised to the power of 0 is 1
Enter Q to quit or any other key to continue. C [Enter]
2 raised to the power of 1 is 2
Enter Q to quit or any other key to continue. C [Enter]
2 raised to the power of 2 is 4
Enter Q to quit or any other key to continue. Q [Enter]
```

Using break in a Nested Loop

In a nested loop, the `break` statement only interrupts the loop in which it is placed. The following program segment displays five rows of asterisks on the screen. The outer loop controls the number of rows, and the inner loop controls the number of asterisks in each row. The inner loop is designed to display 20 asterisks, but the `break` statement stops it during the eleventh iteration.

```
for (int row = 0; row < 5; row++)
{
     for (int star = 0; star < 20; star++)
     {
          cout << '*';
          if (star == 10)
               break;
     }
     cout << endl;
}
```

The output of the program segment above is:

```
***********
***********
***********
***********
***********
```

The continue Statement

The `continue` statement causes the current iteration of a loop to end immediately. When `continue` is encountered, all the statements in the body of the loop that appear after it are ignored, and the loop prepares for the next iteration.

In a `while` loop, this means the program jumps to the test expression at the top of the loop. As usual, if the expression is still true, the next iteration begins. In a `do-while` loop, the program jumps to the test expression at the bottom of the loop, which determines whether the next iteration will begin. In a `for` loop, `continue` causes the update expression to be executed, then the test expression to be evaluated.

The following program segment demonstrates the use of `continue` in a `while` loop:

```
int testVal = 0;
while (testVal++ < 10)
{
    if (testVal == 4)
        continue;
    cout << testVal << " ";
}
```

This loop looks like it displays the integers 1 through 10. When `testVal` is equal to 4, however, the `continue` statement causes the loop to skip the `cout` statement and begin the next iteration. The output of the loop is

```
1 2 3 5 6 7 8 9 10
```

Program 26 demonstrates the `continue` statement. The program calculates the charges for DVD rentals, where current releases cost $3.50 and all others cost $2.50. If a customer rents several DVDs, every third one is free. The `continue` statement is used to skip the part of the loop that calculates the charges for every third DVD.

Program 26

```
// This program calculates the charges for DVD rentals.
// Every third DVD is free.
#include <iostream>
#include <iomanip>
using namespace std;

int main()
{
    int dvdCount = 1;      // DVD counter
    int numDVDs;           // Number of DVDs rented
    double total = 0.0;    // Accumulator
    char current;          // Current release, Y or N

    // Get the number of DVDs.
    cout << "How many DVDs are being rented? ";
    cin >> numDVDs;

    // Determine the charges.
    do
    {
        if ((dvdCount % 3) == 0)
        {
            cout << "DVD #" << dvdCount << " is free!\n";
            continue; // Immediately start the next iteration
        }
        cout << "Is DVD #" << dvdCount;
        cout << " a current release? (Y/N) ";
        cin >> current;
        if (current == 'Y' || current == 'y')
            total += 3.50;
        else
            total += 2.50;
    } while (dvdCount++ < numDVDs);

```

(program continues)

Program 26 *(continued)*

```
        // Display the total.
        cout << fixed << showpoint << setprecision(2);
        cout << "The total is $" << total << endl;
        return 0;
}
```

Program Output with Example Input Shown in Bold

```
How many DVDs are being rented? 6 [Enter]
Is DVD #1 a current release? (Y/N) y [Enter]
Is DVD #2 a current release? (Y/N) n [Enter]
DVD #3 is free!
Is DVD #4 a current release? (Y/N) n [Enter]
Is DVD #5 a current release? (Y/N) y [Enter]
DVD #6 is free!
The total is $12.00
```

Case Study: See the Loan Amortization Case Study on the Computer Science Portal at www.pearsonhighered.com/gaddis.

Review Questions and Exercises

Short Answer

1. Why should you indent the statements in the body of a loop?
2. Describe the difference between pretest loops and posttest loops.
3. Why are the statements in the body of a loop called conditionally executed statements?
4. What is the difference between the `while` loop and the `do-while` loop?
5. Which loop should you use in situations where you wish the loop to repeat until the test expression is false, and the loop should not execute if the test expression is false to begin with?
6. Which loop should you use in situations where you wish the loop to repeat until the test expression is false, but the loop should execute at least one time?
7. Which loop should you use when you know the number of required iterations?
8. Why is it critical that counter variables be properly initialized?
9. Why is it critical that accumulator variables be properly initialized?
10. Why should you be careful not to place a statement in the body of a `for` loop that changes the value of the loop's counter variable?
11. What header file do you need to include in a program that performs file operations?
12. What data type do you use when you want to create a file stream object that can write data to a file?
13. What data type do you use when you want to create a file stream object that can read data from a file?
14. Why should a program close a file when it's finished using it?

15. What is a file's read position? Where is the read position when a file is first opened for reading?

Fill-in-the-Blank

16. To __________ a value means to increase it by one, and to __________ a value means to decrease it by one.
17. When the increment or decrement operator is placed before the operand (or to the operand's left), the operator is being used in __________ mode.
18 When the increment or decrement operator is placed after the operand (or to the operand's right), the operator is being used in __________ mode.
19. The statement or block that is repeated is known as the __________ of the loop.
20. Each repetition of a loop is known as a(n) __________.
21. A loop that evaluates its test expression before each repetition is a(n) __________ loop.
22. A loop that evaluates its test expression after each repetition is a(n) __________ loop.
23. A loop that does not have a way of stopping is a(n) __________ loop.
24. A(n) __________ is a variable that "counts" the number of times a loop repeats.
25. A(n) __________ is a sum of numbers that accumulates with each iteration of a loop.
26. A(n) __________ is a variable that is initialized to some starting value, usually zero, then has numbers added to it in each iteration of a loop.
27. A(n) __________ is a special value that marks the end of a series of values.
28. The __________ loop always iterates at least once.
29. The __________ and __________ loops will not iterate at all if their test expressions are false to start with.
30. The __________ loop is ideal for situations that require a counter.
31. Inside the `for` loop's parentheses, the first expression is the __________, the second expression is the __________, and the third expression is the __________.
32. A loop that is inside another is called a(n) __________ loop.
33. The __________ statement causes a loop to terminate immediately.
34. The __________ statement causes a loop to skip the remaining statements in the current iteration.

Algorithm Workbench

35. Write a `while` loop that lets the user enter a number. The number should be multiplied by 10, and the result stored in the variable `product`. The loop should iterate as long as `product` contains a value less than 100.
36. Write a `do-while` loop that asks the user to enter two numbers. The numbers should be added and the sum displayed. The user should be asked if he or she wishes to perform the operation again. If so, the loop should repeat; otherwise, it should terminate.
37. Write a `for` loop that displays the following set of numbers:

    `0, 10, 20, 30, 40, 50 . . . 1000`
38. Write a loop that asks the user to enter a number. The loop should iterate 10 times and keep a running total of the numbers entered.
39. Write a nested loop that displays 10 rows of '#' characters. There should be 15 '#' characters in each row.

40. Convert the following `while` loop to a `do-while` loop:

```
int x = 1;
while (x > 0)
{
    cout << "enter a number: ";
    cin >> x;
}
```

41. Convert the following `do-while` loop to a `while` loop:

```
char sure;
do
{
    cout << "Are you sure you want to quit? ";
    cin >> sure;
} while (sure != 'Y' && sure != 'N');
```

42. Convert the following `while` loop to a `for` loop:

```
int count = 0;
while (count < 50)
{
    cout << "count is " << count << endl;
    count++;
}
```

43. Convert the following `for` loop to a `while` loop:

```
for (int x = 50; x > 0; x--)
{
    cout << x << " seconds to go.\n";
}
```

44. Write code that does the following: Opens an output file with the filename Numbers.txt, uses a loop to write the numbers 1 through 100 to the file, then closes the file.

45. Write code that does the following: Opens the Numbers.txt file that was created by the code you wrote in Question 44, reads all of the numbers from the file and displays them, then closes the file.

46. Modify the code that you wrote in Question 45 so it adds all of the numbers read from the file and displays their total.

True or False

47. T F The operand of the increment and decrement operators can be any valid mathematical expression.

48. T F The `cout` statement in the following program segment will display 5:

```
int x = 5;
cout << x++;
```

49. T F The `cout` statement in the following program segment will display 5:

```
int x = 5;
cout << ++x;
```

50. T F The `while` loop is a pretest loop.

51. T F The `do-while` loop is a pretest loop.

52. T F The `for` loop is a posttest loop.

53. T F It is not necessary to initialize counter variables.

54. T F All three of the `for` loop's expressions may be omitted.
55. T F One limitation of the `for` loop is that only one variable may be initialized in the initialization expression.
56. T F Variables may be defined inside the body of a loop.
57. T F A variable may be defined in the initialization expression of the `for` loop.
58. T F In a nested loop, the outer loop executes faster than the inner loop.
59. T F In a nested loop, the inner loop goes through all of its iterations for every single iteration of the outer loop.
60. T F To calculate the total number of iterations of a nested loop, add the number of iterations of all the loops.
61. T F The `break` statement causes a loop to stop the current iteration and begin the next one.
62. T F The `continue` statement causes a terminated loop to resume.
63. T F In a nested loop, the `break` statement only interrupts the loop in which it is placed.
64. T F When you call an `ofstream` object's open member function, the specified file will be erased if it already exists.

Find the Errors

Each of the following programs has errors. Find as many as you can.

65.
```
// Find the error in this program.
#include <iostream>
using namespace std;

int main()
{
    int num1 = 0, num2 = 10, result;

    num1++;
    result = ++(num1 + num2);
    cout << num1 << " " << num2 << " " << result;
    return 0;
}
```

66.
```
// This program adds two numbers entered by the user.
#include <iostream>
using namespace std;

int main()
{
    int num1, num2;
    char again;

    while (again == 'y' || again == 'Y')
        cout << "Enter a number: ";
        cin >> num1;
        cout << "Enter another number: ";
        cin >> num2;
        cout << "Their sum is << (num1 + num2) << endl;
        cout << "Do you want to do this again? ";
        cin >> again;
     return 0;
}
```

67.
```
// This program uses a loop to raise a number to a power.
#include <iostream>
using namespace std;

int main()
{
    int num, bigNum, power, count;

    cout << "Enter an integer: ";
    cin >> num;
    cout << "What power do you want it raised to? ";
    cin >> power;
    bigNum = num;
    while (count++ < power);
        bigNum *= num;
    cout << "The result is << bigNum << endl;
    return 0;
}
```

68.
```
// This program averages a set of numbers.
#include <iostream>
using namespace std;

int main()
{
    int numCount, total;
    double average;

    cout << "How many numbers do you want to average? ";
    cin >> numCount;
    for (int count = 0; count < numCount; count++)
    {
        int num;
        cout << "Enter a number: ";
        cin >> num;
        total += num;
        count++;
    }
    average = total / numCount;
    cout << "The average is << average << endl;
    return 0;
}
```

69.
```
// This program displays the sum of two numbers.
#include <iostream>
using namespace std;

int main()
{
    int choice, num1, num2;
```

```
        do
        {
            cout << "Enter a number: ";
            cin >> num1;
            cout << "Enter another number: ";
            cin >> num2;
            cout << "Their sum is " << (num1 + num2) << endl;
            cout << "Do you want to do this again?\n";
            cout << "1 = yes, 0 = no\n";
            cin >> choice;
         } while (choice = 1)
         return 0;
    }
```

70.
```
// This program displays the sum of the numbers 1-100.
#include <iostream>
using namespace std;

int main()
{
    int count = 1, total;

    while (count <= 100)
        total += count;
    cout << "The sum of the numbers 1-100 is ";
    cout << total << endl;
    return 0;
}
```

Programming Challenges

1. **Sum of Numbers**

   Write a program that asks the user for a positive integer value. The program should use a loop to get the sum of all the integers from 1 up to the number entered. For example, if the user enters 50, the loop will find the sum of 1, 2, 3, 4, . . ., 50.

   Input Validation: Do not accept a negative starting number.

2. **Characters for the ASCII Codes**

   Write a program that uses a loop to display the characters for the ASCII codes 0 through 127. Display 16 characters on each line.

3. **Ocean Levels**

   Assuming the ocean's level is currently rising at about 1.5 millimeters per year, write a program that displays a table showing the number of millimeters that the ocean will have risen each year for the next 25 years.

VideoNote
Solving the Calories Burned Problem

4. **Calories Burned**

   Running on a particular treadmill you burn 3.6 calories per minute. Write a program that uses a loop to display the number of calories burned after 5, 10, 15, 20, 25, and 30 minutes.

5. **Membership Fees Increase**

   A country club, which currently charges $2,500 per year for membership, has announced it will increase its membership fee by 4 percent each year for the next 6 years. Write a program that uses a loop to display the projected rates for the next 6 years.

6. Distance Traveled

The distance a vehicle travels can be calculated as follows:

```
distance = speed * time
```

For example, if a train travels 40 miles per hour for 3 hours, the distance traveled is 120 miles.

Write a program that asks the user for the speed of a vehicle (in miles per hour) and how many hours it has traveled. The program should then use a loop to display the distance the vehicle has traveled for each hour of that time period. Here is an example of the output:

```
What is the speed of the vehicle in mph? 40
How many hours has it traveled? 3
Hour  Distance Traveled
--------------------------------
 1          40
 2          80
 3         120
```

Input Validation: Do not accept a negative number for speed and do not accept any value less than 1 for time traveled.

7. Pennies for Pay

Write a program that calculates how much a person would earn over a period of time if his or her salary is one penny the first day and two pennies the second day, and continues to double each day. The program should ask the user for the number of days. Display a table showing how much the salary was for each day, and then show the total pay at the end of the period. The output should be displayed in a dollar amount, not the number of pennies.

Input Validation: Do not accept a number less than 1 for the number of days worked.

8. Math Tutor

This program started in Programming Challenge 17, of the chapter "Expressions and Interactivity", and was modified in Programming Challenge 11 of the chapter "Making Decisions". Modify the program again so it displays a menu allowing the user to select an addition, subtraction, multiplication, or division problem. The final selection on the menu should let the user quit the program. After the user has finished the math problem, the program should display the menu again. This process is repeated until the user chooses to quit the program.

Input Validation: If the user selects an item not on the menu, display an error message and display the menu again.

9. Hotel Occupancy

Write a program that calculates the occupancy rate for a hotel. The program should start by asking the user how many floors the hotel has. A loop should then iterate once for each floor. In each iteration, the loop should ask the user for the number of rooms on the floor and how many of them are occupied. After all the iterations, the program should display how many rooms the hotel has, how many of them are occupied, how many are unoccupied, and the percentage of rooms that are occupied. The percentage may be calculated by dividing the number of rooms occupied by the number of rooms.

> **NOTE:** It is traditional that most hotels do not have a thirteenth floor. The loop in this program should skip the entire thirteenth iteration.

Input Validation: Do not accept a value less than 1 for the number of floors. Do not accept a number less than 10 for the number of rooms on a floor.

10. Average Rainfall

Write a program that uses nested loops to collect data and calculate the average rainfall over a period of years. The program should first ask for the number of years. The outer loop will iterate once for each year. The inner loop will iterate 12 times, once for each month. Each iteration of the inner loop will ask the user for the inches of rainfall for that month.

After all iterations, the program should display the number of months, the total inches of rainfall, and the average rainfall per month for the entire period.

Input Validation: Do not accept a number less than 1 for the number of years. Do not accept negative numbers for the monthly rainfall.

11. Population

Write a program that will predict the size of a population of organisms. The program should ask the user for the starting number of organisms, their average daily population increase (as a percentage), and the number of days they will multiply. A loop should display the size of the population for each day.

Input Validation: Do not accept a number less than 2 for the starting size of the population. Do not accept a negative number for average daily population increase. Do not accept a number less than 1 for the number of days they will multiply.

12. Celsius to Fahrenheit Table

In Programming Challenge 12 of the chapter "Expressions and Interactivity", you were asked to write a program that converts a Celsius temperature to Fahrenheit. Modify that program so that it uses a loop to display a table of the Celsius temperatures 0–20, and the Fahrenheit equivalents.

13. The Greatest and Least of These

Write a program with a loop that lets the user enter a series of integers. The user should enter −99 to signal the end of the series. After all the numbers have been entered, the program should display the largest and smallest numbers entered.

14. Student Line Up

A teacher has asked all her students to line up according to their first name. For example, in one class Amy will be at the front of the line, and Yolanda will be at the end. Write a program that prompts the user to enter the number of students in the class, then loops to read that many names. Once all the names have been read, it reports which student would be at the front of the line and which one would be at the end of the line. You may assume that no two students have the same name.

Input Validation: Do not accept a number less than 1 or greater than 25 for the number of students.

15. Payroll Report

Write a program that displays a weekly payroll report. A loop in the program should ask the user for the employee number, gross pay, state tax, federal tax, and FICA withholdings. The loop will terminate when 0 is entered for the employee number. After the data is entered, the program should display totals for gross pay, state tax, federal tax, FICA withholdings, and net pay.

Input Validation: Do not accept negative numbers for any of the items entered. Do not accept values for state, federal, or FICA withholdings that are greater than the gross pay. If the sum of state tax + federal tax + FICA withholdings for any employee is greater than gross pay, print an error message and ask the user to reenter the data for that employee.

16. Savings Account Balance

Write a program that calculates the balance of a savings account at the end of a period of time. It should ask the user for the annual interest rate, the starting balance, and the number of months that have passed since the account was established. A loop should then iterate once for every month, performing the following:

A) Ask the user for the amount deposited into the account during the month. (Do not accept negative numbers.) This amount should be added to the balance.
B) Ask the user for the amount withdrawn from the account during the month. (Do not accept negative numbers.) This amount should be subtracted from the balance.
C) Calculate the monthly interest. The monthly interest rate is the annual interest rate divided by 12. Multiply the monthly interest rate by the balance, and add the result to the balance.

After the last iteration, the program should display the ending balance, the total amount of deposits, the total amount of withdrawals, and the total interest earned.

> **NOTE:** If a negative balance is calculated at any point, a message should be displayed indicating the account has been closed and the loop should terminate.

17. Sales Bar Chart

Write a program that asks the user to enter today's sales for five stores. The program should then display a bar graph comparing each store's sales. Create each bar in the bar graph by displaying a row of asterisks. Each asterisk should represent $100 of sales.

Here is an example of the program's output:

```
Enter today's sales for store 1: 1000 [Enter]
Enter today's sales for store 2: 1200 [Enter]
Enter today's sales for store 3: 1800 [Enter]
Enter today's sales for store 4: 800 [Enter]
Enter today's sales for store 5: 1900 [Enter]

SALES BAR CHART
(Each * = $100)
Store 1: **********
Store 2: ************
Store 3: ******************
Store 4: ********
Store 5: *******************
```

18. Population Bar Chart

Write a program that produces a bar chart showing the population growth of Prairieville, a small town in the Midwest, at 20-year intervals during the past 100 years. The program should read in the population figures (rounded to the nearest 1,000 people) for 1900, 1920, 1940, 1960, 1980, and 2000 from a file. For each year, it should display the date and a bar consisting of one asterisk for each 1,000 people. The data can be found in the `People.txt` file.

Here is an example of how the chart might begin:

```
PRAIRIEVILLE POPULATION GROWTH
(each * represents 1,000 people)
1900 **
1920 ****
1940 *****
```

19. Budget Analysis

Write a program that asks the user to enter the amount that he or she has budgeted for a month. A loop should then prompt the user to enter each of his or her expenses for the month and keep a running total. When the loop finishes, the program should display the amount that the user is over or under budget.

20. Random Number Guessing Game

Write a program that generates a random number and asks the user to guess what the number is. If the user's guess is higher than the random number, the program should display "Too high, try again." If the user's guess is lower than the random number, the program should display "Too low, try again." The program should use a loop that repeats until the user correctly guesses the random number.

21. Random Number Guessing Game Enhancement

Enhance the program that you wrote for Programming Challenge 20 so it keeps a count of the number of guesses the user makes. When the user correctly guesses the random number, the program should display the number of guesses.

22. Square Display

Write a program that asks the user for a positive integer no greater than 15. The program should then display a square on the screen using the character 'X'. The number entered by the user will be the length of each side of the square. For example, if the user enters 5, the program should display the following:

```
XXXXX
XXXXX
XXXXX
XXXXX
XXXXX
```

If the user enters 8, the program should display the following:

```
XXXXXXXX
XXXXXXXX
XXXXXXXX
XXXXXXXX
XXXXXXXX
XXXXXXXX
XXXXXXXX
XXXXXXXX
```

23. Pattern Displays

Write a program that uses a loop to display Pattern A below, followed by another loop that displays Pattern B.

Pattern A	Pattern B
+	++++++++++
++	+++++++++
+++	++++++++
++++	+++++++
+++++	++++++
++++++	+++++
+++++++	++++
++++++++	+++
+++++++++	++
++++++++++	+

24. Using Files—Numeric Processing

If you have downloaded this chapter's source code from the Computer Science Portal, you will find a file named Random.txt in the Chapter 05 folder. (The Portal can be found at www.pearsonhighered.com/gaddis.) This file contains a long list of random numbers. Copy the file to your system, then write a program that opens the file, reads all the numbers from the file, and calculates the following:

A) The number of numbers in the file
B) The sum of all the numbers in the file (a running total)
C) The average of all the numbers in the file

The program should display the number of numbers found in the file, the sum of the numbers, and the average of the numbers.

25. Using Files—Student Line Up

Modify the Student Line Up program described in Programming Challenge 14 so it gets the names from a file. Names should be read in until there is no more data to read. If you have downloaded this chapter's source code you will find a file named LineUp.txt in the Chapter 05 folder. You can use this file to test the program.

26. Personal Web Page Generator

Write a program that asks the user for his or her name, then asks the user to enter a sentence that describes himself or herself. Here is an example of the program's screen:

```
Enter your name: Julie Taylor [Enter]
Describe yourself: I am a computer science major, a member of the Jazz club,
and I hope to work as a mobile app developer after I graduate. [Enter]
```

Once the user has entered the requested input, the program should create an HTML file, containing the input, for a simple webpage. Here is an example of the HTML content, using the sample input previously shown:

```
<html>
<head>
</head>
<body>
   <center>
      <h1>Julie Taylor</h1>
   </center>
   <hr />
   I am a computer science major, a member of the Jazz club,
   and I hope to work as a mobile app developer after I graduate.
   <hr />
</body>
</html>
```

27. **Average Steps Taken**

A Personal Fitness Tracker is a wearable device that tracks your physical activity, calories burned, heart rate, sleeping patterns, and so on. One common physical activity that most of these devices track is the number of steps you take each day.

If you have downloaded this chapter's source code, you will find a file named steps.txt in the Chapter 05 folder. The steps.txt file contains the number of steps a person has taken each day for a year. There are 365 lines in the file, and each line contains the number of steps taken during a day. (The first line is the number of steps taken on January 1, the second line is the number of steps taken on January 2, and so forth.) Write a program that reads the file, then displays the average number of steps taken for each month. (The data is from a year that was not a leap year, so February has 28 days.)

Answers to Checkpoints

1 A) 32
B) 33
C) 23
D) 34
E) It is true!
F) It is true!

2
```
int number;
cout << "Enter a number in the range 10 through 25: ";
cin >> number;
while (number < 10 || number > 25)
{
    cout << "Error! The number must be in the range "
         << "of 10 through 25. Enter a valid number: ";
    cin >> number;
}
```

3
```
char letter;
cout << "Enter Y for yes or N for no: ";
cin >> letter;
while (letter != 'Y' && letter != 'y' &&
       letter != 'N' && letter != 'n')
{
    cout << "Error! Enter either Y or N: ";
    cin >> letter;
}
```

4
```
string input;
cout << "Enter Yes or No: ";
cin >> input;
while ( (input != "Yes") && (input != "No") )
{
    cout << "Error! Enter either Yes or No: ";
    cin >> input;
}
```

5 A) `Hello World`
B) `10`
C) `8 4`

6 Initialization, test, and update

7 A) `int count = 1;`
B) `count <= 50;`
C) `count++`
D)
```
for (int count = 1; count <= 50; count++)
    cout << "I love to program\n";
```

8 A) `0246810`
B) `-5-4-3-2-101234`
C)
```
5
8
11
14
17
```

9
```
for (int count = 1; count <= 10; count++)
    cout << "Chris Coder\n";
```

10
```
for (int count = 1; count <= 49; count += 2)
    cout << count << endl;
```

11
```
for (int count = 0; count <= 100; count += 5)
    cout << count << endl;
```

12
```
int number, total = 0;
for (int count = 0; count < 7; count++)
{
    cout << "Enter a number: ";
    cin >> number;
    total += number;
}
```

13 The variable x is the counter variable. The variable y is the accumulator.

14 You must be sure to choose a sentinel value that could not be mistaken as a member of the data list.

15 Change the `while` loop to read:

```
while (points >= 0)
```

16 An output file is a file to which data is written. An input file is a file from which data is read.

17
1. Open the file
2. Process the file
3. Close the file

18 A text file contains data that has been encoded as text, using a scheme such ASCII or Unicode. Even if the file contains numbers, those numbers are stored in the file as a series of characters. As a result, the file may be opened and viewed in a text editor such as Notepad. A binary file contains data that has not been converted to text. As a consequence, you cannot view the contents of a binary file with a text editor.

19 When you work with a sequential access file, you access data from the beginning of the file to the end of the file. When you work with a random access file, you can jump directly to any piece of data in the file without reading the data that comes before it.

20 `ofstream`

21 `ifstream`

22
```
ofstream outputFile("num.txt");
for (int num = 1; num <= 10; num++)
     outputFile << num << endl;
outputFile.close();
```

23
```
ifstream inputFile("num.txt");
int num;
while (inputFile >> num)
       cout << num << endl;
inputFile.close();
```

Answers to Odd Numbered Review Questions

1. By indenting the statements, you make them stand out from the surrounding code. This helps you to identify at a glance the statements that are conditionally executed by a loop.
3. Because they are only executed when a condition is true.
5. The `while` loop
7. The `for` loop
9. An accumulator is used to keep a running total of numbers. In a loop, a value is usually added to the current value of the accumulator. If it is not properly initialized, it will not contain the correct total.

11. `fstream`

13. `ifstream`

15. A file's read position marks the location of the next byte that will be read from the file. When an input file is opened, its read position is initially set to the first byte in the file.

17. prefix

19. body

21. pretest

23. infinite or endless

25. running total

27. sentinel

29. `while` and `for`

31. initialization, test, update

33. `break`

35.
```
int product = 0, num;
while (product < 100)
{
    cin >> num;
    product = num * 10;
}
```

37.
```
for (int x = 0; x <= 1000; x += 10)
     cout << x;
```

39.
```
for (int row = 0; row < 10; row++)
{
    for (int col = 0; col < 15; col++)
         cout << '#';
    cout << endl;
}
```

41.
```
char sure = 'x';
while (sure != 'Y' && sure != 'N')
{
    cout << "Are you sure you want quit? "
    cin >> sure;
}
```

43.
```
int x = 50;
while (x > 0)
{
    cout << x << " seconds to go.\n";
    x--;
}
```

45.
```
ifstream inputFile("Numbers.txt");
int number;
while (inputFile >> number)
    cout << number << endl;
inputFile.close();
```

47. False
49. False
51. False
53. False
55. False
57. True
59. True
61. False
63. True
65. The statement `result = ++(num1 + num2);` is invalid.
67. The `while` statement should not end with a semicolon.
It could also be argued that `bigNum` should be defined a `long`.
`count` should be initialized to 1.
69. The expression tested by the `do-while` loop should be `choice == 1` instead of `choice = 1`.

Credits

Functions

TOPICS

1 Focus on Software Engineering: Modular Programming

CONCEPT: A program may be broken up into manageable functions.

A function is a collection of statements that performs a specific task. In this chapter, you will learn how to create your own functions that can be used like library functions.

Functions are commonly used to break a problem down into small, manageable pieces. Instead of writing one long function that contains all of the statements necessary to solve a problem, several small functions that each solve a specific part of the problem can be written. These small functions can then be executed in the desired order to solve the problem. This approach is sometimes called *divide and conquer* because a large problem is divided

From Chapter 6 of *Starting Out with C++: From Control Structures through Objects*, Ninth Edition. Tony Gaddis.

into several smaller problems that are easily solved. Figure 1 illustrates this idea by comparing two programs: one that uses a long, complex function containing all of the statements necessary to solve a problem, and another that divides a problem into smaller problems, each of which is handled by a separate function.

Figure 1 Modular programming

This program has one long, complex function containing all of the statements necessary to solve a problem.

```
int main()
{
   statement;
   statement;
   statement;
   statement;
   statement;
   statement;
   statement;
   statement;
   statement;
   statement;
   statement;
   statement;
   statement;
   statement;
   statement;
   statement;
   statement;
   statement;
   statement;
   statement;
   statement;
   statement;
   statement;
   statement;
}
```

In this program, the problem has been divided into smaller problems, each of which is handled by a separate function.

```
int main()
{
   statement;
   statement;
   statement;
}
```

main function

```
void function2()
{
   statement;
   statement;
   statement;
}
```

function 2

```
void function3()
{
   statement;
   statement;
   statement;
}
```

function 3

```
void function4()
{
   statement;
   statement;
   statement;
}
```

function 4

Another reason to write functions is that they simplify programs. If a specific task is performed in several places in a program, a function can be written once to perform that task, then be executed anytime it is needed. This benefit of using functions is known as *code reuse* because you are writing the code to perform a task once, then reusing it each time you need to perform the task.

2 Defining and Calling Functions

CONCEPT: A function call is a statement that causes a function to execute. A function definition contains the statements that make up the function.

When creating a function, you must write its *definition.* All function definitions have the following parts:

Return type: A function can send a value to the part of the program that executed it. The return type is the data type of the value that is sent from the function.

Name: You should give each function a descriptive name. In general, the same rules that apply to variable names also apply to function names.

Parameter list: The program can send data into a function. The parameter list is a list of variables that hold the values being passed to the function.

Body: The body of a function is the set of statements that perform the function's operation. They are enclosed in a set of braces.

Figure 2 shows the definition of a simple function with the various parts labeled.

Figure 2 Function definition

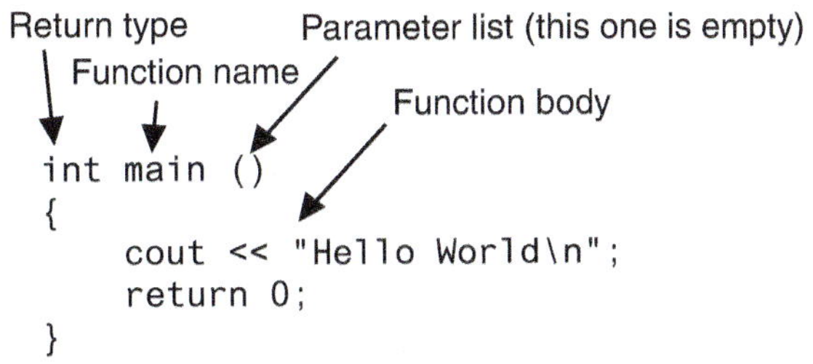

The line in the definition that reads `int main()` is called the *function header.*

`void` Functions

A function can return a value. The `main` function you have seen in this chapter is declared to return an `int` value to the operating system. The `return 0;` statement causes the value 0 to be returned when the `main` function finishes executing.

It isn't necessary for all functions to return a value, however. Some functions simply perform one or more statements, and then terminate. These are called `void` *functions.* The `displayMessage` function, which follows, is an example.

```
void displayMessage()
{
   cout << "Hello from the function displayMessage.\n";
}
```

The function's name is `displayMessage`. This name gives an indication of what the function does: It displays a message. You should always give functions names that reflect their purpose. Notice the function's return type is `void`. This means the function does not return a value to the part of the program that executed it. Also notice the function has no `return` statement. It simply displays a message on the screen and exits.

Calling a Function

A function is executed when it is *called*. Function `main` is called automatically when a program starts, but all other functions must be executed by *function call* statements. When a function is called, the program branches to that function and executes the statements in its body. Let's look at Program 1, which contains two functions: `main` and `displayMessage`.

Program 1

```
1  // This program has two functions: main and displayMessage
2  #include <iostream>
3  using namespace std;
4
5  //*****************************************
6  // Definition of function displayMessage  *
7  // This function displays a greeting.     *
8  //*****************************************
9
10 void displayMessage()
11 {
12     cout << "Hello from the function displayMessage.\n";
13 }
14
15 //*****************************************
16 // Function main                          *
17 //*****************************************
18
19 int main()
20 {
21     cout << "Hello from main.\n";
22     displayMessage();
23     cout << "Back in function main again.\n";
24     return 0;
25 }
```

Program Output

```
Hello from main.
Hello from the function displayMessage.
Back in function main again.
```

The function `displayMessage` is called by the following statement in line 22:

```
displayMessage();
```

This statement is the function call. It is simply the name of the function followed by a set of parentheses and a semicolon. Let's compare this with the function header:

Function Header ——→ `void displayMessage()`

Function Call ——→ `displayMessage();`

The function header is part of the function definition. It declares the function's return type, name, and parameter list. It is not terminated with a semicolon because the definition of the function's body follows it.

The function call is a statement that executes the function, so it is terminated with a semicolon like all other C++ statements. The return type is not listed in the function call, and, if the program is not passing data into the function, the parentheses are left empty.

> **NOTE:** Later in this chapter, you will see how data can be passed into a function by being listed inside the parentheses.

Even though the program starts executing at `main`, the function `displayMessage` is defined first. This is because the compiler must know the function's return type, the number of parameters, and the type of each parameter before the function is called. One way to ensure the compiler will know this information is to place the function definition before all calls to that function. (Later, you will see an alternative, preferred method of accomplishing this.)

> **NOTE:** You should always document your functions by writing comments that describe what they do. These comments should appear just before the function definition.

Notice how Program 1 flows. It starts, of course, in function `main`. When the call to `displayMessage` is encountered, the program branches to that function and performs its statements. Once `displayMessage` has finished executing, the program branches back to function `main` and resumes with the line that follows the function call. This is illustrated in Figure 3.

Figure 3 A function call

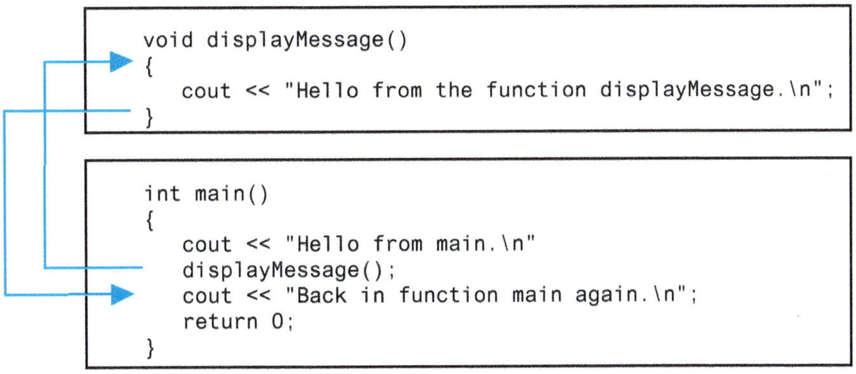

Function call statements may be used in control structures like loops, `if` statements, and `switch` statements. Program 2 places the `displayMessage` function call inside a loop.

Program 2

```
// The function displayMessage is repeatedly called from a loop.
#include <iostream>
using namespace std;

//******************************************
// Definition of function displayMessage  *
// This function displays a greeting.     *
//******************************************

void displayMessage()
{
    cout << "Hello from the function displayMessage.\n";
}

//******************************************
// Function main                          *
//******************************************

int main()
{
    cout << "Hello from main.\n";
    for (int count = 0; count < 5; count++)
        displayMessage(); // Call displayMessage
    cout << "Back in function main again.\n";
    return 0;
}
```

Program Output

```
Hello from main.
Hello from the function displayMessage.
Hello from the function displayMessage.
Hello from the function displayMessage.
Hello from the function displayMessage.
Hello from the function displayMessage.
Back in function main again.
```

It is possible to have many functions and function calls in a program. Program 3 has three functions: `main`, `first`, and `second`.

Program 3

```
// This program has three functions: main, first, and second.
#include <iostream>
using namespace std;

```

```
5  //*******************************************
6  // Definition of function first            *
7  // This function displays a message.       *
8  //*******************************************
9
10 void first()
11 {
12     cout << "I am now inside the function first.\n";
13 }
14
15 //*******************************************
16 // Definition of function second           *
17 // This function displays a message.       *
18 //*******************************************
19
20 void second()
21 {
22     cout << "I am now inside the function second.\n";
23 }
24
25 //*******************************************
26 // Function main                           *
27 //*******************************************
28
29 int main()
30 {
31     cout << "I am starting in function main.\n";
32     first();     // Call function first
33     second();    // Call function second
34     cout << "Back in function main again. \n";
35     return 0;
36 }
```

Program Output

```
I am starting in function main.
I am now inside the function first.
I am now inside the function second.
Back in function main again.
```

In lines 32 and 33 of Program 3, function `main` contains a call to `first` and a call to `second`:

```
first();
second();
```

Each call statement causes the program to branch to a function then back to `main` when the function is finished. Figure 4 illustrates the paths taken by the program.

Figure 4 Paths taken by the program

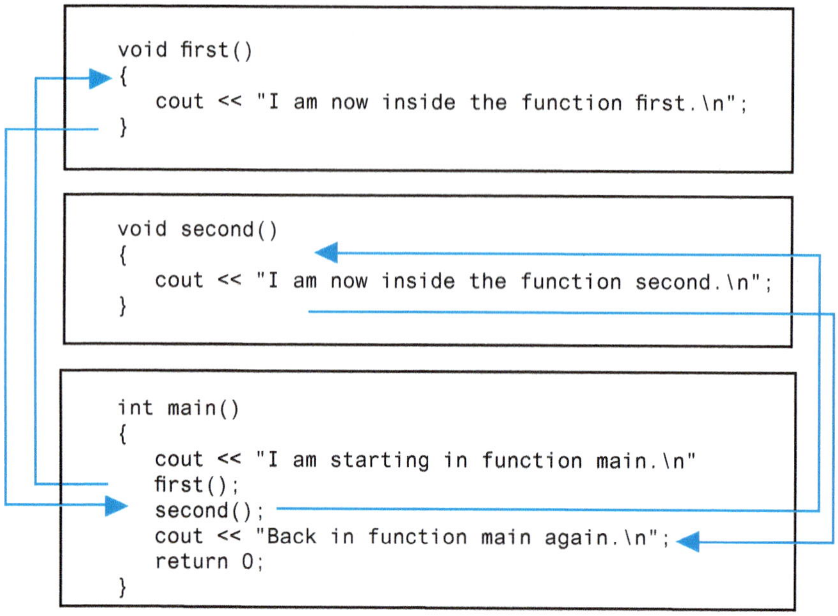

Functions may also be called in a hierarchical, or layered, fashion. This is demonstrated by Program 4, which has three functions: `main`, `deep`, and `deeper`.

Program 4

```
// This program has three functions: main, deep, and deeper
#include <iostream>
using namespace std;

//*****************************************
// Definition of function deeper          *
// This function displays a message.      *
//*****************************************

void deeper()
{
     cout << "I am now inside the function deeper.\n";
}

//*****************************************
// Definition of function deep            *
// This function displays a message.      *
//*****************************************

```

```
void deep()
{
    cout << "I am now inside the function deep.\n";
    deeper();     // Call function deeper
    cout << "Now I am back in deep.\n";
}

//*****************************************
// Function main                          *
//*****************************************

int main()
{
    cout << "I am starting in function main.\n";
    deep();     // Call function deep
    cout << "Back in function main again.\n";
    return 0;
}
```

Program Output

```
I am starting in function main.
I am now inside the function deep.
I am now inside the function deeper.
Now I am back in deep.
Back in function main again.
```

In Program 4, function main only calls the function deep. In turn, deep calls deeper. The paths taken by the program are shown in Figure 5.

Figure 5 Layered function calls

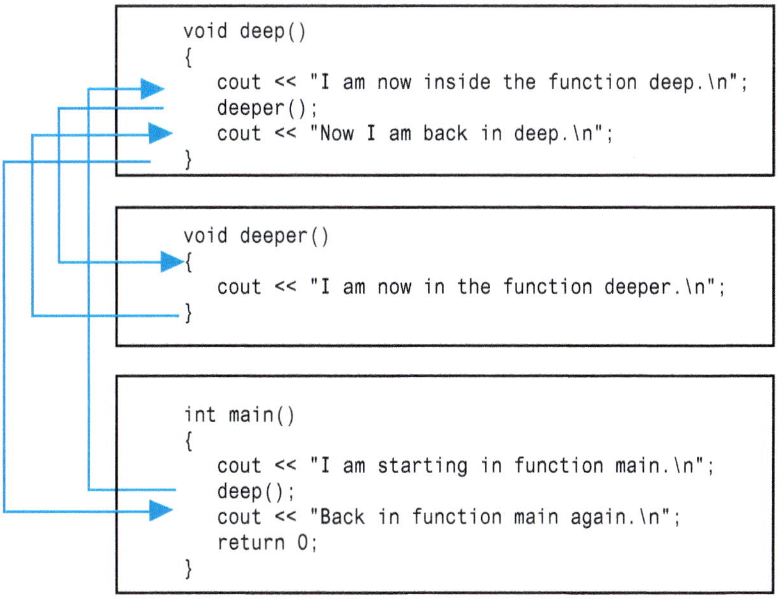

Checkpoint

1 Is the following a function header or a function call?

```
calcTotal();
```

2 Is the following a function header or a function call?

```
void showResults()
```

3 What will the output of the following program be if the user enters 10?

```
#include <iostream>
using namespace std;

void func1()
{
    cout << "Able was I\n";
}

void func2()
{
    cout << "I saw Elba\n";
}

int main()
{
    int input;
    cout << "Enter a number: ";
    cin >> input;
    if (input < 10)
    {
        func1();
        func2();
    }
    else
    {
        func2();
        func1();
    }
    return 0;
}
```

4 The following program skeleton determines whether a person qualifies for a credit card. To qualify, the person must have worked on his or her current job for at least 2 years, and make at least $17,000 per year. Finish the program by writing the definitions of the functions `qualify` and `noQualify`. The function `qualify` should explain that the applicant qualifies for the card, and that the annual interest rate is 12 percent. The function `noQualify` should explain that the applicant does not qualify for the card and give a general explanation why.

```
#include <iostream>
using namespace std;

// You must write definitions for the two functions qualify
// and noQualify.
```

```
int main()
{
   double salary;
   int years;

   cout << "This program will determine if you qualify\n";
   cout << "for our credit card.\n";
   cout << "What is your annual salary? ";
   cin >> salary;
   cout << "How many years have you worked at your ";
   cout << "current job? ";
   cin >> years;
   if (salary >= 17000.0 && years >= 2)
      qualify();
   else
      noQualify();
   return 0;
}
```

3 Function Prototypes

CONCEPT: A function prototype eliminates the need to place a function definition before all calls to the function.

Before the compiler encounters a call to a particular function, it must already know the function's return type, the number of parameters it uses, and the type of each parameter. (You will learn how to use parameters in the next section.)

One way of ensuring that the compiler has this information is to place the function definition before all calls to that function. This was the approach taken in Programs 1, 2, 3, and 4. Another method is to declare the function with a *function prototype*. Here is a prototype for the `displayMessage` function in Program 1:

```
void displayMessage();
```

The prototype looks similar to the function header, except there is a semicolon at the end. The statement above tells the compiler that the function `displayMessage` has a `void` return type (it doesn't return a value) and uses no parameters.

NOTE: Function prototypes are also known as *function declarations*.

WARNING! You must place either the function definition or the function prototype ahead of all calls to the function. Otherwise, the program will not compile.

Function prototypes are usually placed near the top of a program so the compiler will encounter them before any function calls. Program 5 is a modification of Program 3. The definitions of the functions `first` and `second` have been placed after `main`, and a function prototype has been placed after the `using namespace std` statement.

Program 5

```
1   // This program has three functions: main, first, and second.
2   #include <iostream>
3   using namespace std;
4
5   // Function Prototypes
6   void first();
7   void second();
8
9   int main()
10  {
11      cout << "I am starting in function main.\n";
12      first();     // Call function first
13      second();    // Call function second
14      cout << "Back in function main again.\n";
15      return 0;
16  }
17
18  //*************************************
19  // Definition of function first.     *
20  // This function displays a message.  *
21  //*************************************
22
23  void first()
24  {
25      cout << "I am now inside the function first.\n";
26  }
27
28  //*************************************
29  // Definition of function second.    *
30  // This function displays a message.  *
31  //*************************************
32
33  void second()
34  {
35      cout << "I am now inside the function second.\n";
36  }
```

Program Output

(The program's output is the same as the output of Program 3.)

When the compiler is reading Program 5, it encounters the calls to the functions `first` and `second` in lines 12 and 13 before it has read the definition of those functions. Because of the function prototypes, however, the compiler already knows the return type and parameter information of `first` and `second`.

NOTE: Although some programmers make `main` the last function in the program, many prefer it to be first because it is the program's starting point.

4 Sending Data into a Function

CONCEPT: When a function is called, the program may send values into the function.

VideoNote
Functions and Arguments

Values sent into a function are called *arguments*. You're already familiar with how to use arguments in a function call. In the following statement, the function `pow` is being called and two arguments, 2.0 and 4.0, are passed to it:

```
result = pow(2.0, 4.0);
```

By using *parameters*, you can design your own functions that accept data this way. A parameter is a special variable that holds a value being passed into a function. Here is the definition of a function that uses a parameter:

```
void displayValue(int num)
{
    cout << "The value is " << num << endl;
}
```

Notice the integer variable definition inside the parentheses (`int num`). The variable `num` is a parameter. This enables the function `displayValue` to accept an integer value as an argument. Program 6 is a complete program using this function.

> **NOTE:** In this text, the values that are passed into a function are called arguments, and the variables that receive those values are called parameters. There are several variations of these terms in use. Some call the arguments *actual parameters* and call the parameters *formal parameters*. Others use the terms *actual argument* and *formal argument*. Regardless of which set of terms you use, it is important to be consistent.

Program 6

```
// This program demonstrates a function with a parameter.
#include <iostream>
using namespace std;

// Function Prototype
void displayValue(int);

int main()
{
    cout << "I am passing 5 to displayValue.\n";
    displayValue(5);  // Call displayValue with argument 5
    cout << "Now I am back in main.\n";
    return 0;
}

```

(program continues)

Program 6 *(continued)*

```
16  //*************************************************************
17  // Definition of function displayValue.                      *
18  // It uses an integer parameter whose value is displayed.*
19  //*************************************************************
20
21  void displayValue(int num)
22  {
23      cout << "The value is " << num << endl;
24  }
```

Program Output

```
I am passing 5 to displayValue.
The value is 5
Now I am back in main.
```

First, notice the function prototype for `displayValue` in line 6:

```
void displayValue(int);
```

It is not necessary to list the name of the parameter variable inside the parentheses. Only its data type is required. The function prototype shown above could optionally have been written as

```
void displayValue(int num);
```

However, the compiler ignores the name of the parameter variable in the function prototype.

In `main`, the `displayValue` function is called with the argument 5 inside the parentheses. The number 5 is passed into `num`, which is `displayValue`'s parameter. This is illustrated in Figure 6.

Figure 6 An argument passed to a function

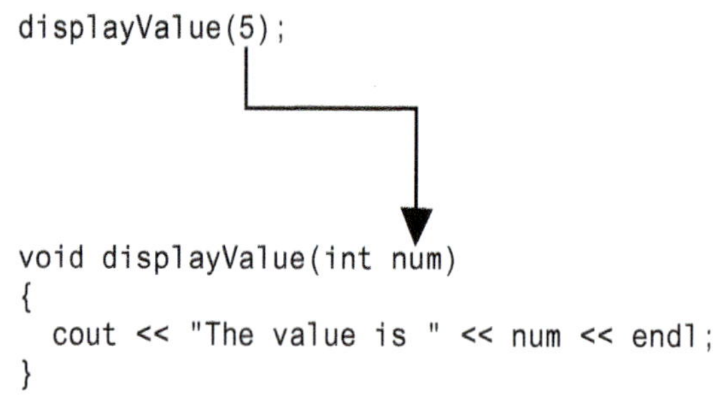

Any argument listed inside the parentheses of a function call is copied into the function's parameter variable. In essence, parameter variables are initialized to the value of their corresponding arguments. Program 7 shows the function `displayValue` being called several times with a different argument being passed each time.

Program 7

```
// This program demonstrates a function with a parameter.
#include <iostream>
using namespace std;

// Function Prototype
void displayValue(int);

int main()
{
    cout << "I am passing several values to displayValue.\n";
    displayValue(5);  // Call displayValue with argument 5
    displayValue(10); // Call displayValue with argument 10
    displayValue(2);  // Call displayValue with argument 2
    displayValue(16); // Call displayValue with argument 16
    cout << "Now I am back in main.\n";
    return 0;
}

//*********************************************************
// Definition of function displayValue.                  *
// It uses an integer parameter whose value is displayed.*
//*********************************************************

void displayValue(int num)
{
    cout << "The value is " << num << endl;
}
```

Program Output

```
I am passing several values to displayValue.
The value is 5
The value is 10
The value is 2
The value is 16
Now I am back in main.
```

WARNING! When passing a variable as an argument, simply write the variable name inside the parentheses of the function call. Do not write the data type of the argument variable in the function call. For example, the following function call will cause an error:

```
displayValue(int x); // Error!
```

The function call should appear as

```
displayValue(x);      // Correct
```

Each time the function is called in Program 7, `num` takes on a different value. Any expression whose value could normally be assigned to `num` may be used as an argument. For example, the following function call would pass the value 8 into `num`:

```
displayValue(3 + 5);
```

If you pass an argument whose type is not the same as the parameter's type, the argument will be promoted or demoted automatically. For instance, the argument in the following function call would be truncated, causing the value 4 to be passed to num:

```
displayValue(4.7);
```

Often, it's useful to pass several arguments into a function. Program 8 shows the definition of a function with three parameters.

Program 8

```
// This program demonstrates a function with three parameters.
#include <iostream>
using namespace std;

// Function Prototype
void showSum(int, int, int);

int main()
{
    int value1, value2, value3;

    // Get three integers.
    cout << "Enter three integers and I will display ";
    cout << "their sum: ";
    cin >> value1 >> value2 >> value3;

    // Call showSum passing three arguments.
    showSum(value1, value2, value3);
    return 0;
}

//**************************************************************
// Definition of function showSum.                             *
// It uses three integer parameters. Their sum is displayed.*
//**************************************************************

void showSum(int num1, int num2, int num3)
{
    cout << (num1 + num2 + num3) << endl;
}
```

Program Output with Example Input Shown in Bold

```
Enter three integers and I will display their sum: 4 8 7 [Enter]
19
```

In the function header for showSum, the parameter list contains three variable definitions separated by commas:

```
void showSum(int num1, int num2, int num3)
```

WARNING! Each parameter variable in a parameter list must have a data type listed before its name. For example, a compiler error would occur if the parameter list for the showSum function were defined as shown in the following header:

```
void showSum(int num1, num2, num3) // Error!
```

A data type for all three of the parameter variables must be listed, as shown here:

```
void showSum(int num1, int num2, int num3) // Correct
```

In the function call in line 18, the variables value1, value2, and value3 are passed as arguments:

```
showSum(value1, value2, value3);
```

When a function with multiple parameters is called, the arguments are passed to the parameters in order. This is illustrated in Figure 7.

Figure 7 Multiple arguments

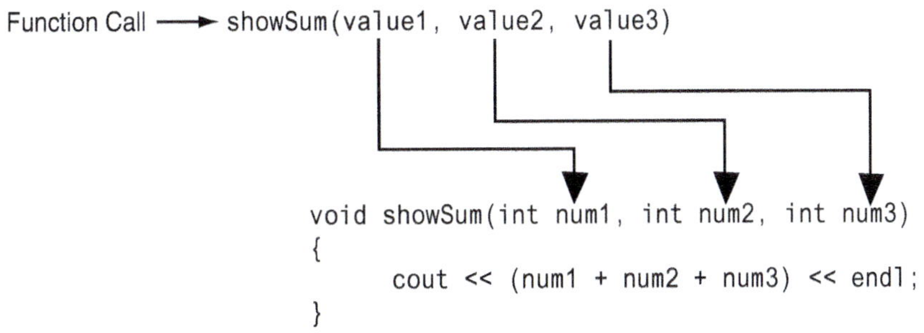

The following function call will cause 5 to be passed into the num1 parameter, 10 to be passed into num2, and 15 to be passed into num3:

```
showSum(5, 10, 15);
```

However, the following function call will cause 15 to be passed into the num1 parameter, 5 to be passed into num2, and 10 to be passed into num3:

```
showSum(15, 5, 10);
```

NOTE: The function prototype must list the data type of each parameter.

NOTE: Like all variables, parameters have a scope. The scope of a parameter is limited to the body of the function that uses it.

5 Passing Data by Value

CONCEPT: When an argument is passed into a parameter, only a copy of the argument's value is passed. Changes to the parameter do not affect the original argument.

As you've seen in this chapter, parameters are special-purpose variables that are defined inside the parentheses of a function definition. They are separate and distinct from the arguments that are listed inside the parentheses of a function call. The values that are stored in the parameter variables are copies of the arguments. Normally, when a parameter's value is changed inside a function, it has no effect on the original argument. Program 9 demonstrates this concept.

Program 9

```
// This program demonstrates that changes to a function parameter
// have no effect on the original argument.
#include <iostream>
using namespace std;

// Function Prototype
void changeMe(int);

int main()
{
    int number = 12;

    // Display the value in number.
    cout << "number is " << number << endl;

    // Call changeMe, passing the value in number
    // as an argument.
    changeMe(number);

    // Display the value in number again.
    cout << "Now back in main again, the value of ";
    cout << "number is " << number << endl;
    return 0;
}

//**************************************************************
// Definition of function changeMe.                            *
// This function changes the value of the parameter myValue.   *
//**************************************************************
```

```

void changeMe(int myValue)
{
    // Change the value of myValue to 0.
    myValue = 0;

    // Display the value in myValue.
    cout << "Now the value is " << myValue << endl;
}
```

Program Output

```
number is 12
Now the value is 0
Now back in main again, the value of number is 12
```

Even though the parameter variable `myValue` is changed in the `changeMe` function, the argument `number` is not modified. The `myValue` variable contains only a copy of the `number` variable.

The `changeMe` function does not have access to the original argument. When only a copy of an argument is passed to a function, it is said to be *passed by value*. This is because the function receives a copy of the argument's value and does not have access to the original argument.

Figure 8 illustrates that a parameter variable's storage location in memory is separate from that of the original argument.

Figure 8 The argument and the parameter are separate

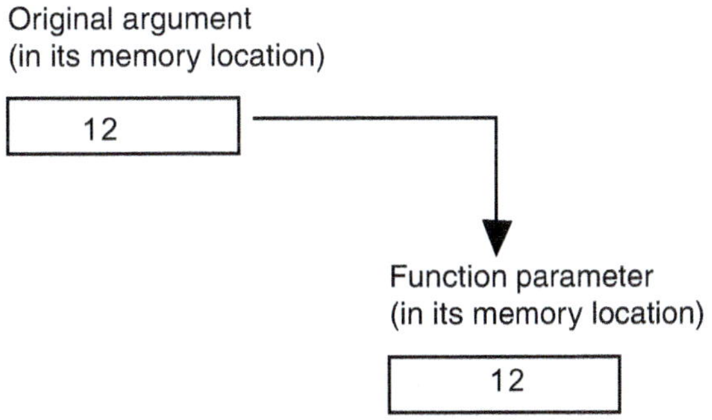

NOTE: Later in this chapter, you will learn ways to give a function access to its original arguments.

6 Focus on Software Engineering: Using Functions in a Menu-Driven Program

CONCEPT: Functions are ideal for use in menu-driven programs. When the user selects an item from a menu, the program can call the appropriate function.

Program 10 shows the program redesigned as a modular program. A *modular* program is broken up into functions that perform specific tasks.

Program 10

```
// This is a menu-driven program that makes a function call
// for each selection the user makes.
#include <iostream>
#include <iomanip>
using namespace std;

// Function prototypes
void showMenu();
void showFees(double, int);

int main()
{
    int choice;       // To hold a menu choice
    int months;       // To hold a number of months

    // Constants for the menu choices
    const int ADULT_CHOICE = 1,
              CHILD_CHOICE = 2,
              SENIOR_CHOICE = 3,
              QUIT_CHOICE = 4;

    // Constants for membership rates
    const double ADULT = 40.0,
                 CHILD = 20.0;
                 SENIOR = 30.0,

    // Set up numeric output formatting.
    cout << fixed << showpoint << setprecision(2);

    do
    {
        // Display the menu and get the user's choice.
        showMenu();
        cin >> choice;

        // Validate the menu selection.
        while (choice < ADULT_CHOICE || choice > QUIT_CHOICE)
        {
```

```
            cout << "Please enter a valid menu choice: ";
            cin >> choice;
        }

        // If the user does not want to quit, proceed.
        if (choice != QUIT_CHOICE)
        {
            // Get the number of months.
            cout << "For how many months? ";
            cin >> months;

            // Display the membership fees.
            switch (choice)
            {
                case ADULT_CHOICE:
                     showFees(ADULT, months);
                     break;
                case CHILD_CHOICE:
                     showFees(CHILD, months);
                     break;
                case SENIOR_CHOICE:
                     showFees(SENIOR, months);
            }
        }
    } while (choice != QUIT_CHOICE);
    return 0;
}

//*****************************************************************
// Definition of function showMenu which displays the menu.       *
//*****************************************************************

void showMenu()
{
    cout << "\n\t\tHealth Club Membership Menu\n\n"
         << "1. Standard Adult Membership\n"
         << "2. Child Membership\n"
         << "3. Senior Citizen Membership\n"
         << "4. Quit the Program\n\n"
         << "Enter your choice: ";
}

//*****************************************************************
// Definition of function showFees. The memberRate parameter holds*
// the monthly membership rate and the months parameter holds the *
// number of months. The function displays the total charges.     *
//*****************************************************************

void showFees(double memberRate, int months)
{
    cout << "The total charges are $"
         << (memberRate * months) << endl;
}
```

(program output continues)

Program 10 *(continued)*

Program Output with Example Input Shown in Bold

```
        Health Club Membership Menu

1. Standard Adult Membership
2. Child Membership
3. Senior Citizen Membership
4. Quit the Program

Enter your choice: 1 [Enter]
For how many months? 12 [Enter]
The total charges are $480.00

        Health Club Membership Menu

1. Standard Adult Membership
2. Child Membership
3. Senior Citizen Membership
4. Quit the Program

Enter your choice: 4 [Enter]
```

Let's take a closer look at this program. First notice the `showMenu` function in lines 71 through 79. This function displays the menu and is called from the `main` function in line 33.

The `showFees` function appears in lines 87 through 91. Its purpose is to display the total fees for a membership lasting a specified number of months. The function accepts two arguments: the monthly membership fee (a `double`) and the number of months of membership (an `int`). The function uses these values to calculate and display the total charges. For example, if we wanted the function to display the fees for an adult membership lasting 6 months, we would pass the `ADULT` constant as the first argument, and 6 as the second argument.

The `showFees` function is called from three different locations in the `switch` statement, which is in the `main` function. The first location is line 54. This statement is executed when the user has selected item 1, standard adult membership, from the menu. The `showFees` function is called with the `ADULT` constant and the `months` variable passed as arguments. The second location is line 57. This statement is executed when the user has selected item 2, child membership, from the menu. The `showFees` function is called in this line with the `CHILD` constant and the `months` variable passed as arguments. The third location is line 60. This statement is executed when the user has selected item 3, senior citizen membership, from the menu. The `showFees` function is called with the `SENIOR` constant and the `months` variable passed as arguments. Each time the `showFees` function is called, it displays the total membership fees for the specified type of membership, for the specified number of months.

Checkpoint

5 Indicate which of the following is the function prototype, the function header, and the function call:

```
void showNum(double num)

void showNum(double);

showNum(45.67);
```

6 Write a function named `timesTen`. The function should have an integer parameter named `number`. When `timesTen` is called, it should display the product of `number` times ten. (*Note*: Just write the function. Do not write a complete program.)

7 Write a function prototype for the `timesTen` function you wrote in Question 6.

8 What is the output of the following program?

```
#include <iostream>
using namespace std;

void showDouble(int); // Function prototype

int main()
{
    int num;

    for (num = 0; num < 10; num++)
        showDouble(num);
    return 0;
}

// Definition of function showDouble.
void showDouble(int value)
{
    cout << value << "\t" << (value * 2) << endl;
}
```

9 What is the output of the following program?

```
#include <iostream>
using namespace std;

void func1(double, int); // Function prototype

int main()
{
    int x = 0;
    double y = 1.5;

    cout << x << " " << y << endl;
    func1(y, x);
    cout << x << " " << y << endl;
    return 0;
}
```

```
void func1(double a, int b)
{
    cout << a << " " << b << endl;
    a = 0.0;
    b = 10;
    cout << a << " " << b << endl;
}
```

10 The following program skeleton asks for the number of hours you've worked and your hourly pay rate. It then calculates and displays your wages. The function showDollars, which you are to write, formats the output of the wages.

```
#include <iostream>
using namespace std;

void showDollars(double); // Function prototype

int main()
{
    double payRate, hoursWorked, wages;

    cout << "How many hours have you worked? "
    cin >> hoursWorked;
    cout << "What is your hourly pay rate? ";
    cin >> payRate;
    wages = hoursWorked * payRate;
    showDollars(wages);
    return 0;
}

// You must write the definition of the function showDollars
// here. It should take one parameter of the type double.
// The function should display the message "Your wages are $"
// followed by the value of the parameter. It should be displayed
// with 2 places of precision after the decimal point, in fixed
// notation, and the decimal point should always display.
```

7 The return Statement

CONCEPT: The return statement causes a function to end immediately.

When the last statement in a void function has finished executing, the function terminates and the program returns to the statement following the function call. It's possible, however, to force a function to return before the last statement has been executed. When the return statement is encountered, the function immediately terminates and control of the program returns to the statement that called the function. This is demonstrated in Program 11. The function divide shows the quotient of arg1 divided by arg2. If arg2 is set to zero, the function returns.

Program 11

```
1   // This program uses a function to perform division. If division
2   // by zero is detected, the function returns.
3   #include <iostream>
4   using namespace std;
5
6   // Function prototype.
7   void divide(double, double);
8
9   int main()
10  {
11      double num1, num2;
12
13      cout << "Enter two numbers and I will divide the first\n";
14      cout << "number by the second number: ";
15      cin >> num1 >> num2;
16      divide(num1, num2);
17      return 0;
18  }
19
20  //***************************************************************
21  // Definition of function divide.                              *
22  // Uses two parameters: arg1 and arg2. The function divides arg1 *
23  // by arg2 and shows the result. If arg2 is zero, however, the   *
24  // function returns.                                            *
25  //***************************************************************
26
27  void divide(double arg1, double arg2)
28  {
29      if (arg2 == 0.0)
30      {
31          cout << "Sorry, I cannot divide by zero.\n";
32          return;
33      }
34      cout << "The quotient is " << (arg1 / arg2) << endl;
35  }
```

Program Output with Example Input Shown in Bold

```
Enter two numbers and I will divide the first
number by the second number: 12 0 [Enter]
Sorry, I cannot divide by zero.
```

In the example running of the program, the user entered 12 and 0 as input. In line 16, the `divide` function was called, passing 12 into the `arg1` parameter and 0 into the `arg2` parameter. Inside the `divide` function, the `if` statement in line 29 executes. Because `arg2` is equal to 0.0, the code in lines 31 and 32 executes. When the `return` statement in line 32 executes, the `divide` function immediately ends. This means the `cout` statement in line 34 does not execute. The program resumes at line 17 in the `main` function.

8 Returning a Value from a Function

CONCEPT: A function may send a value back to the part of the program that called the function.

You've seen that data may be passed into a function by way of parameter variables. Data may also be returned from a function, back to the statement that called it. Functions that return a value are appropriately known as *value-returning functions*.

The pow function, which you have already seen, is an example of a value-returning function. Here is an example:

VideoNote
Value-Returning Functions

```
double x;
x = pow(4.0, 2.0);
```

The second line in this code calls the pow function, passing 4.0 and 2.0 as arguments. The function calculates the value of 4.0 raised to the power of 2.0 and returns that value. The value, which is 16.0, is assigned to the x variable by the = operator.

Although several arguments may be passed into a function, only one value may be returned from it. Think of a function as having multiple communication channels for receiving data (parameters), but only one channel for sending data (the return value). This is illustrated in Figure 9.

Figure 9 A function returns one value

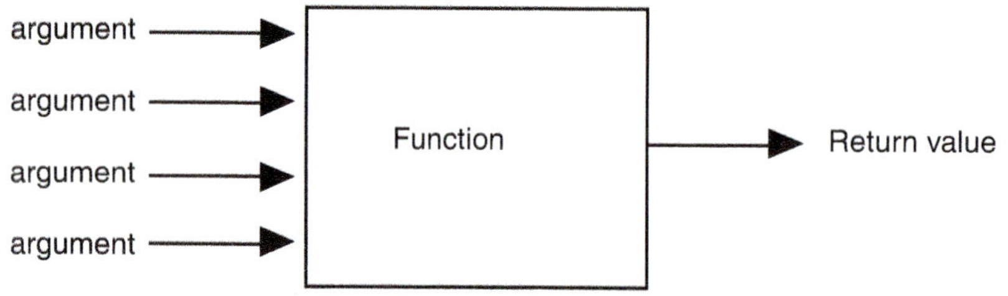

NOTE: It is possible to return multiple values from a function, but they must be "packaged" in such a way that they are treated as a single value.

Defining a Value-Returning Function

When you are writing a value-returning function, you must decide what type of value the function will return. This is because you must specify the data type of the return value in the function header and in the function prototype. Recall that a void function, which does not return a value, uses the key word void as its return type in the function header.

A value-returning function will use `int`, `double`, `bool`, or any other valid data type in its header. Here is an example of a function that returns an `int` value:

```
int sum(int num1, int num2)
{
    int result;
    result = num1 + num2;
    return result;
}
```

The name of this function is `sum`. Notice in the function header the return type is `int`, as illustrated in Figure 10.

Figure 10 Function return type

Return type
↓
```
int sum(int num1, int num2)
```

This code defines a function named `sum` that accepts two `int` arguments. The arguments are passed into the parameter variables `num1` and `num2`. Inside the function, a variable, `result`, is defined. Variables that are defined inside a function are called *local variables*. After the variable definition, the parameter variables `num1` and `num2` are added, and their sum is assigned to the `result` variable. The last statement in the function is

```
return result;
```

This statement causes the function to end, and it sends the value of the `result` variable back to the statement that called the function. A value-returning function must have a `return` statement written in the following general format:

```
return expression;
```

In the general format, *`expression`* is the value to be returned. It can be any expression that has a value, such as a variable, literal, or mathematical expression. The value of the expression is converted to the data type that the function returns, and is sent back to the statement that called the function. In this case, the `sum` function returns the value in the `result` variable.

However, we could have eliminated the `result` variable and returned the expression `num1 + num2`, as shown in the following code:

```
int sum(int num1, int num2)
{
    return num1 + num2;
}
```

When writing the prototype for a value-returning function, follow the same conventions we have covered earlier. Here is the prototype for the `sum` function:

```
int sum(int, int);
```

Calling a Value-Returning Function

Program 12 shows an example of how to call the `sum` function.

Program 12

```
1  // This program uses a function that returns a value.
2  #include <iostream>
3  using namespace std;
4
5  // Function prototype
6  int sum(int, int);
7
8  int main()
9  {
10     int value1 = 20,     // The first value
11         value2 = 40,     // The second value
12         total;           // To hold the total
13
14     // Call the sum function, passing the contents of
15     // value1 and value2 as arguments. Assign the return
16     // value to the total variable.
17     total = sum(value1, value2);
18
19     // Display the sum of the values.
20     cout << "The sum of " << value1 << " and "
21          << value2 << " is " << total << endl;
22     return 0;
23 }
24
25 //*****************************************************
26 // Definition of function sum. This function returns *
27 // the sum of its two parameters.                     *
28 //*****************************************************
29
30 int sum(int num1, int num2)
31 {
32     return num1 + num2;
33 }
```

Program Output

```
The sum of 20 and 40 is 60
```

Here is the statement in line 17 that calls the `sum` function, passing `value1` and `value2` as arguments:

```
total = sum(value1, value2);
```

This statement assigns the value returned by the `sum` function to the `total` variable. In this case, the function will return 60. Figure 11 shows how the arguments are passed into the function, and how a value is passed back from the function.

Figure 11 A function's arguments and return value

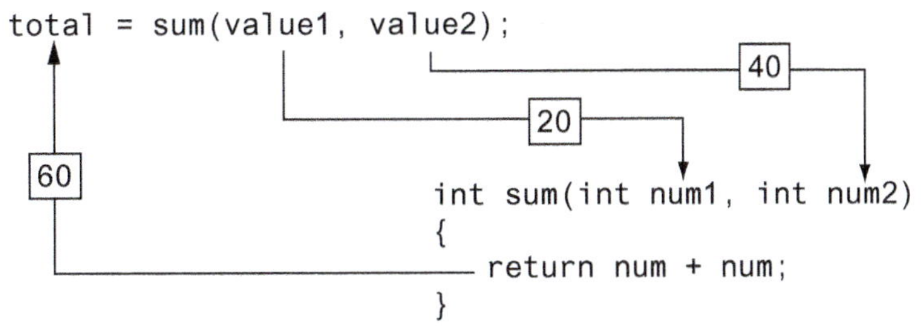

When you call a value-returning function, you usually want to do something meaningful with the value it returns. Program 12 shows a function's return value being assigned to a variable. This is commonly how return values are used, but you can do many other things with them. For example, the following code shows a mathematical expression that uses a call to the `sum` function:

```
int x = 10, y = 15;
double average;
average = sum(x, y) / 2.0;
```

In the last statement, the `sum` function is called with `x` and `y` as its arguments. The function's return value, which is 25, is divided by 2.0. The result, 12.5, is assigned to `average`. Here is another example:

```
int x = 10, y = 15;
cout << "The sum is " << sum(x, y) << endl;
```

This code sends the `sum` function's return value to `cout` so it can be displayed on the screen. The message "The sum is 25" will be displayed.

Remember, a value-returning function returns a value of a specific data type. You can use the function's return value anywhere that you can use a regular value of the same data type. This means anywhere an `int` value can be used, a call to an `int` value-returning function can be used. Likewise, anywhere a `double` value can be used, a call to a `double` value-returning function can be used. The same is true for all other data types.

Let's look at another example. Program 13, which calculates the area of a circle, has two functions in addition to `main`. One of the functions is named `square`, and it returns the square of any number passed to it as an argument. The `square` function is called in a mathematical statement. The program also has a function named `getRadius`, which prompts the user to enter the circle's radius. The value entered by the user is returned from the function.

Program 13

```
// This program demonstrates two value-returning functions.
// The square function is called in a mathematical statement.
#include <iostream>
#include <iomanip>
using namespace std;
```

(program continues)

Program 13 *(continued)*

```

//Function prototypes
double getRadius();
double square(double);

int main()
{
    const double PI = 3.14159; // Constant for pi
    double radius;             // To hold the circle's radius
    double area;               // To hold the circle's area

    // Set the numeric output formatting.
    cout << fixed << showpoint << setprecision(2);

    // Get the radius of the circle.
    cout << "This program calculates the area of ";
    cout << "a circle.\n";
    radius = getRadius();

    // Calculate the area of the circle.
    area = PI * square(radius);

    // Display the area.
    cout << "The area is " << area << endl;
    return 0;
}

//*******************************************************
// Definition of function getRadius.                    *
// This function asks the user to enter the radius of   *
// the circle and then returns that number as a double.*
//*******************************************************

double getRadius()
{
    double rad;

    cout << "Enter the radius of the circle: ";
    cin >> rad;
    return rad;
}

//*******************************************************
// Definition of function square.                       *
// This function accepts a double argument and returns  *
// the square of the argument as a double.              *
//*******************************************************

double square(double number)
```

```
55  {
56      return number * number;
57  }
```

Program Output with Example Input Shown in Bold

```
This program calculates the area of a circle.
Enter the radius of the circle: 10 [Enter]
The area is 314.16
```

First, look at the `getRadius` function defined in lines 39 through 46. The purpose of the function is to prompt the user to enter the radius of a circle. In line 41, the function defines a local variable, `rad`. Lines 43 and 44 prompt the user to enter the circle's radius, which is stored in the `rad` variable. In line 45, the value of the `rad` value is returned. The `getRadius` function is called in the `main` function, in line 23. The value that is returned from the function is assigned to the `radius` variable.

Next, look at the `square` function, which is defined in lines 54 through 57. When the function is called, a `double` argument is passed to it. The function stores the argument in the `number` parameter. The `return` statement in line 56 returns the value of the expression `number * number`, which is the square of the `number` parameter. The `square` function is called in the `main` function, in line 26, with the value of `radius` passed as an argument. The function will return the square of the `radius` variable, and that value will be used in the mathematical expression.

Assuming the user has entered 10 as the radius, and this value is passed as an argument to the `square` function, the `square` function will return the value 100. Figure 12 illustrates how the value 100 is passed back to the mathematical expression in line 26. The value 100 will then be used in the mathematical expression.

Figure 12 The square function

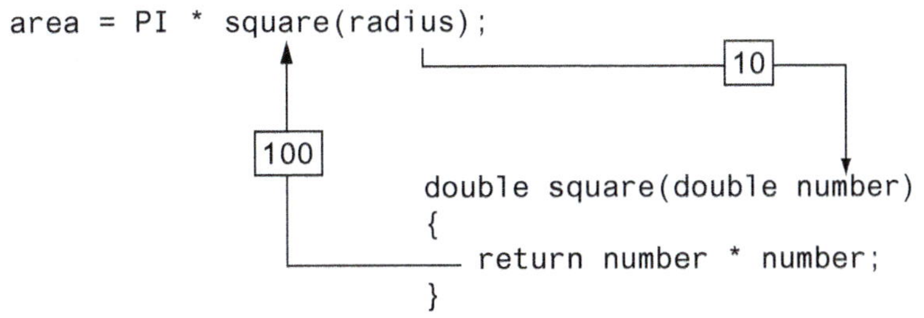

Functions can return values of any type. Both the `getRadius` and `square` functions in Program 13 return a `double`. The `sum` function you saw in Program 12 returned an `int`. When a statement calls a value-returning function, it should properly handle the return value. For example, if you assign the return value of the `square` function to a variable, the variable should be a `double`. If the return value of the function has a fractional portion and you assign it to an `int` variable, the value will be truncated.

In the Spotlight:

Using Functions

Your friend Michael runs a catering company. Some of the ingredients that his recipes require are measured in cups. When he goes to the grocery store to buy those ingredients, however, they are sold only by the fluid ounce. He has asked you to write a simple program that converts cups to fluid ounces.

You design the following algorithm:

1. *Display an introductory screen that explains what the program does.*
2. *Get the number of cups.*
3. *Convert the number of cups to fluid ounces and display the result.*

This algorithm lists the top level of tasks that the program needs to perform and becomes the basis of the program's `main` function. The hierarchy chart shown in Figure 13 shows how the program will be broken down into functions.

Figure 13 Hierarchy chart for the program

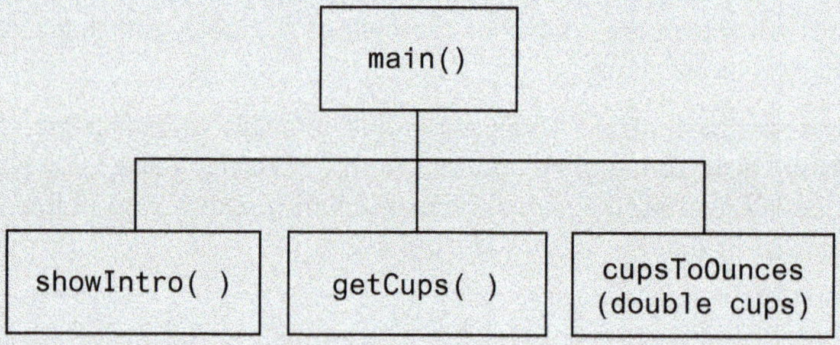

As shown in the hierarchy chart, the `main` function will call three other functions. Here are summaries of those functions:

- `showIntro`—This function will display a message on the screen that explains what the program does.
- `getCups`—This function will prompt the user to enter the number of cups, then will return that value as a `double`.
- `cupsToOunces`—This function will accept the number of cups as an argument, then return an equivalent number of fluid ounces as a `double`.

Program 14 shows the code for the program.

Program 14

```
// This program converts cups to fluid ounces.
#include <iostream>
#include <iomanip>
using namespace std;
```

```

// Function prototypes
void showIntro();
double getCups();
double cupsToOunces(double);

int main()
{
    // Variables for the cups and ounces.
    double cups, ounces;

    // Set up numeric output formatting.
    cout << fixed << showpoint << setprecision(1);

    // Display an intro screen.
    showIntro();

    // Get the number of cups.
    cups = getCups();

    // Convert cups to fluid ounces.
    ounces = cupsToOunces(cups);

    // Display the number of ounces.
    cout << cups << " cups equals "
         << ounces << " ounces.\n";

    return 0;
}

//******************************************
// The showIntro function displays an     *
// introductory screen.                   *
//******************************************

void showIntro()
{
    cout << "This program converts measurements\n"
         << "in cups to fluid ounces. For your\n"
         << "reference the formula is:\n"
         << " 1 cup = 8 fluid ounces\n\n";
}

//******************************************
// The getCups function prompts the user  *
// to enter the number of cups and then   *
// returns that value as a double.        *
//******************************************

double getCups()
```

(program continues)

Program 14 *(continued)*

```
{
    double numCups;

    cout << "Enter the number of cups: ";
    cin >> numCups;
    return numCups;
}

//******************************************
// The cupsToOunces function accepts a     *
// number of cups as an argument and       *
// returns the equivalent number of fluid  *
// ounces as a double.                     *
//******************************************

double cupsToOunces(double numCups)
{
    return numCups * 8.0;
}
```

Program Output with Example Input Shown in Bold

```
This program converts measurements
in cups to fluid ounces. For your
reference the formula is:
   1 cup = 8 fluid ounces
Enter the number of cups: 2 [Enter]
2.0 cups equals 16.0 ounces.
```

9 Returning a Boolean Value

CONCEPT: Functions may return `true` or `false` values.

Frequently, there is a need for a function that tests an argument and returns a `true` or `false` value indicating whether or not a condition exists. Such a function would return a `bool` value. For example, the following function accepts an `int` argument and returns `true` if the argument is within the range of 1 through 100, or `false` otherwise:

```
bool isValid(int number)
{
   bool status;
   if (number >= 1 && number <= 100)
      status = true;
   else
      status = false;
   return status;
}
```

The following code shows an `if/else` statement that uses a call to the function:

```
int value = 20;
if (isValid(value))
   cout << "The value is within range.\n";
else
   cout << "The value is out of range.\n";
```

When this code executes, the message "The value is within range." will be displayed.

Program 15 shows another example. This program has a function named `isEven` which returns `true` if its argument is an even number. Otherwise, the function returns `false`.

Program 15

```
// This program uses a function that returns true or false.
#include <iostream>
using namespace std;

// Function prototype
bool isEven(int);

int main()
{
    int val;

    // Get a number from the user.
    cout << "Enter an integer and I will tell you ";
    cout << "if it is even or odd: ";
    cin >> val;

    // Indicate whether it is even or odd.
    if (isEven(val))
       cout << val << " is even.\n";
    else
       cout << val << " is odd.\n";
    return 0;
}

//*****************************************************************
// Definition of function isEven. This function accepts an       *
// integer argument and tests it to be even or odd. The function *
// returns true if the argument is even or false if the argument *
// is odd. The return value is a bool.                           *
//*****************************************************************

bool isEven(int number)
{
    bool status;

    if (number % 2 == 0)
       status = true;  // The number is even if there is no remainder.
    else
```

(program continues)

Program 15 *(continued)*

```
39          status = false; // Otherwise, the number is odd.
40      return status;
41  }
```

Program Output with Example Input Shown in Bold

```
Enter an integer and I will tell you if it is even or odd: 5 [Enter]
5 is odd.
```

The `isEven` function is called in line 18, in the following statement:

```
if (isEven(val))
```

When the `if` statement executes, `isEven` is called with `val` as its argument. If `val` is even, `isEven` returns `true`; otherwise, it returns `false`.

Checkpoint

11 How many return values may a function have?

12 Write a header for a function named `distance`. The function should return a `double` and have two `double` parameters: `rate` and `time`.

13 Write a header for a function named `days`. The function should return an `int` and have three `int` parameters: `years`, `months`, and `weeks`.

14 Write a header for a function named `getKey`. The function should return a `char` and use no parameters.

15 Write a header for a function named `lightYears`. The function should return a `long` and have one `long` parameter: `miles`.

10 Local and Global Variables

CONCEPT: A local variable is defined inside a function and is not accessible outside the function. A global variable is defined outside all functions and is accessible to all functions in its scope.

Local Variables

Variables defined inside a function are *local* to that function. They are hidden from the statements in other functions, which normally cannot access them. Program 16 shows that because the variables defined in a function are hidden, other functions may have separate, distinct variables with the same name.

Program 16

```
// This program shows that variables defined in a function
// are hidden from other functions.
#include <iostream>
using namespace std;
```

```

void anotherFunction(); // Function prototype

int main()
{
    int num = 1; // Local variable

    cout << "In main, num is " << num << endl;
    anotherFunction();
    cout << "Back in main, num is " << num << endl;
    return 0;
}

//*****************************************************
// Definition of anotherFunction                      *
// It has a local variable, num, whose initial value *
// is displayed.                                       *
//*****************************************************

void anotherFunction()
{
    int num = 20; // Local variable

    cout << "In anotherFunction, num is " << num << endl;
}
```

Program Output

```
In main, num is 1
In anotherFunction, num is 20
Back in main, num is 1
```

Even though there are two variables named num, the program can only "see" one of them at a time because they are in different functions. When the program is executing in main, the num variable defined in main is visible. When anotherFunction is called, however, only variables defined inside it are visible, so the num variable in main is hidden. Figure 14 illustrates the closed nature of the two functions. The boxes represent the scope of the variables.

Figure 14 Visibility of local variables

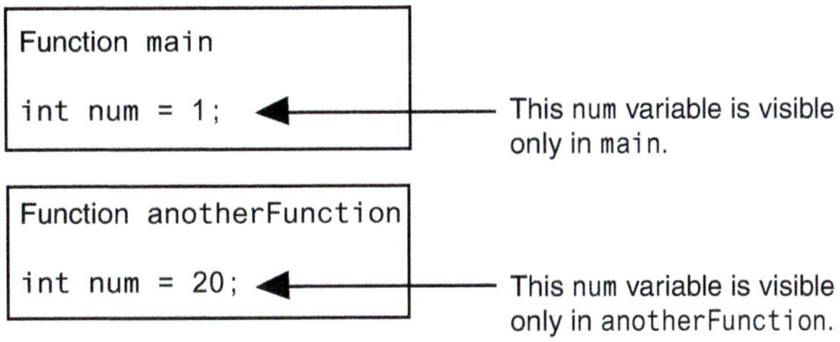

Local Variable Lifetime

A function's local variables exist only while the function is executing. This is known as the *lifetime* of a local variable. When the function begins, its local variables and its parameter variables are created in memory, and when the function ends, the local variables and parameter variables are destroyed. This means that any value stored in a local variable is lost between calls to the function in which the variable is declared.

Initializing Local Variables with Parameter Values

It is possible to use a parameter variable to initialize a local variable. Sometimes this simplifies the code in a function. For example, recall the first version of the sum function we discussed earlier:

```
int sum(int num1, int num2)
{
    int result;

    result = num1 + num2;
    return result;
}
```

In the body of the function, the result variable is defined and then a separate assignment statement assigns num1 + num2 to result. We can combine these statements into one, as shown in the following modified version of the function.

```
int sum(int num1, int num2)
{
    int result = num1 + num2;
    return result;
}
```

Because the scope of a parameter variable is the entire function in which it is declared, we can use parameter variables to initialize local variables.

Global Variables

A global variable is any variable defined outside all the functions in a program. The scope of a global variable is the portion of the program from the variable definition to the end. This means a global variable can be accessed by all functions that are defined after the global variable is defined. Program 17 shows two functions, main and anotherFunction, that access the same global variable, num.

Program 17

```
// This program shows that a global variable is visible
// to all the functions that appear in a program after
// the variable's declaration.
#include <iostream>
using namespace std;

void anotherFunction(); // Function prototype
int num = 2;            // Global variable

int main()
```

```
{
    cout << "In main, num is " << num << endl;
    anotherFunction();
    cout << "Back in main, num is " << num << endl;
    return 0;
}

//*********************************************************
// Definition of anotherFunction                          *
// This function changes the value of the                 *
// global variable num.                                   *
//*********************************************************

void anotherFunction()
{
    cout << "In anotherFunction, num is " << num << endl;
    num = 50;
    cout << "But, it is now changed to " << num << endl;
}
```

Program Output

```
In main, num is 2
In anotherFunction, num is 2
But, it is now changed to 50
Back in main, num is 50
```

In Program 17, num is defined outside of all the functions. Because its definition appears before the definitions of `main` and `anotherFunction`, both functions have access to it.

Unless you explicitly initialize numeric global variables, they are automatically initialized to zero. Global character variables are initialized to NULL.* The variable `globalNum` in Program 18 is never set to any value by a statement, but because it is global, it is automatically set to zero.

Program 18

```
// This program has an uninitialized global variable.
#include <iostream>
using namespace std;

int globalNum; // Global variable, automatically set to zero

int main()
{
    cout << "globalNum is " << globalNum << endl;
    return 0;
}
```

Program Output

```
globalNum is 0
```

*The NULL character is stored as ASCII code 0.

Now that you've had a basic introduction to global variables, I must warn you to restrict your use of them. When beginning students first learn to write programs with multiple functions, they are sometimes tempted to make all their variables global. This is usually because global variables can be accessed by any function in the program without being passed as arguments. Although this approach might make a program easier to create, it usually causes problems later. The reasons are as follows:

- **Global variables make debugging difficult.** Any statement in a program can change the value of a global variable. If you find that the wrong value is being stored in a global variable, you have to track down every statement that accesses it to determine where the bad value is coming from. In a program with thousands of lines of code, this can be difficult.
- **Functions that use global variables are usually dependent on those variables.** If you want to use such a function in a different program, most likely you will have to redesign it so it does not rely on the global variable.
- **Global variables make a program hard to understand.** A global variable can be modified by any statement in the program. If you are to understand any part of the program that uses a global variable, you have to be aware of all the other parts of the program that access the global variable.

Because of this, you should not use global variables for the conventional purposes of storing, manipulating, and retrieving data. In most cases, you should declare variables locally and pass them as arguments to the functions that need to access them.

Global Constants

Although you should try to avoid the use of global variables, it is generally permissible to use global constants in a program. A *global constant* is a named constant that is available to every function in a program. Because a global constant's value cannot be changed during the program's execution, you do not have to worry about the potential hazards that are associated with the use of global variables.

Global constants are typically used to represent unchanging values that are needed throughout a program. For example, suppose a banking program uses a named constant to represent an interest rate. If the interest rate is used in several functions, it is easier to create a global constant, rather than a local named constant in each function. This also simplifies maintenance. If the interest rate changes, only the declaration of the global constant has to be changed, instead of several local declarations.

Program 19 shows an example of how global constants might be used. The program calculates an employee's gross pay, including overtime. In addition to `main`, this program has two functions: `getBasePay` and `getOvertimePay`. The `getBasePay` function accepts the number of hours worked and returns the amount of pay for the non-overtime hours. The `getOvertimePay` function accepts the number of hours worked and returns the amount of pay for the overtime hours, if any.

Program 19

```
// This program calculates gross pay.
#include <iostream>
#include <iomanip>
```

```
using namespace std;

// Global constants
const double PAY_RATE = 22.55;      // Hourly pay rate
const double BASE_HOURS = 40.0;     // Max non-overtime hours
const double OT_MULTIPLIER = 1.5;  // Overtime multiplier

// Function prototypes
double getBasePay(double);
double getOvertimePay(double);

int main()
{
    double hours,              // Hours worked
           basePay,            // Base pay
           overtime = 0.0,     // Overtime pay
           totalPay;           // Total pay

    // Get the number of hours worked.
    cout << "How many hours did you work? ";
    cin >> hours;

    // Get the amount of base pay.
    basePay = getBasePay(hours);

    // Get overtime pay, if any.
    if (hours > BASE_HOURS)
       overtime = getOvertimePay(hours);

    // Calculate the total pay.
    totalPay = basePay + overtime;

    // Set up numeric output formatting.
    cout << setprecision(2) << fixed << showpoint;

    // Display the pay.
    cout << "Base pay: $" << basePay << endl
         << "Overtime pay $" << overtime << endl
         << "Total pay $" << totalPay << endl;
    return 0;
}

//**************************************************
// The getBasePay function accepts the number of  *
// hours worked as an argument and returns the    *
// employee's pay for non-overtime hours.         *
//**************************************************

double getBasePay(double hoursWorked)
{
    double basePay; // To hold base pay

```

(program continues)

Program 19 *(continued)*

```
56        // Determine base pay.
57        if (hoursWorked > BASE_HOURS)
58           basePay = BASE_HOURS * PAY_RATE;
59        else
60           basePay = hoursWorked * PAY_RATE;
61
62        return basePay;
63    }
64
65    //*****************************************************
66    // The getOvertimePay function accepts the number   *
67    // of hours worked as an argument and returns the   *
68    // employee's overtime pay.                         *
69    //*****************************************************
70
71    double getOvertimePay(double hoursWorked)
72    {
73        double overtimePay; // To hold overtime pay
74
75        // Determine overtime pay.
76        if (hoursWorked > BASE_HOURS)
77        {
78           overtimePay = (hoursWorked - BASE_HOURS) *
79                    PAY_RATE * OT_MULTIPLIER;
80        }
81        else
82           overtimePay = 0.0;
83
84        return overtimePay;
85    }
```

Program Output with Example Input Shown in Bold

How many hours did you work? **48** [Enter]
Base pay: $902.00
Overtime pay: $270.60
Total pay: $1172.60

Let's take a closer look at the program. Three global constants are defined in lines 7, 8, and 9. The PAY_RATE constant is set to the employee's hourly pay rate, which is 22.55. The BASE_HOURS constant is set to 40, which is the number of hours an employee can work in a week without getting paid overtime. The OT_MULTIPLIER constant is set to 1.5, which is the pay rate multiplier for overtime hours. This means that the employee's hourly pay rate is multiplied by 1.5 for all overtime hours.

Because these constants are global and are defined before all of the functions in the program, all the functions may access them. For example, the getBasePay function accesses the BASE_HOURS constant in lines 57 and 58 and accesses the PAY_RATE constant in lines 58 and 60. The getOvertimePay function accesses the BASE_HOURS constant in lines 76 and 78, the PAY_RATE constant in line 79, and the OT_MULTIPLIER constant in line 79.

Local and Global Variables with the Same Name

You cannot have two local variables with the same name in the same function. This applies to parameter variables as well. A parameter variable is, in essence, a local variable. So, you cannot give a parameter variable and a local variable in the same function the same name.

However, you can have a local variable or a parameter variable with the same name as a global variable, or a global constant. When you do, the name of the local or parameter variable *shadows* the name of the global variable or global constant. This means that the global variable or constant's name is hidden by the name of the local or parameter variable. For example, look at Program 20. This program has a global constant named `BIRDS`, set to 500. The `california` function has a local constant named `BIRDS`, set to 10000.

Program 20

```
1  // This program demonstrates how a local variable
2  // can shadow the name of a global constant.
3  #include <iostream>
4  using namespace std;
5
6  // Global constant.
7  const int BIRDS = 500;
8
9  // Function prototype
10 void california();
11
12 int main()
13 {
14     cout << "In main there are " << BIRDS
15          << " birds.\n";
16     california();
17     return 0;
18 }
19
20 //********************************************
21 // california function                       *
22 //********************************************
23
24 void california()
25 {
26     const int BIRDS = 10000;
27     cout << "In california there are " << BIRDS
28          << " birds.\n";
29 }
```

Program Output

```
In main there are 500 birds.
In california there are 10000 birds.
```

When the program is executing in the `main` function, the global constant `BIRDS`, which is set to 500, is visible. The cout statement in lines 14 and 15 displays "In main there are 500 birds." (My apologies to folks living in Maine for the difference in spelling.)

When the program is executing in the `california` function, however, the local constant `BIRDS` shadows the global constant `BIRDS`. When the `california` function accesses `BIRDS`, it accesses the local constant. That is why the `cout` statement in lines 27 and 28 displays "In california there are 10000 birds."

11 Static Local Variables

If a function is called more than once in a program, the values stored in the function's local variables do not persist between function calls. This is because the local variables are destroyed when the function terminates, and are then re-created when the function starts again. This is shown in Program 21.

Program 21

```
1  // This program shows that local variables do not retain
2  // their values between function calls.
3  #include <iostream>
4  using namespace std;
5
6  // Function prototype
7  void showLocal();
8
9  int main()
10 {
11     showLocal();
12     showLocal();
13     return 0;
14 }
15
16 //***********************************************************
17 // Definition of function showLocal.                        *
18 // The initial value of localNum, which is 5, is displayed. *
19 // The value of localNum is then changed to 99 before the   *
20 // function returns.                                        *
21 //***********************************************************
22
23 void showLocal()
24 {
25     int localNum = 5; // Local variable
26
27     cout << "localNum is " << localNum << endl;
28     localNum = 99;
29 }
```

Program Output

```
localNum is 5
localNum is 5
```

Even though in line 28, the last statement in the `showLocal` function stores 99 in `localNum`, the variable is destroyed when the function returns. The next time the function is called, `localNum` is re-created and initialized to 5 again.

Sometimes it's desirable for a program to "remember" what value is stored in a local variable between function calls. This can be accomplished by making the variable `static`. Static local variables are not destroyed when a function returns. They exist for the lifetime of the program, even though their scope is only the function in which they are defined. Program 22 demonstrates some characteristics of `static` local variables:

Program 22

```
1   // This program uses a static local variable.
2   #include <iostream>
3   using namespace std;
4
5   void showStatic(); // Function prototype
6
7   int main()
8   {
9       // Call the showStatic function five times.
10      for (int count = 0; count < 5; count++)
11         showStatic();
12      return 0;
13  }
14
15  //**************************************************************
16  // Definition of function showStatic.                          *
17  // statNum is a static local variable. Its value is displayed *
18  // and then incremented just before the function returns.      *
19  //**************************************************************
20
21  void showStatic()
22  {
23      static int statNum;
24
25      cout << "statNum is " << statNum << endl;
26      statNum++;
27  }
```

Program Output

```
statNum is 0
statNum is 1
statNum is 2
statNum is 3
statNum is 4
```

In line 26 of Program 22, `statNum` is incremented in the `showStatic` function, and it retains its value between each function call. Notice even though `statNum` is not explicitly initialized, it starts at zero. Like global variables, all `static` local variables are initialized to zero by default. (Of course, you can provide your own initialization value, if necessary.)

If you do provide an initialization value for a `static` local variable, the initialization only occurs once. This is because initialization normally happens when the variable is created, and `static` local variables are only created once during the running of a program. Program 23, which is a slight modification of Program 22, illustrates this point.

Program 23

```
1  // This program shows that a static local variable is only
2  // initialized once.
3  #include <iostream>
4  using namespace std;
5
6  void showStatic(); // Function prototype
7
8  int main()
9  {
10     // Call the showStatic function five times.
11     for (int count = 0; count < 5; count++)
12        showStatic();
13     return 0;
14 }
15
16 //**************************************************************
17 // Definition of function showStatic.                           *
18 // statNum is a static local variable. Its value is displayed   *
19 // and then incremented just before the function returns.       *
20 //**************************************************************
21
22 void showStatic()
23 {
24     static int statNum = 5;
25
26     cout << "statNum is " << statNum << endl;
27     statNum++;
28 }
```

Program Output

```
statNum is 5
statNum is 6
statNum is 7
statNum is 8
statNum is 9
```

Even though the statement that defines `statNum` in line 24 initializes it to 5, the initialization does not happen each time the function is called. If it did, the variable would not be able to retain its value between function calls.

Checkpoint

16 What is the difference between a static local variable and a global variable?

17 What is the output of the following program?

```
#include <iostream>
using namespace std;

void myFunc();    // Function prototype

int main()
{
```

```
    int var = 100;

    cout << var << endl;
    myFunc();
    cout << var << endl;
    return 0;
}

// Definition of function myFunc
void myFunc()
{
    int var = 50;

    cout << var << endl;
}
```

18 What is the output of the following program?

```
#include <iostream>
using namespace std;

void showVar(); // Function prototype

int main()
{
    for (int count = 0; count < 10; count++)
        showVar();
    return 0;
}

// Definition of function showVar
void showVar()
{
    static int var = 10;

    cout << var << endl;
    var++;
}
```

12 Default Arguments

CONCEPT: Default arguments are passed to parameters automatically if no argument is provided in the function call.

It's possible to assign *default arguments* to function parameters. A default argument is passed to the parameter when the actual argument is left out of the function call. The default arguments are usually listed in the function prototype. Here is an example:

```
void showArea(double = 20.0, double = 10.0);
```

Default arguments are literal values or constants with an = operator in front of them, appearing after the data types listed in a function prototype. Since parameter names are optional in function prototypes, the example prototype could also be declared as

```
void showArea(double length = 20.0, double width = 10.0);
```

In both example prototypes, the function showArea has two double parameters. The first is assigned the default argument 20.0, and the second is assigned the default argument 10.0. Here is the definition of the function:

```
void showArea(double length, double width)
{
   double area = length * width;
   cout << "The area is " << area << endl;
}
```

The default argument for length is 20.0, and the default argument for width is 10.0. Because both parameters have default arguments, they may optionally be omitted in the function call, as shown here:

```
showArea();
```

In this function call, both default arguments will be passed to the parameters. The parameter length will take the value 20.0 and width will take the value 10.0. The output of the function will be

```
The area is 200
```

The default arguments are only used when the actual arguments are omitted from the function call. In the call below, the first argument is specified, but the second is omitted:

```
showArea(12.0);
```

The value 12.0 will be passed to length, while the default value 10.0 will be passed to width. The output of the function will be

```
The area is 120
```

Of course, all the default arguments may be overridden. In the function call below, arguments are supplied for both parameters:

```
showArea(12.0, 5.5);
```

The output of the function call above will be

```
The area is 66
```

NOTE: If a function does not have a prototype, default arguments may be specified in the function header. The showArea function could be defined as follows:

```
void showArea(double length = 20.0, double width = 10.0)
{
   double area = length * width;
   cout << "The area is " << area << endl;
}
```

WARNING! A function's default arguments should be assigned in the earliest occurrence of the function name. This will usually be the function prototype.

Program 24 uses a function that displays asterisks on the screen. Arguments are passed to the function specifying how many columns and rows of asterisks to display. Default arguments are provided to display one row of 10 asterisks.

Program 24

```
// This program demonstrates default function arguments.
#include <iostream>
using namespace std;

// Function prototype with default arguments
void displayStars(int = 10, int = 1);

int main()
{
    displayStars();        // Use default values for cols and rows.
    cout << endl;
    displayStars(5);       // Use default value for rows.
    cout << endl;
    displayStars(7, 3);    // Use 7 for cols and 3 for rows.
    return 0;
}

//***********************************************************
// Definition of function displayStars.                      *
// The default argument for cols is 10 and for rows is 1.*
// This function displays a square made of asterisks.      *
//***********************************************************

void displayStars(int cols, int rows)
{
    // Nested loop. The outer loop controls the rows
    // and the inner loop controls the columns.
    for (int down = 0; down < rows; down++)
    {
        for (int across = 0; across < cols; across++)
            cout << "*";
        cout << endl;
    }
}
```

Program Output

```
**********

*****

*******
*******
*******
```

Although C++'s default arguments are very convenient, they are not totally flexible in their use. When an argument is left out of a function call, all arguments that come after it must be left out as well. In the `displayStars` function in Program 24, it is not possible to omit the argument for `cols` without also omitting the argument for `rows`. For example, the following function call would be illegal:

```
displayStars(, 3); // Illegal function call.
```

It's possible for a function to have some parameters with default arguments, and some without. For example, in the following function (which displays an employee's gross pay), only the last parameter has a default argument:

```
// Function prototype
void calcPay(int empNum, double payRate, double hours = 40.0);

// Definition of function calcPay
void calcPay(int empNum, double payRate, double hours)
{
    double wages;

    wages = payRate * hours;
    cout << fixed << showpoint << setprecision(2);
    cout << "Gross pay for employee number ";
    cout << empNum << " is " << wages << endl;
}
```

When calling this function, arguments must always be specified for the first two parameters (empNum and payRate) since they have no default arguments. Here are examples of valid calls:

```
calcPay(769, 15.75);       // Use default arg for 40 hours
calcPay(142, 12.00, 20);   // Specify number of hours
```

When a function uses a mixture of parameters with and without default arguments, the parameters with default arguments must be defined last. In the calcPay function, hours could not have been defined before either of the other parameters. The following prototypes are illegal:

```
// Illegal prototype
void calcPay(int empNum, double hours = 40.0, double payRate);

// Illegal prototype
void calcPay(double hours = 40.0, int empNum, double payRate);
```

Here is a summary of the important points about default arguments:

- The value of a default argument must be a literal value or a named constant.
- When an argument is left out of a function call (because it has a default value), all the arguments that come after it must be left out too.
- When a function has a mixture of parameters both with and without default arguments, the parameters with default arguments must be declared last.

13 Using Reference Variables as Parameters

CONCEPT: When used as parameters, reference variables allow a function to access the parameter's original argument. Changes to the parameter are also made to the argument.

Earlier you saw that arguments are normally passed to a function by value, and that the function cannot change the source of the argument. C++ provides a special type of variable called a *reference variable* that, when used as a function parameter, allows access to the original argument.

A reference variable is an alias for another variable. Any changes made to the reference variable are actually performed on the variable for which it is an alias. By using a reference variable as a parameter, a function may change a variable that is defined in another function.

Reference variables are defined like regular variables, except you place an ampersand (&) in front of the name. For example, the following function definition makes the parameter `refVar` a reference variable:

```
void doubleNum(int &refVar)
{
    refVar *= 2;
}
```

> **NOTE:** The variable `refVar` is called "a reference to an `int`."

This function doubles `refVar` by multiplying it by 2. Since `refVar` is a reference variable, this action is actually performed on the variable that was passed to the function as an argument. When prototyping a function with a reference variable, be sure to include the ampersand after the data type. Here is the prototype for the `doubleNum` function:

```
void doubleNum(int &);
```

> **NOTE:** Some programmers prefer not to put a space between the data type and the ampersand. The following prototype is equivalent to the one above:
>
> ```
> void doubleNum(int &);
> ```

> **NOTE:** The ampersand must appear in both the prototype and the header of any function that uses a reference variable as a parameter. It does not appear in the function call.

Program 25 demonstrates how the `doubleNum` function works.

Program 25

```
// This program uses a reference variable as a function
// parameter.
#include <iostream>
using namespace std;

// Function prototype. The parameter is a reference variable.
void doubleNum(int &);
```

(program continues)

Program 25 *(continued)*

```
int main()
{
    int value = 4;

    cout << "In main, value is " << value << endl;
    cout << "Now calling doubleNum..." << endl;
    doubleNum(value);
    cout << "Now back in main. value is " << value << endl;
    return 0;
}

//**********************************************************
// Definition of doubleNum.                               *
// The parameter refVar is a reference variable. The value *
// in refVar is doubled.                                  *
//**********************************************************

void doubleNum (int &refVar)
{
    refVar *= 2;
}
```

Program Output

```
In main, value is 4
Now calling doubleNum...
Now back in main. value is 8
```

The parameter `refVar` in Program 25 "points" to the `value` variable in function `main`. When a program works with a reference variable, it is actually working with the variable it references, or to which it points. This is illustrated in Figure 15.

Figure 15 Reference variable

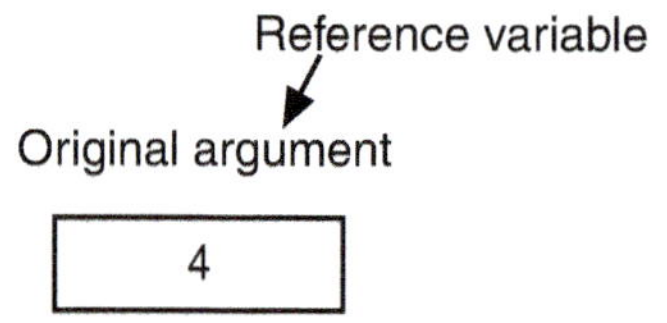

Recall that function arguments are normally passed by value, which means a copy of the argument's value is passed into the parameter variable. When a reference parameter is used, it is said that the argument is *passed by reference.*

Program 26 is a modification of Program 25. The function `getNum` has been added. The function asks the user to enter a number, which is stored in `userNum`. `userNum` is a reference to `main`'s variable `value`.

Program 26

```
// This program uses reference variables as function parameters.
#include <iostream>
using namespace std;

// Function prototypes. Both functions use reference variables
// as parameters.
void doubleNum(int &);
void getNum(int &);

int main()
{
    int value;

    // Get a number and store it in value.
    getNum(value);

    // Double the number stored in value.
    doubleNum(value);

    // Display the resulting number.
    cout << "That value doubled is " << value << endl;
    return 0;
}

//*****************************************************************
// Definition of getNum.                                          *
// The parameter userNum is a reference variable. The user is     *
// asked to enter a number, which is stored in userNum.           *
//*****************************************************************

void getNum(int &userNum)
{
    cout << "Enter a number: ";
    cin >> userNum;
}

//**************************************************************
// Definition of doubleNum.                                    *
// The parameter refVar is a reference variable. The value     *
// in refVar is doubled.                                       *
//**************************************************************

void doubleNum (int &refVar)
{
    refVar *= 2;
}
```

Program Output with Example Input Shown in Bold

Enter a number: **12** [Enter]
That value doubled is 24

NOTE: Only variables may be passed by reference. If you attempt to pass a nonvariable argument, such as a literal, a constant, or an expression, into a reference parameter, an error will result. Using the `doubleNum` function as an example, the following statements will generate an error:

```
doubleNum(5);              // Error
doubleNum(userNum + 10);   // Error
```

If a function uses more than one reference variable as a parameter, be sure to place the ampersand before each reference variable name. Here is the prototype and definition for a function that uses four reference variable parameters:

```
// Function prototype with four reference variables
// as parameters.
void addThree(int &, int &, int &, int &);

// Definition of addThree.
// All four parameters are reference variables.
void addThree(int &sum, int &num1, int &num2, int &num3)
{
   cout << "Enter three integer values: ";
   cin >> num1 >> num2 >> num3;
   sum = num1 + num2 + num3;
}
```

WARNING! Don't get carried away with using reference variables as function parameters. Any time you allow a function to alter a variable that's outside the function, you are creating potential debugging problems. Reference variables should only be used as parameters when the situation requires them.

Checkpoint

19 What kinds of values may be specified as default arguments?

20 Write the prototype and header for a function called `compute`. The function should have three parameters: an `int`, a `double`, and a `long` (not necessarily in that order). The `int` parameter should have a default argument of 5, and the `long` parameter should have a default argument of 65536. The `double` parameter should not have a default argument.

21 Write the prototype and header for a function called `calculate`. The function should have three parameters: an `int`, a reference to a `double`, and a `long` (not necessarily in that order.) Only the `int` parameter should have a default argument, which is 47.

22 What is the output of the following program?

```
#include <iostream>
using namespace std;

void test(int = 2, int = 4, int = 6);
int main()
```

```
{
   test();
   test(6);
   test(3, 9);
   test(1, 5, 7);
   return 0;
}
void test (int first, int second, int third)
{
   first += 3;
   second += 6;
   third += 9;
   cout << first << " " << second << " " << third << endl;
}
```

23 The following program asks the user to enter two numbers. What is the output of the program if the user enters 12 and 14?

```
#include <iostream>
using namespace std;

void func1(int &, int &);
void func2(int &, int &, int &);
void func3(int, int, int);

int main()
{
   int x = 0, y = 0, z = 0;

   cout << x << " " << y << " " << z << endl;
   func1(x, y);
   cout << x << " " << y << " " << z << endl;
   func2(x, y, z);
   cout << x << " " << y << " " << z << endl;
   func3(x, y, z);
   cout << x << " " << y << " " << z << endl;
   return 0;
}
void func1(int &a, int &b)
{
   cout << "Enter two numbers: ";
   cin >> a >> b;
}
void func2(int &a, int &b, int &c)
{
   b++;
   c--;
   a = b + c;
}
void func3(int a, int b, int c)
{
   a = b - c;
}
```

14 Overloading Functions

CONCEPT: Two or more functions may have the same name, as long as their parameter lists are different.

Sometimes, you will create two or more functions that perform the same operation, but use a different set of parameters or parameters of different data types. For instance, in Program 13 there is a `square` function that uses a `double` parameter. But, suppose you also wanted a `square` function that works exclusively with integers, accepting an `int` as its argument. Both functions would do the same thing: return the square of their argument. The only difference is the data type involved in the operation. If you were to use both these functions in the same program, you could assign a unique name to each function. For example, the function that squares an `int` might be named `squareInt`, and the one that squares a `double` might be named `squareDouble`. C++, however, allows you to *overload* functions. That means you may assign the same name to multiple functions, as long as their parameter lists are different. Program 27 uses two overloaded `square` functions.

Program 27

```
// This program uses overloaded functions.
#include <iostream>
#include <iomanip>
using namespace std;

// Function prototypes
int square(int);
double square(double);

int main()
{
    int userInt;
    double userFloat;

    // Get an int and a double.
    cout << fixed << showpoint << setprecision(2);
    cout << "Enter an integer and a floating-point value: ";
    cin >> userInt >> userFloat;

    // Display their squares.
    cout << "Here are their squares: ";
    cout << square(userInt) << " and " << square(userFloat);
    return 0;
}

//**************************************************************
// Definition of overloaded function square.                   *
// This function uses an int parameter, number. It returns the *
// square of number as an int.                                 *
//**************************************************************
```

```

int square(int number)
{
    return number * number;
}

//*****************************************************************
// Definition of overloaded function square.                      *
// This function uses a double parameter, number. It returns      *
// the square of number as a double.                              *
//*****************************************************************

double square(double number)
{
    return number * number;
}
```

Program Output with Example Input Shown in Bold

```
Enter an integer and a floating-point value: 12 4.2 [Enter]
Here are their squares: 144 and 17.64
```

Here are the headers for the square functions used in Program 27:

```
int square(int number)
double square(double number)
```

In C++, each function has a signature. The *function signature* is the name of the function and the data types of the function's parameters in the proper order. The square functions in Program 27 would have the following signatures:

```
square(int)
square(double)
```

When an overloaded function is called, C++ uses the function signature to distinguish it from other functions with the same name. In Program 27, when an int argument is passed to square, the version of the function that has an int parameter is called. Likewise, when a double argument is passed to square, the version with a double parameter is called.

Note the function's return value is not part of the signature. The following functions could not be used in the same program because their parameter lists aren't different:

```
int square(int number)
{
   return number * number
}
double square(int number) // Wrong! Parameter lists must differ
{
   return number * number
}
```

Overloading is also convenient when there are similar functions that use a different number of parameters. For example, consider a program with functions that return the sum of integers. One returns the sum of two integers, another returns the sum of three integers, and yet another returns the sum of four integers. Here are their function headers:

```
int sum(int num1, int num2)

int sum(int num1, int num2, int num3)

int sum(int num1, int num2, int num3, int num4)
```

Because the number of parameters is different in each, they all may be used in the same program. Program 28 is an example that uses two functions, each named `calcWeeklyPay`, to determine an employee's gross weekly pay. One version of the function uses an `int` and a `double` parameter, while the other version only uses a `double` parameter.

Program 28

```
// This program demonstrates overloaded functions to calculate
// the gross weekly pay of hourly paid or salaried employees.
#include <iostream>
#include <iomanip>
using namespace std;

// Function prototypes
void getChoice(char &);
double calcWeeklyPay(int, double);
double calcWeeklyPay(double);

int main()
{
    char selection;    // Menu selection
    int worked;        // Hours worked
    double rate;       // Hourly pay rate
    double yearly;     // Yearly salary

    // Set numeric output formatting.
    cout << fixed << showpoint << setprecision(2);

    // Display the menu and get a selection.
    cout << "Do you want to calculate the weekly pay of\n";
    cout << "(H) an hourly paid employee, or \n";
    cout << "(S) a salaried employee?\n";
    getChoice(selection);

    // Process the menu selection.
    switch (selection)
    {
        // Hourly paid employee
        case 'H' :
        case 'h' : cout << "How many hours were worked? ";
```

```
                        cin >> worked;
                        cout << "What is the hourly pay rate? ";
                        cin >> rate;
                        cout << "The gross weekly pay is $";
                        cout << calcWeeklyPay(worked, rate) << endl;
                        break;

            // Salaried employee
            case 'S' :
            case 's' :  cout << "What is the annual salary? ";
                        cin >> yearly;
                        cout << "The gross weekly pay is $";
                        cout << calcWeeklyPay(yearly) << endl;
                        break;
        }
        return 0;
}

//****************************************************************
// Definition of function getChoice.                             *
// The parameter letter is a reference to a char.                *
// This function asks the user for an H or an S and returns     *
// the validated input.                                          *
//****************************************************************

void getChoice(char & letter)
{
    // Get the user's selection.
    cout << "Enter your choice (H or S): ";
    cin >> letter;

    // Validate the selection.
    while (letter != 'H' && letter != 'h' &&
           letter != 'S' && letter != 's')
    {
        cout << "Please enter H or S: ";
        cin >> letter;
    }
}

//**************************************************************
// Definition of overloaded function calcWeeklyPay.            *
// This function calculates the gross weekly pay of            *
// an hourly paid employee. The parameter hours holds the      *
// number of hours worked. The parameter payRate holds the     *
// hourly pay rate. The function returns the weekly salary.*
//**************************************************************

double calcWeeklyPay(int hours, double payRate)
{
```

(program continues)

Program 28 *(continued)*

```
    return hours * payRate;
}

//***************************************************************
// Definition of overloaded function calcWeeklyPay.            *
// This function calculates the gross weekly pay of            *
// a salaried employee. The parameter holds the employee's     *
// annual salary. The function returns the weekly salary.      *
//***************************************************************

double calcWeeklyPay(double annSalary)
{
    return annSalary / 52;
}
```

Program Output with Example Input Shown in Bold

```
Do you want to calculate the weekly pay of
(H) an hourly paid employee, or
(S) a salaried employee?
Enter your choice (H or S): H [Enter]
How many hours were worked? 40 [Enter]
What is the hourly pay rate? 18.50 [Enter]
The gross weekly pay is $740.00
```

Program Output with Example Input Shown in Bold

```
Do you want to calculate the weekly pay of
(H) an hourly paid employee, or
(S) a salaried employee?
Enter your choice (H or S): S [Enter]
What is the annual salary? 68000.00 [Enter]
The gross weekly pay is $1307.69
```

15 The `exit()` Function

CONCEPT: The `exit()` function causes a program to terminate, regardless of which function or control mechanism is executing.

A C++ program stops executing when the `return` statement in function `main` is encountered. When other functions end, however, the program does not stop. Control of the program goes back to the place immediately following the function call. Sometimes rare circumstances make it necessary to terminate a program in a function other than `main`. To accomplish this, the `exit` function is used.

When the `exit` function is called, it causes the program to stop, regardless of which function contains the call. Program 29 demonstrates its use.

Program 29

```
// This program shows how the exit function causes a program
// to stop executing.
#include <iostream>
#include <cstdlib>  // Needed for the exit function
using namespace std;

void function();     // Function prototype

int main()
{
   function();
   return 0;
}

//***********************************************************
// This function simply demonstrates that exit can be used *
// to terminate a program from a function other than main. *
//***********************************************************

void function()
{
    cout << "This program terminates with the exit function.\n";
    cout << "Bye!\n";
    exit(0);
    cout << "This message will never be displayed\n";
    cout << "because the program has already terminated.\n";
}
```

Program Output

```
This program terminates with the exit function.
Bye!
```

To use the exit function, you must include the <cstdlib> header file. Notice the function takes an integer argument. This argument is the exit code you wish the program to pass back to the computer's operating system. This code is sometimes used outside of the program to indicate whether the program ended successfully or as the result of a failure. In Program 29, the exit code zero is passed, which commonly indicates a successful exit. If you are unsure which code to use with the exit function, there are two named constants, EXIT_FAILURE and EXIT_SUCCESS, defined in <cstdlib> for you to use. The constant EXIT_FAILURE is defined as the termination code that commonly represents an unsuccessful exit under the current operating system. Here is an example of its use:

```
exit(EXIT_FAILURE);
```

The constant EXIT_SUCCESS is defined as the termination code that commonly represents a successful exit under the current operating system. Here is an example:

```
exit(EXIT_SUCCESS);
```

NOTE: Generally, the exit code is important only if you know it will be tested outside the program. If it is not used, just pass zero, or EXIT_SUCCESS.

> **WARNING!** The `exit()` function unconditionally shuts down your program. Because it bypasses a program's normal logical flow, you should use it with caution.

Checkpoint

24 What is the output of the following program?

```
#include <iostream>
#include <cstdlib>
using namespace std;

void showVals(double, double);

int main()
{
   double x = 1.2, y = 4.5;

   showVals(x, y);
   return 0;
}
void showVals(double p1, double p2)
{
   cout << p1 << endl;
   exit(0);
   cout << p2 << endl;
}
```

25 What is the output of the following program?

```
#include <iostream>
using namespace std;

int manip(int);
int manip(int, int);
int manip(int, double);

int main()
{
   int x = 2, y= 4, z;
   double a = 3.1;

   z = manip(x) + manip(x, y) + manip(y, a);
   cout << z << endl;
   return 0;
}
int manip(int val)
{
   return val + val * 2;
}
int manip(int val1, int val2)
{
   return (val1 + val2) * 2;
}
int manip(int val1, double val2)
{
   return val1 * static_cast<int>(val2);
}
```

16 Stubs and Drivers

Stubs and *drivers* are very helpful tools for testing and debugging programs that use functions. They allow you to test the individual functions in a program, in isolation from the parts of the program that call the functions.

A *stub* is a dummy function that is called instead of the actual function it represents. It usually displays a test message acknowledging that it was called, and nothing more. For example, if a stub were used for the showFees function in Program 10 (the modular health club membership program), it might look like this:

```
void showFees(double memberRate, int months)
{
    cout << "The showFees function was called with "
         << "the following arguments:\n"
         << "memberRate: " << memberRate << endl
         << "months: " << months << endl;
}
```

The following is an example output of the program if it were run with the stub instead of the actual showFees function. (A version of the health club program using this stub function is available from Computer Science Portal at www.pearsonhighered.com/gaddis. The program is named HealthClubWithStub.cpp.)

```
                    Health Club Membership Menu

1. Standard Adult Membership
2. Child Membership
3. Senior Citizen Membership
4. Quit the Program

Enter your choice: 1 [Enter]
For how many months? 4 [Enter]
The showFees function was called with the following arguments:
memberRate: 40.00
months: 4
                    Health Club Membership Menu

1. Standard Adult Membership
2. Child Membership
3. Senior Citizen Membership
4. Quit the Program

Enter your choice: 4 [Enter]
```

As you can see, by replacing an actual function with a stub, you can concentrate your testing efforts on the parts of the program that call the function. Primarily, the stub allows you to determine whether your program is calling a function when you expect it to, and to confirm that valid values are being passed to the function. If the stub represents a function that returns a value, then the stub should return a test value. This helps you confirm that the return value is being handled properly. When the parts of the program that call a function are debugged to your satisfaction, you can move on to testing and debugging the actual functions themselves. This is where *drivers* become useful.

A driver is a program that tests a function by simply calling it. If the function accepts arguments, the driver passes test data. If the function returns a value, the driver displays the return value on the screen. This allows you to see how the function performs in isolation from the rest of the program it will eventually be part of. Program 30 shows a driver for testing the showFees function in the health club membership program.

Program 30

```
// This program is a driver for testing the showFees function.
#include <iostream>
using namespace std;

// Prototype
void showFees(double, int);

int main()
{
    // Constants for membership rates
    const double ADULT = 40.0;
    const double SENIOR = 30.0;
    const double CHILD = 20.0;

    // Perform a test for adult membership.
    cout << "Testing an adult membership...\n"
         << "Calling the showFees function with arguments "
         << ADULT << " and 10.\n";
    showFees(ADULT, 10);

    // Perform a test for senior citizen membership.
    cout << "\nTesting a senior citizen membership...\n"
         << "Calling the showFees function with arguments "
         << SENIOR << " and 10.\n";
    showFees(SENIOR, 10);

    // Perform a test for child membership.
    cout << "\nTesting a child membership...\n"
         << "Calling the showFees function with arguments "
         << CHILD << " and 10.\n";
    showFees(CHILD, 10);
    return 0;
}

//*****************************************************************
// Definition of function showFees. The memberRate parameter holds *
// the monthly membership rate and the months parameter holds the  *
// number of months. The function displays the total charges.      *
//*****************************************************************

void showFees(double memberRate, int months)
{
    cout << "The total charges are $"
         << (memberRate * months) << endl;
}
```

Program Output

```
Testing an adult membership...
Calling the showFees function with arguments 40 and 10.
The total charges are $400

Testing a senior citizen membership...
Calling the showFees function with arguments 30 and 10.
The total charges are $300

Testing a child membership...
Calling the showFees function with arguments 20 and 10.
The total charges are $200
```

As shown in Program 30, a driver can be used to thoroughly test a function. It can repeatedly call the function with different test values as arguments. When the function performs as desired, it can be placed into the actual program it will be part of.

Case Study: See High Adventure Travel Agency Part 1 Case Study on the Computer Science Portal at www.pearsonhighered.com/gaddis.

Review Questions and Exercises

Short Answer

1. Why do local variables lose their values between calls to the function in which they are defined?
2. What is the difference between an argument and a parameter variable?
3. Where do you define parameter variables?
4. If you are writing a function that accepts an argument and you want to make sure the function cannot change the value of the argument, what do you do?
5. When a function accepts multiple arguments, does it matter in what order the arguments are passed?
6. How do you return a value from a function?
7. What is the advantage of breaking your application's code into several small procedures?
8. How would a `static` local variable be useful?
9. Give an example where passing an argument by reference would be useful.

Fill-in-the-Blank

10. The ________ is the part of a function definition that shows the function name, return type, and parameter list.
11. If a function doesn't return a value, the word ________ will appear as its return type.
12. Either a function's ________ or its ________ must precede all calls to the function.
13. Values that are sent into a function are called ________.

14. Special variables that hold copies of function arguments are called ________.
15. When only a copy of an argument is passed to a function, it is said to be passed by ________.
16. A(n) ________ eliminates the need to place a function definition before all calls to the function.
17. A(n) ________ variable is defined inside a function and is not accessible outside the function.
18. ________ variables are defined outside all functions and are accessible to any function within their scope.
19. ________ variables provide an easy way to share large amounts of data among all the functions in a program.
20. Unless you explicitly initialize global variables, they are automatically initialized to ________.
21. If a function has a local variable with the same name as a global variable, only the ________ variable can be seen by the function.
22. ________ local variables retain their value between function calls.
23. The ________ statement causes a function to end immediately.
24. ________ arguments are passed to parameters automatically if no argument is provided in the function call.
25. When a function uses a mixture of parameters with and without default arguments, the parameters with default arguments must be defined ________.
26. The value of a default argument must be a(n) ________.
27. When used as parameters, ________ variables allow a function to access the parameter's original argument.
28. Reference variables are defined like regular variables, except there is a(n) ________ in front of the name.
29. Reference variables allow arguments to be passed by ____________.
30. The ________ function causes a program to terminate.
31. Two or more functions may have the same name, as long as their ________ are different.

Algorithm Workbench

32. Examine the following function header, then write an example call to the function:

```
void showValue(int quantity)
```

33. The following statement calls a function named `half`. The `half` function returns a value that is half that of the argument. Write the function.

```
result = half(number);
```

34. A program contains the following function:

```
int cube(int num)
{
   return num * num * num;
}
```

Write a statement that passes the value 4 to this function and assigns its return value to the variable `result`.

35. Write a function named `timesTen` that accepts an argument. When the function is called, it should display the product of its argument multiplied by 10.

36. A program contains the following function:

```
void display(int arg1, double arg2, char arg3)
{
   cout << "Here are the values: "
        << arg1 << " " << arg2 << " "
        << arg3 << endl;
}
```

Write a statement that calls the procedure and passes the following variables to it:

```
int age;
double income;
char initial;
```

37. Write a function named `getNumber` that uses a reference parameter variable to accept an integer argument. The function should prompt the user to enter a number in the range of 1 through 100. The input should be validated and stored in the parameter variable.

True or False

38. T F Functions should be given names that reflect their purpose.
39. T F Function headers are terminated with a semicolon.
40. T F Function prototypes are terminated with a semicolon.
41. T F If other functions are defined before `main`, the program still starts executing at function `main`.
42. T F When a function terminates, it always branches back to `main`, regardless of where it was called from.
43. T F Arguments are passed to the function parameters in the order they appear in the function call.
44. T F The scope of a parameter is limited to the function that uses it.
45. T F Changes to a function parameter always affect the original argument as well.
46. T F In a function prototype, the names of the parameter variables may be left out.
47. T F Many functions may have local variables with the same name.
48. T F Overuse of global variables can lead to problems.
49. T F Static local variables are not destroyed when a function returns.
50. T F All static local variables are initialized to –1 by default.
51. T F Initialization of static local variables only happens once, regardless of how many times the function in which they are defined is called.
52. T F When a function with default arguments is called and an argument is left out, all arguments that come after it must be left out as well.

53. T F It is not possible for a function to have some parameters with default arguments and some without.

54. T F The `exit` function can only be called from `main`.

55. T F A stub is a dummy function that is called instead of the actual function it represents.

Find the Errors

Each of the following functions has errors. Locate as many errors as you can.

56.
```
void total(int value1, value2, value3)
{
   return value1 + value2 + value3;
}
```

57.
```
double average(int value1, int value2, int value3)
{
   double average;

   average = value1 + value2 + value3 / 3;
}
```

58.
```
void area(int length = 30, int width)
{
   return length * width;
}
```

59.
```
void getValue(int value&)
{
   cout << "Enter a value: ";
   cin >> value&;
}
```

60. *(Overloaded functions)*
```
int getValue()
{
   int inputValue;
   cout << "Enter an integer: ";
   cin >> inputValue;
   return inputValue;
}
double getValue()
{
   double inputValue;
   cout << "Enter a floating-point number: ";
   cin >> inputValue;
   return inputValue;
}
```

Programming Challenges

1. Markup

VideoNote
Solving the Markup Problem

Write a program that asks the user to enter an item's wholesale cost and its markup percentage. It should then display the item's retail price. For example:

- If an item's wholesale cost is 5.00 and its markup percentage is 100 percent, then the item's retail price is 10.00.

- If an item's wholesale cost is 5.00 and its markup percentage is 50 percent, then the item's retail price is 7.50.

The program should have a function named `calculateRetail` that receives the wholesale cost and the markup percentage as arguments and returns the retail price of the item.

Input Validation: Do not accept negative values for either the wholesale cost of the item or the markup percentage.

2. Rectangle Area—Complete the Program

If you have downloaded this chapter's source code, you will find a partially written program named AreaRectangle.cpp in the Chapter 06 folder. Your job is to complete the program. When it is complete, the program will ask the user to enter the width and length of a rectangle, then display the rectangle's area. The program calls the following functions, which have not been written:

- `getLength`—This function should ask the user to enter the rectangle's length then return that value as a `double`.
- `getWidth`—This function should ask the user to enter the rectangle's width then return that value as a `double`.
- `getArea`—This function should accept the rectangle's length and width as arguments and return the rectangle's area. The area is calculated by multiplying the length by the width.
- `displayData`—This function should accept the rectangle's length, width, and area as arguments and display them in an appropriate message on the screen.

3. Winning Division

Write a program that determines which of a company's four divisions (Northeast, Southeast, Northwest, and Southwest) had the greatest sales for a quarter. It should include the following two functions, which are called by `main`:

- `double getSales()` is passed the name of a division. It asks the user for a division's quarterly sales figure, validates the input, then returns it. It should be called once for each division.
- `void findHighest()` is passed the four sales totals. It determines which is the largest and prints the name of the high-grossing division, along with its sales figure.

Input Validation: Do not accept dollar amounts less than $0.00.

4. Safest Driving Area

Write a program that determines which of five geographic regions within a major city (north, south, east, west, and central) had the fewest reported automobile accidents last year. It should have the following two functions, which are called by `main`:

- `int getNumAccidents()` is passed the name of a region. It asks the user for the number of automobile accidents reported in that region during the last year, validates the input, then returns it. It should be called once for each city region.
- `void findLowest()` is passed the five accident totals. It determines which is the smallest and prints the name of the region, along with its accident figure.

Input Validation: Do not accept an accident number that is less than 0.

5. Falling Distance

When an object is falling because of gravity, the following formula can be used to determine the distance the object falls in a specific time period:

$d = \frac{1}{2}gt^2$

The variables in the formula are as follows: d is the distance in meters, g is 9.8, and t is the amount of time, in seconds, that the object has been falling.

Write a function named `fallingDistance` that accepts an object's falling time (in seconds) as an argument. The function should return the distance, in meters, that the object has fallen during that time interval. Write a program that demonstrates the function by calling it in a loop that passes the values 1 through 10 as arguments and displays the return value.

6. Kinetic Energy

In physics, an object that is in motion is said to have kinetic energy. The following formula can be used to determine a moving object's kinetic energy:

$KE = \frac{1}{2}\, mv^2$

The variables in the formula are as follows: KE is the kinetic energy, m is the object's mass in kilograms, and v is the object's velocity, in meters per second.

Write a function named `kineticEnergy` that accepts an object's mass (in kilograms) and velocity (in meters per second) as arguments. The function should return the amount of kinetic energy that the object has. Demonstrate the function by calling it in a program that asks the user to enter values for mass and velocity.

7. Celsius Temperature Table

The formula for converting a temperature from Fahrenheit to Celsius is

$$C = \frac{5}{9}(F - 32)$$

where F is the Fahrenheit temperature and C is the Celsius temperature. Write a function named `celsius` that accepts a Fahrenheit temperature as an argument. The function should return the temperature, converted to Celsius. Demonstrate the function by calling it in a loop that displays a table of the Fahrenheit temperatures 0 through 20 and their Celsius equivalents.

8. Coin Toss

Write a function named `coinToss` that simulates the tossing of a coin. When you call the function, it should generate a random number in the range of 1 through 2. If the random number is 1, the function should display "heads." If the random number is 2, the function should display "tails." Demonstrate the function in a program that asks the user how many times the coin should be tossed, then simulates the tossing of the coin that number of times.

9. Present Value

Suppose you want to deposit a certain amount of money into a savings account and then leave it alone to draw interest for the next 10 years. At the end of 10 years, you would like to have $10,000 in the account. How much do you need to deposit today to make that happen? You can use the following formula, which is known as the present value formula, to find out:

$$P = \frac{F}{(1 + r)^n}$$

The terms in the formula are as follows:

- P is the **present value**, or the amount that you need to deposit today.
- F is the **future value** that you want in the account. (In this case, F is $10,000.)
- r is the **annual interest rate.**
- n is the **number of years** that you plan to let the money sit in the account.

Write a program that has a function named `presentValue` that performs this calculation. The function should accept the future value, annual interest rate, and number of years as arguments. It should return the present value, which is the amount that you need to deposit today. Demonstrate the function in a program that lets the user experiment with different values for the formula's terms.

10. Future Value

Suppose you have a certain amount of money in a savings account that earns compound monthly interest, and you want to calculate the amount that you will have after a specific number of months. The formula, which is known as the future value formula, is

$$F = P \times (1 + i)^t$$

The terms in the formula are as follows:

- F is the **future value** of the account after the specified time period.
- P is the **present value** of the account.
- i is the **monthly interest rate.**
- t is the **number of months.**

Write a program that prompts the user to enter the account's present value, monthly interest rate, and the number of months that the money will be left in the account. The program should pass these values to a function named `futureValue` that returns the future value of the account, after the specified number of months. The program should display the account's future value.

11. Lowest Score Drop

Write a program that calculates the average of a group of test scores, where the lowest score in the group is dropped. It should use the following functions:

- `void getScore()` should ask the user for a test score, store it in a reference parameter variable, and validate it. This function should be called by `main` once for each of the five scores to be entered.
- `void calcAverage()` should calculate and display the average of the four highest scores. This function should be called just once by `main` and should be passed the five scores.
- `int findLowest()` should find and return the lowest of the five scores passed to it. It should be called by `calcAverage`, which uses the function to determine which of the five scores to drop.

Input Validation: Do not accept test scores lower than 0 or higher than 100.

12. Star Search

A particular talent competition has five judges, each of whom awards a score between 0 and 10 to each performer. Fractional scores, such as 8.3, are allowed. A performer's final score is determined by dropping the highest and lowest score received, then averaging the three remaining scores. Write a program that uses this method to calculate a contestant's score. It should include the following functions:

- `void getJudgeData()` should ask the user for a judge's score, store it in a reference parameter variable, and validate it. This function should be called by `main` once for each of the five judges.
- `void calcScore()` should calculate and display the average of the three scores that remain after dropping the highest and lowest scores the performer received. This function should be called just once by `main` and should be passed the five scores.

The last two functions, described below, should be called by `calcScore`, which uses the returned information to determine which of the scores to drop.

- `int findLowest()` should find and return the lowest of the five scores passed to it.
- `int findHighest()` should find and return the highest of the five scores passed to it.

Input Validation: Do not accept judge scores lower than 0 or higher than 10.

13. Days Out

Write a program that calculates the average number of days a company's employees are absent. The program should have the following functions:

- A function called by `main` that asks the user for the number of employees in the company. This value should be returned as an `int`. (The function accepts no arguments.)
- A function called by `main` that accepts one argument: the number of employees in the company. The function should ask the user to enter the number of days each employee missed during the past year. The total of these days should be returned as an `int`.
- A function called by `main` that takes two arguments: the number of employees in the company and the total number of days absent for all employees during the year. The function should return, as a `double`, the average number of days absent. (This function does not perform screen output and does not ask the user for input.)

Input Validation: Do not accept a number less than 1 for the number of employees. Do not accept a negative number for the days any employee missed.

14. Order Status

The Middletown Wholesale Copper Wire Company sells spools of copper wiring for $100 each. Write a program that displays the status of an order. The program should have a function that asks for the following data:

- The number of spools ordered
- The number of spools in stock
- Whether there are special shipping and handling charges

(Shipping and handling is normally $10 per spool.) If there are special charges, the program should ask for the special charges per spool.

The gathered data should be passed as arguments to another function that displays:

- The number of spools ready to ship from current stock
- The number of spools on backorder (if the number ordered is greater than what is in stock)
- Subtotal of the portion ready to ship (the number of spools ready to ship times $100)
- Total shipping and handling charges on the portion ready to ship
- Total of the order ready to ship

The shipping and handling parameter in the second function should have the default argument 10.00.

Input Validation: Do not accept numbers less than 1 for spools ordered. Do not accept a number less than 0 for spools in stock or shipping and handling charges.

15. Overloaded Hospital

Write a program that computes and displays the charges for a patient's hospital stay. First, the program should ask if the patient was admitted as an inpatient or an outpatient. If the patient was an inpatient, the following data should be entered:

- The number of days spent in the hospital
- The daily rate
- Hospital medication charges
- Charges for hospital services (lab tests, etc.)

The program should ask for the following data if the patient was an outpatient:

- Charges for hospital services (lab tests, etc.)
- Hospital medication charges

The program should use two overloaded functions to calculate the total charges. One of the functions should accept arguments for the inpatient data, while the other function accepts arguments for outpatient information. Both functions should return the total charges.

Input Validation: Do not accept negative numbers for any data.

16. Population

In a population, the birth rate is the percentage increase of the population due to births, and the death rate is the percentage decrease of the population due to deaths. Write a program that displays the size of a population for any number of years. The program should ask for the following data:

- The starting size of a population
- The annual birth rate
- The annual death rate
- The number of years to display

Write a function that calculates the size of the population for a year. The formula is

```
N = P + BP - DP
```

where `N` is the new population size, `P` is the previous population size, `B` is the birth rate, and `D` is the death rate.

Input Validation: Do not accept numbers less than 2 for the starting size. Do not accept negative numbers for birth rate or death rate. Do not accept numbers less than 1 for the number of years.

17. Transient Population

Modify Programming Challenge 16 to also consider the effect on population caused by people moving into or out of a geographic area. Given as input a starting population size, the annual birth rate, the annual death rate, the number of individuals who typically move into the area each year, and the number of individuals who typically leave the area each year, the program should project what the population will be `numYears` from now. You can either prompt the user to input a value for `numYears`, or you can set it within the program.

Input Validation: Do not accept numbers less than 2 for the starting size. Do not accept negative numbers for birth rate, death rate, arrivals, or departures.

18. Paint Job Estimator

A painting company has determined that for every 110 square feet of wall space, 1 gallon of paint and 8 hours of labor will be required. The company charges $25.00 per hour for labor. Write a modular program that allows the user to enter the number of rooms that are to be painted and the price of the paint per gallon. It should also ask for the square feet of wall space in each room. It should then display the following data:

- The number of gallons of paint required
- The hours of labor required
- The cost of the paint
- The labor charges
- The total cost of the paint job

Input validation: Do not accept a value less than 1 for the number of rooms. Do not accept a value less than $10.00 for the price of paint. Do not accept a negative value for square footage of wall space.

19. Using Files—Hospital Report

Modify Programming Challenge 15 (Overloaded Hospital) to write the report it creates to a file.

20. Stock Profit

The profit from the sale of a stock can be calculated as follows:

$$\text{Profit} = ((NS \times SP) - SC) - ((NS \times PP) + PC)$$

where *NS* is the number of shares, *SP* is the sale price per share, *SC* is the sale commission paid, *PP* is the purchase price per share, and *PC* is the purchase commission paid. If the calculation yields a positive value, then the sale of the stock resulted in a profit. If the calculation yields a negative number, then the sale resulted in a loss.

Write a function that accepts as arguments the number of shares, the purchase price per share, the purchase commission paid, the sale price per share, and the sale commission paid. The function should return the profit (or loss) from the sale of stock.

Demonstrate the function in a program that asks the user to enter the necessary data and displays the amount of the profit or loss.

21. Multiple Stock Sales

Use the function that you wrote for Programming Challenge 20 (Stock Profit) in a program that calculates the total profit or loss from the sale of multiple stocks. The program should ask the user for the number of stock sales and the necessary data for each stock sale. It should accumulate the profit or loss for each stock sale, then display the total.

22. `isPrime` Function

A prime number is a number that is only evenly divisible by itself and 1. For example, the number 5 is prime because it can only be evenly divided by 1 and 5. The number 6, however, is not prime because it can be divided evenly by 1, 2, 3, and 6.

Write a function name `isPrime`, which takes an integer as an argument and returns `true` if the argument is a prime number, or `false` otherwise. Demonstrate the function in a complete program.

> **TIP:** Recall that the % operator divides one number by another, and returns the remainder of the division. In an expression such as `num1 % num2`, the % operator will return 0 if `num1` is evenly divisible by `num2`.

23. Prime Number List

Use the `isPrime` function that you wrote in Programming Challenge 22 (`isPrime` function) in a program that stores a list of all the prime numbers from 1 through 100 in a file.

24. Rock, Paper, Scissors Game

Write a program that lets the user play the game of Rock, Paper, Scissors against the computer. The program should work as follows:

1. When the program begins, a random number in the range of 1 through 3 is generated. If the number is 1, then the computer has chosen rock. If the number is 2, then the computer has chosen paper. If the number is 3, then the computer has chosen scissors. (Don't display the computer's choice yet.)
2. The user enters his or her choice of "rock", "paper", or "scissors" at the keyboard. (You can use a menu if you prefer.)
3. The computer's choice is displayed.
4. A winner is selected according to the following rules:

   - If one player chooses rock and the other player chooses scissors, then rock wins. (The rock smashes the scissors.)
   - If one player chooses scissors and the other player chooses paper, then scissors wins. (Scissors cuts paper.)
   - If one player chooses paper and the other player chooses rock, then paper wins. (Paper wraps rock.)
   - If both players make the same choice, the game must be played again to determine the winner.

Be sure to divide the program into functions that perform each major task.

Group Project

25. Travel Expenses

This program should be designed and written by a team of students. Here are some suggestions:

- One student should design function `main`, which will call the other functions in the program. The remainder of the functions will be designed by other members of the team.
- The requirements of the program should be analyzed so each student is given about the same workload.
- The parameters and return types of each function should be decided in advance.
- Stubs and drivers should be used to test and debug the program.
- The program can be implemented as a multi-file program, or all the functions can be cut and pasted into the main file.

Here is the assignment: Write a program that calculates and displays the total travel expenses of a businessperson on a trip. The program should have functions that ask for and return the following:

- The total number of days spent on the trip
- The time of departure on the first day of the trip, and the time of arrival back home on the last day of the trip
- The amount of any round-trip airfare
- The amount of any car rentals
- Miles driven, if a private vehicle was used. Calculate the vehicle expense as $0.27 per mile driven
- Parking fees (The company allows up to $6 per day. Anything in excess of this must be paid by the employee.)
- Taxi fees, if a taxi was used anytime during the trip (The company allows up to $10 per day, for each day a taxi was used. Anything in excess of this must be paid by the employee.)
- Conference or seminar registration fees
- Hotel expenses (The company allows up to $90 per night for lodging. Anything in excess of this must be paid by the employee.)
- The amount of *each* meal eaten. On the first day of the trip, breakfast is allowed as an expense if the time of departure is before 7 a.m. Lunch is allowed if the time of departure is before 12 noon. Dinner is allowed on the first day if the time of departure is before 6 p.m. On the last day of the trip, breakfast is allowed if the time of arrival is after 8 a.m. Lunch is allowed if the time of arrival is after 1 p.m. Dinner is allowed on the last day if the time of arrival is after 7 p.m. The program should only ask for the amounts of allowable meals. (The company allows up to $9 for breakfast, $12 for lunch, and $16 for dinner. Anything in excess of this must be paid by the employee.)

The program should calculate and display the total expenses incurred by the businessperson, the total allowable expenses for the trip, the excess that must be reimbursed by the businessperson, if any, and the amount saved by the businessperson if the expenses were under the total allowed.

Input Validation: Do not accept negative numbers for any dollar amount or for miles driven in a private vehicle. Do not accept numbers less than 1 for the number of days. Only accept valid times for the time of departure and the time of arrival.

Answers to Checkpoints

1 Function call

2 Function header

3
```
I saw Elba
Able was I
```

4
```
void qualify()
{
     cout << "Congratulations, you qualify for\n";
     cout << "the loan. The annual interest rate\n";
     cout << "is 12%\n";
}

void noQualify()
{
     cout << "You do not qualify. In order to\n";
     cout << "qualify you must have worked on\n";
     cout << "your current job for at least two\n";
     cout << "years and you must earn at least\n";
     cout << "$17,000 per year.\n";
}
```

5 Header
Prototype
Function call

6
```
void timesTen(int number)
{
     cout << (number * 10);
}
```

7
```
void timesTen(int);
```

8
```
0    0
1    2
2    4
3    6
4    8
5    10
6    12
7    14
8    16
9    18
```

9
```
0 1.5
1.5 0
0 10
0 1.5
```

10
```
void showDollars(double amount)
{
    cout << "Your wages are $";
    cout << setprecision(2);
    cout << fixed << showpoint;
    cout << amount << endl;
}
```

11 One

12 `double distance(double rate, double time)`

13 `int days(int years, int months, int weeks)`

14 `char getKey()`

15 `long lightYears(long miles)`

16 A static local variable's scope is limited to the function in which it is declared. A global variable's scope is the portion of the program beginning at its declaration to the end.

17
```
100
50
100
```

18
```
10
11
12
13
14
15
16
17
18
19
```

19 Literals or constants

20 *Prototype:*
`void compute(double, int = 5, long = 65536);`

Header:
`void compute(double x, int y, long z)`

21 *Prototype:*
`void calculate(long, double&, int = 47);`

Header:
`void calculate(long x, double &y, int z)`

22
```
5 10 15
9 10 15
6 15 15
4 11 16
```

23
```
0 00
Enter two numbers: 12 14
12 140
14 15-1
14 15-1
```

24
```
1.2
```

25
```
30
```

Answers to Odd Numbered Review Questions

1. Because they are created in memory when the function begins execution, and are destroyed when the function ends.
3. Inside the parentheses of a function header
5. Yes. The first argument is passed into the parameter variable that appears first inside the function header's parentheses. Likewise, the second argument is passed into the second parameter, and so on.
7. It makes the program easier to manage. Imagine a book that has a thousand pages, but isn't divided into chapters or sections. Trying to find a single topic in the book would be very difficult. Real-world programs can easily have thousands of lines of code, and unless they are modularized, they can be very difficult to modify and maintain.
9. A function such as the following could be written to get user input. The input is stored in the variables that are passed as arguments.

```
void getValues(int &x, int &y)
{
    cout << "Enter a number: ";
    cin >> x;
    cout << "Enter another number: ";
    cin >> y;
}
```

11. `void`
13. arguments
15. value
17. local
19. global
21. local
23. `return`
25. last
27. reference

29. reference

31. parameter lists

33.
```
double half(double num)
{
    return num / 2;
}
```

35.
```
void timesTen(int num)
{
    cout << (num * 10) << endl;
}
```

37.
```
void getNumber(int &num)
{
    cout << "Enter a number in the range 1 - 100 : ";
    cin >> num;
    while (num < 1 || num > 100)
    {
        cout << "That number is out of range.\n";
        cout << "Enter a number in the range 1 - 100 : ";
        cin >> num;
    }
}
```

39. False

41. True

43. True

45. False

47. True

49. True

51. True

53. False

55. True

57. The assignment statement should read:

```
average = (value1 + value2 + value3) / 3.0;
```

The function is defined as a `double` but returns no value.

59. The parameter should be defined as:

```
int &value
```

The `cin` statement should read:

```
cin >> value;
```

Arrays and Vectors

TOPICS

1 Arrays Hold Multiple Values

CONCEPT: An array allows you to store and work with multiple values of the same data type.

Each of the variable definitions in Figure 1 causes only enough memory to be reserved to hold one value of the specified data type.

Figure 1 Variables can hold one value at a time

Definition	Memory	Value
`int count;`	Enough memory for 1 `int`	12314
`float price;`	Enough memory for 1 float	56.981
`char letter;`	Enough memory for 1 char	A

An array works like a variable that can store a group of values, all of the same type. The values are stored together in consecutive memory locations. Here is a definition of an array of integers:

```
int days[6];
```

The name of this array is `days`. The number inside the brackets is the array's *size declarator.* It indicates the number of *elements*, or values, the array can hold. The `days` array can store six elements, each one an integer. This is depicted in Figure 2.

Figure 2 An array with six elements

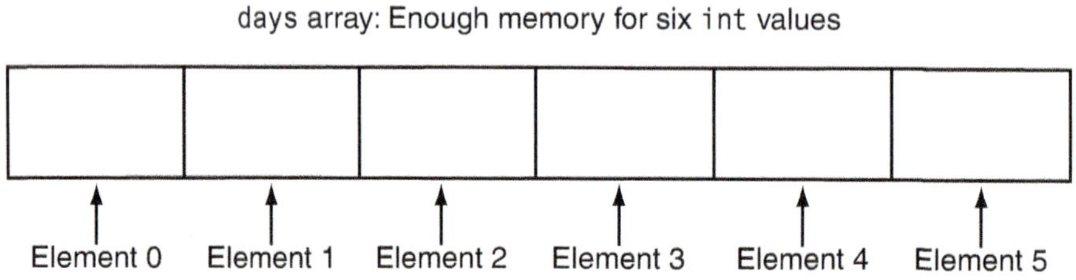

An array's size declarator must be a constant integer expression with a value greater than zero. It can be either a literal, as in the previous example, or a named constant, as shown in the following:

```
const int NUM_DAYS = 6;
int days[NUM_DAYS];
```

Arrays of any data type can be defined. The following are all valid array definitions:

```
float temperatures[100];     // Array of 100 floats
string names[10];            // Array of 10 string objects
long units[50];              // Array of 50 long integers
double sizes[1200];          // Array of 1200 doubles
```

Memory Requirements of Arrays

The amount of memory used by an array depends on the array's data type and the number of elements. The `hours` array, defined here, is an array of six `shorts`.

```
short hours[6];
```

On a typical system, a `short` uses 2 bytes of memory, so the `hours` array would occupy 12 bytes. This is shown in Figure 3.

Figure 3 Array memory usage

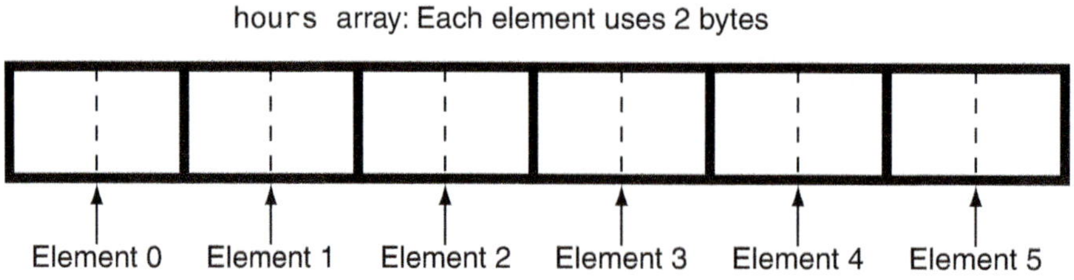

The size of an array can be calculated by multiplying the size of an individual element by the number of elements in the array. Table 1 shows the typical sizes of various arrays.

Table 1 Arrays and Their sizes

Array Definition	Number of Elements	Size of Each Element	Size of the Array
`char letters[25];`	25	1 byte	25 bytes
`short rings[100];`	100	2 bytes	200 bytes
`int miles[84];`	84	4 bytes	336 bytes
`float temp[12];`	12	4 bytes	48 bytes
`double distance[1000];`	1000	8 bytes	8000 bytes

2 Accessing Array Elements

CONCEPT: The individual elements of an array are assigned unique subscripts. These subscripts are used to access the elements.

Even though an entire array has only one name, the elements may be accessed and used as individual variables. This is possible because each element is assigned a number known as a *subscript*. A subscript is used as an index to pinpoint a specific element within an array. The first element is assigned the subscript 0, the second element is assigned 1, and so forth. The six elements in the array `hours` would have the subscripts 0 through 5. This is shown in Figure 4.

Figure 4 Subscripts

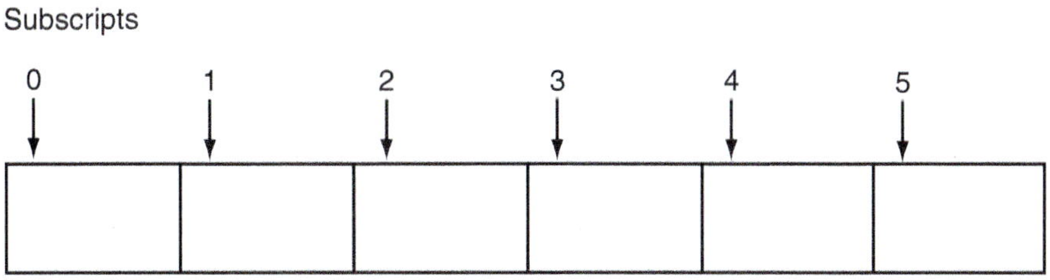

NOTE: Subscript numbering in C++ always starts at zero. The subscript of the last element in an array is one less than the total number of elements in the array. This means that in the array shown in Figure 4, the element `hours[6]` does not exist. `hours[5]` is the last element in the array.

Each element in the `hours` array, when accessed by its subscript, can be used as a `short` variable. Here is an example of a statement that stores the number 20 in the first element of the array:

```
hours[0] = 20;
```

> **NOTE:** The expression `hours[0]` is pronounced "hours sub zero." You would read this assignment statement as "hours sub zero is assigned twenty."

Figure 5 shows the contents of the `hours` array after the statement assigns 20 to `hours[0]`.

Figure 5 Contents of the `hours` array

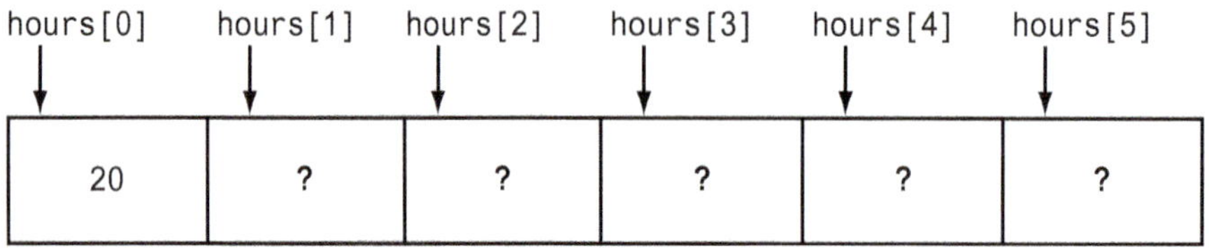

> **NOTE:** Because values have not been assigned to the other elements of the array, question marks will be used to indicate that the contents of those elements are unknown. If an array is defined globally, all of its elements are initialized to zero by default. Local arrays, however, have no default initialization value.

The following statement stores the integer 30 in `hours[3]`:

```
hours[3] = 30;
```

Figure 6 shows the contents of the array after the previous statement executes.

Figure 6 Contents of the `hours` array

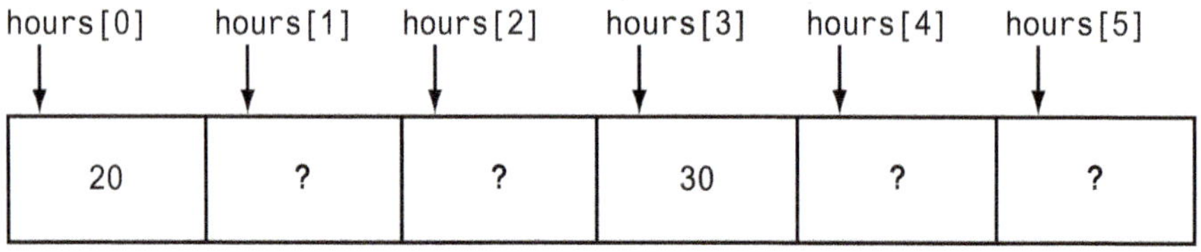

> **NOTE:** Understand the difference between the array size declarator and a subscript. The number inside the brackets of an array definition is the size declarator. The number inside the brackets of an assignment statement or any statement that works with the contents of an array is a subscript.

Inputting and Outputting Array Contents

Array elements may be used with the `cin` and `cout` objects like any other variable. Program 1 shows the array `hours` being used to store and display values entered by the user.

Program 1

```cpp
// This program asks for the number of hours worked
// by six employees. It stores the values in an array.
#include <iostream>
using namespace std;

int main()
{
    const int NUM_EMPLOYEES = 6;
    int hours[NUM_EMPLOYEES];

    // Get the hours worked by each employee.
    cout << "Enter the hours worked by "
         << NUM_EMPLOYEES << " employees: ";
    cin >> hours[0];
    cin >> hours[1];
    cin >> hours[2];
    cin >> hours[3];
    cin >> hours[4];
    cin >> hours[5];

    // Display the values in the array.
    cout << "The hours you entered are:";
    cout << " " << hours[0];
    cout << " " << hours[1];
    cout << " " << hours[2];
    cout << " " << hours[3];
    cout << " " << hours[4];
    cout << " " << hours[5] << endl;
    return 0;
}
```

Program Output with Example Input Shown in Bold

Enter the hours worked by 6 employees: **20 12 40 30 30 15** [Enter]
The hours you entered are: 20 12 40 30 30 15

Figure 7 shows the contents of the array hours with the values entered by the user in the example output above.

Figure 7 Contents of the hours array

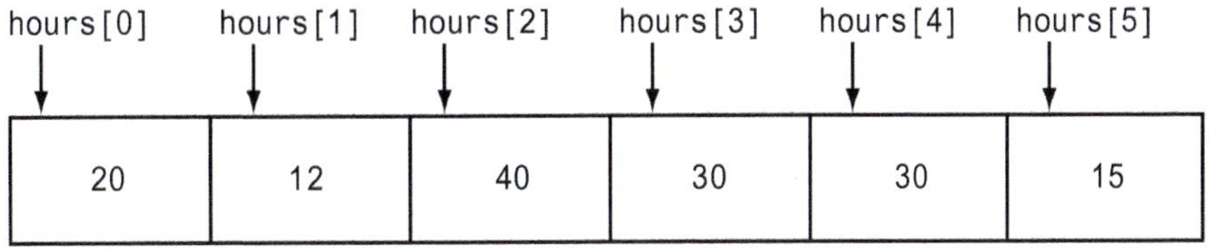

Even though the size declarator of an array definition must be a constant or a literal, subscript numbers can be stored in variables. This makes it possible to use a loop to "step through" an entire array, performing the same operation on each element. For example, look at the following code:

```
const int ARRAY_SIZE = 5;
int numbers[ARRAY_SIZE];

for (int count = 0; count < ARRAY_SIZE; count++)
   numbers[count] = 99;
```

VideoNote
Accessing Array Elements with a Loop

This code first defines a constant `int` named `ARRAY_SIZE` and initializes it with the value 5. Then, it defines an `int` array named `numbers`, using `ARRAY_SIZE` as the size declarator. As a result, the `numbers` array will have five elements. The `for` loop uses a counter variable named `count`. This loop will iterate five times, and during the loop iterations the `count` variable will take on the values 0 through 4.

Notice the statement inside the loop uses the `count` variable as a subscript. It assigns 99 to `numbers[count]`. During the first iteration, 99 is assigned to `numbers[0]`. During the next iteration, 99 is assigned to `numbers[1]`. This continues until 99 has been assigned to all of the array's elements. Figure 8 illustrates that the loop's initialization, test, and update expressions have been written so that the loop starts and ends the counter variable with valid subscript values (0 through 4). This ensures that only valid subscripts are used in the body of the loop.

Figure 8 Initialization, test, and update expressions

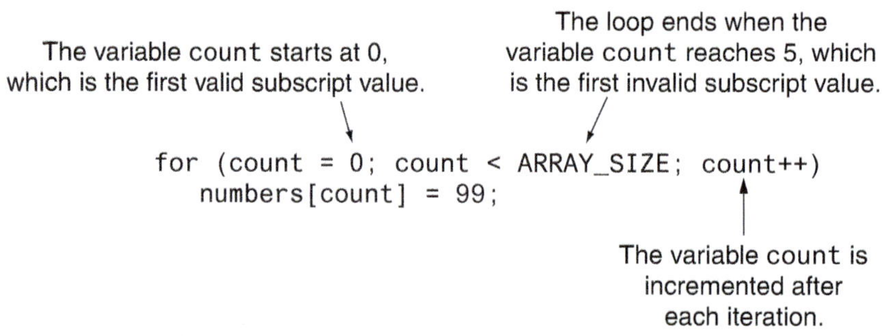

Program 1 could be simplified by using two `for` loops: one for inputting the values into the array, and another for displaying the contents of the array. This is shown in Program 2.

Program 2

```
// This program asks for the number of hours worked
// by six employees. It stores the values in an array.
#include <iostream>
using namespace std;

```

```
6  int main()
7  {
8      const int NUM_EMPLOYEES = 6; // Number of employees
9      int hours[NUM_EMPLOYEES];    // Each employee's hours
10     int count;                   // Loop counter
11
12     // Input the hours worked.
13     for (count = 0; count < NUM_EMPLOYEES; count++)
14     {
15         cout << "Enter the hours worked by employee "
16              << (count + 1) << ": ";
17         cin >> hours[count];
18     }
19
20     // Display the contents of the array.
21     cout << "The hours you entered are:";
22     for (count = 0; count < NUM_EMPLOYEES; count++)
23         cout << " " << hours[count];
24     cout << endl;
25     return 0;
26 }
```

Program Output with Example Input Shown in Bold

```
Enter the hours worked by employee 1: 20 [Enter]
Enter the hours worked by employee 2: 12 [Enter]
Enter the hours worked by employee 3: 40 [Enter]
Enter the hours worked by employee 4: 30 [Enter]
Enter the hours worked by employee 5: 30 [Enter]
Enter the hours worked by employee 6: 15 [Enter]
The hours you entered are: 20 12 40 30 30 15
```

The first `for` loop, in lines 13 through 18, prompts the user for each employee's hours. Take a closer look at lines 15 through 17:

```
cout << "Enter the hours worked by employee "
     << (count + 1) << ": ";
cin >> hours[count];
```

Notice the `cout` statement uses the expression `count + 1` to display the employee number, but the `cin` statement uses `count` as the array subscript. This is because the hours for employee number 1 are stored in `hours[0]`, the hours for employee number 2 are stored in `hours[1]`, and so forth.

The loop in lines 22 and 23 also uses the `count` variable to step through the array, displaying each element.

NOTE: You can use any integer expression as an array subscript. For example, the first loop in Program 2 could have been written like this:

```
for (count = 1; count <= NUM_EMPLOYEES; count++)
{
   cout << "Enter the hours worked by employee "
        << count << ": ";
   cin >> hours[count - 1];
}
```

In this code, the `cin` statement uses the expression `count - 1` as a subscript.

Inputting data into an array must normally be done one element at a time. For example, the following `cin` statement will not input data into the `hours` array:

```
cin >> hours;   // Wrong! This will NOT work.
```

Instead, you must use multiple `cin` statements to read data into each array element, or use a loop to step through the array, reading data into its elements. Also, outputting an array's contents must normally be done one element at a time. For example, the following `cout` statement will not display the contents of the `hours` array:

```
cout << hours;   // Wrong! This will NOT work.
```

Instead, you must output each element of the array separately.

Array Initialization

Like regular variables, C++ allows you to initialize an array's elements when you create the array. Here is an example:

```
const int MONTHS = 12;
int days[MONTHS] = {31, 28, 31, 30, 31, 30, 31, 31, 30, 31, 30, 31};
```

The series of values inside the braces and separated with commas is called an *initialization list*. These values are stored in the array elements in the order they appear in the list. (The first value, 31, is stored in `days[0]`, the second value, 28, is stored in `days[1]`, and so forth.) Figure 9 shows the contents of the array after the initialization.

Figure 9 The array after initialization

Subscripts

0	1	2	3	4	5	6	7	8	9	10	11
31	28	31	30	31	30	31	31	30	31	30	31

Program 3 demonstrates how an array may be initialized.

Program 3

```
// This program displays the number of days in each month.
#include <iostream>
using namespace std;

int main()
{
   const int MONTHS = 12;
   int days[MONTHS] = { 31, 28, 31, 30,
                        31, 30, 31, 31,
                        30, 31, 30, 31 };

   for (int count = 0; count < MONTHS; count++)
   {
      cout << "Month " << (count + 1) << " has ";
      cout << days[count] << " days.\n";
   }
   return 0;
}
```

Program Output

```
Month 1 has 31 days.
Month 2 has 28 days.
Month 3 has 31 days.
Month 4 has 30 days.
Month 5 has 31 days.
Month 6 has 30 days.
Month 7 has 31 days.
Month 8 has 31 days.
Month 9 has 30 days.
Month 10 has 31 days.
Month 11 has 30 days.
Month 12 has 31 days.
```

NOTE: C++ allows you to spread the initialization list across multiple lines. Both of the following array definitions are equivalent:

```
double coins[5] = {0.05, 0.1, 0.25, 0.5, 1.0};
double coins[5] = {0.05,
                   0.1,
                   0.25,
                   0.5,
                   1.0};
```

Program 4 shows an example with a `string` array that is initialized with strings.

Program 4

```
// This program initializes a string array.
#include<iostream>
#include<string>
using namespace std;

int main()
{
    const int SIZE = 9;
    string planets[SIZE] = { "Mercury", "Venus", "Earth", "Mars",
                             "Jupiter", "Saturn", "Uranus",
                             "Neptune", "Pluto (a dwarf planet)" };

    cout << "Here are the planets:\n";

    for (int count = 0; count < SIZE; count++)
       cout << planets[count] << endl;
    return 0;
}
```

Program Output

```
Here are the planets:
Mercury
Venus
Earth
Mars
Jupiter
Saturn
Uranus
Neptune
Pluto (a dwarf planet)
```

Program 5 shows a character array being initialized with the first ten letters of the alphabet. The array is then used to display those characters' ASCII codes.

Program 5

```
// This program uses an array of ten characters to store the
// first ten letters of the alphabet. The ASCII codes of the
// characters are displayed.
#include <iostream>
using namespace std;

int main()
{
    const int NUM_LETTERS = 10;
    char letters[NUM_LETTERS] = {'A', 'B', 'C', 'D', 'E',
                                 'F', 'G', 'H', 'I', 'J'};

```

```
    cout << "Character" << "\t" << "ASCII Code\n";
    cout << "---------" << "\t" << "----------\n";
    for (int count = 0; count < NUM_LETTERS; count++)
    {
       cout << letters[count] << "\t\t";
       cout << static_cast<int>(letters[count]) << endl;
    }
    return 0;
}
```

Program Output

```
Character    ASCII Code
---------    ----------
A            65
B            66
C            67
D            68
E            69
F            70
G            71
H            72
I            73
J            74
```

NOTE: An array's initialization list cannot have more values than the array has elements.

Partial Array Initialization

When an array is being initialized, C++ does not require a value for every element. It's possible to only initialize part of an array, such as:

```
int numbers[7] = {1, 2, 4, 8};
```

This definition initializes only the first four elements of a 7-element array, as illustrated in Figure 10.

Figure 10 Partial array initialization

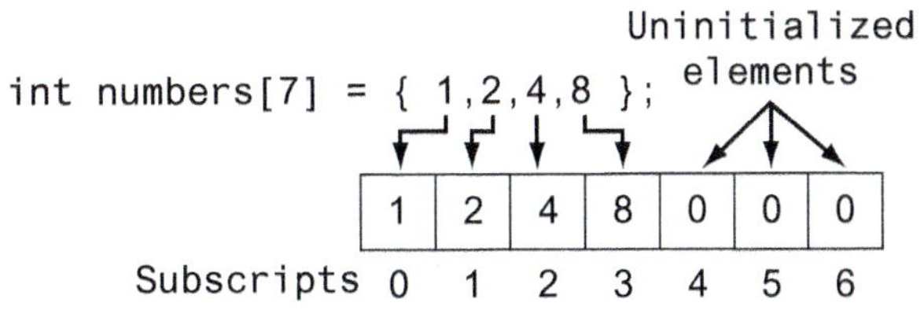

It's important to note that if an array is partially initialized, the uninitialized elements will be set to zero. The uninitialized elements of a `string` array will contain empty strings. This is true even if the array is defined locally. (If a local array is completely uninitialized, its elements will contain "garbage," like all other local variables.) Program 6 shows the contents of the numbers array after it is partially initialized.

Program 6

```
// This program has a partially initialized array.
#include <iostream>
using namespace std;

int main()
{
   const int SIZE = 7;
   int numbers[SIZE] = {1, 2, 4, 8}; // Initialize first 4 elements

   cout << "Here are the contents of the array:\n";
   for (int index = 0; index < SIZE; index++)
      cout << numbers[index] << " ";

   cout << endl;
   return 0;
}
```

Program Output

```
Here are the contents of the array:
1 2 4 8 0 0 0
```

If you leave an element uninitialized, you must leave all the elements that follow it uninitialized as well. C++ does not provide a way to skip elements in the initialization list. For example, the following is *not* legal:

```
int numbers[6] = {2, 4, , 8, , 12}; // NOT Legal!
```

Implicit Array Sizing

It's possible to define an array without specifying its size, as long as you provide an initialization list. C++ automatically makes the array large enough to hold all the initialization values. For example, the following definition creates an array with five elements:

```
double ratings[] = {1.0, 1.5, 2.0, 2.5, 3.0};
```

Because the size declarator is omitted, C++ counts the number of items in the initialization list and gives the array that many elements.

> **NOTE:** You *must* provide an initialization list if you leave out an array's size declarator. Otherwise, the compiler doesn't know how large to make the array.

Reading Data from a File into an Array

Reading the contents of a file into an array is straightforward: Open the file and use a loop to read each item from the file, storing each item in an array element. The loop should iterate until either the array is filled or the end of the file is reached. Program 7 demonstrates by opening a file that has 10 numbers stored in it then reading the file's contents into an array.

Program 7

```
1  // This program reads data from a file into an array.
2  #include <iostream>
3  #include <fstream>
4  using namespace std;
5
6  int main()
7  {
8      const int ARRAY_SIZE = 10; // Array size
9      int numbers[ARRAY_SIZE];   // Array with 10 elements
10     int count = 0;             // Loop counter variable
11     ifstream inputFile;        // Input file stream object
12
13     // Open the file.
14     inputFile.open("TenNumbers.txt");
15
16     // Read the numbers from the file into the array.
17     while (count < ARRAY_SIZE && inputFile >> numbers[count])
18         count++;
19
20     // Close the file.
21     inputFile.close();
22
23     // Display the numbers read:
24     cout << "The numbers are: ";
25     for (count = 0; count < ARRAY_SIZE; count++)
26         cout << numbers[count] << " ";
27     cout << endl;
28     return 0;
29 }
```

Program Output

```
The numbers are: 101 102 103 104 105 106 107 108 109 110
```

The `while` loop in lines 17 and 18 reads items from the file and assigns them to elements of the `numbers` array. Notice the loop tests two Boolean expressions, connected by the && operator:

- The first expression is `count < ARRAY_SIZE`. The purpose of this expression is to prevent the loop from writing beyond the end of the array. If the expression is true, the second Boolean expression is tested. If this expression is false, however, the loop stops.
- The second expression is `inputFile >> numbers[count]`. This expression reads a value from the file and stores it in the `numbers[count]` array element. If a value is successfully read from the file, the expression is true and the loop continues. If no value can be read from the file, however, the expression is false and the loop stops.

Each time the loop iterates, it increments `count` in line 18.

Writing the Contents of an Array to a File

Writing the contents of an array to a file is also a straightforward matter. Use a loop to step through each element of the array, writing its contents to a file. Program 8 demonstrates this.

Program 8

```
// This program writes the contents of an array to a file.
#include <iostream>
#include <fstream>
using namespace std;

int main()
{
    const int ARRAY_SIZE = 10;  // Array size
    int numbers[ARRAY_SIZE];    // Array with 10 elements
    int count;                  // Loop counter variable
    ofstream outputFile;        // Output file stream object

    // Store values in the array.
    for (count = 0; count < ARRAY_SIZE; count++)
       numbers[count] = count;

    // Open a file for output.
    outputFile.open("SavedNumbers.txt");

    // Write the array contents to the file.
    for (count = 0; count < ARRAY_SIZE; count++)
       outputFile << numbers[count] << endl;

    // Close the file.
    outputFile.close();

    // That's it!
    cout << "The numbers were saved to the file.\n ";
    return 0;
}
```

Program Output

```
The numbers were saved to the file.
```

Contents of the File `SavedNumbers.txt`

```
0
1
2
3
4
5
6
7
8
9
```

3 No Bounds Checking in C++

CONCEPT: C++ does not prevent you from overwriting an array's bounds.

C++ is a popular language for software developers who have to write fast, efficient code. To increase runtime efficiency, C++ does not provide many of the common safeguards to prevent unsafe memory access found in other languages. For example, C++ does not perform array bounds checking. This means you can write programs with subscripts that go beyond the boundaries of a particular array. Program 9 demonstrates this capability.

> **WARNING!** Program 9 will attempt to write to an area of memory outside the array. This is an invalid operation and will most likely cause the program to crash.

Program 9

```
// This program unsafely accesses an area of memory by writing
// values beyond an array's boundary.
// WARNING: If you compile and run this program, it could crash.
#include <iostream>
using namespace std;

int main()
{
    const int SIZE = 3;   // Constant for the array size
    int values[SIZE];     // An array of 3 integers
    int count;            // Loop counter variable

    // Attempt to store five numbers in the 3-element array.
    cout << "I will store 5 numbers in a 3-element array!\n";
    for (count = 0; count < 5; count++)
        values[count] = 100;

    // If the program is still running, display the numbers.
    cout << "If you see this message, it means the program\n";
    cout << "has not crashed! Here are the numbers:\n";
    for (count = 0; count < 5; count++)
        cout << values[count] << endl;
    return 0;
}
```

The `values` array has three integer elements, with the subscripts 0, 1, and 2. The loop, however, stores the number 100 in elements 0, 1, 2, 3, and 4. The elements with subscripts 3 and 4 do not exist, but C++ allows the program to write beyond the boundary of the array, as if those elements were there. Figure 11 depicts the way the array is set up in memory when the program first starts to execute, and what happens when the loop writes data beyond the boundary of the array.

Figure 11 Writing data beyond the bounds of an array

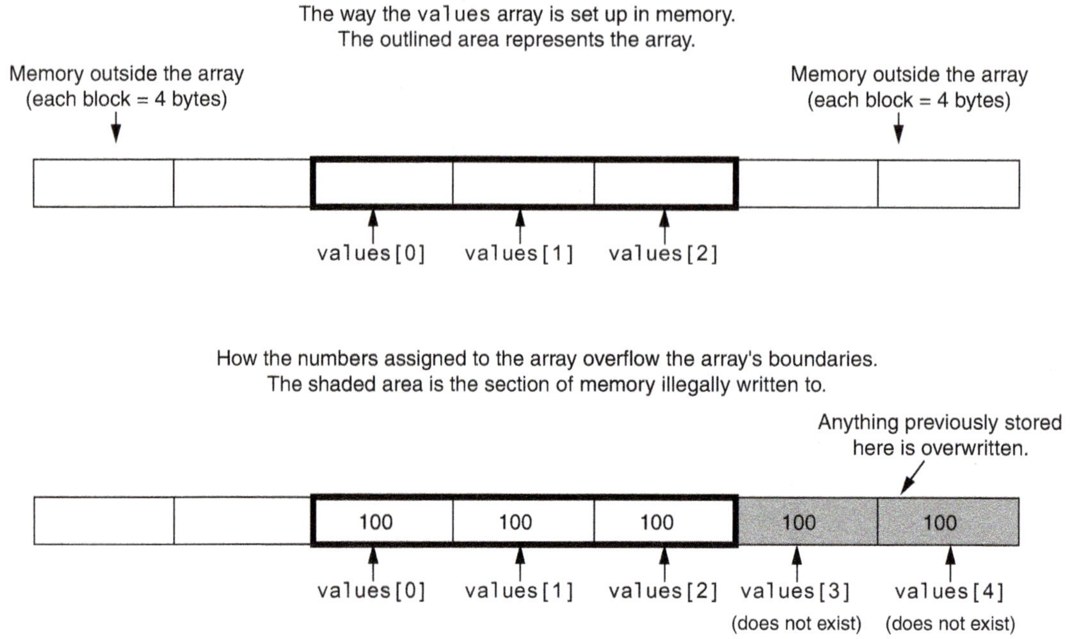

Although C++ programs are fast and efficient, the absence of safeguards such as array bounds checking usually proves to be a bad thing. It's easy for C++ programmers to make careless mistakes that allow programs to access areas of memory that are supposed to be off-limits. You must always make sure that any time you assign values to array elements, the values are written within the array's boundaries.

Watch for Off-by-One Errors

In working with arrays, a common type of mistake is the *off-by-one error*. This is an easy mistake to make because array subscripts start at 0 rather than 1. For example, look at the following code:

```
// This code has an off-by-one error.
const int SIZE = 100;
int numbers[SIZE];
for (int count = 1; count <= SIZE; count++)
   numbers[count] = 0;
```

The intent of this code is to create an array of integers with 100 elements, and store the value 0 in each element. However, this code has an off-by-one error. The loop uses its counter variable, `count`, as a subscript with the `numbers` array. During the loop's execution, the variable `count` takes on the values 1 through 100, when it should take on the values 0 through 99. As a result, the first element, which is at subscript 0, is skipped. In addition, the loop attempts to use 100 as a subscript during the last iteration. Because 100 is an invalid subscript, the program will write data beyond the array's boundaries.

Checkpoint

1 Define the following arrays:

A) `empNums`, a 100-element array of `int`s
B) `payRates`, a 25-element array of `float`s
C) `miles`, a 14-element array of `long`s
D) `cityName`, a 26-element array of `string` objects
E) `lightYears`, a 1,000-element array of `double`s

2 What's wrong with the following array definitions?

```
int readings[-1];
float measurements[4.5];
int size;
string names[size];
```

3 What would the valid subscript values be in a 4-element array of `double`s?

4 What is the difference between an array's size declarator and a subscript?

5 What is "array bounds checking"? Does C++ perform it?

6 What is the output of the following code?

```
int values[5], count;
for (count = 0; count < 5; count++)
     values[count] = count + 1;
for (count = 0; count < 5; count++)
     cout << values[count] << endl;
```

7 The following program skeleton contains a 20-element array of `int`s called `fish`. When completed, the program should ask how many fish were caught by fishermen 1 through 20, and store this data in the array. Complete the program.

```
#include <iostream>
using namespace std;
int main()
{
   const int NUM_FISH = 20;
   int fish[NUM_FISH];
   // You must finish this program. It should ask how
   // many fish were caught by fishermen 1-20, and
   // store this data in the array fish.
   return 0;
}
```

8 Define the following arrays:

A) `ages`, a 10-element array of `int`s initialized with the values 5, 7, 9, 14, 15, 17, 18, 19, 21, and 23.
B) `temps`, a 7-element array of `float`s initialized with the values 14.7, 16.3, 18.43, 21.09, 17.9, 18.76, and 26.7.
C) `alpha`, an 8-element array of `char`s initialized with the values ‘J’, ‘B’, ‘L’, ‘A’, ‘*’, ‘$’, ‘H’, and ‘M’.

9 Is each of the following a valid or invalid array definition? (If a definition is invalid, explain why.)

A) `int numbers[10] = {0, 0, 1, 0, 0, 1, 0, 0, 1, 1};`
B) `int matrix[5] = {1, 2, 3, 4, 5, 6, 7};`
C) `double radii[10] = {3.2, 4.7};`
D) `int table[7] = {2, , , 27, , 45, 39};`
E) `char codes[] = {'A', 'X', '1', '2', 's'};`
F) `int blanks[];`

11 4 The Range-Based `for` Loop

CONCEPT: The range-based `for` loop is a loop that iterates once for each element in an array. Each time the loop iterates, it copies an element from the array to a variable. The range-based `for` loop was introduced in C++ 11.

C++ 11 provides a specialized version of the `for` loop that, in many circumstances, simplifies array processing. It is known as the *range-based `for` loop*. When you use the range-based `for` loop with an array, the loop automatically iterates once for each element in the array. For example, if you use the range-based `for` loop with an 8-element array, the loop will iterate 8 times. Because the range-based `for` loop automatically knows the number of elements in an array, you do not have to use a counter variable to control its iterations, as with a regular `for` loop. Additionally, you do not have to worry about stepping outside the bounds of an array when you use the range-based `for` loop.

The range-based `for` loop is designed to work with a built-in variable known as the *range variable*. Each time the range-based `for` loop iterates, it copies an array element to the range variable. For example, the first time the loop iterates, the range variable will contain the value of element 0, the second time the loop iterates, the range variable will contain the value of element 1, and so forth.

Here is the general format of the range-based `for` loop:

```
for (dataType rangeVariable : array)
    statement;
```

Let's look at the syntax more closely as follows:

- *`dataType`* is the data type of the range variable. It must be the same as the data type of the array elements, or a type to which the elements can automatically be converted.
- *`rangeVariable`* is the name of the range variable. This variable will receive the value of a different array element during each loop iteration. During the first loop iteration, it receives the value of the first element; during the second iteration, it receives the value of the second element, and so forth.
- *`array`* is the name of an array on which you wish the loop to operate. The loop will iterate once for every element in the array.
- *`statement`* is a statement that executes during a loop iteration. If you need to execute more than one statement in the loop, enclose the statements in a set of braces.

For example, assume that you have the following array definition:

```
int numbers[] = { 3, 6, 9 };
```

You can use the following range-based `for` loop to display the contents of the `numbers` array:

```
for (int val : numbers)
   cout << val << endl;
```

Because the `numbers` array has three elements, this loop will iterate three times. The first time it iterates, the `val` variable will receive the value in `numbers[0]`. During the second iteration, `val` will receive the value in `numbers[1]`. During the third iteration, `val` will receive the value in `numbers[2]`. The code's output will be as follows:

```
3
6
9
```

Here is an example of a range-based `for` loop that executes more than one statement in the body of the loop:

```
int[] numbers = { 3, 6, 9 };
for (int val : numbers)
{
   cout << "The next value is ";
   cout << val << endl;
}
```

This code will produce the following output:

```
The next value is 3
The next value is 6
The next value is 9
```

If you wish, you can use the `auto` key word to specify the range variable's data type. Here is an example:

```
int[] numbers = { 3, 6, 9 };
for (auto val : numbers)
    cout << val << endl;
```

Program 10 demonstrates the range-based `for` loop by displaying the elements of an `int` array.

Program 10

```
// This program demonstrates the range-based for loop.
#include <iostream>
using namespace std;

int main()
{
     // Define an array of integers.
     int numbers[] = { 10, 20, 30, 40, 50 };

     // Display the values in the array.
     for (int val : numbers)
         cout << val << endl;

     return 0;
}
```

(program output continues)

Program 10 *(continued)*

Program Output

```
10
20
30
40
50
```

Program 11 shows another example of the range-based `for` loop. This program displays the elements of a `string` array.

Program 11

```
// This program demonstrates the range-based for loop.
#include <iostream>
#include <string>
using namespace std;

int main()
{
    string planets[] = { "Mercury", "Venus", "Earth", "Mars",
                         "Jupiter", "Saturn", "Uranus",
                         "Neptune", "Pluto (a dwarf planet)" };

    cout << "Here are the planets:\n";

    // Display the values in the array.
    for (string val : planets)
        cout << val << endl;

    return 0;
}
```

Program Output

```
Here are the planets:
Mercury
Venus
Earth
Mars
Jupiter
Saturn
Uranus
Neptune
Pluto (a dwarf planet)
```

Modifying an Array with a Range-Based `for` Loop

As the range-based `for` loop executes, its range variable contains only a copy of an array element. As a consequence, you cannot use a range-based `for` loop to modify the contents of an array unless you declare the range variable as a reference. A reference variable is an alias for another value. Any changes made to the reference variable are actually made to the value for which it is an alias.

To declare the range variable as a reference variable, simply write an ampersand (&) in front of its name in the loop header. Program 12 shows an example.

Program 12

```
1  // This program uses a range-based for loop to
2  // modify the contents of an array.
3  #include <iostream>
4  using namespace std;
5
6  int main()
7  {
8     const int SIZE = 5;
9     int numbers[5];
10
11    // Get values for the array.
12    for (int &val : numbers)
13    {
14       cout << "Enter an integer value: ";
15       cin >> val;
16    }
17
18    // Display the values in the array.
19    cout << "Here are the values you entered:\n";
20    for (int val : numbers)
21       cout << val << endl;
22
23    return 0;
24 }
```

Program Output with Example Input Shown in Bold

```
Enter an integer value: 1 [Enter]
Enter an integer value: 2 [Enter]
Enter an integer value: 3 [Enter]
Enter an integer value: 4 [Enter]
Enter an integer value: 5 [Enter]

Here are the values you entered:
1
2
3
4
5
```

Notice in line 12 the range variable, `val`, has an ampersand (&) written in front of its name. This declares `val` as a reference variable. As the loop executes, the `val` variable will not merely contain a copy of an array element, but it will be an alias for the element. Any changes made to the `val` variable will actually be made to the array element it references.

Also notice in line 20, we did not declare `val` as a reference variable (there is no ampersand written in front of the variable's name). Because the loop is simply displaying the array elements, and does not need to change the array's contents, there is no need to make `val` a reference variable.

The Range-Based `for` Loop versus the Regular `for` Loop

The range-based `for` loop can be used in any situation where you need to step through the elements of an array, and you do not need to use the element subscripts. It will not work, however, in situations where you need the element subscript for some purpose. In those situations, you need to use the regular `for` loop.

NOTE: You can use the `auto` key word with a reference range variable. For example, the code in lines 12 through 16 in Program 12 could have been written like this:

```
for (auto &val : numbers)
{
    cout << "Enter an integer value: ";
    cin >> val;
}
```

5 Processing Array Contents

CONCEPT: Individual array elements are processed like any other type of variable.

Processing array elements is no different than processing other variables. For example, the following statement multiplies `hours[3]` by the variable `rate`:

```
pay = hours[3] * rate;
```

And the following are examples of pre-increment and post-increment operations on array elements:

```
int score[5] = {7, 8, 9, 10, 11};
++score[2];    // Pre-increment operation on the value in score[2]
score[4]++;    // Post-increment operation on the value in score[4]
```

NOTE: When using increment and decrement operators, be careful not to confuse the subscript with the array element. For example, the following statement decrements the variable `count`, but does nothing to the value in `amount[count]`.

```
amount[count--];
```

To decrement the value stored in `amount[count]`, use the following statement:

```
amount[count]--;
```

Program 13 demonstrates the use of array elements in a simple mathematical statement. A loop steps through each element of the array, using the elements to calculate the gross pay of five employees.

Program 13

```
// This program stores, in an array, the hours worked by
// employees who all make the same hourly wage.
#include <iostream>
#include <iomanip>
using namespace std;

int main()
{
    const int NUM_EMPLOYEES = 5;  // Number of employees
    int hours[NUM_EMPLOYEES];     // Array to hold hours
    double payrate;               // Hourly pay rate
    double grossPay;              // To hold the gross pay

    // Input the hours worked.
    cout << "Enter the hours worked by ";
    cout << NUM_EMPLOYEES << " employees who all\n";
    cout << "earn the same hourly rate.\n";
    for (int index = 0; index < NUM_EMPLOYEES; index++)
    {
        cout << "Employee #" << (index + 1) << ": ";
        cin >> hours[index];
    }

    // Input the hourly rate for all employees.
    cout << "Enter the hourly pay rate for all the employees:  ";
    cin >> payrate;

    // Display each employee's gross pay.
    cout << "Here is the gross pay for each employee:\n";
    cout << fixed << showpoint << setprecision(2);
    for (int index = 0; index < NUM_EMPLOYEES; index++)
    {
        grossPay = hours[index] * payrate;
        cout << "Employee #" << (index + 1);
        cout << ": $" << grossPay << endl;
    }
    return 0;
}
```

Program Output with Example Input Shown in Bold

```
Enter the hours worked by 5 employees who all
earn the same hourly rate.
Employee #1: 5 [Enter]
Employee #2: 10 [Enter]
```

(program output continues)

Program 13 *(continued)*

```
Employee #3: 15 [Enter]
Employee #4: 20 [Enter]
Employee #5: 40 [Enter]
Enter the hourly pay rate for all the employees: 12.75 [Enter]
Here is the gross pay for each employee:
Employee #1: $63.75
Employee #2: $127.50
Employee #3: $191.25
Employee #4: $255.00
Employee #5: $510.00
```

The following statement in line 33 assigns the value of `hours[index]` times `payRate` to the `grossPay` variable:

```
grossPay = hours[index] * payRate;
```

Array elements may also be used in relational expressions. For example, the following `if` statement tests `cost[20]` to determine whether it is less than `cost[0]`:

```
if (cost[20] < cost[0])
```

And the following statement sets up a `while` loop to iterate as long as `value[place]` does not equal 0:

```
while (value[place] != 0)
```

Thou Shall Not Assign

The following code defines two integer arrays: `newValues` and `oldValues`. `newValues` is uninitialized, and `oldValues` is initialized with 10, 100, 200, and 300.

```
const int SIZE = 4;
int oldValues[SIZE] = {10, 100, 200, 300};
int newValues[SIZE];
```

At first glance, it might appear that the following statement assigns the contents of the array `oldValues` to `newValues`:

```
newValues = oldValues; // Wrong!
```

Unfortunately, this statement will not work. The only way to assign one array to another is to assign the individual elements in the arrays. Usually, this is best done with a loop, such as:

```
for (int count = 0; count < SIZE; count++)
    newValues[count] = oldValues[count];
```

The reason the assignment operator will not work with an entire array at once is complex, but important to understand. Anytime the name of an array is used without brackets and a subscript, *it is seen as the array's beginning memory address*. To illustrate this, consider the definition of the arrays `newValues` and `oldValues` above. Figure 12 depicts the two arrays in memory.

Figure 12 The newValues and oldValues arrays

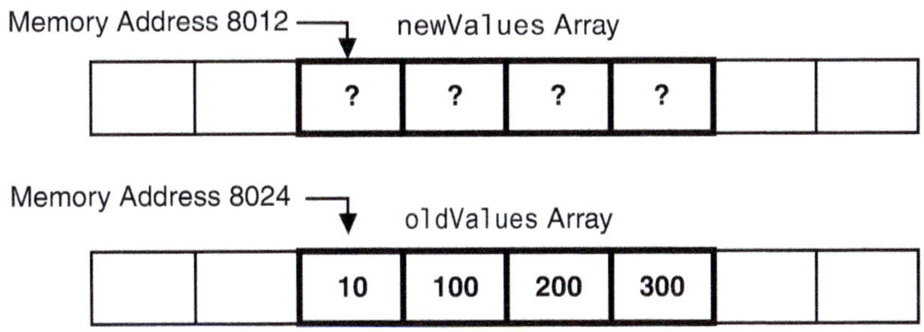

In the figure, newValues is shown starting at memory address 8012 and oldValues is shown starting at 8024. (Of course, these are just arbitrary addresses, picked for illustration purposes. In reality, the addresses would probably be different.) Table 2 shows various expressions that use the names of these arrays and their values.

Table 2 Array Expressions

Expression	Value
`oldValues[0]`	10 (Contents of Element 0 of `oldValues`)
`oldValues[1]`	100 (Contents of Element 1 of `oldValues`)
`oldValues[2]`	200 (Contents of Element 2 of `oldValues`)
`oldValues[3]`	300 (Contents of Element 3 of `oldValues`)
`newValues`	8012 (Memory Address of `newValues`)
`oldValues`	8024 (Memory Address of `oldValues`)

Because the name of an array without the brackets and subscript stands for the array's starting memory address, the statement

```
newValues = oldValues;
```

is interpreted by C++ as

```
8012 = 8024;
```

The statement will not work, because you cannot change the starting memory address of an array.

Printing the Contents of an Array

Suppose we have the following array definition:

```
const int SIZE = 5;
int numbers [SIZE] = {10, 20, 30, 40, 50};
```

You now know that an array's name is seen as the array's beginning memory address. This explains why the following statement cannot be used to display the contents of the numbers array.

```
cout << numbers << endl;   //Wrong!
```

When this statement executes, cout will display the array's memory address, not the array's contents. You must use a loop to display the contents of each of the array's elements, as follows:

```
for (int count = 0; count < SIZE; count++)
    cout << numbers[count] << endl;
```

11 In C++ 11, you can use the range-based for loop to display an array's contents, as shown here:

```
for (int val : numbers)
    cout << val << endl;
```

Summing the Values in a Numeric Array

To sum the values in an array, you must use a loop with an accumulator variable. The loop adds the value in each array element to the accumulator. For example, assume the following statements appear in a program, and values have been stored in the units array:

```
const int NUM_UNITS = 24;
int units[NUM_UNITS];
```

The following code uses a regular for loop to add the values of each element in the array to the total variable. When the code is finished, total will contain the sum of the units array's elements.

```
int total = 0;   // Initialize accumulator
for (int count = 0; count < NUM_UNITS; count++)
    total += units[count];
```

11 In C++ 11, you can use the range-based for loop, as shown below. When the code is finished, total will contain the sum of the units array's elements.

```
int total = 0;   // Initialize accumulator
for (int val : units)
    total += val;
```

NOTE: The first statement in both of these code segments sets total to 0. An accumulator variable must be set to 0 before it is used to keep a running total, or the sum will not be correct.

Getting the Average of the Values in a Numeric Array

The first step in calculating the average of all the values in an array is to sum the values. The second step is to divide the sum by the number of elements in the array. Assume the following statements appear in a program, and values have been stored in the scores array:

```
const int NUM_SCORES = 10;
double scores[NUM_SCORES];
```

The following code calculates the average of the values in the scores array. When the code completes, the average will be stored in the average variable.

```
double total = 0;    // Initialize accumulator
double average;      // Will hold the average
for (int count = 0; count < NUM_SCORES; count++)
    total += scores[count];
average = total / NUM_SCORES;
```

Notice the last statement, which divides `total` by `NUM_SCORES`, is not inside the loop. This statement should only execute once, after the loop has finished its iterations.

In C++ 11, you can use the range-based `for` loop, as shown below. When the code completes, the average will be stored in the `average` variable.

```
double total = 0;   // Initialize accumulator
double average;     // Will hold the average
for (int val : scores)
    total += val;
average = total / NUM_SCORES;
```

Finding the Highest and Lowest Values in a Numeric Array

The algorithms for finding the highest and lowest values in an array are very similar. First, let's look at code for finding the highest value in an array. Assume the following code exists in a program, and values have already been stored in the `numbers` array:

```
const int SIZE = 50;
int numbers[SIZE];
```

The code to find the highest value in the array is as follows:

```
int count;
int highest;

highest = numbers[0];
for (count = 1; count < SIZE; count++)
{
   if (numbers[count] > highest)
      highest = numbers[count];
}
```

First, we copy the value in the first array element to the variable `highest`. Then, the loop compares all of the remaining array elements, beginning at subscript 1, to the value in `highest`. Each time it finds a value in the array that is greater than `highest`, it copies that value to `highest`. When the loop has finished, `highest` will contain the highest value in the array.

The following code finds the lowest value in the array. As you can see, it is nearly identical to the code for finding the highest value.

```
int count;
int lowest;

lowest = numbers[0];
for (count = 1; count < SIZE; count++)
{
   if (numbers[count] < lowest)
      lowest = numbers[count];
}
```

When the loop has finished, `lowest` will contain the lowest value in the array.

Partially Filled Arrays

Sometimes you need to store a series of items in an array, but you do not know the number of items that there are. As a result, you do not know the exact number of elements needed for the array. One solution is to make the array large enough to hold the largest possible number of items. This can lead to another problem, however. If the actual number of items stored in the array is less than the number of elements, the array will be only partially filled. When you process a partially filled array, you must only process the elements that contain valid data items.

A partially filled array is normally used with an accompanying integer variable that holds the number of items stored in the array. For example, suppose a program uses the following code to create an array with 100 elements, and an `int` variable named `count` that will hold the number of items stored in the array.

```
const int SIZE = 100;
int numbers[SIZE];
int count = 0;
```

Each time we add an item to the array, we must increment `count`. The following code demonstrates this:

```
int num;
cout << "Enter a number or -1 to quit: ";
cin >> num;
while (num != -1 && count < SIZE)
{
    count++;
    numbers[count - 1] = num;
    cout << "Enter a number or -1 to quit: ";
    cin >> num;
}
```

Each iteration of this sentinel-controlled loop allows the user to enter a number to be stored in the array, or –1 to quit. The `count` variable is incremented then used to calculate the subscript of the next available element in the array. When the user enters –1, or `count` exceeds 99, the loop stops. The following code displays all of the valid items in the array:

```
for (int index = 0; index < count; index++)
{
    cout << numbers[index] << endl;
}
```

Notice this code uses `count` to determine the maximum array subscript to use.

Program 14 shows how this technique can be used to read an unknown number of items from a file into an array. The program reads values from the file numbers.txt.

Program 14

```
//This program reads data from a file into an array.
#include <iostream>
#include <fstream>
using namespace std;

int main()
{
    const int ARRAY_SIZE = 100; // Array size
    int numbers[ARRAY_SIZE];    // Array with 100 elements
```

```
10        int count = 0;                 // Loop counter variable
11        ifstream inputFile;            // Input file stream object
12
13        inputFile.open("numbers.txt"); // Open the file.
14
15        // Read the numbers from the file into the array.
16        // After this loop executes, the count variable will hold
17        // the number of values that were stored in the array.
18        while (count < ARRAY_SIZE && inputFile >> numbers[count])
19            count++;
20
21        // Close the file.
22        inputFile.close();
23
24        // Display the numbers read.
25        cout << "The numbers are: ";
26        for (int index = 0; index < count; index++)
27            cout << numbers[index] << " ";
28        cout << endl;
29        return 0;
30    }
```

Program Output

```
The numbers are: 47 89 65 36 12 25 17 8 62 10 87 62
```

Look closer at the `while` loop that begins in line 18. It repeats as long as `count` is less than `ARRAY_SIZE` and the end of the file has not been encountered. The first part of the `while` loop's test expression, `count < ARRAY_SIZE`, prevents the loop from writing outside the array boundaries. The `&&` operator performs short-circuit evaluation, so the second part of the `while` loop's test expression, `inputFile >> values[count]`, will be executed only if `count` is less than `ARRAY_SIZE`.

Comparing Arrays

We have already noted that you cannot simply assign one array to another array. You must assign each element of the first array to an element of the second array. In addition, you cannot use the `==` operator with the names of two arrays to determine whether the arrays are equal. For example, the following code appears to compare two arrays, but in reality it does not:

```
int firstArray[] = { 5, 10, 15, 20, 25 };
int secondArray[] = { 5, 10, 15, 20, 25 };
if (firstArray == secondArray)        // This is a mistake.
   cout << "The arrays are the same.\n";
else
   cout << "The arrays are not the same.\n";
```

When you use the `==` operator with array names, the operator compares the beginning memory addresses of the arrays, not the contents of the arrays. The two array names in this code will obviously have different memory addresses. Therefore, the result of the expression `firstArray == secondArray` is false, and the code reports that the arrays are not the same.

To compare the contents of two arrays, you must compare the elements of the two arrays. For example, look at the following code:

```
const int SIZE = 5;
int firstArray[SIZE] = { 5, 10, 15, 20, 25 };
int secondArray[SIZE] = { 5, 10, 15, 20, 25 };
bool arraysEqual = true; // Flag variable
int count = 0;           // Loop counter variable

// Determine whether the elements contain the same data.
while (arraysEqual && count < SIZE)
{
    if (firstArray[count] != secondArray[count])
        arraysEqual = false;
    count++;
}

if (arraysEqual)
    cout << "The arrays are equal.\n";
else
    cout << "The arrays are not equal.\n";
```

This code determines whether `firstArray` and `secondArray` contain the same values. A `bool` variable, `arraysEqual`, which is initialized to `true`, is used to signal whether the arrays are equal. Another variable, `count`, which is initialized to 0, is used as a loop counter variable.

Then a `while` loop begins. The loop executes as long as `arraysEqual` is `true` and the counter variable `count` is less than `SIZE`. During each iteration, it compares a different set of corresponding elements in the arrays. When it finds two corresponding elements that have different values, the `arraysEqual` variable is set to `false`. After the loop finishes, an `if` statement examines the `arraysEqual` variable. If the variable is `true`, then the arrays are equal and a message indicating so is displayed. Otherwise, they are not equal, so a different message is displayed.

6 Focus on Software Engineering: Using Parallel Arrays

CONCEPT: By using the same subscript, you can build relationships between data stored in two or more arrays.

Sometimes it's useful to store related data in two or more arrays. It's especially useful when the related data is of unlike types. For example, Program 15 is another variation of the payroll program. It uses two arrays: one to store the hours worked by each employee (as `int`s), and another to store each employee's hourly pay rate (as `double`s).

Program 15

```
// This program uses two parallel arrays: one for hours
// worked and one for pay rate.
#include <iostream>
```

```
#include <iomanip>
using namespace std;

int main()
{
    const int NUM_EMPLOYEES = 5;   // Number of employees
    int hours[NUM_EMPLOYEES];      // Holds hours worked
    double payRate[NUM_EMPLOYEES]; // Holds pay rates

    // Input the hours worked and the hourly pay rate.
    cout << "Enter the hours worked by " << NUM_EMPLOYEES
         << " employees and their\n"
         << "hourly pay rates.\n";
    for (int index = 0; index < NUM_EMPLOYEES; index++)
    {
        cout << "Hours worked by employee #" << (index+1) << ": ";
        cin >> hours[index];
        cout << "Hourly pay rate for employee #" << (index+1) << ": ";
        cin >> payRate[index];
    }

    // Display each employee's gross pay.
    cout << "Here is the gross pay for each employee:\n";
    cout << fixed << showpoint << setprecision(2);
    for (int index = 0; index < NUM_EMPLOYEES; index++)
    {
        double grossPay = hours[index] * payRate[index];
        cout << "Employee #" << (index + 1);
        cout << ": $" << grossPay << endl;
    }
    return 0;
}
```

Program Output with Example Input Shown in Bold

```
Enter the hours worked by 5 employees and their
hourly pay rates.
Hours worked by employee #1: 10 [Enter]
Hourly pay rate for employee #1: 9.75 [Enter]
Hours worked by employee #2: 15 [Enter]
Hourly pay rate for employee #2: 8.62 [Enter]
Hours worked by employee #3: 20 [Enter]
Hourly pay rate for employee #3: 10.50 [Enter]
Hours worked by employee #4: 40 [Enter]
Hourly pay rate for employee #4: 18.75 [Enter]
Hours worked by employee #5: 40 [Enter]
Hourly pay rate for employee #5: 15.65 [Enter]
Here is the gross pay for each employee:
Employee #1: $97.50
Employee #2: $129.30
Employee #3: $210.00
Employee #4: $750.00
Employee #5: $626.00
```

Notice in the loops the same subscript is used to access both arrays. That's because the data for one employee is stored in the same relative position in each array. For example, the hours worked by employee #1 are stored in `hours[0]`, and the same employee's pay rate is stored in `payRate[0]`. The subscript relates the data in both arrays.

This concept is illustrated in Figure 13.

Figure 13 Parallel arrays

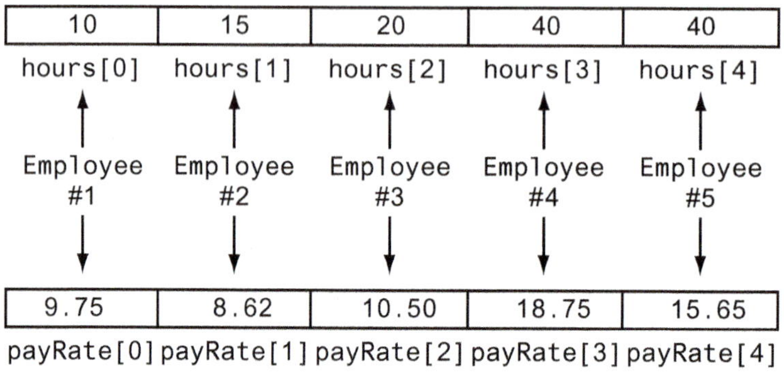

Checkpoint

10 Given the following array definition:

```
int values[] = {2, 6, 10, 14};
```

What does each of the following display?

A) `cout << values[2];`

B) `cout << ++values[0];`

C) `cout << values[1]++;`

D)
```
x = 2;
cout << values[++x];
```

11 Given the following array definition:

```
int nums[5] = {1, 2, 3};
```

What will the following statement display?

```
cout << nums[3];
```

12 What is the output of the following code? (You may need to use a calculator.)

```
double balance[5] = {100.0, 250.0, 325.0, 500.0, 1100.0};
const double INTRATE = 0.1;

cout << fixed << showpoint << setprecision(2);
for (int count = 0; count < 5; count++)
    cout << (balance[count] * INTRATE) << endl;
```

13 What is the output of the following code? (You may need to use a calculator.)

```
const int SIZE = 5;
int time[SIZE] = {1, 2, 3, 4, 5},
    speed[SIZE] = {18, 4, 27, 52, 100},
    dist[SIZE];
for (int count = 0; count < SIZE; count++)
    dist[count] = time[count] * speed[count];
for (int count = 0; count < SIZE; count++)
{
    cout << time[count] << " ";
    cout << speed[count] << " ";
    cout << dist[count] << endl;
}
```

7 Arrays as Function Arguments

CONCEPT: To pass an array as an argument to a function, pass the name of the array.

VideoNote
Passing an Array to a Function

Quite often, you'll want to write functions that process the data in arrays. For example, functions could be written to put values in an array, display an array's contents on the screen, total all of an array's elements, or calculate their average. Usually, such functions accept an array as an argument.

When a single element of an array is passed to a function, it is handled like any other variable. For example, Program 16 shows a loop that passes one element of the array `numbers` to the function `showValue` each time the loop iterates.

Program 16

```
// This program demonstrates that an array element is passed
// to a function like any other variable.
#include <iostream>
using namespace std;

void showValue(int); // Function prototype

int main()
{
    const int SIZE = 8;
    int numbers[SIZE] = {5, 10, 15, 20, 25, 30, 35, 40};

    for (int index = 0; index < SIZE; index++)
        showValue(numbers[index]);
    return 0;
}
```

(program continues)

Program 16 *(continued)*

```
17
18  //**************************************************
19  // Definition of function showValue.                *
20  // This function accepts an integer argument.      *
21  // The value of the argument is displayed.         *
22  //**************************************************
23
24  void showValue(int num)
25  {
26      cout << num << " ";
27  }
```

Program Output

```
5 10 15 20 25 30 35 40
```

Each time `showValue` is called in line 14, a copy of an array element is passed into the parameter variable `num`. The `showValue` function simply displays the contents of `num` and doesn't work directly with the array element itself. (In other words, the array element is passed by value.)

If the function were written to accept the entire array as an argument, however, the parameter would be set up differently. In the following function definition, the parameter `nums` is followed by an empty set of brackets. This indicates that the argument will be an array, not a single value.

```
void showValues(int nums[], int size)
{
   for (int index = 0; index < size; index++)
       cout << nums[index] << " ";
   cout << endl;
}
```

The reason there is no size declarator inside the brackets of `nums` is because `nums` is not actually an array. It's a special variable that can accept the address of an array. When an entire array is passed to a function, it is not passed by value, but passed by reference. Imagine the CPU time and memory that would be necessary if a copy of a 10,000-element array were created each time it was passed to a function! Instead, only the starting memory address of the array is passed. Program 17 shows the function `showValues` in use.

> **NOTE:** Notice in the function prototype, empty brackets appear after the data type of the array parameter. This indicates that `showValues` accepts the address of an array of integers.

Program 17

```
1  // This program demonstrates an array being passed to a function.
2  #include <iostream>
3  using namespace std;
4
5  void showValues(int [], int); // Function prototype
6
7  int main()
8  {
9      const int ARRAY_SIZE = 8;
10     int numbers[ARRAY_SIZE] = {5, 10, 15, 20, 25, 30, 35, 40};
11
12     showValues(numbers, ARRAY_SIZE);
13     return 0;
14 }
15
16 //**************************************************
17 // Definition of function showValue.               *
18 // This function accepts an array of integers and  *
19 // the array's size as its arguments. The contents *
20 // of the array are displayed.                     *
21 //**************************************************
22
23 void showValues(int nums[], int size)
24 {
25     for (int index = 0; index < size; index++)
26         cout << nums[index] << " ";
27     cout << endl;
28 }
```

Program Output

```
5 10 15 20 25 30 35 40
```

In Program 17, the function `showValues` is called in the following statement that appears in line 12:

```
showValues(numbers, ARRAY_SIZE);
```

The first argument is the name of the array. Remember, in C++ the name of an array without brackets and a subscript is actually the beginning address of the array. In this function call, the address of the `numbers` array is being passed as the first argument to the function. The second argument is the size of the array.

In the `showValues` function, the beginning address of the `numbers` array is copied into the `nums` parameter variable. The `nums` variable is then used to reference the `numbers` array. Figure 14 illustrates the relationship between the `numbers` array and the `nums` parameter variable. When the contents of `nums[0]` are displayed, it is actually the contents of `numbers[0]` that appear on the screen.

Figure 14 Relationship between the `numbers` array and the `nums` parameter

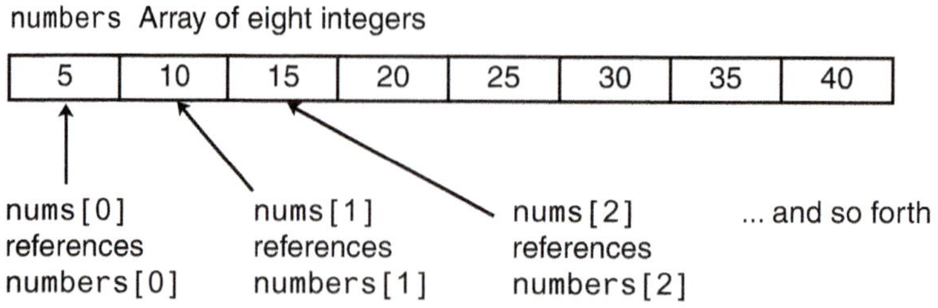

> **NOTE:** Although `nums` is not a reference variable, it works like one.

The `nums` parameter variable in the `showValues` function can accept the address of any integer array, and can be used to reference that array. So, we can use the `showValues` function to display the contents of any integer array by passing the name of the array and its size as arguments. Program 18 uses the function to display the contents of two different arrays.

Program 18

```
// This program demonstrates the showValues function being
// used to display the contents of two arrays.
#include <iostream>
using namespace std;

void showValues(int [], int); // Function prototype

int main()
{
    const int SIZE1 = 8; // Size of set1 array
    const int SIZE2 = 5; // Size of set2 array
    int set1[SIZE1] = {5, 10, 15, 20, 25, 30, 35, 40};
    int set2[SIZE2] = {2, 4, 6, 8, 10};

    // Pass set1 to showValues.
    showValues(set1, SIZE1);

    // Pass set2 to showValues.
    showValues(set2, SIZE2);
    return 0;
}

//**************************************************
// Definition of function showValues.              *
// This function accepts an array of integers and  *
// the array's size as its arguments. The contents *
// of the array are displayed.                     *
//**************************************************

```

```
void showValues(int nums[], int size)
{
    for (int index = 0; index < size; index++)
        cout << nums[index] << " ";
    cout << endl;
}
```

Program Output

```
5 10 15 20 25 30 35 40
2 4 6 8 10
```

When a reference variable is used as a parameter, it gives the function access to the original argument. Any changes made to the reference variable are actually performed on the argument referenced by the variable. Array parameters work very much like reference variables. They give the function direct access to the original array. Any changes made with the array parameter are actually made on the original array used as the argument. The function `doubleArray` in Program 19 uses this capability to double the contents of each element in the array.

Program 19

```
// This program uses a function to double the value of
// each element of an array.
#include <iostream>
using namespace std;

// Function prototypes
void doubleArray(int [], int);
void showValues(int [], int);

int main()
{
    const int ARRAY_SIZE = 7;
    int set[ARRAY_SIZE] = {1, 2, 3, 4, 5, 6, 7};

    // Display the initial values.
    cout << "The array's values are:\n";
    showValues(set, ARRAY_SIZE);

    // Double the values in the array.
    doubleArray(set, ARRAY_SIZE);

    // Display the resulting values.
    cout << "After calling doubleArray the values are:\n";
    showValues(set, ARRAY_SIZE);

    return 0;
}

```

(program continues)

Program 19 *(continued)*

```
//*****************************************************
// Definition of function doubleArray                 *
// This function doubles the value of each element    *
// in the array passed into nums. The value passed    *
// into size is the number of elements in the array.  *
//*****************************************************

void doubleArray(int nums[], int size)
{
    for (int index = 0; index < size; index++)
        nums[index] *= 2;
}

//**************************************************
// Definition of function showValues.              *
// This function accepts an array of integers and  *
// the array's size as its arguments. The contents *
// of the array are displayed.                     *
//**************************************************

void showValues(int nums[], int size)
{
    for (int index = 0; index < size; index++)
        cout << nums[index] << " ";
    cout << endl;
}
```

Program Output

```
The array's values are:
1 2 3 4 5 6 7
After calling doubleArray the values are:
2 4 6 8 10 12 14
```

Using const Array Parameters

Sometimes you want a function to be able to modify the contents of an array that is passed to it as an argument, and sometimes you don't. You can prevent a function from making changes to an array argument by using the `const` key word in the parameter declaration. Here is an example of the `showValues` function, shown previously, rewritten with a `const` array parameter:

```
void showValues(const int nums[], int size)
{
    for (int index = 0; index < size; index++)
        cout << nums[index] << " ";
    cout << endl;
}
```

When an array parameter is declared as `const`, the function is not allowed to make changes to the array's contents. If a statement in the function attempts to modify the array, an error will occur at compile time. As a precaution, you should always use `const` array parameters in any function that is not intended to modify its array argument. That way, the function will fail to compile if you inadvertently write code in it that modifies the array.

Some Useful Array Functions

Section 5 introduced you to algorithms such as summing an array and finding the highest and lowest values in an array. Now that you know how to pass an array as an argument to a function, you can write general purpose functions that perform those operations. The following *In the Spotlight* section shows an example.

In the Spotlight:

Processing an Array

Dr. LaClaire gives four exams during the semester in her chemistry class. At the end of the semester, she drops each student's lowest test score before averaging the scores. She has asked you to write a program that will read a student's four test scores as input, and calculate the average with the lowest score dropped. Here is the pseudocode algorithm that you developed:

Read the student's four test scores.
Calculate the total of the scores.
Find the lowest score.
Subtract the lowest score from the total. This gives the adjusted total.
Divide the adjusted total by 3. This is the average.
Display the average.

Program 20 shows the program, which is modularized. Rather than presenting the entire program at once, let's first examine the `main` function, then each additional function separately. Here is the first part of the program, including the `main` function:

Program 20 **(`main` function)**

```
// This program gets a series of test scores and
// calculates the average of the scores with the
// lowest score dropped.
#include <iostream>
#include <iomanip>
using namespace std;

// Function prototypes
void getTestScores(double[], int);
double getTotal(const double[], int);
double getLowest(const double[], int);

```

(program continues)

Program 20 *(continued)*

```
13 int main()
14 {
15     const int SIZE = 4;       // Array size
16     double testScores[SIZE], // Array of test scores
17            total,             // Total of the scores
18            lowestScore,       // Lowest test score
19            average;           // Average test score
20
21     // Set up numeric output formatting.
22     cout << fixed << showpoint << setprecision(1);
23
24     // Get the test scores from the user.
25     getTestScores(testScores, SIZE);
26
27     // Get the total of the test scores.
28     total = getTotal(testScores, SIZE);
29
30     // Get the lowest test score.
31     lowestScore = getLowest(testScores, SIZE);
32
33     // Subtract the lowest score from the total.
34     total -= lowestScore;
35
36     // Calculate the average. Divide by 3 because
37     // the lowest test score was dropped.
38     average = total / (SIZE - 1);
39
40     // Display the average.
41     cout << "The average with the lowest score "
42          << "dropped is " << average << ".\n";
43
44     return 0;
45 }
46
```

Lines 15 through 19 define the following items:

- `SIZE`—an `int` constant that is used as an array size declarator
- `testScores`—a `double` array to hold the test scores
- `tOtal`—a `double` variable that will hold the test score totals
- `lowestScore`—a `double` variable that will hold the lowest test score
- `average`—a `double` variable that will hold the average of the test scores

Line 25 calls the `getTestScores` function, passing the `testScores` array and the value of the `SIZE` constant as arguments. The function gets the test scores from the user and stores them in the array.

Line 28 calls the `getTotal` function, passing the `testScores` array and the value of the `SIZE` constant as arguments. The function returns the total of the values in the array. This value is assigned to the `total` variable.

Line 31 calls the getLowest function, passing the testScores array and the value of the SIZE constant as arguments. The function returns the lowest value in the array. This value is assigned to the lowestScore variable.

Line 34 subtracts the lowest test score from the total variable. Then, line 38 calculates the average by dividing total by SIZE - 1. (The program divides by SIZE - 1 because the lowest test score was dropped.) Lines 41 and 42 display the average.

The getTestScores function appears next, as shown here:

Program 20 (getTestScores **function)**

```
47 //***************************************************************
48 // The getTestScores function accepts an array and its size *
49 // as arguments. It prompts the user to enter test scores,  *
50 // which are stored in the array.                           *
51 //***************************************************************
52
53 void getTestScores(double scores[], int size)
54 {
55     // Loop counter
56     int index;
57
58     // Get each test score.
59     for(index = 0; index <= size - 1; index++)
60     {
61         cout << "Enter test score number "
62              << (index + 1) << ": ";
63         cin >> scores[index];
64     }
65 }
66
```

The getTestScores function has two parameters:

- scores[]—A double array
- size—An int specifying the size of the array that is passed into the scores[] parameter

The purpose of this function is to get a student's test scores from the user and store them in the array that is passed as an argument into the scores[] parameter.

The getTotal function appears next, as shown here:

Program 20 (getTotal **function)**

```
67 //*****************************************************
68 // The getTotal function accepts a double array       *
69 // and its size as arguments. The sum of the array's *
70 // elements is returned as a double.                  *
71 //*****************************************************
72
```

(program continues)

Program 20 *(continued)*

```
double getTotal(const double numbers[], int size)
{
    double total = 0; // Accumulator

    // Add each element to total.
    for (int count = 0; count < size; count++)
        total += numbers[count];

    // Return the total.
    return total;
}
```

The `getTotal` function has two parameters:

- `numbers[]`—A `const double` array
- `size`—An `int` specifying the size of the array that is passed into the `numbers[]` parameter

This function returns the total of the values in the array that is passed as an argument into the `numbers[]` parameter.

The `getLowest` function appears next, as shown here:

Program 20 **(`getLowest` function)**

```
//*****************************************************
// The getLowest function accepts a double array and *
// its size as arguments. The lowest value in the    *
// array is returned as a double.                    *
//*****************************************************

double getLowest(const double numbers[], int size)
{
    double lowest; // To hold the lowest value

    // Get the first array's first element.
    lowest = numbers[0];

    // Step through the rest of the array. When a
    // value less than lowest is found, assign it
    // to lowest.
    for (int count = 1; count < size; count++)
    {
        if (numbers[count] < lowest)
            lowest = numbers[count];
    }

    // Return the lowest value.
    return lowest;
}
```

The `getLowest` function has two parameters:

- `numbers[]`—A `const double` array
- `size`—An `int` specifying the size of the array that is passed into the `numbers[]` parameter

This function returns the lowest value in the array that is passed as an argument into the `numbers[]` parameter. Here is an example of the program's output:

Program 20

Program Output with Example Input Shown in Bold

```
Enter test score number 1: 92 [Enter]
Enter test score number 2: 67 [Enter]
Enter test score number 3: 75 [Enter]
Enter test score number 4: 88 [Enter]
The average with the lowest score dropped is 85.0.
```

Checkpoint

14 Given the following array definitions:

```
double array1[4] = {1.2, 3.2, 4.2, 5.2};
double array2[4];
```

Will the following statement work? If not, why?

```
array2 = array1;
```

15 When an array name is passed to a function, what is actually being passed?

16 When used as function arguments, are arrays passed by value?

17 What is the output of the following program? (You may need to consult the ASCII table in Appendix: The ASCII Character Set.)

```
#include <iostream>
using namespace std;

// Function prototypes
void fillArray(char [], int);
void showArray(const char [], int);

int main ()
{
   const int SIZE = 8;
   char prodCode[SIZE] = {'0', '0', '0', '0', '0', '0', '0', '0'};
   fillArray(prodCode, SIZE);
   showArray(prodCode, SIZE);
   return 0;
}

// Definition of function fillArray.
// (Hint: 65 is the ASCII code for 'A')
```

```
void fillArray(char arr[], int size)
{
    char code = 65;
    for (int k = 0; k < size; code++, k++)
        arr[k] = code;
}

// Definition of function showArray.

void showArray(const char codes[], int size)
{
    for (int k = 0; k < size; k++)
        cout << codes[k];
    cout << endl;
}
```

18 The following program skeleton, when completed, will ask the user to enter 10 integers, which are stored in an array. The function `avgArray`, which you must write, is to calculate and return the average of the numbers entered.

```
#include <iostream>
using namespace std;

// Write your function prototype here

int main()
{
    const int SIZE = 10;
    int userNums[SIZE];

    cout << "Enter 10 numbers: ";
    for (int count = 0; count < SIZE; count++)
    {
        cout << "#" << (count + 1) << " ";
        cin >> userNums[count];
    }
    cout << "The average of those numbers is ";
    cout << avgArray(userNums, SIZE) << endl;
    return 0;
}
//
// Write the function avgArray here.
//
```

8 Two-Dimensional Arrays

CONCEPT: A two-dimensional array is like several identical arrays put together. It is useful for storing multiple sets of data.

An array is useful for storing and working with a set of data. Sometimes, though, it's necessary to work with multiple sets of data. For example, in a grade-averaging program, a teacher might record all of one student's test scores in an array of `double`s. If the teacher has 30 students, that means he or she will need 30 arrays of `double`s to record the scores for the entire class. Instead of defining 30 individual arrays, however, it would be better to define a two-dimensional array.

The arrays you have studied so far are one-dimensional arrays. They are called *one-dimensional* because they can only hold one set of data. Two-dimensional arrays, which are sometimes called *2D arrays*, can hold multiple sets of data. It's best to think of a two-dimensional array as having rows and columns of elements, as shown in Figure 15. This figure shows an array of test scores, having three rows and four columns.

Figure 15 Two-dimensional array

	Column 0	Column 1	Column 2	Column 3
Row 0	scores[0] [0]	scores[0] [1]	scores[0] [2]	scores[0] [3]
Row 1	scores[1] [0]	scores[1] [1]	scores[1] [2]	scores[1] [3]
Row 2	scores[2] [0]	scores[2] [1]	scores[2] [2]	scores[2] [3]

The array depicted in Figure 15 has three rows (numbered 0 through 2) and four columns (numbered 0 through 3). There are a total of 12 elements in the array.

To define a two-dimensional array, two size declarators are required. The first one is for the number of rows, and the second one is for the number of columns. Here is an example definition of a two-dimensional array with three rows and four columns:

```
double scores[3][4];

  Rows   Columns
```

The first size declarator specifies the number of rows, and the second size declarator specifies the number of columns. Notice each number is enclosed in its own set of brackets.

When processing the data in a two-dimensional array, each element has two subscripts: one for its row, and another for its column. In the `scores` array defined above, the elements in row 0 are referenced as

```
scores[0][0]
scores[0][1]
scores[0][2]
scores[0][3]
```

The elements in row 1 are

```
scores[1][0]
scores[1][1]
scores[1][2]
scores[1][3]
```

And the elements in row 2 are

```
scores[2][0]
scores[2][1]
scores[2][2]
scores[2][3]
```

The subscripted references are used in a program just like the references to elements in a single-dimensional array, except now you use two subscripts. The first subscript represents the row position, and the second subscript represents the column position. For example, the following statement assigns the value 92.25 to the element at row 2, column 1 of the `scores` array:

```
scores[2][1] = 92.25;
```

And the following statement displays the element at row 0, column 2:

```
cout << scores[0][2];
```

Programs that step through each element of a two-dimensional array usually do so with nested loops. Program 21 is an example.

Program 21

```
// This program demonstrates a two-dimensional array.
#include <iostream>
#include <iomanip>
using namespace std;

int main()
{
    const int NUM_DIVS = 3;          // Number of divisions
    const int NUM_QTRS = 4;          // Number of quarters
    double sales[NUM_DIVS][NUM_QTRS]; // Array with 3 rows and 4 columns.
    double totalSales = 0;           // To hold the total sales.
    int div, qtr;                    // Loop counters.

    cout << "This program will calculate the total sales of\n";
    cout << "all the company's divisions.\n";
    cout << "Enter the following sales information:\n\n";

    // Nested loops to fill the array with quarterly
    // sales figures for each division.
    for (div = 0; div < NUM_DIVS; div++)
    {
        for (qtr = 0; qtr < NUM_QTRS; qtr++)
        {
            cout << "Division " << (div + 1);
            cout << ", Quarter " << (qtr + 1) << ": $";
            cin >> sales[div][qtr];
        }
        cout << endl; // Print blank line.
    }

    // Nested loops used to add all the elements.
    for (div = 0; div < NUM_DIVS; div++)
    {
        for (qtr = 0; qtr < NUM_QTRS; qtr++)
            totalSales += sales[div][qtr];
    }

```

```
    cout << fixed << showpoint << setprecision(2);
    cout << "The total sales for the company are: $";
    cout << totalSales << endl;
    return 0;
}
```

Program Output with Example Input Shown in Bold

```
This program will calculate the total sales of
all the company's divisions.
Enter the following sales data:

Division 1, Quarter 1: $31569.45 [Enter]
Division 1, Quarter 2: $29654.23 [Enter]
Division 1, Quarter 3: $32982.54 [Enter]
Division 1, Quarter 4: $39651.21 [Enter]

Division 2, Quarter 1: $56321.02 [Enter]
Division 2, Quarter 2: $54128.63 [Enter]
Division 2, Quarter 3: $41235.85 [Enter]
Division 2, Quarter 4: $54652.33 [Enter]

Division 3, Quarter 1: $29654.35 [Enter]
Division 3, Quarter 2: $28963.32 [Enter]
Division 3, Quarter 3: $25353.55 [Enter]
Division 3, Quarter 4: $32615.88 [Enter]

The total sales for the company are: $456782.34
```

When initializing a two-dimensional array, it helps to enclose each row's initialization list in a set of braces. Here is an example:

```
int hours[3][2] = {{8, 5}, {7, 9}, {6, 3}};
```

The same definition could also be written as:

```
int hours[3][2] = {{8, 5},
                   {7, 9},
                   {6, 3}};
```

In either case, the values are assigned to hours in the following manner:

```
hours[0][0] is set to 8
hours[0][1] is set to 5
hours[1][0] is set to 7
hours[1][1] is set to 9
hours[2][0] is set to 6
hours[2][1] is set to 3
```

Figure 16 illustrates the initialization.

Figure 16 Two-dimensional array initialization

	Column 0	Column 1
Row 0	8	5
Row 1	7	9
Row 2	6	3

The extra braces that enclose each row's initialization list are optional. Both of the following statements perform the same initialization:

```
int hours[3][2] = {{8, 5}, {7, 9}, {6, 3}};
int hours[3][2] = {8, 5, 7, 9, 6, 3};
```

Because the extra braces visually separate each row, however, it's a good idea to use them. In addition, the braces give you the ability to leave out initializers within a row without omitting the initializers for the rows that follow it. For instance, look at the following array definition:

```
int table[3][2] = {{1}, {3, 4}, {5}};
```

`table[0][0]` is initialized to 1, `table[1][0]` is initialized to 3, `table[1][1]` is initialized to 4, and `table[2][0]` is initialized to 5. `table[0][1]` and `table[2][1]` are not initialized. Because some of the array elements are initialized, these two initialized elements are automatically set to zero.

Passing Two-Dimensional Arrays to Functions

Program 22 demonstrates passing a two-dimensional array to a function. When a two-dimensional array is passed to a function, the parameter type must contain a size declarator for the number of columns. Here is the header for the function `showArray`, from Program 22:

```
void showArray(const int numbers[][COLS], int rows)
```

`COLS` is a global named constant that is set to 4. The function can accept any two-dimensional integer array, as long as it consists of four columns. In the program, the contents of two separate arrays are displayed by the function.

Program 22

```
// This program demonstrates accepting a 2D array argument.
#include <iostream>
#include <iomanip>
using namespace std;

// Global constants
const int COLS = 4;        // Number of columns in each array
const int TBL1_ROWS = 3; // Number of rows in table1
const int TBL2_ROWS = 4; // Number of rows in table2

void showArray(const int [][COLS], int); // Function prototype

int main()
{
    int table1[TBL1_ROWS][COLS] = {{1, 2, 3, 4},
                                   {5, 6, 7, 8},
                                   {9, 10, 11, 12}};
    int table2[TBL2_ROWS][COLS] = {{10, 20, 30, 40},
                                   {50, 60, 70, 80},
                                   {90, 100, 110, 120},
                                   {130, 140, 150, 160}};
```

```

    cout << "The contents of table1 are:\n";
    showArray(table1, TBL1_ROWS);
    cout << "The contents of table2 are:\n";
    showArray(table2, TBL2_ROWS);
    return 0;
}

//*****************************************************************
// Function Definition for showArray                              *
// The first argument is a two-dimensional int array with COLS    *
// columns. The second argument, rows, specifies the number of    *
// rows in the array. The function displays the array's contents. *
//*****************************************************************

void showArray(const int numbers[][COLS], int rows)
{
    for (int x = 0; x < rows; x++)
    {
        for (int y = 0; y < COLS; y++)
        {
            cout << setw(4) << numbers[x][y] << " ";
        }
        cout << endl;
    }
}
```

Program Output

```
The contents of table1 are:
   1    2    3    4
   5    6    7    8
   9   10   11   12
The contents of table2 are:
  10   20   30   40
  50   60   70   80
  90  100  110  120
 130  140  150  160
```

C++ requires the columns to be specified in the function prototype and header because of the way two-dimensional arrays are stored in memory. One row follows another, as shown in Figure 17.

Figure 17 Memory organization of a two-dimensional array

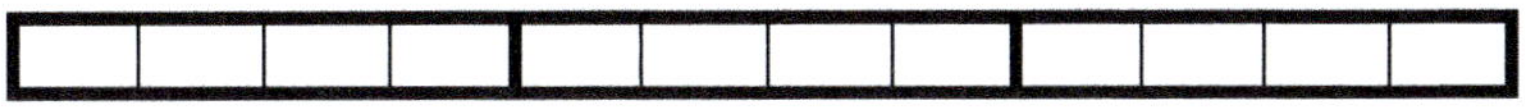

When the compiler generates code for accessing the elements of a two-dimensional array, it needs to know how many bytes separate the rows in memory. The number of columns is a critical factor in this calculation.

Summing All the Elements of a Two-Dimensional Array

To sum all the elements of a two-dimensional array, you can use a pair of nested loops to add the contents of each element to an accumulator. The following code is an example:

```
const int NUM_ROWS = 5;   // Number of rows
const int NUM_COLS = 5;   // Number of columns
int total = 0;            // Accumulator
int numbers[NUM_ROWS][NUM_COLS] = {{2, 7, 9, 6, 4},
                                   {6, 1, 8, 9, 4},
                                   {4, 3, 7, 2, 9},
                                   {9, 9, 0, 3, 1},
                                   {6, 2, 7, 4, 1}};

// Sum the array elements.
for (int row = 0; row < NUM_ROWS; row++)
{
   for (int col = 0; col < NUM_COLS; col++)
        total += numbers[row][col];
}

// Display the sum.
cout << "The total is " << total << endl;
```

Summing the Rows of a Two-Dimensional Array

Sometimes you may need to calculate the sum of each row in a two-dimensional array. For example, suppose a two-dimensional array is used to hold a set of test scores for a set of students. Each row in the array is a set of test scores for one student. To get the sum of a student's test scores (perhaps so an average may be calculated), you use a loop to add all the elements in one row. The following code shows an example.

```
const int NUM_STUDENTS = 3;        // Number of students
const int NUM_SCORES = 5;          // Number of test scores
double total;                      // Accumulator is set in the loops
double average;                    // To hold each student's average
double scores[NUM_STUDENTS][NUM_SCORES] = {{88, 97, 79, 86, 94},
                                           {86, 91, 78, 79, 84},
                                           {82, 73, 77, 82, 89}};

// Get each student's average score.
for (int row = 0; row < NUM_STUDENTS; row++)
{
   // Set the accumulator.
   total = 0;

   // Sum a row.
   for (int col = 0; col < NUM_SCORES; col++)
        total += scores[row][col];

   // Get the average.
   average = total / NUM_SCORES;

   // Display the average.
   cout << "Score average for student "
        << (row + 1) << " is " << average <<endl;
}
```

Notice the `total` variable, which is used as an accumulator, is set to zero just before the inner loop executes. This is because the inner loop sums the elements of a row and stores the sum in `total`. Therefore, the `total` variable must be set to zero before each iteration of the inner loop.

Summing the Columns of a Two-Dimensional Array

Sometimes you may need to calculate the sum of each column in a two-dimensional array. In the previous example, a two-dimensional array is used to hold a set of test scores for a set of students. Suppose you wish to calculate the class average for each of the test scores. To do this, you calculate the average of each column in the array. This is accomplished with a set of nested loops. The outer loop controls the column subscript, and the inner loop controls the row subscript. The inner loop calculates the sum of a column, which is stored in an accumulator. The following code demonstrates this:

```
const int NUM_STUDENTS = 3;    // Number of students
const int NUM_SCORES = 5;      // Number of test scores
double total;                  // Accumulator is set in the loops
double average;                // To hold each score's class average
double scores[NUM_STUDENTS][NUM_SCORES] = {{88, 97, 79, 86, 94},
                                           {86, 91, 78, 79, 84},
                                           {82, 73, 77, 82, 89}};

// Get the class average for each score.
for (int col = 0; col < NUM_SCORES; col++)
{
   // Reset the accumulator.
   total = 0;

   // Sum a column.
   for (int row = 0; row < NUM_STUDENTS; row++)
        total += scores[row][col];

   // Get the average.
   average = total / NUM_STUDENTS;

   // Display the class average.
   cout << "Class average for test " << (col + 1)
        << " is " << average << endl;
}
```

9 Arrays with Three or More Dimensions

CONCEPT: C++ does not limit the number of dimensions that an array may have. It is possible to create arrays with multiple dimensions, to model data that occur in multiple sets.

C++ allows you to create arrays with virtually any number of dimensions. Here is an example of a three-dimensional array definition:

```
double seats[3][5][8];
```

This array can be thought of as three sets of five rows, with each row containing eight elements. The array might be used to store the prices of seats in an auditorium, where there are eight seats in a row, five rows in a section, and a total of three sections.

Figure 18 illustrates the concept of a three-dimensional array as "pages" of two-dimensional arrays.

Figure 18 A three-dimensional array

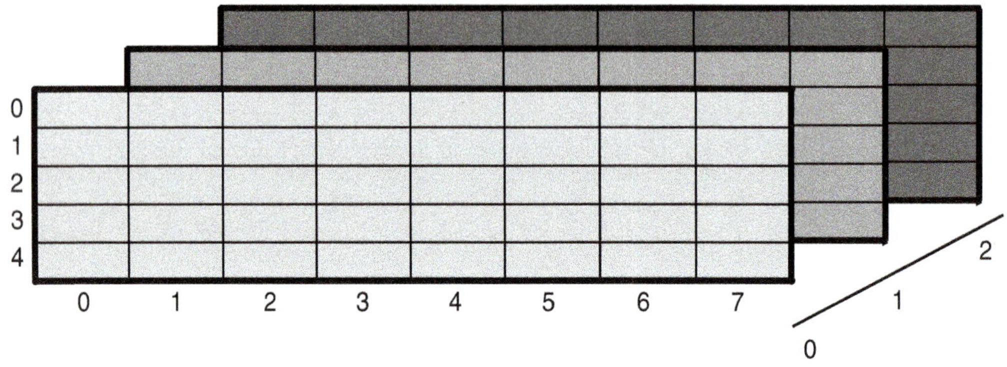

Arrays with more than three dimensions are difficult to visualize, but can be useful in some programming problems. For example, in a factory warehouse where cases of widgets are stacked on pallets, an array with four dimensions could be used to store a part number for each widget. The four subscripts of each element could represent the pallet number, case number, row number, and column number of each widget. Similarly, an array with five dimensions could be used if there were multiple warehouses.

NOTE: When writing functions that accept multi-dimensional arrays as arguments, all but the first dimension must be explicitly stated in the parameter list.

Checkpoint

19 Define a two-dimensional array of `int`s named `grades`. It should have 30 rows and 10 columns.

20 How many elements are in the following array?

```
double sales[6][4];
```

21 Write a statement that assigns the value 56893.12 to the first column of the first row of the array defined in Question 20.

22 Write a statement that displays the contents of the last column of the last row of the array defined in Question 20.

23 Define a two-dimensional array named `settings` large enough to hold the table of data below. Initialize the array with the values in the table.

12	24	32	21	42
14	67	87	65	90
19	1	24	12	8

24 Fill in the table below so that it shows the contents of the following array:

```
int table[3][4] = {{2, 3}, {7, 9, 2}, {1}};
```


25 Write a function called `displayArray7`. The function should accept a two-dimensional array as an argument and display its contents on the screen. The function should work with any of the following arrays:

```
int hours[5][7];
int stamps[8][7];
int autos[12][7];
int cats[50][7];
```

26 A video rental store keeps DVDs on 50 racks with 10 shelves each. Each shelf holds 25 DVDs. Define a three-dimensional array large enough to represent the store's storage system.

10 Focus on Problem Solving and Program Design: A Case Study

The National Commerce Bank has hired you as a contract programmer. Your first assignment is to write a function that will be used by the bank's automated teller machines (ATMs) to validate a customer's personal identification number (PIN).

Your function will be incorporated into a larger program that asks the customer to input his or her PIN on the ATM's numeric keypad. (PINs are seven-digit numbers. The program stores each digit in an element of an integer array.) The program also retrieves a copy of the customer's actual PIN from a database. (The PINs are also stored in the database as 7-element arrays.) If these two numbers match, then the customer's identity is validated. Your function is to compare the two arrays and determine whether they contain the same numbers.

Here are the specifications your function must meet:

Parameters The function is to accept as arguments two integer arrays of seven elements each. The first argument will contain the number entered by the customer. The second argument will contain the number retrieved from the bank's database.

Return value The function should return a Boolean `true` value, if the two arrays are identical. Otherwise, it should return `false`.

Here is the pseudocode for the function:

```
For each element in the first array
    Compare the element with the element in the second array
    that is in the corresponding position.
    If the two elements contain different values
       Return false.
    End If.
End For.
Return true.
```

The C++ code is shown below.

```
bool testPIN(const int custPIN[], const int databasePIN[], int size)
{
    for (int index = 0; index < size; index++)
    {
        if (custPIN[index] != databasePIN[index])
            return false; // We've found two different values.
    }
    return true; // If we make it this far, the values are the same.
}
```

Because you have only been asked to write a function that performs the comparison between the customer's input and the PIN that was retrieved from the database, you will also need to design a driver. Program 23 shows the complete program.

Program 23

```
// This program is a driver that tests a function comparing the
// contents of two int arrays.
#include <iostream>
using namespace std;

// Function Prototype
bool testPIN(const int [], const int [], int);

int main ()
{
    const int NUM_DIGITS = 7; // Number of digits in a PIN
    int pin1[NUM_DIGITS] = {2, 4, 1, 8, 7, 9, 0}; // Base set of values.
    int pin2[NUM_DIGITS] = {2, 4, 6, 8, 7, 9, 0}; // Only 1 element is
                                                  // different from pin1.
    int pin3[NUM_DIGITS] = {1, 2, 3, 4, 5, 6, 7}; // All elements are
                                                  // different from pin1.
    if (testPIN(pin1, pin2, NUM_DIGITS))
       cout << "ERROR: pin1 and pin2 report to be the same.\n";
    else
       cout << "SUCCESS: pin1 and pin2 are different.\n";

    if (testPIN(pin1, pin3, NUM_DIGITS))
       cout << "ERROR: pin1 and pin3 report to be the same.\n";
    else
       cout << "SUCCESS: pin1 and pin3 are different.\n";

    if (testPIN(pin1, pin1, NUM_DIGITS))
       cout << "SUCCESS: pin1 and pin1 report to be the same.\n";
    else
       cout << "ERROR: pin1 and pin1 report to be different.\n";
    return 0;
}
```

```
//*********************************************************************
// The following function accepts two int arrays. The arrays are    *
// compared. If they contain the same values, true is returned.     *
// If they contain different values, false is returned.             *
//*********************************************************************

bool testPIN(const int custPIN[], const int databasePIN[], int size)
{
    for (int index = 0; index < size; index++)
    {
        if (custPIN[index] != databasePIN[index])
           return false; // We've found two different values.
    }
    return true; // If we make it this far, the values are the same.
}
```

Program Output

```
SUCCESS: pin1 and pin2 are different.
SUCCESS: pin1 and pin3 are different.
SUCCESS: pin1 and pin1 report to be the same.
```

Case Study: See the Intersection of Sets Case Study on the Computer Science Portal at www.pearsonhighered.com/gaddis.

11 Introduction to the STL vector

CONCEPT: The Standard Template Library offers a vector data type, which in many ways, is superior to standard arrays.

The *Standard Template Library* (STL) is a collection of data types and algorithms that you may use in your programs. These data types and algorithms are *programmer-defined*. They are not part of the C++ language, but were created in addition to the built-in data types. If you plan to continue your studies in the field of computer science, you should become familiar with the STL. This section introduces one of the STL data types.

In this section, you will learn to use the vector data type. A vector is a container that can store data. It is like an array in the following ways:

- A vector holds a sequence of values or elements.
- A vector stores its elements in contiguous memory locations.
- You can use the array subscript operator [] to read the individual elements in the vector.

However, a vector offers several advantages over arrays. Here are just a few:

- You do not have to declare the number of elements that the vector will have.
- If you add a value to a vector that is already full, the vector will automatically increase its size to accommodate the new value.
- vectors can report the number of elements they contain.

Defining a vector

To use vectors in your program, you must include the <vector> header file with the following statement:

```
#include <vector>
```

> **NOTE:** To use the vector data type, you should also have the using namespace std; statement in your program.

Now you are ready to define an actual vector object. The syntax for defining a vector is somewhat different from the syntax used in defining a regular variable or array. Here is an example:

```
vector<int> numbers;
```

This statement defines numbers as a vector of ints. Notice the data type is enclosed in angled brackets, immediately after the word vector. Because the vector expands in size as you add values to it, there is no need to declare a size. You can define a starting size, if you prefer. Here is an example:

```
vector<int> numbers(10);
```

This statement defines numbers as a vector of 10 ints. This is only a starting size, however. Although the vector has 10 elements, its size will expand if you add more than 10 values to it.

> **NOTE:** If you specify a starting size for a vector, the size declarator is enclosed in parentheses, not in square brackets.

When you specify a starting size for a vector, you may also specify an initialization value. The initialization value is copied to each element. Here is an example:

```
vector<int> numbers(10, 2);
```

In this statement, numbers is defined as a vector of 10 ints. Each element in numbers is initialized to the value 2.

You may also initialize a vector with the values in another vector. For example, look at the following statement. Assume set1 is a vector of ints that already has values stored in it.

```
vector<int> set2(set1);
```

After this statement executes, set2 will be a copy of set1.

Table 3 summarizes the vector definition procedures we have discussed.

Table 3 vector Definitions

Definition Format	Description
`vector<float> amounts;`	Defines `amounts` as an empty `vector` of `floats`.
`vector<string> names;`	Defines `names` as an empty `vector` of `string` objects.
`vector<int> scores(15);`	Defines `scores` as a `vector` of 15 `ints`.
`vector<char> letters(25, 'A');`	Defines `letters` as a `vector` of 25 characters. Each element is initialized with `'A'`.
`vector<double> values2(values1);`	Defines `values2` as a `vector` of `doubles`. All the elements of `values1`, which is also a `vector` of `doubles`, are copied to `value2`.

Using an Initialization List with a vector in C++ 11

If you are using C++ 11, you can initialize a `vector` with a list of values, as shown in this example:

```
vector<int> numbers { 10, 20, 30, 40 };
```

This statement defines a `vector` of `ints` named `numbers`. The `vector` will have four elements, initialized with the values 10, 20, 30, and 40. Notice the initialization list is enclosed in a set of braces, but you do not use an = operator before the list.

Storing and Retrieving Values in a vector

To store a value in an element that already exists in a `vector`, you may use the array subscript operator `[]`. For example, look at Program 24.

Program 24

```
// This program stores, in two vectors, the hours worked by 5
// employees, and their hourly pay rates.
#include <iostream>
#include <iomanip>
#include <vector>
using namespace std;

int main()
{
    const int NUM_EMPLOYEES = 5;           // Number of employees
    vector<int> hours(NUM_EMPLOYEES);      // A vector of integers
    vector<double> payRate(NUM_EMPLOYEES); // A vector of doubles
    int index;                             // Loop counter

    // Input the data.
    cout << "Enter the hours worked by " << NUM_EMPLOYEES;
    cout << " employees and their hourly rates.\n";
    for (index = 0; index < NUM_EMPLOYEES; index++)
```

(program continues)

Program 24 *(continued)*

```
19        {
20            cout << "Hours worked by employee #" << (index + 1);
21            cout << ": ";
22            cin >> hours[index];
23            cout << "Hourly pay rate for employee #";
24            cout << (index + 1) << ": ";
25            cin >> payRate[index];
26        }
27
28        // Display each employee's gross pay.
29        cout << "\nHere is the gross pay for each employee:\n";
30        cout << fixed << showpoint << setprecision(2);
31        for (index = 0; index < NUM_EMPLOYEES; index++)
32        {
33            double grossPay = hours[index] * payRate[index];
34            cout << "Employee #" << (index + 1);
35            cout << ": $" << grossPay << endl;
36        }
37        return 0;
38    }
```

Program Output with Example Input Shown in Bold

```
Enter the hours worked by 5 employees and their hourly rates.
Hours worked by employee #1: 10 [Enter]
Hourly pay rate for employee #1: 9.75 [Enter]
Hours worked by employee #2: 15 [Enter]
Hourly pay rate for employee #2: 8.62 [Enter]
Hours worked by employee #3: 20 [Enter]
Hourly pay rate for employee #3: 10.50 [Enter]
Hours worked by employee #4: 40 [Enter]
Hourly pay rate for employee #4: 18.75 [Enter]
Hours worked by employee #5: 40 [Enter]
Hourly pay rate for employee #5: 15.65 [Enter]

Here is the gross pay for each employee:
Employee #1: $97.50
Employee #2: $129.30
Employee #3: $210.00
Employee #4: $750.00
Employee #5: $626.00
```

Notice Program 24 uses the following statements in lines 11 and 12 to define two vectors:

```
vector<int> hours(NUM_EMPLOYEES);      // A vector of integers
vector<double> payRate(NUM_EMPLOYEES); // A vector of doubles
```

Both of the vectors are defined with the starting size 5, which is the value of the named constant NUM_EMPLOYEES. The program uses the following loop in lines 18 through 26 to store a value in each element of both vectors:

```
for (index = 0; index < NUM_EMPLOYEES; index++)
{
    cout << "Hours worked by employee #" << (index + 1);
    cout << ": ";
    cin >> hours[index];
    cout << "Hourly pay rate for employee #";
    cout << (index + 1) << ": ";
    cin >> payRate[index];
}
```

Because the values entered by the user are being stored in vector elements that already exist, the program uses the array subscript operator [], as shown in the following statements, which appear in lines 22 and 25:

```
cin >> hours[index];
cin >> payRate[index];
```

Using the Range-Based for Loop with a vector in C++ 11

With C++ 11, you can use a range-based for loop to step through the elements of a vector, as shown in Program 25.

Program 25

```
// This program demonstrates the range-based for loop with a vector.
include <iostream>
#include <vector>
using namespace std;

int main()
{
    // Define and initialize a vector.
    vector<int> numbers { 10, 20, 30, 40, 50 };

    // Display the vector elements.
    for (int val : numbers)
        cout << val << endl;

    return 0;
}
```

Program Output

```
10
20
30
40
50
```

Program 26 shows how you can use a reference variable with the range-based `for` loop to store items in a `vector`.

Program 26

```
1  // This program demonstrates the range-based for loop with a vector.
2  #include <iostream>
3  #include <vector>
4  using namespace std;
5  
6  int main()
7  {
8      // Define a vector.
9      vector<int> numbers(5);
10 
11     // Get values for the vector elements.
12     for (int &val : numbers)
13     {
14         cout << "Enter an integer value: ";
15         cin >> val;
16     }
17 
18     // Display the vector elements.
19     cout << "Here are the values you entered:\n";
20     for (int val : numbers)
21         cout << val << endl;
22 
23     return 0;
24 }
```

Program Output with Example Input Shown in Bold

Enter an integer value: **1** [Enter]
Enter an integer value: **2** [Enter]
Enter an integer value: **3** [Enter]
Enter an integer value: **4** [Enter]
Enter an integer value: **5** [Enter]
Here are the values you entered:
1
2
3
4
5

In line 9, we define `numbers` as a `vector` of `ints`, with five elements. Notice in line 12 the range variable, `val`, has an ampersand (&) written in front of its name. This declares `val` as a reference variable. As the loop executes, the `val` variable will be an alias for a `vector` element. Any changes made to the `val` variable will actually be made to the `vector` element it references.

Also notice in line 20 we did not declare `val` as a reference variable (there is no ampersand written in front of the variable's name). Because the loop is simply displaying the `vector` elements, and does not need to change the `vector`'s contents, there is no need to make `val` a reference variable.

Using the push_back Member Function

You cannot use the `[]` operator to access a `vector` element that does not exist. To store a value in a `vector` that does not have a starting size, or that is already full, use the `push_back` member function. The `push_back` member function accepts a value as an argument and stores that value after the last element in the `vector`. (It pushes the value onto the back of the `vector`.) Here is an example:

```
numbers.push_back(25);
```

Assuming `numbers` is a `vector` of `int`s, this statement stores 25 as the last element. If `numbers` is full, the statement creates a new last element and stores 25 in it. If there are no elements in `numbers`, this statement creates an element and stores 25 in it.

Program 27 is a modification of Program 24. This version, however, allows the user to specify the number of employees. The two `vector`s, `hours` and `payRate`, are defined without starting sizes. Because these `vector`s have no starting elements, the `push_back` member function is used to store values in the `vector`s.

Program 27

```
// This program stores, in two arrays, the hours worked by 5
// employees, and their hourly pay rates.
#include <iostream>
#include <iomanip>
#include <vector>
using namespace std;

int main()
{
    vector<int> hours;       // hours is an empty vector
    vector<double> payRate;  // payRate is an empty vector
    int numEmployees;        // The number of employees
    int index;               // Loop counter

    // Get the number of employees.
    cout << "How many employees do you have? ";
    cin >> numEmployees;

    // Input the payroll data.
    cout << "Enter the hours worked by " << numEmployees;
    cout << " employees and their hourly rates.\n";
    for (index = 0; index < numEmployees; index++)
    {
        int tempHours;           // To hold the number of hours entered
        double tempRate;         // To hold the pay rate entered

```

(program continues)

Program 27 *(continued)*

```
27             cout << "Hours worked by employee #" << (index + 1);
28             cout << ": ";
29             cin >> tempHours;
30             hours.push_back(tempHours);       // Add an element to hours
31             cout << "Hourly pay rate for employee #";
32             cout << (index + 1) << ": ";
33             cin >> tempRate;
34             payRate.push_back(tempRate); // Add an element to payRate
35         }
36 
37         // Display each employee's gross pay.
38         cout << "Here is the gross pay for each employee:\n";
39         cout << fixed << showpoint << setprecision(2);
40         for (index = 0; index < numEmployees; index++)
41         {
42              double grossPay = hours[index] * payRate[index];
43              cout << "Employee #" << (index + 1);
44              cout << ": $" << grossPay << endl;
45         }
46         return 0;
47     }
```

Program Output with Example Input Shown in Bold

```
How many employees do you have? 3 [Enter]
Enter the hours worked by 3 employees and their hourly rates.
Hours worked by employee #1: 40 [Enter]
Hourly pay rate for employee #1: 12.63 [Enter]
Hours worked by employee #2: 25 [Enter]
Hourly pay rate for employee #2: 10.35 [Enter]
Hours worked by employee #3: 45 [Enter]
Hourly pay rate for employee #3: 22.65 [Enter]

Here is the gross pay for each employee:
Employee #1: $505.20
Employee #2: $258.75
Employee #3: $1019.2
```

Notice in lines 40 through 45, the second loop, which calculates and displays each employee's gross pay, uses the `[]` operator to access the elements of the `hours` and `payRate` vectors.

```
for (index = 0; index < numEmployees; index++)
{
   double grossPay = hours[index] * payRate[index];
   cout << "Employee #" << (index + 1);
   cout << ": $" << grossPay << endl;
}
```

This is possible because the first loop in lines 22 through 35 uses the `push_back` member function to create the elements in the two vectors.

Determining the Size of a vector

Unlike arrays, vectors can report the number of elements they contain. This is accomplished with the size member function. Here is an example of a statement that uses the size member function:

```
numValues = set.size();
```

In this statement, assume numValues is an int, and set is a vector. After the statement executes, numValues will contain the number of elements in set.

The size member function is especially useful when you are writing functions that accept vectors as arguments. For example, look at the following code for the showValues function:

```
void showValues(vector<int> vect)
{
    for (int count = 0; count < vect.size(); count++)
        cout << vect[count] << endl;
}
```

Because the vector can report its size, this function does not need to accept a second argument indicating the number of elements in the vector. Program 28 demonstrates this function.

Program 28

```
// This program demonstrates the vector size
// member function.
#include <iostream>
#include <vector>
using namespace std;

// Function prototype
void showValues(vector<int>);

int main()
{
    vector<int> values;

    // Put a series of numbers in the vector.
    for (int count = 0; count < 7; count++)
        values.push_back(count * 2);

    // Display the numbers.
    showValues(values);
    return 0;
}

//****************************************************
// Definition of function showValues.                *
// This function accepts an int vector as its        *
// argument. The value of each of the vector's       *
// elements is displayed.                            *
//****************************************************
```

(program continues)

Program 28 *(continued)*

```

void showValues(vector<int> vect)
{
   for (int count = 0; count < vect.size(); count++)
      cout << vect[count] << endl;
}
```

Program Output

```
0
2
4
6
8
10
12
```

Removing Elements from a vector

Use the pop_back member function to remove the last element from a vector. In the following statement, assume collection is the name of a vector:

```
collection.pop_back();
```

This statement removes the last element from the collection vector. Program 29 demonstrates the function.

Program 29

```
// This program demonstrates the vector pop_back member function.
#include <iostream>
#include <vector>
using namespace std;

int main()
{
    vector<int> values;

    // Store values in the vector.
    values.push_back(1);
    values.push_back(2);
    values.push_back(3);
    cout << "The size of values is " << values.size() << endl;

    // Remove a value from the vector.
    cout << "Popping a value from the vector ... \n";
    values.pop_back();
    cout << "The size of values is now " << values.size() << endl;

```

```
    // Now remove another value from the vector.
    cout << "Popping a value from the vector ... \n";
    values.pop_back();
    cout << "The size of values is now " << values.size() << endl;

    // Remove the last value from the vector.
    cout << "Popping a value from the vector ... \n";
    values.pop_back();
    cout << "The size of values is now " << values.size() << endl;
    return 0;
}
```

Program Output

```
The size of values is 3
Popping a value from the vector...
The size of values is now 2
Popping a value from the vector...
The size of values is now 1
Popping a value from the vector...
The size of values is now 0
```

Clearing a vector

To completely clear the contents of a `vector`, use the `clear` member function, as shown in the following statement:

```
numbers.clear();
```

After this statement executes, `numbers` will be cleared of all its elements. Program 30 demonstrates the function.

Program 30

```
// This program demonstrates the vector clear member function.
#include <iostream>
#include <vector>
using namespace std;

int main()
{
    vector<int> values(100);

    cout << "The values vector has "
         << values.size() << " elements.\n";
    cout << "I will call the clear member function ... \n";
    values.clear();
    cout << "Now, the values vector has "
         << values.size() << " elements.\n";
   return 0;
}
```

(program output continues)

Program 30 *(continued)*

Program Output

```
The values vector has 100 elements.
I will call the clear member function...
Now, the values vector has 0 elements.
```

Detecting an Empty vector

To determine if a vector is empty, use the empty member function. The function returns true if the vector is empty, and false if the vector has elements stored in it. Assuming numberVector is a vector, here is an example of its use:

```
if (numberVector.empty())
    cout << "No values in numberVector.\n";
```

Program 31 uses a function named avgVector, which demonstrates the empty member function.

Program 31

```
// This program demonstrates the vector's empty member function.
#include <iostream>
#include <vector>
using namespace std;

// Function prototype
double avgVector(vector<int>);

int main()
{
    vector<int> values;   // A vector to hold values
    int numValues;        // The number of values
    double average;       // To hold the average

    // Get the number of values to average.
    cout << "How many values do you wish to average? ";
    cin >> numValues;

    // Get the values and store them in the vector.
    for (int count = 0; count < numValues; count++)
    {
        int tempValue;
        cout << "Enter a value: ";
        cin >> tempValue;
        values.push_back(tempValue);
    }

    // Get the average of the values and display it.
    average = avgVector(values);
    cout << "Average: " << average << endl;
```

```
    return 0;
}

//****************************************************************
// Definition of function avgVector.                             *
// This function accepts an int vector as its argument. If       *
// the vector contains values, the function returns the          *
// average of those values. Otherwise, an error message is       *
// displayed and the function returns 0.0.                       *
//****************************************************************

double avgVector(vector<int> vect)
{
    int total = 0;      // accumulator
    double avg;         // average

    if (vect.empty())   // Determine if the vector is empty
    {
        cout << "No values to average.\n";
        avg = 0.0;
    }
    else
    {
        for (int count = 0; count < vect.size(); count++)
            total += vect[count];
        avg = total / vect.size();
    }
    return avg;
}
```

Program Output with Example Input Shown in Bold

```
How many values do you wish to average? 5 [Enter]
Enter a value: 12
Enter a value: 18
Enter a value: 3
Enter a value: 7
Enter a value: 9
Average: 9
```

Program Output with Different Example Input Shown in Bold

```
How many values do you wish to average? 0 [Enter]
No values to average.
Average: 0
```

Summary of `vector` Member Functions

Table 4 provides a summary of the `vector` member function we have discussed, as well as some additional ones.

Table 4 Some of the vector Member Functions

Member Function	Description
`at(element)`	Returns the value of the element located at *element* in the vector. *Example:* `x = vect.at(5);` This statement assigns the value of the fifth element of vect to x.
`clear()`	Clears a vector of all its elements. *Example:* `vect.clear();` This statement removes all the elements from vect.

`empty()`	Returns true if the vector is empty. Otherwise, it returns false.
	Example:
	`if (vect.empty())`
	`cout << "The vector is empty.";`
	This statement displays the message if vect is empty.

`pop_back()`	Removes the last element from the vector. *Example:* `vect.pop_back();` This statement removes the last element of vect, thus reducing its size by 1.
`push_back(value)`	Stores *value* in the last element of the vector. If the vector is full or empty, a new element is created. *Example:* `vect.push_back(7);` This statement stores 7 in the last element of vect.
`resize(elements, value)`	Resizes a vector by *elements* elements. Each of the new elements is initialized with the value in *value*. *Example:* `vect.resize(5, 1);` This statement increases the size of vect by five elements. The five new elements are initialized to the value 1.
`swap(vector2)`	Swaps the contents of the vector with the contents of *vector2*. *Example:* `vect1.swap(vect2);` This statement swaps the contents of vect1 and vect2.

Checkpoint

27 What header file must you `#include` in order to define `vector` objects?

28 Write a definition statement for a `vector` named `frogs`. `frogs` should be an empty `vector` of `int`s.

29 Write a definition statement for a `vector` named `lizards`. `lizards` should be a `vector` of 20 `float`s.

30 Write a definition statement for a `vector` named `toads`. `toads` should be a `vector` of 100 `char`s, with each element initialized to `'Z'`.

31 `gators` is an empty `vector` of `int`s. Write a statement that stores the value 27 in `gators`.

32 `snakes` is a `vector` of `double`s, with 10 elements. Write a statement that stores the value 12.897 in element 4 of the `snakes vector`.

Review Questions and Exercises

Short Answer

1. What is the difference between a size declarator and a subscript?
2. Look at the following array definition:

   ```
   int values[10];
   ```

   How many elements does the array have?

   What is the subscript of the first element in the array?

   What is the subscript of the last element in the array?

   Assuming that an `int` uses 4 bytes of memory, how much memory does the array use?
3. Why should a function that accepts an array as an argument, and processes that array, also accept an argument specifying the array's size?
4. Consider the following array definition:

   ```
   int values[5] = { 4, 7, 6, 8, 2 };
   ```

   What does each of the following statements display?

   ```
   cout << values[4] << endl; __________
   cout << (values[2] + values[3]) << endl; __________
   cout << ++values[1] << endl; __________
   ```
5. How do you define an array without providing a size declarator?
6. Look at the following array definition:

   ```
   int numbers[5] = { 1, 2, 3 };
   ```

   What value is stored in `numbers[2]`?

   What value is stored in `numbers[4]`?

7. Assuming that `array1` and `array2` are both arrays, why is it not possible to assign the contents of `array2` to `array1` with the following statement?

   ```
   array1 = array2;
   ```

8. Assuming that `numbers` is an array of `doubles`, will the following statement display the contents of the array?

   ```
   cout << numbers << endl;
   ```

9. Is an array passed to a function by value or by reference?
10. When you pass an array name as an argument to a function, what is actually being passed?
11. How do you establish a parallel relationship between two or more arrays?
12. Look at the following array definition:

    ```
    double sales[8][10];
    ```

    How many rows does the array have?

    How many columns does the array have?

    How many elements does the array have?

    Write a statement that stores a number in the last column of the last row in the array.

13. When writing a function that accepts a two-dimensional array as an argument, which size declarator must you provide in the parameter for the array?
14. What advantages does a `vector` offer over an array?

Fill-in-the-Blank

15. The ________ indicates the number of elements, or values, an array can hold.
16. The size declarator must be a(n) ________ with a value greater than ________.
17. Each element of an array is accessed and indexed by a number known as a(n) ________.
18. Subscript numbering in C++ always starts at ________.
19. The number inside the brackets of an array definition is the ________, but the number inside an array's brackets in an assignment statement, or any other statement that works with the contents of the array, is the ________.
20. C++ has no array ________ checking, which means you can inadvertently store data past the end of an array.
21. Starting values for an array may be specified with a(n) ________ list.
22. If an array is partially initialized, the uninitialized elements will be set to ________.
23. If the size declarator of an array definition is omitted, C++ counts the number of items in the ________ to determine how large the array should be.
24. By using the same ________ for multiple arrays, you can build relationships between the data stored in the arrays.

25. You cannot use the ________ operator to copy data from one array to another in a single statement.
26. Any time the name of an array is used without brackets and a subscript, it is seen as ________.
27. To pass an array to a function, pass the ________ of the array.
28. A(n) ________ array is like several arrays of the same type put together.
29. It's best to think of a two-dimensional array as having ________ and ________.
30. To define a two-dimensional array, ________ size declarators are required.
31. When initializing a two-dimensional array, it helps to enclose each row's initialization list in ________.
32. When a two-dimensional array is passed to a function, the ________ size must be specified.
33. The ________________ is a collection of programmer-defined data types and algorithms that you may use in your programs.
34. The two types of containers defined by the STL are __________ and ____________.
35. The `vector` data type is a(n) ____________ container.
36. To define a `vector` in your program, you must `#include` the __________ header file.
37. To store a value in a `vector` that does not have a starting size, or that is already full, use the ______________ member function.
38. To determine the number of elements in a `vector`, use the ____________ member function.
39. Use the ______________ member function to remove the last element from a `vector`.
40. To completely clear the contents of a `vector`, use the __________ member function.

Algorithm Workbench

41. `names` is an integer array with 20 elements. Write a regular `for` loop, as well as a range-based `for` loop that prints each element of the array.
42. The arrays `numberArray1` and `numberArray2` have 100 elements. Write code that copies the values in `numberArray1` to `numberArray2`.
43. In a program, you need to store the identification numbers of ten employees (as `int`s) and their weekly gross pay (as `double`s).
    A) Define two arrays that may be used in parallel to store the ten employee identification numbers and gross pay amounts.
    B) Write a loop that uses these arrays to print each employee's identification number and weekly gross pay.
44. Define a two-dimensional array of integers named `grades`. It should have 30 rows and 10 columns.

45. In a program, you need to store the populations of 12 countries.

    A) Define two arrays that may be used in parallel to store the names of the countries and their populations.

    B) Write a loop that uses these arrays to print each country's name and its population.

46. The following code totals the values in two arrays: `numberArray1` and `numberArray2`. Both arrays have 25 elements. Will the code print the correct sum of values for both arrays? Why or why not?

```
int total = 0;          // Accumulator
int count;              // Loop counter
// Calculate and display the total of the first array.
for (count = 0; count < 24; count++)
   total += numberArray1[count];
cout << "The total for numberArray1 is " << total << endl;
// Calculate and display the total of the second array.
for (count = 0; count < 24; count++)
   total += numberArray2[count];
cout << "The total for numberArray2 is " << total << endl;
```

47. Look at the following array definition:

```
int numberArray[9][11];
```

    Write a statement that assigns 145 to the first column of the first row of this array.

    Write a statement that assigns 18 to the last column of the last row of this array.

48. `values` is a two-dimensional array of `floats` with 10 rows and 20 columns. Write code that sums all the elements in the array and stores the sum in the variable `total`.

49. An application uses a two-dimensional array defined as follows:

```
int days[29][5];
```

    Write code that sums each row in the array and displays the results.

    Write code that sums each column in the array and displays the results.

True or False

50. T F An array's size declarator can be either a literal, a named constant, or a variable.

51. T F To calculate the amount of memory used by an array, multiply the number of elements by the number of bytes each element uses.

52. T F The individual elements of an array are accessed and indexed by unique numbers.

53. T F The first element in an array is accessed by the subscript 1.

54. T F The subscript of the last element in a single-dimensional array is one less than the total number of elements in the array.

55. T F The contents of an array element cannot be displayed with `cout`.

56. T F Subscript numbers may be stored in variables.

57. T F You can write programs that use invalid subscripts for an array.

58. T F Arrays cannot be initialized when they are defined. A loop or other means must be used.

59. T F The values in an initialization list are stored in the array in the order they appear in the list.

60. T F C++ allows you to partially initialize an array.

61. T F If an array is partially initialized, the uninitialized elements will contain "garbage."

62. T F If you leave an element uninitialized, you do not have to leave all the ones that follow it uninitialized.

63. T F If you leave out the size declarator of an array definition, you do not have to include an initialization list.

64. T F The uninitialized elements of a `string` array will automatically be set to the value `"0"`.

65. T F You cannot use the assignment operator to copy one array's contents to another in a single statement.

66. T F When an array name is used without brackets and a subscript, it is seen as the value of the first element in the array.

67. T F To pass an array to a function, pass the name of the array.

68. T F When defining a parameter variable to hold a single-dimensional array argument, you do not have to include the size declarator.

69. T F When an array is passed to a function, the function has access to the original array.

70. T F A two-dimensional array is like several identical arrays put together.

71. T F It's best to think of two-dimensional arrays as having rows and columns.

72. T F The first size declarator (in the declaration of a two-dimensional array) represents the number of columns. The second size definition represents the number of rows.

73. T F Two-dimensional arrays may be passed to functions, but the row size must be specified in the definition of the parameter variable.

74. T F C++ allows you to create arrays with three or more dimensions.

75. T F A `vector` is an associative container.

76. T F To use a `vector`, you must include the `vector` header file.

77. T F `vectors` can report the number of elements they contain.

78. T F You can use the `[]` operator to insert a value into a `vector` that has no elements.

79. T F If you add a value to a `vector` that is already full, the `vector` will automatically increase its size to accommodate the new value.

Find the Errors

Each of the following definitions and program segments has errors. Locate as many as you can.

80.
```
int size;
double values[size];
```

81.
```
int collection[-20];
```

82.
```
int table[10];
for (int x = 0; x < 20; x++)
{
    cout << "Enter the next value: ";
    cin >> table[x];
}
```

83.
```
int hours[3] = 8, 12, 16;
```

84.
```
int numbers[8] = {1, 2, , 4, , 5};
```

85.
```
float ratings[];
```

86.
```
char greeting[] = {'H', 'e', 'l', 'l', 'o'};
cout << greeting;
```

87.
```
int array1[4], array2[4] = {3, 6, 9, 12};
array1 = array2;
```

88.
```
void showValues(int nums)
{
    for (int count = 0; count < 8; count++)
       cout << nums[count];
}
```

89.
```
void showValues(int nums[4][])
{
   for (rows = 0; rows < 4; rows++)
      for (cols = 0; cols < 5; cols++)
         cout << nums[rows][cols];
}
```

90.
```
vector<int> numbers = { 1, 2, 3, 4 };
```

Programming Challenges

1. **Largest/Smallest Array Values**

   Write a program that lets the user enter ten values into an array. The program should then display the largest and smallest values stored in the array.

2. **Rainfall Statistics**

   Write a program that lets the user enter the total rainfall for each of 12 months into an array of `double`s. The program should calculate and display the total rainfall for the year, the average monthly rainfall, and the months with the highest and lowest amounts.

   Input Validation: Do not accept negative numbers for monthly rainfall figures.

VideoNote
Solving the Chips and Salsa Problem

3. **Chips and Salsa**

   Write a program that lets a maker of chips and salsa keep track of sales for five different types of salsa: mild, medium, sweet, hot, and zesty. The program should use two parallel 5-element arrays: an array of strings that holds the five salsa names, and an array of integers that holds the number of jars sold during the past month for each salsa type. The salsa names should be stored using an initialization list at the time the name array is created. The program should prompt the user to enter the number of jars sold for each type. Once this sales data has been entered, the program should produce a report that displays sales for each salsa type, total sales, and the names of the highest selling and lowest selling products.

   Input Validation: Do not accept negative values for number of jars sold.

4. **Larger than *n***

   In a program, write a function that accepts three arguments: an array, the size of the array, and a number *n*. Assume the array contains integers. The function should display all of the numbers in the array that are greater than the number *n*.

5. **Monkey Business**

   A local zoo wants to keep track of how many pounds of food each of its three monkeys eats each day during a typical week. Write a program that stores this information in a two-dimensional 3 × 5 array, where each row represents a different monkey, and each column represents a different day of the week. The program should first have the user input the data for each monkey. Then, it should create a report that includes the following information:

   - Average amount of food eaten per day by the whole family of monkeys.
   - The least amount of food eaten during the week by any one monkey.
   - The greatest amount of food eaten during the week by any one monkey.

   Input Validation: Do not accept negative numbers for pounds of food eaten.

6. **Rain or Shine**

   An amateur meteorologist wants to keep track of weather conditions during the past year's three-month summer season, and has designated each day as either rainy ('R'), cloudy ('C'), or sunny ('S'). Write a program that stores this information in a 3 × 30 array of characters, where the row indicates the month (0 = June, 1 = July, 2 = August) and the column indicates the day of the month. Note data are not being collected for the 31st of any month. The program should begin by reading the weather data in from a file. Then it should create a report that displays, for each month and for the whole three-month period, how many days were rainy, how many were cloudy, and how many were sunny. It should also report which of the three months had the largest number of rainy days. Data for the program can be found in the RainOrShine.txt file.

7. **Number Analysis Program**

   Write a program that asks the user for a file name. Assume the file contains a series of numbers, each written on a separate line. The program should read the contents of the file into an array then display the following data:

   - The lowest number in the array
   - The highest number in the array

- The total of the numbers in the array
- The average of the numbers in the array

If you have downloaded this chapter's source code from the Computer Science Portal at www.pearsonhighered.com/gaddis, you will find a file named numbers.txt in the Chapter 07 folder. You can use the file to test the program.

8. **Lo Shu Magic Square**

The Lo Shu Magic Square is a grid with 3 rows and 3 columns shown in Figure 19. The Lo Shu Magic Square has the following properties:

- The grid contains the numbers 1 through 9 exactly.
- The sum of each row, each column, and each diagonal all add up to the same number. This is shown in Figure 20.

In a program, you can simulate a magic square using a two-dimensional array. Write a function that accepts a two-dimensional array as an argument, and determines whether the array is a Lo Shu Magic Square. Test the function in a program.

Figure 19 Lo Shu Magic Square

4	9	2
3	5	7
8	1	6

Figure 20 Sums of the rows, columns, and diagonals

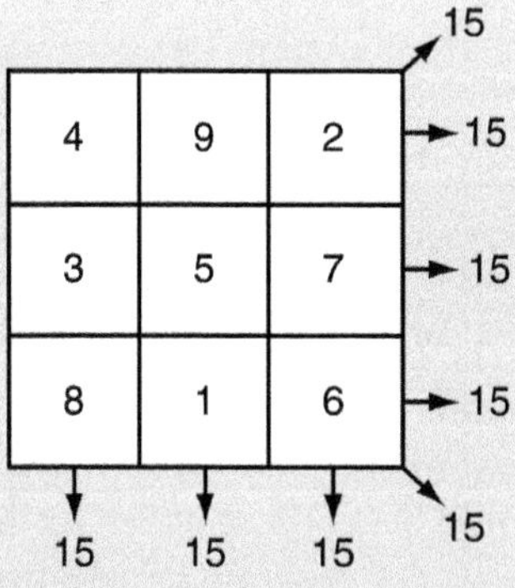

9. **Payroll**

Write a program that uses the following arrays:

- `empId`: an array of seven long integers to hold employee identification numbers. The array should be initialized with the following numbers:

```
5658845   4520125   7895122   8777541
8451277   1302850   7580489
```

- `hours`: an array of seven integers to hold the number of hours worked by each employee
- `payRate`: an array of seven `double`s to hold each employee's hourly pay rate
- `wages`: an array of seven `double`s to hold each employee's gross wages

The program should relate the data in each array through the subscripts. For example, the number in element 0 of the `hours` array should be the number of hours worked by the employee whose identification number is stored in element 0 of the `empId` array. That same employee's pay rate should be stored in element 0 of the `payRate` array.

The program should display each employee number and ask the user to enter that employee's hours and pay rate. It should then calculate the gross wages for that employee (hours times pay rate) and store them in the `wages` array. After the data has been entered for all the employees, the program should display each employee's identification number and gross wages.

Input Validation: Do not accept negative values for hours or numbers less than 15.00 for pay rate.

10. Driver's License Exam

The local Driver's License Office has asked you to write a program that grades the written portion of the driver's license exam. The exam has 20 multiple-choice questions. Here are the correct answers:

1. A	6. B	11. A	16. C
2. D	7. A	12. C	17. C
3. B	8. B	13. D	18. A
4. B	9. C	14. B	19. D
5. C	10. D	15. D	20. B

Your program should store the correct answers shown above in an array. It should ask the user to enter the student's answers for each of the 20 questions, and the answers should be stored in another array. After the student's answers have been entered, the program should display a message indicating whether the student passed or failed the exam. (A student must correctly answer 15 of the 20 questions to pass the exam.) It should then display the total number of correctly answered questions, the total number of incorrectly answered questions, and a list showing the question numbers of the incorrectly answered questions.

Input Validation: Only accept the letters A, B, C, or D as answers.

11. Exam Grader

One of your professors has asked you to write a program to grade her final exams, which consist of only 20 multiple-choice questions. Each question has one of four possible answers: A, B, C, or D. The file CorrectAnswers.txt contains the correct answers for all of the questions, with each answer written on a separate line. The first line contains the answer to the first question, the second line contains the answer to the second question, and so forth. (Download the chapter's source code from the Computer Science Portal at www.pearsonhighered.com/gaddis. You will find the file in the Chapter 07 folder.)

Write a program that reads the contents of the CorrectAnswers.txt file into a `char` array, then reads the contents of another file, containing a student's answers, into a second `char` array. (You can use the file StudentAnswers.txt for testing purposes. This file is also in the Chapter 07 source code folder.) The program should determine the number of questions that the student missed, then display the following:

- A list of the questions missed by the student, showing the correct answer and the incorrect answer provided by the student for each missed question
- The total number of questions missed
- The percentage of questions answered correctly. This can be calculated as

  Correctly Answered Questions ÷ Total Number of Questions

- If the percentage of correctly answered questions is 70 percent or greater, the program should indicate that the student passed the exam. Otherwise, it should indicate that the student failed the exam.

12. Grade Book

A teacher has five students who have taken four tests. The teacher uses the following grading scale to assign a letter grade to a student, based on the average of his or her four test scores:

Test Score	Letter Grade
90–100	A
80–89	B
70–79	C
60–69	D
0–59	F

Write a program that uses an array of `string` objects to hold the five student names, an array of five characters to hold the five students' letter grades, and five arrays of four `double`s to hold each student's set of test scores.

The program should allow the user to enter each student's name and his or her four test scores. It should then calculate and display each student's average test score, and a letter grade based on the average.

Input Validation: Do not accept test scores less than 0 or greater than 100.

13. Grade Book Modification

Modify the grade book application in Programming Challenge 12 so it drops each student's lowest score when determining the test score averages and letter grades.

14. Lottery Application

Write a program that simulates a lottery. The program should have an array of five integers named `lottery` and should generate a random number in the range of 0 through 9 for each element in the array. The user should enter five digits, which should be stored in an integer array named `user`. The program is to compare the corresponding elements in the two arrays and keep a count of the digits that match. For example, the following shows the `lottery` array and the `user` array with sample numbers stored in each. There are two matching digits (elements 2 and 4).

Lottery array:

7	4	9	1	3

User array:

4	2	9	7	3

The program should display the random numbers stored in the `lottery` array and the number of matching digits. If all of the digits match, display a message proclaiming the user as a grand prize winner.

15. `vector` Modification

Modify the National Commerce Bank case study presented in Program 23 so `pin1`, `pin2`, and `pin3` are `vector`s instead of arrays. You must also modify the `testPIN` function to accept a `vector` instead of an array.

16. World Series Champions

If you have downloaded this chapter's source code, you will find the following files in this chapter's folder:

- Teams.txt—This file contains a list of several Major League baseball teams in alphabetical order. Each team listed in the file has won the World Series at least once.
- WorldSeriesWinners.txt—This file contains a chronological list of the World Series' winning teams from 1903 to 2012. (The first line in the file is the name of the team that won in 1903, and the last line is the name of the team that won in 2012. Note the World Series was not played in 1904 or 1994.)

Write a program that displays the contents of the Teams.txt file on the screen and prompts the user to enter the name of one of the teams. The program should then display the number of times that team has won the World Series in the time period from 1903 to 2012.

> **TIP:** Read the contents of the WorldSeriesWinners.txt file into an array or `vector`. When the user enters the name of a team, the program should step through the array or `vector` counting the number of times the selected team appears.

17. Name Search

If you have downloaded this chapter's source code, you will find the following files in this chapter's folder:

- GirlNames.txt—This file contains a list of the 200 most popular names given to girls born in the United States from 2000 to 2009.
- BoyNames.txt—This file contains a list of the 200 most popular names given to boys born in the United States from 2000 to 2009.

Write a program that reads the contents of the two files into two separate arrays or `vector`s. The user should be able to enter a boy's name, a girl's name, or both, and the application should display messages indicating whether the names were among the most popular.

18. Tic-Tac-Toe Game

Write a program that allows two players to play a game of tic-tac-toe. Use a two-dimensional `char` array with three rows and three columns as the game board. Each element of the array should be initialized with an asterisk (*). The program should run a loop that does the following:

- Displays the contents of the board array.
- Allows player 1 to select a location on the board for an X. The program should ask the user to enter the row and column numbers.
- Allows player 2 to select a location on the board for an O. The program should ask the user to enter the row and column numbers.
- Determines whether a player has won, or a tie has occurred. If a player has won, the program should declare that player the winner and end. If a tie has occurred, the program should display an appropriate message and end.

Player 1 wins when there are three Xs in a row on the game board. The Xs can appear in a row, in a column, or diagonally across the board. Player 2 wins when there are three Os in a row on the game board. The Os can appear in a row, in a column, or diagonally across the board. A tie occurs when all of the locations on the board are full, but there is no winner.

19. Magic 8 Ball

Write a program that simulates a Magic 8 Ball, which is a fortune-telling toy that displays a random response to a yes or no question. In the student sample programs for this chapter, you will find a text file named 8_ball_responses.txt. The file contains 12 responses, such as "I don't think so", "Yes, of course!", "I'm not sure", and so forth. The program should read the responses from the file into an array or `vector`. It should prompt the user to ask a question, and then display one of the responses, randomly selected from the array or `vector`. The program should repeat until the user is ready to quit.

Contents of 8_ball_responses.txt:

```
Yes, of course!
Without a doubt, yes.
You can count on it.
For sure!
Ask me later.
I'm not sure.
I can't tell you right now.
I'll tell you after my nap.
No way!
I don't think so.
Without a doubt, no.
The answer is clearly NO.
```

20. 1994 Gas Prices

In the student sample programs for this chapter, you will find a text file named 1994_Weekly_Gas_Averages.txt. The file contains the average gas price for each week in the year 1994 (There are 52 lines in the file. Line 1 contains the average price for week 1, line 2 contains the average price for week 2, and so forth.) Write a program that reads the gas prices from the file into an array or a `vector`. The program should do the following:

- Display the lowest average price of the year, along with the week number for that price, and the name of the month in which it occurred.

- Display the highest average price of the year, along with the week number for that price, and the name of the month in which it occurred.
- Display the average gas price for each month. (To get the average price for a given month, calculate the average of the average weekly prices for that month.)

21. 2D Array Operations

Write a program that creates a two-dimensional array initialized with test data. Use any data type you wish. The program should have the following functions:

- `getTotal`—This function should accept a two-dimensional array as its argument and return the total of all the values in the array.
- `getAverage`—This function should accept a two-dimensional array as its argument and return the average of all the values in the array.
- `getRowTotal`—This function should accept a two-dimensional array as its first argument and an integer as its second argument. The second argument should be the subscript of a row in the array. The function should return the total of the values in the specified row.
- `getColumnTotal`—This function should accept a two-dimensional array as its first argument and an integer as its second argument. The second argument should be the subscript of a column in the array. The function should return the total of the values in the specified column.
- `getHighestInRow`—This function should accept a two-dimensional array as its first argument and an integer as its second argument. The second argument should be the subscript of a row in the array. The function should return the highest value in the specified row of the array.
- `getLowestInRow`—This function should accept a two-dimensional array as its first argument and an integer as its second argument. The second argument should be the subscript of a row in the array. The function should return the lowest value in the specified row of the array.

Demonstrate each of the functions in this program.

Group Project

22. Theater Seating

This program should be designed and written by a team of students. Here are some suggestions:

- One student should design function `main`, which will call the other functions in the program. The remainder of the functions will be designed by other members of the team.
- The requirements of the program should be analyzed so that each student is given about the same workload.
- The parameters and return types of each function should be decided in advance.
- The program can be implemented as a multi-file program, or all the functions can be cut and pasted into the main file.

Here is the assignment: Write a program that can be used by a small theater to sell tickets for performances. The theater's auditorium has 15 rows of seats, with 30 seats in each row. The program should display a screen that shows which seats are available and which are taken. For example, the following screen shows a chart depicting each seat in the theater. Seats that are taken are represented by an * symbol, and seats that are available are represented by a # symbol.

```
                Seats
         123456789012345678901234567890
Row  1   ***###***###*########*****####
Row  2   ####*************####*******##
Row  3   **###**********########****###
Row  4   **######**************##******
Row  5   ********#####*********########
Row  6   ##############************####
Row  7   #######************###########
Row  8   ************##****############
Row  9   #########*****############****
Row 10   #####*************############
Row 11   #**********#################**
Row 12   #############********########*
Row 13   ###***********########**######
Row 14   ##############################
Row 15   ##############################
```

Here is a list of tasks this program must perform:

- When the program begins, it should ask the user to enter the seat prices for each row. The prices can be stored in a separate array. (Alternatively, the prices may be read from a file.)
- Once the prices are entered, the program should display a seating chart similar to the one shown above. The user may enter the row and seat numbers for tickets being sold. Every time a ticket or group of tickets is purchased, the program should display the total ticket prices and update the seating chart.
- The program should keep a total of all ticket sales. The user should be given an option of viewing this amount.
- The program should also give the user an option to see a list of how many seats have been sold, how many seats are available in each row, and how many seats are available in the entire auditorium.

Input Validation: When tickets are being sold, do not accept row or seat numbers that do not exist. When someone requests a particular seat, the program should make sure that seat is available before it is sold.

Answers to Checkpoints

1 A) `int empNums[100];`
  B) `float payRates[25];`
  C) `long miles[14];`
  D) `string cityNames[26];`
  E) `double lightYears[1000];`

2
```
int readings[-1]; // Size declarator cannot be negative
float measurements[4.5]; // Size declarator must be an integer
int size;
string names[size]; // Size declarator must be a constant
```

3 0 through 3

4 The size declarator is used in the array declaration statement. It specifies the number of elements in the array. A subscript is used to access an individual element in an array.

5 Array bounds checking is a safeguard provided by some languages. It prevents a program from using a subscript that is beyond the boundaries of an array. C++ does not perform array bounds checking.

6
```
1
2
3
4
5
```

7
```
#include <iostream>
using namespace std;

int main()
{
    const int NUM_FISH = 20;
    int fish[NUM_FISH], count;
    cout << "Enter the number of fish caught\n";
    cout << "by each fisherman.\n";
    for (count = 0; count < NUM_FISH; count++)
    {
        cout << "fisherman " << (count+1) << ": ";
        cin >> fish[count];
    }
    return 0;
}
```

8 A) `int ages[10] = {5, 7, 9, 14, 15, 17, 18, 19, 21, 23};`
B) `float temps[7] = {14.7, 16.3, 18.43, 21.09, 17.9, 18.76, 26.7};`
C) `char alpha[8] = {'J', 'B', 'L', 'A', '*', '$', 'H', 'M'};`

9 The definition of `numbers` is valid.

The declaration of `matrix` is invalid because there are too many values in the initialization list.

The definition of `radii` is valid.

The definition of `table` is invalid. Values cannot be skipped in the initialization list.

The definition of `codes` is valid.

The definition of `blanks` is invalid. An initialization list must be provided when an array is implicitly sized.

10 A) 0
B) 3
C) 6
D) 14

11 0

12
```
10.00
25.00
32.50
50.00
110.00
```

13
```
1 18 18
2 4 8
3 27 81
4 52 208
5 100 500
```

14 No. An entire array cannot be copied in a single statement with the = operator. The array must be copied element-by-element.

15 The address of the array

16 No

17 ABCDEFGH

18 *(The entire program is shown here.)*

```
#include <iostream>
using namespace std;

// Function prototype here
double avgArray(int []);

int main()
{
    const int SIZE = 10;
    int userNums[SIZE];
    cout << "Enter 10 numbers: ";
    for (int count = 0; count < SIZE; count++)
    {
        cout << "#" << (count + 1) << " ";
        cin >> userNums[count];
    }
    cout << "The average of those numbers is ";
    cout << avgArray(userNums, SIZE) << endl;
    return 0;
}

// Function avgArray
double avgArray(int arr[])
{
    double total = 0.0, average;
    for (int count = 0; count < 10; count++)
        total += arr[count];
    average = total / 10;
    return average;
}
```

19 `int grades[30][10];`

20 24

21 `sales[0][0] = 56893.12;`

22 `cout << sales[5][3];`

23
```
int settings[3][5] = {{12, 24, 32, 21, 42},
                      {14, 67, 87, 65, 90},
                      {19, 1, 24, 12, 8}};
```

24

2	3	0	0
7	9	2	0
1	0	0	0

25
```
void displayArray7(int arr[][7], int rows)
{
    for (int x = 0; x < rows; x++)
    {
        for (int y = 0; y < 7; y++)
        {
            cout << arr[x][y] << " ";
        }
        cout << endl;
    }
}
```

26 `int vidNum[50][10][25];`

27 `vector`

28 `vector <int> frogs;`

29 `vector <float> lizards(20);`

30 `vector <char> toads(100, 'Z');`

31
```
vector <int> gators;
gators.push_back(27);
```

32 `snakes[4] = 12.897;`

Answers to Odd Numbered Review Questions

1. The size declarator is used in a definition of an array to indicate the number of elements the array will have. A subscript is used to access a specific element in an array.
3. Because, with the array alone, the function has no way of determining the number of elements it has.
5. By providing an initialization list. The array is sized to hold the number of values in the list.

7. Because an array name without brackets and a subscript represents the array's beginning memory address. The statement shown attempts to assign the address of `array2` to `array1`, which is not permitted.
9. By reference
11. By using the same subscript value for each array
13. The second size declarator, which is for the number of columns
15. size declarator
17. subscript
19. size declarator, subscript
21. initialization
23. initialization list
25. =
27. address, or name
29. rows, columns
31. braces
33. Standard Template Library (or STL)
35. sequence
37. `push_back`
39. `pop_back`
41.
```
for (int i = 0; i < 20; i++)
   cout << names[i] << endl;
```
43.
```
const int SIZE = 10;
int id[SIZE];                  // To hold ID numbers
double weeklyPay[SIZE];        // To hold weekly pay
   // Display each employee's gross weekly pay.
for (int i = 0; i < SIZE; i++)
{
    cout << "The pay for employee "
         << id[i] << " is $" << fixed
         << showpoint << setprecision(2)
         << weeklyPay[i] << endl;
}
```
45.
```
const int SIZE = 12;
// A 2D array to hold the country names
string countries[SIZE];
// An array to hold populations
long populations[SIZE];
// Display each country's name and population.
for (int i = 0; i < SIZE; i++)
```

```
{
    cout << "The population of " << countries[i]
         << " is " << populations[i] << endl;
}
```

47.
```
numberArray[0][0] = 145;
numberArray[8][10] = 18;
```

49.
```
const int NUM_ROWS = 29;
const int NUM_COLS = 5;
int row, col,  // Loop counters
    total;     // Accumulator
// Display the sum of each row.
for (row = 0; row < NUM_ROWS; row++)
{
    // Set the accumulator.
    total = 0;
    // Sum a row.
    for (col = 0; col < NUM_COLS; col++)
        total += days[row][col];
    // Display the row's total.
    cout << "The total for row " << row
         << " is " << total << endl;
}
// Display the sum of each column.
for (col = 0; col < NUM_COLS; col++)
{
    // Set the accumulator.
    total = 0;
    // Sum a column.
    for (row = 0; row < NUM_ROWS; row++)
        total += days[row][col];
    // Display the column's total.
    cout << "The total for column "
         << col << " is " << total << endl;
}
```

51. True
53. False
55. False
57. True
59. True
61. False
63. False
65. True

67. True
69. True
71. True
73. False
75. False
77. True
79. True
81. The size declarator cannot be negative.
83. The initialization list must be enclosed in braces.
85. For the array to be implicitly sized, there must be an initialization list.
87. The assignment operator cannot be used to assign the contents of one array to another, in a single statement.
89. The parameter must specify the number of columns, not the number of rows.

Searching and Sorting Arrays

TOPICS

1 Focus on Software Engineering: Introduction to Search Algorithms

CONCEPT: A search algorithm is a method of locating a specific item in a larger collection of data. This section discusses two algorithms for searching the contents of an array.

It's very common for programs not only to store and process data stored in arrays, but also to search arrays for specific items. This section will show you two methods of searching an array: the linear search and the binary search. Each has its advantages and disadvantages.

The Linear Search

The *linear search* is a very simple algorithm. Also known as the *sequential search* algorithm, it uses a loop to sequentially step through an array, starting with the first element. It compares each element with the value being searched for, and stops when either the value is found or the end of the array is encountered. If the value being searched for is not in the array, the algorithm will unsuccessfully search to the end of the array.

Here is the pseudocode for a function that performs the linear search:

```
Set found to false
Set position to -1
Set index to 0
```

From Chapter 8 of *Starting Out with C++: From Control Structures through Objects*, Ninth Edition. Tony Gaddis.

```
While found is false and index < number of elements
    If list[index] is equal to search value
        found = true
        position = index
    End If
    Add 1 to index
End While
Return position
```

The `linearSearch` function shown below is an example of C++ code used to perform a linear search on an integer array. The array `arr`, which has a maximum of `size` elements, is searched for an occurrence of the number stored in `value`. If the number is found, its array subscript is returned. Otherwise, –1 is returned, indicating the value did not appear in the array.

```
int linearSearch (const int arr[], int size, int value)
{
   int index = 0;         // Used as a subscript to search the array
   int position = -1;     // To record the position of the search value
   bool found = false;    // Flag to indicate if the value was found

   while (index < size && !found)
   {
      if (arr[index] == value)       // If the value is found
      {
         found = true;               // Set the flag
         position = index;           // Record the value's subscript
      }
      index++;                       // Go to the next element
   }
   return position;                  // Return the position, or -1
}
```

NOTE: The reason –1 is returned when the search value is not found in the array is because –1 is not a valid subscript.

Program 1 is a complete program that uses the `linearSearch` function. It searches the five-element array `tests` to find a score of 100.

Program 1

```
// This program demonstrates the linear search algorithm.
#include <iostream>
using namespace std;

// Function prototype
int linearSearch(const int[], int, int);

int main()
{
    const int SIZE = 5;
    int tests[SIZE] = { 87, 75, 98, 100, 82 };
    int results;
```

```
   // Search the array for 100.
   results = linearSearch(tests, SIZE, 100);

   // If linearSearch returned -1, then 100 was not found.
   if (results == -1)
      cout << "You did not earn 100 points on any test\n";
   else
   {
      // Otherwise results contains the subscript of
      // the first 100 in the array.
      cout << "You earned 100 points on test ";
      cout << (results + 1) << endl;
   }
   return 0;
}

//*******************************************************************
// The linearSearch function performs a linear search on an         *
// integer array. The array arr, which has a maximum of size        *
// elements, is searched for the number stored in value. If the     *
// number is found, its array subscript is returned. Otherwise,     *
// -1 is returned indicating the value was not in the array.        *
//*******************************************************************
int linearSearch(const int arr[], int size, int value)
{
   int index = 0;        // Used as a subscript to search array
   int position = -1;    // To record position of search value
   bool found = false;   // Flag to indicate if the value was found

   while (index < size && !found)
   {
      if (arr[index] == value)     // If the value is found
      {
         found = true;             // Set the flag
         position = index;         // Record the value's subscript
      }
      index++;                     // Go to the next element
   }
   return position;                // Return the position, or -1
}
```

Program Output

```
You earned 100 points on test 4
```

Inefficiency of the Linear Search

The advantage of the linear search is its simplicity. It is very easy to understand and implement. Furthermore, it doesn't require the data in the array to be stored in any particular order. Its disadvantage, however, is its inefficiency. If the array being searched contains 20,000 elements, the algorithm will have to look at all 20,000 elements in order to find a value stored in the last element (so the algorithm actually reads an element of the array 20,000 times).

In an average case, an item is just as likely to be found near the beginning of the array as near the end. Typically, for an array of N items, the linear search will locate an item in N/2 attempts. If an array has 50,000 elements, the linear search will make a comparison with 25,000 of them in a typical case. This is assuming, of course, that the search item is consistently found in the array. (N/2 is the average number of comparisons. The maximum number of comparisons is always N.)

When the linear search fails to locate an item, it must make a comparison with every element in the array. As the number of failed search attempts increases, so does the average number of comparisons. Obviously, the linear search should not be used on large arrays if the speed is important.

The Binary Search

VideoNote
The Binary Search

The *binary search* is a clever algorithm that is much more efficient than the linear search. Its only requirement is that the values in the array be sorted in order. Instead of testing the array's first element, this algorithm starts with the element in the middle. If that element happens to contain the desired value, then the search is over. Otherwise, the value in the middle element is either greater than or less than the value being searched for. If it is greater, then the desired value (if it is in the list) will be found somewhere in the first half of the array. If it is less, then the desired value (again, if it is in the list) will be found somewhere in the last half of the array. In either case, half of the array's elements have been eliminated from further searching.

If the desired value wasn't found in the middle element, the procedure is repeated for the half of the array that potentially contains the value. For instance, if the last half of the array is to be searched, the algorithm immediately tests *its* middle element. If the desired value isn't found there, the search is narrowed to the quarter of the array that resides before or after that element. This process continues until either the value being searched for is found, or there are no more elements to test.

Here is the pseudocode for a function that performs a binary search on an array:

```
Set first to 0
Set last to the last subscript in the array
Set found to false
Set position to -1
While found is not true and first is less than or equal to last
    Set middle to the subscript halfway between array[first]
    and array[last]
    If array[middle] equals the desired value
        Set found to true
        Set position to middle
    Else If array[middle] is greater than the desired value
        Set last to middle - 1
    Else
        Set first to middle + 1
    End If
End While
Return position
```

This algorithm uses three index variables: `first`, `last`, and `middle`. The `first` and `last` variables mark the boundaries of the portion of the array currently being searched. They are initialized with the subscripts of the array's first and last elements. The subscript of the element halfway between `first` and `last` is calculated and stored in the `middle` variable. If the element in the middle of the array does not contain the search value, the `first` or `last` variables are adjusted so only the top or bottom half of the array is searched during the next iteration. This cuts the portion of the array being searched in half each time the loop fails to locate the search value.

The function `binarySearch` shown in the following example is used to perform a binary search on an integer array. The first parameter, `array`, which has a maximum of `numElems` elements, is searched for an occurrence of the number stored in `value`. If the number is found, its array subscript is returned. Otherwise, –1 is returned indicating the value did not appear in the array.

```
int binarySearch(const int array[], int numElems, int value)
{
   int first = 0,                      // First array element
       last = numElems - 1,            // Last array element
       middle,                         // Midpoint of search
       position = -1;                  // Position of search value
   bool found = false;                 // Flag

   while (!found && first <= last)
   {
       middle = (first + last) / 2;    // Calculate midpoint
       if (array[middle] == value)     // If value is found at mid
       {
          found = true;
          position = middle;
       }
       else if (array[middle] > value) // If value is in lower half
          last = middle - 1;
       else
          first = middle + 1;          // If value is in upper half
   }
   return position;
}
```

Program 2 is a complete program using the `binarySearch` function. It searches an array of employee ID numbers for a specific value.

Program 2

```
// This program demonstrates the binarySearch function, which
// performs a binary search on an integer array.
#include <iostream>
using namespace std;

// Function prototype
int binarySearch(const int [], int, int);
const int SIZE = 20;
```

(program continues)

Program 2 *(continued)*

```

int main()
{
    // Array with employee IDs sorted in ascending order.
    int idNums[SIZE] = {101, 142, 147, 189, 199, 207, 222,
                        234, 289, 296, 310, 319, 388, 394,
                        417, 429, 447, 521, 536, 600};
    int results;  // To hold the search results
    int empID;    // To hold an employee ID

    // Get an employee ID to search for.
    cout << "Enter the employee ID you wish to search for: ";
    cin >> empID;

    // Search for the ID.
    results = binarySearch(idNums, SIZE, empID);

    // If results contains -1 the ID was not found.
    if (results == -1)
       cout << "That number does not exist in the array. \n";
    else
    {
         // Otherwise results contains the subscript of
         // the specified employee ID in the array.
         cout << "That ID is found at element " << results;
         cout << " in the array.\n";
    }
    return 0;
}

//*****************************************************************
// The binarySearch function performs a binary search on an      *
// integer array. array, which has a maximum of size elements,   *
// is searched for the number stored in value. If the number is  *
// found, its array subscript is returned. Otherwise, -1 is      *
// returned indicating the value was not in the array.           *
//*****************************************************************

int binarySearch(const int array[], int size, int value)
{
      int first = 0,            // First array element
          last = size - 1,      // Last array element
          middle,               // Midpoint of search
          position = -1;        // Position of search value
      bool found = false;       // Flag

    while (!found && first <= last)
    {
       middle = (first + last) / 2;     // Calculate midpoint
       if (array[middle] == value)      // If value is found at mid
```

```
            {
                found = true;
                position = middle;
            }
            else if (array[middle] > value)// If value is in lower half
                last = middle - 1;
            else
                first = middle + 1; // If value is in upper half
        }
        return position;
    }
```

Program Output with Example Input Shown in Bold

```
Enter the employee ID you wish to search for: 199 [Enter]
That ID is found at element 4 in the array.
```

WARNING! Notice the array in Program 2 is initialized with its values already sorted in ascending order. The binary search algorithm will not work properly unless the values in the array are sorted.

The Efficiency of the Binary Search

Obviously, the binary search is much more efficient than the linear search. Every time it makes a comparison and fails to find the desired item, it eliminates half of the remaining portion of the array that must be searched. For example, consider an array with 1,000 elements. If the binary search fails to find an item on the first attempt, the number of elements that remains to be searched is 500. If the item is not found on the second attempt, the number of elements that remains to be searched is 250. This process continues until the binary search has either located the desired item or determined that it is not in the array. With 1,000 elements, this takes no more than 10 comparisons. (Compare this to the linear search, which would make an average of 500 comparisons!)

Powers of 2 are used to calculate the maximum number of comparisons the binary search will make on an array of any size. (A power of 2 is 2 raised to the power of some number.) Simply find the smallest power of 2 that is greater than or equal to the number of elements in the array. For example, a maximum of 16 comparisons will be made on an array of 50,000 elements ($2^{16} = 65{,}536$), and a maximum of 20 comparisons will be made on an array of 1,000,000 elements ($2^{20} = 1{,}048{,}576$).

2 Focus on Problem Solving and Program Design: A Case Study

The Demetris Leadership Center (DLC, Inc.) publishes the books, DVDs, and audio CDs listed in Table 1.

Table 1 Products

Product Title	Product Description	Product Number	Unit Price
Six Steps to Leadership	Book	914	$12.95
Six Steps to Leadership	Audio CD	915	$14.95
The Road to Excellence	DVD	916	$18.95
Seven Lessons of Quality	Book	917	$16.95
Seven Lessons of Quality	Audio CD	918	$21.95
Seven Lessons of Quality	DVD	919	$31.95
Teams Are Made, Not Born	Book	920	$14.95
Leadership for the Future	Book	921	$14.95
Leadership for the Future	Audio CD	922	$16.95

The manager of the Telemarketing Group has asked you to write a program that will help order-entry operators look up product prices. The program should prompt the user to enter a product number, and will then display the title, description, and price of the product.

Variables

Table 2 lists the variables needed:

Table 2 Variables

Variable	Description
`NUM_PRODS`	A constant integer initialized with the number of products the Demetris Leadership Center sells. This value will be used in the definition of the program's array.
`MIN_PRODNUM`	A constant integer initialized with the lowest product number.
`MAX_PRODNUM`	A constant integer initialized with the highest product number.
`id`	Array of integers. Holds each product's number.
`title`	Array of strings, initialized with the titles of products.
`description`	Array of strings, initialized with the descriptions of each product.
`prices`	Array of `double`s. Holds each product's price.

Modules

The program will consist of the functions listed in Table 3.

Table 3 Functions

Function	Description
`main`	The program's `main` function. It calls the program's other functions.
`getProdNum`	Prompts the user to enter a product number. The function validates input and rejects any value outside the range of correct product numbers.
`binarySearch`	A standard binary search routine. Searches an array for a specified value. If the value is found, its subscript is returned. If the value is not found, –1 is returned.
`displayProd`	Uses a common subscript into the `title`, `description`, and `prices` arrays to display the title, description, and price of a product.

Function `main`

Function `main` contains the variable definitions and calls the other functions. Here is its pseudocode:

```
do
   Call getProdNum
   Call binarySearch
   If binarySearch returned -1
      Inform the user that the product number was not found
   else
      Call displayProd
   End If
   Ask the user if the program should repeat
While the user wants to repeat the program
```

Here is its actual C++ code:

```
do
{
   // Get the desired product number.
   prodNum = getProdNum();

   // Search for the product number.
   index = binarySearch(id, NUM_PRODS, prodNum);

   // Display the results of the search.
   if (index == -1)
      cout << "That product number was not found.\n";
   else
      displayProd(title, description, prices, index);

   // Does the user want to do this again?
   cout << "Would you like to look up another product? (y/n) ";
   cin >> again;
} while (again == 'y' || again == 'Y');
```

The named constant `NUM_PRODS` is defined globally and initialized with the value 9. The arrays `id`, `title`, `description`, and `prices` will already be initialized with data.

The `getProdNum` Function

The `getProdNum` function prompts the user to enter a product number. It tests the value to ensure it is in the range of 914–922 (which are the valid product numbers). If an invalid value is entered, it is rejected and the user is prompted again. When a valid product number is entered, the function returns it. The pseudocode is shown below.

```
Display a prompt to enter a product number
Read prodNum
While prodNum is invalid
   Display an error message
   Read prodNum
End While
Return prodNum
```

Here is the actual C++ code:

```
int getProdNum()
{
    int prodNum;

    cout << "Enter the item's product number: ";
    cin >> prodNum;
    // Validate input.
    while (prodNum < MIN_PRODNUM || prodNum > MAX_PRODNUM)
    {
       cout << "Enter a number in the range of " << MIN_PRODNUM;
       cout <<" through " << MAX_PRODNUM << ".\n";
       cin >> prodNum;
    }
    return prodNum;
}
```

The binarySearch Function

The binarySearch function is identical to the function discussed earlier in this chapter.

The displayProd Function

The displayProd function has parameter variables named title, desc, price, and index. These accept as arguments (respectively) the title, description, and price arrays, and a subscript value. The function displays the data stored in each array at the subscript passed into index. Here is the C++ code:

```
void displayProd(const string title[], const string desc[],
                 const double price[], int index)
{
    cout << "Title: " << title[index] << endl;
    cout << "Description: " << desc[index] << endl;
    cout << "Price: $" << price[index] << endl;
}
```

The Entire Program

Program 3 shows the entire program's source code.

Program 3

```
// Demetris Leadership Center (DLC) product lookup program
// This program allows the user to enter a product number
// and then displays the title, description, and price of
// that product.
#include <iostream>
#include <string>
using namespace std;

```

```
const int NUM_PRODS = 9;         // The number of products produced
const int MIN_PRODNUM = 914;     // The lowest product number
const int MAX_PRODNUM = 922;     // The highest product number

// Function prototypes
int getProdNum();
int binarySearch(const int [], int, int);
void displayProd(const string [], const string [], const double [], int);

int main()
{
    // Array of product IDs
    int id[NUM_PRODS] = {914, 915, 916, 917, 918, 919, 920,
                         921, 922};

    // Array of product titles
    string title[NUM_PRODS] =
        { "Six Steps to Leadership",
          "Six Steps to Leadership",
          "The Road to Excellence",
          "Seven Lessons of Quality",
          "Seven Lessons of Quality",
          "Seven Lessons of Quality",
          "Teams Are Made, Not Born",
          "Leadership for the Future",
          "Leadership for the Future"
        };

    // Array of product descriptions
    string description[NUM_PRODS] =
        { "Book", "Audio CD", "DVD",
          "Book", "Audio CD", "DVD",
          "Book", "Book", "Audio CD"
        };

    // Array of product prices
    double prices[NUM_PRODS] = {12.95, 14.95, 18.95, 16.95, 21.95,
                                31.95, 14.95, 14.95, 16.95};

    int prodNum; // To hold a product number
    int index;   // To hold search results
    char again;  // To hold a Y or N answer

    do
    {
        // Get the desired product number.
        prodNum = getProdNum();

        // Search for the product number.
        index = binarySearch(id, NUM_PRODS, prodNum);

        // Display the results of the search.
        if (index == -1)
```

(program continues)

Program 3 *(continued)*

```
            cout << "That product number was not found.\n";
        else
            displayProd(title, description, prices, index);

        // Does the user want to do this again?
        cout << "Would you like to look up another product? (y/n) ";
        cin >> again;
    } while (again == 'y' || again == 'Y');
    return 0;
}

//****************************************************
// Definition of getProdNum function                 *
// The getProdNum function asks the user to enter a *
// product number. The input is validated, and when *
// a valid number is entered, it is returned.        *
//****************************************************

int getProdNum()
{
    int prodNum; // Product number

    cout << "Enter the item's product number: ";
    cin >> prodNum;
    // Validate input
    while (prodNum < MIN_PRODNUM || prodNum > MAX_PRODNUM)
    {
        cout << "Enter a number in the range of " << MIN_PRODNUM;
        cout <<" through " << MAX_PRODNUM << ".\n";
        cin >> prodNum;
    }
    return prodNum;
}

//***************************************************************
// Definition of binarySearch function                          *
// The binarySearch function performs a binary search on an     *
// integer array. array, which has a maximum of numElems        *
// elements, is searched for the number stored in value. If the *
// number is found, its array subscript is returned. Otherwise, *
// -1 is returned indicating the value was not in the array.    *
//***************************************************************

int binarySearch(const int array[], int numElems, int value)
{
    int first = 0,              // First array element
        last = numElems - 1,    // Last array element
        middle,                 // Midpoint of search
        position = -1;          // Position of search value
    bool found = false;         // Flag
```

```

    while (!found && first <= last)
    {
        middle = (first + last) / 2; // Calculate midpoint
        if (array[middle] == value)  // If value is found at mid
        {
            found = true;
            position = middle;
        }
        else if (array[middle] > value) // If value is in lower half
            last = middle - 1;
        else
            first = middle + 1;         // If value is in upper half
    }
    return position;
}

//*****************************************************************
// The displayProd function accepts three arrays and an int.      *
// The arrays parameters are expected to hold the title,          *
// description, and prices arrays defined in main. The index      *
// parameter holds a subscript. This function displays the        *
// information in each array contained at the subscript.          *
//*****************************************************************

void displayProd(const string title[], const string desc[],
                 const double price[], int index)
{
    cout << "Title: " << title[index] << endl;
    cout << "Description: " << desc[index] << endl;
    cout << "Price: $" << price[index] << endl;
}
```

Program Output with Example Input Shown in Bold

```
Enter the item's product number: 916 [Enter]
Title: The Road to Excellence
Description: DVD
Price: $18.95
Would you like to look up another product? (y/n) y [Enter]
Enter the item's product number: 920 [Enter]
Title: Teams Are Made, Not Born
Description: Book
Price: $14.95
Would you like to look up another product? (y/n) n [Enter]
```

Checkpoint

1 Describe the difference between the linear search and the binary search.

-2 On average, with an array of 20,000 elements, how many comparisons will the linear search perform? (Assume the items being searched for are consistently found in the array.)

3 With an array of 20,000 elements, what is the maximum number of comparisons the binary search will perform?

4 If a linear search is performed on an array, and it is known that some items are searched for more frequently than others, how can the contents of the array be reordered to improve the average performance of the search?

3 Focus on Software Engineering: Introduction to Sorting Algorithms

CONCEPT: Sorting algorithms are used to arrange data into some order.

Sorting Algorithms

Many programming tasks require the data in an array be sorted in some order. Customer lists, for instance, are commonly sorted in alphabetical order. Student grades might be sorted from highest to lowest, and product codes could be sorted so that all the products of the same color are stored together. To sort the data in an array, the programmer must use an appropriate sorting algorithm. A *sorting algorithm* is a technique for stepping through an array and rearranging its contents in some order.

The data in an array can be sorted in either ascending or descending order. If an array is sorted in *ascending order,* it means the values in the array are stored from lowest to highest. If the values are sorted in *descending order*, they are stored from highest to lowest. This section will introduce two simple sorting algorithms: the *bubble sort* and the *selection sort.*

The Bubble Sort

The bubble sort is an easy way to arrange data in ascending or descending order. It is called the *bubble sort* algorithm because as it makes passes through and compares the elements of the array, certain values "bubble" toward the end of the array with each pass. For example, if you are using the algorithm to sort an array in ascending order, the larger values move toward the end. If you are using the algorithm to sort an array in descending order, the smaller values move toward the end. In this section, you will see how the bubble sort algorithm can be used to sort an array in ascending order.

Suppose we have the array shown in Figure 1. Let's see how the bubble sort can be used in arranging the array's elements in ascending order.

Figure 1 An array

7	2	3	8	9	1
Element 0	Element 1	Element 2	Element 3	Element 4	Element 5

The bubble sort starts by comparing the first two elements in the array. If element 0 is greater than element 1, they are swapped. The array would then appear as shown in Figure 2.

Figure 2 Elements 0 and 1 are swapped

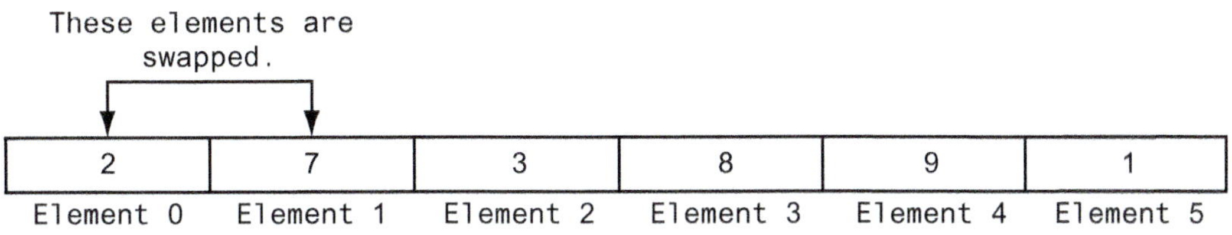

This method is repeated with elements 1 and 2. If element 1 is greater than element 2, they are swapped. The array would then appear as shown in Figure 3.

Figure 3 Elements 1 and 2 are swapped

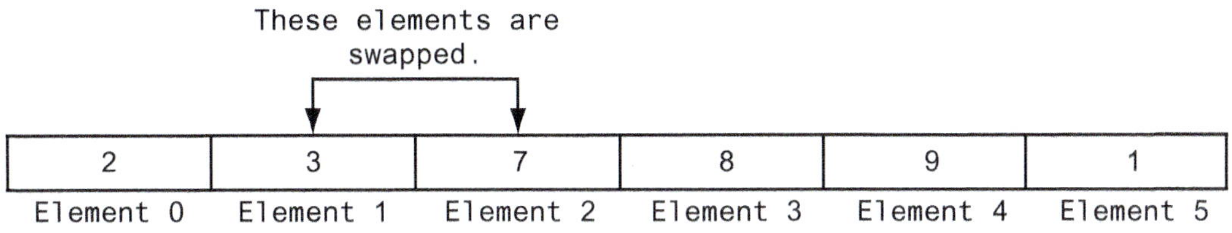

Next, elements 2 and 3 are compared. In this array, these elements are already in the proper order (element 2 is less than element 3), so no values are swapped. As the cycle continues, elements 3 and 4 are compared. Once again, it is not necessary to swap the values because they are already in the proper order.

When elements 4 and 5 are compared, however, they must be swapped because element 4 is greater than element 5. The array now appears as shown in Figure 4.

Figure 4 Elements 4 and 5 are swapped

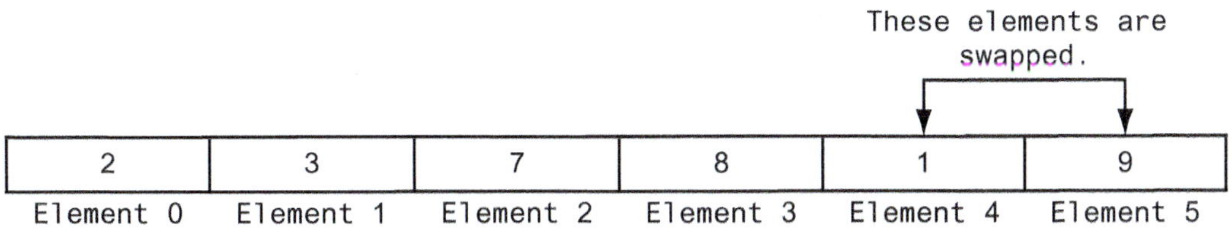

At this point, the entire array has been scanned once, and the largest value, 9, is in the correct position. There are other elements, however, that are not yet in their final positions. So, the algorithm will make another pass through the array, comparing each element with its neighbor. In the next pass, it will stop comparing after reaching the next-to-last element because the last element already contains the correct value.

The second pass starts by comparing elements 0 and 1. Because those two are in the proper order, they are not swapped. Elements 1 and 2 are compared next, but once again, they are not swapped. This continues until elements 3 and 4 are compared. Because element 3 is greater than element 4, they are swapped. Element 4 is the last element that is compared during this pass, so this pass stops. The array now appears as shown in Figure 5.

Figure 5 Elements 3 and 4 are swapped

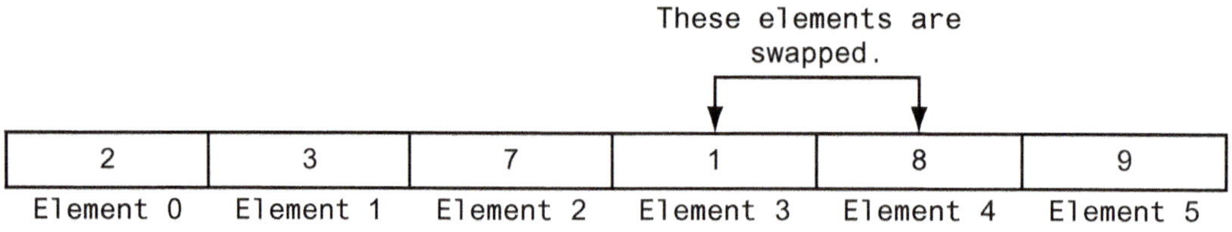

At the end of the second pass, the last two elements in the array contain the correct values. The third pass starts now, comparing each element with its neighbor. The third pass will not involve the last two elements, however, because they have already been sorted. When the third pass is finished, the last three elements will hold the correct values, as shown in Figure 6.

Figure 6 The array after the third pass

2	3	1	7	8	9
Element 0	Element 1	Element 2	Element 3	Element 4	Element 5

Each time the algorithm makes a pass through the array, the portion of the array that is scanned is decreased in size by one element, and the largest value in the scanned portion of the array is moved to its final position. When all of the passes have been made, the array will appear as shown in Figure 7.

Figure 7 The array with all elements sorted

1	2	3	7	8	9
Element 0	Element 1	Element 2	Element 3	Element 4	Element 5

Here is the bubble sort algorithm in pseudocode:

```
For maxElement = each subscript in the array, from the last to the first
    For index = 0 To maxElement - 1
        If array[index] > array[index + 1]
            swap array[index] with array[index + 1]
        End If
    End For
End For
```

And here is the C++ code for the bubble sort algorithm written as a function that sorts an array of integers. The function accepts two arguments: the array to sort, and the size of the array.

```
void bubbleSort(int array[], int size)
{
    int maxElement;
    int index;

    for (maxElement = size - 1; maxElement > 0; maxElement--)
    {
        for (index = 0; index < maxElement; index++)
```

```
9          {
10            if (array[index] > array[index + 1])
11            {
12               swap(array[index], array[index + 1]);
13            }
14         }
15      }
16   }
```

In lines 3 and 4, the following local variables are defined:

- The `maxElement` variable will hold the subscript of the last element that is to be compared to its immediate neighbor.
- The `index` variable is used as an array subscript in one of the loops.

The function uses two `for` loops, one nested inside another. The outer loop begins in line 6 as follows:

```
for (maxElement = size - 1; maxElement > 0; maxElement--)
```

This loop will iterate once for each element in the array. It causes the `maxElement` variable to take on all of the array's subscripts, from the highest subscript down to 0. After each iteration, `maxElement` is decremented by one.

The second loop, which is nested inside the first loop, begins in line 8 as follows:

```
for (index = 0; index < maxElement; index++)
```

This loop iterates once for each of the unsorted array elements. It starts `index` at 0 and increments it up through `maxElement` – 1. During each iteration, the comparison in line 10 is performed:

```
if (array[index] > array[index + 1])
```

This `if` statement compares the element at `array [index]` with its neighbor `array [index + 1]`. If the element's neighbor is greater, the `swap` function is called in line 12 to swap the two elements.

Swapping Array Elements

As you saw in the description of the bubble sort algorithm, certain elements are swapped as the algorithm steps through the array. Let's briefly discuss the process of swapping two items in computer memory. Assume we have the following variable declarations:

```
int a = 1;
int b = 9;
```

Suppose we want to swap the values in these variables so the variable `a` contains 9, and the variable `b` contains 1. At first, you might think that we only need to assign the variables to each other, like this:

```
// ERROR! The following does NOT swap the variables.
a = b;
b = a;
```

To understand why this doesn't work, let's step through the two lines of code. The first statement

```
a = b;
```

causes the value 9 to be assigned to a. But what happens to the value 1 that was previously stored in a? Remember, when you assign a new value to a variable, the new value replaces any value that was previously stored in the variable. So, the old value, 1, will be thrown away.

Then, the next statement is

```
b = a;
```

Because the variable a contains 9, this assigns 9 to b. After these statements execute, the variables a and b will both contain the value 9.

To successfully swap the contents of two variables, we need a third variable that can serve as a temporary storage location:

```
int temp;
```

Then, we can perform the following steps to swap the values in the variables a and b:

- Assign the value of a to temp.
- Assign the value of b to a.
- Assign the value of temp to b.

Here is the code for a swap function that swaps two int arguments:

```
void swap(int &a, int &b)
{
    int temp = a;
    a = b;
    b = temp;
}
```

NOTE: It is critical that we use reference parameters in the swap function, because the function must be able to change the values of the items that are passed to it as arguments.

Program 4 demonstrates the bubbleSort function in a complete program.

Program 4

```
// This program demonstrates the Bubble Sort algorithm.
#include <iostream>
using namespace std;

// Function prototypes
void bubbleSort(int[], int);
void swap(int &, int &);

int main()
{
    const int SIZE = 6;

    // Array of unsorted values
    int values[SIZE] = { 6, 1, 5, 2, 4, 3 };

```

```
   // Display the unsorted array.
   cout << "The unsorted values:\n";
   for (auto element : values)
     cout << element << " ";
   cout << endl;

   // Sort the array.
   bubbleSort(values, SIZE);

   // Display the sorted array.
   cout << "The sorted values:\n";
   for (auto element : values)
      cout << element << " ";
   cout << endl;

   return 0;
}

//***********************************************************************
// The bubbleSort function sorts an int array in ascending order. *
//***********************************************************************
void bubbleSort(int array[], int size)
{
   int maxElement;
   int index;

   for (maxElement = size - 1; maxElement > 0; maxElement--)
   {
      for (index = 0; index < maxElement; index++)
      {
         if (array[index] > array[index + 1])
         {
            swap(array[index], array[index + 1]);
         }
      }
   }
}

//*****************************************************
// The swap function swaps a and b in memory.        *
//*****************************************************
void swap(int &a, int &b)
{
   int temp = a;
   a = b;
   b = temp;
}
```

Program Output

```
The unsorted values:
6 1 5 2 4 3
The sorted values:
1 2 3 4 5 6
```

VideoNote
The Selection Sort

The Selection Sort Algorithm

The bubble sort algorithm is simple, but it is inefficient because values move by only one element at a time toward their final destination in the array. The *selection sort algorithm* usually performs fewer swaps because it moves items immediately to their final position in the array. The selection sort works like this: The smallest value in the array is located and moved to element 0. Then, the next smallest value is located and moved to element 1. This process continues until all of the elements have been placed in their proper order. Let's see how the selection sort works when arranging the elements of the array in Figure 8.

Figure 8 Values in an array

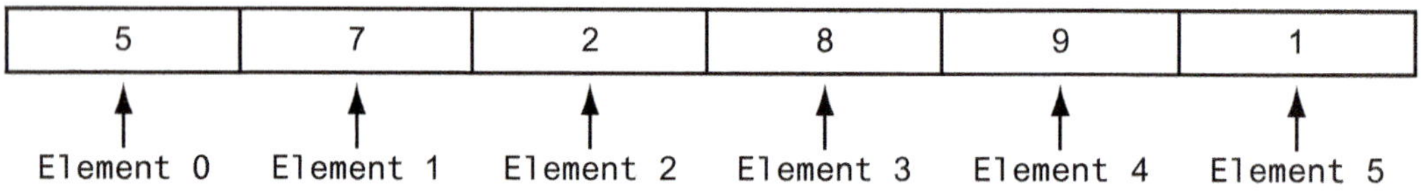

The selection sort scans the array, starting at element 0, and locates the element with the smallest value. Then, the contents of this element are swapped with the contents of element 0. In this example, the 1 stored in element 5 is swapped with the 5 stored in element 0. After the swap, the array appears as shown in Figure 9.

Figure 9 Values in the array after the first swap

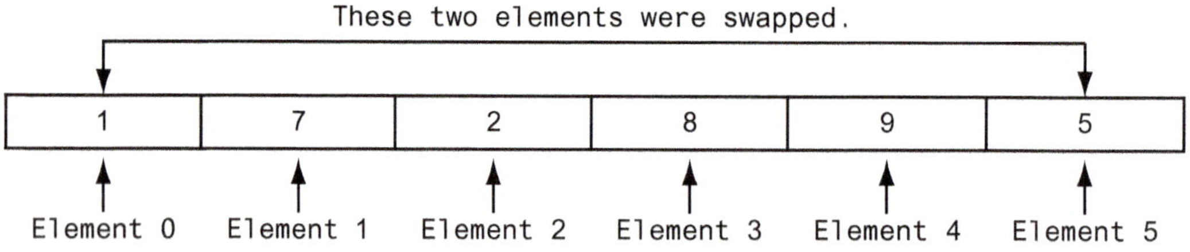

Then, the algorithm repeats the process, but because element 0 already contains the smallest value in the array, it can be left out of the procedure. This time, the algorithm begins the scan at element 1. In this example, the value in element 2 is swapped with the value in element 1. Then, the array appears as shown in Figure 10.

Figure 10 Values in the array after the second swap

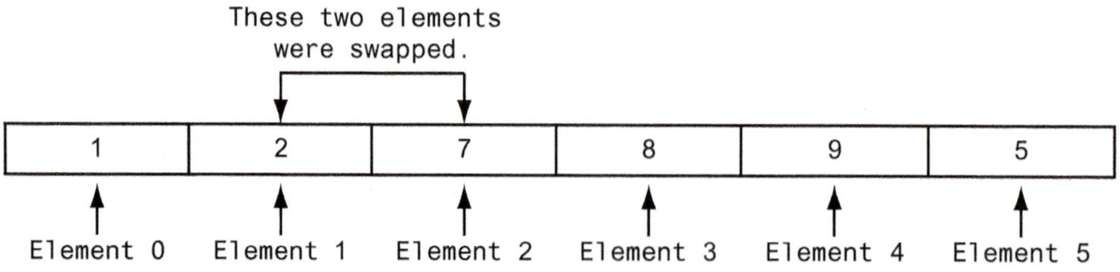

Once again the process is repeated, but this time the scan begins at element 2. The algorithm will find that element 5 contains the next smallest value. This element's value is swapped with that of element 2, causing the array to appear as shown in Figure 11.

Figure 11 Values in the array after the third swap

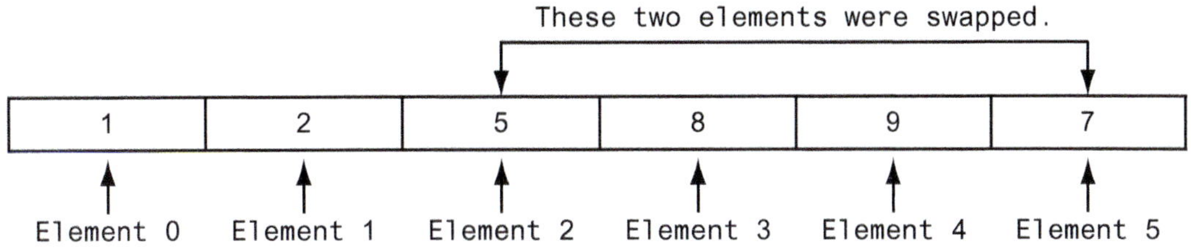

Next, the scanning begins at element 3. Its value is swapped with that of element 5, causing the array to appear as shown in Figure 12.

Figure 12 Values in the array after the fourth swap

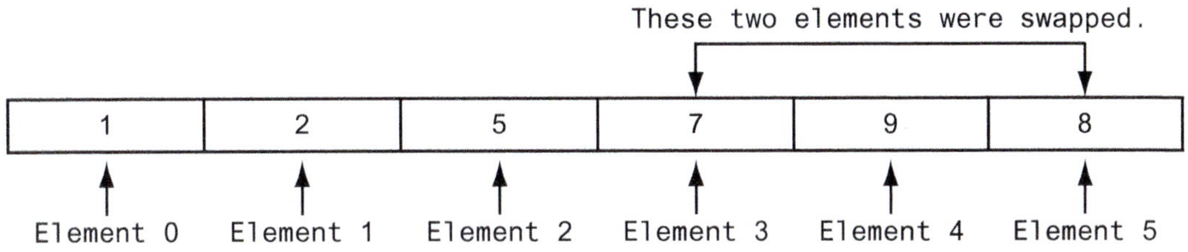

At this point, there are only two elements left to sort. The algorithm finds that the value in element 5 is smaller than that of element 4, so the two are swapped. This puts the array in its final arrangement, as shown in Figure 13.

Figure 13 Values in the array after the fifth swap

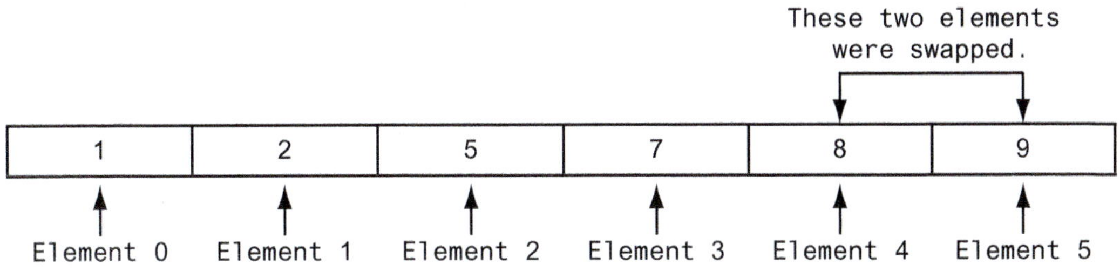

Here is the selection sort algorithm in pseudocode:

```
For start = each array subscript, from the first to the next-to-last
    minIndex = start
    minValue = array[start]
    For index = start + 1 To size - 1
        If array[index] < minValue
            minValue = array[index]
```

```
            minIndex = index
         End If
      End For
      swap array[minIndex] with array[start]
   End For
```

The following C++ code implements the selection sort in a function. It accepts two arguments: an integer array, and the size of the array. The function uses the selection sort algorithm to arrange the values in the array in ascending order.

```
1  void selectionSort(int array[], int size)
2  {
3     int minIndex, minValue;
4
5     for (int start = 0; start < (size - 1); start++)
6     {
7        minIndex = start;
8        minValue = array[start];
9        for (int index = start + 1; index < size; index++)
10       {
11          if (array[index] < minValue)
12          {
13             minValue = array[index];
14             minIndex = index;
15          }
16       }
17       swap(array[minIndex], array[start]);
18    }
19 }
```

Inside the function are two `for` loops, one nested inside the other. The inner loop (in lines 9 through 16) sequences through the array, starting at `array[start + 1]`, searching for the element with the smallest value. When the element is found, its subscript is stored in the variable `minIndex`, and its value is stored in `minValue`. The outer loop (lines 5 through 18) then exchanges the contents of this element with `array[start]` and increments `start`. This procedure repeats until the contents of every element have been moved to their proper location.

Program 5 demonstrates the `selectionSort` function in a complete program.

Program 5

```
// This program demonstrates the Selection Sort algorithm.
#include <iostream>
using namespace std;

// Function prototypes
void selectionSort(int[], int);
void swap(int &, int &);

```

```
int main()
{
   const int SIZE = 6;

   // Array of unsorted values
   int values[SIZE] = { 6, 1, 5, 2, 4, 3 };

   // Display the unsorted array.
   cout << "The unsorted values:\n";
   for (auto element : values)
      cout << element << " ";
   cout << endl;

   // Sort the array.
   selectionSort(values, SIZE);

   // Display the sorted array.
   cout << "The sorted values:\n";
   for (auto element : values)
      cout << element << " ";
   cout << endl;

   return 0;
}

//**********************************************************************
// The selectionSort function sorts an int array in ascending order. *
//**********************************************************************
void selectionSort(int array[], int size)
{
   int minIndex, minValue;

   for (int start = 0; start < (size - 1); start++)
   {
      minIndex = start;
      minValue = array[start];
      for (int index = start + 1; index < size; index++)
      {
         if (array[index] < minValue)
         {
            minValue = array[index];
            minIndex = index;
         }
      }
      swap(array[minIndex], array[start]);
   }
}

//*****************************************************
// The swap function swaps a and b in memory.        *
//*****************************************************
void swap(int &a, int &b)
{
```

(program continues)

Program 5 *(continued)*

```
    int temp = a;
    a = b;
    b = temp;
}
```

Program Output

```
The unsorted values:
6 1 5 2 4 3
The sorted values:
1 2 3 4 5 6
```

4 Focus on Problem Solving and Program Design: A Case Study

Like the previous case study, this is a program developed for the Demetris Leadership Center. Recall that DLC, Inc., publishes books, DVDs, and audio CDs. (See Table 1 for a complete list of products, with title, description, product number, and price.) Table 4 shows the number of units of each product sold during the past six months.

Table 4 Units Sold

Product Number	Units Sold
914	842
915	416
916	127
917	514
918	437
919	269
920	97
921	492
922	212

The vice president of sales has asked you to write a sales-reporting program that displays the following information:

- A list of the products in the order of their sales dollars (NOT units sold), from highest to lowest
- The total number of all units sold
- The total sales for the 6-month period

Variables

Table 5 lists the variables needed.

Table 5 Variables

Variable	Description
NUM_PRODS	A constant integer initialized with the number of products that DLC, Inc., sells. This value will be used in the definition of the program's array.
prodNum	Array of ints. Holds each product's number.
units	Array of ints. Holds each product's number of units sold.
prices	Array of doubles. Holds each product's price.
sales	Array of doubles. Holds the computed sales amounts (in dollars) of each product.

The elements of the four arrays, prodNum, units, prices, and sales, will correspond with each other. For example, the product whose number is stored in prodNum[2] will have sold the number of units stored in units[2]. The sales amount for the product will be stored in sales[2].

Modules

The program will consist of the functions listed in Table 6.

Table 6 Functions

Function	Description
main	The program's main function. It calls the program's other functions.
calcSales	Calculates each product's sales.
dualSort	Sorts the sales array so the elements are ordered from highest to lowest. The prodNum array is ordered so the product numbers correspond with the correct sales figures in the sorted sales array.
swap	Swaps the values of two doubles that are passed by reference (overloaded).
swap	Swaps the values of two ints that are passed by reference (overloaded).
showOrder	Displays a list of the product numbers and sales amounts from the sorted sales and prodNum arrays.
showTotals	Displays the total number of units sold and the total sales amount for the period.

Function main

Function main is very simple. It contains the variable definitions and calls the other functions. Here is the pseudocode for its executable statements:

```
Call calcSales
Call dualSort
Set display mode to fixed point with two decimal places of precision
Call showOrder
Call showTotals
```

Here is its actual C++ code:

```
// Calculate each product's sales.
calcSales(units, prices, sales, NUM_PRODS);
```

```
// Sort the elements in the sales array in descending
// order and shuffle the ID numbers in the id array to
// keep them in parallel.
dualSort(id, sales, NUM_PRODS);

// Set the numeric output formatting.
cout << setprecision(2) << fixed << showpoint;

// Display the products and sales amounts.
showOrder(sales, id, NUM_PRODS);

// Display total units sold and total sales.
showTotals(sales, units, NUM_PRODS);
```

The named constant `NUM_PRODS` will be defined globally and initialized to the value 9.

The arrays `id`, `units`, and `prices` will already be initialized with data. (It will be left as an exercise for you to modify this program so the user may enter these values.)

The `calcSales` Function

The `calcSales` function multiplies each product's units sold by its price. The resulting amount is stored in the `sales` array. Here is the function's pseudocode:

```
For index = each array subscript from 0 through the last subscript
   sales[index] = units[index] * prices[index]
End For
```

And here is the function's actual C++ code:

```
void calcSales(const int units[], const double prices[],
               double sales[], int num)
{
   for (int index = 0; index < num; index++)
     sales[index] = units[index] * prices[index];
}
```

The `dualSort` Function

The `dualSort` function is a modified version of the selection sort algorithm shown in Program 5. The `dualSort` function accepts two arrays as arguments: the `sales` array and the `id` array. The function actually performs the selection sort on the `sales` array. When the function moves an element in the `sales` array, however, it also moves the corresponding element in the `id` array. This is to ensure that the product numbers in the `id` array still have subscripts that match their sales figures in the `sales` array.

The `dualSort` function is also different in another way: It sorts the array in descending order. Here is the pseudocode for the `dualSort` function:

```
For start = each array subscript, from the first to the next-to-last
   index = start
   maxIndex = start
   tempId = id[start]
   maxValue = sales[start]
   For index = start + 1 To size - 1
```

```
        If sales[index] > maxValue
            maxValue = sales[index]
            tempId = id[index]
            maxIndex = index
        End If
    End For
    swap sales[maxIndex] with sales[start]
    swap id[maxIndex] with id[start]
End For
```

Here is the actual C++ code for the `dualSort` function:

```
void dualSort(int id[], double sales[], int size)
{
    int start, maxIndex, tempid;
    double maxValue;

    for (start = 0; start < (size - 1); start++)
    {
        maxIndex = start;
        maxValue = sales[start];
        tempid = id[start];
        for (int index = start + 1; index < size; index++)
        {
            if (sales[index] > maxValue)
            {
                maxValue = sales[index];
                tempid = id[index];
                maxIndex = index;
            }
        }
        swap(sales[maxIndex], sales[start]);
        swap(id[maxIndex], id[start]);
    }
}
```

NOTE: Once the `dualSort` function is called, the `id` and `sales` arrays are no longer synchronized with the `units` and `prices` arrays. Because this program doesn't use `units` and `prices` together with `id` and `sales` after this point, it will not be noticed in the final output. However, it is never a good programming practice to sort parallel arrays in such a way that they are out of synchronization. It will be left as an exercise for you to modify the program so all the arrays are synchronized and used in the final output of the program.

The Overloaded swap Functions

We have two overloaded versions of the `swap` function in this program: one that swaps `double` values, and another that swaps `int` values. We need two different versions of the `swap` function because the `dualSort` function swaps two elements of the `sales` array, which are `doubles`, then it swaps two elements of the `id` array, which are `ints`. Here is the C++ code for both functions:

```
//**************************************************************
// The swap function swaps doubles a and b in memory. *
//**************************************************************
void swap(double &a, double &b)
{
   double temp = a;
   a = b;
   b = temp;
}

//**************************************************************
// The swap function swaps ints a and b in memory.     *
//**************************************************************
void swap(int &a, int &b)
{
   int temp = a;
   a = b;
   b = temp;
}
```

The showOrder Function

The showOrder function displays a heading and the sorted list of product numbers and their sales amounts. It accepts the id and sales arrays as arguments. Here is its pseudocode:

```
Display heading
For index = each subscript of the arrays from 0 through the last subscript
   Display id[index]
   Display sales[index]
End For
```

Here is the function's actual C++ code:

```
void showOrder(const double sales[], const int id[], int num)
{
   cout << "Product Number\tSales\n";

   cout << "----------------------------------\n";
   for (int index = 0; index < num; index++)
   {
      cout << id[index] << "\t\t$";
      cout << setw(8) << sales[index] << endl;
   }
   cout << endl;
}
```

The showTotals Function

The showTotals function displays the total number of units of all products sold and the total sales for the period. It accepts the units and sales arrays as arguments. Here is its pseudocode:

```
totalUnits = 0
totalSales = 0.0
```

```
For index = each array subscript from 0 through the last subscript
   Add units[index] to totalUnits[index]
   Add sales[index] to totalSales
End For
Display totalUnits with appropriate heading
Display totalSales with appropriate heading
```

Here is the function's actual C++ code:

```
void showTotals(const double sales[], const int units[], int num)
{
   int totalUnits = 0;
   double totalSales = 0.0;
   for (int index = 0; index < num; index++)
   {
      totalUnits += units[index];
      totalSales += sales[index];
   }
   cout << "Total Units Sold: " << totalUnits << endl;
   cout << "Total Sales:      $" << totalSales << endl;
}
```

The Entire Program

Program 6 shows the entire program's source code.

Program 6

```
// This program produces a sales report for DLC, Inc.
#include <iostream>
#include <iomanip>
using namespace std;

// Function prototypes
void calcSales(const int[], const double[], double[], int);
void showOrder(const double[], const int[], int);
void dualSort(int[], double[], int);
void showTotals(const double[], const int[], int);
void swap(double&, double&);
void swap(int&, int&);

int main()
{
   // NUM_PRODS is the number of products produced.
   const int NUM_PRODS = 9;

   // Array with product ID numbers
   int id[NUM_PRODS] = { 914, 915, 916, 917, 918,
                         919, 920, 921, 922 };

   // Array with number of units sold for each product
   int units[NUM_PRODS] = { 842, 416, 127, 514, 437,
                            269, 97,  492, 212 };
```

(program continues)

Program 6 *(continued)*

```

    // Array with product prices
    double prices[NUM_PRODS] = { 12.95, 14.95, 18.95, 16.95, 21.95,
                                 31.95, 14.95, 14.95, 16.95 };

    // Array to hold the computed sales amounts
    double sales[NUM_PRODS];

    // Calculate each product's sales.
    calcSales(units, prices, sales, NUM_PRODS);

    // Sort the elements in the sales array in descending
    // order and shuffle the ID numbers in the id array to
    // keep them in parallel.
    dualSort(id, sales, NUM_PRODS);

    // Set the numeric output formatting.
    cout << setprecision(2) << fixed << showpoint;

    // Display the products and sales amounts.
    showOrder(sales, id, NUM_PRODS);

    // Display total units sold and total sales.
    showTotals(sales, units, NUM_PRODS);
    return 0;
}

//****************************************************************
// Definition of calcSales. Accepts units, prices, and sales    *
// arrays as arguments. The size of these arrays is passed      *
// into the num parameter. This function calculates each        *
// product's sales by multiplying its units sold by each unit's *
// price. The result is stored in the sales array.              *
//****************************************************************

void calcSales(const int units[], const double prices[], double sales[], int num)
{
    for (int index = 0; index < num; index++)
        sales[index] = units[index] * prices[index];
}

//****************************************************************
// Definition of function dualSort. Accepts id and sales arrays *
// as arguments. The size of these arrays is passed into size.  *
// This function performs a descending order selection sort on  *
// the sales array. The elements of the id array are exchanged  *
// identically as those of the sales array. size is the number  *
// of elements in each array.                                   *
//****************************************************************

```

```
void dualSort(int id[], double sales[], int size)
{
   int start, maxIndex, tempid;
   double maxValue;

   for (start = 0; start < (size - 1); start++)
   {
      maxIndex = start;
      maxValue = sales[start];
      tempid = id[start];
      for (int index = start + 1; index < size; index++)
      {
         if (sales[index] > maxValue)
         {
            maxValue = sales[index];
            tempid = id[index];
            maxIndex = index;
         }
      }
      swap(sales[maxIndex], sales[start]);
      swap(id[maxIndex], id[start]);
   }
}

//*****************************************************
// The swap function swaps doubles a and b in memory. *
//*****************************************************
void swap(double &a, double &b)
{
   double temp = a;
   a = b;
   b = temp;
}

//*****************************************************
// The swap function swaps ints a and b in memory.    *
//*****************************************************
void swap(int &a, int &b)
{
   int temp = a;
   a = b;
   b = temp;
}

//****************************************************************
// Definition of showOrder function. Accepts sales and id arrays *
// as arguments. The size of these arrays is passed into num.    *
// The function first displays a heading, then the sorted list   *
// of product numbers and sales.                                 *
//****************************************************************
```

(program continues)

Program 6 *(continued)*

```
void showOrder(const double sales[], const int id[], int num)
{
   cout << "Product Number\tSales\n";
   cout << "----------------------------------\n";
   for (int index = 0; index < num; index++)
   {
      cout << id[index] << "\t\t$";
      cout << setw(8) << sales[index] << endl;
   }
   cout << endl;
}

//****************************************************************
// Definition of showTotals function. Accepts sales and id arrays *
// as arguments. The size of these arrays is passed into num.     *
// The function first calculates the total units (of all          *
// products) sold and the total sales. It then displays these     *
// amounts.                                                       *
//****************************************************************

void showTotals(const double sales[], const int units[], int num)
{
   int totalUnits = 0;
   double totalSales = 0.0;

   for (int index = 0; index < num; index++)
   {
      totalUnits += units[index];
      totalSales += sales[index];
   }
   cout << "Total units Sold:  " << totalUnits << endl;
   cout << "Total sales:      $" << totalSales << endl;
}
```

Program Output

```
Product Number          Sales
----------------------------------
914                  $10903.90
918                  $ 9592.15
917                  $ 8712.30
919                  $ 8594.55
921                  $ 7355.40
915                  $ 6219.20
922                  $ 3593.40
916                  $ 2406.65
920                  $ 1450.15

Total Units Sold:      3406
Total Sales:         $58827.70
```

5 Sorting and Searching vectors (Continued from Section 11 of the chapter "Arrays and Vectors")

CONCEPT: **The sorting and searching algorithms you have studied in this chapter may be applied to STL `vectors` as well as arrays.**

Once you have properly defined an STL `vector` and populated it with values, you may sort and search the `vector` with the algorithms presented in this chapter. Simply substitute the `vector` syntax for the array syntax when necessary. Program 7 demonstrates how to use the selection sort and binary search algorithms with a `vector` of strings.

Program 7

```
// This program demonstrates how to sort and search a
// string vector using selection sort and binary search.
#include <iostream>
#include <string>
#include <vector>
using namespace std;

// Function prototypes
void selectionSort(vector<string>&);
void swap(string &, string &);
int binarySearch(const vector<string>&, string);

int main()
{
   string searchValue;  // Value to search for
   int position;        // Position of found value

   // Define a vector of strings.
   vector<string> names{ "Lopez", "Smith", "Pike", "Jones",
                         "Abernathy", "Hall", "Wilson", "Kimura",
                         "Alvarado", "Harrison", "Geddes", "Irvine" };

   // Sort the vector.
   selectionSort(names);

   // Display the vector's elements.
   cout << "Here are the sorted names:\n";
   for (auto element : names)
      cout << element << endl;
   cout << endl;

   // Search for a name.
   cout << "Enter a name to search for: ";
   getline(cin, searchValue);
   position = binarySearch(names, searchValue);
```

(program continues)

Program 7 *(continued)*

```

    // Display the results.
    if (position != -1)
       cout << "That name is found at position " << position << endl;
    else
       cout << "That name is not found.\n";

    return 0;
}

//***********************************************************************
// The selectionSort function sorts a string vector in ascending order.*
//***********************************************************************
void selectionSort(vector<string> &v)
{
    int minIndex;
    string minValue;

    for (int start = 0; start < (v.size() - 1); start++)
    {
       minIndex = start;
       minValue = v[start];
       for (int index = start + 1; index < v.size(); index++)
       {
          if (v[index] < minValue)
          {
             minValue = v[index];
             minIndex = index;
          }
       }
       swap(v[minIndex], v[start]);
    }
}

//****************************************************
// The swap function swaps a and b in memory.        *
//****************************************************
void swap(string &a, string &b)
{
    string temp = a;
    a = b;
    b = temp;
}

//******************************************************************
// The binarySearch function performs a binary search on a        *
// string vector. array, which has a maximum of size elements,    *
// is searched for the number stored in value. If the number is   *
// found, its vector subscript is returned. Otherwise, -1 is      *
// returned indicating the value was not in the vector.           *
//******************************************************************
```

```

int binarySearch(const vector<string> &v, string str)
{
    int first = 0,                // First vector element
        last = v.size() - 1,      // Last vector element
        middle,                   // Mid point of search
        position = -1;            // Position of search value
    bool found = false;           // Flag

    while (!found && first <= last)
    {
       middle = (first + last) / 2; // Calculate mid point
       if (v[middle] == str)         // If value is found at mid
       {
          found = true;
          position = middle;
       }
       else if (v[middle] > str)     // If value is in lower half
          last = middle - 1;
       else
          first = middle + 1;        // If value is in upper half
    }
    return position;
}
```

Program Output with Example Input Shown in Bold

Here are the sorted names:

Abernathy
Alvarado
Geddes
Hall
Harrison
Irvine
Jones
Kimura
Lopez
Pike
Smith
Wilson

Enter a name to search for: **Lopez** [Enter]
That name is found at position 8

Program Output with Example Input Shown in Bold

Here are the sorted names:
Abernathy
Alvarado
Geddes
Hall

(program output continues)

Program 7 *(continued)*

```
Harrison
Irvine
Jones
Kimura
Lopez
Pike
Smith
Wilson

Enter a name to search for: Carter [Enter]
That name is not found.
```

Review Questions and Exercises

Short Answer

1. Why is the linear search also called "sequential search"?
2. If a linear search function is searching for a value that is stored in the last element of a 10,000-element array, how many elements will the search code have to read to locate the value?
3. In an average case involving an array of N elements, how many times will a linear search function have to read the array to locate a specific value?
4. A binary search function is searching for a value that is stored in the middle element of an array. How many times will the function read an element in the array before finding the value?
5. What is the maximum number of comparisons that a binary search function will make when searching for a value in a 1,000-element array?
6. Why is the bubble sort inefficient for large arrays?
7. Why is the selection sort more efficient than the bubble sort on large arrays?

Fill-in-the-Blank

8. The ________ search algorithm steps sequentially through an array, comparing each item with the search value.
9. The ________ search algorithm repeatedly divides the portion of an array being searched in half.
10. The ________ search algorithm is adequate for small arrays but not large arrays.
11. The ________ search algorithm requires that the array's contents be sorted.
12. If an array is sorted in ________ order, the values are stored from lowest to highest.
13. If an array is sorted in ________ order, the values are stored from highest to lowest.

True or False

14. T F If data are sorted in ascending order, it means they are ordered from lowest value to highest value.
15. T F If data are sorted in descending order, it means they are ordered from lowest value to highest value.
16. T F The *average* number of comparisons performed by the linear search on an array of N elements is N/2 (assuming the search values are consistently found).
17. T F The *maximum* number of comparisons performed by the linear search on an array of N elements is N/2 (assuming the search values are consistently found).
18. Complete the following table calculating the average and maximum number of comparisons the linear search will perform, and the maximum number of comparisons the binary search will perform.

Array Size →	50 Elements	500 Elements	10,000 Elements	100,000 Elements	10,000,000 Elements
Linear Search (Average Comparisons)					
Linear Search (Maximum Comparisons)					
Binary Search (Maximum Comparisons)					

Programming Challenges

1. **Charge Account Validation**

   Write a program that lets the user enter a charge account number. The program should determine if the number is valid by checking for it in the following list:

```
5658845  4520125  7895122  8777541  8451277  1302850
8080152  4562555  5552012  5050552  7825877  1250255
1005231  6545231  3852085  7576651  7881200  4581002
```

   The list of numbers above should be initialized in a single-dimensional array. A simple linear search should be used to locate the number entered by the user. If the user enters a number that is in the array, the program should display a message saying the number is valid. If the user enters a number that is not in the array, the program should display a message indicating the number is invalid.

2. **Lottery Winners**

   A lottery ticket buyer purchases ten tickets a week, always playing the same ten 5-digit "lucky" combinations. Write a program that initializes an array or a `vector` with these numbers, then lets the player enter this week's winning 5-digit number. The program should perform a linear search through the list of the player's numbers and report whether or not one of the tickets is a winner this week. Here are the numbers:

```
13579   26791   26792   33445   55555
62483   77777   79422   85647   93121
```

3. **Lottery Winners Modification**

   Modify the program you wrote for Programming Challenge 2 (Lottery Winners) so it performs a binary search instead of a linear search.

VideoNote
Solving the Charge Account Validation Modification Problem

4. **Charge Account Validation Modification**

   Modify the program you wrote for Problem 1 (Charge Account Validation) so it performs a binary search to locate valid account numbers. Use the selection sort algorithm to sort the array before the binary search is performed.

5. **Rainfall Statistics Modification**

   Modify the Rainfall Statistics program you wrote for Programming Challenge 2 of the chapter "Arrays and Vectors" (Rainfall Statistics). The program should display a list of months, sorted in order of rainfall, from highest to lowest.

6. **String Selection Sort**

   Modify the `selectionSort` function presented in this chapter so it sorts an array of strings instead of an array of `int`s. Test the function with a driver program. Use Program 8 as a skeleton to complete.

Program 8

```
#include <iostream>
#include <string>
using namespace std;

int main()
{
    const int NUM_NAMES = 20;
    string names[NUM_NAMES] = {"Collins, Bill", "Smith, Bart", "Allen, Jim",
                               "Griffin, Jim", "Stamey, Marty", "Rose, Geri",
                               "Taylor, Terri", "Johnson, Jill",
                               "Allison, Jeff", "Looney, Joe", "Wolfe, Bill",
                               "James, Jean", "Weaver, Jim", "Pore, Bob",
                               "Rutherford, Greg", "Javens, Renee",
                               "Harrison, Rose", "Setzer, Cathy",
                               "Pike, Gordon", "Holland, Beth" };
    // Insert your code to complete this program

    return 0;
}
```

7. **Binary String Search**

   Modify the `binarySearch` function presented in this chapter so it searches an array of strings instead of an array of `int`s. Test the function with a driver program. Use

Program 8 as a skeleton to complete. (The array must be sorted before the binary search will work.)

8. **Search Benchmarks**

   Write a program that has an array of at least 20 integers. It should call a function that uses the linear search algorithm to locate one of the values. The function should keep a count of the number of comparisons it makes until it finds the value. The program then should call a function that uses the binary search algorithm to locate the same value. It should also keep count of the number of comparisons it makes. Display these values on the screen.

9. **Sorting Benchmarks**

   Write a program that uses two identical arrays of at least 20 integers. It should call a function that uses the bubble sort algorithm to sort one of the arrays in ascending order. The function should keep a count of the number of exchanges it makes. The program then should call a function that uses the selection sort algorithm to sort the other array. It should also keep count of the number of exchanges it makes. Display these values on the screen.

10. **Sorting Orders**

    Write a program that uses two identical arrays of just eight integers. It should display the contents of the first array, then call a function to sort the array using an ascending order bubble sort modified to print out the array contents after each pass of the sort. Next, the program should display the contents of the second array, then call a function to sort the array using an ascending order selection sort modified to print out the array contents after each pass of the sort.

11. **Using Files—String Selection Sort Modification**

    Modify the program you wrote for Programming Challenge 6 (String Selection Sort) so it reads in 20 strings from a file. The data can be found in the names.txt file.

12. **Sorted List of 1994 Gas Prices**

    In the student sample programs for this chapter, you will find a text file named 1994_Weekly_Gas_Averages.txt. The file contains the average gas price for each week in the year 1994. (There are 52 lines in the file. Line 1 contains the average price for week 1; line 2 contains the average price for week 2, and so forth.) Write a program that reads the gas prices from the file, and calculates the average gas price for each month. (To get the average price for a given month, calculate the average of the average weekly prices for that month.) Then, the program should create another file that lists the names of the months, along with each month's average gas price, sorted from lowest to highest.

Answers to Checkpoints

1 The linear search algorithm simply uses a loop to step through each element of an array, comparing each element's value with the value being searched for. The binary search algorithm, which requires the values in the array to be sorted in order, starts searching at the element in the middle of the array. If the middle element's value is greater than the value being searched for, the algorithm next tests

the element in the middle of the first half of the array. If the middle element's value is less than the value being searched for, the algorithm next tests the element in the middle of the last half of the array. Each time the array tests an array element and does not find the value being searched for, it eliminates half of the remaining portion of the array. This method continues until the value is found, or there are no more elements to test. The binary search is more efficient than the linear search.

2 10,000

3 15

4 The items frequently searched for can be stored near the beginning of the array.

Answers to Odd Numbered Review Questions

1. Because it uses a loop to sequentially step through an array, starting with the first element. It compares each element with the value being searched for, and stops when either the value is found or the end of the array is encountered.
3. N/2 times
5. Ten
7. The selection sort usually performs fewer exchanges because it moves items immediately to their final position in the array.
9. binary
11. binary
13. descending
15. False
17. False

Pointers

TOPICS

1 Getting the Address of a Variable

CONCEPT: The address operator (&) returns the memory address of a variable.

Every variable is allocated a section of memory large enough to hold a value of the variable's data type. On a PC, for instance, it's common for 1 byte to be allocated for `char`s, 2 bytes for `short`s, 4 bytes for `int`s, `long`s, and `float`s, and 8 bytes for `double`s.

Each byte of memory has a unique *address*. A variable's address is the address of the first byte allocated to that variable. Suppose the following variables are defined in a program:

```
char letter;
short number;
float amount;
```

Figure 1 illustrates how they might be arranged in memory and shows their addresses.

From Chapter 9 of *Starting Out with C++: From Control Structures through Objects*, Ninth Edition. Tony Gaddis.

Figure 1 Variables and their addresses

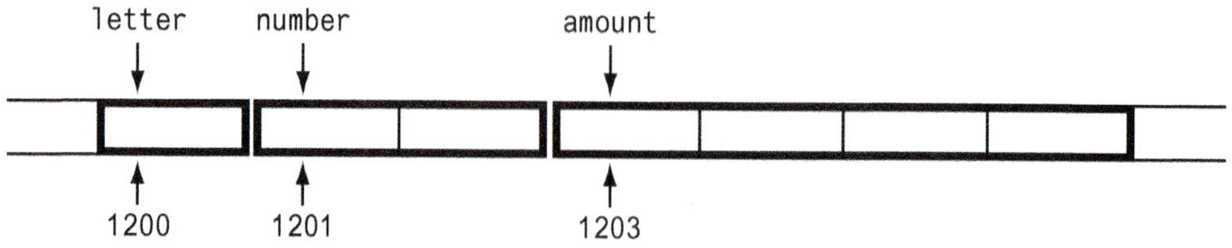

In Figure 1, the variable `letter` is shown at address 1200, `number` is at address 1201, and `amount` is at address 1203.

> **NOTE:** The addresses of the variables shown in Figure 1 are arbitrary values used only for illustration purposes.

Getting the address of a variable is accomplished with an operator in C++. When the address operator (`&`) is placed in front of a variable name, it returns the address of that variable. Here is an expression that returns the address of the variable `amount`:

```
&amount
```

And here is a statement that displays the variable's address on the screen:

```
cout << &amount;
```

> **NOTE:** Do not confuse the address operator with the `&` symbol used when defining a reference variable.

Program 1 demonstrates the use of the address operator to display the address, size, and contents of a variable.

Program 1

```
// This program uses the & operator to determine a variable's
// address and the sizeof operator to determine its size.
#include <iostream>
using namespace std;

int main()
{
    int x = 25;

    cout << "The address of x is " << &x << endl;
    cout << "The size of x is " << sizeof(x) << " bytes\n";
    cout << "The value in x is " << x << endl;
    return 0;
}
```

Program Output

```
The address of x is 0x8f05
The size of x is 4 bytes
The value in x is 25
```

NOTE: The address of the variable x is displayed in hexadecimal. This is the way addresses are normally shown in C++.

2 Pointer Variables

CONCEPT: ***Pointer variables*, which are often just called *pointers*, are designed to hold memory addresses. With pointer variables, you can indirectly manipulate data stored in other variables.**

A *pointer variable*, which often is just called a *pointer*, is a special variable that holds a memory address. Just as `int` variables are designed to hold integers, and `double` variables are designed to hold floating-point numbers, pointer variables are designed to hold memory addresses.

Memory addresses identify specific locations in the computer's memory. Because a pointer variable holds a memory address, it can be used to hold the location of some other piece of data. This should give you a clue as to why it is called a pointer: It "points" to some piece of data that is stored in the computer's memory. Pointer variables also allow you to work with the data that they point to.

When we pass an array as an argument to a function, we are actually passing the array's beginning address. For example, suppose we have an array named `numbers`, and we call the `showValues` function as shown here:

```
const int SIZE = 5;
int numbers[SIZE] = { 1, 2, 3, 4, 5 };
showValues(numbers, SIZE);
```

In this code, we are passing the name of the array, `numbers`, and its size as arguments to the `showValues` function. Here is the definition for the `showValues` function:

```
void showValues(int values[], int size)
{
    for (int count = 0; count < size; count++)
        cout << values[count] << endl;
}
```

In the function, the `values` parameter receives the address of the `numbers` array. It works like a pointer because it "points" to the `numbers` array, as shown in Figure 2.

Figure 2 Passing an array to a function

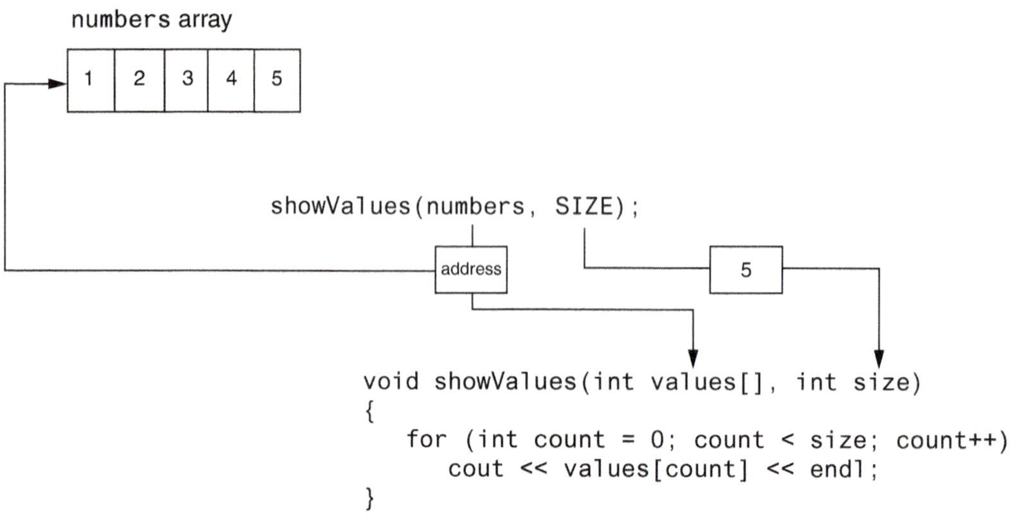

Inside the showValues function, anything done to the values parameter is actually done to the numbers array. We can say that the values parameter references the numbers array.

A reference variable acts as an alias for another variable. It is called a reference variable because it references another variable in the program. Anything you do to the reference variable is actually done to the variable it references. For example, suppose we have the variable jellyDonuts, and we pass the variable to the getOrder function, as shown here:

```
int jellyDonuts;
getOrder(jellyDonuts);
```

Here is the definition for the getOrder function:

```
void getOrder(int &donuts)
{
    cout << "How many doughnuts do you want? ";
    cin >> donuts;
}
```

In the function, the donuts parameter is a reference variable, and it receives the address of the jellyDonuts variable. It works like a pointer because it "points" to the jellyDonuts variable as shown in Figure 3.

Inside the getOrder function, the donuts parameter references the jellyDonuts variable. Anything done to the donuts parameter is actually done to the jellyDonuts variable. When the user enters a value, the cin statement uses the donuts reference variable to indirectly store the value in the jellyDonuts variable.

Notice the connection between the donuts reference variable and the jellyDonuts argument is automatically established by C++ when the function is called. When you are writing this code, you don't have to go through the trouble of finding the memory address of the jellyDonuts variable then properly storing that address in the donuts reference variable.

Figure 3 Passing an argument by reference

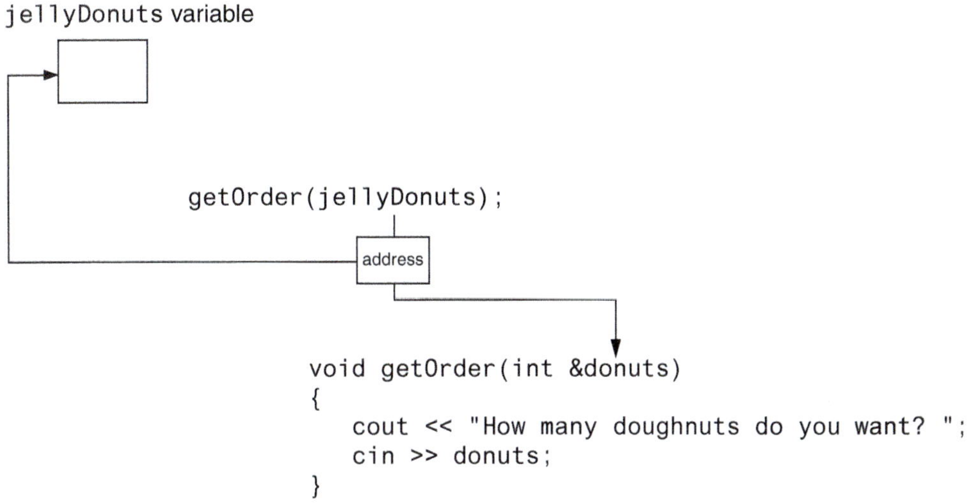

When you are storing a value in the donuts variable, you don't have to specify that the value should actually be stored in the jellyDonuts variable. C++ handles all of that automatically.

In C++, pointer variables are yet another mechanism for using memory addresses to work with pieces of data. Pointer variables are similar to reference variables, but pointer variables operate at a lower level. By this, I mean that C++ does not automatically do as much work for you with pointer variables as it does with reference variables. In order to make a pointer variable reference another item in memory, you have to write code that fetches the memory address of that item and assigns the address to the pointer variable. Also, when you use a pointer variable to store a value in the memory location that the pointer references, your code has to specify that the value should be stored in the location referenced by the pointer variable, and not in the pointer variable itself.

Because reference variables are easier to work with, you might be wondering why you would ever use pointers at all. In C++, pointers are useful, and even necessary, for many operations. One such operation is dynamic memory allocation. When you are writing a program that will need to work with an unknown amount of data, dynamic memory allocation allows you to create variables, arrays, and more complex data structures in memory while the program is running. We will discuss dynamic memory allocation in greater detail in this chapter. Pointers are also very useful in algorithms that manipulate arrays and work with certain types of strings. In object-oriented programming, pointers are very useful for creating and working with objects, and for sharing access to those objects.

Creating and Using Pointer Variables

The definition of a pointer variable looks pretty much like any other definition. Here is an example:

```
int *ptr;
```

The asterisk in front of the variable name indicates that `ptr` is a pointer variable. The `int` data type indicates that `ptr` can be used to hold the address of an integer variable. The definition statement above would read "`ptr` is a pointer to an `int`."

> **NOTE:** In this definition, the word `int` does not mean `ptr` is an integer variable. It means `ptr` can hold the address of an integer variable. Remember, pointers only hold one kind of value: an address.

Some programmers prefer to define pointers with the asterisk next to the type name, rather than the variable name. For example, the previous definition shown above could be written as:

```
int* ptr;
```

This style of definition might visually reinforce the fact that `ptr`'s data type is not `int`, but pointer-to-`int`. Both definition styles are correct.

It is never a good idea to define a pointer variable without initializing it with a valid memory address. If you inadvertently use an uninitialized pointer variable, you will be affecting some unknown location in memory. For that reason, it is a good idea to initialize pointer variables with the special value `nullptr`.

In C++ 11, the `nullptr` key word was introduced to represent the address 0. So, assigning `nullptr` to a pointer variable makes the variable point to the address 0. When a pointer is set to the address 0, it is referred to as a *null pointer* because it points to "nothing." Here is an example of how you define a pointer variable and initialize it with the value `nullptr`:

```
int *ptr = nullptr;
```

> **NOTE:** If you are using an older compiler that does not support the C++ 11 standard, you should initialize pointers with the integer 0, or the value `NULL`. The value `NULL` is defined in the `<iostream>` header file (as well as other header files) to represent the value 0.

Program 2 demonstrates a very simple usage of a pointer: storing and printing the address of another variable.

Program 2

```
// This program stores the address of a variable in a pointer.
#include <iostream>
using namespace std;

int main()
{
    int x = 25;          // int variable
    int *ptr = nullptr;  // Pointer variable, can point to an int

    ptr = &x;            // Store the address of x in ptr
    cout << "The value in x is " << x << endl;
    cout << "The address of x is " << ptr << endl;
    return 0;
}
```

Program Output

```
The value in x is 25
The address of x is 0x7e00
```

In Program 2, two variables are defined: `x` and `ptr`. The variable `x` is an `int`, and the variable `ptr` is a pointer to an `int`. The variable `x` is initialized with the value 25, and `ptr` is initialized with `nullptr`. Then, the variable `ptr` is assigned the address of `x` with the following statement in line 10:

```
ptr = &x;
```

Figure 4 illustrates the relationship between `ptr` and `x`.

Figure 4 `ptr` points to `x`

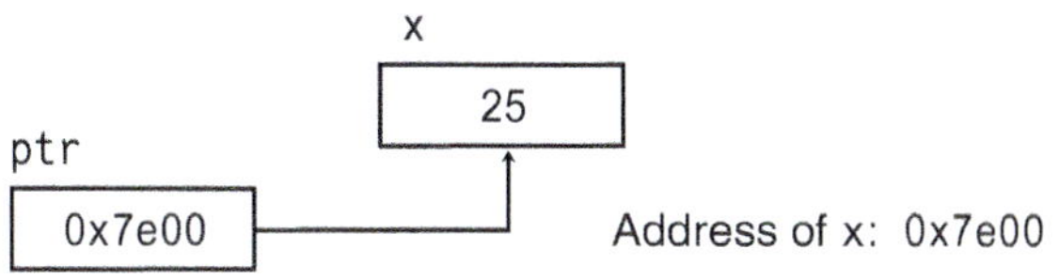

As shown in Figure 4, `x`, which is located at memory address 0x7e00, contains the number 25. The `ptr` pointer contains the address 0x7e00. In essence, it "points" to the variable `x`.

The real benefit of pointers is that they allow you to indirectly access and modify the variable being pointed to. In Program 2, for instance, `ptr` could be used to change the contents of the variable `x`. This is done with the *indirection operator*, which is an asterisk (*). When the indirection operator is placed in front of a pointer variable name, it *dereferences* the pointer. When you are working with a dereferenced pointer, you are actually working with the value the pointer is pointing to. This is demonstrated in Program 3.

Program 3

```
// This program demonstrates the use of the indirection operator.
#include <iostream>
using namespace std;

int main()
{
    int x = 25;            // int variable
    int *ptr = nullptr;    // Pointer variable, can point to an int

    ptr = &x;              // Store the address of x in ptr

    // Use both x and ptr to display the value in x.
    cout << "Here is the value in x, printed twice:\n";
    cout << x << endl;     // Displays the contents of x
    cout << *ptr << endl; // Displays the contents of x

    // Assign 100 to the location pointed to by ptr. This
    // will actually assign 100 to x.
    *ptr = 100;
```

(program continues)

Program 3 *(continued)*

```
20
21        // Use both x and ptr to display the value in x.
22        cout << "Once again, here is the value in x:\n";
23        cout << x << endl;     // Displays the contents of x
24        cout << *ptr << endl; // Displays the contents of x
25        return 0;
26  }
```

Program Output

```
Here is the value in x, printed twice:
25
25
Once again, here is the value in x:
100
100
```

Take a closer look at the statement in line 10:

```
ptr = &x;
```

This statement assigns the address of the `x` variable to the `ptr` variable. Now look at line 15:

```
cout << *ptr << endl; // Displays the contents of x
```

When you apply the indirection operator (`*`) to a pointer variable, you are working not with the pointer variable itself, but with the item it points to. Because this statement sends the expression `*ptr` to the `cout` object, it does not display the value in `ptr`, but the value that `ptr` points to. Since `ptr` points to the `x` variable, this statement displays the contents of the `x` variable.

Suppose the statement did not use the indirection operator. Suppose that statement had been written as:

```
cout << ptr << endl;  // Displays an address
```

Because the indirection operator is not applied to `ptr` in this statement, it works directly with the `ptr` variable. This statement would display the address that is stored in `ptr`.

Now take a look at the following statement, which appears in line 19:

```
*ptr = 100;
```

Notice the indirection operator being used with `ptr`. That means the statement is not affecting `ptr`, but the item that `ptr` points to. This statement assigns 100 to the item `ptr` points to, which is the `x` variable. After this statement executes, 100 will be stored in the `x` variable.

Program 4 demonstrates that pointers can point to different variables.

Program 4

```
// This program demonstrates a pointer variable referencing
// different variables.
#include <iostream>
using namespace std;
```

```
5
6  int main()
7  {
8      int x = 25, y = 50, z = 75;  // Three int variables
9      int *ptr = nullptr;          // Pointer variable
10
11     // Display the contents of x, y, and z.
12     cout << "Here are the values of x, y, and z:\n";
13     cout << x << " " << y << " " << z << endl;
14
15     // Use the pointer to manipulate x, y, and z.
16
17     ptr = &x;        // Store the address of x in ptr.
18     *ptr += 100;     // Add 100 to the value in x.
19
20     ptr = &y;        // Store the address of y in ptr.
21     *ptr += 100;     // Add 100 to the value in y.
22
23     ptr = &z;        // Store the address of z in ptr.
24     *ptr += 100;     // Add 100 to the value in z.
25
26     // Display the contents of x, y, and z.
27     cout << "Once again, here are the values of x, y, and z:\n";
28     cout << x << " " << y << " " << z << endl;
29     return 0;
30 }
```

Program Output

```
Here are the values of x, y, and z:
25  50  75
Once again, here are the values of x, y, and z:
125 150 175
```

Take a closer look at the statement in line 17:

```
ptr = &x;
```

This statement assigns the address of the x variable to the ptr variable. Now look at line 18:

```
*ptr += 100;
```

In this statement, notice the indirection operator (*) is used with the ptr variable. When we apply the indirection operator to ptr, we are working not with ptr, but with the item that ptr points to. When this statement executes, ptr is pointing at x, so the statement in line 18 adds 100 to the contents of x. Then the following statement, in line 20, executes:

```
ptr = &y;
```

This statement assigns the address of the y variable to the ptr variable. After this statement executes, ptr is no longer pointing at x. Rather, it will be pointing at y. The statement in line 21, shown here, adds 100 to the y variable:

```
*ptr += 100;
```

These steps are repeated with the z variable in lines 23 and 24.

NOTE: So far, you've seen three different uses of the asterisk in C++:

- As the multiplication operator, in statements such as

```
distance = speed * time;
```

- In the definition of a pointer variable, such as

```
int *ptr = nullptr;
```

- As the indirection operator, in statements such as

```
*ptr = 100;
```

3 The Relationship between Arrays and Pointers

CONCEPT: Array names can be used as constant pointers, and pointers can be used as array names.

An array name, without brackets and a subscript, actually represents the starting address of the array. This means that an array name is really a pointer. Program 5 illustrates this by showing an array name being used with the indirection operator.

Program 5

```
// This program shows an array name being dereferenced with the *
// operator.
#include <iostream>
using namespace std;

int main()
{
    short numbers[] = {10, 20, 30, 40, 50};

    cout << "The first element of the array is ";
    cout << *numbers << endl;
    return 0;
}
```

Program Output

```
The first element of the array is 10
```

Because `numbers` works like a pointer to the starting address of the array, the first element is retrieved when `numbers` is dereferenced. So how could the entire contents of an array be retrieved using the indirection operator? Remember, array elements are stored together in memory, as illustrated in Figure 5.

It makes sense that if `numbers` is the address of `numbers[0]`, values could be added to `numbers` to get the addresses of the other elements in the array. It's important to know, however, that pointers do not work like regular variables when used in mathematical statements. In C++, when you add a value to a pointer, you are actually adding that value *times*

Figure 5 Array elements are stored in contiguous memory locations

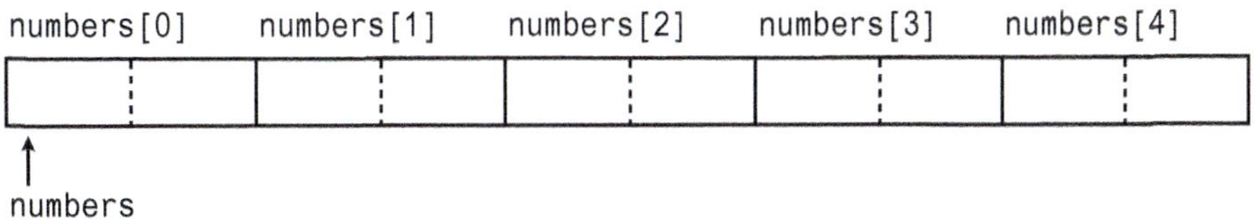

the size of the data type being referenced by the pointer. In other words, if you add one to `numbers`, you are actually adding `1 * sizeof(short)` to `numbers`. If you add 2 to `numbers`, the result is `numbers + 2 * sizeof(short)`, and so forth. On a typical system, this means the following are true, because `short` integers typically use 2 bytes:

```
*(numbers + 1) is actually *(numbers + 1 * 2)
*(numbers + 2) is actually *(numbers + 2 * 2)
*(numbers + 3) is actually *(numbers + 3 * 2)
```

and so forth.

This automatic conversion means an element in an array can be retrieved by using its subscript, or by adding its subscript to a pointer to the array. If the expression `*numbers`, which is the same as `*(numbers + 0)`, retrieves the first element in the array, then `*(numbers + 1)` retrieves the second element. Likewise, `*(numbers + 2)` retrieves the third element, and so forth. Figure 6 shows the equivalence of subscript notation and pointer notation.

Figure 6 Subscript notation and pointer notation

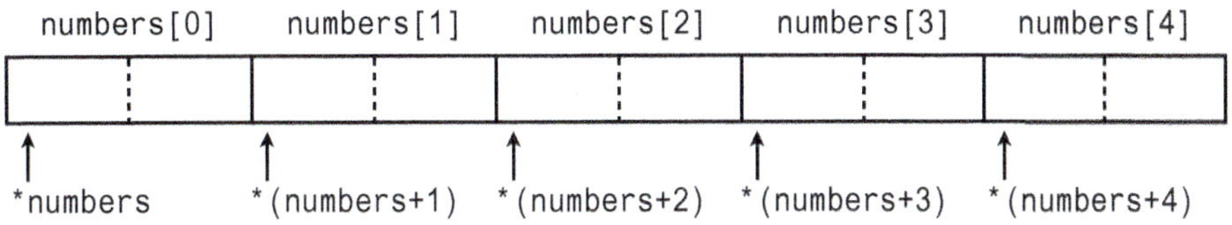

> **NOTE:** The parentheses are critical when adding values to pointers. The * operator has precedence over the + operator, so the expression `*number + 1` is not equivalent to `*(number + 1)`. `*number + 1` adds one to the contents of the first element of the array, while `*(number + 1)` adds one to the address in `number`, then dereferences it.

Program 6 shows the entire contents of the array being accessed, using pointer notation.

Program 6

```
// This program processes an array using pointer notation.
#include <iostream>
using namespace std;

```

(program continues)

Program 6 *(continued)*

```
int main()
{
    const int SIZE = 5; // Size of the array
    int numbers[SIZE];  // Array of integers
    int count;          // Counter variable

    // Get values to store in the array.
    // Use pointer notation instead of subscripts.
    cout << "Enter " << SIZE << " numbers: ";
    for (count = 0; count < SIZE; count++)
        cin >> *(numbers + count);

    // Display the values in the array.
    // Use pointer notation instead of subscripts.
    cout << "Here are the numbers you entered:\n";
    for (count = 0; count < SIZE; count++)
        cout << *(numbers + count)<< " ";
    cout << endl;
    return 0;
}
```

Program Output with Example Input Shown in Bold

Enter 5 numbers: **5 10 15 20 25** [Enter]
Here are the numbers you entered:
5 10 15 20 25

When working with arrays, remember the following rule:

`array[index]` is equivalent to `*(array + index)`

WARNING! Remember that C++ performs no bounds checking with arrays. When stepping through an array with a pointer, it's possible to give the pointer an address outside of the array.

To demonstrate just how close the relationship is between array names and pointers, look at Program 7. It defines an array of `double`s and a `double` pointer, which is assigned the starting address of the array. Not only is pointer notation then used with the array name, but subscript notation is also used with the pointer!

Program 7

```
// This program uses subscript notation with a pointer variable and
// pointer notation with an array name.
#include <iostream>
using namespace std;

int main()
```

```
{
    const int NUM_COINS = 5;
    double coins[NUM_COINS] = {0.05, 0.1, 0.25, 0.5, 1.0};
    double *doublePtr;    // Pointer to a double
    int count;            // Array index

    // Assign the address of the coins array to doublePtr.
    doublePtr = coins;

    // Display the contents of the coins array. Use subscripts
    // with the pointer!
    cout << "Here are the values in the coins array:\n";
    for (count = 0; count < NUM_COINS; count++)
       cout << doublePtr[count] << " ";

    // Display the contents of the array again, but this time
    // use pointer notation with the array name!
    cout << "\nAnd here they are again:\n";
    for (count = 0; count < NUM_COINS; count++)
       cout << *(coins + count) << " ";
    cout << endl;
    return 0;
}
```

Program Output

```
Here are the values in the coins array:
0.05 0.1 0.25 0.5 1
And here they are again:
0.05 0.1 0.25 0.5 1
```

Notice the address operator is not needed when an array's address is assigned to a pointer. Because the name of an array is already an address, use of the & operator would be incorrect. You can, however, use the address operator to get the address of an individual element in an array. For instance, `&numbers[1]` gets the address of `numbers[1]`. This technique is used in Program 8.

Program 8

```
// This program uses the address of each element in the array.
#include <iostream>
using namespace std;

int main()
{
    const int NUM_COINS = 5;
    double coins[NUM_COINS] = {0.05, 0.1, 0.25, 0.5, 1.0};
    double *doublePtr = nullptr;     // Pointer to a double
    int count;                       // Array index

```

(program continues)

Program 8 *(continued)*

```
    // Use the pointer to display the values in the array.
    cout << "Here are the values in the coins array:\n";
    for (count = 0; count < NUM_COINS; count++)
    {
       // Get the address of an array element.
       doublePtr = &coins[count];

       // Display the contents of the element.
       cout << *doublePtr << " ";
    }
    cout << endl;
    return 0;
}
```

Program Output

```
Here are the values in the coins array:
0.05 0.1 0.25 0.5 1
```

The only difference between array names and pointer variables is that you cannot change the address an array name points to. For example, consider the following definitions:

```
double readings[20], totals[20];
double *dptr = nullptr;
```

These statements are legal:

```
dptr = readings;  // Make dptr point to readings.
dptr = totals;    // Make dptr point to totals.
```

But these are illegal:

```
readings = totals;  // ILLEGAL! Cannot change readings.
totals = dptr;      // ILLEGAL! Cannot change totals.
```

Array names are *pointer constants*. You can't make them point to anything but the array they represent.

4 Pointer Arithmetic

CONCEPT: **Some mathematical operations may be performed on pointers.**

The contents of pointer variables may be changed with mathematical statements that perform addition or subtraction. This is demonstrated in Program 9. The first loop increments the pointer variable, stepping it through each element of the array. The second loop decrements the pointer, stepping it backwards through the array.

Program 9

```
// This program uses a pointer to display the contents of an array.
#include <iostream>
using namespace std;

int main()
{
    const int SIZE = 8;
    int set[SIZE] = {5, 10, 15, 20, 25, 30, 35, 40};
    int *numPtr = nullptr;  // Pointer
    int count;              // Counter variable for loops

    // Make numPtr point to the set array.
    numPtr = set;

    // Use the pointer to display the array contents.
    cout << "The numbers in set are:\n";
    for (count = 0; count < SIZE; count++)
    {
        cout << *numPtr << " ";
        numPtr++;
    }

    // Display the array contents in reverse order.
    cout << "\nThe numbers in set backward are:\n";
    for (count = 0; count < SIZE; count++)
    {
        numPtr--;
        cout << *numPtr << " ";
    }
    return 0;
}
```

Program Output

```
The numbers in set are:
5 10 15 20 25 30 35 40
The numbers in set backward are:
40 35 30 25 20 15 10 5
```

NOTE: Because `numPtr` is a pointer to an integer, the increment operator adds the size of one integer to `numPtr`, so it points to the next element in the array. Likewise, the decrement operator subtracts the size of one integer from the pointer.

Not all arithmetic operations may be performed on pointers. For example, you cannot multiply or divide a pointer. The following operations are allowable:

- The ++ and -- operators may be used to increment or decrement a pointer variable.
- An integer may be added to or subtracted from a pointer variable. This may be performed with the + and - operators, or the += and -= operators.
- A pointer may be subtracted from another pointer.

5 Initializing Pointers

CONCEPT: Pointers may be initialized with the address of an existing object.

Remember a pointer is designed to point to an object of a specific data type. When a pointer is initialized with an address, it must be the address of an object the pointer can point to. For instance, the following definition of `pint` is legal because `myValue` is an integer:

```
int myValue;
int *pint = &myValue;
```

The following is also legal because `ages` is an array of integers:

```
int ages[20];
int *pint = ages;
```

But the following definition of `pint` is illegal because `myFloat` is not an `int`:

```
float myFloat;
int *pint = &myFloat;   // Illegal!
```

Pointers may be defined in the same statement as other variables of the same type. The following statement defines an integer variable, `myValue`, then defines a pointer, `pint`, which is initialized with the address of `myValue`:

```
int myValue, *pint = &myValue;
```

And the following statement defines an array, `readings`, and a pointer, `marker`, which is initialized with the address of the first element in the array:

```
double readings[50], *marker = readings;
```

Of course, a pointer can only be initialized with the address of an object that has already been defined. The following is illegal, because `pint` is being initialized with the address of an object that does not exist yet:

```
int *pint = &myValue;   // Illegal!
int myValue;
```

Checkpoint

1 Write a statement that displays the address of the variable `count`.

2 Write the definition statement for a variable `fltPtr`. The variable should be a pointer to a `float`.

3 List three uses of the * symbol in C++.

4 What is the output of the following code?

```
int x = 50, y = 60, z = 70;
int *ptr = nullptr;

cout << x << " " << y << " " << z << endl;
ptr = &x;
```

```
*ptr *= 10;
ptr = &y;
*ptr *= 5;
ptr = &z;
*ptr *= 2;
cout << x << " " << y << " " << z << endl;
```

5 Rewrite the following loop so it uses pointer notation (with the indirection operator) instead of subscript notation.

```
for (int x = 0; x < 100; x++)
   cout << arr[x] << endl;
```

6 Assume `ptr` is a pointer to an `int` and holds the address 12000. On a system with 4-byte integers, what address will be in `ptr` after the following statement?

```
ptr += 10;
```

7 Assume `pint` is a pointer variable. Is each of the following statements valid or invalid? If any is invalid, why?

A) `pint++;`
B) `--pint;`
C) `pint /= 2;`
D) `pint *= 4;`
E) `pint += x; // Assume x is an int.`

8 Is each of the following definitions valid or invalid? If any is invalid, why?

A)
```
int ivar;
int *iptr = &ivar;
```
B)
```
int ivar, *iptr = &ivar;
```
C)
```
float fvar;
int *iptr = &fvar;
```
D)
```
int nums[50], *iptr = nums;
```
E)
```
int *iptr = &ivar;
int ivar;
```

6 Comparing Pointers

CONCEPT: If one address comes before another address in memory, the first address is considered "less than" the second. C++'s relational operators may be used to compare pointer values.

Pointers may be compared by using any of C++'s relational operators:

```
>> < == != >= <=
```

In an array, all the elements are stored in consecutive memory locations, so the address of element 1 is greater than the address of element 0. This is illustrated in Figure 7.

Figure 7 Array elements

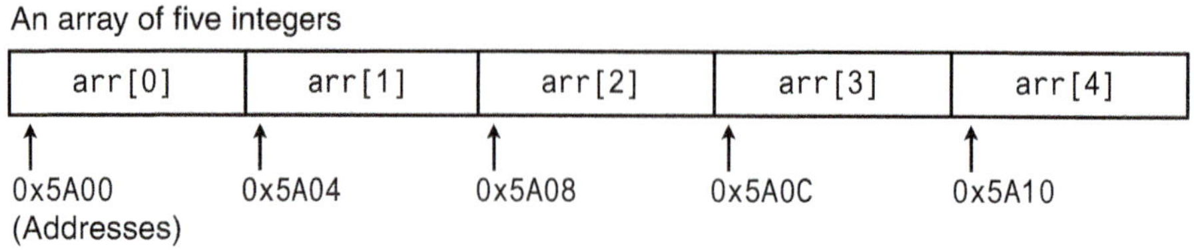

Because the addresses grow larger for each subsequent element in the array, the expressions tested by the following `if` statements are all true:

```
if (&arr[1] > &arr[0])
if (arr < &arr[4])
if (arr == &arr[0])
if (&arr[2] != &arr[3])
```

> **NOTE:** Comparing two pointers is not the same as comparing the values the two pointers point to. For example, the following `if` statement compares the addresses stored in the pointer variables `ptr1` and `ptr2`:
>
> `if (ptr1 < ptr2)`
>
> The following statement, however, compares the values that `ptr1` and `ptr2` point to:
>
> `if (*ptr1 < *ptr2)`

The capability of comparing addresses gives you another way to be sure a pointer does not go beyond the boundaries of an array. Program 10 initializes the pointer `ptr` with the starting address of the array `numbers`. The `ptr` pointer is then stepped through the `numbers` array until the address it contains is equal to the address of the last element of the array. Then, the pointer is stepped backward through the array until it points to the first element.

Program 10

```
// This program uses a pointer to display the contents
// of an integer array.
#include <iostream>
using namespace std;

int main()
{
    const int SIZE = 8;
    int numbers[SIZE] = {5, 10, 15, 20, 25, 30, 35, 40};
    int *ptr = numbers;       // Make ptr point to numbers

    // Display the numbers in the array.
    cout << "The numbers are:\n";
    cout << *ptr << " ";      // Display first element
```

```
    while (ptr < &numbers[SIZE - 1])
    {
       // Advance ptr to point to the next element.
       ptr++;
       // Display the value pointed to by ptr.
       cout << *ptr << " ";
    }

    // Display the numbers in reverse order.
    cout << "\nThe numbers backward are:\n";
    cout << *ptr << " ";    // Display first element
    while (ptr > numbers)
    {
       // Move backward to the previous element.
       ptr--;
       // Display the value pointed to by ptr.
       cout << *ptr << " ";
    }
    return 0;
}
```

Program Output

```
The numbers are:
5 10 15 20 25 30 35 40
The numbers backward are:
40 35 30 25 20 15 10 5
```

7 Pointers as Function Parameters

CONCEPT: A pointer can be used as a function parameter. It gives the function access to the original argument, much like a reference parameter does.

Reference variables can be used as function parameters. A reference variable acts as an alias to the original variable used as an argument. This gives the function access to the original argument variable, allowing it to change the variable's contents. When a variable is passed into a reference parameter, the argument is said to be passed by reference.

Another way to pass an argument by reference is to use a pointer variable as the parameter. Admittedly, reference variables are much easier to work with than pointers. Reference variables hide all the "mechanics" of dereferencing and indirection. You should still learn to use pointers as function arguments, however, because some tasks (especially when you are dealing with strings) are best done with pointers.* Also, the C++ library has many functions that use pointers as parameters.

*It is also important to learn this technique in case you ever need to write a C program. In C, the only way to pass a variable by reference is to use a pointer.

Here is the definition of a function that uses a pointer parameter:

```
void doubleValue(int *val)
{
    *val *= 2;
}
```

The purpose of this function is to double the variable pointed to by `val` with the following statement:

```
*val *= 2;
```

When `val` is dereferenced, the `*=` operator works on the variable pointed to by `val`. This statement multiplies the original variable, whose address is stored in `val`, by 2. Of course, when the function is called, the address of the variable that is to be doubled must be used as the argument, not the variable itself. Here is an example of a call to the `doubleValue` function:

```
doubleValue(&number);
```

This statement uses the address operator (&) to pass the address of `number` into the `val` parameter. After the function executes, the contents of `number` will have been multiplied by 2. The use of this function is illustrated in Program 11.

Program 11

```
// This program uses two functions that accept addresses of
// variables as arguments.
#include <iostream>
using namespace std;

// Function prototypes
void getNumber(int *);
void doubleValue(int *);

int main()
{
    int number;

    // Call getNumber and pass the address of number.
    getNumber(&number);

    // Call doubleValue and pass the address of number.
    doubleValue(&number);

    // Display the value in number.
    cout << "That value doubled is " << number << endl;
    return 0;
}
```

```
25 //*****************************************************************
26 // Definition of getNumber. The parameter, input, is a pointer. *
27 // This function asks the user for a number. The value entered  *
28 // is stored in the variable pointed to by input.               *
29 //*****************************************************************
30 
31 void getNumber(int *input)
32 {
33     cout << "Enter an integer number: ";
34     cin >> *input;
35 }
36 
37 //*****************************************************************
38 // Definition of doubleValue. The parameter, val, is a pointer. *
39 // This function multiplies the variable pointed to by val by   *
40 // two.                                                          *
41 //*****************************************************************
42 
43 void doubleValue(int *val)
44 {
45     *val *= 2;
46 }
```

Program Output with Example Input Shown in Bold

Enter an integer number: **10** [Enter]
That value doubled is 20

Program 11 has two functions that use pointers as parameters. Notice the function prototypes:

```
void getNumber(int *);
void doubleValue(int *);
```

Each one uses the notation `int *` to indicate the parameter is a pointer to an `int`. As with all other types of parameters, it isn't necessary to specify the name of the variable in the prototype. The `*` is required, though.

The `getNumber` function asks the user to enter an integer value. The following `cin` statement, in line 34, stores the value entered by the user in memory:

```
cin >> *input;
```

The indirection operator causes the value entered by the user to be stored, not in `input`, but in the variable pointed to by `input`.

WARNING! It's critical that the indirection operator be used in the statement above. Without it, `cin` would store the value entered by the user in `input`, as if the value were an address. If this happens, `input` will no longer point to the `number` variable in function `main`. Subsequent use of the pointer will result in erroneous, if not disastrous, results.

When the `getNumber` function is called in line 15, the address of the `number` variable in function `main` is passed as the argument. After the function executes, the value entered by the user is stored in `number`. Next, the `doubleValue` function is called in line 18, with the address of `number` passed as the argument. This causes `number` to be multiplied by 2.

Pointer variables can also be used to accept array addresses as arguments. Either subscript or pointer notation may then be used to work with the contents of the array. This is demonstrated in Program 12.

Program 12

```
// This program demonstrates that a pointer may be used as a
// parameter to accept the address of an array.
#include <iostream>
#include <iomanip>
using namespace std;

// Function prototypes
void getSales(double *, int);
double totalSales(double *, int);

int main()
{
    const int QTRS = 4;
    double sales[QTRS];

    // Get the sales data for all quarters.
    getSales(sales, QTRS);

    // Set the numeric output formatting.
    cout << fixed << showpoint << setprecision(2);

    // Display the total sales for the year.
    cout << "The total sales for the year are $";
    cout << totalSales(sales, QTRS) << endl;
    return 0;
}

//*****************************************************************
// Definition of getSales. This function uses a pointer to accept *
// the address of an array of doubles. The function asks the user *
// to enter sales figures and stores them in the array.           *
//*****************************************************************
void getSales(double *arr, int size)
{
    for (int count = 0; count < size; count++)
    {
        cout << "Enter the sales figure for quarter ";
        cout << (count + 1) << ": ";
        cin >> arr[count];
    }
}

```

```
43  //*****************************************************************
44  // Definition of totalSales. This function uses a pointer to      *
45  // accept the address of an array. The function returns the total *
46  // of the elements in the array.                                  *
47  //*****************************************************************
48  double totalSales(double *arr, int size)
49  {
50      double sum = 0.0;
51
52      for (int count = 0; count < size; count++)
53      {
54          sum += *arr;
55          arr++;
56      }
57      return sum;
58  }
```

Program Output with Example Input Shown in Bold

```
Enter the sales figure for quarter 1: 10263.98 [Enter]
Enter the sales figure for quarter 2: 12369.69 [Enter]
Enter the sales figure for quarter 3: 11542.13 [Enter]
Enter the sales figure for quarter 4: 14792.06 [Enter]
The total sales for the year are $48967.86
```

Notice in the `getSales` function in Program 12, even though the parameter `arr` is defined as a pointer, subscript notation is used in the `cin` statement in line 39:

```
cin >> arr[count];
```

In the `totalSales` function, `arr` is used with the indirection operator in line 54:

```
sum += *arr;
```

And in line 55, the address in `arr` is incremented to point to the next element:

```
arr++;
```

> **NOTE:** The two previous statements could be combined into the following statement:
>
> `sum += *arr++;`
>
> The `*` operator will first dereference `arr`, then the `++` operator will increment the address in `arr`.

Pointers to Constants

You have seen how an item's address can be passed into a pointer parameter, and how the pointer can be used to modify the item that was passed as an argument. Sometimes it is necessary to pass the address of a `const` item into a pointer. When this is the case, the pointer must be defined as a pointer to a `const` item. For example, consider the following array definition:

```
const int SIZE = 6;
const double payRates[SIZE] = { 18.55, 17.45,
                                12.85, 14.97,
                                10.35, 18.89 };
```

In this code, payRates is an array of const doubles. This means each element in the array is a const double, and the compiler will not allow us to write code that changes the array's contents. If we want to pass the payRates array into a pointer parameter, the parameter must be declared as a pointer to const double. The following function shows such an example:

```
void displayPayRates(const double *rates, int size)
{
    // Set numeric output formatting.
    cout << setprecision(2) << fixed << showpoint;

    // Display all the pay rates.
    for (int count = 0; count < size; count++)
    {
        cout << "Pay rate for employee " << (count + 1)
             << " is $" << *(rates + count) << endl;
    }
}
```

In the function header, notice the rates parameter is defined as a pointer to const double. It should be noted the word const is applied to the thing that rates points to, not rates itself. This is illustrated in Figure 8.

Figure 8 rates is a pointer to const double

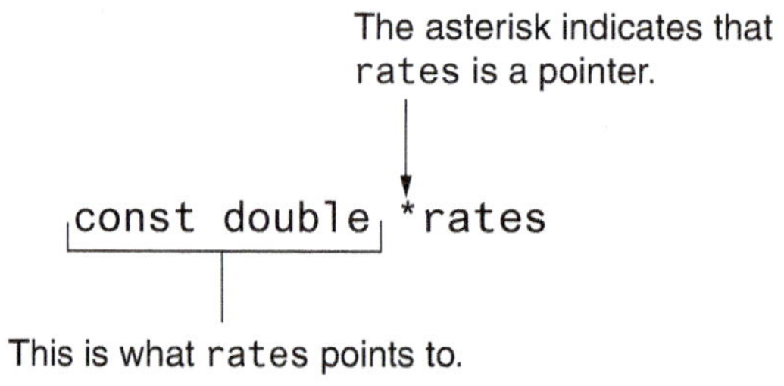

Because rates is a pointer to a const, the compiler will not allow us to write code that changes the thing that rates points to.

In passing the address of a constant into a pointer variable, the variable must be defined as a pointer to a constant. If the word const had been left out of the definition of the rates parameter, a compiler error would have resulted.

Passing a Nonconstant Argument into a Pointer to a Constant

Although a constant's address can be passed only to a pointer to const, a pointer to const can also receive the address of a nonconstant item. For example, look at Program 13.

Program 13

```
// This program demonstrates a pointer to const parameter
#include <iostream>
using namespace std;

void displayValues(const int *, int);

int main()
{
    // Array sizes
    const int SIZE = 6;

    // Define an array of const ints.
    const int array1[SIZE] = { 1, 2, 3, 4, 5, 6 };

    // Define an array of nonconst ints.
    int array2[SIZE] = { 2, 4, 6, 8, 10, 12 };

    // Display the contents of the const array.
    displayValues(array1, SIZE);

    // Display the contents of the nonconst array.
    displayValues(array2, SIZE);
    return 0;
}

//*****************************************************
// The displayValues function uses a pointer to     *
// parameter to display the contents of an array.   *
//*****************************************************

void displayValues(const int *numbers, int size)
{
    // Display all the values.
    for (int count = 0; count < size; count++)
    {
        cout << *(numbers + count) << " ";
    }
    cout << endl;
}
```

Program Output

```
1 2 3 4 5 6
2 4 6 8 10 12
```

NOTE: When you are writing a function that uses a pointer parameter, and the function is not intended to change the data the parameter points to, it is always a good idea to make the parameter a pointer to `const`. Not only will this protect you from writing code in the function that accidentally changes the argument, but the function will be able to accept the addresses of both constant and nonconstant arguments.

Constant Pointers

In the previous section, we discussed pointers to const, that is, pointers that point to const data. You can also use the const key word to define a constant pointer. Here are the differences between a pointer to const and a const pointer:

- A pointer to const points to a constant item. The data that the pointer points to cannot change, but the pointer itself can change.
- With a const pointer, it is the pointer itself that is constant. Once the pointer is initialized with an address, it cannot point to anything else.

The following code shows an example of a const pointer:

```
int value = 22;
int * const ptr = &value;
```

Notice in the definition of ptr, the word const appears after the asterisk. This means that ptr is a const pointer. This is illustrated in Figure 9. In the code, ptr is initialized with the address of the value variable. Because ptr is a constant pointer, a compiler error will result if we write code that makes ptr point to anything else. An error will not result, however, if we use ptr to change the contents of value. This is because value is not constant, and ptr is not a pointer to const.

Figure 9 ptr is a const pointer to int

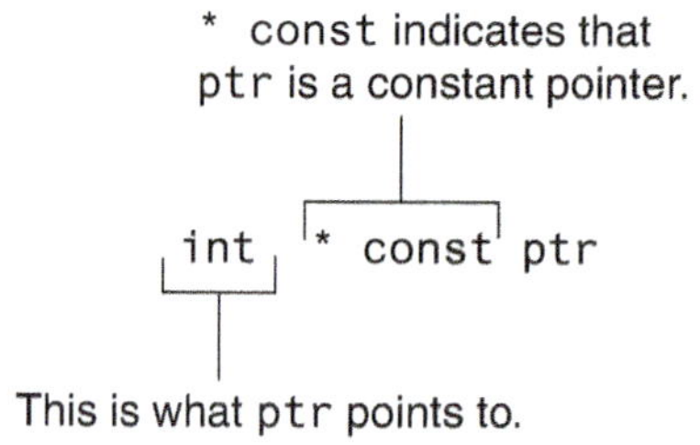

Constant pointers must be initialized with a starting value, as shown in the previous example code. If a constant pointer is used as a function parameter, the parameter will be initialized with the address that is passed as an argument into it, and cannot be changed to point to anything else while the function is executing. Here is an example that attempts to violate this rule:

```
void setToZero(int * const ptr)
{
   ptr = 0; // ERROR!! Cannot change the contents of ptr.
}
```

This function's parameter, ptr, is a const pointer. It will not compile because we cannot have code in the function that changes the contents of ptr. However, ptr does not point to a const, so we can have code that changes the data that ptr points to. Here is an example of the function that will compile:

```
void setToZero(int * const ptr)
{
   *ptr = 0;
}
```

Although the parameter is const pointer, we can call the function multiple times with different arguments. The following code will successfully pass the addresses of x, y, and z to the setToZero function:

```
int x, y, z;
// Set x, y, and z to 0.
setToZero(&x);
setToZero(&y);
setToZero(&z);
```

Constant Pointers to Constants

So far, when using const with pointers, we've seen pointers to constants and we've seen constant pointers. You can also have constant pointers to constants. For example, look at the following code:

```
int value = 22;
const int * const ptr = &value;
```

In this code, ptr is a const pointer to a const int. Notice the word const appears before int, indicating that ptr points to a const int, and it appears after the asterisk, indicating that ptr is a constant pointer. This is illustrated in Figure 10.

Figure 10 ptr is a const pointer to const int

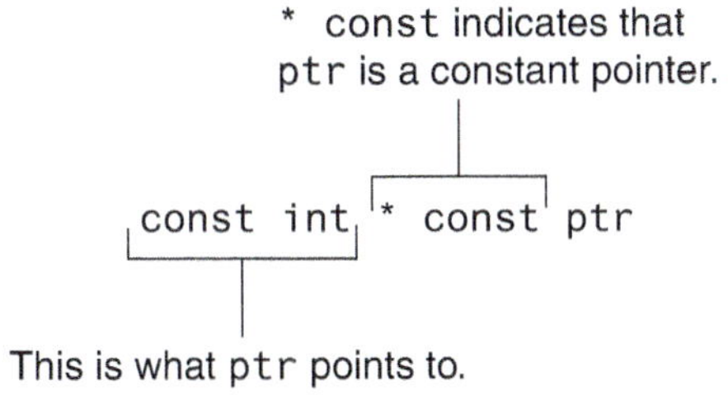

In the code, ptr is initialized with the address of value. Because ptr is a const pointer, we cannot write code that makes ptr point to anything else. Because ptr is a pointer to const, we cannot use it to change the contents of value. The following code shows one more example of a const pointer to a const. This is another version of the displayValues function in Program 13.

```
void displayValues(const int * const numbers, int size)
{
   // Display all the values.
   for (int count = 0; count < size; count++)
   {
      cout << *(numbers + count) << " ";
   }
   cout << endl;
}
```

In this code, the parameter numbers is a const pointer to a const int. Although we can call the function with different arguments, the function itself cannot change what numbers points to, and it cannot use numbers to change the contents of an argument.

8 Dynamic Memory Allocation

CONCEPT: **Variables may be created and destroyed while a program is running.**

As long as you know how many variables you will need during the execution of a program, you can define those variables up front. For example, a program to calculate the area of a rectangle will need three variables: one for the rectangle's length, one for the rectangle's width, and one to hold the area. If you are writing a program to compute the payroll for 30 employees, you'll probably create an array of 30 elements to hold the amount of pay for each person.

But what about those times when you don't know how many variables you need? For instance, suppose you want to write a test-averaging program that will average any number of tests. Obviously the program would be very versatile, but how do you store the individual test scores in memory if you don't know how many variables to define? Quite simply, you allow the program to create its own variables "on the fly." This is called *dynamic memory allocation*, and is only possible through the use of pointers.

To dynamically allocate memory means that a program, while running, asks the computer to set aside a chunk of unused memory large enough to hold a variable of a specific data type. Let's say a program needs to create an integer variable. It will make a request to the computer that it allocate enough bytes to store an `int`. When the computer fills this request, it finds and sets aside a chunk of unused memory large enough for the variable. It then gives the program the starting address of the chunk of memory. The program can access the newly allocated memory only through its address, so a pointer is required to use those bytes.

The way a C++ program requests dynamically allocated memory is through the `new` operator. Assume a program has a pointer to an `int` defined as

```
int *iptr = nullptr;
```

Here is an example of how this pointer may be used with the `new` operator:

```
iptr = new int;
```

This statement is requesting that the computer allocate enough memory for a new `int` variable. The operand of the `new` operator is the data type of the variable being created. Once the statement executes, `iptr` will contain the address of the newly allocated memory. This is illustrated in Figure 11. A value may be stored in this new variable by dereferencing the pointer:

```
*iptr = 25;
```

Any other operation may be performed on the new variable by simply using the dereferenced pointer. Here are some example statements:

```
cout << *iptr;    // Display the contents of the new variable.
cin >> *iptr;     // Let the user input a value.
total += *iptr;   // Use the new variable in a computation.
```

Figure 11 iptr points to a chunk of dynamically allocated memory

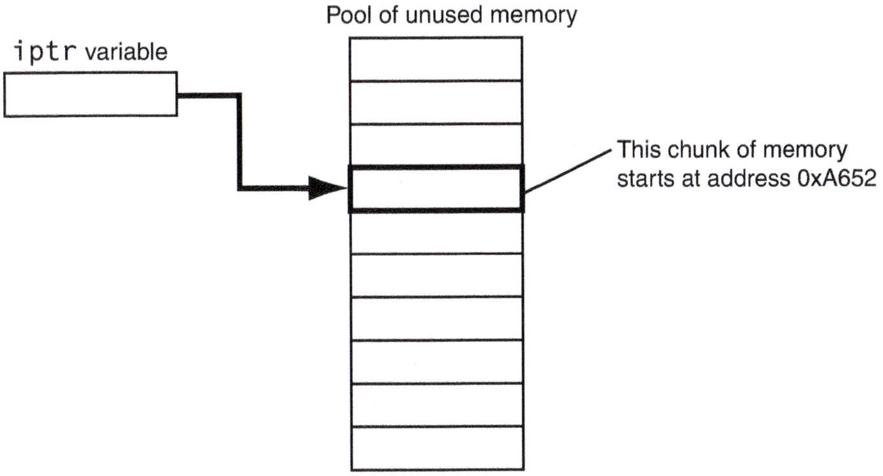

Although the statements above illustrate the use of the new operator, there's little purpose in dynamically allocating a single variable. A more practical use of the new operator is to dynamically create an array. Here is an example of how a 100-element array of integers may be allocated:

```
iptr = new int[100];
```

VideoNote
Dynamically Allocating an Array

Once the array is created, the pointer may be used with subscript notation to access it. For instance, the following loop could be used to store the value 1 in each element:

```
for (int count = 0; count < 100; count++)
    iptr[count] = 1;
```

But what if there isn't enough free memory to accommodate the request? What if the program asks for a chunk large enough to hold a 100,000-element array of `floats`, and that much memory isn't available? When memory cannot be dynamically allocated, C++ throws an exception and terminates the program. *Throwing an exception* means the program signals that an error has occurred.

When a program is finished using a dynamically allocated chunk of memory, it should release it for future use. The `delete` operator is used to free memory that was allocated with new. Here is an example of how `delete` is used to free a single variable, pointed to by `iptr`:

```
delete iptr;
```

If `iptr` points to a dynamically allocated array, the `[]` symbol must be placed between `delete` and `iptr`:

```
delete [] iptr;
```

Failure to release dynamically allocated memory can cause a program to have a *memory leak*. For example, suppose the following grabMemory function is in a program:

```
void grabMemory()
{
    const int SIZE = 100;
    // Allocate space for a 100-element
    // array of integers.
    int *iptr = new int[SIZE];
    // The function ends without deleting the memory!
}
```

Notice the function dynamically allocates a 100-element int array and assigns its address to the iptr pointer variable. But then, the function ends without deleting the memory. Once the function has ended, the iptr pointer variable no longer exists. As a result, the program does not have a pointer to the dynamically allocated memory; therefore, the memory cannot be accessed or deleted. It will sit unused as long as the program is running.

WARNING! Only use pointers with delete that were previously used with new. If you use a pointer with delete that does not reference dynamically allocated memory, unexpected problems could result!

Program 14 demonstrates the use of new and delete. It asks for sales amounts for any number of days. The amounts are stored in a dynamically allocated array, then totaled and averaged.

Program 14

```
// This program totals and averages the sales amounts for any
// number of days. The amounts are stored in a dynamically
// allocated array.
#include <iostream>
#include <iomanip>
using namespace std;

int main()
{
    double *sales = nullptr, // To dynamically allocate an array
           total = 0.0,      // Accumulator
           average;          // To hold average sales
    int numDays,             // To hold the number of days of sales
        count;               // Counter variable

    // Get the number of days of sales.
    cout << "How many days of sales amounts do you wish ";
    cout << "to process? ";
    cin >> numDays;
```

```
20
21        // Dynamically allocate an array large enough to hold
22        // that many days of sales amounts.
23        sales = new double[numDays];
24
25        // Get the sales amounts for each day.
26        cout << "Enter the sales amounts below.\n";
27        for (count = 0; count < numDays; count++)
28        {
29            cout << "Day " << (count + 1) << ": ";
30            cin >> sales[count];
31        }
32
33        // Calculate the total sales
34        for (count = 0; count < numDays; count++)
35        {
36            total += sales[count];
37        }
38
39        // Calculate the average sales per day
40        average = total / numDays;
41
42        // Display the results
43        cout << fixed << showpoint << setprecision(2);
44        cout << "\n\nTotal Sales: $" << total << endl;
45        cout << "Average Sales: $" << average << endl;
46
47        // Free dynamically allocated memory
48        delete [] sales;
49        sales = nullptr;    // Make sales a null pointer.
50
51        return 0;
52    }
```

Program Output with Example Input Shown in Bold

```
How many days of sales amounts do you wish to process? 5 [Enter]
Enter the sales amounts below.
Day 1: 898.63 [Enter]
Day 2: 652.32 [Enter]
Day 3: 741.85 [Enter]
Day 4: 852.96 [Enter]
Day 5: 921.37 [Enter]

Total Sales: $4067.13
Average Sales: $813.43
```

The statement in line 23 dynamically allocates memory for an array of `double`s, using the value in `numDays` as the number of elements. The `new` operator returns the starting address of the chunk of memory, which is assigned to the `sales` pointer variable. The `sales` variable is then used throughout the program to store the sales amounts in the array and perform the necessary calculations. In line 48, the `delete` operator is used to free the allocated memory.

Notice in line 49, the value nullptr is assigned to the sales pointer. It is a good practice to set a pointer variable to nullptr after using delete on it. First, it prevents code from inadvertently using the pointer to access the area of memory that was freed. Second, it prevents errors from occurring if delete is accidentally called on the pointer again. The delete operator is designed to have no effect when used on a null pointer.

9 Returning Pointers from Functions

CONCEPT: Functions can return pointers, but you must be sure the item the pointer references still exists.

Like any other data type, functions may return pointers. For example, the following function locates the null terminator that appears at the end of a string (such as a string literal) and returns a pointer to it:

```
char *findNull(char *str)
{
   char *ptr = str;

   while (*ptr != '\0')
     ptr++;
   return ptr;
}
```

The char * return type in the function header indicates the function returns a pointer to a char.

```
char *findNull(char *str)
```

When writing functions that return pointers, you should take care not to create elusive bugs. For instance, see if you can determine what's wrong with the following function:

```
string *getFullName()
{
   string fullName[3];
   cout << "Enter your first name: ";
   getline(cin, fullName[0]);
   cout << "Enter your middle name: ";
   getline(cin, fullName[1]);
   cout << "Enter your last name: ";
   getline(cin, fullName[2]);
   return fullName;
}
```

The problem, of course, is that the function returns a pointer to an array that no longer exists. Because the fullName array is defined locally, it is destroyed when the function terminates. Attempting to use the pointer will result in erroneous and unpredictable results.

You should return a pointer from a function only if it is:

- A pointer to an item that was passed into the function as an argument.
- A pointer to a dynamically allocated chunk of memory.

For instance, the following function is acceptable:

```
string *getFullName(string fullName[])
{
   cout << "Enter your first name: ";
   getline(cin, fullName[0]);
   cout << "Enter your middle name: ";
   getline(cin, fullName[1]);
   cout << "Enter your last name: ";
   getline(cin, fullName[2]);
   return fullName;
}
```

This function accepts a pointer to the memory location where the user's input is to be stored. Because the pointer references a memory location that was valid prior to the function being called, it is safe to return a pointer to the same location. Here is another acceptable function:

```
string *getFullName()
{
   string *fullName = new string[3];

   cout << "Enter your first name: ";
   getline(cin, fullName[0]);
   cout << "Enter your middle name: ";
   getline(cin, fullName[1]);
   cout << "Enter your last name: ";
   getline(cin, fullName[2]);
   return fullName;
}
```

This function uses the `new` operator to allocate a section of memory. This memory will remain allocated until the `delete` operator is used or the program ends, so it's safe to return a pointer to it.

Program 15 shows another example. This program uses a function, `getRandomNumbers`, to get a pointer to an array of random numbers. The function accepts an integer argument that is the number of random numbers in the array. The function dynamically allocates an array, uses the system clock to seed the random number generator, populates the array with random values, then returns a pointer to the array.

Program 15

```
// This program demonstrates a function that returns
// a pointer.
#include <iostream>
#include <cstdlib>   // For rand and srand
#include <ctime>     // For the time function
using namespace std;

// Function prototype
int *getRandomNumbers(int);

```

(program continues)

Program 15 *(continued)*

```
int main()
{
    int *numbers = nullptr;   // To point to the numbers

    // Get an array of five random numbers.
    numbers = getRandomNumbers(5);

    // Display the numbers.
    for (int count = 0; count < 5; count++)
        cout << numbers[count] << endl;

    // Free the memory.
    delete [] numbers;
    numbers = nullptr;
    return 0;
}

//**************************************************
// The getRandomNumbers function returns a pointer *
// to an array of random integers. The parameter   *
// indicates the number of numbers requested.      *
//**************************************************

int *getRandomNumbers(int num)
{
    int *arr = nullptr;   // Array to hold the numbers

    // Return a null pointer if num is zero or negative.
    if (num <= 0)
        return nullptr;

    // Dynamically allocate the array.
    arr = new int[num];

    // Seed the random number generator by passing
    // the return value of time(0) to srand.
    srand( time(0) );

    // Populate the array with random numbers.
    for (int count = 0; count < num; count++)
        arr[count] = rand();

    // Return a pointer to the array.
    return arr;
}
```

Program Output

```
2712
9656
24493
12483
7633
```

In the Spotlight:

Suppose you are developing a program that works with arrays of integers, and you find that you frequently need to duplicate the arrays. Rather than rewriting the array-duplicating code each time you need it, you decide to write a function that accepts an array and its size as arguments, creates a new array that is a copy of the argument array, and returns a pointer to the new array. The function will work as follows:

Accept an array and its size as arguments.
Dynamically allocate a new array that is the same size as the argument array.
Copy the elements of the argument array to the new array.
Return a pointer to the new array.

Program 16 demonstrates the function, which is named `duplicateArray`.

Program 16

```
// This program uses a function to duplicate
// an int array of any size.
#include <iostream>
using namespace std;

// Function prototype
int *duplicateArray(const int *, int);
void displayArray(const int[], int);

int main()
{
    // Define constants for the array sizes.
    const int SIZE1 = 5, SIZE2 = 7, SIZE3 = 10;

    // Define three arrays of different sizes.
    int array1[SIZE1] = { 100, 200, 300, 400, 500 };
    int array2[SIZE2] = { 10, 20, 30, 40, 50, 60, 70 };
    int array3[SIZE3] = { 1, 2, 3, 4, 5, 6, 7, 8, 9, 10 };

    // Define three pointers for the duplicate arrays.
    int *dup1 = nullptr, *dup2 = nullptr, *dup3 = nullptr;

    // Duplicate the arrays.
    dup1 = duplicateArray(array1, SIZE1);
    dup2 = duplicateArray(array2, SIZE2);
    dup3 = duplicateArray(array3, SIZE3);

    // Display the original arrays.
    cout << "Here are the original array contents:\n";
    displayArray(array1, SIZE1);
    displayArray(array2, SIZE2);
    displayArray(array3, SIZE3);

    // Display the new arrays.
```

(program continues)

Program 16 *(continued)*

```
    cout << "\nHere are the duplicate arrays: \n";
    displayArray(dup1, SIZE1);
    displayArray(dup2, SIZE2);
    displayArray(dup3, SIZE3);

    // Free the dynamically allocated memory and
    // set the pointers to 0.
    delete [] dup1;
    delete [] dup2;
    delete [] dup3;
    dup1 = nullptr;
    dup2 = nullptr;
    dup3 = nullptr;
    return 0;
}
//*****************************************************
// The duplicateArray function accepts an int array   *
// and an int that indicates the array's size. The    *
// function creates a new array that is a duplicate   *
// of the argument array and returns a pointer to the *
// new array. If an invalid size is passed, the       *
// function returns a null pointer.                   *
//*****************************************************

int *duplicateArray(const int *arr, int size)
{
    int *newArray = nullptr;

    // Validate the size. If 0 or a negative
    // number was passed, return a null pointer.
    if (size <= 0)
       return nullptr;

    // Allocate a new array.
    newArray = new int[size];

    // Copy the array's contents to the
    // new array.
    for (int index = 0; index < size; index++)
       newArray[index] = arr[index];

    // Return a pointer to the new array.
    return newArray;
}

//**************************************************
// The displayArray function accepts an int array *
// and its size as arguments and displays the     *
// contents of the array.                         *
//**************************************************

```

```
86    void displayArray(const int arr[], int size)
87    {
88       for (int index = 0; index < size; index++)
89          cout << arr[index] << " ";
90       cout << endl;
91    }
```

Program Output

```
Here are the original array contents:
100 200 300 400 500
10 20 30 40 50 60 70
1 2 3 4 5 6 7 8 9 10
Here are the duplicate arrays:
100 200 300 400 500
10 20 30 40 50 60 70
1 2 3 4 5 6 7 8 9 10
```

The `duplicateArray` function appears in lines 59 and 78. The `if` statement in lines 65 and 66 validates that `size` contains a valid array size. If `size` is 0 or less, the function immediately returns `nullptr` to indicate that an invalid size was passed.

Line 69 allocates a new array and assigns its address to the `newArray` pointer. Then, the loop in lines 73 and 74 copies the elements of the `arr` parameter to the new array. Then, the `return` statement in line 77 returns a pointer to the new array.

Checkpoint

9 Assuming `arr` is an array of `int`s, will each of the following program segments display "True" or "False"?

A)
```
if (arr < &arr[1])
   cout << "True";
else
   cout << "False";
```

B)
```
if (&arr[4] < &arr[1])
   cout << "True";
else
   cout << "False";
```

C)
```
if (arr != &arr[2])
   cout << "True";
else
   cout << "False";
```

D)
```
if (arr != &arr[0])
   cout << "True";
else
   cout << "False";
```

10 Give an example of the proper way to call the following function:

```
void makeNegative(int *val)
{
   if (*val > 0)
```

```
    *val = -(*val);
}
```

11 Complete the following program skeleton. When finished, the program will ask the user for a length (in inches), then convert that value to centimeters, and display the result. You are to write the function `convert`. (*Note:* 1 inch = 2.54 cm. Do not modify function `main`.)

```
#include <iostream>
#include <iomanip>
using namespace std;

// Write your function prototype here.

int main()
{
    double measurement;

    cout << "Enter a length in inches, and I will convert\n";
    cout << "it to centimeters: ";
    cin >> measurement;
    convert(&measurement);
    cout << fixed << setprecision(4);
    cout << "Value in centimeters: " << measurement << endl;
    return 0;
}
//
// Write the function convert here.
//
```

12 Look at the following array definition:

```
const int numbers[SIZE] = { 18, 17, 12, 14 };
```

Suppose we want to pass the array to the function `processArray` in the following manner:

```
processArray(numbers, SIZE);
```

Which of the following function headers is the correct one for the `processArray` function?

A) `void processArray(const int *arr, int size)`
B) `void processArray(int * const arr, int size)`

13 Assume `ip` is a pointer to an `int`. Write a statement that will dynamically allocate an integer variable and store its address in `ip`. Write a statement that will free the memory allocated in the statement you wrote above.

14 Assume `ip` is a pointer to an `int`. Then, write a statement that will dynamically allocate an array of 500 integers and store its address in `ip`. Write a statement that will free the memory allocated in the statement you just wrote.

15 What is a null pointer?

16 Give an example of a function that correctly returns a pointer.

17 Give an example of a function that incorrectly returns a pointer.

10 Using Smart Pointers to Avoid Memory Leaks

CONCEPT: C++ 11 introduces smart pointers, objects that work like pointers, but have the ability to automatically delete dynamically allocated memory that is no longer being used.

In C++ 11, you can use *smart pointers* to dynamically allocate memory and not worry about deleting the memory when you are finished using it. A smart pointer automatically deletes a chunk of dynamically allocated memory when the memory is no longer being used. This helps to prevent memory leaks from occurring.

C++ 11 provides three types of smart pointer: unique_ptr, shared_ptr, and weak_ptr. These smart pointers are described in Table 1.

Table 1 Smart Pointer Types

Smart Pointer Type	Description
unique_ptr	A unique_ptr is the sole owner of a piece of dynamically allocated memory. No two unique_ptrs can point to the same piece of memory. When a unique_ptr goes out of scope, it automatically deallocates the piece of memory that it points to.
shared_ptr	A shared_ptr can share ownership of a piece of dynamically allocated memory. Multiple pointers of the shared_ptr type can point to the same piece of memory. The memory is deallocated when the last shared_ptr that is pointing to it is destroyed.
weak_ptr	A weak_ptr does not own the memory it points to, and cannot be used to access the memory's contents. It is used in special situations where the memory pointed to by a shared_ptr must be referenced without increasing the number of shared_ptrs that own it.

To use any of the smart pointers, you must #include the <memory> header file with the following directive:

```
#include <memory>
```

In this chapter, we introduce unique_ptr. The syntax for defining a unique_ptr is somewhat different from the syntax used in defining a regular pointer. Here is an example:

```
unique_ptr<int> ptr( new int );
```

This statement defines a unique_ptr named ptr that points to a dynamically allocated int. Here are some details about the statement:

- The notation <int> that appears immediately after unique_ptr indicates that the pointer can point to an int.
- The name of the pointer is ptr.
- The expression new int that appears inside the parentheses allocates a chunk of memory to hold an int. The address of the chunk of memory will be assigned to the ptr pointer.

Figure 12 shows the different parts of the definition statement.

Figure 12 Definition of a `unique_ptr`

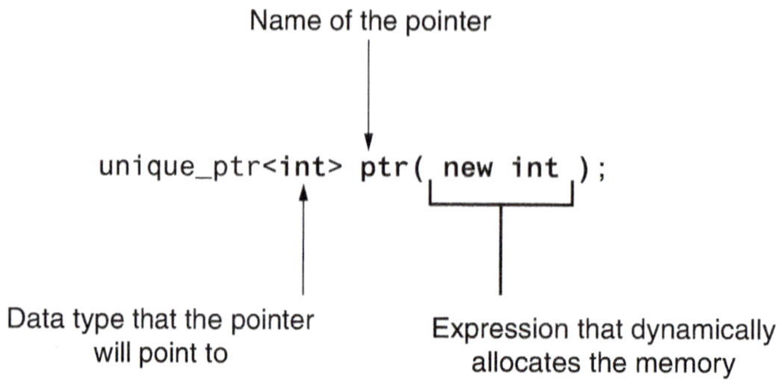

Once you have defined a `unique_ptr`, you can use it in a similar way as a regular pointer. This is demonstrated in Program 17.

Program 17

```
1  // This program demonstrates a unique_ptr.
2  #include <iostream>
3  #include <memory>
4  using namespace std;
5
6  int main()
7  {
8       // Define a unique_ptr smart pointer, pointing
9       // to a dynamically allocated int.
10      unique_ptr<int> ptr( new int );
11
12      // Assign 99 to the dynamically allocated int.
13      *ptr = 99;
14
15      // Display the value of the dynamically allocated int.
16      cout << *ptr << endl;
17      return 0;
18 }
```

Program Output

```
99
```

In line 3, we have a `#include` directive for the `<memory>` header file. Line 10 defines a `unique_ptr` named `ptr`, pointing to a dynamically allocated `int`. Line 13 assigns the value 99 to the dynamically allocated `int`. Notice the indirection operator (`*`) is used with the `unique_ptr`, just as if it were a regular pointer. Line 16 displays the value stored in the dynamically allocated `int`, once again using the indirection operator with the `unique_ptr`. Notice there is no `delete` statement to free the dynamically allocated memory. It is unnecessary to delete the memory, because the smart pointer will automatically delete it as the function comes to an end.

Program 17 demonstrates a unique_ptr, but it isn't very practical. Dynamically allocating an array is more useful than allocating a single integer. The following code shows an example of how to use a unique_ptr to dynamically allocate an array of integers:

```
const int SIZE = 100;
unique_ptr<int[]> ptr( new int[SIZE] );
```

The first statement defines an int constant named SIZE, set to the value 100. The second statement defines a unique_ptr named ptr that points to a dynamically allocated array of 100 ints. Notice the following things about the definition statement:

- Following unique_ptr, the notation <int[]> indicates that the pointer will point to an array of ints.
- The expression inside the parentheses, new int[SIZE], allocates an array of ints.

The address of the dynamically allocated array of ints will be assigned to the ptr pointer. After the definition statement, you can use the [] operator with subscripts to access the array elements. Here is an example:

```
ptr[0] = 99;
cout << ptr[0] << endl;
```

The first statement assigns the value 99 to ptr[0], and the second statement displays the value of ptr[0]. Program 18 gives a more complete demonstration.

Program 18

```
// This program demonstrates a unique_ptr pointing
// to a dynamically allocated array of integers.
#include <iostream>
#include <memory>
using namespace std;

int main()
{
    int max; // Max size of the array

    // Get the number of values to store.
    cout << "How many numbers do you want to enter? ";
    cin >> max;

    // Define a unique_ptr smart pointer, pointing
    // to a dynamically allocated array of ints.
    unique_ptr<int[]> ptr( new int[max]);

    // Get values for the array.
    for (int index = 0; index < max; index++)
    {
        cout << "Enter an integer number: ";
        cin >> ptr[index];
    }

```

(program continues)

Program 18 *(continued)*

```
    // Display the values in the array.
    cout << "Here are the values you entered:\n";
    for (int index = 0; index < max; index++)
        cout << ptr[index] << endl;

    return 0;
}
```

Program Output with Example Input Shown in Bold

```
How many numbers do you want to enter? 5 [Enter]
Enter an integer number: 1 [Enter]
Enter an integer number: 2 [Enter]
Enter an integer number: 3 [Enter]
Enter an integer number: 4 [Enter]
Enter an integer number: 5 [Enter]
Here are the values you entered:
1
2
3
4
5
```

You can define an uninitialized `unique_ptr`, then assign it a value in a later statement. Here is an example:

```
unique_ptr<int> ptr;
ptr = unique_ptr<int>(new int);
```

Smart pointers support the same `*` and `->` dereferencing operators as regular pointers, but smart pointers do not support pointer arithmetic. The following code will result in a compile-time error:

```
unique_ptr<int[]> ptr( new int[max]);
ptr++;     // ERROR!
```

11 Focus on Problem Solving and Program Design: A Case Study

CONCEPT: **This case study demonstrates how an array of pointers can be used to display the contents of a second array in sorted order, without sorting the second array.**

The United Cause, a charitable relief agency, solicits donations from businesses. The local United Cause office received the following donations from the employees of CK Graphics, Inc.:

```
$5, $100, $5, $25, $10, $5, $25, $5, $5, $100, $10, $15, $10, $5, $10
```

The donations were received in the order they appear. The United Cause manager has asked you to write a program that displays the donations in ascending order, as well as in their original order.

Variables

Table 2 shows the major variables needed.

Table 2 Variables

Variable	Description
NUM_DONATIONS	A constant integer initialized with the number of donations received from CK Graphics, Inc. This value will be used in the definition of the program's arrays.
donations	An array of integers containing the donation amounts.
arrPtr	An array of pointers to integers. This array has the same number of elements as the donations array. Each element of arrPtr will be initialized to point to an element of the donations array.

Programming Strategy

In this program, the donations array will contain the donations in the order they were received. The elements of the arrPtr array are pointers to integers. They will point to the elements of the donations array, as illustrated in Figure 13.

Figure 13 Relationship between the arrays

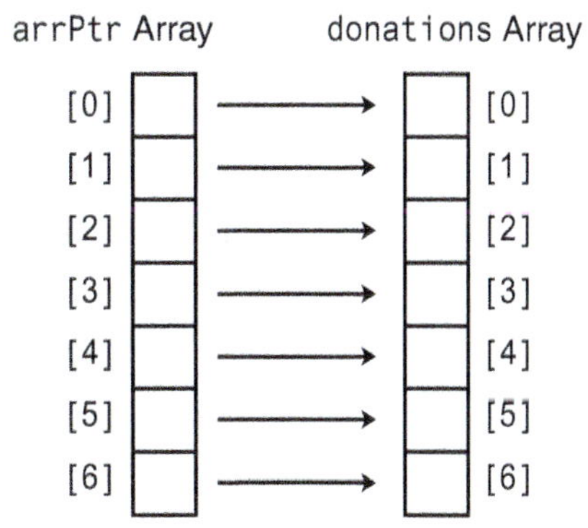

The arrPtr array will initially be set up to point to the elements of the donations array in their natural order. In other words, arrPtr[0] will point to donations[0], arrPtr[1] will point to donations[1], and so forth. In that arrangement, the following statement would cause the contents of donations[5] to be displayed:

```
cout << *(arrPtr[5]) << endl;
```

After the arrPtr array is sorted, however, arrPtr[0] will point to the smallest element of donations, arrPtr[1] will point to the next-to-smallest element of donations, and so forth. This is illustrated in Figure 14.

Figure 14 Accessing the donations array elements in sorted order

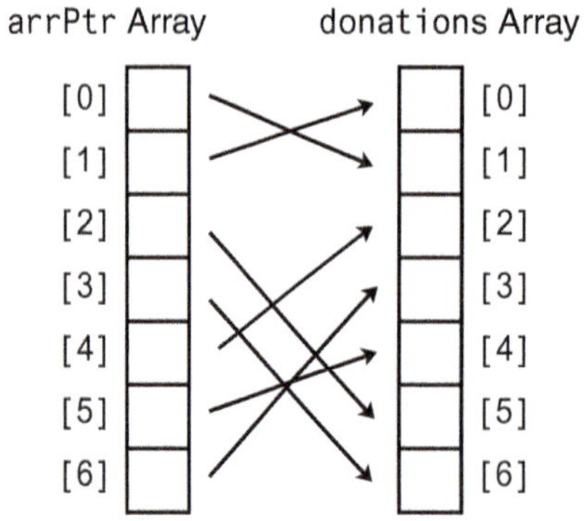

This technique gives us access to the elements of the donations array in a sorted order without actually disturbing the contents of the donations array itself.

Functions

The program will consist of the functions listed in Table 3.

Table 3 Functions

Function	Description
main	The program's main function. It calls the program's other functions.
arrSelectSort	Performs an ascending order selection sort on its parameter, arr, which is an array of pointers. Each element of arr points to an element of a second array. After the sort, arr will point to the elements of the second array in ascending order.
showArray	Displays the contents of its parameter, arr, which is an array of integers. This function is used to display the donations in their original order.
showArrPtr	Accepts an array of pointers to integers as an argument. Displays the contents of what each element of the array points to. This function is used to display the contents of the donations array in sorted order.

Function main

In addition to containing the variable definitions, function main sets up the arrPtr array to point to the elements of the donations array. Then, the function arrSelectSort is called to sort the elements of arrPtr. Last, the functions showArrPtr and showArray are called to display the donations. Here is the pseudocode for main's executable statements:

```
For count is set to the values 0 through the number of donations
    Set arrPtr[count] to the address of donations[count].
End For
Call arrSelectSort
Call showArrPtr
Call showArray
```

The arrSelectSort Function

The arrSelectSort function is a modified version of the selection sort algorithm. The only difference is that arr is now an array of pointers. Instead of sorting on the contents of arr's elements, arr is sorted on the contents of what its elements point to. Here is the pseudocode:

```
For startScan is set to the values 0 up to (but not including) the
        next-to-last subscript in arr
  Set index variable to startScan
  Set minIndex variable to startScan
  Set minElem pointer to arr[startScan]
  For index variable is set to the values from (startScan + 1) through
             the last subscript in arr
     If *(arr[index]) is less than *minElem
       Set minElem to arr[index]
       Set minIndex to index
     End If
  End For
  Set arr[minIndex] to arr[startScan]
  Set arr[startScan] to minElem
End For
```

The showArrPtr Function

The showArrPtr function accepts an array of pointers as its argument. It displays the values pointed to by the elements of the array. Here is its pseudocode:

```
For every element in the arr
   Dereference the element and display what it points to
End For.
```

The showArray Function

The showArray function simply displays the contents of arr sequentially. Here is its pseudocode:

```
For every element in arr
   Display the element's contents
End For.
```

The Entire Program

Program 19 shows the entire program's source code.

Program 19

```
// This program shows the donations made to the United Cause
// by the employees of CK Graphics, Inc. It displays
// the donations in order from lowest to highest
```

(program continues)

Program 19 *(continued)*

```
// and in the original order they were received.
#include <iostream>
using namespace std;

// Function prototypes
void arrSelectSort(int *[], int);
void showArray(const int [], int);
void showArrPtr(int *[], int);

int main()
{
    const int NUM_DONATIONS = 15;    // Number of donations

    // An array containing the donation amounts.
    int donations[NUM_DONATIONS] = { 5,  100, 5,  25, 10,
                                     5,  25,  5,  5,  100,
                                     10, 15,  10, 5,  10 };

    // An array of pointers to int.
     int *arrPtr[NUM_DONATIONS] = { nullptr, nullptr, nullptr, nullptr, nullptr,
                                    nullptr, nullptr, nullptr, nullptr, nullptr,
                                    nullptr, nullptr, nullptr, nullptr, nullptr};

    // Each element of arrPtr is a pointer to int. Make each
    // element point to an element in the donations array.
    for (int count = 0; count < NUM_DONATIONS; count++)
        arrPtr[count] = &donations[count];

    // Sort the elements of the array of pointers.
    arrSelectSort(arrPtr, NUM_DONATIONS);

    // Display the donations using the array of pointers. This
    // will display them in sorted order.
    cout << "The donations, sorted in ascending order, are: \n";
    showArrPtr(arrPtr, NUM_DONATIONS);

    // Display the donations in their original order.
    cout << "The donations, in their original order, are: \n";
    showArray(donations, NUM_DONATIONS);
    return 0;
}

//****************************************************************
// Definition of function arrSelectSort.                          *
// This function performs an ascending order selection sort on   *
// arr, which is an array of pointers. Each element of array     *
// points to an element of a second array. After the sort,       *
// arr will point to the elements of the second array in         *
// ascending order.                                              *
//****************************************************************

```

```
void arrSelectSort(int *arr[], int size)
{
    int startScan, minIndex;
    int *minElem;

    for (startScan = 0; startScan < (size - 1); startScan++)
    {
        minIndex = startScan;
        minElem = arr[startScan];
        for(int index = startScan + 1; index < size; index++)
        {
            if (*(arr[index]) < *minElem)
            {
                minElem = arr[index];
                minIndex = index;
            }
        }
        arr[minIndex] = arr[startScan];
        arr[startScan] = minElem;
    }
}

//************************************************************
// Definition of function showArray.                         *
// This function displays the contents of arr. size is the *
// number of elements.                                       *
//************************************************************

void showArray(const int arr[], int size)
{
    for (int count = 0; count < size; count++)
        cout << arr[count] << " ";
    cout << endl;
}

//****************************************************************
// Definition of function showArrPtr.                            *
// This function displays the contents of the array pointed to *
// by arr. size is the number of elements.                       *
//****************************************************************

void showArrPtr(int *arr[], int size)
{
    for (int count = 0; count < size; count++)
        cout << *(arr[count]) << " ";
    cout << endl;
}
```

Program Output

```
The donations, sorted in ascending order, are:
5 5 5 5 5 5 10 10 10 10 15 25 25 100 100
The donations, in their original order, are:
5 100 5 25 10 5 25 5 5 100 10 15 10 5 10
```

Review Questions and Exercises

Short Answer

1. What does the indirection operator do?
2. Look at the following code.

```
int x = 7;
int *iptr = &x;
```

What will be displayed if you send the expression `*iptr` to `cout`? What happens if you send the expression `ptr` to `cout`?
3. So far you have learned three different uses for the * operator. What are they?
4. What math operations are allowed on pointers?
5. Assuming `ptr` is a pointer to an `int`, what happens when you add 4 to `ptr`?
6. Look at the following array definition.

```
int numbers[] = { 2, 4, 6, 8, 10 };
```

What will the following statement display?

```
cout << *(numbers + 3) << endl;
```

7. What is the purpose of the `new` operator?
8. What happens when a program uses the `new` operator to allocate a block of memory, but the amount of requested memory isn't available? How do programs written with older compilers handle this?
9. What is the purpose of the `delete` operator?
10. Under what circumstances can you successfully return a pointer from a function?
11. What is the difference between a pointer to a constant and a constant pointer?
12. What are two advantages of declaring a pointer parameter as a constant pointer?

Fill-in-the-Blank

13. Each byte in memory is assigned a unique __________.
14. The __________ operator can be used to determine a variable's address.
15. __________ variables are designed to hold addresses.
16. The __________ operator can be used to work with the variable a pointer points to.
17. Array names can be used as __________, and vice versa.
18. Creating variables while a program is running is called __________.
19. The __________ operator is used to dynamically allocate memory.
20. Under older compilers, if the `new` operator cannot allocate the amount of memory requested, it returns __________.
21. A pointer that contains the address 0 is called a(n) __________ pointer.
22. When a program is finished with a chunk of dynamically allocated memory, it should free it with the __________ operator.
23. You should only use pointers with `delete` that were previously used with __________.

Algorithm Workbench

24. Look at the following code:

```
double value = 29.7;
double *ptr = &value;
```

Write a cout statement that uses the ptr variable to display the contents of the value variable.

25. Look at the following array definition:

```
int set[10];
```

Write a statement using pointer notation that stores the value 99 in set[7];

26. Write code that dynamically allocates an array of 20 integers, then uses a loop to allow the user to enter values for each element of the array.
27. Assume tempNumbers is a pointer that points to a dynamically allocated array. Write code that releases the memory used by the array.
28. Look at the following function definition:

```
void getNumber(int &n)
{
    cout << "Enter a number: ";
    cin >> n;
}
```

In this function, the parameter n is a reference variable. Rewrite the function so n is a pointer.

29. Write the definition of ptr, a pointer to a constant int.
30. Write the definition of ptr, a constant pointer to an int.

True or False

31. T F Each byte of memory is assigned a unique address.
32. T F The * operator is used to get the address of a variable.
33. T F Pointer variables are designed to hold addresses.
34. T F The & symbol is called the indirection operator.
35. T F The & operator dereferences a pointer.
36. T F When the indirection operator is used with a pointer variable, you are actually working with the value the pointer is pointing to.
37. T F Array names cannot be dereferenced with the indirection operator.
38. T F When you add a value to a pointer, you are actually adding that number times the size of the data type referenced by the pointer.
39. T F The address operator is not needed to assign an array's address to a pointer.
40. T F You can change the address that an array name points to.
41. T F Any mathematical operation, including multiplication and division, may be performed on a pointer.
42. T F Pointers may be compared using the relational operators.
43. T F When used as function parameters, reference variables are much easier to work with than pointers.

44. T F The new operator dynamically allocates memory.

45. T F A pointer variable that has not been initialized is called a null pointer.

46. T F The address 0 is generally considered unusable.

47. T F In using a pointer with the `delete` operator, it is not necessary for the pointer to have been previously used with the new operator.

Find the Error

Each of the following definitions and program segments has errors. Locate as many as you can.

48.
```
int ptr* = nullptr;
```

49.
```
int x, *ptr = nullptr;
&x = ptr;
```

50.
```
int x, *ptr = nullptr;
*ptr = &x;
```

51.
```
int x, *ptr = nullptr;
ptr = &x;
ptr = 100; // Store 100 in x
cout << x << endl;
```

52.
```
int numbers[] = {10, 20, 30, 40, 50};
cout << "The third element in the array is ";
cout << *numbers + 3 << endl;
```

53.
```
int values[20], *iptr = nullptr;
iptr = values;
iptr *= 2;
```

54.
```
float level;
int fptr = &level;
```

55.
```
int *iptr = &ivalue;
int ivalue;
```

56.
```
void doubleVal(int val)
{
   *val *= 2;
}
```

57.
```
int *pint = nullptr;
new pint;
```

58.
```
int *pint = nullptr;
pint = new int;
if (pint == nullptr)
    *pint = 100;
else
    cout << "Memory allocation error\n";
```

59.
```
int *pint = nullptr;
pint = new int[100]; // Allocate memory
    .
    .
```
Code that processes the array.
```
    .
    .
delete pint; // Free memory
```
60.
```
int *getNum()
{
    int wholeNum;
    cout << "Enter a number: ";
    cin >> wholeNum;
    return &wholeNum;
}
```
61.
```
const int arr[] = { 1, 2, 3 };
int *ptr = arr;
```
62.
```
void doSomething(int * const ptr)
{
    int localArray[] = { 1, 2, 3 };
    ptr = localArray;
}
```

Programming Challenges

1. **Array Allocator**

   Write a function that dynamically allocates an array of integers. The function should accept an integer argument indicating the number of elements to allocate. The function should return a pointer to the array.

2. **Test Scores #1**

   Write a program that dynamically allocates an array large enough to hold a user-defined number of test scores. Once all the scores are entered, the array should be passed to a function that sorts them in ascending order. Another function should be called that calculates the average score. The program should display the sorted list of scores and averages with appropriate headings. Use pointer notation rather than array notation whenever possible.

   Input Validation: Do not accept negative numbers for test scores.

3. **Drop Lowest Score**

   Modify Problem 2 above so the lowest test score is dropped. This score should not be included in the calculation of the average.

4. Test Scores #2

Modify the program of Programming Challenge 2 (Test Scores #1) to allow the user to enter name–score pairs. For each student taking a test, the user types the student's name followed by the student's integer test score. Modify the sorting function so it takes an array holding the student names, and an array holding the student test scores. When the sorted list of scores is displayed, each student's name should be displayed along with his or her score. In stepping through the arrays, use pointers rather than array subscripts.

5. Pointer Rewrite

VideoNote
Solving the Pointer Rewrite Problem

The following function uses reference variables as parameters. Rewrite the function so it uses pointers instead of reference variables, then demonstrate the function in a complete program.

```
int doSomething(int &x, int &y)
{
    int temp = x;
    x = y * 10;
    y = temp * 10;
    return x + y;
}
```

6. Case Study Modification #1

Modify Program 19 (the United Cause case study program) so it can be used with any set of donations. The program should dynamically allocate the `donations` array and ask the user to input its values.

7. Case Study Modification #2

Modify Program 19 (the United Cause case study program) so the `arrptr` array is sorted in descending order instead of ascending order.

8. Mode Function

In statistics, the *mode* of a set of values is the value that occurs most often or with the greatest frequency. Write a function that accepts as arguments the following:

A) An array of integers

B) An integer that indicates the number of elements in the array

The function should determine the mode of the array. That is, it should determine which value in the array occurs most often. The mode is the value the function should return. If the array has no mode (none of the values occur more than once), the function should return −1. (Assume the array will always contain nonnegative values.)

Demonstrate your pointer prowess by using pointer notation instead of array notation in this function.

9. Median Function

In statistics, when a set of values is sorted in ascending or descending order, its *median* is the middle value. If the set contains an even number of values, the median is the mean, or average, of the two middle values. Write a function that accepts as arguments the following:

A) An array of integers

B) An integer that indicates the number of elements in the array

The function should determine the median of the array. This value should be returned as a `double`. (Assume the values in the array are already sorted.)

Demonstrate your pointer prowess by using pointer notation instead of array notation in this function.

10. Reverse Array

Write a function that accepts an `int` array and the array's size as arguments. The function should create a copy of the array, except that the element values should be reversed in the copy. The function should return a pointer to the new array. Demonstrate the function in a complete program.

11. Array Expander

Write a function that accepts an `int` array and the array's size as arguments. The function should create a new array that is twice the size of the argument array. The function should copy the contents of the argument array to the new array and initialize the unused elements of the second array with 0. The function should return a pointer to the new array.

12. Element Shifter

Write a function that accepts an `int` array and the array's size as arguments. The function should create a new array that is one element larger than the argument array. The first element of the new array should be set to 0. Element 0 of the argument array should be copied to element 1 of the new array, element 1 of the argument array should be copied to element 2 of the new array, and so forth. The function should return a pointer to the new array.

13. Movie Statistics

Write a program that can be used to gather statistical data about the number of movies college students see in a month. The program should perform the following steps:

A) Ask the user how many students were surveyed. An array of integers with this many elements should then be dynamically allocated.

B) Allow the user to enter the number of movies each student saw into the array.

C) Calculate and display the average, median, and mode of the values entered. (Use the functions you wrote in Programming Challenges 8 and 9 to calculate the median and mode.)

Input Validation: Do not accept negative numbers for input.

Answers to Checkpoints

1 `cout << &count;`

2 `float *fltPtr;`

3 Multiplication operator, pointer definition, indirection operator

4
```
50  60  70
500  300  140
```

5
```
for (int x = 0; x < 100; x++)
     cout << *(array + x) << endl;
```

6 12040

7 A) Valid
B) Valid
C) Invalid. Only addition and subtraction are valid arithmetic operations with pointers.
D) Invalid. Only addition and subtraction are valid arithmetic operations with pointers.
E) Valid

8 A) Valid
B) Valid
C) Invalid. `fvar` is a float and `iptr` is a pointer to an `int`.
D) Valid
E) Invalid. `ivar` must be declared before `iptr`.

9 A) True
B) False
C) True
D) False

10
```
makeNegative (&num);
```

11
```
void convert(double *val)
{
     *val *= 2.54;
}
```

12 A

13
```
ip = new int;
delete ip;
```

14
```
ip = new int[500];
delete [] ip;
```

15 A pointer that contains the address 0.

16
```
char *getInitials()
{
     char *initials = new char[3];
     cout << "Enter your three initials: ";
     cin >> initials[0] >> initials[1] >> initials[2];
     return initials;
}
```

17

```
char *getInitials()
{
     char[3] initials;
     cout << "Enter your three initials: ";
     cin >> initials[0] >> initials[1] >> initials[2];
     return initials;
}
```

Answers to Odd Numbered Review Questions

1. It dereferences a pointer, allowing code to work with the value that the pointer points to.
3. Multiplication operator, definition of a pointer variable, and the indirection operator.
5. It adds 4 times the size of an `int` to the address stored in `ptr`.
7. To dynamically allocate memory.
9. To free memory that has been dynamically allocated with the `new` operator.
11. A pointer to a constant points to a constant item. The data to which the pointer points cannot change, but the pointer itself can change. With a constant pointer, it is the pointer itself that is constant. Once the pointer is initialized with an address, it cannot point to anything else.
13. address
15. pointer
17. pointers
19. `new`
21. null
23. `new`
25. `*(set + 7) = 99;`
27. `delete [] tempNumbers;`
29. `const int *ptr;`
31. True
33. True
35. False
37. False
39. True
41. False

43. True
45. False
47. False
49. The assignment statement should read `ptr = &x;`
51. The assignment statement should read `*ptr = 100;`
53. Multiplication cannot be performed on pointers.
55. `iptr` cannot be initialized with the address of `ivalue`. `ivalue` is defined after `iptr`.
57. The second statement should read `pint = new int;`
59. The last line should read `delete [] pint;`
61. The pointer definition should read:
    ```
    const int *ptr = array;
    ```

Characters, C-Strings, and More about the `string` Class

TOPICS

1 Character Testing

CONCEPT: The C++ library provides several functions for testing characters. To use these functions you must include the `<cctype>` header file.

The C++ library provides several functions that allow you to test the value of a character. These functions test a single `char` argument and return either `true` or `false`.* For example, the following program segment uses the `isupper` function to determine whether the character passed as an argument is an uppercase letter. If it is, the function returns `true`. Otherwise, it returns `false`.

```
char letter = 'a';
if (isupper(letter))
   cout << "Letter is uppercase.\n";
else
   cout << "Letter is lowercase.\n";
```

Because the variable `letter`, in this example, contains a lowercase character, `isupper` returns `false`. The `if` statement will cause the message `"Letter is lowercase"` to be displayed.

* These functions actually return an `int` value. The return value is nonzero to indicate `true`, or zero to indicate `false`.

From Chapter 10 of *Starting Out with C++: From Control Structures through Objects*, Ninth Edition. Tony Gaddis.

Table 1 lists several character-testing functions. Each of these is prototyped in the `<cctype>` header file, so be sure to include that file when using the functions.

Table 1 Character-Testing Functions in <cctype>

Character Function	Description
`isalpha`	Returns `true` (a nonzero number) if the argument is a letter of the alphabet. Returns 0 if the argument is not a letter.
`isalnum`	Returns `true` (a nonzero number) if the argument is a letter of the alphabet or a digit. Otherwise, it returns 0.
`isdigit`	Returns `true` (a nonzero number) if the argument is a digit from 0 through 9. Otherwise, it returns 0.
`islower`	Returns `true` (a nonzero number) if the argument is a lowercase letter. Otherwise, it returns 0.
`isprint`	Returns `true` (a nonzero number) if the argument is a printable character (including a space). Returns 0 otherwise.
`ispunct`	Returns `true` (a nonzero number) if the argument is a printable character other than a digit, letter, or space. Returns 0 otherwise.
`isupper`	Returns `true` (a nonzero number) if the argument is an uppercase letter. Otherwise, it returns 0.
`isspace`	Returns `true` (a nonzero number) if the argument is a whitespace character. Whitespace characters are any of the following: space `' '` vertical tab `'\v'` newline `'\n'` tab `'\t'` Otherwise, it returns 0.

Program 1 uses several of the functions shown in Table 1. It asks the user to input a character then displays various messages, depending upon the return value of each function.

Program 1

```
// This program demonstrates some character-testing functions.
#include <iostream>
#include <cctype>
using namespace std;

int main()
{
    char input;

    cout << "Enter any character: ";
    cin.get(input);
    cout << "The character you entered is: " << input << endl;
```

```
    if (isalpha(input))
       cout << "That's an alphabetic character.\n";
    if (isdigit(input))
       cout << "That's a numeric digit.\n";
    if (islower(input))
       cout << "The letter you entered is lowercase.\n";
    if (isupper(input))
       cout << "The letter you entered is uppercase.\n";
    if (isspace(input))
       cout << "That's a whitespace character.\n";
    return 0;
}
```

Program Output with Example Input Shown in Bold

```
Enter any character: A [Enter]
The character you entered is: A
That's an alphabetic character.
The letter you entered is uppercase.
```

Program Output with Different Example Input Shown in Bold

```
Enter any character: 7 [Enter]
The character you entered is: 7
That's a numeric digit.
```

Program 2 shows a more practical application of the character-testing functions. It tests a seven-character customer number to determine whether it is in the proper format.

Program 2

```
// This program tests a customer number to determine whether
// it is in the proper format.
#include <iostream>
#include <cctype>
using namespace std;

// Function prototype
bool testNum(char [], int);

int main()
{
    const int SIZE = 8;    // Array size
    char customer[SIZE];   // To hold a customer number

    // Get the customer number.
    cout << "Enter a customer number in the form ";
    cout << "LLLNNNN\n";
    cout << "(LLL = letters and NNNN = numbers): ";
    cin.getline(customer, SIZE);

```

(program continues)

Program 2 *(continued)*

```
    // Determine whether it is valid.
    if (testNum(customer, SIZE))
        cout << "That's a valid customer number.\n";
    else
    {
        cout << "That is not the proper format of the ";
        cout << "customer number.\nHere is an example:\n";
        cout << "   ABC1234\n";
    }
    return 0;
}

//**********************************************************
// Definition of function testNum.                         *
// This function determines whether the custNum parameter  *
// holds a valid customer number. The size parameter is    *
// the size of the custNum array.                          *
//**********************************************************

bool testNum(char custNum[], int size)
{
    int count; // Loop counter

    // Test the first three characters for alphabetic letters.
    for (count = 0; count < 3; count++)
    {
        if (!isalpha(custNum[count]))
            return false;
    }

    // Test the remaining characters for numeric digits.
    for (count = 3; count < size - 1; count++)
    {
        if (!isdigit(custNum[count]))
            return false;
    }
    return true;
}
```

Program Output with Example Input Shown in Bold

```
Enter a customer number in the form LLLNNNN
(LLL = letters and NNNN = numbers): RQS4567 [Enter]
That's a valid customer number.
```

Program Output with Different Example Input Shown in Bold

```
Enter a customer number in the form LLLNNNN
(LLL = letters and NNNN = numbers): AX467T9 [Enter]
That is not the proper format of the customer number.
Here is an example:
    ABC1234
```

In this program, the customer number is expected to consist of three alphabetic letters followed by four numeric digits. The testNum function accepts an array argument and tests the first three characters with the following loop in lines 45 through 49:

```
for (count = 0; count < 3; count++)
{
    if (!isalpha(custNum[count]))
       return false;
}
```

The isalpha function returns true if its argument is an alphabetic character. The ! operator is used in the if statement to determine whether the tested character is NOT alphabetic. If this is so for any of the first three characters, the function testNum returns false. Likewise, the next four characters are tested to determine whether they are numeric digits with the following loop in lines 52 through 56:

```
for (count = 3; count < size - 1; count++)
{
    if (!isdigit(custNum[count]))
       return false;
}
```

The isdigit function returns true if its argument is the character representation of any of the digits 0 through 9. Once again, the ! operator is used to determine whether the tested character is *not* a digit. If this is so for any of the last four characters, the function testNum returns false. If the customer number is in the proper format, the function will cycle through both the loops without returning false. In that case, the last line in the function is the return true statement, which indicates the customer number is valid.

2 Character Case Conversion

CONCEPT: The C++ library offers functions for converting a character to uppercase or lowercase.

The C++ library provides two functions, toupper and tolower, for converting the case of a character. The functions are described in Table 2. (These functions are prototyped in the header file <cctype>, so be sure to include it.)

Table 2 Case-Conversion Functions in <cctype>

Function	Description
toupper	Returns the uppercase equivalent of its argument.
tolower	Returns the lowercase equivalent of its argument.

Each of the functions in Table 2 accepts a single character argument. If the argument is a lowercase letter, the toupper function returns its uppercase equivalent. For example, the following statement will display the character A on the screen:

```
cout << toupper('a');
```

If the argument is already an uppercase letter, `toupper` returns it unchanged. The following statement causes the character `Z` to be displayed:

```
cout << toupper('Z');
```

Any nonletter argument passed to `toupper` is returned as it is. Each of the following statements displays `toupper`'s argument without any change:

```
cout << toupper('*');    // Displays *
cout << toupper ('&');   // Displays &
cout << toupper('%');    // Displays %
```

`toupper` and `tolower` don't actually cause the character argument to change; they simply return the uppercase or lowercase equivalent of the argument. For example, in the following program segment, the variable `letter` is set to the value 'A'. The `tolower` function returns the character 'a', but `letter` still contains 'A'.

```
char letter = 'A';
cout << tolower(letter) << endl;
cout << letter << endl;
```

These statements will cause the following to be displayed:

```
a
A
```

Program 3 demonstrates the `toupper` function in an input validation loop.

Program 3

```
// This program calculates the area of a circle. It asks the user
// if he or she wishes to continue. A loop that demonstrates the
// toupper function repeats until the user enters 'y', 'Y',
// 'n', or 'N'.
#include <iostream>
#include <cctype>
#include <iomanip>
using namespace std;

int main()
{
    const double PI = 3.14159;  // Constant for pi
    double radius;              // The circle's radius
    char goAgain;               // To hold Y or N

    cout << "This program calculates the area of a circle.\n";
    cout << fixed << setprecision(2);

    do
    {
        // Get the radius and display the area.
        cout << "Enter the circle's radius: ";
        cin >> radius;
        cout << "The area is " << (PI * radius * radius);
        cout << endl;
```

```
26
27          // Does the user want to do this again?
28          cout << "Calculate another? (Y or N) ";
29          cin >> goAgain;
30
31          // Validate the input.
32          while (toupper(goAgain) != 'Y' && toupper(goAgain) != 'N')
33          {
34              cout << "Please enter Y or N: ";
35              cin >> goAgain;
36          }
37
38      } while (toupper(goAgain) == 'Y');
39      return 0;
40  }
```

Program Output with Example Input Shown in Bold

```
This program calculates the area of a circle.
Enter the circle's radius: 10 [Enter]
The area is 314.16
Calculate another? (Y or N) b [Enter]
Please enter Y or N: y [Enter]
Enter the circle's radius: 1 [Enter]
The area is 3.14
Calculate another? (Y or N) n [Enter]
```

In lines 28 and 29, the user is prompted to enter either Y or N to indicate whether he or she wants to calculate another area. We don't want the program to be so picky that it accepts only uppercase Y or uppercase N. Lowercase y or lowercase n is also acceptable. The input validation loop must be written to reject anything except `'Y'`, `'y'`, `'N'`, or `'n'`. One way to do this would be to test the `goAgain` variable in four relational expressions, as shown here:

```
while (goAgain != 'Y' && goAgain != 'y' &&
       goAgain != 'N' && goAgain != 'N')
```

Although there is nothing wrong with this code, we could use the `toupper` function to get the uppercase equivalent of `goAgain` and make only two comparisons. This is the approach taken in line 32:

```
while (toupper(goAgain) != 'Y' && toupper(goAgain) != 'N')
```

Another approach would have been to use the `tolower` function to get the lowercase equivalent of `goAgain`. Here is an example:

```
while (tolower(goAgain) != 'y' && tolower(goAgain) != 'n')
```

Either approach will yield the same results.

Checkpoint

1 Write a short description of each of the following functions:

```
isalpha
isalnum
isdigit
islower
isprint
ispunct
isupper
isspace
toupper
tolower
```

2 Write a statement that will convert the contents of the `char` variable `big` to lowercase. The converted value should be assigned to the variable `little`.

3 Write an `if` statement that will display the word "digit" if the variable `ch` contains a numeric digit. Otherwise, it should display "Not a digit."

4 What is the output of the following statement?

```
cout << toupper(tolower('A'));
```

5 Write a loop that asks the user "Do you want to repeat the program or quit? (R/Q)". The loop should repeat until the user has entered an R or a Q (either uppercase or lowercase).

3 C-Strings

CONCEPT: In C++, a C-string is a sequence of characters stored in consecutive memory locations, terminated by a null character.

String is a generic term that describes any consecutive sequence of characters. A word, a sentence, a person's name, and the title of a song are all strings. In the C++ language, there are two primary ways that strings are stored in memory: as `string` objects or as C-strings. You have already been introduced to the `string` class, and by now, you have written several programs that use `string` objects. In this section, we will use C-strings, which are an alternative method for storing and working with strings.

A *C-string* is a string whose characters are stored in consecutive memory locations and are followed by a null character, or null terminator. A null character or null terminator is a byte holding the ASCII code 0. Strings that are stored this way are called C-strings because this is the way strings are handled in the C programming language.

In C++, all string literals are stored in memory as C-strings. A string literal (or string constant) is the literal representation of a string in a program. In C++, string literals are enclosed in double quotation marks, such as:

```
"Bailey"
```

Figure 1 illustrates how the string literal "Bailey" is stored in memory, as a C-string.

Figure 1 A C-string stored in memory

B	a	i	l	e	y	\0

> **NOTE:** Remember that \0 ("slash zero") is the escape sequence representing the null terminator. It stands for the ASCII code 0.

The purpose of the null terminator is to mark the end of the C-string. Without it, there would be no way for a program to know the length of a C-string.

More about String Literals

A string literal or string constant is enclosed in a set of double quotation marks (" "). For example, here are five string literals:

```
"Have a nice day."
"What is your name?"
"John Smith"
"Please enter your age:"
"Part Number 45Q1789"
```

All of a program's string literals are stored in memory as C-strings, with the null terminator automatically appended. For example, look at Program 4.

Program 4

```
// This program contains string literals.
#include <iostream>
using namespace std;

int main()
{
    char again;

    do
    {
          cout << "C++ programming is great fun!" << endl;
          cout << "Do you want to see the message again? ";
          cin >> again;
    } while (again == 'Y' || again == 'y');
    return 0;
}
```

This program contains two string literals:

```
"C++ programming is great fun!"
"Do you want to see the message again? "
```

The first string occupies 30 bytes of memory (including the null terminator), and the second string occupies 39 bytes. They appear in memory in the following forms:

C	+	+		p	r	o	g	r	a	m	m	i	n	g		i	s		g	r	e	a	t		f	u	n	!	\0

D	o		y	o	u		w	a	n	t		t	o		s	e	e		t	h	e		m	e	s	s	a	g
e		a	g	a	i	n	?		\0																			

It's important to realize that a string literal has its own storage location, just like a variable or an array. When a string literal appears in a statement, it's actually its memory address that C++ uses. Look at the following example:

```
cout << "Do you want to see the message again? ";
```

In this statement, the memory address of the string literal "Do you want to see the message again?" is passed to the `cout` object. `cout` displays the consecutive characters found at this address. It stops displaying the characters when a null terminator is encountered.

C-Strings Stored in Arrays

The C programming language does not provide a `string` class like that which C++ provides. In the C language, all strings are treated as C-strings. When a C programmer wants to store a string in memory, he or she has to create a `char` array that is large enough to hold the string, plus one extra element for the null character.

You might be wondering why this should matter to anyone learning C++. You need to know about C-strings for the following reasons:

- The `string` class has not always existed in the C++ language. Several years ago, C++ stored strings as C-strings. As a professional programmer, you might encounter older C++ code (known as *legacy code*) that uses C-strings.
- Some of the C++ library functions work only with C-strings.
- In the workplace, it is not unusual for C++ programmers to work with specialized libraries that are written in C. Any strings with which C libraries work will be C-strings.

As previously mentioned, if you want to store a C-string in memory, you have to define a `char` array that is large enough to hold the string, plus one extra element for the null character. Here is an example:

```
const int SIZE = 21;
char name[SIZE];
```

This code defines a `char` array that has 21 elements, so it is big enough to hold a C-string that is no more that 20 characters long.

You can initialize a `char` array with a string literal, as shown here:

```
const int SIZE = 21;
char name[SIZE] = "Jasmine";
```

After this code executes, the `name` array will be created with 21 elements. The first eight elements will be initialized with the characters `'J'`, `'a'`, `'s'`, `'m'`, `'i'`, `'n'`, `'e'`, and `'\0'`. The null character is automatically added as the last character. You can implicitly size a `char` array by initializing it with a string literal, as shown here:

```
char name[] = "Jasmine";
```

After this code executes, the name array will be created with eight elements, initialized with the characters 'J','a', 's', 'm', 'i', 'n', 'e', and '\0'.

C-string input can be performed by the cin object. For example, the following code allows the user to enter a string (with no whitespace characters) into the name array:

```
const int SIZE = 21;
char name[SIZE];
cin >> name;
```

An array name with no brackets and no subscript is converted into the beginning address of the array. In the previous statement, name indicates the address in memory where the string is to be stored. Of course, cin has no way of knowing that name has 21 elements. If the user enters a string of 30 characters, cin will write past the end of the array. This can be prevented by using cin's getline member function. Assume the following array has been defined in a program:

```
const int SIZE = 80;
char line[SIZE];
```

The following statement uses cin's getline member function to get a line of input (including whitespace characters) and store it in the line array:

```
cin.getline(line, SIZE);
```

The first argument tells getline where to store the string input. This statement indicates the starting address of the line array as the storage location for the string. The second argument indicates the maximum length of the string, including the null terminator. In this example, the SIZE constant is equal to 80, so cin will read 79 characters, or until the user presses the [Enter] key, whichever comes first. cin will automatically append the null terminator to the end of the string.

Once a string is stored in an array, it can be processed using standard subscript notation. For example, Program 5 displays a string stored in an array. It uses a loop to display each character in the array until the null terminator is encountered.

Program 5

```
// This program displays a string stored in a char array.
#include <iostream>
using namespace std;

int main()
{
    const int SIZE = 80;    // Array size
    char line[SIZE];        // To hold a line of input
    int count = 0;          // Loop counter variable

    // Get a line of input.
    cout << "Enter a sentence of no more than "
         << (SIZE - 1) << " characters:\n";
    cin.getline(line, SIZE);

```

(program continues)

Program 5 *(continued)*

```
    // Display the input one character at a time.
    cout << "The sentence you entered is:\n";
    while (line[count] != '\0')
    {
        cout << line[count];
        count++;
    }
    return 0;
}
```

Program Output with Example Input Shown in Bold

```
Enter a sentence of no more than 79 characters:
C++ is challenging but fun! [Enter]
The sentence you entered is:
C++ is challenging but fun!
```

4 Library Functions for Working with C-Strings

CONCEPT: The C++ library has numerous functions for handling C-strings. These functions perform various tests and manipulations, and require the `<cstring>` header file be included.

The `strlen` Function

Because C-strings are stored in arrays, working with them is quite different from working with `string` objects. Fortunately, the C++ library provides many functions for manipulating and testing C-strings. These functions all require the `<cstring>` header file to be included, as shown here:

```
#include <cstring>
```

For instance, the following code segment uses the `strlen` function to determine the length of the string stored in the `name` array:

```
char name[] = "Thomas Edison";
int length;
length = strlen(name);
```

The `strlen` function accepts a pointer to a C-string as its argument. It returns the length of the string, which is the number of characters up to, but not including, the null terminator. As a result, the variable `length` will have the number 13 stored in it. The length of a string isn't to be confused with the size of the array holding it. Remember, the only information being passed to `strlen` is the beginning address of a C-string. It doesn't know where the array ends, so it looks for the null terminator to indicate the end of the string.

When using a C-string-handling function, you must pass one or more C-strings as arguments. This means passing the address of the C-string, which may be accomplished by using any of the following as arguments:

- The name of the array holding the C-string
- A pointer variable that holds the address of the C-string
- A literal string

Anytime a literal string is used as an argument to a function, the address of the literal string is passed. Here is an example of the strlen function being used with such an argument:

```
length = strlen("Thomas Edison");
```

The strcat Function

The strcat function accepts two pointers to C-strings as its arguments. The function *concatenates*, or appends one string to another. The following code shows an example of its use:

```
const int SIZE = 13;
char string1[SIZE] = "Hello ";
char string2[] = "World!";

cout << string1 << endl;
cout << string2 << endl;
strcat(string1, string2);
cout << string1 << endl;
```

These statements will cause the following output:

```
Hello
World!
Hello World!
```

The strcat function copies the contents of string2 to the end of string1. In this example, string1 contains the string "Hello " before the call to strcat. After the call, it contains the string "Hello World!". Figure 2 shows the contents of both arrays before and after the function call.

Figure 2 Using strcat

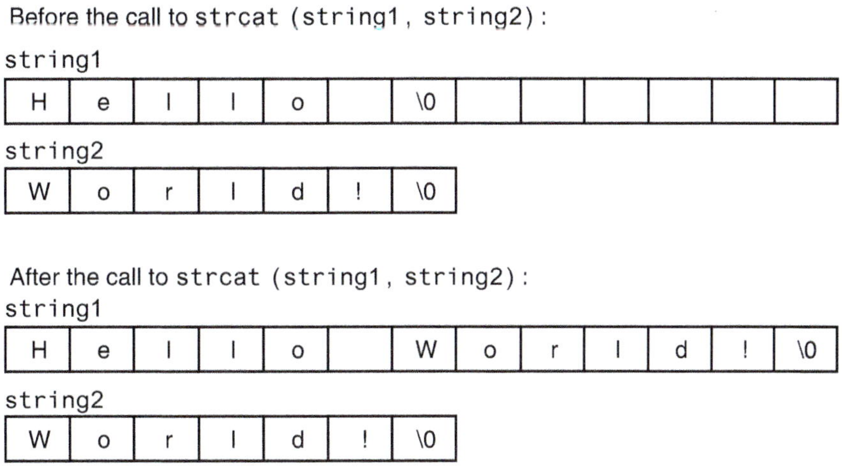

Notice the last character in string1 (before the null terminator) is a space. The strcat function doesn't insert a space, so it's the programmer's responsibility to make sure one is already there, if needed. It's also the programmer's responsibility to make sure the array holding string1 is large enough to hold string1 plus string2 plus a null terminator.

Here is a program segment that uses the sizeof operator to test an array's size before strcat is called:

```
if (sizeof(string1) >= (strlen(string1) + strlen(string2) + 1))
    strcat(string1, string2);
else
    cout << "String1 is not large enough for both strings.\n";
```

WARNING! If the array holding the first string isn't large enough to hold both strings, strcat will overflow the boundaries of the array.

The strcpy Function

One array cannot be assigned to another with the = operator. Each individual element must be assigned, usually inside a loop. The strcpy function can be used to copy one string to another. Here is an example of its use:

```
const int SIZE = 13;
char name[SIZE];
strcpy(name, "Albert Einstein");
```

The strcpy function's two arguments are C-string addresses. The contents of the second argument are copied to the memory location specified by the first argument, including the null terminator. (The first argument usually references an array.) In this example, the strcpy function will copy the string "Albert Einstein" to the name array.

If anything is already stored in the location referenced by the first argument, it is overwritten, as shown in the following program segment:

```
const int SIZE = 10;
char string1[SIZE] = "Hello", string2[SIZE] = "World!";
cout << string1 << endl;
cout << string2 << endl;
strcpy(string1, string2);
cout << string1 << endl;
cout << string2 << endl;
```

Here is the output:

```
Hello
World!
World!
World!
```

WARNING! Being true to C++'s nature, strcpy performs no bounds checking. The array specified by the first argument will be overflowed if it isn't large enough to hold the string specified by the second argument.

The strncat and strncpy Functions

Because the strcat and strcpy functions can potentially overwrite the bounds of an array, they make it possible to write unsafe code. As an alternative, you should use strncat and strncpy whenever possible.

The strncat functions works like strcat, except it takes a third argument specifying the maximum number of characters from the second string to append to the first. Here is an example call to strncat:

```
strncat(string1, string2, 10);
```

When this statement executes, strncat will append no more than 10 characters from string2 to string1. The following code shows an example of calculating the maximum number of characters that can be appended to an array:

```
1   int maxChars;
2   const int SIZE_1 = 17;
3   const int SIZE_2 = 18;
4
5   char string1[SIZE_1] = "Welcome ";
6   char string2[SIZE_2] = "to North Carolina";
7
8   cout << string1 << endl;
9   cout << string2 << endl;
10  maxChars = sizeof(string1) - (strlen(string1) + 1);
11  strncat(string1, string2, maxChars);
12  cout << string1 << endl;
```

The statement in line 10 calculates the number of empty elements in string1. It does this by subtracting the length of the string stored in the array plus 1 for the null terminator. This code will cause the following output:

```
Welcome
to North Carolina
Welcome to North
```

The strncpy function allows you to copy a specified number of characters from a string to a destination. Calling strncpy is similar to calling strcpy, except you pass a third argument specifying the maximum number of characters from the second string to copy to the first. Here is an example call to strncpy:

```
strncpy(string1, string2, 5);
```

When this statement executes, strncpy will copy no more than five characters from string2 to string1. However, if the specified number of characters is less than or equal to the length of string2, a null terminator is not appended to string1. If the specified number of characters is greater than the length of string2, then string1 is padded with null terminators, up to the specified number of characters. The following code shows an example using the strncpy function:

```
int maxChars;
const int SIZE = 11;

char string1[SIZE];
char string2[] = "I love C++ programming!";

```

```
7   maxChars = sizeof(string1) - 1;
8   strncpy(string1, string2, maxChars);
9   // Put the null terminator at the end.
10  string1[maxChars] = '\0';
11  cout << string1 << endl;
```

Notice a statement was written in line 10 to put the null terminator at the end of `string1`. This is because `maxChars` was less than the length of `string2`, and `strncpy` did not automatically place a null terminator there.

The `strstr` Function

The `strstr` function searches for a string inside of a string. For instance, it could be used to search for the string "seven" inside the larger string "Four score and seven years ago." The function's first argument is the string to be searched, and the second argument is the string for which to look. If the function finds the second string inside the first, it returns the address of the occurrence of the second string within the first string. Otherwise, it returns `nullptr` (the address 0). Here is an example:

```
char arr[] = "Four score and seven years ago";
char *strPtr = nullptr;
cout << arr << endl;
strPtr = strstr(arr, "seven"); // search for "seven"
cout << strPtr << endl;
```

In this code, `strstr` will locate the string "seven" inside the string "Four score and seven years ago." It will return the address of the first character in "seven" which will be stored in the pointer variable `strPtr`. If run as part of a complete program, this segment will display the following:

```
Four score and seven years ago
seven years ago
```

> **NOTE:** The `nullptr` key word was introduced in C++ 11. If you are using a previous version of the C++ language, use the constant `NULL` instead.

The `strstr` function can be useful in any program that must locate data inside one or more strings. Program 6, for example, stores a list of product numbers and descriptions in an array of C-strings. It allows the user to look up a product description by entering all or part of its product number.

Program 6

```
// This program uses the strstr function to search an array.
#include <iostream>
#include <cstring>     // For strstr
using namespace std;

int main()
{
    // Constants for array lengths
    const int NUM_PRODS = 5;    // Number of products
    const int LENGTH = 27;      // String length
```

```
11
12        // Array of products
13        char products[NUM_PRODS][LENGTH] =
14                         { "TV327 31-inch Television",
15                           "CD257 CD Player",
16                           "TA677 Answering Machine",
17                           "CS109 Car Stereo",
18                           "PC955 Personal Computer" };
19
20        char lookUp[LENGTH];       // To hold user's input
21        char *strPtr = nullptr;    // To point to the found product
22        int index;                 // Loop counter
23
24        // Prompt the user for a product number.
25        cout << "\tProduct Database\n\n";
26        cout << "Enter a product number to search for: ";
27        cin.getline(lookUp, LENGTH);
28
29        // Search the array for a matching substring
30        for (index = 0; index < NUM_PRODS; index++)
31        {
32            strPtr = strstr(products[index], lookUp);
33            if (strPtr != nullptr)
34                break;
35        }
36
37        // If a matching substring was found, display the product info.
38        if (strPtr != nullptr)
39            cout << products[index] << endl;
40        else
41            cout << "No matching product was found.\n";
42
43        return 0;
44    }
```

Program Output with Example Input Shown in Bold

        Product Database

Enter a product to search for: **CS** [Enter]
CS109 Car Stereo

Program Output with Different Example Input Shown in Bold

        Product Database

Enter a product to search for: **AB** [Enter]
No matching product was found.

Table 3 summarizes the string-handling functions discussed here, as well as the `strcmp` function that was discussed in the chapter "Making Decisions". (All the functions listed require the `<cstring>` header file.)

In Program 6, the `for` loop in lines 30 through 35 steps through each C-string in the array calling the following statement:

```
strPtr = strstr(prods[index], lookUp);
```

The `strstr` function searches the string referenced by `prods[index]` for the name entered by the user, which is stored in `lookUp`. If `lookUp` is found inside `prods[index]`, the function returns its address. In that case, the following `if` statement causes the `for` loop to terminate:

```
if (strPtr != nullptr)
     break;
```

Outside the loop, the following `if else` statement in lines 38 through 41 determines whether the string entered by the user was found in the array. If not, it informs the user that no matching product was found. Otherwise, the product number and description are displayed.

```
if (strPtr == nullptr)
     cout << "No matching product was found.\n";
else
     cout << prods[index] << endl;
```

The strcmp Function

Because C-strings are stored in `char` arrays, you cannot use the relational operators to compare two C-strings. To compare C-strings, you should use the library function `strcmp`. This function takes two C-strings as arguments and returns an integer that indicates how the two strings compare to each other. Here is the function's prototype:

```
int strcmp(char *string1, char *string2);
```

The function takes two C-strings as parameters (actually, pointers to C-strings) and returns an integer result. The value of the result is set accordingly:

- The result is *zero* if the two strings are *equal* on a character-by-character basis.
- The result is *negative* if `string1` comes *before* `string2` in alphabetical order.
- The result is *positive* if `string1` comes *after* `string2` in alphabetical order.

Here is an example of the use of `strcmp` to determine if two strings are equal:

```
if (strcmp(string1, string2) == 0)
     cout << "The strings are equal.\n";
else
     cout << "The strings are not equal.\n";
```

Program 7 shows a complete example.

Program 7

```
// This program tests two C-strings for equality
// using the strcmp function.
#include <iostream>
#include <string>
using namespace std;

int main()
{
    // Two arrays for two strings.
    const int LENGTH = 40;
    char firstString[LENGTH], secondString[LENGTH];

```

```
    // Read two strings.
    cout << "Enter a string: ";
    cin.getline(firstString, LENGTH);
    cout << "Enter another string: ";
    cin.getline(secondString, LENGTH);

    // Compare the strings for equality with strcmp.
    if (strcmp(firstString, secondString) == 0)
        cout << "You entered the same string twice.\n";
    else
        cout << "The strings are not the same.\n";

    return 0;
}
```

Program Output with Example Input Shown in Bold

Enter a string: **Alfonso** [Enter]
Enter another string: **Alfonso** [Enter]
You entered the same string twice.

The strcmp function is case sensitive when it compares strings. If the user enters "Dog" and "dog" in Program 7, it will report they are not the same. Most compilers provide nonstandard versions of strcmp that perform case-insensitive comparisons. For instance, some compilers provide a function named stricmp that works identically to strcmp, except the case of the characters is ignored.

Program 8 is a more practical example of how strcmp can be used. It asks the user to enter the part number of the MP3 player they wish to purchase. The part number contains digits, letters, and a hyphen, so it must be stored as a string. Once the user enters the part number, the program displays the price of the stereo.

Program 8

```
// This program uses strcmp to compare the string entered
// by the user with the valid MP3 player part numbers.
#include <iostream>
#include <cstring>
#include <iomanip>
using namespace std;

int main()
{
    // Price of parts.
    const double A_PRICE = 99.0,
                 B_PRICE = 199.0;

    // Character array for part number.
    const int PART_LENGTH = 9;
    char partNum[PART_LENGTH];

```

(program continues)

Program 8 *(continued)*

```
    // Instruct the user to enter a part number.
    cout << "The MP3 player part numbers are:\n"
         << "\t16 Gigabyte, part number S147-29A\n"
         << "\t32 Gigabyte, part number S147-29B\n"
         << "Enter the part number of the MP3 player you\n"
         << "wish to purchase: ";

    // Read a part number of at most 8 characters.
    cin >> partNum;

    // Determine what user entered using strcmp
    // and print its price.
    cout << showpoint << fixed << setprecision(2);
    if (strcmp(partNum, "S147-29A") == 0)
        cout << "The price is $" << A_PRICE << endl;
    else if (strcmp(partNum, "S147-29B") == 0)
        cout << "The price is $" << B_PRICE << endl;
    else
        cout << partNum << " is not a valid part number.\n";
    return 0;
}
```

Program Output with Example Input Shown in Bold

```
The MP3 player part numbers are:
    16 Gigabyte, part number S147-29A
    32 Gigabyte, part number S147-29B
Enter the part number of the stereo you
wish to purchase: S147-29B [Enter]
The price is $199.00
```

Using ! with strcmp

Some programmers prefer to use the logical NOT operator with strcmp when testing strings for equality. Because 0 is considered logically false, the ! operator converts that value to true. The expression !strcmp(string1, string2) returns true when both strings are the same, and false when they are different. The two following statements perform the same operation:

```
if (strcmp(firstString, secondString) == 0)
if (!strcmp(firstString, secondString))
```

Sorting Strings

Programs are frequently written to print alphabetically sorted lists of items. For example, consider a department store computer system that keeps customers' names and addresses in a file. The names do not appear in the file alphabetically, but in the order the operator entered them. If a list were to be printed in this order, it would be very difficult to locate any specific name. The list would have to be sorted before it was printed.

Because the value returned by strcmp is based on the relative alphabetic order of the two strings being compared, it can be used in programs that sort strings. Program 9 asks the user to enter two names, which are then printed in alphabetic order.

Program 9

```
// This program uses the return value of strcmp to
// alphabetically sort two strings entered by the user.
#include <iostream>
#include <string>
using namespace std;

int main()
{
    // Two arrays to hold two strings.
    const int NAME_LENGTH = 30;
    char name1[NAME_LENGTH], name2[NAME_LENGTH];

    // Read two strings.
    cout << "Enter a name (last name first): ";
    cin.getline(name1, NAME_LENGTH);
    cout << "Enter another name: ";
    cin.getline(name2, NAME_LENGTH);

    // Print the two strings in alphabetical order.
    cout << "Here are the names sorted alphabetically:\n";
    if (strcmp(name1, name2) < 0)
        cout << name1 << endl << name2 << endl;
    else if (strcmp(name1, name2) > 0)
        cout << name2 << endl << name1 << endl;
    else
        cout << "You entered the same name twice!\n";

    return 0;
}
```

Program Output with Example Input Shown in Bold

```
Enter a name (last name first): Smith, Richard [Enter]
Enter another name: Jones, John [Enter]
Here are the names sorted alphabetically:
Jones, John
Smith, Richard
```

Table 3 provides a summary of the C-string-handling functions we have discussed. All of the functions listed require the `<cstring>` header file.

Table 3 Some of the C-String Functions in `<cstring>`

Function	Description
`strlen`	Accepts a C-string or a pointer to a C-string as an argument. Returns the length of the C-string (not including the null terminator.) *Example Usage:* `len = strlen(name);`
`strcat`	Accepts two C-strings or pointers to two C-strings as arguments. The function appends the contents of the second string to the first C-string. (The first string is altered, the second string is left unchanged.) *Example Usage:* `strcat(string1, string2);`

(table continues)

Table 3 *(continued)*

Function	Description
strcpy	Accepts two C-strings or pointers to two C-strings as arguments. The function copies the second C-string to the first C-string. The second C-string is left unchanged. *Example Usage:* `strcpy(string1, string2);`
strncat	Accepts two C-strings or pointers to two C-strings, and an integer argument. The third argument, an integer, indicates the maximum number of characters to copy from the second C-string to the first C-string. *Example Usage:* `strncat(string1, string2, n);`
strncpy	Accepts two C-strings or pointers to two C-strings, and an integer argument. The third argument, an integer, indicates the maximum number of characters to copy from the second C-string to the first C-string. If n is less than the length of string2, the null terminator is not automatically appended to string1. If n is greater than the length of string2, string1 is padded with '\0' characters. *Example Usage:* `strncpy(string1, string2, n);`
strcmp	Accepts two C-strings or pointers to two C-strings arguments. If string1 and string2 are the same, this function returns 0. If string2 is alphabetically greater than string1, it returns a negative number. If string2 is alphabetically less than string1, it returns a positive number. *Example Usage:* `if (strcmp(string1, string2))`
strstr	Accepts two C-strings or pointers to two C-strings as arguments. Searches for the first occurrence of string2 in string1. If an occurrence of string2 is found, the function returns a pointer to it. Otherwise, it returns nullptr (address 0). *Example Usage:* `cout << strstr(string1, string2);`

Checkpoint

6 Write a short description of each of the following functions:

```
strlen
strcat
strcpy
strncat
strncpy
strcmp
strstr
```

7 What will the following program segment display?

```
char dog[] = "Fido";
cout << strlen(dog) << endl;
```

8 What will the following program segment display?

```
char string1[16] = "Have a ";
char string2[9] = "nice day";
strcat(string1, string2);
cout << string1 << endl;
cout << string2 << endl;
```

9 Write a statement that will copy the string "Beethoven" to the array `composer`.

10 When complete, the following program skeleton will search for the string "Windy" in the array `place`. If `place` contains "Windy" the program will display the message "Windy found." Otherwise, it will display "Windy not found."

```
#include <iostream>
// include any other necessary header files
using namespace std;

int main()
{
    char place[] = "The Windy City";
    // Complete the program. It should search the array place
    // for the string "Windy" and display the message "Windy
    // found" if it finds the string. Otherwise, it should
    // display the message "Windy not found."
    return 0;
}
```

5 String/Numeric Conversion Functions

CONCEPT: The C++ library provides functions for converting C-strings and `string` objects to numeric data types and vice versa.

There is a great difference between a number that is stored as a string, and one stored as a numeric value. The string "26792" isn't actually a number, but a series of ASCII codes representing the individual digits of the number. It uses 6 bytes of memory (including the null terminator). Because it isn't an actual number, it's not possible to perform mathematical operations with it, unless it is first converted to a numeric value.

Several functions exist in the C++ library for converting C-string representations of numbers into numeric values. Table 4 shows some of these. Note all of these functions require the `<cstdlib>` header file.

Table 4 C-String/Numeric Conversion Functions in `<cstdlib>`

Function	Description
`atoi`	Accepts a C-string as an argument. The function converts the C-string to an integer and returns that value. *Example Usage:* `int num = atoi("4569");`
`atol`	Accepts a C-string as an argument. The function converts the C-string to a `long` integer and returns that value. *Example Usage:* `long lnum = atol("500000");`
`atof`	Accepts a C-string as an argument. The function converts the C-string to a `double` and returns that value. *Example Usage:* `double fnum = atof("3.14159");`

NOTE: If a C-string that cannot be converted to a numeric value is passed to any of the functions in Table 4, the function's behavior is undefined by C++. Many compilers, however, will perform the conversion process until an invalid character is encountered. For example, `atoi("123x5")` might return the integer 123. It is possible that these functions will return 0 if they cannot successfully convert their argument.

The `string` to Number Functions

11

C++ 11 introduced several new functions that convert `string` objects to numeric values. Table 5 lists the functions. To use any of the functions in Table 5, you must `#include` the `<string>` header file.

Table 5 `string` to Number Functions

Function	Description
`stoi(string str)`	Accepts a `string` argument and returns that argument's value converted to an `int`.
`stol(string str)`	Accepts a `string` argument and returns that argument's value converted to a `long`.
`stoul(string str)`	Accepts a `string` argument and returns that argument's value converted to an `unsigned long`.
`stoll(string str)`	Accepts a `string` argument and returns that argument's value converted to a `long long`.
`stoull(string str)`	Accepts a `string` argument and returns that argument's value converted to an `unsigned long long`.
`stof(string str)`	Accepts a `string` argument and returns that argument's value converted to a `float`.
`stod(string str)`	Accepts a `string` argument and returns that argument's value converted to a `double`.
`stold(string str)`	Accepts a `string` argument and returns that argument's value converted to a `long double`.

NOTE: If a `string` that cannot be converted to a numeric value is passed to any of the functions in Table 5, the function will throw an `invalid_argument` exception. If the `string` argument converts to a value that is out of range for the target data type, the function will throw an `out_of_range` exception.

The functions shown in Table 5 can accept either a `string` object or a C-string as an argument. For example, each of the following code snippets use the `stoi` function to convert the string "99" to an `int`:

```
// Convert a string object to an int.
string str = "99";
int i = stoi(str);

// Convert a string literal to an int.
int i = stoi("99");
```

```
// Convert a C-String in a char array to an int.
char cstr[] = "99";
int i = stoi(cstr);
```

The to_string Function

C++ 11 introduces a function named to_string that converts a numeric value to a string object. There are nine overloaded versions of the to_string function listed in Table 6. Note the to_string function requires the <string> header file to be included.

Each version of the function accepts an argument of a numeric data type and returns the value of that argument converted to a string object. Here is an example:

```
int number = 99;
string output = to_string(number);
```

Table 6 Overloaded Versions of the to_string Function

Function	Description
to_string(int *value*);	Accepts an int argument and returns that argument converted to a string object.
to_string(long *value*);	Accepts a long argument and returns that argument converted to a string object.
to_string(long long *value*);	Accepts a long long argument and returns that argument converted to a string object.
to_string(unsigned *value*);	Accepts an unsigned argument and returns that argument converted to a string object.
to_string(unsigned long *value*);	Accepts an unsigned long argument and returns that argument converted to a string object.
to_string(unsigned long long *value*);	Accepts an unsigned long long argument and returns that argument converted to a string object.
to_string(float *value*);	Accepts a float argument and returns that argument converted to a string object.
to_string(double *value*);	Accepts a double argument and returns that argument converted to a string object.
to_string(long double *value*);	Accepts a long double argument and returns that argument converted to a string object.

The first statement initializes the number variable (an int) to the value 99. In the second statement, the number variable is passed as an argument to the to_string function. The to_string function returns the value "99", which is assigned to the output variable.

Here is another example:

```
double number = 3.14159;
cout << to_string(number) << endl;
```

The first statement initializes the number variable (a double) to the value 3.14159. In the second statement, the number variable is passed as an argument to the to_string function, and the value "3.14159" is returned from the function and displayed on the screen.

Now let's look at Program 10, which uses one of the C++ 11 `string`-to-number conversion functions, `stoi`. It allows the user to enter a series of values, or the letter `Q` or `q` to quit. The average of the numbers is then calculated and displayed.

Program 10

```cpp
// This program demonstrates the tolower and stoi functions.
#include <iostream>
#include <cctype>          // For tolower
#include <string>
using namespace std;

int main()
{
   string input;           // To hold user input
   int total = 0;          // Accumulator
   int count = 0;          // Loop counter
   double average;         // To hold the average of numbers

   // Get the first number.
   cout << "This program will average a series of numbers.\n";
   cout << "Enter the first number or Q to quit: ";
   getline(cin, input);

   // Process the number and subsequent numbers.
   while (tolower(input[0]) != 'q')
   {
      total += stoi(input);     // Keep a running total
      count++;                  // Count the numbers entered
      // Get the next number.
      cout << "Enter the next number or Q to quit: ";
      getline(cin, input);
   }

   // If any numbers were entered, display their average.
   if (count != 0)
   {
      average = static_cast<double>(total) / count;
      cout << "Average: " << average << endl;
   }
   return 0;
}
```

Program Output with Example Input Shown in Bold

```
This program will average a series of numbers.
Enter the first number or Q to quit: 1 [Enter]
Enter the next number or Q to quit: 2 [Enter]
Enter the next number or Q to quit: 3 [Enter]
Enter the next number or Q to quit: 4 [Enter]
Enter the next number or Q to quit: 5 [Enter]
Enter the next number or Q to quit: q [Enter]
Average: 3
```

In line 20, the following `while` statement uses the `tolower` function to determine whether the first character entered by the user is "q" or "Q".

```
while (tolower(input[0]) != 'q')
```

If the user hasn't entered 'Q' or 'q', the loop performs an iteration. The following statement, in line 22, uses `stoi` to convert `input` to an integer, and adds its value to `total`:

```
total += stoi(input);     // Keep a running total
```

The counter is updated in line 23, then the user is asked for the next number. When all the numbers are entered, the user terminates the loop by entering 'Q' or 'q'. If one or more numbers are entered, their average is displayed.

The string-to-numeric conversion functions can also help with a common input problem. Using `cin >>` then calling `cin.get` causes problems because the `>>` operator leaves the newline character in the keyboard buffer. When the `cin.get` function executes, the first character it sees in the keyboard buffer is the newline character, so it reads no further.

The same problem exists when a program uses `cin >>` then calls `getline` to read a line of input. For example, look at the following code. (Assume `idNumber` is an `int` and name is a `string` object.)

```
1  // Get the user's ID number.
2  cout << "What is your ID number? ";
3  cin >> idNumber;
4
5  // Get the user's name.
6  cout << "What is your name? ";
7  getline(cin, name);
```

Let's say the user enters 25 and presses [Enter] when the `cin >>` statement in line 3 executes. The value 25 will be stored in `idNumber`, and the newline character will be left in the keyboard buffer. When the `getline` function is called in line 7, the first character it sees in the keyboard buffer is the newline character, so it reads no further. It will appear that the statement in line 7 was skipped.

One work-around that we have used in this chapter is to call `cin.ignore` to skip over the newline character just before calling `getline`. Another approach is to use `getline` to read *all* of a program's input, including numbers. When numeric input is needed, it is read into a `string` object as a string then converted to the appropriate numeric data type. Because you aren't mixing `cin >>` with `getline`, the problem of the remaining newline character doesn't exist. Program 11 shows an example.

Program 11

```
// This program demonstrates how the getline function can
// be used for all of a program's input.
#include <iostream>
#include <string>
#include <iomanip>
using namespace std;

```

(program continues)

Program 11 *(continued)*

```
int main()
{
   string input;          // To hold a line of input
   string name;           // To hold a name
   int idNumber;          // To hold an ID number.
   int age;               // To hold an age
   double income;         // To hold income

   // Get the user's ID number.
   cout << "What is your ID number? ";
   getline(cin, input);                // Read as a string
   idNumber = stoi(input);             // Convert to int

   // Get the user's name. No conversion necessary.
   cout << "What is your name? ";
   getline(cin, name);

   // Get the user's age.
   cout << "How old are you? ";
   getline(cin, input);                // Read as a string
   age = stoi(input);                  // Convert to int

   // Get the user's income.
   cout << "What is your annual income? ";
   getline(cin, input);                // Read as a string
   income = stod(input);               // Convert to double

   // Show the resulting data.
   cout << setprecision(2) << fixed << showpoint;
   cout << "Your name is " << name
        <<", you are " << age
        << " years old,\nand you make $"
        << income << " per year.\n";

   return 0;
}
```

Program Output with Example Input Shown in Bold

What is your ID number? **1234** [Enter]
What is your name? **Janice Smith** [Enter]
How old are you? **25** [Enter]
What is your annual income? **60000** [Enter]
Your name is Janice Smith, you are 25 years old,
and you make $60000.00 per year.

Checkpoint

11 Write a short description of each of the following functions:

`atoi`	`stoi`
`atol`	`stol`
`atof`	`stof`
`itoa`	`stod`

12 Write a statement that will convert the string "`10`" to an integer and store the result in the variable `num`.

13 Write a statement that will convert the string "`100000`" to a `long` and store the result in the variable `num`.

14 Write a statement that will convert the string "`7.2389`" to a `double` and store the result in the variable `num`.

15 Write a statement that will convert the integer 127 to a string, and assign the result to a `string` object named `str`.

6 Focus on Software Engineering: Writing Your Own C-String-Handling Functions

CONCEPT: You can design your own specialized functions for manipulating strings.

VideoNote
Writing a C-String-Handling Function

By being able to pass arrays as arguments, you can write your own functions for processing C-strings. For example, Program 12 uses a function to copy a C-string from one array to another.

Program 12

```
// This program uses a function to copy a C-string into an array.
#include <iostream>
using namespace std;

void stringCopy(char [], char []); // Function prototype

int main()
{
    const int LENGTH = 30;  // Size of the arrays
    char first[LENGTH];     // To hold the user's input
    char second[LENGTH];    // To hold the copy

    // Get a string from the user and store in first.
    cout << "Enter a string with no more than "
         << (LENGTH - 1) << " characters:\n";
    cin.getline(first, LENGTH);

```

(program continues)

Program 12 *(continued)*

```
    // Copy the contents of first to second.
    stringCopy(first, second);

    // Display the copy.
    cout << "The string you entered is:\n" << second << endl;
    return 0;
}

//*********************************************************
// Definition of the stringCopy function.                 *
// This function copies the C-string in string1 to string2.*
//*********************************************************

void stringCopy(char string1[], char string2[])
{
    int index = 0;   // Loop counter

    // Step through string1, copying each element to
    // string2. Stop when the null character is encountered.
    while (string1[index] != '\0')
    {
        string2[index] = string1[index];
        index++;
    }

    // Place a null character in string2.
    string2[index] = '\0';
}
```

Program Output with Example Input Shown in Bold

```
Enter a string with no more than 29 characters:
Thank goodness it's Friday! [Enter]
The string you entered is:
Thank goodness it's Friday!
```

Notice the function `stringCopy` does not accept an argument indicating the size of the arrays. It simply copies the characters from `string1` into `string2` until it encounters a null terminator in `string1`. When the null terminator is found, the loop has reached the end of the C-string. The last statement in the function assigns a null terminator (the `'\0'` character) to the end of `string2`, so it is properly terminated.

> **WARNING!** Because the `stringCopy` function doesn't know the size of the second array, it's the programmer's responsibility to make sure the second array is large enough to hold the string in the first array.

Program 13 uses another C-string-handling function: `nameSlice`. The program asks the user to enter his or her first and last names, separated by a space. The function searches the string for the space and replaces it with a null terminator. In effect, this "cuts" the last name off of the string.

Program 13

```
 1 // This program uses the function nameSlice to cut the last
 2 // name off of a string that contains the user's first and
 3 // last names.
 4 #include <iostream>
 5 using namespace std;
 6
 7 void nameSlice(char []);  // Function prototype
 8
 9 int main()
10 {
11     const int SIZE = 41; // Array size
12     char name[SIZE];     // To hold the user's name
13
14     cout << "Enter your first and last names, separated ";
15     cout << "by a space:\n";
16     cin.getline(name, SIZE);
17     nameSlice(name);
18     cout << "Your first name is: " << name << endl;
19     return 0;
20 }
21
22 //****************************************************************
23 // Definition of function nameSlice. This function accepts a    *
24 // character array as its argument. It scans the array looking *
25 // for a space. When it finds one, it replaces it with a null  *
26 // terminator.                                                 *
27 //****************************************************************
28
29 void nameSlice(char userName[])
30 {
31     int count = 0; // Loop counter
32
33     // Locate the first space, or the null terminator if there
34     // are no spaces.
35     while (userName[count] != ' ' && userName[count] != '\0')
36         count++;
37
38     // If a space was found, replace it with a null terminator.
39     if (userName[count] == ' ')
40         userName[count] = '\0';
41 }
```

Program Output with Example Input Shown in Bold

```
Enter your first and last names, separated by a space:
Jimmy Jones [Enter]
Your first name is: Jimmy
```

The following loop in lines 35 and 36 starts at the first character in the array and scans the string searching for either a space or a null terminator:

```
while (userName[count] != ' ' && userName[count] != '\0')
    count++;
```

If the character in `userName[count]` isn't a space or the null terminator, `count` is incremented, and the next character is examined. With the example input "`Jimmy Jones`," the loop finds the space separating "`Jimmy`" and "`Jones`" at `userName[5]`. When the loop stops, `count` is set to 5. This is illustrated in Figure 3.

Figure 3 Scanning for a space in a string

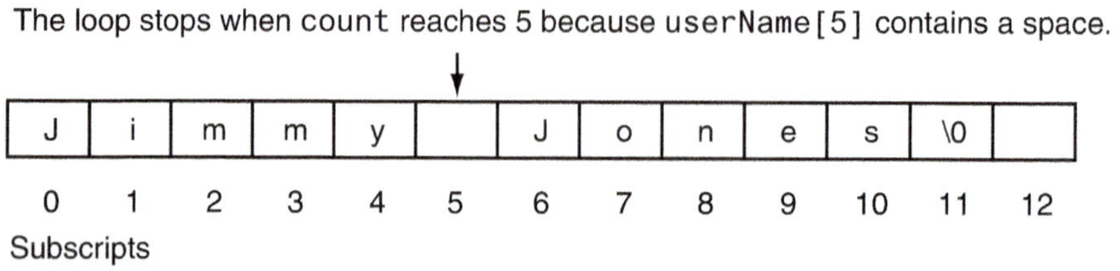

> **NOTE:** The loop will also stop if it encounters a null terminator. This is so it will not go beyond the boundary of the array if the user didn't enter a space.

Once the loop has finished, `userName[count]` will either contain a space or a null terminator. If it contains a space, the following `if` statement (in lines 39 and 40) replaces it with a null terminator:

```
if (userName[count] == ' ')
    userName[count] = '\0';
```

This is illustrated in Figure 4.

Figure 4 Replacing a space with a null terminator

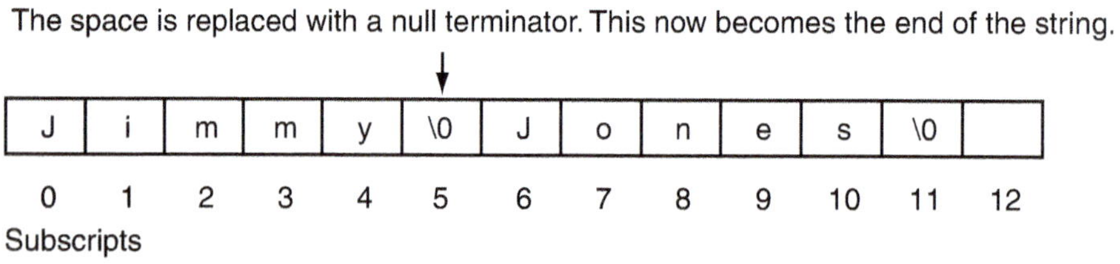

The new null terminator now becomes the end of the string.

Using Pointers to Pass C-String Arguments

Pointers are extremely useful for writing functions that process C-strings. If the starting address of a string is passed into a pointer parameter variable, it can be assumed that all the characters, from that address up to the byte that holds the null terminator, are part of the string. (It isn't necessary to know the length of the array that holds the string.)

Program 14 demonstrates a function, `countChars`, that uses a pointer to count the number of times a specific character appears in a C-string.

Program 14

```
// This program demonstrates a function, countChars, that counts
// the number of times a specific character appears in a string.
#include <iostream>
```

```
using namespace std;

int countChars(char *, char); // Function prototype

int main()
{
    const int SIZE = 51;     // Array size
    char userString[SIZE];   // To hold a string
    char letter;             // The character to count

    // Get a string from the user.
    cout << "Enter a string (up to 50 characters): ";
    cin.getline(userString, SIZE);

    // Choose a character whose occurrences within the string will be counted.
    cout << "Enter a character and I will tell you how many\n";
    cout << "times it appears in the string: ";
    cin >> letter;

    // Display the number of times the character appears.
    cout << letter << " appears ";
    cout << countChars(userString, letter) << " times.\n";
    return 0;
}

//****************************************************************
// Definition of countChars. The parameter strPtr is a pointer   *
// that points to a string. The parameter Ch is a character that *
// the function searches for in the string. The function returns *
// the number of times the character appears in the string.      *
//****************************************************************

int countChars(char *strPtr, char ch)
{
    int times = 0;  // Number of times ch appears in the string

    // Step through the string counting occurrences of ch.
    while (*strPtr != '\0')
    {
        if (*strPtr == ch)      // If the current character equals ch...
            times++;            // ... increment the counter
        strPtr++;               // Go to the next char in the string.
    }

    return times;
}
```

Program Output with Example Input Shown in Bold

Enter a string (up to 50 characters): **Starting Out with C++** [Enter]
Enter a character and I will tell you how many
times it appears in the string: **t** [Enter]
t appears 4 times.

In the function countChars, strPtr points to the C-string that is to be searched, and ch contains the character for which to look. The while loop in lines 41 through 46 repeats as long as the character that strPtr points to is not the null terminator:

```
while (*strPtr != '\0')
```

Inside the loop, the if statement in line 43 compares the character that strPtr points to with the character in ch:

```
if (*strPtr == ch)
```

If the two are equal, the variable times is incremented in line 44. (times keeps a running total of the number of times the character appears.) The last statement in the loop is

```
strPtr++;
```

This statement increments the address in strPtr. This causes strPtr to point to the next character in the string. Then, the loop starts over. When strPtr finally reaches the null terminator, the loop terminates, and the function returns the value in times.

For another example, see the String Manipulation Case Study, available for download from the Computer Science Portal at www.pearsonhighered.com/gaddis.

Checkpoint

16 What is the output of the following program?

```
#include <iostream>
using namespace std;

// Function Prototype
void mess(char []);

int main()
{
   char stuff[] = "Tom Talbert Tried Trains";
   cout << stuff << endl;
   mess(stuff);
   cout << stuff << endl;
   return 0;
}

// Definition of function mess
void mess(char str[])
{
   int step = 0;

   while (str[step] != '\0')
   {
      if (str[step] == 'T')
         str[step] = 'D';
      step++;
   }
}
```

7 More about the C++ `string` Class

CONCEPT: Standard C++ provides a special data type for storing and working with strings.

VideoNote
More about the `string` Class

The `string` class is an abstract data type. This means it is not a built-in, primitive data type like `int` or `char`. Instead, it is a programmer-defined data type that accompanies the C++ language. It provides many capabilities that make storing and working with strings easy and intuitive.

Using the `string` Class

The first step in using the `string` class is to `#include` the `<string>` header file. This is accomplished with the following preprocessor directive:

```
#include <string>
```

Now you are ready to define a `string` object. Defining a `string` object is similar to defining a variable of a primitive type. For example, the following statement defines a `string` object named `movieTitle`:

```
string movieTitle;
```

You assign a string value to the `movieTitle` object with the assignment operator, as shown in the following statement:

```
movieTitle = "Wheels of Fury";
```

The contents of `movieTitle` are displayed on the screen with the `cout` object, as shown in the next statement:

```
cout << "My favorite movie is " << movieTitle << endl;
```

Program 15 is a complete program that demonstrates the statements shown above.

Program 15

```
// This program demonstrates the string class.
#include <iostream>
#include <string>     // Required for the string class.
using namespace std;

int main()
{
    string movieTitle;

    movieTitle = "Wheels of Fury";
    cout << "My favorite movie is " << movieTitle << endl;
    return 0;
}
```

Program Output

```
My favorite movie is Wheels of Fury
```

As you can see, working with string objects is similar to working with variables of other types. For example, Program 16 demonstrates how you can use cin to read a value from the keyboard into a string object.

Program 16

```
// This program demonstrates how cin can read a string into
// a string class object.
#include <iostream>
#include <string>
using namespace std;

int main()
{
    string name;

    cout << "What is your name? ";
    cin >> name;
    cout << "Good morning " << name << endl;
    return 0;
}
```

Program Output with Example Input Shown in Bold

```
What is your name? Peggy [Enter]
Good morning Peggy
```

Reading a Line of Input into a string Object

If you want to read a line of input (with spaces) into a string object, use the getline() function. Here is an example:

```
string name;
cout << "What is your name? ";
getline(cin, name);
```

The getline() function's first argument is the name of a stream object from which you wish to read the input. The function call above passes the cin object to getline(), so the function reads a line of input from the keyboard. The second argument is the name of a string object. This is where getline() stores the input that it reads.

Comparing and Sorting string Objects

There is no need to use a function such as strcmp to compare string objects. You may use the <, >, <=, >=, ==, and != relational operators. For example, assume the following definitions exist in a program:

```
string set1 = "ABC";
string set2 = "XYZ";
```

The object set1 is considered less than the object set2 because the characters "ABC" alphabetically precede the characters "XYZ." So, the following if statement will cause the message "set1 is less than set2" to be displayed on the screen:

```
if (set1 < set2)
   cout << "set1 is less than set2.\n";
```

Relational operators perform comparisons on string objects in a fashion similar to the way the strcmp function compares C-strings. One by one, each character in the first operand is compared with the character in the corresponding position in the second operand. If all the characters in both strings match, the two strings are equal. Other relationships can be determined if two characters in corresponding positions do not match. The first operand is less than the second operand if the mismatched character in the first operand is less than its counterpart in the second operand. Likewise, the first operand is greater than the second operand if the mismatched character in the first operand is greater than its counterpart in the second operand.

For example, assume a program has the following definitions:

```
string name1 = "Mary";
string name2 = "Mark";
```

The value in name1, "Mary," is greater than the value in name2, "Mark." This is because the "y" in "Mary" has a greater ASCII value than the "k" in "Mark."

string objects can also be compared to C-strings with relational operators. Assuming str is a string object, all of the following are valid relational expressions:

```
str > "Joseph"
"Kimberly" < str
str == "William"
```

Program 17 demonstrates string objects and relational operators.

Program 17

```
// This program uses the == operator to compare a string entered
// by the user with the valid part numbers.
#include <iostream>
#include <iomanip>
#include <string>
using namespace std;

int main()
{
   const double APRICE = 249.0;    // Price for part A
   const double BPRICE = 199.0;    // Price for part B
   string partNum;                 // Part mumber

   cout << "The headphone part numbers are:\n";
   cout << "\tNoise canceling, part number S147-29A\n";
   cout << "\tWireless, part number S147-29B\n";
   cout << "Enter the part number of the desired headphones: ";
   cin >> partNum;
   cout << fixed << showpoint << setprecision(2);

   if (partNum == "S147-29A")
      cout << "The price is $" << APRICE << endl;
   else if (partNum == "S147-29B")
      cout << "The price is $" << BPRICE << endl;
   else
      cout << partNum << " is not a valid part number.\n";
```

(program continues)

Program 17 *(continued)*

```
    return 0;
}
```

Program Output with Example Input Shown in Bold

```
The headphone part numbers are:
        Noise canceling, part number S147-29A
        Wireless, part number S147-29B
Enter the part number of the desired headphones: S147-29B [Enter]
The price is $199.00
```

You may also use relational operators to sort string objects. Program 18 demonstrates this.

Program 18

```
// This program uses relational operators to alphabetically
// sort two strings entered by the user.
#include <iostream>
#include <string>
using namespace std;

int main ()
{
    string name1, name2;

    // Get a name.
    cout << "Enter a name (last name first): ";
    getline(cin, name1);

    // Get another name.
    cout << "Enter another name: ";
    getline(cin, name2);

    // Display them in alphabetical order.
    cout << "Here are the names sorted alphabetically:\n";
    if (name1 < name2)
        cout << name1 << endl << name2 << endl;
    else if (name1 > name2)
        cout << name2 << endl << name1 << endl;
    else
        cout << "You entered the same name twice!\n";
    return 0;
}
```

Program Output with Example Input Shown in Bold

```
Enter a name (last name first): Smith, Richard [Enter]
Enter another name: Jones, John [Enter]
Here are the names sorted alphabetically:
Jones, John
Smith, Richard
```

Other Ways to Define `string` Objects

There are a variety of ways to initialize a `string` object when you define it. Table 7 shows several example definitions and describes each. Program 19 demonstrates a `string` object initialized with the string "William Smith."

Program 19

```
1  // This program initializes a string object.
2  #include <iostream>
3  #include <string>
4  using namespace std;
5
6  int main()
7  {
8     string greeting;
9     string name("William Smith");
10
11    greeting = "Hello ";
12    cout << greeting << name << endl;
13    return 0;
14 }
```

Program Output

```
Hello William Smith
```

Table 7 Examples of `string` Object Definitions

Definition	Description
`string address;`	Defines an empty `string` object named `address`.
`string name("William Smith");`	Defines a `string` object named `name`, initialized with "William Smith."
`string person1(person2);`	Defines a `string` object named `person1`, which is a copy of `person2`. `person2` may be either a `string` object or character array.
`string str1(str2, 5);`	Defines a `string` object named `str1`, which is initialized to the first five characters in the character array `str2`.
`string lineFull('z', 10);`	Defines a `string` object named `lineFull` initialized with 10 `'z'` characters.
`string firstName(fullName, 0, 7);`	Defines a `string` object named `firstName`, initialized with a substring of the `string fullName`. The substring is seven characters long, beginning at position 0.

Notice in Program 19 the use of the = operator to assign a value to the `string` object (line 11). The `string` class supports several operators, which are described in Table 8.

Table 8 string Class Operators

Supported Operator	Description
>>	Extracts characters from a stream and inserts them into the string. Characters are copied until a whitespace or the end of the string is encountered.
<<	Inserts the string into a stream.
=	Assigns the string on the right to the string object on the left.
+=	Appends a copy of the string on the right to the string object on the left.
+	Returns a string that is the concatenation of the two string operands.
[]	Implements array-subscript notation, as in name[x]. A reference to the character in the x position is returned.
Relational Operators	Each of the relational operators is implemented: `< > <= >= == ! =`

Program 20 demonstrates some of the string operators.

Program 20

```
// This program demonstrates the C++ string class.
#include <iostream>
#include <string>
using namespace std;

int main ()
{
    // Define three string objects.
    string str1, str2, str3;

    // Assign values to all three.
    str1 = "ABC";
    str2 = "DEF";
    str3 = str1 + str2;

    // Display all three.
    cout << str1 << endl;
    cout << str2 << endl;
    cout << str3 << endl;

    // Concatenate a string onto str3 and display it.
    str3 += "GHI";
    cout << str3 << endl;
    return 0;
}
```

Program Output

```
ABC
DEF
ABCDEF
ABCDEFGHI
```

Using string Class Member Functions

The string class also has member functions. For example, the length member function returns the length of the string stored in the object. The value is returned as an unsigned integer.

Assume the following string object definition exists in a program:

```
string town = "Charleston";
```

The following statement in the same program would assign the value 10 to the variable x.

```
x = town.length();
```

Program 21 further demonstrates the length member function.

Program 21

```
// This program demonstrates a string
// object's length member function.
#include <iostream>
#include <string>
using namespace std;

int main ()
{
    string town;

    cout << "Where do you live? ";
    cin >> town;
    cout << "Your town's name has " << town.length() ;
    cout << " characters\n";
    return 0;
}
```

Program Output with Example Input Shown in Bold

```
Where do you live? Jacksonville [Enter]
Your town's name has 12 characters
```

The size function also returns the length of the string. It is demonstrated in the for loop in Program 22.

Program 22

```
// This program demonstrates the C++ string class.
#include <iostream>
#include <string>
using namespace std;

int main()
{
    // Define three string objects.
    string str1, str2, str3;

    // Assign values to all three.
```

(program continues)

Program 22 *(continued)*

```
    str1 = "ABC";
    str2 = "DEF";
    str3 = str1 + str2;

    // Use subscripts to display str3 one character
    // at a time.
    for (int x = 0; x < str3.size(); x++)
        cout << str3[x];
    cout << endl;

    // Compare str1 with str2.
    if (str1 < str2)
        cout << "str1 is less than str2\n";
    else
        cout << "str1 is not less than str2\n";
    return 0;
}
```

Program Output

```
ABCDEF
str1 is less than str2
```

Table 9 lists many of the `string` class member functions and their overloaded variations. In the examples, assume `mystring` is the name of a `string` object.

Table 9 `string` Class Member Functions

Member Function Example	Description
`mystring.append(n, 'z')`	Appends n copies of `'z'` to `mystring`.
`mystring.append(str)`	Appends `str` to `mystring`. `str` can be a `string` object or character array.
`mystring.append(str, n)`	The first n characters of the character array `str` are appended to `mystring`.
`mystring.append(str, x, n)`	n number of characters from `str`, starting at position x, are appended to `mystring`. If `mystring` is too small, the function will copy as many characters as possible.
`mystring.assign(n, 'z')`	Assigns n copies of `'z'` to `mystring`.
`mystring.assign(str)`	Assigns `str` to `mystring`. `str` can be a `string` object or character array.
`mystring.assign(str, n)`	The first n characters of the character array `str` are assigned to `mystring`.
`mystring.assign(str, x, n)`	n number of characters from `str`, starting at position x, are assigned to `mystring`. If `mystring` is too small, the function will copy as many characters as possible.
`mystring.at(x)`	Returns the character at position x in the `string`.
`mystring.back()`	Returns the last character in the `string`. (This member function was introduced in C++ 11.)

Table 9 *(continued)*

Member Function Example	Description
`mystring.begin()`	Returns an iterator pointing to the first character in the `string`.
`mystring.c_str()`	Converts the contents of `mystring` to a C-string, and returns a pointer to the C-string.
`mystring.capacity()`	Returns the size of the storage allocated for the `string`.
`mystring.clear()`	Clears the `string` by deleting all the characters stored in it.
`mystring.compare(str)`	Performs a comparison like the `strcmp` function), with the same return values. `str` can be a `string` object or a character array.
`mystring.compare(x, n, str)`	Compares `mystring` and `str`, starting at position `x`, and continuing for `n` characters. The return value is like `strcmp`. `str` can be a `string` object or character array.
`mystring.copy(str, x, n)`	Copies the character array `str` to `mystring`, beginning at position `x`, for `n` characters. If `mystring` is too small, the function will copy as many characters as possible.
`mystring.empty()`	Returns `true` if `mystring` is empty.
`mystring.end()`	Returns an iterator pointing to the last character of the string in `mystring`.
`mystring.erase(x, n)`	Erases `n` characters from `mystring`, beginning at position `x`.
`mystring.find(str, x)`	Returns the first position at or beyond position `x` where the string `str` is found in `mystring`. `str` may be either a `string` object or a character array.
`mystring.find('z', x)`	Returns the first position at or beyond position `x` where `'z'` is found in `mystring`. If `'z'` is not found, the function returns the special value `string::npos`.
11 `mystring.front()`	Returns the first character in the `string`. (This member function was introduced in C++ 11.)
`mystring.insert(x, n, 'z')`	Inserts `'z'` `n` times into `mystring` at position `x`.
`mystring.insert(x, str)`	Inserts a copy of `str` into `mystring`, beginning at position `x`. `str` may be either a `string` object or a character array.
`mystring.length()`	Returns the length of the string in `mystring`.
`mystring.replace(x, n, str)`	Replaces the `n` characters in `mystring` beginning at position `x` with the characters in string object `str`.
`mystring.resize(n, 'z')`	Changes the size of the allocation in `mystring` to `n`. If `n` is less than the current size of the string, the string is truncated to `n` characters. If `n` is greater, the string is expanded and `'z'` is appended at the end enough times to fill the new spaces.
`mystring.size()`	Returns the length of the string in `mystring`.
`mystring.substr(x, n)`	Returns a copy of a substring. The substring is `n` characters long and begins at position `x` of `mystring`.
`mystring.swap(str)`	Swaps the contents of `mystring` with `str`.

In the Spotlight:

String Tokenizing

Sometimes a string will contain a series of words or other items of data separated by spaces or other characters. For example, look at the following string:

```
"peach raspberry strawberry vanilla"
```

This string contains the following four items of data: `peach`, `raspberry`, `strawberry`, and `vanilla`. In programming terms, items such as these are known as *tokens*. Notice a space appears between the items. The character that separates tokens is known as a *delimiter*. Here is another example:

```
"17;92;81;12;46;5"
```

This string contains the following tokens: `17`, `92`, `81`, `12`, `46`, and `5`. Notice a semicolon appears between each item. In this example, the semicolon is used as a delimiter. Some programming problems require you to read a string that contains a list of items then extract all of the tokens from the string for processing. For example, look at the following string that contains a date:

```
"3-22-2018"
```

The tokens in this string are `3`, `22`, and `2018`, and the delimiter is the hyphen character. Perhaps a program needs to extract the month, day, and year from such a string. Another example is an operating system pathname, such as the following:

```
/home/rsullivan/data
```

The tokens in this string are `home`, `rsullivan`, and `data`, and the delimiter is the '`/`' character. Perhaps a program needs to extract all of the directory names from such a pathname. The process of breaking a string into tokens is known as *tokenizing*, or *splitting* a string.

The following function, `split`, shows an example of how we can split a string into tokens. The function has three parameters:

- `s`—the string that we want to split into tokens
- `delim`—the character that is used as a delimiter
- `tokens`—a vector that will hold the tokens once they are extracted

```
void split(const string& s, char delim, vector<string>& tokens)
{
    int tokenStart = 0;  // Starting position of the next token

    // Find the first occurrence of the delimiter.
    int delimPosition = s.find(delim);

    // While we haven't run out of delimiters...
    while (delimPosition != string::npos)
    {
        // Extract the token.
        string tok = s.substr(tokenStart, delimPosition - tokenStart);

        // Push the token onto the tokens vector.
        tokens.push_back(tok);
```

```
16
17         // Move delimPosition to the next character position.
18         delimPosition++;
19
20         // Move tokenStart to delmiPosition.
21         tokenStart = delimPosition;
22
23         // Find the next occurrence of the delimiter.
24         delimPosition = s.find(delim, delimPosition);
25
26         // If no more delimiters, extract the last token.
27         if (delimPosition == string::npos)
28         {
29             // Extract the token.
30             string tok = s.substr(tokenStart, delimPosition - tokenStart);
31
32             // Push the token onto the vector.
33             tokens.push_back(tok);
34         }
35     }
36 }
```

Let's take a closer look at the code:

- The `tokenStart` variable defined in line 3 will be used to hold the starting position of the next token. This variable is initialized with 0, assuming the first token starts at position 0.
- In line 6, we call the `s.find()` function, passing `delim` as an argument. The function will return the position of the first occurrence of `delim` in `s`. That value is assigned to the `delimPosition` variable. Note if the `find()` member function does not find the specified delimiter, it will return the special constant `string::npos` (which is defined as –1).
- The `while` loop that begins in line 9 iterates as long as `delimPosition` is not equal to `string::npos`.
- Inside the `while` loop, line 12 extracts the substring beginning at `tokenStart`, and continuing up to the delimiter. The substring, which is a token, is assigned to the `tok` object.
- In line 15, we push the `tok` object to the back of the `tokens` vector.
- Now we are ready to find the next token. Line 18 increments `delimPosition`, and line 21 sets `tokenStart` to the same value as `delimPosition`.
- Line 24 calls the `s.find()` function, passing `delim` and `delimPosition` as arguments. The function will return the position of the next occurrence of `delim`, appearing at or after `delimPosition`. That value is assigned to the `delimPosition` variable. If the specified delimiter is not found, the `find()` member function will return the constant `string::npos`. When that happens in this statement, it means we are processing the last token in the string.
- The `if` statement that starts in line 27 determines whether `delimPosition` is equal to `string::npos`. As previously stated, if this is true, it means we are processing the last token. If that is the case, line 30 extracts the token and assigns it to `tok`, and line 33 pushes `tok` to the back of the `tokens` vector.

Program 23 demonstrates the `split` function.

Program 23

```
#include <iostream>
#include <string>
#include <vector>
using namespace std;

// Function prototype
void split(const string&, char, vector<string>&);

int main()
{
   // Strings to tokenize
   string str1 = "one two three four";
   string str2 = "10:20:30:40:50";
   string str3 = "a/b/c/d/e/f";

   // vector to hold the tokens.
   vector<string> tokens;

   // Tokenize str1, using ' ' as the delimiter.
   split(str1, ' ', tokens);
   for (auto e : tokens)
      cout << e << " ";
   cout << endl;
   tokens.clear();

   // Tokenize str2, using ':' as the delimiter.
   split(str2, ':', tokens);
   for (auto e : tokens)
      cout << e << " ";
   cout << endl;
   tokens.clear();

   // Tokenize str3, using '/' as the delimiter.
   split(str3, '/', tokens);
   for (auto e : tokens)
      cout << e << " ";
   cout << endl;
   return 0;
}
```

The split function is not shown here.

Program Output

```
one two three four
10 20 30 40 50
a b c d e f
```

8 Focus on Problem Solving and Program Design: A Case Study

As a programmer for the Home Software Company, you are asked to develop a function named `dollarFormat` that inserts commas and a $ sign at the appropriate locations in a `string` object containing an unformatted dollar amount. As an argument, the function should accept a reference to a `string` object. You may assume the `string` object contains a value such as 1084567.89. The function should modify the `string` object so it contains a formatted dollar amount, such as $1,084,567.89.

The code for the `dollarFormat` function is as follows:

```
void dollarFormat(string &currency)
{
   int dp;
   dp = currency.find('.');    // Find decimal point
   if (dp > 3)                 // Insert commas
   {
      for (int x = dp - 3; x > 0; x -= 3)
         currency.insert(x, ",");
   }
   currency.insert(0, "$");    // Insert dollar sign
}
```

The function defines an `int` variable named `dp`. This variable is used to hold the position of the unformatted number's decimal point. This is accomplished with the statement:

```
dp = currency.find('.');
```

The `string` class's `find` member function returns the position number in the string where the '.' character is found. An `if` statement determines if the number has more than three numbers preceding the decimal point:

```
if (dp > 3)
```

If the decimal point is at a position greater than 3, then the function inserts commas in the string with the following loop:

```
for (int x = dp - 3; x > 0; x -= 3)
    currency.insert(x, ",");
```

Finally, a $ symbol is inserted at position 0 (the first character in the `string`).

Program 24 demonstrates the function.

Program 24

```
// This program lets the user enter a number. The
// dollarFormat function formats the number as
// a dollar amount.
#include <iostream>
#include <string>
using namespace std;

// Function prototype
```

(program continues)

Program 24 *(continued)*

```
void dollarFormat(string &);

int main ()
{
    string input;

    // Get the dollar amount from the user.
    cout << "Enter a dollar amount in the form nnnnn.nn : ";
    cin >> input;
    dollarFormat(input);
    cout << "Here is the amount formatted:\n";
    cout << input << endl;
    return 0;
}

//************************************************************
// Definition of the dollarFormat function. This function   *
// accepts a string reference object, which is assumed      *
// to hold a number with a decimal point. The function      *
// formats the number as a dollar amount with commas and    *
// a $ symbol.                                              *
//************************************************************

void dollarFormat(string &currency)
{
    int dp;

    dp = currency.find('.');     // Find decimal point
    if (dp > 3)                  // Insert commas
    {
       for (int x = dp - 3; x > 0; x -= 3)
           currency.insert(x, ",");
    }
    currency.insert(0, "$");     // Insert dollar sign
}
```

Program Output with Example Input Shown in Bold

```
Enter a dollar amount in the form nnnnn.nn: 1084567.89 [Enter]
Here is the amount formatted:
$1,084,567.89
```

Review Questions and Exercises

Short Answer

1. What header file must you include in a program using character-testing functions such as `isalpha` and `isdigit`?
2. What header file must you include in a program using the character conversion functions `toupper` and `tolower`?

3. Assume c is a char variable. What value does c hold after each of the following statements executes?

Statement	Contents of c
`c = toupper('a');`	________
`c = toupper('B');`	________
`c = tolower('D');`	________
`c = toupper('e');`	________

4. Look at the following code. What value will be stored in s after the code executes?

```
char name[10];
int s;
strcpy(name, "Jimmy");
s = strlen(name);
```

5. What header file must you include in a program using string functions such as strlen and strcpy?
6. What header file must you include in a program using string/numeric conversion functions such as atoi and atof?
7. What header file must you include in a program using string class objects?
8. How do you compare string class objects?

Fill-in-the-Blank

9. The ________ function returns true if the character argument is uppercase.
10. The ________ function returns true if the character argument is a letter of the alphabet.
11. The ________ function returns true if the character argument is a digit.
12. The ________ function returns true if the character argument is a whitespace character.
13. The ________ function returns the uppercase equivalent of its character argument.
14. The ________ function returns the lowercase equivalent of its character argument.
15. The ________ file must be included in a program that uses character-testing functions.
16. The ________ function returns the length of a string.
17. To ________ two strings means to append one string to the other.
18. The ________ function concatenates two strings.
19. The ________ function copies one string to another.
20. The ________ function searches for a string inside of another one.
21. The ________ function compares two strings.
22. The ________ function copies, at most, *n* number of characters from one string to another.
23. The ________ function returns the value of a string converted to an integer.
24. The ________ function returns the value of a string converted to a long integer.
25. The ________ function returns the value of a string converted to a float.
26. The ________ function converts an integer to a string.

Algorithm Workbench

27. The following `if` statement determines whether choice is equal to `'Y'` or `'y'`:

```
if (choice == 'Y' || choice == 'y')
```

Simplify this statement by using either the `toupper` or `tolower` function.

28. Assume `input` is a `char` array holding a C-string. Write code that counts the number of elements in the array that contain an alphabetic character.

29. Look at the following array definition:

```
char str[10];
```

Assume `name` is also a `char` array, and it holds a C-string. Write code that copies the contents of `name` to `str` if the C-string in `name` is not too big to fit in `str`.

30. Look at the following statements:

```
char str[] = "237.89";
double value;
```

Write a statement that converts the string in `str` to a `double` and stores the result in `value`.

31. Write a function that accepts a pointer to a C-string as its argument. The function should count the number of times the character 'w' occurs in the argument and return that number.

32. Assume `str1` and `str2` are string class objects. Write code that displays "They are the same!" if the two objects contain the same string.

True or False

33. T F Character-testing functions, such as `isupper`, accept strings as arguments and test each character in the string.
34. T F If `toupper`'s argument is already uppercase, it is returned as is, with no changes.
35. T F If `tolower`'s argument is already lowercase, it will be inadvertently converted to uppercase.
36. T F The `strlen` function returns the size of the array containing a string.
37. T F If the starting address of a C-string is passed into a pointer parameter, it can be assumed that all the characters, from that address up to the byte that holds the null terminator, are part of the string.
38. T F C-string-handling functions accept as arguments pointers to strings (array names or pointer variables), or literal strings.
39. T F The `strcat` function checks to make sure the first string is large enough to hold both strings before performing the concatenation.
40. T F The `strcpy` function will overwrite the contents of its first string argument.
41. T F The `strcpy` function performs no bounds checking on the first argument.
42. T F There is no difference between "847" and 847.

Find the Errors

Each of the following programs or program segments has errors. Find as many as you can.

43.
```
char str[] = "Stop";
if (isupper(str) == "STOP")
    exit(0);
```

44.
```
char numeric[5];
int x = 123;
numeric = atoi(x);
```

45.
```
char string1[] = "Billy";
char string2[] = " Bob Jones";
strcat(string1, string2);
```

46.
```
char x = 'a', y = 'a';
if (strcmp(x, y) == 0)
    exit(0);
```

Programming Challenges

1. String Length

Write a function that returns an integer and accepts a pointer to a C-string as an argument. The function should count the number of characters in the string and return that number. Demonstrate the function in a simple program that asks the user to input a string, passes it to the function, then displays the function's return value.

VideoNote
Solving the Backward String Problem

2. Backward String

Write a function that accepts a pointer to a C-string as an argument and displays its contents backward. For instance, if the string argument is `"Gravity"` the function should display `"ytivarG"`. Demonstrate the function in a program that asks the user to input a string then passes it to the function.

3. Word Counter

Write a function that accepts a pointer to a C-string as an argument and returns the number of words contained in the string. For instance, if the string argument is "Four score and seven years ago" the function should return the number 6. Demonstrate the function in a program that asks the user to input a string then passes it to the function. The number of words in the string should be displayed on the screen. *Optional Exercise:* Write an overloaded version of this function that accepts a `string` class object as its argument.

4. Average Number of Letters

Modify the program you wrote for Programming Challenge 3 (Word Counter), so it also displays the average number of letters in each word.

5. Sentence Capitalizer

Write a function that accepts a pointer to a C-string as an argument and capitalizes the first character of each sentence in the string. For instance, if the string argument is `"hello. my name is Joe. what is your name?"` the function should manipulate the string so that it contains `"Hello. My name is Joe. What is your name?"`

Demonstrate the function in a program that asks the user to input a string then passes it to the function. The modified string should be displayed on the screen. *Optional Exercise:* Write an overloaded version of this function that accepts a `string` class object as its argument.

6. Vowels and Consonants

Write a function that accepts a pointer to a C-string as its argument. The function should count the number of vowels appearing in the string and return that number.

Write another function that accepts a pointer to a C-string as its argument. This function should count the number of consonants appearing in the string and return that number.

Demonstrate these two functions in a program that performs the following steps:

1. The user is asked to enter a string.
2. The program displays the following menu:
   A) Count the number of vowels in the string
   B) Count the number of consonants in the string
   C) Count both the vowels and consonants in the string
   D) Enter another string
   E) Exit the program
3. The program performs the operation selected by the user and repeats until the user selects E to exit the program.

7. Name Arranger

Write a program that asks for the user's first, middle, and last names. The names should be stored in three different character arrays. The program should then store, in a fourth array, the name arranged in the following manner: the last name followed by a comma and a space, followed by the first name and a space, followed by the middle name. For example, if the user entered `"Carol Lynn Smith"`, it should store `"Smith, Carol Lynn"` in the fourth array. Display the contents of the fourth array on the screen.

8. Sum of Digits in a String

Write a program that asks the user to enter a series of single-digit numbers with nothing separating them. Read the input as a C-string or a `string` object. The program should display the sum of all the single-digit numbers in the string. For example, if the user enters 2514, the program should display 12, which is the sum of 2, 5, 1, and 4. The program should also display the highest and lowest digits in the string.

9. Most Frequent Character

Write a function that accepts either a pointer to a C-string, or a `string` object, as its argument. The function should return the character that appears most frequently in the string. Demonstrate the function in a complete program.

10. `replaceSubstring` Function

Write a function named `replaceSubstring`. The function should accept three C-string or `string` object arguments. Let's call them *`string1`*, *`string2`*, and *`string3`*. It should search *`string1`* for all occurrences of *`string2`*. When it finds an occurrence of *string2*, it should replace it with *string3*. For example, suppose the three arguments have the following values:

string1:	"the dog jumped over the fence"
string2:	"the"
string3:	"that"

With these three arguments, the function would return a `string` object with the value "that dog jumped over that fence." Demonstrate the function in a complete program.

11. Case Manipulator

Write a program with three functions: `upper`, `lower`, and `reverse`. The `upper` function should accept a pointer to a C-string as an argument. It should step through each character in the string, converting it to uppercase. The `lower` function, too, should accept a pointer to a C-string as an argument. It should step through each character in the string, converting it to lowercase. Like `upper` and `lower`, `reverse` should also accept a pointer to a string. As it steps through the string, it should test each character to determine whether it is uppercase or lowercase. If a character is uppercase, it should be converted to lowercase. Likewise, if a character is lowercase, it should be converted to uppercase.

Test the functions by asking for a string in function `main`, then passing it to them in the following order: `reverse`, `lower`, and `upper`.

12. Password Verifier

Imagine you are developing a software package that requires users to enter their own passwords. Your software requires that users' passwords meet the following criteria:

- The password should be at least six characters long.
- The password should contain at least one uppercase and at least one lowercase letter.
- The password should have at least one digit.

Write a program that asks for a password then verifies that it meets the stated criteria. If it doesn't, the program should display a message telling the user why.

13. Date Printer

Write a program that reads a string from the user containing a date in the form mm/dd/yyyy. It should print the date in the form March 12, 2018.

14. Word Separator

Write a program that accepts as input a sentence in which all of the words are run together, but the first character of each word is uppercase. Convert the sentence to a string in which the words are separated by spaces and only the first word starts with an uppercase letter. For example, the string "StopAndSmellTheRoses." would be converted to "Stop and smell the roses."

15. Character Analysis

If you have downloaded this chapter's source code, you will find a file named text.txt in the Chapter 10 folder. Write a program that reads the file's contents and determines the following:

- The number of uppercase letters in the file
- The number of lowercase letters in the file
- The number of digits in the file

16. Pig Latin

Write a program that reads a sentence as input and converts each word to "Pig Latin." In one version, to convert a word to Pig Latin, you remove the first letter and place that letter at the end of the word. Then you append the string "ay" to the word. Here is an example:

English: I SLEPT MOST OF THE NIGHT
Pig Latin: IAY LEPTSAY OSTMAY FOAY HETAY IGHTNAY

17. Morse Code Converter

Morse code is a code where each letter of the English alphabet, each digit, and various punctuation characters are represented by a series of dots and dashes. Table 10 shows part of the code.

Write a program that asks the user to enter a string then converts that string to Morse code.

Table 10 Morse Code

Character	Code	Character	Code	Character	Code	Character	Code
space	*space*	6	-....	G	--.	Q	--.-
comma	--..--	7	--...	H	....	R	.-.
period	.-.-.-	8	---..	I	..	S	...
question mark	..--..	9	----.	J	.---	T	-
0	-----	A	.-	K	-.-	U	..-
1	.----	B	-...	L	.-..	V	...-
2	..---	C	-.-.	M	--	W	.--
3	...--	D	-..	N	-.	X	-..-
4	....-	E	.	O	---	Y	-.--
5	.....	F	..-.	P	.--.	Z	--..

18. Phone Number List

Write a program that has an array of at least 10 `string` objects that hold people's names and phone numbers. You may make up your own strings, or use the following:

```
"Alejandra Cruz, 555-1223"
"Joe Looney, 555-0097"
"Geri Palmer, 555-8787"
"Li Chen, 555-1212"
"Holly Gaddis, 555-8878"
"Sam Wiggins, 555-0998"
"Bob Kain, 555-8712"
"Tim Haynes, 555-7676"
"Warren Gaddis, 555-9037"
"Jean James, 555-4939"
"Ron Palmer, 555-2783"
```

The program should ask the user to enter a name or partial name to search for in the array. Any entries in the array that match the string entered should be displayed. For example, if the user enters `"Palmer"` the program should display the following names from the list:

```
Geri Palmer, 555-8787
Ron Palmer, 555-2783
```

19. Check Writer

Write a program that displays a simulated paycheck. The program should ask the user to enter the date, the payee's name, and the amount of the check (up to $10,000). It should then display a simulated check with the dollar amount spelled out, as shown here:

```
                                                     Date: 11/24/2018

Pay to the Order of: John Phillips                  $1920.85

One thousand nine hundred twenty and 85 cents
```

Be sure to format the numeric value of the check in fixed-point notation with two decimal places of precision. Be sure the decimal place always displays, even when the number is zero or has no fractional part. Use either C-strings or `string` class objects in this program.

Input Validation: Do not accept negative dollar amounts, or amounts over $10,000.

20. Lottery Statistics

To play the PowerBall lottery, you buy a ticket that has five numbers in the range of 1–69, and a "PowerBall" number in the range of 1-26. (You can pick the numbers yourself, or you can let the ticket machine randomly pick them for you.) Then, on a specified date, a winning set of numbers are randomly selected by a machine. If your first five numbers match the first five winning numbers in any order, and your PowerBall number matches the winning PowerBall number, then you win the jackpot, which is a very large amount of money. If your numbers match only some of the winning numbers, you win a lesser amount, depending on how many of the winning numbers you have matched.

In the student sample programs for this chapter, you will find a file named pbnumbers.txt, containing the winning lottery numbers that were selected between February 3, 2010 and May 11, 2016 (the file contains 654 sets of winning numbers). Here is an example of the first few lines of the file's contents:

```
17 22 36 37 52 24
14 22 52 54 59 04
05 08 29 37 38 34
10 14 30 40 51 01
07 08 19 26 36 15
```
and so on ...

Each line in the file contains the set of six numbers that were selected on a given date. The numbers are separated by a space, and the last number in each line is the PowerBall number for that day. For example, the first line in the file shows the numbers for February 3, 2010, which are 17, 22, 36, 37, 52, and the PowerBall number 24.

Write one or more programs that work with this file to perform the following:

- Display the 10 most common numbers, ordered by frequency.
- Display the 10 least common numbers, ordered by frequency.
- Display the 10 most overdue numbers (numbers that haven't been drawn in a long time), ordered from most overdue to least overdue.
- Display the frequency of each number 1-69, and the frequency of each Powerball number 1-26.

Answers to Checkpoints

1

`isalpha`	Returns true (a nonzero number) if the argument is a letter of the alphabet. Returns 0 if the argument is not a letter.
`isalnum`	Returns true (a nonzero number) if the argument is a letter of the alphabet or a digit. Otherwise it returns 0.
`isdigit`	Returns true (a nonzero number) if the argument is a digit 0–9. Otherwise it returns 0.
`islower`	Returns true (a nonzero number) if the argument is a lowercase letter. Otherwise, it returns 0.
`isprint`	Returns true (a nonzero number) if the argument is a printable character (including a space). Returns 0 otherwise.
`ispunct`	Returns true (a nonzero number) if the argument is a printable character other than a digit, letter, or space. Returns 0 otherwise.
`isupper`	Returns true (a nonzero number) if the argument is an uppercase letter. Otherwise, it returns 0.
`isspace`	Returns true (a nonzero number) if the argument is a whitespace character. Whitespace characters are any of the following: space................ `' '` newline.............. `'\n'` tab................. `'\t'` vertical tab......... `'\v'` Otherwise, it returns 0.
`toupper`	Returns the uppercase equivalent of its argument.
`tolower`	Returns the lowercase equivalent of its argument.

2
```
little = tolower(big);
```

3
```
if (isdigit(ch))
   cout << "digit";
else
   cout << "Not a digit.";
```

4 A

5
```
char choice;
do
{
      cout << "Do you want to repeat the program or quit? (R/Q) ";
      cin >> choice;
} while (toupper(choice) != 'R' && toupper(choice) != 'Q');
```

6

strlen	Accepts a pointer to a string as an argument. Returns the length of the string (not including the null terminator).
strcat	Accepts pointers to two strings as arguments. The function appends the contents of the second string to the first string. (The first string is altered, the second string is left unchanged.)
strcpy	Accepts pointers to two strings as arguments. The function copies the second string to the first string. The second string is left unchanged.
strncpy	Accepts pointers to two strings and an integer argument. The third argument, an integer, indicates how many characters to copy from the second string to the first string. If the String2 has fewer than n characters, String1 is padded with '\0' characters.
strcmp	Accepts pointers to two string arguments. If String1 and String2 are the same, this function returns 0. If String2 is alphabetically greater than String1, it returns a positive number. If String2 is alphabetically less than String1, it returns a negative number.
strstr	Searches for the first occurrence of String2 in String1. If an occurrence of String2 is found, the function returns a pointer to it. Otherwise, it returns a NULL pointer (address 0).

7 4

8
```
Have a nice day
nice day
```

9
```
strcpy(composer, "Beethoven");
```

10
```
#include <iostream>
#include <cstring>
using namespace std;

int main()
{
    char place[] = "The Windy City";
    if (strstr(place, "Windy"))
       cout << "Windy found.\n";
    else
       cout << "Windy not found.\n";
    return 0;
}
```

11

`atoi`	Accepts a string as an argument. The function converts the string to an integer and returns that value.
`atol`	Accepts a string as an argument. The function converts the string to a long integer and returns that value.
`atof`	Accepts a string as an argument. The function converts the string to a `float` and returns that value.
`itoa`	Converts an integer to a string. The first argument is the integer. The result will be stored at the location pointed to by the second argument. The third argument is an integer. It specifies the numbering system that the converted integer should be expressed in. (8 = octal, 10 = decimal, 16 = hexadecimal, etc.)

12 `num = atoi("10");`

13 `num = atol("10000");`

14 `num = atof("7.2389");`

15 `itoa(127, Value, 10);`

16
```
Tom Talbert Tried Trains
Dom Dalbert Dried Drains
```

Answers to Odd Numbered Review Questions

1. `cctype`
3. 'A'
   'B'
   'd'
   'E'
5. `cstring`
7. `string`
9. `isupper`
11. `isdigit`
13. `toupper`
15. `cctype`
17. concatenate
19. `strcpy`
21. `strcmp`
23. `atoi`
25. `atof`

27. `if (toupper(choice) == 'Y')`

29.
```
if (strlen(name) <= 9)
            strcpy(str, name);
```

31.
```
int wCount(char *str)
{
    int num = 0;
    while (*str != '\0')
    {
         if (*str == 'w')
             num++;
    }
    return num;
}
```

33. False

35. False

37. True

39. False

41. True

43. The `isupper` function can only be used to test a character, not a string.

45. The compiler will not allocate enough space in `string1` to accommodate both strings.

Structured Data

TOPICS

1 Abstract Data Types

CONCEPT: Abstract data types (ADTs) are data types created by the programmer. ADTs have their own range (or domain) of data and their own sets of operations that may be performed on them.

The term *abstract data type*, or ADT, is very important in computer science and is especially significant in object-oriented programming. This chapter introduces you to the structure, which is one of C++'s mechanisms for creating abstract data types.

Abstraction

An *abstraction* is a general model of something. It is a definition that includes only the general characteristics of an object. For example, the term "dog" is an abstraction. It defines a general type of animal. The term captures the essence of what all dogs are without specifying the detailed characteristics of any particular type of dog. According to *Webster's New Collegiate Dictionary*, a dog is a highly variable carnivorous domesticated mammal (*Canis familiaris*) probably descended from the common wolf.

In real life, however, there is no such thing as a mere "dog." There are specific types of dogs, each with its own set of characteristics. There are poodles, cocker spaniels, Great

From Chapter 11 of *Starting Out with C++: From Control Structures through Objects*, Ninth Edition. Tony Gaddis.

Danes, rottweilers, and many other breeds. There are small dogs and large dogs. There are gentle dogs and ferocious dogs. They come in all shapes, sizes, and dispositions. A real-life dog is not abstract. It is concrete.

Data Types

C++ has several *primitive data types*, or data types that are defined as a basic part of the language, as shown in Table 1.

Table 1 Primitive Data Types

`bool`	`short int`	`long long int`
`char`	`unsigned short int`	`unsigned long long int`
`char_16_t`	`int`	
`char_32_t`	`unsigned int`	`float`
`wchar_t`	`long int`	`double`
`unsigned char`	`unsigned long int`	`long double`

A data type defines what values a variable may hold. Each data type listed in Table 1 has its own range of values, such as –32,768 to +32,767 for `short`s, and so forth. Data types also define what values a variable may not hold. For example, integer variables may not be used to hold fractional numbers.

In addition to defining a range or domain of values that a variable may hold, data types also define the operations that may be performed on a value. All of the data types listed in Table 1 allow the following mathematical and relational operators to be used with them:

```
+  -  *  /  >  <  >=  <=  ==  !=
```

Only the integer data types, however, allow operations with the modulus operator (%). So, a data type defines what values an object may hold, and the operations that may be performed on the object.

The primitive data types are abstract in the sense that a data type and a variable of that data type are not the same thing. For example, consider the following variable definition:

```
int x = 1, y = 2, z = 3;
```

In the statement above, the integer variables `x`, `y`, and `z` are defined. They are three separate instances of the data type `int`. Each variable has its own characteristics (`x` is set to 1, `y` is set to 2, and `z` is set to 3). In this example, the data type `int` is the abstraction, and the variables `x`, `y`, and `z` are concrete occurrences.

Abstract Data Types

An abstract data type (ADT) is a data type created by the programmer and is composed of one or more primitive data types. The programmer decides what values are acceptable for the data type, as well as what operations may be performed on the data type. In many cases, the programmer designs his or her own specialized operations.

For example, suppose a program is created to simulate a 12-hour clock. The program could contain three ADTs: `Hours`, `Minutes`, and `Seconds`. The range of values for the `Hours` data type would be the integers 1 through 12. The range of values for the `Minutes` and `Seconds` data types would be 0 through 59. If an `Hours` object is set to 12 and then incremented, it will then take on the value 1. Likewise, if a `Minutes` object or a `Seconds` object is set to 59 then incremented, it will take on the value 0.

Abstract data types often combine several values. In the clock program, the `Hours`, `Minutes`, and `Seconds` objects could be combined to form a single `Clock` object. In this chapter, you will learn how to combine variables of primitive data types to form your own data structures, or ADTs.

2 Structures

CONCEPT: C++ allows you to group several variables together into a single item known as a structure.

So far, you've written programs that keep data in individual variables. If you need to group items together, C++ allows you to create arrays. The limitation of arrays, however, is that all the elements must be of the same data type. Sometimes a relationship exists between items of different types. For example, a payroll system might keep the variables shown in Table 2. These variables hold data for a single employee.

Table 2 Variables in a Payroll System

Variable Definition	Data Held
`int empNumber;`	Employee number
`string name;`	Employee's name
`double hours;`	Hours worked
`double payRate;`	Hourly pay rate
`double grossPay;`	Gross pay

VideoNote
Creating a Structure

All of the variables listed in Table 2 are related because they can hold data about the same employee. Their definition statements, though, do not make it clear that they belong together. To create a relationship between variables, C++ gives you the ability to package them together into a *structure*.

Before a structure can be used, it must be declared. Here is the general format of a structure declaration:

```
struct tag
{
   variable declaration;
   // ... more declarations
   //     may follow...
};
```

The *tag* is the name of the structure. As you will see later, it's used like a data type name. The variable declarations that appear inside the braces declare *members* of the structure. Here is an example of a structure declaration that holds the payroll data listed in Table 2:

```
struct PayRoll
{
    int empNumber;        // Employee number
    string name;          // Employee's name
    double hours;         // Hours worked
    double payRate;       // Hourly pay rate
    double grossPay;      // Gross pay
};
```

This declaration declares a structure named `PayRoll`. The structure has five members: `empNumber`, `name`, `hours`, `payRate`, and `grossPay`.

> **WARNING!** Notice a semicolon is required after the closing brace of the structure declaration.

> **NOTE:** In this text, we begin the names of structure tags with an uppercase letter. This visually differentiates these names from the names of variables.

> **NOTE:** The structure declaration shown contains three `double` members, each declared on a separate line. The three could also have been declared on the same line, as
>
> ```
> struct PayRoll
> {
>     int empNumber;
>     string name;
>     double hours, payRate, grossPay;
> };
> ```
>
> Many programmers prefer to place each member declaration on a separate line, however, for increased readability.

It's important to note the structure declaration in our example does not define a variable. It simply tells the compiler what a `PayRoll` structure is made of. In essence, it creates a new data type named `PayRoll`. You can define variables of this type with simple definition statements, just as you would with any other data type. For example, the following statement defines a variable named `deptHead`:

```
PayRoll deptHead;
```

The data type of `deptHead` is the `PayRoll` structure. The structure tag, `PayRoll`, is listed before the variable name, just as the word `int` or `double` would be listed to define variables of those types.

Remember that structure variables are actually made up of other variables known as members. Because `deptHead` is a `PayRoll` structure, it contains the following members:

```
empNumber, an int
name, astring object
hours, adouble
payRate, adouble
grossPay, adouble
```

Figure 1 illustrates this.

Figure 1 A structure and its members

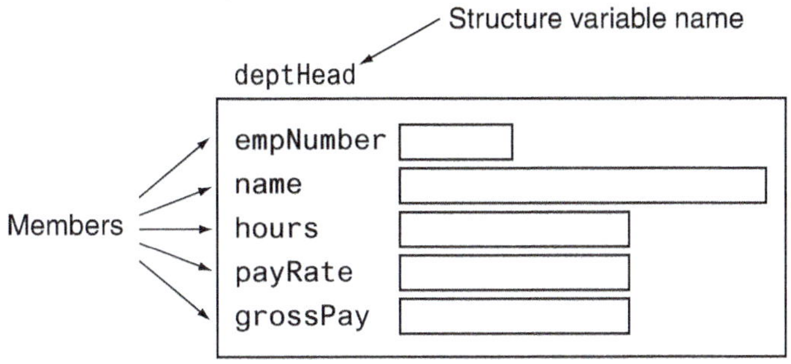

Just as it's possible to define multiple `int` or `double` variables, it's possible to define multiple structure variables in a program. The following statement defines three `PayRoll` variables: `deptHead`, `foreman`, and `associate`:

```
PayRoll deptHead, foreman, associate;
```

Figure 2 illustrates the existence of these three variables.

Figure 2 Multiple structure variables

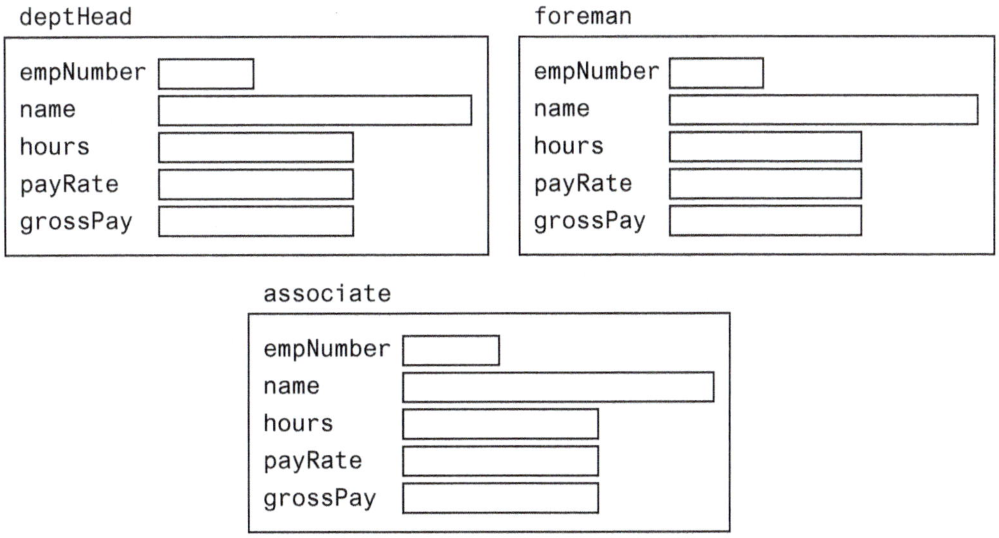

Each of the variables defined in this example is a separate *instance* of the `PayRoll` structure and contains its own members. An instance of a structure is a variable that exists in memory. It contains within it all the members described in the structure declaration.

Although the structure variables in the example are separate, each contains members with the same name. (In the next section, you'll see how to access these members.) Here are some other examples of structure declarations and variable definitions:

```
struct Time
{
    int hour;
    int minutes;
    int seconds;
};

// Definition of the
// structure variable now.
Time now;
```

```
struct Date
{
    int day;
    int month;
    int year;
};

// Definition of the structure
// variable today.
Date today;
```

In review, there are typically two steps to implementing structures in a program:

- Create the structure declaration. This establishes the tag (or name) of the structure and a list of items that are members.
- Define variables (or instances) of the structure and use them in the program to hold data.

3 Accessing Structure Members

CONCEPT: The *dot operator* (.) allows you to access structure members in a program.

C++ provides the dot operator (a period) to access the individual members of a structure. Using our example of `deptHead` as a `PayRoll` structure variable, the following statement demonstrates how to access the `empNumber` member:

```
deptHead.empNumber = 475;
```

In this statement, the number 475 is assigned to the `empNumber` member of `deptHead`. The dot operator connects the name of the member variable with the name of the structure variable it belongs to. The following statements assign values to the `empNumber` members of the `deptHead`, `foreman`, and `associate` structure variables:

```
deptHead.empNumber = 475;
foreman.empNumber = 897;
associate.empNumber = 729;
```

With the dot operator, you can use member variables just like regular variables. For example, these statements display the contents of `deptHead`'s members:

```
cout << deptHead.empNumber << endl;
cout << deptHead.name << endl;
cout << deptHead.hours << endl;
cout << deptHead.payRate << endl;
cout << deptHead.grossPay << endl;
```

Program 1 is a complete program that uses the `PayRoll` structure.

Program 1

```
// This program demonstrates the use of structures.
#include <iostream>
#include <string>
#include <iomanip>
using namespace std;

struct PayRoll
{
   int empNumber;     // Employee number
   string name;       // Employee's name
   double hours;      // Hours worked
   double payRate;    // Hourly payRate
   double grossPay;   // Gross pay
};

int main()
{
    PayRoll employee; // employee is a PayRoll structure.

    // Get the employee's number.
    cout << "Enter the employee's number: ";
    cin >> employee.empNumber;

    // Get the employee's name.
    cout << "Enter the employee's name: ";
    cin.ignore();    // To skip the remaining '\n' character
    getline(cin, employee.name);

    // Get the hours worked by the employee.
    cout << "How many hours did the employee work? ";
    cin >> employee.hours;

    // Get the employee's hourly pay rate.
    cout << "What is the employee's hourly payRate? ";
    cin >> employee.payRate;

    // Calculate the employee's gross pay.
    employee.grossPay = employee.hours * employee.payRate;

    // Display the employee data.
    cout << "Here is the employee's payroll data:\n";
    cout << "Name: " << employee.name << endl;
    cout << "Number: " << employee.empNumber << endl;
    cout << "Hours worked: " << employee.hours << endl;
    cout << "Hourly payRate: " << employee.payRate << endl;
    cout << fixed << showpoint << setprecision(2);
    cout << "Gross Pay: $" << employee.grossPay << endl;
    return 0;
}
```

(program continues)

Program 1 *(continued)*

Program Output with Example Input Shown in Bold

```
Enter the employee's number: 489 [Enter]
Enter the employee's name: Jill Smith [Enter]
How many hours did the employee work? 40 [Enter]
What is the employee's hourly pay rate? 20 [Enter]
Here is the employee's payroll data:
Name: Jill Smith
Number: 489
Hours worked: 40
Hourly pay rate: 20
Gross pay: $800.00
```

NOTE: Program 1 has the following call, in line 26, to `cin`'s `ignore` member function:

```
cin.ignore();
```

Recall that the `ignore` function causes `cin` to ignore the next character in the input buffer. This is necessary for the `getline` function to work properly in the program.

NOTE: The contents of a structure variable cannot be displayed by passing the entire variable to `cout`. For example, assuming `employee` is a `PayRoll` structure variable, the following statement will not work:

```
cout << employee << endl;   // Will not work!
```

Instead, each member must be separately passed to `cout`.

As you can see from Program 1, structure members that are of a primitive data type can be used with `cin`, `cout`, mathematical statements, and any operation that can be performed with regular variables. The only difference is that the structure variable name and the dot operator must precede the name of a member. Program 2 shows the member of a structure variable being passed to the pow function.

Program 2

```
// This program stores data about a circle in a structure.
#include <iostream>
#include <cmath> // For the pow function
#include <iomanip>
using namespace std;

// Constant for pi.
const double PI = 3.14159;
```

```

// Structure declaration
struct Circle
{
    double radius;        // A circle's radius
    double diameter;      // A circle's diameter
    double area;          // A circle's area
};

int main()
{
    Circle c;     // Define a structure variable

    // Get the circle's diameter.
    cout << "Enter the diameter of a circle: ";
    cin >> c.diameter;

    // Calculate the circle's radius.
    c.radius = c.diameter / 2;

    // Calculate the circle's area.
    c.area = PI * pow(c.radius, 2.0);

    // Display the circle data.
    cout << fixed << showpoint << setprecision(2);
    cout << "The radius and area of the circle are:\n";
    cout << "Radius: " << c.radius << endl;
    cout << "Area: " << c.area << endl;
    return 0;
}
```

Program Output with Example Input Shown in Bold

```
Enter the diameter of a circle: 10 [Enter]
The radius and area of the circle are:
Radius: 5
Area: 78.54
```

Comparing Structure Variables

You cannot perform comparison operations directly on structure variables. For example, assume `circle1` and `circle2` are `Circle` structure variables. The following statement will cause an error:

```
if (circle1 == circle2)   // Error!
```

In order to compare two structures, you must compare the individual members, as shown in the following code:

```
if (circle1.radius == circle2.radius &&
    circle1.diameter == circle2.diameter &&
    circle1.area == circle2.area)
```

4 Initializing a Structure

CONCEPT: The members of a structure variable may be initialized with starting values when the structure variable is defined.

A structure variable may be initialized when it is defined, in a fashion similar to the initialization of an array. Assume the following structure declaration exists in a program:

```
struct CityInfo
{
    string cityName;
    string state;
    long population;
    int distance;
};
```

A variable may then be defined with an initialization list, as shown in the following:

```
CityInfo location = {"Asheville", "NC", 80000, 28};
```

This statement defines the variable `location`. The first value in the initialization list is assigned to the first declared member, the second value in the initialization list is assigned to the second member, and so on. The `location` variable is initialized in the following manner:

The string "Asheville" is assigned to `location.cityName`
The string "NC" is assigned to `location.state`
80000 is assigned to `location.population`
28 is assigned to `location.distance`

You do not have to provide initializers for all the members of a structure variable. For example, the following statement only initializes the `cityName` member of `location`:

```
CityInfo location = {"Tampa"};
```

The `state`, `population`, and `distance` members are left uninitialized. The following statement only initializes the `cityName` and `state` members, while leaving `population` and `distance` uninitialized:

```
CityInfo location = {"Atlanta", "GA"};
```

If you leave a structure member uninitialized, you must leave all the members that follow it uninitialized as well. C++ does not provide a way to skip members in a structure. For example, the following statement, which attempts to skip the initialization of the `population` member, is *not* legal:

```
CityInfo location = {"Knoxville", "TN", , 90};   // Illegal!
```

Program 3 demonstrates the use of partially initialized structure variables.

Program 3

```
// This program demonstrates partially initialized
// structure variables.
#include <iostream>
```

```cpp
#include <string>
#include <iomanip>
using namespace std;

struct EmployeePay
{
    string name;          // Employee name
    int empNum;           // Employee number
    double payRate;       // Hourly pay rate
    double hours;         // Hours worked
    double grossPay;      // Gross pay
};

int main()
{
    EmployeePay employee1 = {"Betty Ross", 141, 18.75};
    EmployeePay employee2 = {"Jill Sandburg", 142, 17.50};

    cout << fixed << showpoint << setprecision(2);

    // Calculate pay for employee1
    cout << "Name: " << employee1.name << endl;
    cout << "Employee Number: " << employee1.empNum << endl;
    cout << "Enter the hours worked by this employee: ";
    cin >> employee1.hours;
    employee1.grossPay = employee1.hours * employee1.payRate;
    cout << "Gross Pay: " << employee1.grossPay << endl << endl;

    // Calculate pay for employee2
    cout << "Name: " << employee2.name << endl;
    cout << "Employee Number: " << employee2.empNum << endl;
    cout << "Enter the hours worked by this employee: ";
    cin >> employee2.hours;
    employee2.grossPay = employee2.hours * employee2.payRate;
    cout << "Gross Pay: " << employee2.grossPay << endl;
    return 0;
}
```

Program Output with Example Input Shown in Bold

Name: Betty Ross
Employee Number: 141
Enter the hours worked by this employee: **40** [Enter]
Gross Pay: 750.00

Name: Jill Sandburg
Employee Number: 142
Enter the hours worked by this employee: **20** [Enter]
Gross Pay: 350.00

Beginning with C++ 11, the = sign is optional when initializing a structure variable. For example, in C++ 11, we could define a `CityInfo` variable and initialize with the following statement:

```
CityInfo location {"Asheville", "NC", 80000, 28};
```

Checkpoint

1 Write a structure declaration to hold the following data about a savings account:

Account Number (`string` object)
Account Balance (`double`)
Interest Rate (`double`)
Average Monthly Balance (`double`)

2 Write a definition statement for a variable of the structure you declared in Question 1. Initialize the members with the following data:

Account Number: ACZ42137-B12-7
Account Balance: $4512.59
Interest Rate: 4%
Average Monthly Balance: $4217.07

3 The following program skeleton, when complete, asks the user to enter these data about his or her favorite movie:

Name of movie
Name of the movie's director
Name of the movie's producer
The year the movie was released

Complete the following program by declaring the structure that holds this data, defining a structure variable, and writing the individual statements necessary.

```
#include <iostream>
using namespace std;
// Write the structure declaration here to hold the movie data.

int main()
{
   // define the structure variable here.

   cout << "Enter the following data about your\n";
   cout << "favorite movie.\n";
   cout << "name: ";
   // Write a statement here that lets the user enter the
   // name of a favorite movie. Store the name in the
   // structure variable.
   cout << "Director: ";
   // Write a statement here that lets the user enter the
   // name of the movie's director. Store the name in the
   // structure variable.
```

```
    cout << "Producer: ";
    // Write a statement here that lets the user enter the
    // name of the movie's producer. Store the name in the
    // structure variable.
    cout << "Year of release: ";
    // Write a statement here that lets the user enter the
    // year the movie was released. Store the year in the
    // structure variable.
    cout << "Here is data on your favorite movie:\n";
    // Write statements here that display the data.
    // just entered into the structure variable.
    return 0;
}
```

5 Arrays of Structures

CONCEPT: Arrays of structures can simplify some programming tasks.

Data can be stored in two or more arrays, with a relationship established between the arrays through their subscripts. Because structures can hold several items of varying data types, a single array of structures can be used in place of several arrays of regular variables.

An array of structures is defined like any other array. Assume the following structure declaration exists in a program:

```
struct BookInfo
{
   string title;
   string author;
   string publisher;
   double price;
};
```

The following statement defines an array, `bookList`, that has 20 elements. Each element is a `BookInfo` structure.

```
BookInfo bookList[20];
```

Each element of the array may be accessed through a subscript. For example, `bookList[0]` is the first structure in the array, `bookList[1]` is the second, and so forth. To access a member of any element, simply place the dot operator and member name after the subscript. For example, the following expression refers to the `title` member of `bookList[5]`:

```
bookList[5].title
```

The following loop steps through the array, displaying the data stored in each element:

```
for (int index = 0; index < 20; index++)
{
   cout << bookList[index].title << endl;
   cout << bookList[index].author << endl;
   cout << bookList[index].publisher << endl;
   cout << bookList[index].price << endl << endl;
}
```

Program 4 calculates and displays payroll data for three employees. It uses a single array of structures.

Program 4

```
// This program uses an array of structures.
#include <iostream>
#include <iomanip>
using namespace std;

struct PayInfo
{
    int hours;          // Hours worked
    double payRate;     // Hourly pay rate
};

int main()
{
    const int NUM_WORKERS = 3;      // Number of workers
    PayInfo workers[NUM_WORKERS];   // Array of structures
    int index;                      // Loop counter

    // Get employee pay data.
    cout << "Enter the hours worked by " << NUM_WORKERS
         << " employees and their hourly rates.\n";

    for (index = 0; index < NUM_WORKERS; index++)
    {
        // Get the hours worked by an employee.
        cout << "Hours worked by employee #" << (index + 1);
        cout << ": ";
        cin >> workers[index].hours;

        // Get the employee's hourly pay rate.
        cout << "Hourly pay rate for employee #";
        cout << (index + 1) << ": ";
        cin >> workers[index].payRate;
        cout << endl;
    }

    // Display each employee's gross pay.
    cout << "Here is the gross pay for each employee:\n";
    cout << fixed << showpoint << setprecision(2);
    for (index = 0; index < NUM_WORKERS; index++)
    {
        double gross;
        gross = workers[index].hours * workers[index].payRate;
        cout << "Employee #" << (index + 1);
        cout << ": $" << gross << endl;
    }
    return 0;
}
```

Program Output with Example Input Shown in Bold

```
Enter the hours worked by 3 employees and their hourly rates.
Hours worked by employee #1: 10 [Enter]
Hourly pay rate for employee #1: 9.75 [Enter]

Hours worked by employee #2: 20 [Enter]
Hourly pay rate for employee #2: 10.00 [Enter]

Hours worked by employee #3: 40 [Enter]
Hourly pay rate for employee #3: 20.00 [Enter]

Here is the gross pay for each employee:
Employee #1: $97.50
Employee #2: $200.00
Employee #3: $800.00
```

Initializing a Structure Array

To initialize a structure array, simply provide an initialization list for one or more of the elements. For example, the array in Program 4 could have been initialized as follows:

```
PayInfo workers[NUM_WORKERS] = {
                                   {10, 9.75 },
                                   {15, 8.62 },
                                   {40, 15.65}
                               };
```

As in all single-dimensional arrays, you can initialize all or part of the elements in an array of structures, as long as you do not skip elements.

6 Focus on Software Engineering: Nested Structures

CONCEPT: It's possible for a structure variable to be a member of another structure variable.

Sometimes it's helpful to nest structures inside other structures. For example, consider the following structure declarations:

```
struct Costs
{
   double wholesale;
   double retail;
};

struct Item
{
   string partNum;
   string description;
   Costs pricing;
};
```

The Costs structure has two members: wholesale and retail, both doubles. Notice the third member of the Item structure, pricing, is a Costs structure. Assume the variable widget is defined as follows:

```
Item widget;
```

The following statements show examples of accessing members of the pricing variable, which is inside widget:

```
widget.pricing.wholesale = 100.0;
widget.pricing.retail = 150.0;
```

Program 5 gives a more elaborate illustration of nested structures.

Program 5

```
// This program uses nested structures.
#include <iostream>
#include <string>
using namespace std;

// The Date structure holds data about a date.
struct Date
{
    int month;
    int day;
    int year;
};

// The Place structure holds a physical address.
struct Place
{
    string address;
    string city;
    string state;
    string zip;
};

// The EmployeeInfo structure holds an employee's data.
struct EmployeeInfo
{
    string name;
    int employeeNumber;
    Date birthDate;                // Nested structure
    Place residence;               // Nested structure
};

int main()
{
    // Define a structure variable to hold info about the manager.
    EmployeeInfo manager;

```

```
    // Get the manager's name and employee number
    cout << "Enter the manager's name: ";
    getline(cin, manager.name);
    cout << "Enter the manager's employee number: ";
    cin >> manager.employeeNumber;

    // Get the manager's birth date
    cout << "Now enter the manager's date of birth.\n";
    cout << "Month (up to 2 digits): ";
    cin >> manager.birthDate.month;
    cout << "Day (up to 2 digits): ";
    cin >> manager.birthDate.day;
    cout << "Year: ";
    cin >> manager.birthDate.year;
    cin.ignore();  // Skip the remaining newline character

    // Get the manager's residence information
    cout << "Enter the manager's street address: ";
    getline(cin, manager.residence.address);
    cout << "City: ";
    getline(cin, manager.residence.city);
    cout << "State: ";
    getline(cin, manager.residence.state);
    cout << "ZIP Code: ";
    getline(cin, manager.residence.zip);

    // Display the information just entered
    cout << "\nHere is the manager's information:\n";
    cout << manager.name << endl;
    cout << "Employee number " << manager.employeeNumber << endl;
    cout << "Date of birth: ";
    cout << manager.birthDate.month << "-";
    cout << manager.birthDate.day << "-";
    cout << manager.birthDate.year << endl;
    cout << "Place of residence:\n";
    cout << manager.residence.address << endl;
    cout << manager.residence.city << ", ";
    cout << manager.residence.state << " ";
    cout << manager.residence.zip << endl;
    return 0;
}
```

Program Output with Example Input Shown in Bold

Enter the manager's name: **John Smith** [Enter]
Enter the manager's employee number: **789** [Enter]
Now enter the manager's date of birth.
Month (up to 2 digits): **10** [Enter]
Day (up to 2 digits): **14** [Enter]
Year: **1970** [Enter]
Enter the manager's street address: **190 Disk Drive** [Enter]
City: **Redmond** [Enter]

(program output continues)

Program 5 *(continued)*

```
State: WA [Enter]
ZIP Code: 98052 [Enter]
Here is the manager's information:
John Smith
Employee number 789
Date of birth: 10-14-1970
Place of residence:
190 Disk Drive
Redmond, WA 98052
```

Checkpoint

For Questions 4–7 below, assume the `Product` structure is declared as follows:

```
struct Product
{
    string description;    // Product description
    int partNum;           // Part number
    double cost;           // Product cost
};
```

4 Write a definition for an array of 100 `Product` structures. Do not initialize the array.

5 Write a loop that will step through the entire array you defined in Question 4, setting all the product descriptions to an empty string, all part numbers to zero, and all costs to zero.

6 Write the statements that will store the following data in the first element of the array you defined in Question 4:

Description: Claw hammer
Part Number: 547
Part Cost: $8.29

7 Write a loop that will display the contents of the entire array you created in Question 4.

8 Write a structure declaration named `Measurement`, with the following members:

`miles`, an integer
`meters`, a `long` integer

9 Write a structure declaration named `Destination`, with the following members:

`city`, a `string` object
`distance`, a `Measurement` structure (declared in Question 8)

Also define a variable of this structure type.

10 Write statements that store the following data in the variable you defined in Question 9:

City: Tupelo
Miles: 375
Meters: 603,375

7 Structures as Function Arguments

CONCEPT: Structure variables may be passed as arguments to functions.

VideoNote
Passing a Structure to a Function

Like other variables, the individual members of a structure variable may be used as function arguments. For example, assume the following structure declaration exists in a program:

```
struct Rectangle
{
   double length;
   double width;
   double area;
};
```

Let's say the following function definition exists in the same program:

```
double multiply(double x, double y)
{
   return x * y;
}
```

Assuming `box` is a variable of the `Rectangle` structure type, the following function call will pass `box.length` into `x` and `box.width` into `y`. The return value will be stored in `box.area`.

```
box.area = multiply(box.length, box.width);
```

Sometimes it's more convenient to pass an entire structure variable into a function instead of individual members. For example, the following function definition uses a `Rectangle` structure variable as its parameter:

```
void showRect(Rectangle r)
{
   cout << r.length << endl;
   cout << r.width << endl;
   cout << r.area << endl;
}
```

The following function call passes the `box` variable into `r`:

```
showRect(box);
```

Inside the function `showRect`, `r's` members contain a copy of `box's` members. This is illustrated in Figure 3.

Once the function is called, `r.length` contains a copy of `box.length`, `r.width` contains a copy of `box.width`, and `r.area` contains a copy of `box.area`.

Structures, like all variables, are normally passed by value into a function. If a function is to access the members of the original argument, a reference variable may be used as the parameter. Program 6 uses two functions that accept structures as arguments. Arguments are passed to the `getItem` function by reference, and to the `showItem` function by value.

Figure 3 Passing a structure variable to a function

```
showRect(box);

void showRect(Rectangle r)
{
     cout << r.length << endl;
     cout << r.width << endl;
     cout << r.area << endl;
}
```

Program 6

```
// This program has functions that accept structure variables
// as arguments.
#include <iostream>
#include <string>
#include <iomanip>
using namespace std;

struct InventoryItem
{
     int partNum;                    // Part number
     string description;             // Item description
     int onHand;                     // Units on hand
     double price;                   // Unit price
};

// Function Prototypes
void getItem(InventoryItem&);        // Argument passed by reference
void showItem(InventoryItem);        // Argument passed by value

int main()
{
     InventoryItem part;

     getItem(part);
     showItem(part);
     return 0;
}

//*****************************************************************
// Definition of function getItem. This function uses            *
// a structure reference variable as its parameter. It asks *
// the user for information to store in the structure.           *
//*****************************************************************

```

```
void getItem(InventoryItem &p)   // Uses a reference parameter
{
    // Get the part number.
    cout << "Enter the part number: ";
    cin >> p.partNum;

    // Get the part description.
    cout << "Enter the part description: ";
    cin.ignore();   // Ignore the remaining newline character
    getline(cin, p.description);

    // Get the quantity on hand.
    cout << "Enter the quantity on hand: ";
    cin >> p.onHand;

    // Get the unit price.
    cout << "Enter the unit price: ";
    cin >> p.price;
}

//***********************************************************
// Definition of function showItem. This function accepts   *
// an argument of the InventoryItem structure type. The     *
// contents of the structure is displayed.                  *
//***********************************************************

void showItem(InventoryItem p)
{
    cout << fixed << showpoint << setprecision(2);
    cout << "Part Number: " << p.partNum << endl;
    cout << "Description: " << p.description << endl;
    cout << "Units On Hand: " << p.onHand << endl;
    cout << "Price: $" << p.price << endl;
}
```

Program Output with Example Input Shown in Bold

Enter the part number: **800** [Enter]
Enter the part description: **Screwdriver** [Enter]
Enter the quantity on hand: **135** [Enter]
Enter the unit price: **1.25** [Enter]
Part Number: 800
Description: Screwdriver
Units on Hand: 135
Price: $1.25

Notice the InventoryItem structure declaration in Program 6 appears before both the prototypes and the definitions of the getItem and showItem functions. This is because both functions use an InventoryItem structure variable as their parameter. The compiler must know what InventoryItem is before it encounters any definitions for variables of that type. Otherwise, an error will occur.

Constant Reference Parameters

Sometimes structures can be quite large. Passing large structures by value can decrease a program's performance because a copy of the structure has to be created. When a structure is passed by reference, however, it isn't copied. A reference that points to the original argument is passed instead. So, it's often preferable to pass large objects such as structures by reference.

Of course, the disadvantage of passing an object by reference is that the function has access to the original argument. It can potentially alter the argument's value. This can be prevented, however, by passing the argument as a constant reference. The `showItem` function from Program 6 is shown here, modified to use a constant reference parameter.

```
void showItem(const InventoryItem &p)
{
   cout << fixed << showpoint << setprecision(2);
   cout << "Part Number: " << p.partNum << endl;
   cout << "Description: " << p.description << endl;
   cout << "Units on Hand: " << p.onHand << endl;
   cout << "Price: $" << p.price << endl;
}
```

This version of the function is more efficient than the original version because the amount of time and memory consumed in the function call is reduced. Because the parameter is defined as a constant, the function cannot accidentally corrupt the value of the argument.

The prototype for this version of the function is as follows:

```
void showItem(const InventoryItem&);
```

8 Returning a Structure from a Function

CONCEPT: A function may return a structure.

Just as functions can be written to return an `int`, `long`, `double`, or other data type, they can also be designed to return a structure. Recall the following structure declaration from Program 2:

```
struct Circle
{
   double radius;
   double diameter;
   double area;
};
```

A function, such as the following, could be written to return a variable of the `Circle` data type:

```
Circle getCircleData()
{
   Circle temp;              // Temporary Circle structure

   temp.radius = 10.0;       // Store the radius
   temp.diameter = 20.0;     // Store the diameter
```

```
    temp.area = 314.159;     // Store the area
    return temp;             // Return the temporary structure
}
```

Notice the `getCircleData` function has a return data type of `Circle`. That means the function returns an entire `Circle` structure when it terminates. The return value can be assigned to any variable that is a `Circle` structure. The following statement, for example, assigns the function's return value to the `Circle` structure variable named `myCircle`:

```
myCircle = getCircleData();
```

After this statement executes, `myCircle.radius` will be set to 10.0, `myCircle.diameter` will be set to 20.0, and `myCircle.area` will be set to 314.159.

When a function returns a structure, it is always necessary for the function to have a local structure variable to hold the member values that are to be returned. In the `getCircleData` function, the values for `diameter`, `radius`, and `area` are stored in the local variable `temp`. The `temp` variable is then returned from the function.

Program 7 is a modification of Program 2. The function `getInfo` gets the circle's diameter from the user and calculates the circle's radius. The diameter and radius are stored in a local structure variable, `round`, which is returned from the function.

Program 7

```
// This program uses a function to return a structure. This
// is a modification of Program 2.
#include <iostream>
#include <iomanip>
#include <cmath>  // For the pow function
using namespace std;

// Constant for pi.
const double PI = 3.14159;

// Structure declaration
struct Circle
{
    double radius;      // A circle's radius
    double diameter;    // A circle's diameter
    double area;        // A circle's area
};

// Function prototype
Circle getInfo();

int main()
{
    Circle c;         // Define a structure variable

    // Get data about the circle.
    c = getInfo();
```

(program continues)

Program 7 *(continued)*

```
    // Calculate the circle's area.
    c.area = PI * pow(c.radius, 2.0);

    // Display the circle data.
    cout << "The radius and area of the circle are:\n";
    cout << fixed << setprecision(2);
    cout << "Radius: " << c.radius << endl;
    cout << "Area: " << c.area << endl;
    return 0;
}

//*****************************************************************
// Definition of function getInfo. This function uses a local     *
// variable, tempCircle, which is a circle structure. The user    *
// enters the diameter of the circle, which is stored in          *
// tempCircle.diameter. The function then calculates the radius,  *
// which is stored in tempCircle.radius. tempCircle is then       *
// returned from the function.                                    *
//*****************************************************************

Circle getInfo()
{
    Circle tempCircle;  // Temporary structure variable

    // Store circle data in the temporary variable.
    cout << "Enter the diameter of a circle: ";
    cin >> tempCircle.diameter;
    tempCircle.radius = tempCircle.diameter / 2.0;

    // Return the temporary variable.
    return tempCircle;
}
```

Program Output with Example Input Shown in Bold

```
Enter the diameter of a circle: 10 [Enter]
The radius and area of the circle are:
Radius: 5.00
Area: 78.54
```

NOTE: C++ only allows you to return a single value from a function. Structures, however, provide a way around this limitation. Even though a structure may have several members, a structure variable is a single value. By packaging multiple values inside a structure, you can return as many variables as you need from a function.

9 Pointers to Structures

CONCEPT: You may take the address of a structure variable and create variables that are pointers to structures.

Defining a variable that is a pointer to a structure is as simple as defining any other pointer variable: The data type is followed by an asterisk and the name of the pointer variable. Here is an example:

```
Circle *cirPtr = nullptr;
```

This statement defines `cirPtr` as a pointer to a `Circle` structure. Look at the following code:

```
Circle myCircle = { 10.0, 20.0, 314.159 };
Circle *cirPtr = nullptr;
cirPtr = &myCircle;
```

The first two lines define `myCircle`, a structure variable, and `cirPtr`, a pointer. The third line assigns the address of `myCircle` to `cirPtr`. After this line executes, `cirPtr` will point to the `myCircle` structure. This is illustrated in Figure 4.

Figure 4 A pointer to a structure

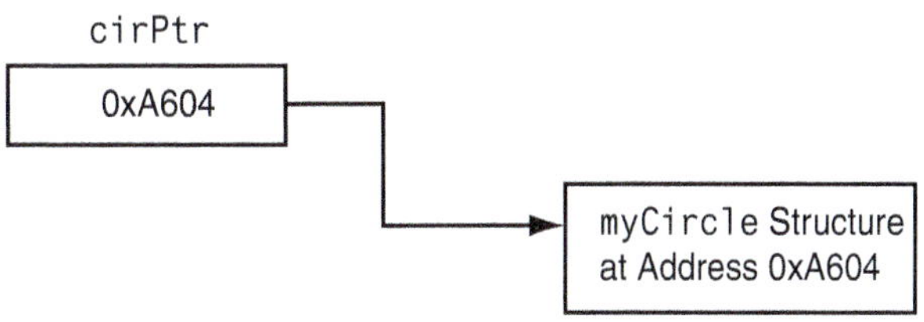

Indirectly accessing the members of a structure through a pointer can be clumsy, however, if the indirection operator is used. One might think the following statement would access the `radius` member of the structure pointed to by `cirPtr`, but it doesn't:

```
*cirPtr.radius = 10;
```

The dot operator has higher precedence than the indirection operator, so the indirection operator tries to dereference `cirPtr.radius`, not `cirPtr`. To dereference the `cirPtr` pointer, a set of parentheses must be used.

```
(*cirPtr).radius = 10;
```

Because of the awkwardness of this notation, C++ has a special operator for dereferencing structure pointers. It's called the *structure pointer operator*, and it consists of a hyphen (-) followed by the greater-than symbol (>). The previous statement, rewritten with the structure pointer operator, looks like this:

```
cirPtr->radius = 10;
```

The structure pointer operator takes the place of the dot operator in statements using pointers to structures. The operator automatically dereferences the structure pointer on its left. There is no need to enclose the pointer name in parentheses.

> **NOTE:** The structure pointer operator is supposed to look like an arrow, thus visually indicating that a "pointer" is being used.

Program 8 shows that a pointer to a structure may be used as a function parameter, allowing the function to access the members of the original structure argument.

Program 8

```
// This program demonstrates a function that uses a
// pointer to a structure variable as a parameter.
#include <iostream>
#include <string>
#include <iomanip>
using namespace std;

struct Student
{
    string name;            // Student's name
    int idNum;              // Student ID number
    int creditHours;        // Credit hours enrolled
    double gpa;             // Current GPA
};

void getData(Student *);    // Function prototype

int main()
{
    Student freshman;

    // Get the student data.
    cout << "Enter the following student data:\n";
    getData(&freshman);      // Pass the address of freshman.
    cout << "\nHere is the student data you entered:\n";

    // Now display the data stored in freshman
    cout << setprecision(3);
    cout << "Name: " << freshman.name << endl;
    cout << "ID Number: " << freshman.idNum << endl;
    cout << "Credit Hours: " << freshman.creditHours << endl;
    cout << "GPA: " << freshman.gpa << endl;
    return 0;
}
```

```
//***************************************************************
// Definition of function getData. Uses a pointer to a         *
// Student structure variable. The user enters student          *
// information, which is stored in the variable.                *
//***************************************************************

void getData(Student *s)
{
    // Get the student name.
    cout << "Student name: ";
    getline(cin, s->name);

    // Get the student ID number.
    cout << "Student ID Number: ";
    cin >> s->idNum;

    // Get the credit hours enrolled.
    cout << "Credit Hours Enrolled: ";
    cin >> s->creditHours;

    // Get the GPA.
    cout << "Current GPA: ";
    cin >> s->gpa;
}
```

Program Output with Example Input Shown in Bold

```
Enter the following student data:
Student Name: Frank Smith [Enter]
Student ID Number: 4876 [Enter]
Credit Hours Enrolled: 12 [Enter]
Current GPA: 3.45 [Enter]

Here is the student data you entered:
Name: Frank Smith
ID Number: 4876
Credit Hours: 12
GPA: 3.45
```

Dynamically Allocating a Structure

You can also use a structure pointer and the new operator to dynamically allocate a structure. For example, the following code defines a `Circle` pointer named `cirPtr` and dynamically allocates a `Circle` structure. Values are then stored in the dynamically allocated structure's members.

```
Circle *cirPtr = nullptr; // Define a Circle pointer
cirPtr = new Circle;      // Dynamically allocate a Circle structure
cirPtr->radius = 10;      // Store a value in the radius member
cirPtr->diameter = 20;    // Store a value in the diameter member
cirPtr->area = 314.159;   // Store a value in the area member
```

You can also dynamically allocate an array of structures. The following code shows an array of five `Circle` structures being allocated:

```
Circle *circles = nullptr;
circles = new Circle[5];
for (int count = 0; count < 5; count++)
{
   cout << "Enter the radius for circle "
        << (count + 1) << ": ";
   cin >> circles[count].radius;
}
```

10 Focus on Software Engineering: When to Use ., When to Use ->, and When to Use *

Sometimes structures contain pointers as members. For example, the following structure declaration has an `int` pointer member:

```
struct GradeInfo
{
   string name;                 // Student names
   int *testScores;             // Dynamically allocated array
   float average;               // Test average
};
```

It is important to remember that the structure pointer operator (`->`) is used to dereference a pointer to a structure, not a pointer that is a member of a structure. If a program dereferences the `testScores` pointer in this structure, the indirection operator must be used. For example, assume that the following variable has been defined:

```
GradeInfo student1;
```

The following statement will display the value pointed to by the `testScores` member:

```
cout << *student1.testScores;
```

It is still possible to define a pointer to a structure that contains a pointer member. For instance, the following statement defines `stPtr` as a pointer to a `GradeInfo` structure:

```
GradeInfo *stPtr = nullptr;
```

Assuming `stPtr` points to a valid `GradeInfo` variable, the following statement will display the value pointed to by its `testScores` member:

```
cout << *stPtr->testScores;
```

In this statement, the * operator dereferences `stPtr->testScores`, while the `->` operator dereferences `stPtr`. It might help to remember that the following expression:

```
stPtr->testScores
```

is equivalent to

```
(*stPtr).testScores
```

So, the expression

```
*stPtr->testScores
```

is the same as

```
*(*stPtr).testScores
```

The awkwardness of this last expression shows the necessity of the -> operator. Table 3 lists some expressions using the *, ->, and . operators and describes what each references.

Table 3 Structure Pointer Expressions

Expression	Description
`s->m`	s is a structure pointer and m is a member. This expression accesses the m member of the structure pointed to by s.
`*a.p`	a is a structure variable and p, a pointer, is a member. This expression dereferences the value pointed to by p.
`(*s).m`	s is a structure pointer and m is a member. The * operator dereferences s, causing the expression to access the m member of the structure pointed to by s. This expression is the same as s->m.
`*s->p`	s is a structure pointer and p, a pointer, is a member of the structure pointed to by s. This expression accesses the value pointed to by p. (The -> operator dereferences s and the * operator dereferences p.)
`*(*s).p`	s is a structure pointer and p, a pointer, is a member of the structure pointed to by s. This expression accesses the value pointed to by p. (*s) dereferences s and the outermost * operator dereferences p. The expression *s->p is equivalent.

Checkpoint

Assume the following structure declaration exists for Questions 11–15:

```
struct Rectangle
{
   int length;
   int width;
};
```

11 Write a function that accepts a Rectangle structure as its argument and displays the structure's contents on the screen.

12 Write a function that uses a Rectangle structure reference variable as its parameter and stores the user's input in the structure's members.

13 Write a function that returns a Rectangle structure. The function should store the user's input in the members of the structure before returning it.

14 Write the definition of a pointer to a Rectangle structure.

15 Assume rptr is a pointer to a Rectangle structure. Which of the expressions, A, B, or C, is equivalent to the following expression:

```
rptr->width
```

A) `*rptr.width`
B) `(*rptr).width`
C) `rptr.(*width)`

11 Enumerated Data Types

CONCEPT: An enumerated data type is a programmer-defined data type. It consists of values known as enumerators, which represent integer constants.

Using the enum key word, you can create your own data type and specify the values that belong to that type. Such a type is known as an *enumerated data type*. Here is an example of an enumerated data type declaration:

```
enum Day { MONDAY, TUESDAY, WEDNESDAY, THURSDAY, FRIDAY };
```

An enumerated type declaration begins with the key word enum, followed by the name of the type, followed by a list of identifiers inside braces, and is terminated with a semicolon. The example declaration creates an enumerated data type named Day. The identifiers MONDAY, TUESDAY, WEDNESDAY, THURSDAY, and FRIDAY, which are listed inside the braces, are known as *enumerators*. They represent the values that belong to the Day data type. Here is the general format of an enumerated type declaration:

```
enum TypeName { One or more enumerators };
```

Note the enumerators are not enclosed in quotation marks; therefore, they are not strings. Enumerators must be legal C++ identifiers.

Once you have created an enumerated data type in your program, you can define variables of that type. For example, the following statement defines workDay as a variable of the Day type:

```
Day workDay;
```

Because workDay is a variable of the Day data type, we may assign any of the enumerators MONDAY, TUESDAY, WEDNESDAY, THURSDAY, or FRIDAY to it. For example, the following statement assigns the value WEDNESDAY to the workDay variable.

```
Day workDay = WEDNESDAY;
```

So just what are these enumerators MONDAY, TUESDAY, WEDNESDAY, THURSDAY, and FRIDAY? You can think of them as integer named constants. Internally, the compiler assigns integer values to the enumerators, beginning with 0. The enumerator MONDAY is stored in memory as the number 0, TUESDAY is stored in memory as the number 1, WEDNESDAY is stored in memory as the number 2, and so forth. To prove this, look at the following code.

```
cout << MONDAY << endl << TUESDAY << endl
     << WEDNESDAY << endl << THURSDAY << endl
     << FRIDAY << endl;
```

This statement will produce the following output:

```
0
1
2
3
4
```

> **NOTE:** When making up names for enumerators, it is not required that they be written in all uppercase letters. For example, we could have written the enumerators of the `Days` type as `monday`, `tuesday`, and so on. Because they represent constant values, however, many programmers prefer to write them in all uppercase letters. This is strictly a preference of style.

Assigning an Integer to an `enum` Variable

Even though the enumerators of an enumerated data type are stored in memory as integers, you cannot directly assign an integer value to an `enum` variable. For example, assuming that `workDay` is a variable of the `Day` data type previously described, the following assignment statement is illegal:

```
workDay = 3;   // Error!
```

Compiling this statement will produce an error message such as "Cannot convert `int` to `Day`." When assigning a value to an `enum` variable, you should use a valid enumerator. However, if circumstances require that you store an integer value in an `enum` variable, you can do so by casting the integer. Here is an example:

```
workDay = static_cast<Day>(3);
```

This statement will produce the same results as:

```
workDay = THURSDAY;
```

Assigning an Enumerator to an `int` Variable

Although you cannot directly assign an integer value to an `enum` variable, you can directly assign an enumerator to an integer variable. For example, the following code will work just fine.

```
enum Day { MONDAY, TUESDAY, WEDNESDAY, THURSDAY, FRIDAY };
int x;
x = THURSDAY;
cout << x << endl;
```

When this code runs, it will display 3. You can also assign a variable of an enumerated type to an integer variable, as shown here:

```
Day workDay = FRIDAY;
int x = workDay;
cout << x << endl;
```

When this code runs, it will display 4.

Comparing Enumerator Values

Enumerator values can be compared using the relational operators. For example, using the `Day` data type we have been discussing, the following expression is `true`:

```
FRIDAY > MONDAY
```

The expression is `true` because the enumerator `FRIDAY` is stored in memory as 4 and the enumerator `MONDAY` is stored as 0. The following code will display the message "Friday is greater than Monday.":

```
if (FRIDAY > MONDAY)
   cout << "Friday is greater than Monday. \n";
```

You can also compare enumerator values with integer values. For example, the following code will display the message "Monday is equal to zero.":

```
if (MONDAY == 0)
   cout << "Monday is equal to zero.\n";
```

Let's look at a complete program that uses much of what we have learned so far. Program 9 uses the Day data type we have been discussing.

Program 9

```
// This program demonstrates an enumerated data type.
#include <iostream>
#include <iomanip>
using namespace std;

enum Day { MONDAY, TUESDAY, WEDNESDAY, THURSDAY, FRIDAY };

int main()
{
    const int NUM_DAYS = 5;      // The number of days
    double sales[NUM_DAYS];      // To hold sales for each day
    double total = 0.0;          // Accumulator
    int index;                   // Loop counter

    // Get the sales for each day.
    for (index = MONDAY; index <= FRIDAY; index++)
    {
        cout << "Enter the sales for day "
             << index << ": ";
        cin >> sales[index];
    }

    // Calculate the total sales.
    for (index = MONDAY; index <= FRIDAY; index++)
       total += sales[index];

    // Display the total.
    cout << "The total sales are $" << setprecision(2)
         << fixed << total << endl;

    return 0;
}
```

Program Output with Example Input Shown in Bold

```
Enter the sales for day 0: 1525.00 [Enter]
Enter the sales for day 1: 1896.50 [Enter]
Enter the sales for day 2: 1975.63 [Enter]
Enter the sales for day 3: 1678.33 [Enter]
Enter the sales for day 4: 1498.52 [Enter]
The total sales are $8573.98
```

Anonymous Enumerated Types

Notice Program 9 does not define a variable of the Day data type. Instead, it uses the Day data type's enumerators in the for loops. The counter variable index is initialized to MONDAY (which is 0), and the loop iterates as long as index is less than or equal to FRIDAY (which is 4). When you do not need to define variables of an enumerated type, you can actually make the type anonymous. An *anonymous enumerated type* is simply one that does not have a name. For example, in Program 9 we could have declared the enumerated type as:

```
enum { MONDAY, TUESDAY, WEDNESDAY, THURSDAY, FRIDAY };
```

This declaration still creates the enumerators. We just can't use the data type to define variables, because the type does not have a name.

Using Math Operators to Change the Value of an enum Variable

Even though enumerators are really integers, and enum variables really hold integer values, you can run into problems when trying to perform math operations with them. For example, look at the following code:

```
Day day1, day2;     // Defines two Day variables.
day1 = TUESDAY;     // Assign TUESDAY to day1.
day2 = day1 + 1;    // ERROR! This will not work!
```

The third statement causes a problem because the expression day1 + 1 results in the integer value 2. The assignment operator then attempts to assign the integer value 2 to the enum variable day2. Because C++ cannot implicitly convert an int to a Day, an error occurs. You can fix this by using a cast to explicitly convert the result to Day, as shown here:

```
day2 = static_cast<Day>(day1 + 1);   // This works.
```

Using an enum Variable to Step through an Array's Elements

Because enumerators are stored in memory as integers, you can use them as array subscripts. For example, look at the following code:

```
enum Day { MONDAY, TUESDAY, WEDNESDAY, THURSDAY, FRIDAY };
const int NUM_DAYS = 5;
double sales[NUM_DAYS];
sales[MONDAY] = 1525.0;       // Stores 1525.0 in sales[0].
sales[TUESDAY] = 1896.5;      // Stores 1896.5 in sales[1].
sales[WEDNESDAY] = 1975.63;   // Stores 1975.63 in sales[2].
sales[THURSDAY] = 1678.33;    // Stores 1678.33 in sales[3].
sales[FRIDAY] = 1498.52;      // Stores 1498.52 in sales[4].
```

This code stores values in all five elements of the `sales` array. Because enumerator values can be used as array subscripts, you can use an `enum` variable in a loop to step through the elements of an array. However, using an `enum` variable for this purpose is not as straightforward as using an `int` variable. This is because you cannot use the `++` or `--` operators directly on an `enum` variable. To understand what I mean, first look at the following code taken from Program 9:

```
for (index = MONDAY; index <= FRIDAY; index++)
{
   cout << "Enter the sales for day "
        << index << ": ";
   cin >> sales[index];
}
```

In this code, `index` is an `int` variable used to step through each element of the array. It is reasonable to expect that we could use a `Day` variable instead, as shown in the following code:

```
Day workDay;   // Define a Day variable

// ERROR!!! This code will NOT work.
for (workDay = MONDAY; workDay <= FRIDAY; workDay++)
{
   cout << "Enter the sales for day "
        << workDay << ": ";
   cin >> sales[workDay];
}
```

Notice the `for` loop's update expression uses the `++` operator to increment `workDay`. Although this works fine with an `int` variable, the `++` operator cannot be used with an `enum` variable. Instead, you must convert `workDay++` to an equivalent expression that will work. The expression `workDay++` attempts to do the same thing as:

```
workDay = workDay + 1;   // Good idea, but still won't work.
```

However, this still will not work. We have to use a cast to explicitly convert the expression `workDay + 1` to the `Day` data type, like this:

```
workDay = static_cast<Day>(workDay + 1);
```

This is the expression that we must use in the `for` loop instead of `workDay++`. The corrected `for` loop looks like this:

```
for (workDay = MONDAY; workDay <= FRIDAY;
                 workDay = static_cast<Day>(workDay + 1))
{
   cout << "Enter the sales for day "
        << workDay << ": ";
   cin >> sales[workDay];
}
```

Program 10 is a version of Program 9 that is modified to use a `Day` variable to step through the elements of the `sales` array.

Program 10

```
// This program demonstrates an enumerated data type.
#include <iostream>
#include <iomanip>
using namespace std;

enum Day { MONDAY, TUESDAY, WEDNESDAY, THURSDAY, FRIDAY };

int main()
{
    const int NUM_DAYS = 5;       // The number of days
    double sales[NUM_DAYS];       // To hold sales for each day
    double total = 0.0;           // Accumulator
    Day workDay;                  // Loop counter

    // Get the sales for each day.
    for (workDay = MONDAY; workDay <= FRIDAY;
                           workDay = static_cast<Day>(workDay + 1))
    {
        cout << "Enter the sales for day "
             << workDay << ": ";
        cin >> sales[workDay];
    }

    // Calculate the total sales.
    for (workDay = MONDAY; workDay <= FRIDAY;
                           workDay = static_cast<Day>(workDay + 1))
        total += sales[workDay];

    // Display the total.
    cout << "The total sales are $" << setprecision(2)
         << fixed << total << endl;

    return 0;
}
```

Program Output with Example Input Shown in Bold

Enter the sales for day 0: **1525.00** [Enter]
Enter the sales for day 1: **1896.50** [Enter]
Enter the sales for day 2: **1975.63** [Enter]
Enter the sales for day 3: **1678.33** [Enter]
Enter the sales for day 4: **1498.52** [Enter]
The total sales are $8573.98

Using Enumerators to Output Values

As you have already seen, sending an enumerator to cout causes the enumerator's integer value to be displayed. For example, assuming we are using the Day type previously described, the following statement displays 0:

```
cout << MONDAY << endl;
```

If you wish to use the enumerator to display a string such as "Monday," you'll have to write code that produces the desired string. For example, in the following code, assume workDay is a Day variable that has been initialized to some value. The switch statement displays the name of a day, based upon the value of the variable.

```
switch(workDay)
{
   case MONDAY    : cout << "Monday";
                    break;
   case TUESDAY   : cout << "Tuesday";
                    break;
   case WEDNESDAY : cout << "Wednesday";
                    break;
   case THURSDAY  : cout << "Thursday";
                    break;
   case FRIDAY    : cout << "Friday";
}
```

Program 11 shows this type of code used in a function. Instead of asking the user to enter the sales for day 0, day 1, and so forth, it displays the names of the days.

Program 11

```
// This program demonstrates an enumerated data type.
#include <iostream>
#include <iomanip>
using namespace std;

enum Day { MONDAY, TUESDAY, WEDNESDAY, THURSDAY, FRIDAY };

// Function prototype
void displayDayName(Day);

int main()
{
    const int NUM_DAYS = 5;     // The number of days
    double sales[NUM_DAYS];     // To hold sales for each day
    double total = 0.0;         // Accumulator
    Day workDay;                // Loop counter

    // Get the sales for each day.
    for (workDay = MONDAY; workDay <= FRIDAY;
                           workDay = static_cast<Day>(workDay + 1))
    {
        cout << "Enter the sales for day ";
        displayDayName(workDay);
        cout << ": ";
        cin >> sales[workDay];
    }

```

```
    // Calculate the total sales.
    for (workDay = MONDAY; workDay <= FRIDAY;
                           workDay = static_cast<Day>(workDay + 1))
        total += sales[workDay];

    // Display the total.
    cout << "The total sales are $" << setprecision(2)
         << fixed << total << endl;

    return 0;
}

//**********************************************************
// Definition of the displayDayName function               *
// This function accepts an argument of the Day type and   *
// displays the corresponding name of the day.             *
//**********************************************************

void displayDayName(Day d)
{
    switch(d)
    {
        case MONDAY    : cout << "Monday";
                         break;
        case TUESDAY   : cout << "Tuesday";
                         break;
        case WEDNESDAY : cout << "Wednesday";
                         break;
        case THURSDAY  : cout << "Thursday";
                         break;
        case FRIDAY    : cout << "Friday";
    }
}
```

Program Output with Example Input Shown in Bold

Enter the sales for Monday: **1525.00** [Enter]
Enter the sales for Tuesday: **1896.50** [Enter]
Enter the sales for Wednesday: **1975.63** [Enter]
Enter the sales for Thursday: **1678.33** [Enter]
Enter the sales for Friday: **1498.52** [Enter]
The total sales are $8573.98

Specifying Integer Values for Enumerators

By default, the enumerators in an enumerated data type are assigned the integer values 0, 1, 2, and so forth. If this is not appropriate, you can specify the values to be assigned, as in the following example:

```
enum Water { FREEZING = 32, BOILING = 212 };
```

In this example, the `FREEZING` enumerator is assigned the integer value 32, and the `BOILING` enumerator is assigned the integer value 212. Program 12 demonstrates how this enumerated type might be used.

Program 12

```
// This program demonstrates an enumerated data type.
#include <iostream>
#include <iomanip>
using namespace std;

int main()
{
    enum Water { FREEZING = 32, BOILING = 212 };
    int waterTemp; // To hold the water temperature

    cout << "Enter the current water temperature: ";
    cin >> waterTemp;
    if (waterTemp <= FREEZING)
        cout << "The water is frozen.\n";
    else if (waterTemp >= BOILING)
        cout << "The water is boiling.\n";
    else
        cout << "The water is not frozen or boiling.\n";

    return 0;
}
```

Program Output with Example Input Shown in Bold

Enter the current water temperature: **10** [Enter]
The water is frozen.

Program Output with Example Input Shown in Bold

Enter the current water temperature: **300** [Enter]
The water is boiling.

Program Output with Example Input Shown in Bold

Enter the current water temperature: **92** [Enter]
The water is not frozen or boiling.

If you leave out the value assignment for one or more of the enumerators, it will be assigned a default value. Here is an example:

```
enum Colors { RED, ORANGE, YELLOW = 9, GREEN, BLUE };
```

In this example, the enumerator `RED` will be assigned the value 0, `ORANGE` will be assigned the value 1, `YELLOW` will be assigned the value 9, `GREEN` will be assigned the value 10, and `BLUE` will be assigned the value 11.

Enumerators Must Be Unique within the Same Scope

Enumerators are identifiers just like variable names, named constants, and function names. As with all identifiers, they must be unique within the same scope. For example, an error will result if both of the following enumerated types are declared within the same scope. In the following example, the reason is that `ROOSEVELT` is declared twice.

```
enum Presidents { MCKINLEY, ROOSEVELT, TAFT };
enum VicePresidents { ROOSEVELT, FAIRBANKS, SHERMAN };   // Error!
```

The following declarations will also cause an error if they appear within the same scope.

```
enum Status { OFF, ON };
const int OFF = 0;          // Error!
```

Declaring the Type and Defining the Variables in One Statement

The following code uses two lines to declare an enumerated data type and define a variable of the type:

```
enum Car { PORSCHE, FERRARI, JAGUAR };
Car sportsCar;
```

C++ allows you to declare an enumerated data type and define one or more variables of the type in the same statement. The previous code could be combined into the following statement:

```
enum Car { PORSCHE, FERRARI, JAGUAR } sportsCar;
```

The following statement declares the `Car` data type and defines two variables: `myCar` and `yourCar`.

```
enum Car { PORSCHE, FERRARI, JAGUAR } myCar, yourCar;
```

Using Strongly Typed `enum`s in C++ 11

Earlier, we mentioned that you cannot have multiple enumerators with the same name, within the same scope. In C++ 11, you can use a new type of `enum`, known as a *strongly typed enum* (also known as an *enum class*), to get around this limitation. Here are two examples of a strongly typed `enum` declaration:

```
enum class Presidents { MCKINLEY, ROOSEVELT, TAFT };
enum class VicePresidents { ROOSEVELT, FAIRBANKS, SHERMAN };
```

These statements declare two strongly typed `enum`s: `Presidents` and `VicePresidents`. Notice they look like regular `enum` declarations, except the word `class` appears after `enum`. Although both `enum`s contain the same enumerator (`ROOSEVELT`), these declarations will compile without an error.

When you use a strongly typed enumerator, you must prefix the enumerator with the name of the `enum`, followed by the `::` operator. Here are two examples:

```
Presidents prez = Presidents::ROOSEVELT;
VicePresidents vp = VicePresidents::ROOSEVELT;
```

The first statement defines a `Presidents` variable named `prez`, and initializes it with the `Presidents::ROOSEVELT` enumerator. The second statement defines a `VicePresidents` variable named `vp`, and initializes it with the `VicePresidents::ROOSEVELT` enumerator. Here is an example of an `if` statement that compares the `prez` variable with an enumerator:

```
if (prez == Presidents::ROOSEVELT)
   cout << "Roosevelt is president!\n";
```

Strongly typed enumerators are stored as integers like regular enumerators. However, if you want to retrieve a strongly typed enumerator's underlying integer value, you must use a cast operator. Here is an example:

```
int x = static_cast<int>(Presidents::ROOSEVELT);
```

This statement assigns the underlying integer value of the `Presidents::ROOSEVELT` enumerator to the variable `x`. Here is another example:

```
cout << static_cast<int>(Presidents::TAFT) << endl
     << static_cast<int>(Presidents::MCKINLEY) << endl;
```

This statement displays the integer values for the `Presidents::TAFT` and the `Presidents::MCKINLEY` enumerators.

When you declare a strongly typed `enum`, you can optionally specify any integer data type as the underlying type. You simply write a colon (:) after the enum name, followed by the desired data type. For example, the following statement declares an `enum` that uses the `char` data type for its enumerators:

```
enum class Day : char { MONDAY, TUESDAY, WEDNESDAY, THURSDAY, FRIDAY };
```

The following statement shows another example. This statement declares an `enum` named `Water` that uses `unsigned` as the data type of its enumerators. Additionally, values are assigned to the enumerators.

```
enum class Water : unsigned { FREEZING = 32, BOILING = 212 };
```

Checkpoint

16 Look at the following declaration:

```
enum Flower { ROSE, DAISY, PETUNIA };
```

In memory, what value will be stored for the enumerator `ROSE`? For `DAISY`? For `PETUNIA`?

17 What will the following code display?

```
enum { HOBBIT, ELF = 7, DRAGON };
cout << HOBBIT << " " << ELF << " " << DRAGON << endl;
```

18 Does the enumerated data type declared in Checkpoint Question 17 have a name, or is it anonymous?

19 What will the following code display?

```
enum Letters { Z, Y, X };
if (Z > X)
    cout << "Z is greater than X. \n";
else
    cout << "Z is not greater than X. \n";
```

20 Will the following code cause an error, or will it compile without any errors? If it causes an error, rewrite it so it compiles.

```
enum Color { RED, GREEN, BLUE };
Color c;
c = 0;
```

21 Will the following code cause an error, or will it compile without any errors? If it causes an error, rewrite it so it compiles.

```
enum Color { RED, GREEN, BLUE };
Color c = RED;
c++;
```

NOTE: For an additional example of this chapter's topics, see the High Adventure Travel Part 2 Case Study on the Computer Science Portal at pearsonhighered.com/gaddis.

Review Questions and Exercises

Short Answer

1. What is a primitive data type?
2. Does a structure declaration cause a structure variable to be created?
3. Both arrays and structures are capable of storing multiple values. What is the difference between an array and a structure?
4. Look at the following structure declaration:

```
struct Point
{
    int x;
    int y;
};
```

   Write statements that

   A) define a `Point` structure variable named `center`.
   B) assign 12 to the `x` member of `center`.
   C) assign 7 to the `y` member of `center`.
   D) display the contents of the `x` and `y` members of `center`.

5. Look at the following structure declaration:

```
struct FullName
{
    string lastName;
    string middleName;
    string firstName;
};
```

   Write statements that

   A) define a `FullName` structure variable named `info`.
   B) assign your last, middle, and first name to the members of the `info` variable.
   C) display the contents of the members of the `info` variable.

6. Look at the following code:

```
struct PartData
{
    string partName;
    int idNumber;
};
PartData inventory[100];
```

Write a statement that displays the contents of the `partName` member of element 49 of the `inventory` array.

7. Look at the following code:

```
struct Town
{
   string townName;
   string countyName;
   double population;
   double elevation;
};

Town t = { "Canton", "Haywood", 9478 };
```

A) What value is stored in `t.townName`?
B) What value is stored in `t.countyName`?
C) What value is stored in `t.population`?
D) What value is stored in `t.elevation`?

8. Look at the following code:

```
structure Rectangle
{
   int length;
   int width;
};
Rectangle *r = nullptr
```

Write statements that

A) dynamically allocate a `Rectangle` structure variable and use `r` to point to it.
B) assign 10 to the structure's `length` member and 14 to the structure's `width` member.

9. What will the following code display?

```
enum { POODLE, BOXER, TERRIER };
cout << POODLE << " " << BOXER << " " << TERRIER << endl;
```

10. Look at the following declaration:

```
enum Person { BILL, JOHN, CLAIRE, BOB };
Person p;
```

Indicate whether each of the following statements or expressions is valid or invalid.

A) `p = BOB;`
B) `p++;`
C) `BILL > BOB`
D) `p = 0;`
E) `int x = BILL;`
F) `p = static_cast<Person>(3);`
G) `cout << CLAIRE << endl;`

Fill-in-the-Blank

11. Before a structure variable can be created, the structure must be ________.
12. The ________ is the name of the structure type.
13. The variables declared inside a structure declaration are called ________.
14. A(n) ________ is required after the closing brace of a structure declaration.
15. In the definition of a structure variable, the ________ is placed before the variable name, just like the data type of a regular variable is placed before its name.
16. The ________ operator allows you to access structure members.

Algorithm Workbench

17. The structure `Car` is declared as follows:

```
struct Car
{
    string carMake;
    string carModel;
    int yearModel;
    double cost;
};
```

Write a definition statement that defines a `Car` structure variable initialized with the following data:

Make: Ford
Model: Mustang
Year Model: 1968
Cost: $20,000

18. Define an array of 25 of the `Car` structure variables (the structure is declared in Question 17).
19. Define an array of 35 of the `Car` structure variables. Initialize the first three elements with the following data:

Make	Model	Year	Cost
Ford	Taurus	1997	$21,000
Honda	Accord	1992	$11,000
Lamborghini	Countach	1997	$200,000

20. Write a loop that will step through the array you defined in Question 19, displaying the contents of each element.
21. Declare a structure named `TempScale`, with the following members:

```
fahrenheit: a double
centigrade: a double
```

Next, declare a structure named `Reading`, with the following members:

```
windSpeed: an int
humidity: a double
temperature: a TempScale structure variable
```

Next, define a `Reading` structure variable.

22. Write statements that will store the following data in the variable you defined in Problem 21:

    Wind Speed: 37 mph
    Humidity: 32%
    Fahrenheit temperature: 32 degrees
    Centigrade temperature: 0 degrees

23. Write a function called `showReading`. It should accept a `Reading` structure variable (see Problem 21) as its argument. The function should display the contents of the variable on the screen.
24. Write a function called `findReading`. It should use a `Reading` structure reference variable (see Problem 21) as its parameter. The function should ask the user to enter values for each member of the structure.
25. Write a function called `getReading`, which returns a `Reading` structure (see Problem 21). The function should ask the user to enter values for each member of a `Reading` structure, then return the structure.
26. Write a function called `recordReading`. It should use a `Reading` structure pointer variable (see Problem 21) as its parameter. The function should ask the user to enter values for each member of the structure pointed to by the parameter.
27. Rewrite the following statement using the structure pointer operator:

```
(*rptr).windSpeed = 50;
```

28. Look at the following statement:

```
enum Color { RED, ORANGE, GREEN, BLUE };
```

    A) What is the name of the data type declared by this statement?
    B) What are the enumerators for this type?
    C) Write a statement that defines a variable of this type and initializes it with a valid value.

29. A pet store sells dogs, cats, birds, and hamsters. Write a declaration for an anonymous enumerated data type that can represent the types of pets the store sells.

True or False

30. T F A semicolon is required after the closing brace of a structure declaration.
31. T F A structure declaration does not define a variable.
32. T F The contents of a structure variable can be displayed by passing the structure variable to the `cout` object.
33. T F Structure variables may not be initialized.
34. T F In a structure variable's initialization list, you do not have to provide initializers for all the members.
35. T F You may skip members in a structure's initialization list.
36. T F The following expression refers to element 5 in the array `carInfo`: `carInfo.model[5]`
37. T F An array of structures may be initialized.

38. T F A structure variable may not be a member of another structure.
39. T F A structure member variable may be passed to a function as an argument.
40. T F An entire structure may not be passed to a function as an argument.
41. T F A function may return a structure.
42. T F When a function returns a structure, it is always necessary for the function to have a local structure variable to hold the member values that are to be returned.
43. T F The indirection operator has higher precedence than the dot operator.
44. T F The structure pointer operator does not automatically dereference the structure pointer on its left.

Find the Errors

Each of the following declarations, programs, and program segments has errors. Locate as many as you can.

45.
```
struct
{
    int x;
    float y;
};
```

46.
```
struct Values
{
    string name;
    int age;
}
```

47.
```
struct TwoVals
{
    int a, b;
};
int main ()
{
    TwoVals.a = 10;
    TwoVals.b = 20;
    return 0;
}
```

48.
```
#include <iostream>
using namespace std;

struct ThreeVals
{
    int a, b, c;
};
int main()
{
    ThreeVals vals = {1, 2, 3};
    cout << vals << endl;
    return 0;
}
```

49.
```
#include <iostream>
#include <string>
using namespace std;

struct names
{
   string first;
   string last;
};
int main ()
{
   names customer = "Smith", "Orley";
   cout << names.first << endl;
   cout << names.last << endl;
   return 0;
}
```

50.
```
struct FourVals
{
   int a, b, c, d;
};
int main ()
{
   FourVals nums = {1, 2, , 4};
   return 0;
}
```

51.
```
struct TwoVals
{
   int a;
   int b;
};
TwoVals getVals()
{
   TwoVals.a = TwoVals.b = 0;
}
```

52.
```
struct ThreeVals
{
   int a, b, c;
};
int main ()
{
   TwoVals s, *sptr = nullptr;
   sptr = &s;
   *sptr.a = 1;
   return 0;
}
```

Programming Challenges

1. Movie Data

Write a program that uses a structure named `MovieData` to store the following information about a movie:

Title
Director
Year Released
Running Time (in minutes)

The program should create two `MovieData` variables, store values in their members, and pass each one, in turn, to a function that displays the information about the movie in a clearly formatted manner.

2. Movie Profit

Modify the program written for Programming Challenge 1 (Movie Data) to include two additional members that hold the movie's production costs and first-year revenues. Modify the function that displays the movie data to display the title, director, release year, running time, and first year's profit or loss.

3. Corporate Sales Data

Write a program that uses a structure to store the following data on a company division:

Division Name (such as East, West, North, or South)
First-Quarter Sales
Second-Quarter Sales
Third-Quarter Sales
Fourth-Quarter Sales
Total Annual Sales
Average Quarterly Sales

The program should use four variables of this structure. Each variable should represent one of the following corporate divisions: East, West, North, and South. The user should be asked for the four quarters' sales figures for each division. Each division's total and average sales should be calculated and stored in the appropriate member of each structure variable. These figures should then be displayed on the screen.

Input Validation: Do not accept negative numbers for any sales figures.

4. Weather Statistics

VideoNote
Solving the Weather Statistics Problem

Write a program that uses a structure to store the following weather data for a particular month:

Total Rainfall
High Temperature
Low Temperature
Average Temperature

The program should have an array of 12 structures to hold weather data for an entire year. When the program runs, it should ask the user to enter data for each month. (The average temperature should be calculated.) Once the data are entered for all the months, the program should calculate and display the average monthly rainfall, the total rainfall for the year, the highest and lowest temperatures for the year (and the months they occurred in), and the average of all the monthly average temperatures.

Input Validation: Only accept temperatures within the range between –100 and +140 degrees Fahrenheit.

5. **Weather Statistics Modification**

   Modify the program that you wrote for Programming Challenge 4 (weather statistics) so it defines an enumerated data type with enumerators for the months (`JANUARY`, `FEBRUARY`, so on). The program should use the enumerated type to step through the elements of the array.

6. **Soccer Scores**

   Write a program that stores the following data about a soccer player in a structure:

   Player's Name
   Player's Number
   Points Scored by Player

   The program should keep an array of 12 of these structures. Each element is for a different player on a team. When the program runs, it should ask the user to enter the data for each player. It should then show a table that lists each player's number, name, and points scored. The program should also calculate and display the total points earned by the team. The number and name of the player who has earned the most points should also be displayed.

   Input Validation: Do not accept negative values for players' numbers or points scored.

7. **Customer Accounts**

   Write a program that uses a structure to store the following data about a customer account:

   Name
   Address
   City, State, and ZIP
   Telephone Number
   Account Balance
   Date of Last Payment

   The program should use an array of at least 10 structures. It should let the user enter data into the array, change the contents of any element, and display all the data stored in the array. The program should have a menu-driven user interface.

   Input Validation: When the data for a new account is entered, be sure the user enters data for all the fields. No negative account balances should be entered.

8. **Search Function for Customer Accounts Program**

   Add a function to Programming Challenge 7 (Customer Accounts) that allows the user to search the structure array for a particular customer's account. It should accept part of the customer's name as an argument then search for an account with a name that matches it. All accounts that match should be displayed. If no account matches, a message saying so should be displayed.

9. Speakers' Bureau

Write a program that keeps track of a speakers' bureau. The program should use a structure to store the following data about a speaker:

Name
Telephone Number
Speaking Topic
Fee Required

The program should use an array of at least 10 structures. It should let the user enter data into the array, change the contents of any element, and display all the data stored in the array. The program should have a menu-driven user interface.

Input Validation: When the data for a new speaker is entered, be sure the user enters data for all the fields. No negative amounts should be entered for a speaker's fee.

10. Search Function for the Speakers' Bureau Program

Add a function to Programming Challenge 9 (Speakers' Bureau) that allows the user to search for a speaker on a particular topic. It should accept a key word as an argument then search the array for a structure with that key word in the Speaking Topic field. All structures that match should be displayed. If no structure matches, a message saying so should be displayed.

11. Monthly Budget

A student has established the following monthly budget:

Housing	$500.00
Utilities	$150.00
Household Expenses	$65.00
Transportation	$50.00
Food	$250.00
Medical	$30.00
Insurance	$100.00
Entertainment	$150.00
Clothing	$75.00
Miscellaneous	$50.00

Write a program that has a `MonthlyBudget` structure designed to hold each of these expense categories. The program should pass the structure to a function that asks the user to enter the amounts spent in each budget category during a month. The program should then pass the structure to a function that displays a report indicating the amount over or under in each category, as well as the amount over or under for the entire monthly budget.

12. Course Grade

Write a program that uses a structure to store the following data:

Member Name	Description
Name	Student name
Idnum	Student ID number
Tests	Pointer to an array of test scores
Average	Average test score
Grade	Course grade

The program should keep a list of test scores for a group of students. It should ask the user how many test scores there are to be and how many students there are. It should then dynamically allocate an array of structures. Each structure's `Tests` member should point to a dynamically allocated array that will hold the test scores.

After the arrays have been dynamically allocated, the program should ask for the ID number and all the test scores for each student. The average test score should be calculated and stored in the `average` member of each structure. The course grade should be computed on the basis of the following grading scale:

Average Test Grade	Course Grade
91–100	A
81–90	B
71–80	C
61–70	D
60 or below	F

The course grade should then be stored in the `Grade` member of each structure. Once all this data is calculated, a table should be displayed on the screen listing each student's name, ID number, average test score, and course grade.

Input Validation: Be sure all the data for each student is entered. Do not accept negative numbers for any test score.

13. Drink Machine Simulator

Write a program that simulates a soft drink machine. The program should use a structure that stores the following data:

Drink Name
Drink Cost
Number of Drinks in Machine

The program should create an array of five structures. The elements should be initialized with the following data:

Drink Name	Cost	Number in Machine
Cola	.75	20
Root Beer	.75	20
Lemon-Lime	.75	20
Grape Soda	.80	20
Cream Soda	.80	20

Each time the program runs, it should enter a loop that performs the following steps: A list of drinks is displayed on the screen. The user should be allowed to either quit the program or pick a drink. If the user selects a drink, he or she will next enter the amount of money that is to be inserted into the drink machine. The program should display the amount of change that would be returned, and subtract one from the number of that drink left in the machine. If the user selects a drink that has sold out, a message should be displayed. The loop then repeats. When the user chooses to quit the program, it should display the total amount of money the machine earned.

Input Validation: When the user enters an amount of money, do not accept negative values or values greater than $1.00.

14. Inventory Bins

Write a program that simulates inventory bins in a warehouse. Each bin holds a number of the same type of parts. The program should use a structure that keeps the following data:

Description of the part kept in the bin
Number of parts in the bin

The program should have an array of 10 bins, initialized with the following data:

Part Description	Number of Parts in the Bin
Valve	10
Bearing	5
Bushing	15
Coupling	21
Flange	7
Gear	5
Gear Housing	5
Vacuum Gripper	25
Cable	18
Rod	12

The program should have the following functions:

`AddParts`—increases a specific bin's part count by a specified number.

`RemoveParts`—decreases a specific bin's part count by a specified number.

When the program runs, it should repeat a loop that performs the following steps: The user should see a list of what each bin holds and how many parts are in each bin. The user can choose to either quit the program or select a bin. When a bin is selected, the user can either add parts to it or remove parts from it. The loop then repeats, showing the updated bin data on the screen.

Input Validation: No bin can hold more than 30 parts, so don't let the user add more than a bin can hold. Also, don't accept negative values for the number of parts being added or removed.

Answers to Checkpoints

1
```
struct Account
{
    string acctNum;
    double acctBal;
    double intRate;
    double avgBal;
};
```

2
```
Account savings = {"ACZ42137-B12-7",
                   4512.59,
                   0.04,
                   4217.07 };
```

3
```
#include <iostream>
#include <string>
using namespace std;
struct Movie
{
    string name;
    string director;
    string producer;
    string year;
};

int main()
{
    Movie favorite;

    cout << "Enter the following information about your\n";
    cout << "favorite movie.\n";
    cout << "Name: ";
    getline(cin, favorite.name);
    cout << "Director: ";
    getline(cin, favorite.director);

    cout << "Producer: ";
    getline(cin, favorite.producer);

    cout << "Year of release: ";
    getline(cin, favorite.year);

    cout << "Here is information on your favorite movie:\n";
    cout << "Name: " << favorite.name << endl;
    cout << "Director: " << favorite.director << endl;
    cout << "Producer: " << favorite.producer << endl;
    cout << "Year of release: " << favorite.year << endl;
    return 0;
}
```

4
```
Product items[100];
```

5
```
for (int x = 0; x < 100; x++)
{
    items[x].description = "";
    items[x].partNum = 0;
    items[x].cost = 0;
}
```

6
```
items[0].description = "Claw Hammer";
items[0].partNum = 547;
items[0].cost = 8.29;
```

7
```
for (int x = 0; x < 100; x++)
{
    cout << items[x].description << endl;
    cout << items[x].partNum << endl;
    cout << items[x].cost << endl << endl;
}
```

8
```
struct Measurement
{
    int miles;
    long meters;
};
```

9
```
struct Destination
{
    string city;
    Measurement distance;
};
Destination place;
```

10
```
place.city = "Tupelo";
place.distance.miles = 375;
place.distance.meters = 603375;
```

11
```
void showRect(Rectangle r)
{
    cout << r.length << endl;
    cout << r.width << endl;
}
```

12
```
void getRect(Rectangle &r)
{
    cout << "Width: ";
    cin >> r.width;
    cout << "length: ";
    cin >> r.length;
}
```

13
```
Rectangle getRect()
{
    Rectangle r;
    cout << "Width: ";
    cin >> r.width;
    cout << "length: ";
    cin >> r.length;
    return r;
}
```

14 `Rectangle *rptr;`

15 B

16 The integers 0, 1, and 2

17 0 7 8

18 It is anonymous.

19 Z is not greater than X.

20 The code will not compile. The assignment statement should be written as:

```
c = static_cast<Color>(0);
```

21 The code will not compile. The statement c++ should be written as:

```
c = static_cast<Color>(c + 1);
```

Answers to Odd Numbered Review Questions

1. A data type that is built into the C++ language, such as `int`, `char`, `float`, etc.
3. The elements of an array must all be of the same data type. The members of a structure may be of different data types.
5. A) `FullName info;`

   B)
   ```
   info.lastName = "Smith";
   info.middleName = "Bart";
   info.firstName = "William";
   ```
   C)
   ```
   cout << info.lastName << endl;
   cout << info.middleName << endl;
   cout << info.firstName << endl;
   ```
7. A) “Canton”

   B) “Haywood”

   C) 9478

   D) uninitialized
9. 0 1 2
11. declared

13. members

15. tag

17. `Car hotRod = {"Ford", "Mustang", 1997, 20000};`

19.
```
Car forSale[35] = {{"Ford", "Taurus", 1997, 21000},
                   {"Honda", "Accord", 1992, 11000},
                   {"Lamborghini", "Countach", 1997, 200000}};
```

21.
```
struct TempScale
{
    double fahrenheit;
    double centigrade;
};
struct Reading
{
    int windSpeed;
    double humidity;
    tempScale temperature;
};
Reading today;
```

23.
```
void showReading(Reading values)
{
    cout << "Wind speed: " << values.windSpeed << endl;
    cout << "Humidity: " << values.humidity << endl;
    cout << "Fahrenheit temperature: " <<
            values.temperature.fahrenheit << endl;
    cout << "Centigrade temperature: " <<
            values.temperature.centigrade << endl;
}
```

25.
```
Reading getReading()
{
    Reading local;
    cout << "Enter the following values:\n";
    cout << "Wind speed: ";
    cin >> local.windSpeed;
    cout << "Humidity: ";
    cin >> local.humidity;
    cout << "Fahrenheit temperature: ";
    cin >> local.temperature.fahrenheit;
    cout << "Centigrade temperature: ";
    cin >> local.temperature.centigrade;
    return local;
}
```

27. `rptr->WindSpeed = 50;`

29. `enum Pets {DOGS, CATS, BIRDS, HAMSTERS};`

31. True
33. False
35. False
37. True
39. True
41. True
43. False
45. The structure declaration has no tag.
47. No structure variable has been declared. `TwoVals` is the structure tag.
49. The initialization list of the `customer` variable must be enclosed in braces.
51. The function must define a variable of the `TwoVals` structure. The variable, then, should be used in the assignment statement.

Advanced File Operations

TOPICS

1 File Operations

CONCEPT: A file is a collection of data that is usually stored on a computer's disk. Data can be saved to files and then later reused.

Almost all real-world programs use files to store and retrieve data. Here are a few examples of familiar software packages that use files extensively:

- **Word Processors:** Word processing programs are used to write letters, memos, reports, and other documents. The documents are then saved in files so they can be edited and reprinted.
- **Database Management Systems:** DBMSs are used to create and maintain databases. Databases are files that contain large collections of data, such as payroll records, inventories, sales statistics, and customer records.
- **Spreadsheets:** Spreadsheet programs are used to work with numerical data. Numbers and mathematical formulas can be inserted into the rows and columns of the spreadsheet. The spreadsheet can then be saved to a file for later use.
- **Compilers:** Compilers translate the source code of a program, which is saved in a file, into an executable file.

This chapter covers more advanced file operations and focuses primarily

From Chapter 12 of *Starting Out with C++: From Control Structures through Objects*, Ninth Edition. Tony Gaddis.

on the `fstream` data type. As a review, Table 1 compares the `ifstream`, `ofstream`, and `fstream` data types. All of these data types require the `<fstream>` header file.

Table 1 File Stream Data Types

Data Type	Description
`ifstream`	Input File Stream. This data type can be used only to read data from files into memory.
`ofstream`	Output File Stream. This data type can be used to create files and write data to them.
`fstream`	File Stream. This data type can be used to create files, write data to them, and read data from them.

Using the `fstream` Data Type

You define an `fstream` object just as you define objects of other data types. The following statement defines an `fstream` object named `dataFile`:

```
fstream dataFile;
```

As with `ifstream` and `ofstream` objects, you use an `fstream` object's `open` function to open a file. An `fstream` object's `open` function requires two arguments, however. The first argument is a string containing the name of the file. The second argument is a file access flag that indicates the mode in which you wish to open the file. Here is an example:

```
dataFile.open("info.txt", ios::out);
```

The first argument in this function call is the name of the file, info.txt. The second argument is the file access flag `ios::out`. This tells C++ to open the file in output mode. Output mode allows data to be written to a file. The following statement uses the `ios::in` access flag to open a file in input mode, which allows data to be read from the file.

```
dataFile.open("info.txt", ios::in);
```

There are many file access flags, as listed in Table 2.

Table 2 File Access Flags

File Access Flag	Meaning
`ios::app`	Append mode. If the file already exists, its contents are preserved and all output is written to the end of the file. By default, this flag causes the file to be created if it does not exist.
`ios::ate`	If the file already exists, the program goes directly to the end of it. Output may be written anywhere in the file.
`ios::binary`	Binary mode. When a file is opened in binary mode, data are written to or read from it in pure binary format. (The default mode is text.)
`ios::in`	Input mode. Data will be read from the file. If the file does not exist, it will not be created, and the open function will fail.
`ios::out`	Output mode. Data will be written to the file. By default, the file's contents will be deleted if it already exists.
`ios::trunc`	If the file already exists, its contents will be deleted (truncated). This is the default mode used by `ios::out`.

Several flags may be used together if they are connected with the | operator. For example, assume `dataFile` is an `fstream` object in the following statement:

```
dataFile.open("info.txt", ios::in | ios::out);
```

This statement opens the file info.txt in both input and output modes. This means data may be written to and read from the file.

> **NOTE:** When used by itself, the `ios::out` flag causes the file's contents to be deleted if the file already exists. When used with the `ios::in` flag, however, the file's existing contents are preserved. If the file does not already exist, it will be created.

The following statement opens the file in such a way that data will only be written to its end:

```
dataFile.open("info.txt", ios::out | ios::app);
```

By using different combinations of access flags, you can open files in many possible modes.

Program 1 uses an `fstream` object to open a file for output, then writes data to the file.

Program 1

```
// This program uses an fstream object to write data to a file.
#include <iostream>
#include <fstream>
using namespace std;

int main()
{
    fstream dataFile;

    cout << "Opening file...\n";
    dataFile.open("demofile.txt", ios::out);     // Open for output
    cout << "Now writing data to the file.\n";
    dataFile << "Jones\n";                       // Write line 1
    dataFile << "Smith\n";                       // Write line 2
    dataFile << "Willis\n";                      // Write line 3
    dataFile << "Davis\n";                       // Write line 4
    dataFile.close();                            // Close the file
    cout << "Done.\n";
    return 0;
}
```

Program Output

```
Opening file...
Now writing data to the file.
Done.
```

Output to File `demofile.txt`

```
Jones
Smith
Willis
Davis
```

The file output is shown for Program 1 the way it would appear if the file contents were displayed on the screen. The `\n` characters cause each name to appear on a separate line. The actual file contents, however, appear as a stream of characters as shown in Figure 1.

Figure 1 File contents

J	o	n	e	s	\n	S	m	i	t	h	\n	W	i	l

l	i	s	\n	D	a	v	i	s	\n	<EOF>

As you can see from the figure, `\n` characters are written to the file along with all the other characters. The characters are added to the file sequentially, in the order they are written by the program. The very last character is an *end-of-file marker*. It is a character that marks the end of the file, and is automatically written when the file is closed. (The actual character used to mark the end of a file depends upon the operating system being used. It is always a nonprinting character. For example, some systems use control-Z, which is ASCII code 26.)

Program 2 is a modification of Program 1 that further illustrates the sequential nature of files. The file is opened, two names are written to it, and it is closed. The file is then reopened by the program in append mode (with the `ios::app` access flag). When a file is opened in append mode, its contents are preserved, and all subsequent output is appended to the file's end. Two more names are added to the file before it is closed and the program terminates.

Program 2

```
// This program writes data to a file, closes the file,
// then reopens the file and appends more data.
#include <iostream>
#include <fstream>
using namespace std;

int main()
{
    ofstream dataFile;

    cout << "Opening file...\n";
    // Open the file in output mode.
    dataFile.open("demofile.txt", ios::out);
    cout << "Now writing data to the file.\n";
    dataFile << "Jones\n";                    // Write line 1
    dataFile << "Smith\n";                    // Write line 2
    cout << "Now closing the file.\n";
    dataFile.close();                         // Close the file

    cout << "Opening the file again...\n";
    // Open the file in append mode.
    dataFile.open("demofile.txt", ios::out | ios::app);
    cout << "Writing more data to the file.\n";
    dataFile << "Willis\n";                   // Write line 3
    dataFile << "Davis\n";                    // Write line 4
    cout << "Now closing the file.\n";
    dataFile.close();                         // Close the file
```

```
    cout << "Done.\n";
    return 0;
}
```

Output to File `demofile.txt`

```
Jones
Smith
Willis
Davis
```

The first time the file is opened, the names are written as shown in Figure 2.

Figure 2 Original file contents

J	o	n	e	s	\n	S	m	i	t	h	\n	<EOF>

The file is closed, and an end-of-file character is automatically written. When the file is reopened, the new output is appended to the end of the file, as shown in Figure 3.

Figure 3 New data appended to the file

J	o	n	e	s	\n	S	m	i	t	h	\n	W	i	l

l	i	s	\n	D	a	v	i	s	\n	<EOF>

NOTE: If the `ios::out` flag had been alone, without `ios::app` the second time the file was opened, the file's contents would have been deleted. If this had been the case, the names Jones and Smith would have been erased, and the file would only have contained the names Willis and Davis.

File Open Modes with `ifstream` and `ofstream` Objects

The `ifstream` and `ofstream` data types each have a default mode in which they open files. This mode determines the operations that may be performed on the file and what happens if the file that is being opened already exists. Table 3 describes each data type's default open mode.

Table 3 Default Open Mode

File Type	Default Open Mode
`ofstream`	The file is opened for output only. Data may be written to the file, but not read from the file. If the file does not exist, it is created. If the file already exists, its contents are deleted (the file is truncated).
`ifstream`	The file is opened for input only. Data may be read from the file, but not written to it. The file's contents will be read from its beginning. If the file does not exist, the open function fails.

You cannot change the fact that `ifstream` files may only be read from, and `ofstream` files may only be written to. You can, however, vary the way operations are carried out on these files by providing a file access flag as an optional second argument to the `open` function. The following code shows an example using an `ofstream` object:

```
ofstream outputFile;
outputFile.open("values.txt", ios::out|ios::app);
```

The `ios::app` flag specifies that data written to the values.txt file should be appended to its existing contents.

Checking for a File's Existence Before Opening It

Sometimes you want to determine whether a file already exists before opening it for output. You can do this by first attempting to open the file for input. If the file does not exist, the open operation will fail. In that case, you can create the file by opening it for output. The following code gives an example:

```
fstream dataFile;
dataFile.open("values.txt", ios::in);
if (dataFile.fail())
{
   // The file does not exist, so create it.
   dataFile.open("values.txt", ios::out);
   //
   // Continue to process the file...
   //
}
else    // The file already exists.
{
   dataFile.close();
   cout << "The file values.txt already exists.\n";
}
```

Opening a File with the File Stream Object Definition Statement

An alternative to using the `open` member function is to use the file stream object definition statement to open the file. Here is an example:

```
fstream dataFile("names.txt", ios::in | ios::out);
```

This statement defines an `fstream` object named `dataFile` and uses it to open the file names.txt. The file is opened in both input and output modes. This technique eliminates the need to call the `open` function when your program knows the name and access mode of the file at the time the object is defined. You may also use this technique with `ifstream` and `ofstream` objects, as shown in the following examples.

```
ifstream inputFile("info.txt");
ofstream outputFile("addresses.txt");
ofstream dataFile("customers.txt", ios::out|ios::app);
```

You may also test for errors after you have opened a file with this technique. The following code shows an example:

```
ifstream inputFile("SalesData.txt");
if (!inputFile)
    cout << "Error opening SalesData.txt.\n";
```

Checkpoint

1 Which file access flag would you use if you want all output to be written to the end of an existing file?

2 How do you use more than one file access flag?

3 Assuming `diskInfo` is an `fstream` object, write a statement that opens the file names.dat for output.

4 Assuming `diskInfo` is an `fstream` object, write a statement that opens the file customers.txt for output, where all output will be written to the end of the file.

5 Assuming `diskInfo` is an `fstream` object, write a statement that opens the file payable.txt for both input and output.

6 Write a statement that defines an `fstream` object named `dataFile` and opens a file named salesfigures.txt for input. (*Note:* The file should be opened with the definition statement, not an `open` function call.)

2 File Output Formatting

CONCEPT: File output may be formatted in the same way that screen output is formatted.

The same output formatting techniques that are used with `cout` may also be used with file stream objects. For example, the `setprecision` and `fixed` manipulators may be called to establish the number of digits of precision to which floating-point values are rounded Program 3 demonstrates this.

Program 3

```
// This program uses the setprecision and fixed
// manipulators to format file output.
#include <iostream>
#include <iomanip>
#include <fstream>
using namespace std;

int main()
{
    fstream dataFile;
    double num = 17.816392;

    dataFile.open("numfile.txt", ios::out);     // Open in output mode

```

(program continues)

Program 3 *(continued)*

```
    dataFile << fixed;              // Format for fixed-point notation
    dataFile << num << endl;        // Write the number

    dataFile << setprecision(4);    // Format for 4 decimal places
    dataFile << num << endl;        // Write the number

    dataFile << setprecision(3);    // Format for 3 decimal places
    dataFile << num << endl;        // Write the number

    dataFile << setprecision(2);    // Format for 2 decimal places
    dataFile << num << endl;        // Write the number

    dataFile << setprecision(1);    // Format for 1 decimal place
    dataFile << num << endl;        // Write the number

    cout << "Done.\n";
    dataFile.close();               // Close the file
    return 0;
}
```

Contents of File numfile.txt

```
17.816392
17.8164
17.816
17.82
17.8
```

Notice the file output is formatted just as cout would format screen output. Program 4 shows the setw stream manipulator being used to format file output into columns.

Program 4

```
// This program writes three rows of numbers to a file.
#include <iostream>
#include <fstream>
#include <iomanip>
using namespace std;

int main()
{
    const int ROWS = 3;    // Rows to write
    const int COLS = 3;    // Columns to write
    int nums[ROWS][COLS] = { 2897, 5, 837,
                             34, 7, 1623,
                             390, 3456, 12 };
    fstream outFile("table.txt", ios::out);

```

```
    // Write the three rows of numbers with each
    // number in a field of 8 character spaces.
    for (int row = 0; row < ROWS; row++)
    {
        for (int col = 0; col < COLS; col++)
        {
            outFile << setw(8) << nums[row][col];
        }
        outFile << endl;
    }
    outFile.close();
    cout << "Done.\n";
    return 0;
}
```

Contents of File `table.txt`

```
    2897       5     837
      34       7    1623
     390    3456      12
```

Figure 4 shows the way the characters appear in the file.

Figure 4 File contents

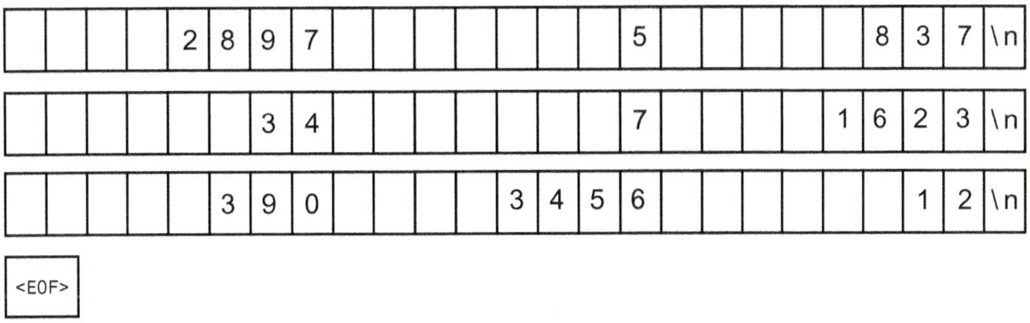

3 Passing File Stream Objects to Functions

CONCEPT: File stream objects may be passed by reference to functions.

VideoNote
Passing File Stream Objects to Functions

When writing actual programs, you'll want to create modularized code for handling file operations. File stream objects may be passed to functions, but they should always be passed by reference. The `openFile` function shown below uses an `fstream` reference object parameter:

```
bool openFileIn(fstream &file, string name)
{
   bool status;
   file.open(name, ios::in);
```

```
    if (file.fail())
       status = false;
    else
       status = true;
    return status;
}
```

The internal state of file stream objects changes with most every operation. They should always be passed to functions by reference to ensure internal consistency. Program 5 shows an example of how file stream objects may be passed as arguments to functions.

Program 5

```
// This program demonstrates how file stream objects may
// be passed by reference to functions.
#include <iostream>
#include <fstream>
#include <string>
using namespace std;

// Function prototypes
bool openFileIn(fstream &, string);
void showContents(fstream &);

int main()
{
    fstream dataFile;

    if (openFileIn(dataFile, "demofile.txt"))
    {
        cout << "File opened successfully.\n";
        cout << "Now reading data from the file.\n\n";
        showContents(dataFile);
        dataFile.close();
        cout << "\nDone.\n";
    }
    else
        cout << "File open error!" << endl;

    return 0;
}

//***********************************************************
// Definition of function openFileIn. Accepts a reference  *
// to an fstream object as an argument. The file is opened  *
// for input. The function returns true upon success, false *
// upon failure.                                            *
//***********************************************************

```

```
bool openFileIn(fstream &file, string name)
{
    file.open(name, ios::in);
    if (file.fail())
        return false;
    else
        return true;
}

//***********************************************************
// Definition of function showContents. Accepts an fstream  *
// reference as its argument. Uses a loop to read each name *
// from the file and displays it on the screen.             *
//***********************************************************

void showContents(fstream &file)
{
    string line;

    while (file >> line)
    {
        cout << line << endl;
    }
}
```

Program Output

```
File opened successfully.
Now reading data from the file.

Jones
Smith
Willis
Davis

Done.
```

4 More Detailed Error Testing

CONCEPT: All stream objects have error state bits that indicate the condition of the stream.

All stream objects contain a set of bits that act as flags. These flags indicate the current state of the stream. Table 4 lists these bits. These bits can be tested by the member functions listed in Table 5. (You've already learned about the `fail()` function.) One of the functions listed in the table, `clear()`, can be used to set a status bit.

Table 4 Stream Bits

Bit	Description
`ios::eofbit`	Set when the end of an input stream is encountered.
`ios::failbit`	Set when an attempted operation has failed.
`ios::hardfail`	Set when an unrecoverable error has occurred.
`ios::badbit`	Set when an invalid operation has been attempted.
`ios::goodbit`	Set when all the flags above are not set. Indicates the stream is in good condition.

Table 5 Functions to Test the State of Stream Bits

Function	Description
`eof()`	Returns true (nonzero) if the `eofbit` flag is set, otherwise returns false.
`fail()`	Returns true (nonzero) if the `failbit` or `hardfail` flags are set, otherwise returns false.
`bad()`	Returns true (nonzero) if the `badbit` flag is set, otherwise returns false.
`good()`	Returns true (nonzero) if the `goodbit` flag is set, otherwise returns false.
`clear()`	When called with no arguments, clears all the flags listed above. Can also be called with a specific flag as an argument.

The function `showState`, shown here, accepts a file stream reference as its argument. It shows the state of the file by displaying the return values of the `eof()`, `fail()`, `bad()`, and `good()` member functions.

```
void showState(fstream &file)
{
   cout << "File Status:\n";
   cout << " eof bit: " << file.eof() << endl;
   cout << " fail bit: " << file.fail() << endl;
   cout << " bad bit: " << file.bad() << endl;
   cout << " good bit: " << file.good() << endl;
   file.clear();      // Clear any bad bits
}
```

Program 6 uses the `showState` function to display `testFile`'s status after various operations. First, the file is created and the integer value 10 is stored in it. The file is then closed and reopened for input. The integer is read from the file, then a second read operation is performed. Because there is only one item in the file, the second read operation will result in an error.

Program 6

```
// This program demonstrates the return value of the stream
// object error testing member functions.
#include <iostream>
#include <fstream>
using namespace std;

```

```
// Function prototype
void showState(fstream &);

int main()
{
    int num = 10;

    // Open the file for output.
    fstream testFile("stuff.dat", ios::out);
    if (testFile.fail())
    {
        cout << "ERROR: Cannot open the file.\n";
        return 0;
    }

    // Write a value to the file.
    cout << "Writing the value " << num << " to the file.\n";
    testFile << num;

    // Show the bit states.
    showState(testFile);

    // Close the file.
    testFile.close();

    // Reopen the file for input.
    testFile.open("stuff.dat", ios::in);
    if (testFile.fail())
    {
        cout << "ERROR: Cannot open the file.\n";
        return 0;
    }

    // Read the only value from the file.
    cout << "Reading from the file.\n";
    testFile >> num;
    cout << "The value " << num << " was read.\n";

    // Show the bit states.
    showState(testFile);

    // No more data in the file, but force an invalid read operation.
    cout << "Forcing a bad read operation.\n";
    testFile >> num;

    // Show the bit states.
    showState(testFile);

    // Close the file.
    testFile.close();
    return 0;
}

```

(program continues)

Program 6 *(continued)*

```
//*******************************************************************
// Definition of function showState. This function uses              *
// an fstream reference as its parameter. The return values of      *
// the eof(), fail(), bad(), and good() member functions are        *
// displayed. The clear() function is called before the function *
// returns.                                                         *
//*******************************************************************

void showState(fstream &file)
{
    cout << "File Status:\n";
    cout << "  eof bit: " << file.eof() << endl;
    cout << "  fail bit: " << file.fail() << endl;
    cout << "  bad bit: " << file.bad() << endl;
    cout << "  good bit: " << file.good() << endl;
    file.clear(); // Clear any bad bits
}
```

Program Output

```
Writing the value 10 to the file.
File Status:
    eof bit: 0
    fail bit: 0
    bad bit: 0
    good bit: 1
Reading from the file.
The value 10 was read.
File Status:
    eof bit: 1
    fail bit: 0
    bad bit: 0
    good bit: 1
Forcing a bad read operation.
File Status:
    eof bit: 1
    fail bit: 1
    bad bit: 0
    good bit: 0
```

5 Member Functions for Reading and Writing Files

CONCEPT: File stream objects have member functions for more specialized file reading and writing.

If whitespace characters are part of the data in a file, a problem arises when the file is read by the >> operator. Because the operator considers whitespace characters as delimiters, it does not read them. For example, consider the file murphy.txt, which contains the following data:

Jayne Murphy
47 Jones Circle
Almond, NC 28702

Figure 5 shows the way the data is recorded in the file.

Figure 5 File contents

J	a	y	n	e		M	u	r	p	h	y	\n	4	7
	J	o	n	e	s		C	i	r	c	l	e	\n	A
l	m	o	n	d	,		N	C			2	8	7	0
2	\n	<EOF>												

The problem that arises from the use of the >> operator is evident in the output of Program 7.

Program 7

```
// This program demonstrates how the >> operator should not
// be used to read data that contain whitespace characters
// from a file.
#include <iostream>
#include <fstream>
#include <string>
using namespace std;

int main()
{
    string input;      // To hold file input
    fstream nameFile;  // File stream object

    // Open the file in input mode.
    nameFile.open("murphy.txt", ios::in);

    // If the file was successfully opened, continue.
    if (nameFile)
    {
        // Read the file contents.
        while (nameFile >> input)
        {
            cout << input;
        }

```

(program continues)

Program 7 *(continued)*

```
        // Close the file.
        nameFile.close();
    }
    else
    {
        cout << "ERROR: Cannot open file.\n";
    }
    return 0;
}
```

Program Output

```
JayneMurphy47JonesCircleAlmond,NC28702
```

The `getline` Function

The problem with Program 7 can be solved by using the `getline` function. The function reads a "line" of data, including whitespace characters. Here is an example of the function call:

```
getline(dataFile, str,'\n');
```

The three arguments in this statement are explained as follows:

`dataFile`	This is the name of the file stream object. It specifies the stream object from which the data is to be read.
`str`	This is the name of a `string` object. The data read from the file will be stored here.
`'\n'`	This is a delimiter character of your choice. If this delimiter is encountered, it will cause the function to stop reading. (This argument is optional. If it's left out, `'\n'` is the default.)

The statement is an instruction to read a line of characters from the file. The function will read until it encounters a `\n`. The line of characters will be stored in the `str` object.

Program 8 is a modification of Program 7. It uses the `getline` function to read whole lines of data from the file.

Program 8

```
// This program uses the getline function to read a line of
// data from the file.
#include <iostream>
#include <fstream>
#include <string>
using namespace std;

int main()
```

```
{
    string input;        // To hold file input
    fstream nameFile;    // File stream object

    // Open the file in input mode.
    nameFile.open("murphy.txt", ios::in);

    // If the file was successfully opened, continue.
    if (nameFile)
    {
        // Read an item from the file.
        getline(nameFile, input);

        // While the last read operation
        // was successful, continue.
        while (nameFile)
        {
            // Display the last item read.
            cout << input << endl;

            // Read the next item.
            getline(nameFile, input);
        }

        // Close the file.
        nameFile.close();
    }
    else
    {
        cout << "ERROR: Cannot open file.\n";
    }
    return 0;
}
```

Program Output

```
Jayne Murphy
47 Jones Circle
Almond, NC 28702
```

Because the third argument of the `getline` function was left out in Program 8, its default value is `\n`. Sometimes you might want to specify another delimiter. For example, consider a file that contains multiple names and addresses, and that is internally formatted in the following manner:

Contents of `names2.txt`

```
Jayne Murphy$47 Jones Circle$Almond, NC 28702\n$Bobbie Smith$
217 Halifax Drive$Canton, NC 28716\n$Bill Hammet$PO Box 121$
Springfield, NC 28357\n$
```

Think of this file as consisting of three records. A record is a complete set of data about a single item. Also, the records in the file above are made of three fields. The first field is the person's name. The second field is the person's street address or PO box number. The third field contains the person's city, state, and ZIP code. Notice each field ends with a $ character, and each record ends with a `\n` character. Program 9 demonstrates how a `getline` function can be used to detect the $ characters.

Program 9

```
// This file demonstrates the getline function with
// a specified delimiter.
#include <iostream>
#include <fstream>
#include <string>
using namespace std;

int main()
{
    string input; // To hold file input

    // Open the file for input.
    fstream dataFile("names2.txt", ios::in);

    // If the file was successfully opened, continue.
    if (dataFile)
    {
        // Read an item using $ as a delimiter.
        getline(dataFile, input, '$');

        // While the last read operation
        // was successful, continue.
        while (dataFile)
        {
            // Display the last item read.
            cout << input << endl;

            // Read an item using $ as a delimiter.
            getline(dataFile, input, '$');
        }

        // Close the file.
        dataFile.close();
    }
    else
    {
        cout << "ERROR: Cannot open file.\n";
    }
    return 0;
}
```

Program Output

```
Jayne Murphy
47 Jones Circle
Almond, NC 28702

Bobbie Smith
217 Halifax Drive
Canton, NC 28716

Bill Hammet
PO Box 121
Springfield, NC 28357
```

Notice the `\n` characters, which mark the end of each record, are also part of the output. They cause an extra blank line to be printed on the screen, separating the records.

> **NOTE:** When using a printable character, such as $, to delimit data in a file, be sure to select a character that will not actually appear in the data itself. Since it's doubtful that anyone's name or address contains a $ character, it's an acceptable delimiter. If the file contained dollar amounts, however, another delimiter would have been chosen.

The get Member Function

The file stream object's `get` member function is also useful. It reads a single character from the file. Here is an example of its usage:

```
inFile.get(ch);
```

In this example, `ch` is a `char` variable. A character will be read from the file and stored in `ch`. Program 10 shows the function used in a complete program. The user is asked for the name of a file. The file is opened and the `get` function is used in a loop to read the file's contents, one character at a time.

Program 10

```
// This program asks the user for a file name. The file is
// opened and its contents are displayed on the screen.
#include <iostream>
#include <fstream>
#include <string>
using namespace std;

int main()
{
    string fileName;   // To hold the file name
    char ch;           // To hold a character
    fstream file;      // File stream object

    // Get the file name
    cout << "Enter a file name: ";
    cin >> fileName;

    // Open the file.
    file.open(filename, ios::in);

    // If the file was successfully opened, continue.
    if (file)
    {
        // Get a character from the file.
        file.get(ch);

        // While the last read operation was
        // successful, continue.
        while (file)
        {
```

(program continues)

Program 10 *(continued)*

```
            // Display the last character read.
            cout << ch;

            // Read the next character
            file.get(ch);
        }

        // Close the file.
        file.close();
    }
    else
        cout << fileName << " could not be opened.\n";
    return 0;
}
```

Program 10 will display the contents of any file. The `get` function even reads whitespaces, so all the characters will be shown exactly as they appear in the file.

The put Member Function

The `put` member function writes a single character to the file. Here is an example of its usage:

```
outFile.put(ch);
```

In this statement, the variable `ch` is assumed to be a `char` variable. Its contents will be written to the file associated with the file stream object `outFile`. Program 11 demonstrates the `put` function.

Program 11

```
// This program demonstrates the put member function.
#include <iostream>
#include <fstream>
using namespace std;

int main()
{
    char ch;   // To hold a character

    // Open the file for output.
    fstream dataFile("sentence.txt", ios::out);

    cout << "Type a sentence and be sure to end it with a ";
    cout << "period.\n";

    // Get a sentence from the user one character at a time
    // and write each character to the file.
    cin.get(ch);
    while (ch != '.')
    {
        dataFile.put(ch);
        cin.get(ch);
    }
```

```
    dataFile.put(ch); // Write the period.

    // Close the file.
    dataFile.close();
    return 0;
}
```

Program Output with Example Input Shown in Bold

```
Type a sentence and be sure to end it with a period.
```

I am on my way to becoming a great programmer. [Enter]

Resulting Contents of the File `sentence.txt`:

```
I am on my way to becoming a great programmer.
```

Checkpoint

7 Assume the file input.txt contains the following characters:

R	u	n		S	p	o	t		r	u	n	\n	S	e

e		S	p	o	t		r	u	n	\n	<EOF>

What will the following program display on the screen?

```
#include <iostream>
#include <fstream>
#include <string>
using namespace std;

int main()
{
    fstream inFile("input.txt", ios::in);
    string item;
    inFile >> item;
    while (inFile)
    {
        cout << item << endl;
        inFile >> item;
    }
    inFile.close();
    return 0;
}
```

8 Describe the difference between reading a file with the >> operator and the `getline` function.

9 What will be stored in the file out.txt after the following program runs?

```
#include <iostream>
#include <fstream>
#include <iomanip>
using namespace std;
```

```
int main()
{
    const int SIZE = 5;
    ofstream outFile("out.txt");
    double nums[SIZE] = {100.279, 1.719, 8.602, 7.777, 5.099};

    outFile << fixed << setprecision(2);
    for (int count = 0; count < 5; count++)
    {
        outFile << setw(8) << nums[count];
    }
    outFile.close();
    return 0;
}
```

6 Focus on Software Engineering: Working with Multiple Files

CONCEPT: It's possible to have more than one file open at once in a program.

VideoNote
Working with Multiple Files

Quite often you will need to have multiple files open at once. In many real-world applications, data about a single item are categorized and written to several different files. For example, a payroll system might keep the following files:

emp.dat	A file that contains the following data about each employee: name, job title, address, telephone number, employee number, and the date hired.
pay.dat	A file that contains the following data about each employee: employee number, hourly pay rate, overtime rate, and number of hours worked in the current pay cycle.
withhold.dat	A file that contains the following data about each employee: employee number, dependents, and extra withholdings.

When the system is writing paychecks, you can see that it will need to open each of the files listed above and read data from them. (Notice each file contains the employee number. This is how the program can locate a specific employee's data.)

In C++, you open multiple files by defining multiple file stream objects. For example, if you need to read from three files, you can define three file stream objects, such as:

```
ifstream file1, file2, file3;
```

Sometimes you will need to open one file for input and another file for output. For example, Program 12 asks the user for a file name. The file is opened and read. Each character is converted to uppercase and written to a second file called out.txt. This type of program can be considered a *filter*. Filters read the input of one file, changing the data in some fashion, and write it out to a second file. The second file is a modified version of the first file.

Program 12

```
// This program demonstrates reading from one file and writing
// to a second file.
#include <iostream>
#include <fstream>
#include <string>
#include <cctype> // Needed for the toupper function.
using namespace std;

int main()
{
    string fileName;     // To hold the file name
    char ch;             // To hold a character
    ifstream inFile;     // Input file

    // Open a file for output.
    ofstream outFile("out.txt");

    // Get the input file name.
    cout << "Enter a file name: ";
    cin >> fileName;

    // Open the file for input.
    inFile.open(filename);

    // If the input file opened successfully, continue.
    if (inFile)
    {
        // Read a char from file 1.
        inFile.get(ch);

        // While the last read operation was
        // successful, continue.
        while (inFile)
        {
            // Write uppercase char to file 2.
            outFile.put(toupper(ch));

            // Read another char from file 1.
            inFile.get(ch);
        }

        // Close the two files.
        inFile.close();
        outFile.close();
        cout << "File conversion done.\n";
    }
    else
        cout << "Cannot open " << fileName << endl;
    return 0;
}
```

(program output continues)

Program 12 *(continued)*

Program Output with Example Input Shown in Bold

```
Enter a file name: hownow.txt [Enter]
File conversion done.
```

Contents of `hownow.txt`

```
how now brown cow.
How Now?
```

Resulting Contents of `out.txt`

```
HOW NOW BROWN COW.
HOW NOW?
```

7 Binary Files

CONCEPT: Binary files contain data that is not necessarily stored as ASCII text.

All the files you've been working with so far have been text files. That means the data stored in the files has been formatted as ASCII text. Even a number, when stored in a file with the << operator, is converted to text. For example, consider the following program segment:

```
ofstream file("num.dat");
short x = 1297;
file << x;
```

The last statement writes the contents of x to the file. When the number is written, however, it is stored as the characters '1', '2', '9', and '7'. This is illustrated in Figure 6.

Figure 6 File contents

'1'	'2'	'9'	'7'	<EOF>

1297 expressed in ASCII

49	50	57	55	<EOF>

The number 1297 isn't stored in memory (in the variable x) in the fashion depicted in the figure above, however. It is formatted as a binary number, occupying 2 bytes on a typical system. Figure 7 shows how the number is represented in memory, using binary or hexadecimal.

Figure 7 The value 1297 stored as a `short int`

1297 as a short integer, in binary

00000101	00010001

1297 as a short integer, in hexadecimal

05	11

The representation of the number shown in Figure 7 is the way the "raw" data is stored in memory. Data can be stored in a file in its pure, binary format. The first step is to open the file in binary mode. This is accomplished by using the `ios::binary` flag. Here is an example:

```
file.open("stuff.dat", ios::out | ios::binary);
```

Notice the `ios::out` and `ios::binary` flags are joined in the statement with the `|` operator. This causes the file to be opened in both output and binary modes.

NOTE: By default, files are opened in text mode.

The `write` and `read` Member Functions

The file stream object's `write` member function is used to write binary data to a file. The general format of the `write` member function is

```
fileObject.write(address, size);
```

Let's look at the parts of this function call format:

- *`fileObject`* is the name of a file stream object.
- *`address`* is the starting address of the section of memory that is to be written to the file. This argument is expected to be the address of a `char` (or a pointer to a `char`).
- *`size`* is the number of bytes of memory to write. This argument must be an integer value.

For example, the following code uses a file stream object named `file` to write a character to a binary file:

```
char letter = 'A';
file.write(&letter, sizeof(letter));
```

The first argument passed to the `write` function is the address of the `letter` variable. This tells the `write` function where the data that is to be written to the file is located. The second argument is the size of the `letter` variable, which is returned from the `sizeof` operator. This tells the `write` function the number of bytes of data to write to the file. Because the sizes of data types can vary among systems, it is best to use the `sizeof` operator to determine the number of bytes to write. After this function call executes, the contents of the `letter` variable will be written to the binary file associated with the `file` object.

The following code shows another example. This code writes an entire `char` array to a binary file.

```
char data[] = {'A', 'B', 'C', 'D'};
file.write(data, sizeof(data));
```

In this code, the first argument is the name of the `data` array. By passing the name of the array, we are passing a pointer to the beginning of the array. Because `data` is an array of `char` values, the name of the array is a pointer to a `char`. The second argument passes the name of the array to the `sizeof` operator. When the name of an array is passed to the `sizeof` operator, the operator returns the number of bytes allocated to the array. After this function call executes, the contents of the `data` array will be written to the binary file associated with the `file` object.

The read member function is used to read binary data from a file into memory. The general format of the read member function is

```
fileObject.read(address, size);
```

Here are the parts of this function call format:

- *fileObject* is the name of a file stream object.
- *address* is the starting address of the section of memory where the data being read from the file is to be stored. This is expected to be the address of a char (or a pointer to a char).
- *size* is the number of bytes of memory to read from the file. This argument must be an integer value.

For example, suppose we want to read a single character from a binary file and store that character in the letter variable. The following code uses a file stream object named file to do just that:

```
char letter;
file.read(&letter, sizeof(letter));
```

The first argument passed to the read function is the address of the letter variable. This tells the read function where to store the value that is read from the file. The second argument is the size of the letter variable. This tells the read function the number of bytes to read from the file. After this function executes, the letter variable will contain a character that was read from the file.

The following code shows another example. This code reads enough data from a binary file to fill an entire char array.

```
char data[4];
file.read(data, sizeof(data));
```

In this code, the first argument is the address of the data array. The second argument is the number of bytes allocated to the array. On a system that uses 1-byte characters, this function will read 4 bytes from the file and store them in the data array.

Program 13 demonstrates writing a char array to a file then reading the data from the file back into memory.

Program 13

```
// This program uses the write and read functions.
#include <iostream>
#include <fstream>
using namespace std;

int main()
{
    const int SIZE = 4;
    char data[SIZE] = {'A', 'B', 'C', 'D'};
    fstream file;

```

```
    // Open the file for output in binary mode.
    file.open("test.dat", ios::out | ios::binary);

    // Write the contents of the array to the file.
    cout << "Writing the characters to the file.\n";
    file.write(data, sizeof(data));

    // Close the file.
    file.close();

    // Open the file for input in binary mode.
    file.open("test.dat", ios::in | ios::binary);

    // Read the contents of the file into the array.
    cout << "Now reading the data back into memory.\n";
    file.read(data, sizeof(data));

    // Display the contents of the array.
    for (int count = 0; count < SIZE; count++)
        cout << data[count] << " ";
    cout << endl;

    // Close the file.
    file.close();
    return 0;
}
```

Program Output

```
Writing the characters to the file.
Now reading the data back into memory.
A B C D
```

Writing Data other than `char` to Binary Files

Because the `write` and `read` member functions expect their first argument to be a pointer to a `char`, you must use a type cast when writing and reading items that are of other data types. To convert a pointer from one type to another, you should use the `reinterpret_cast` type cast. The general format of the type cast is

```
reinterpret_cast<dataType>(value)
```

where *`dataType`* is the data type that you are converting to, and *`value`* is the value that you are converting. For example, the following code uses the type cast to store the address of an `int` in a `char` pointer variable:

```
int x = 65;
char *ptr = nullptr;
ptr = reinterpret_cast<char *>(&x);
```

The following code shows how to use the type cast to pass the address of an integer as the first argument to the `write` member function:

```
int x = 27;
file.write(reinterpret_cast<char *>(&x), sizeof(x));
```

After the function executes, the contents of the variable `x` will be written to the binary file associated with the `file` object. The following code shows an `int` array being written to a binary file:

```
const int SIZE = 10;
int numbers[SIZE] = {1, 2, 3, 4, 5, 6, 7, 8, 9, 10};
file.write(reinterpret_cast<char *>(numbers), sizeof(numbers));
```

After this function call executes, the contents of the `numbers` array will be written to the binary file. The following code shows values being read from the file and stored into the `numbers` array:

```
const int SIZE = 10;
int numbers[SIZE];
file.read(reinterpret_cast<char *>(numbers), sizeof(numbers));
```

Program 14 demonstrates writing an `int` array to a file then reading the data from the file back into memory.

Program 14

```
// This program uses the write and read functions.
#include <iostream>
#include <fstream>
using namespace std;

int main()
{
    const int SIZE = 10;
    fstream file;
    int numbers[SIZE] = {1, 2, 3, 4, 5, 6, 7, 8, 9, 10};

    // Open the file for output in binary mode.
    file.open("numbers.dat", ios::out | ios::binary);

    // Write the contents of the array to the file.
    cout << "Writing the data to the file.\n";
    file.write(reinterpret_cast<char *>(numbers), sizeof(numbers));

    // Close the file.
    file.close();

    // Open the file for input in binary mode.
    file.open("numbers.dat", ios::in | ios::binary);

    // Read the contents of the file into the array.
    cout << "Now reading the data back into memory.\n";
    file.read(reinterpret_cast<char *>(numbers), sizeof(numbers));

    // Display the contents of the array.
    for (int count = 0; count < SIZE; count++)
        cout << numbers[count] << " ";
    cout << endl;

    // Close the file.
    file.close();
    return 0;
}
```

Program Output

```
Writing the data to the file.
Now reading the data back into memory.
1 2 3 4 5 6 7 8 9 10
```

8 Creating Records with Structures

CONCEPT: Structures may be used to store fixed-length records to a file.

Earlier in this chapter, the concept of fields and records was introduced. A field is an individual piece of data pertaining to a single item. A record is made up of fields and is a complete set of data about a single item. For example, a set of fields might be a person's name, age, address, and phone number. Together, all those fields that pertain to one person make up a record.

In C++, structures provide a convenient way to organize data into fields and records. For example, the following code could be used to create a record containing data about a person:

```
const int NAME_SIZE = 51, ADDR_SIZE = 51, PHONE_SIZE = 14;

struct Info
{
     char name[NAME_SIZE];
     int age;
     char address1[ADDR_SIZE];
     char address2[ADDR_SIZE];
     char phone[PHONE_SIZE];
};
```

Besides providing an organizational structure for data, structures also package data into a single unit. For example, assume the structure variable `person` is defined as

```
Info person;
```

Once the members (or fields) of `person` are filled with data, the entire variable may be written to a file using the `write` function:

```
file.write(reinterpret_cast<char *>(&person), sizeof(person));
```

The first argument is the address of the `person` variable. The `reinterpret_cast` operator is used to convert the address to a `char` pointer. The second argument is the `sizeof` operator with `person` as its `argument`. This returns the number of bytes used by the `person` structure. Program 15 demonstrates this technique.

NOTE: Because structures can contain a mixture of data types, you should always use the `ios::binary` mode when opening a file to store them.

Program 15

```
// This program uses a structure variable to store a record to a file.
#include <iostream>
#include <fstream>
using namespace std;

// Array sizes
const int NAME_SIZE = 51, ADDR_SIZE = 51, PHONE_SIZE = 14;

// Declare a structure for the record.
struct Info
{
    char name[NAME_SIZE];
    int age;
    char address1[ADDR_SIZE];
    char address2[ADDR_SIZE];
    char phone[PHONE_SIZE];
};

int main()
{
    Info person;    // To hold info about a person
    char again;     // To hold Y or N

    // Open a file for binary output.
    fstream people("people.dat", ios::out | ios::binary);

    do
    {
        // Get data about a person.
        cout << "Enter the following data about a "
             << "person:\n";
        cout << "Name: ";
        cin.getline(person.name, NAME_SIZE);
        cout << "Age: ";
        cin >> person.age;
        cin.ignore(); // Skip over the remaining newline.
        cout << "Address line 1: ";
        cin.getline(person.address1, ADDR_SIZE);
        cout << "Address line 2: ";
        cin.getline(person.address2, ADDR_SIZE);
        cout << "Phone: ";
        cin.getline(person.phone, PHONE_SIZE);

        // Write the contents of the person structure to the file.
        people.write(reinterpret_cast<char *>(&person),
                     sizeof(person));

        // Determine whether the user wants to write another record.
        cout << "Do you want to enter another record? ";
        cin >> again;
        cin.ignore(); // Skip over the remaining newline.
    } while (again == 'Y' || again == 'y');

```

```
    // Close the file.
    people.close();
    return 0;
}
```

Program Output with Example Input Shown in Bold

Enter the following data about a person:
Name: **Charlie Baxter** [Enter]
Age: **42** [Enter]
Address line 1: **67 Kennedy Blvd.** [Enter]
Address line 2: **Perth, SC 38754** [Enter]
Phone: **(803)555-1234** [Enter]
Do you want to enter another record? **Y** [Enter]
Enter the following data about a person:
Name: **Merideth Murney** [Enter]
Age: **22** [Enter]
Address line 1: **487 Lindsay Lane** [Enter]
Address line 2: **Hazelwood, NC 28737** [Enter]
Phone: **(828)555-9999** [Enter]
Do you want to enter another record? **N** [Enter]

Program 15 allows you to build a file by filling the members of the person variable, then writing the variable to the file. Program 16 opens the file and reads each record into the person variable, then displays the data on the screen.

Program 16

```
// This program uses a structure variable to read a record from a file.
#include <iostream>
#include <fstream>
using namespace std;

const int NAME_SIZE = 51, ADDR_SIZE = 51, PHONE_SIZE = 14;

// Declare a structure for the record.
struct Info
{
    char name[NAME_SIZE];
    int age;
    char address1[ADDR_SIZE];
    char address2[ADDR_SIZE];
    char phone[PHONE_SIZE];
};

int main()
{
    Info person;      // To hold info about a person
    char again;       // To hold Y or N
    fstream people;   // File stream object

    // Open the file for input in binary mode.
    people.open("people.dat", ios::in | ios::binary);

```

(program continues)

Program 16 *(continued)*

```
    // Test for errors.
    if (!people)
    {
        cout << "Error opening file. Program aborting.\n";
        return 0;
    }


    cout << "Here are the people in the file:\n\n";
    // Read the first record from the file.
    people.read(reinterpret_cast<char *>(&person),
                sizeof(person));

    // While not at the end of the file, display
    // the records.
    while (!people.eof())
    {
        // Display the record.
        cout << "Name: ";
        cout << person.name << endl;
        cout << "Age: ";
        cout << person.age << endl;
        cout << "Address line 1: ";
        cout << person.address1 << endl;
        cout << "Address line 2: ";
        cout << person.address2 << endl;
        cout << "Phone: ";
        cout << person.phone << endl;

        // Wait for the user to press the Enter key.
        cout << "\nPress the Enter key to see the next record.\n";
        cin.get(again);

        // Read the next record from the file.
        people.read(reinterpret_cast<char *>(&person),
                    sizeof(person));
    }

    cout << "That's all the data in the file!\n";
    people.close();
    return 0;
}
```

Program Output (Using the same file created by Program 15 as input)

```
Here are the people in the file:

Name: Charlie Baxter
Age: 42
Address line 1: 67 Kennedy Blvd.
Address line 2: Perth, SC 38754
Phone: (803)555-1234
```

```
Press the Enter key to see the next record.

Name: Merideth Murney
Age: 22
Address line 1: 487 Lindsay Lane
Address line 2: Hazelwood, NC 28737
Phone: (828)555-9999

Press the Enter key to see the next record.

That's all the data in the file!
```

NOTE: Structures containing pointers cannot be correctly stored to disk using the techniques of this section. This is because if the structure is read into memory on a subsequent run of the program, it cannot be guaranteed that all program variables will be at the same memory locations. Because `string` class objects contain implicit pointers, they cannot be a part of a structure that has to be stored.

9 Random-Access Files

CONCEPT: Random access means nonsequentially accessing data in a file.

All of the programs created so far in this chapter have performed *sequential file access*. When a file is opened, the position where reading and/or writing will occur is at the file's beginning (unless the `ios::app` mode is used, which causes data to be written to the end of the file). If the file is opened for output, bytes are written to it one after the other. If the file is opened for input, data is read beginning at the first byte. As the reading or writing continues, the file stream object's read/write position advances sequentially through the file's contents.

The problem with sequential file access is that in order to read a specific byte from the file, all the bytes that precede it must be read first. For instance, if a program needs data stored at the hundredth byte of a file, it will have to read the first 99 bytes to reach it. If you've ever listened to a cassette tape player, you understand sequential access. To listen to a song at the end of the tape, you have to listen to all the songs that come before it, or fast-forward over them. There is no way to immediately jump to that particular song.

Although sequential file access is useful in many circumstances, it can slow a program down tremendously. If the file is very large, locating data buried deep inside it can take a long time. Alternatively, C++ allows a program to perform *random file access*. In random file access, a program may immediately jump to any byte in the file without first reading the preceding bytes. The difference between sequential and random file access is like the difference between a cassette tape and a compact disc. When listening to a CD, there is no need to listen to or fast forward over unwanted songs. You simply jump to the track that you want to listen to. This is illustrated in Figure 8.

The seekp and seekg Member Functions

File stream objects have two member functions that are used to move the read/write position to any byte in the file. They are `seekp` and `seekg`. The `seekp` function is used with

Figure 8 Sequential versus random access

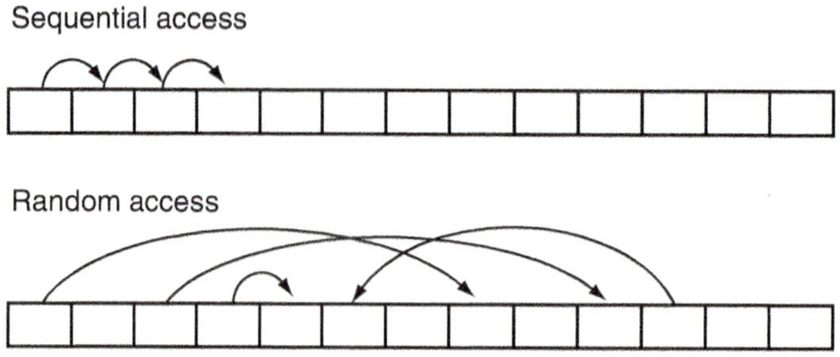

files opened for output, and `seekg` is used with files opened for input. (It makes sense if you remember that "p" stands for "put" and "g" stands for "get." `seekp` is used with files into which you put data, and `seekg` is used with files from which you get data out.)

Here is an example of `seekp`'s usage:

```
file.seekp(20L, ios::beg);
```

The first argument is a `long` integer representing an offset into the file. This is the number of the byte to which you wish to move. In this example, `20L` is used. (Remember, the L suffix forces the compiler to treat the number as a long integer.) This statement moves the file's write position to byte number 20. (All numbering starts at 0, so byte number 20 is actually the twenty-first byte.)

The second argument is called the mode, and it designates where to calculate the offset *from*. The flag `ios::beg` means the offset is calculated from the beginning of the file. Alternatively, the offset can be calculated from the end of the file or the current position in the file. Table 6 lists the flags for all three of the random-access modes.

Table 6 Offset Modes

Mode Flag	Description
`ios::beg`	The offset is calculated from the beginning of the file.
`ios::end`	The offset is calculated from the end of the file.
`ios::cur`	The offset is calculated from the current position.

Table 7 shows examples of `seekp` and `seekg` using the various mode flags.

Notice some of the examples in Table 7 use a negative offset. Negative offsets result in the read or write position being moved backward in the file, while positive offsets result in a forward movement.

Assume the file letters.txt contains the following data:

```
abcdefghijklmnopqrstuvwxyz
```

Program 17 uses the `seekg` function to jump around to different locations in the file, retrieving a character after each stop.

Table 7 Mode Examples

Statement	How It Affects the Read/Write Position
`file.seekp(32L, ios::beg);`	Sets the write position to the 33rd byte (byte 32) from the beginning of the file.
`file.seekp(-10L, ios::end);`	Sets the write position to the 10th byte from the end of the file.
`file.seekp(120L, ios::cur);`	Sets the write position to the 121st byte (byte 120) from the current position.
`file.seekg(2L, ios::beg);`	Sets the read position to the 3rd byte (byte 2) from the beginning of the file.
`file.seekg(-100L, ios::end);`	Sets the read position to the 100th byte from the end of the file.
`file.seekg(40L, ios::cur);`	Sets the read position to the 41st byte (byte 40) from the current position.
`file.seekg(0L, ios::end);`	Sets the read position to the end of the file.

Program 17

```
// This program demonstrates the seekg function.
#include <iostream>
#include <fstream>
using namespace std;

int main()
{
    char ch; // To hold a character

    // Open the file for input.
    fstream file("letters.txt", ios::in);

    // Move to byte 5 from the beginning of the file
    // (the 6th byte) and read the character there.
    file.seekg(5L, ios::beg);
    file.get(ch);
    cout << "Byte 5 from beginning: " << ch << endl;

    // Move to the 10th byte from the end of the file
    // and read the character there.
    file.seekg(-10L, ios::end);
    file.get(ch);
    cout << "10th byte from end: " << ch << endl;

    // Move to byte 3 from the current position
    // (the 4th byte) and read the character there.
    file.seekg(3L, ios::cur);
    file.get(ch);
    cout << "Byte 3 from current: " << ch << endl;

    file.close();
    return 0;
}
```

(program output continues)

Program 17 *(continued)*

Program Screen Output

```
Byte 5 from beginning: f
10th byte from end: q
Byte 3 from current: u
```

Program 18 shows a more robust example of the `seekg` function. It opens the people.dat file created by Program 15. The file contains two records. Program 18 displays record 1 (the second record) first, then displays record 0.

The program has two important functions other than `main`. The first, `byteNum`, takes a record number as its argument and returns that record's starting byte. It calculates the record's starting byte by multiplying the record number by the size of the `Info` structure. This returns the offset of that record from the beginning of the file. The second function, `showRec`, accepts an `Info` structure as its argument and displays its contents on the screen.

Program 18

```
// This program randomly reads a record of data from a file.
#include <iostream>
#include <fstream>
using namespace std;

const int NAME_SIZE = 51, ADDR_SIZE = 51, PHONE_SIZE = 14;

// Declare a structure for the record.
struct Info
{
    char name[NAME_SIZE];
    int age;
    char address1[ADDR_SIZE];
    char address2[ADDR_SIZE];
    char phone[PHONE_SIZE];
};

// Function Prototypes
long byteNum(int);
void showRec(Info);

int main()
{
    Info person;      // To hold info about a person
    fstream people;   // File stream object

    // Open the file for input in binary mode.
    people.open("people.dat", ios::in | ios::binary);

```

```
    // Test for errors.
    if (!people)
    {
        cout << "Error opening file. Program aborting.\n";
        return 0;
    }

    // Read and display record 1 (the second record).
    cout << "Here is record 1:\n";
    people.seekg(byteNum(1), ios::beg);
    people.read(reinterpret_cast<char *>(&person), sizeof(person));
    showRec(person);

    // Read and display record 0 (the first record).
    cout << "\nHere is record 0:\n";
    people.seekg(byteNum(0), ios::beg);
    people.read(reinterpret_cast<char *>(&person), sizeof(person));
    showRec(person);

    // Close the file.
    people.close();
    return 0;
}

//************************************************************
// Definition of function byteNum. Accepts an integer as    *
// its argument. Returns the byte number in the file of the *
// record whose number is passed as the argument.           *
//************************************************************

long byteNum(int recNum)
{
    return sizeof(Info) * recNum;
}

//************************************************************
// Definition of function showRec. Accepts an Info structure *
// as its argument, and displays the structure's contents.  *
//************************************************************

void showRec(Info record)
{
    cout << "Name: ";
    cout << record.name << endl;
    cout << "Age: ";
    cout << record.age << endl;
    cout << "Address line 1: ";
    cout << record.address1 << endl;
    cout << "Address line 2: ";
    cout << record.address2 << endl;
```

(program continues)

Program 18 *(continued)*

```
        cout << "Phone: ";
        cout << record.phone << endl;
}
```

Program Output (Using the same file created by Program 12–15 as input)

```
Here is record 1:
Name: Merideth Murney
Age: 22
Address line 1: 487 Lindsay Lane
Address line 2: Hazelwood, NC 28737
Phone: (828)555-9999

Here is record 0:
Name: Charlie Baxter
Age: 42
Address line 1: 67 Kennedy Blvd.
Address line 2: Perth, SC 38754
Phone: (803)555-1234
```

WARNING! If a program has read to the end of a file, you must call the file stream object's `clear` member function before calling `seekg` or `seekp`. This clears the file stream object's `eof` flag. Otherwise, the `seekg` or `seekp` function will not work.

The `tellp` and `tellg` Member Functions

File stream objects have two more member functions that may be used for random file access: `tellp` and `tellg`. Their purpose is to return, as a long integer, the current byte number of a file's read and write position. As you can guess, `tellp` returns the write position and `tellg` returns the read position. Assuming `pos` is a long integer, here is an example of the functions' usage:

```
pos = outFile.tellp();
pos = inFile.tellg();
```

One application of these functions is to determine the number of bytes that a file contains. The following example demonstrates how to do this using the `tellg` function:

```
file.seekg(0L, ios::end);
numBytes = file.tellg();
cout << "The file has " << numBytes << " bytes.\n";
```

First, the `seekg` member function is used to move the read position to the last byte in the file. Then, the `tellg` function is used to get the current byte number of the read position.

Program 19 demonstrates the `tellg` function. It opens the letters.txt file, which was also used in Program 17. The file contains the following characters:

```
abcdefghijklmnopqrstuvwxyz
```

Program 19

```
// This program demonstrates the tellg function.
#include <iostream>
#include <fstream>
using namespace std;

int main()
{
    long offset;      // To hold an offset amount
    long numBytes;    // To hold the file size
    char ch;          // To hold a character
    char again;       // To hold Y or N

    // Open the file for input.
    fstream file("letters.txt", ios::in);

    // Determine the number of bytes in the file.
    file.seekg(0L, ios::end);
    numBytes = file.tellg();
    cout << "The file has " << numBytes << " bytes.\n";

    // Go back to the beginning of the file.
    file.seekg(0L, ios::beg);

    // Let the user move around within the file.
    do
    {
        // Display the current read position.
        cout << "Currently at position " << file.tellg() << endl;

        // Get a byte number from the user.
        cout << "Enter an offset from the beginning of the file: ";
        cin >> offset;

        // Move the read position to that byte, read the
        // character there, and display it.
        if (offset >= numBytes)   // Past the end of the file?
            cout << "Cannot read past the end of the file.\n";
        else
        {
            file.seekg(offset, ios::beg);
            file.get(ch);
            cout << "Character read: " << ch << endl;
        }

        // Does the user want to try this again?
        cout << "Do it again? ";
        cin >> again;
    } while (again == 'Y' || again == 'y');

    // Close the file.
    file.close();
    return 0;
}
```

(program output continues)

Program 19 *(continued)*

Program Output with Example Input Shown in Bold

```
The file has 26 bytes.
Currently at position 0
Enter an offset from the beginning of the file: 5 [Enter]
Character read: f
Do it again? y [Enter]
Currently at position 6
Enter an offset from the beginning of the file: 0 [Enter]
Character read: a
Do it again? y [Enter]
Currently at position 1
Enter an offset from the beginning of the file: 26 [Enter]
Cannot read past the end of the file.
Do it again? n [Enter]
```

Rewinding a Sequential-Access File with seekg

Sometimes when processing a sequential file, it is necessary for a program to read the contents of the file more than one time. For example, suppose a program searches a file for an item specified by the user. The program must open the file, read its contents, and determine if the specified item is in the file. If the user needs to search the file again for another item, the program must read the file's contents again.

One simple approach for reading a file's contents more than once is to close and reopen the file, as shown in the following code example:

```
dataFile.open("file.txt", ios::in);      // Open the file.

//
// Read and process the file's contents.
//

dataFile.close();                        // Close the file.
dataFile.open("file.txt", ios::in);      // Open the file again.

//
// Read and process the file's contents again.
//

dataFile.close();                        // Close the file.
```

Each time the file is reopened, its read position is located at the beginning of the file. The read position is the byte in the file that will be read with the next read operation.

Another approach is to "rewind" the file. This means moving the read position to the beginning of the file without closing and reopening it. This is accomplished with the file stream object's `seekg` member function to move the read position back to the beginning of the file. The following example code demonstrates this.

```
dataFile.open("file.txt", ios::in);      // Open the file.

//
// Read and process the file's contents.
//
```

```
dataFile.clear();                      // Clear the eof flag.
dataFile.seekg(0L, ios::beg);          // Rewind the read position.
//
// Read and process the file's contents again.
//
dataFile.close();                      // Close the file.
```

Notice prior to calling the `seekg` member function, the `clear` member function is called. As previously mentioned, this clears the file object's `eof` flag and is necessary only if the program has read to the end of the file. This approach eliminates the need to close and reopen the file each time the file's contents are processed.

10 Opening a File for Both Input and Output

CONCEPT: You may perform input and output on an `fstream` file without closing it and reopening it.

Sometimes you'll need to perform both input and output on a file without closing and reopening it. For example, consider a program that allows you to search for a record in a file then make changes to it. A read operation is necessary to copy the data from the file to memory. After the desired changes have been made to the data in memory, a write operation is necessary to replace the old data in the file with the new data in memory.

Such operations are possible with `fstream` objects. The `ios::in` and `ios::out` file access flags may be joined with the `|` operator, as shown in the following statement:

```
fstream file("data.dat", ios::in | ios::out)
```

The same operation may be accomplished with the `open` member function.

```
file.open("data.dat", ios::in | ios::out);
```

You may also specify the `ios::binary` flag if binary data is to be written to the file. Here is an example:

```
file.open("data.dat", ios::in | ios::out | ios::binary);
```

When an `fstream` file is opened with both the `ios::in` and `ios::out` flags, the file's current contents are preserved, and the read/write position is initially placed at the beginning of the file. If the file does not exist, it is created.

Programs 20, 21, and 22 demonstrate many of the techniques we have discussed. Program 20 sets up a file with five blank inventory records. Each record is a structure with members for holding a part description, quantity on hand, and price. Program 21 displays the contents of the file on the screen. Program 22 opens the file in both input and output modes and allows the user to change the contents of a specific record.

Program 20

```
// This program sets up a file of blank inventory records.
#include <iostream>
#include <fstream>
using namespace std;

// Constants
const int DESC_SIZE = 31;     // Description size
const int NUM_RECORDS = 5;    // Number of records

// Declaration of InventoryItem structure
struct InventoryItem
{
    char desc[DESC_SIZE];
    int qty;
    double price;
};

int main()
{
    // Create an empty InventoryItem structure.
    InventoryItem record = { "", 0, 0.0 };

    // Open the file for binary output.
    fstream inventory("Inventory.dat", ios::out | ios::binary);

    // Write the blank records
    for (int count = 0; count < NUM_RECORDS; count++)
    {
        cout << "Now writing record " << count << endl;
        inventory.write(reinterpret_cast<char *>(&record),
                        sizeof(record));
    }

    // Close the file.
    inventory.close();
    return 0;
}
```

Program Output

```
Now writing record 0
Now writing record 1
Now writing record 2
Now writing record 3
Now writing record 4
```

Program 21 simply displays the contents of the inventory file on the screen. It can be used to verify that Program 20 successfully created the blank records, and that Program 22 correctly modified the designated record.

Program 21

```
// This program displays the contents of the inventory file.
#include <iostream>
#include <fstream>
using namespace std;

const int DESC_SIZE = 31; // Description size

// Declaration of InventoryItem structure
struct InventoryItem
{
    char desc[DESC_SIZE];
    int qty;
    double price;
};

int main()
{
    InventoryItem record; // To hold an inventory record

    // Open the file for binary input.
    fstream inventory("Inventory.dat", ios::in | ios::binary);

    // Now read and display the records
    inventory.read(reinterpret_cast<char *>(&record),
                   sizeof(record));
    while (!inventory.eof())
    {
        cout << "Description: ";
        cout << record.desc << endl;
        cout << "Quantity: ";
        cout << record.qty << endl;
        cout << "Price: ";
        cout << record.price << endl << endl;
        inventory.read(reinterpret_cast<char *>(&record),
                       sizeof(record));
    }

    // Close the file.
    inventory.close();
    return 0;
}
```

Here is the screen output of Program 21 if it is run immediately after Program 20 sets up the file of blank records.

Program 21

Program Output

```
Description:
Quantity: 0
Price: 0.0
```

(program output continues)

Program 21 *(continued)*

```
Description:
Quantity: 0
Price: 0.0

Description:
Quantity: 0
Price: 0.0

Description:
Quantity: 0
Price: 0.0

Description:
Quantity: 0
Price: 0.0
```

Program 22 allows the user to change the contents of an individual record in the inventory file.

Program 22

```
// This program allows the user to edit a specific record.
#include <iostream>
#include <fstream>
using namespace std;

const int DESC_SIZE = 31; // Description size

// Declaration of InventoryItem structure
struct InventoryItem
{
    char desc[DESC_SIZE];
    int qty;
    double price;
};

int main()
{
    InventoryItem record;   // To hold an inventory record
    long recNum;            // To hold a record number

    // Open the file in binary mode for input and output
    fstream inventory("Inventory.dat",
                      ios::in | ios::out | ios::binary);

    // Get the record number of the desired record.
    cout << "Which record do you want to edit? ";
    cin >> recNum;

    // Move to the record and read it.
    inventory.seekg(recNum * sizeof(record), ios::beg);
    inventory.read(reinterpret_cast<char *>(&record),
                   sizeof(record));
```

```

        // Display the record contents.
        cout << "Description: ";
        cout << record.desc << endl;
        cout << "Quantity: ";
        cout << record.qty << endl;
        cout << "Price: ";
        cout << record.price << endl;

        // Get the new record data.
        cout << "Enter the new data:\n";
        cout << "Description: ";
        cin.ignore();
        cin.getline(record.desc, DESC_SIZE);
        cout << "Quantity: ";
        cin >> record.qty;
        cout << "Price: ";
        cin >> record.price;

        // Move back to the beginning of this record's position.
        inventory.seekp(recNum * sizeof(record), ios::beg);

        // Write the new record over the current record.
        inventory.write(reinterpret_cast<char *>(&record),
                        sizeof(record));

        // Close the file.
        inventory.close();
        return 0;
}
```

Program Output with Example Input Shown in Bold

```
Which record do you want to edit? 2 [Enter]
Description:
Quantity: 0
Price: 0.0
Enter the new data:
Description: Wrench [Enter]
Quantity: 10 [Enter]
Price: 4.67 [Enter]
```

Checkpoint

10 Describe the difference between the `seekg` and the `seekp` functions.

11 Describe the difference between the `tellg` and the `tellp` functions.

12 Describe the meaning of the following file access flags:

```
ios::beg
ios::end
ios::cur
```

13 What is the number of the first byte in a file?

14 Briefly describe what each of the following statements does:

```
file.seekp(100L, ios::beg);
file.seekp(-10L, ios::end);
file.seekg(-25L, ios::cur);
file.seekg(30L, ios::cur);
```

15 Describe the mode that each of the following statements causes a file to be opened in:

```
file.open("info.dat", ios::in | ios::out);
file.open("info.dat", ios::in | ios::app);
file.open("info.dat", ios::in | ios::out | ios::ate);
file.open("info.dat", ios::in | ios::out | ios::binary);
```

For another example of this chapter's topics, see the High Adventure Travel Part 3 Case Study, available on the Computer Science Portal at www.pearsonhighered.com/gaddis.

Review Questions and Exercises

Short Answer

1. What capability does the `fstream` data type provide that the `ifstream` and `ofstream` data types do not?
2. Which file access flag do you use to open a file when you want all output written to the end of the file's existing contents?
3. Assume the file data.txt already exists, and the following statement executes. What happens to the file?

   ```
   fstream file("data.txt", ios::out);
   ```
4. How do you combine multiple file access flags when opening a file?
5. Should file stream objects be passed to functions by value or by reference? Why?
6. Under what circumstances is a file stream object's `ios::hardfail` bit set? What member function reports the state of this bit?
7. Under what circumstances is a file stream object's `ios::eofbit` bit set? What member function reports the state of this bit?
8. Under what circumstances is a file stream object's `ios::badbit` bit set? What member function reports the state of this bit?
9. How do you read the contents of a text file that contains whitespace characters as part of its data?
10. What arguments do you pass to a file stream object's `write` member function?
11. What arguments do you pass to a file stream object's `read` member function?
12. What type cast do you use to convert a pointer from one type to another?
13. What is the difference between the `seekg` and `seekp` member functions?
14. How do you get the byte number of a file's current read position? How do you get the byte number of a file's current write position?
15. If a program has read to the end of a file, what must you do before using either the `seekg` or `seekp` member function?

16. How do you determine the number of bytes that a file contains?
17. How do you rewind a sequential-access file?

Fill-in-the-Blank

18. The __________ file stream data type is for output files, input files, or files that perform both input and output.
19. If a file fails to open, the file stream object will be set to __________.
20. The same formatting techniques used with __________ may also be used when writing data to a file.
21. The __________ function reads a line of text from a file.
22. The __________ member function reads a single character from a file.
23. The __________ member function writes a single character to a file.
24. __________ files contain data that is unformatted and not necessarily stored as ASCII text.
25. __________ files contain data formatted as __________.
26. A(n) __________ is a complete set of data about a single item and is made up of __________.
27. In C++, __________ provide a convenient way to organize data into fields and records.
28. The __________ member function writes "raw" binary data to a file.
29. The __________ member function reads "raw" binary data from a file.
30. The __________ operator is necessary if you pass anything other than a pointer-to-char as the first argument of the two functions mentioned in Questions 26 and 27.
31. In __________ file access, the contents of the file are read in the order they appear in the file, from the file's start to its end.
32. In __________ file access, the contents of a file may be read in any order.
33. The __________ member function moves a file's read position to a specified byte in the file.
34. The __________ member function moves a file's write position to a specified byte in the file.
35. The __________ member function returns a file's current read position.
36. The __________ member function returns a file's current write position.
37. The __________ mode flag causes an offset to be calculated from the beginning of a file.
38. The __________ mode flag causes an offset to be calculated from the end of a file.
39. The __________ mode flag causes an offset to be calculated from the current position in the file.
40. A negative offset causes the file's read or write position to be moved __________ in the file from the position specified by the mode.

Algorithm Workbench

41. Write a statement that defines a file stream object named `places`. The object will be used for both output and input.

42. Write two statements that use a file stream object named `people` to open a file named people.dat. (Show how to open the file with a member function and at the definition of the file stream object.) The file should be opened for output.
43. Write two statements that use a file stream object named `pets` to open a file named pets.dat. (Show how to open the file with a member function and at the definition of the file stream object.) The file should be opened for input.
44. Write two statements that use a file stream object named `places` to open a file named places.dat. (Show how to open the file with a member function and at the definition of the file stream object.) The file should be opened for both input and output.
45. Write a program segment that defines a file stream object named `employees`. The file should be opened for both input and output (in binary mode). If the file fails to open, the program segment should display an error message.
46. Write code that opens the file data.txt for both input and output, but first determines if the file exists. If the file does not exist, the code should create it, then open it for both input and output.
47. Write code that determines the number of bytes contained in the file associated with the file stream object `dataFile`.
48. The `infoFile` file stream object is used to sequentially access data. The program has already read to the end of the file. Write code that rewinds the file.

True or False

49. T F Different operating systems have different rules for naming files.
50. T F `fstream` objects are only capable of performing file output operations.
51. T F `ofstream` objects, by default, delete the contents of a file if it already exists when opened.
52. T F `ifstream` objects, by default, create a file if it doesn't exist when opened.
53. T F Several file access flags may be joined by using the `|` operator.
54. T F A file may be opened in the definition of the file stream object.
55. T F If a file is opened in the definition of the file stream object, no mode flags may be specified.
56. T F A file stream object's `fail` member function may be used to determine if the file was successfully opened.
57. T F The same output formatting techniques used with `cout` may also be used with file stream objects.
58. T F The `>>` operator expects data to be delimited by whitespace characters.
59. T F The `getline` member function can be used to read text that contains whitespaces.
60. T F It is not possible to have more than one file open at once in a program.
61. T F Binary files contain unformatted data, not necessarily stored as text.
62. T F Binary is the default mode in which files are opened.
63. T F The `tellp` member function tells a file stream object which byte to move its write position to.
64. T F It is possible to open a file for both input and output.

Find the Error

Each of the following programs or program segments has errors. Find as many as you can.

65.
```
fstream file(ios::in | ios::out);
file.open("info.dat");
if (!file)
{
   cout << "Could not open file.\n";
}
```

66.
```
ofstream file;
file.open("info.dat", ios::in);
if (file)
{
   cout << "Could not open file.\n";
}
```

67.
```
fstream file("info.dat");
if (!file)
{
   cout << "Could not open file.\n";
}
```

68.
```
fstream dataFile("info.dat", ios:in | ios:binary);
int x = 5;
dataFile << x;
```

69.
```
fstream dataFile("info.dat", ios:in);
char stuff[81];
dataFile.get(stuff);
```

70.
```
fstream dataFile("info.dat", ios:in);
char stuff[81] = "abcdefghijklmnopqrstuvwxyz";
dataFile.put(stuff);
```

71.
```
fstream dataFile("info.dat", ios:out);
struct Date
{
   int month;
   int day;
   int year;
};
Date dt = { 4, 2, 98 };
dataFile.write(&dt, sizeof(int));
```

72.
```
fstream inFile("info.dat", ios:in);
int x;
inFile.seekp(5);
inFile >> x;
```

Programming Challenges

1. **File Head Program**

   Write a program that asks the user for the name of a file. The program should display the first ten lines of the file on the screen (the "head" of the file). If the file has fewer than ten lines, the entire file should be displayed, with a message indicating the entire file has been displayed.

> **NOTE:** Using an editor, you should create a simple text file that can be used to test this program.

2. **File Display Program**

   Write a program that asks the user for the name of a file. The program should display the contents of the file on the screen. If the file's contents won't fit on a single screen, the program should display 24 lines of output at a time, then pause. Each time the program pauses, it should wait for the user to strike a key before the next 24 lines are displayed.

> **NOTE:** Using an editor, you should create a simple text file that can be used to test this program.

3. **Punch Line**

   Write a program that reads and prints a joke and its punch line from two different files. The first file contains a joke, but not its punch line. The second file has the punch line as its last line, preceded by "garbage." The `main` function of your program should open the two files then call two functions, passing each one the file it needs. The first function should read and display each line in the file it is passed (the joke file). The second function should display only the last line of the file it is passed (the punch line file). It should find this line by seeking to the end of the file and then backing up to the beginning of the last line. Data to test your program can be found in the joke.txt and punchline.txt files.

4. **Tail Program**

   Write a program that asks the user for the name of a file. The program should display the last ten lines of the file on the screen (the "tail" of the file). If the file has fewer than ten lines, the entire file should be displayed, with a message indicating the entire file has been displayed.

> **NOTE:** Using an editor, you should create a simple text file that can be used to test this program.

5. **Line Numbers**

   (This assignment could be done as a modification of the program in Programming Challenge 2.) Write a program that asks the user for the name of a file. The program should display the contents of the file on the screen. Each line of screen output should be preceded with a line number, followed by a colon. The line numbering should start at 1. Here is an example:

```
1:George Rolland
2:127 Academy Street
3:Brasstown, NC 28706
```

If the file's contents won't fit on a single screen, the program should display 24 lines of output at a time, and then pause. Each time the program pauses, it should wait for the user to strike a key before the next 24 lines are displayed.

> **NOTE:** Using an editor, you should create a simple text file that can be used to test this program.

6. **String Search**

   Write a program that asks the user for a file name and a string for which to search. The program should search the file for every occurrence of a specified string. When the string is found, the line that contains it should be displayed. After all the occurrences have been located, the program should report the number of times the string appeared in the file.

> **NOTE:** Using an editor, you should create a simple text file that can be used to test this program.

7. **Sentence Filter**

   Write a program that asks the user for two file names. The first file will be opened for input, and the second file will be opened for output. (It will be assumed the first file contains sentences that end with a period.) The program will read the contents of the first file and change all the letters to lowercase except the first letter of each sentence, which should be made uppercase. The revised contents should be stored in the second file.

> **NOTE:** Using an editor, you should create a simple text file that can be used to test this program.

8. **Array/File Functions**

   Write a function named `arrayToFile`. The function should accept three arguments: the name of a file, a pointer to an `int` array, and the size of the array. The function should open the specified file in binary mode, write the contents of the array to the file, and then close the file.

   Write another function named `fileToArray`. This function should accept three arguments: the name of a file, a pointer to an `int` array, and the size of the array. The function should open the specified file in binary mode, read its contents into the array, and then close the file.

   Write a complete program that demonstrates these functions by using the `arrayToFile` function to write an array to a file, then using the `fileToArray` function to read the data from the same file. After the data are read from the file into the array, display the array's contents on the screen.

9. **File Encryption Filter**

VideoNote
Solving the File Encryption Filter Problem

File encryption is the science of writing the contents of a file in a secret code. Your encryption program should work like a filter, reading the contents of one file, modifying the data into a code, then writing the coded contents out to a second file. The second file will be a version of the first file, but written in a secret code.

Although there are complex encryption techniques, you should come up with a simple one of your own. For example, you could read the first file one character at a time, and add 10 to the ASCII code of each character before it is written to the second file.

10. **File Decryption Filter**

Write a program that decrypts the file produced by the program in Programming Challenge 9. The decryption program should read the contents of the coded file, restore the data to its original state, and write it to another file.

11. **Corporate Sales Data Output**

Write a program that uses a structure to store the following data on a company division:

- Division Name (such as East, West, North, or South)
- Quarter (1, 2, 3, or 4)
- Quarterly Sales

The user should be asked for the four quarters' sales figures for the East, West, North, and South divisions. The data for each quarter for each division should be written to a file.

Input Validation: Do not accept negative numbers for any sales figures.

12. **Corporate Sales Data Input**

Write a program that reads the data in the file created by the program in Programming Challenge 11. The program should calculate and display the following figures:

- Total corporate sales for each quarter
- Total yearly sales for each division
- Total yearly corporate sales
- Average quarterly sales for the divisions
- The highest and lowest quarters for the corporation

13. **Inventory Program**

Write a program that uses a structure to store the following inventory data in a file:

- Item Description
- Quantity on Hand
- Wholesale Cost
- Retail Cost
- Date Added to Inventory

The program should have a menu that allows the user to perform the following tasks:

- Add new records to the file
- Display any record in the file
- Change any record in the file

Input Validation: The program should not accept quantities, or wholesale or retail costs, less than 0. The program should not accept dates that the programmer determines are unreasonable.

14. Inventory Screen Report

Write a program that reads the data in the file created by the program in Programming Challenge 13. The program should calculate and display the following data:

- The total wholesale value of the inventory
- The total retail value of the inventory
- The total quantity of all items in the inventory

15. Average Number of Words

If you have downloaded this chapter's source code, you will find a file named text.txt in the Chapter 12 folder. The text that is in the file is stored as one sentence per line. Write a program that reads the file's contents and calculates the average number of words per sentence.

Group Project

16. Customer Accounts

This program should be designed and written by a team of students. Here are some suggestions:

- One student should design function `main`, which will call other program functions. The remainder of the functions will be designed by other members of the team.
- The requirements of the program should be analyzed so that each student is given about the same workload.

Write a program that uses a structure to store the following data about a customer account:

- Name
- Address
- City, State, and ZIP
- Telephone Number
- Account Balance
- Date of Last Payment

The structure should be used to store customer account records in a file. The program should have a menu that lets the user perform the following operations:

- Enter new records into the file
- Search for a particular customer's record and display it
- Search for a particular customer's record and delete it
- Search for a particular customer's record and change it
- Display the contents of the entire file

Input Validation: When the data for a new account is entered, be sure the user enters data for all the fields. No negative account balances should be entered.

Answers to Checkpoints

1 `ios::app`

2 Place the | operator between them.

3 `diskInfo.open("names.dat", ios::out);`

4 `diskInfo.open("customers.dat", ios::out | ios::app);`

5 `diskInfo.open("payable.dat", ios::in | ios::out);`

6 `fstream dataFile("salesfigures.txt", ios::in);`

7
```
Run
Spot
run
See
spot
run
```

8 The >> operator considers whitespace characters as delimiters, and does not read them. The `getline()` member function does read whitespace characters.

9
```
100.28        1.72        8.60        7.78        5.10
```

10 `seekg` moves the file's read position (for input) and `seekp` moves the file's write position (for output).

11 `tellg` reports the file's read position and `tellp` reports the files write position.

12

`ios::beg`	The offset is calculated from the beginning of the file
`ios::end`	The offset is calculated from the end of the file
`ios::curr`	The offset is calculated from the current position

13 0

14 `file.seekp(100L, ios::beg);`
Moves the write position to the 101st byte (byte 100) from the beginning of the file.

`file.seekp(-10L, ios::end);`
Moves the write position to the 11th byte (byte 10) from the end of the file.

`file.seekp(-25L, ios::cur);`
Moves the write position backward to the 26th byte from the current position.

`file.seekp(30L, ios::cur);`
Moves the write position to the 30th byte (byte 31) from the current position.

15 `file.open("info.dat", ios::in | ios::out);`
Input and output

`file.open("info.dat", ios::in | ios::app);`
Input and output. Output will be appended to the end of the file.

`file.open("info.dat", ios::in | ios::out | ios::ate);`
Input and output. If the file already exists, the program goes immediately to the end of the file.

`file.open("info.dat", ios::in | ios::out);`
Input and output, binary mode

Answers to Odd Numbered Review Questions

1. The `fstream` data type allows both reading and writing, while the `ifstream` data type allows only for reading, and the `ofstream` data type allows only for writing.
3. Its contents are erased. (In other words, the file is truncated.)
5. By reference because the internal state of file stream objects changes with most every operation. They should always be passed to functions by reference to ensure internal consistency.
7. When the end of the file has been encountered. The `eof` member function reports the state of this bit.
9. By using the `getline` member function
11. Two arguments: The starting address of the section of memory where the data will be stored, and the number of bytes to read.
13. The `seekg` function moves a file's write position, and the `seekp` function moves a file's read position.
15. Call the file object's `clear` member function.
17. Use the `seekg` member function to move the read position back to the beginning of the file.
19. NULL or 0
21. `getline`
23. `put`
25. text, ASCII text
27. structures
29. `read`
31. sequential
33. `seekg`
35. `tellg`
37. `ios::beg`
39. `ios::cur`

41. `fstream places("places.dat", ios::in | ios::out);`

43.
```
pets.open("pets.dat", ios::in);
fstream pets("pets.dat" ios::in);
```

45.
```
fstream employees;
employees.open("emp.dat", ios::in | ios::out | ios::binary);
if (!employees)
    cout << "Failed to open file.\n";
```

47.
```
dataFile.seekg(0L, ios::end);
numBytes = dataFile.tellg();
cout << "The file has " << numBytes << " bytes.\n";
```

49. True

51. True

53. True

55. False

57. True

59. True

61. True

63. False

65. File should be opened as

```
fstream file("info.dat", ios::in | ios::out);
```

or

```
fstream file;
        file.open("info.dat", ios::in | ios::out);
```

67. File access flags must be specified with `fstream` objects.

69. The file access flag should be `ios::in`. Also, the `get` member function cannot be used to read a string.

71. The file access flag should be `ios::out`. Also, the last line should read

```
dataFile.write(reinterpret_cast<char *>(&dt), sizeof(dt));
```

Introduction to Classes

TOPICS

1 Procedural and Object-Oriented Programming

CONCEPT: Procedural programming is a method of writing software. It is a programming practice centered on the procedures or actions that take place in a program. Object-oriented programming is centered around the object. Objects are created from abstract data types that encapsulate data and functions together.

There are two common programming methods in practice today: procedural programming and object-oriented programming (or OOP).

In a procedural program, you typically have data stored in a collection of variables and/or structures, coupled with a set of functions that perform operations on the data. The data and the functions are separate entities. For example, in a program that works with the geometry of a rectangle you might have the variables in Table 1.

Table 1 Variables Related to a Rectangle

Variable Definition	Description
`double width;`	Holds the rectangle's width
`double length;`	Holds the rectangle's length

In addition to the variables listed in Table 1, you might also have the functions listed in Table 2.

Table 2 Functions Related to a Rectangle

Function Name	Description
`setData()`	Stores values in `width` and `length`
`displayWidth()`	Displays the rectangle's width
`displayLength()`	Displays the rectangle's length
`displayArea()`	Displays the rectangle's area

Usually the variables and data structures in a procedural program are passed to the functions that perform the desired operations. As you might imagine, the focus of procedural programming is on creating the functions that operate on the program's data.

Procedural programming has worked well for software developers for many years. However, as programs become larger and more complex, the separation of a program's data and the code that operates on the data can lead to problems. For example, the data in a procedural program are stored in variables, as well as more complex structures that are created from variables. The procedures that operate on the data must be designed with those variables and data structures in mind. But what happens if the format of the data is altered? Quite often, a program's specifications change, resulting in redesigned data structures. When the structure of the data changes, the code that operates on the data must also change to accept the new format. This results in additional work for programmers and a greater opportunity for bugs to appear in the code.

This problem has helped influence the shift from procedural programming to object-oriented programming (OOP). Whereas procedural programming is centered on creating procedures or functions, object-oriented programming is centered on creating objects. An *object* is a software entity that contains both data and procedures. The data contained in an object are known as the object's *attributes*. The procedures an object performs are called *member functions*. The object is, conceptually, a self-contained unit consisting of attributes (data) and procedures (functions). This is illustrated in Figure 1.

OOP addresses the problems that can result from the separation of code and data through encapsulation and data hiding. *Encapsulation* refers to the combining of data and code into a single object. *Data hiding* refers to an object's ability to hide its data from code

Figure 1 An object contains data and procedures

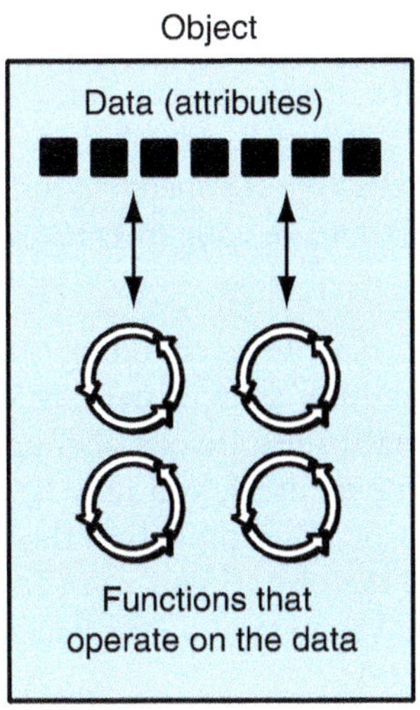

NOTE: In other programming languages, the procedures an object performs are often called *methods*.

that is outside the object. Only the object's member functions may directly access and make changes to the object's data. An object typically hides its data, but allows outside code to access its member functions. As shown in Figure 2, the object's member functions provide programming statements outside the object with indirect access to the object's data.

Figure 2 Only an object's member functions may access the object's data

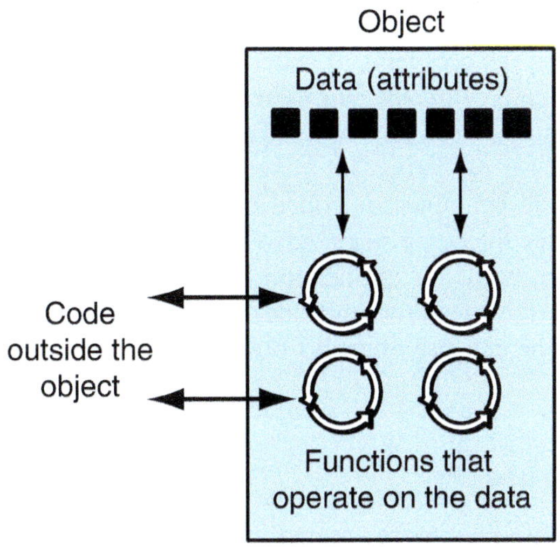

When an object's internal data are hidden from outside code, and access to that data is restricted to the object's member functions, the data are protected from accidental corruption. In addition, the programming code outside the object does not need to know about the format or internal structure of the object's data. The code only needs to interact with the object's functions. When a programmer changes the structure of an object's internal data, he or she also modifies the object's member functions so they may properly operate on the data. The way in which outside code interacts with the member functions, however, does not change.

An everyday example of object-oriented technology is the automobile. It has a rather simple interface that consists of an ignition switch, steering wheel, gas pedal, brake pedal, and a gear shift. Vehicles with manual transmissions also provide a clutch pedal. If you want to drive an automobile (to become its user), you only have to learn to operate these elements of its interface. To start the motor, you simply turn the key in the ignition switch. What happens internally is irrelevant to the user. If you want to steer the auto to the left, you rotate the steering wheel left. The movements of all the linkages connecting the steering wheel to the front tires occur transparently.

Because automobiles have simple user interfaces, they can be driven by people who have no mechanical knowledge. This is good for the makers of automobiles because it means more people are likely to become customers. It's good for the users of automobiles because they can learn just a few simple procedures and operate almost any vehicle.

These are also valid concerns in software development. A real-world program is rarely written by only one person. Even the programs you have created so far weren't written entirely by you. If you incorporated C++ library functions, or objects like `cin` and `cout`, you used code written by someone else. In the world of professional software development, programmers commonly work in teams, buy and sell their code, and collaborate on projects. With OOP, programmers can create objects with powerful engines tucked away "under the hood," protected by simple interfaces that safeguard the object's algorithms.

Object Reusability

In addition to solving the problems of code/data separation, the use of OOP has also been encouraged by the trend of *object reusability*. An object is not a stand-alone program, but is used by programs that need its service. For example, Sharon is a programmer who has developed an object for rendering 3D images. She is a math whiz and knows a lot about computer graphics, so her object is coded to perform all the necessary 3D mathematical operations and handle the computer's video hardware. Tom, who is writing a program for an architectural firm, needs his application to display 3D images of buildings. Because he is working under a tight deadline and does not possess a great deal of knowledge about computer graphics, he can use Sharon's object to perform the 3D rendering (for a small fee, of course!).

Classes and Objects

Now let's discuss how objects are created in software. Before an object can be created, it must be designed by a programmer. The programmer determines the attributes and functions that are necessary then creates a class. A *class* is code that specifies the attributes and member functions that a particular type of object may have. Think of a class as a "blueprint" from which objects may be created. It serves a similar purpose as the blueprint for a house. The blueprint itself is not a house, but is a detailed description of a house. When we use the blueprint to build an actual house, we could say we are building an instance of the house described by the blueprint. If we so desire, we can build several identical houses from the same blueprint. Each house is a separate instance of the house described by the blueprint. This idea is illustrated in Figure 3.

Figure 3 A blueprint describes a house

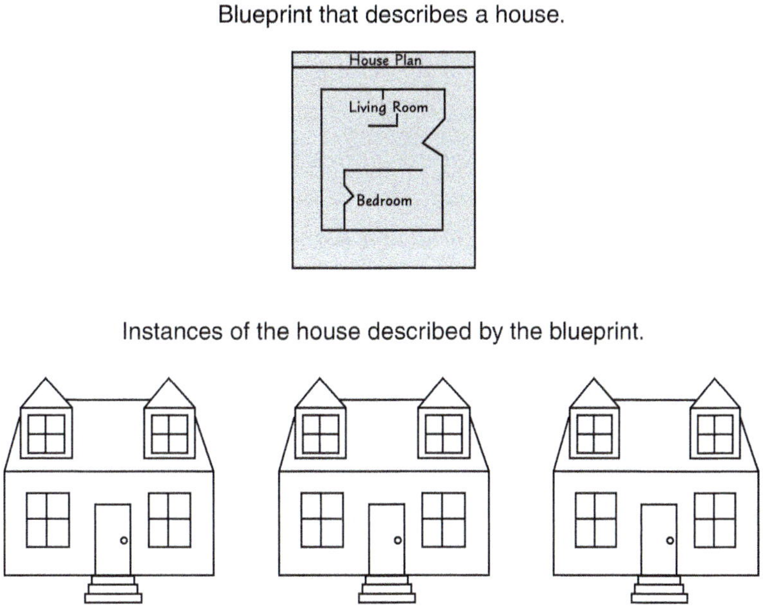

So, a class is not an object, but it is a description of an object. When the program is running, it uses the class to create, in memory, as many objects of a specific type as needed. Each object that is created from a class is called an *instance* of the class.

For example, Jessica is an entomologist (someone who studies insects), and she also enjoys writing computer programs. She designs a program to catalog different types of insects. As part of the program, she creates a class named `Insect`, which specifies attributes and member functions for holding and manipulating data common to all types of insects. The `Insect` class is not an object, but a specification that objects may be created from. Next, she writes programming statements that create a `housefly` object, which is an instance of the `Insect` class. The `housefly` object is an entity that occupies computer memory and stores data about a housefly. It has the attributes and member functions specified by the `Insect` class. Then she writes programming statements that create a `mosquito` object. The `mosquito` object is also an instance of the `Insect` class. It has its own area in memory and stores data about a mosquito. Although the `housefly` and `mosquito` objects are two separate entities in the computer's memory, they were both created from the `Insect` class. This means that each of the objects has the attributes and member functions described by the `Insect` class. This is illustrated in Figure 4.

Figure 4 Instances of a class

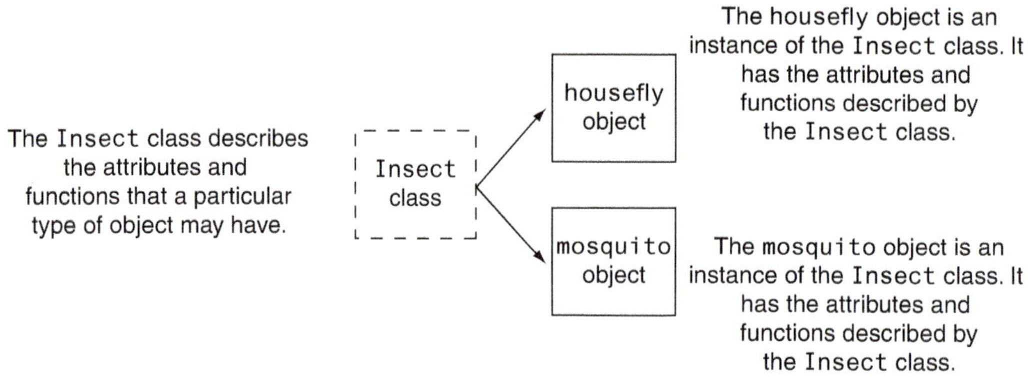

At the beginning of this section, we discussed how a procedural program that works with rectangles might have variables to hold the rectangle's width and length and separate functions to do things like store values in the variables and make calculations. The program would pass the variables to the functions as needed. In an object-oriented program, we would create a `Rectangle` class, which would encapsulate the data (width and length) and the functions that work with the data. Figure 5 shows a representation of such a class.

Figure 5 A class encapsulates data and functions

Member Variables

```
double width;
double length;
```

Member Functions

```
void setWidth(double w)
{ ... function code ...}

void setLength(double len)
{ ... function code ...}

double getWidth()
{ ... function code ...}

double getLength()
{ ... function code ...}

double getArea()
{ ... function code ...}
```

In the object-oriented approach, the variables and functions are all members of the `Rectangle` class. When we need to work with a rectangle in our program, we create a `Rectangle` object, which is an instance of the `Rectangle` class. When we need to perform an operation on the `Rectangle` object's data, we use that object to call the appropriate member function. For example, if we need to get the area of the rectangle, we use the object to call the `getArea` member function. The `getArea` member function would be designed to calculate the area of that object's rectangle and return the value.

Using a Class You Already Know

Before we go any further, let's review the basics of a class that you have already learned something about: the `string` class. First, recall that you must have the following `#include` directive in any program that uses the `string` class:

```
#include <string>
```

This is necessary because the `string` class is declared in the `<string>` header file. Next, you can define a `string` object with a statement such as

```
string cityName;
```

This creates a `string` object named `cityName`. The `cityName` object is an instance of the `string` class.

Once a `string` object has been created, you can store data in it. Because the `string` class is designed to work with the assignment operator, you can assign a string literal to a `string` object. Here is an example:

```
cityName = "Charleston";
```

After this statement executes, the string `"Charleston"` will be stored in the `cityName` object. `"Charleston"` will become the object's data.

The `string` class specifies numerous member functions that perform operations on the data that a `string` object holds. For example, it has a member function named `length`, which returns the length of the string stored in a `string` object. The following code demonstrates:

```
string cityName;               // Create a string object named cityName
int strSize;                   // To hold the length of a string
cityName = "Charleston";       // Assign "Charleston" to cityName
strSize = cityName.length();   // Store the string length in strSize
```

The last statement calls the `length` member function, which returns the length of a string. The expression `cityName.length()` returns the length of the string stored in the `cityName` object. After this statement executes, the `strSize` variable will contain the value 10, which is the length of the string `"Charleston"`.

The `string` class also specifies a member function named `append`, which appends an additional string onto the string already stored in an object. The following code demonstrates this:

```
string cityName;
cityName = "Charleston";
cityName.append(" South Carolina");
```

In the second line, the string `"Charleston"` is assigned to the `cityName` object. In the third line, the `append` member function is called and `" South Carolina"` is passed as an argument. The argument is appended to the string that is already stored in `cityName`. After this statement executes, the `cityName` object will contain the string `"Charleston South Carolina"`.

2 Introduction to Classes

CONCEPT: In C++, the class is the construct primarily used to create objects.

A *class* is similar to a structure. It is a data type defined by the programmer, consisting of variables and functions. Here is the general format of a class declaration:

VideoNote
Writing a Class

```
class ClassName
{
    declaration;
    // ... more declarations
    // may follow...
};
```

The declaration statements inside a class declaration are for the variables and functions that are members of that class. For example, the following code declares a class named `Rectangle` with two member variables: `width` and `length`.

```
class Rectangle
{
    double width;
    double length;
};                      // Don't forget the semicolon.
```

There is a problem with this class, however. Unlike structures, the members of a class are *private* by default. Private class members cannot be accessed by programming statements outside the class. So, no statements outside this `Rectangle` class can access the `width` and `length` members.

Recall from our earlier discussion on object-oriented programming that an object can perform data hiding, which means that critical data stored inside the object are protected from code outside the object. In C++, a class's private members are hidden and can be accessed only by functions that are members of the same class. A class's *public* members may be accessed by code outside the class.

Access Specifiers

C++ provides the key words `private` and `public`, which you may use in class declarations. These key words are known as *access specifiers* because they specify how class members may be accessed. The following is the general format of a class declaration that uses the `private` and `public` access specifiers:

```
class ClassName
{
    private:
      // Declarations of private
      // members appear here.
    public:
      // Declarations of public
      // members appear here.
};
```

Notice the access specifiers are followed by a colon (:) then followed by one or more member declarations. In this general format, the `private` access specifier is used first. All of the declarations that follow it, up to the `public` access specifier, are for private members. Then, all of the declarations that follow the `public` access specifier are for public members.

Public Member Functions

To allow access to a class's private member variables, you create public member functions that work with the private member variables. For example, consider the `Rectangle` class. To allow access to a `Rectangle` object's `width` and `length` member variables, we will add the member functions listed in Table 3.

Table 3 The `Rectangle` Class's Member Functions

Member Function	Description
`setWidth`	This function accepts an argument, which is assigned to the `width` member variable.
`setLength`	This function accepts an argument, which is assigned to the `length` member variable.
`getWidth`	This function returns the value stored in the `width` member variable.
`getLength`	This function returns the value stored in the `length` member variable.
`getArea`	This function returns the product of the `width` member variable multiplied by the `length` member variable. This value is the area of the rectangle.

For the moment, we will not actually define the functions described in Table 3. We leave that for later. For now, we will only include declarations, or prototypes, for the functions in the class declaration.

```
class Rectangle
{
   private:
     double width;
     double length;
   public:
     void setWidth(double);
     void setLength(double);
     double getWidth() const;
     double getLength() const;
     double getArea() const;
};
```

In this declaration, the member variables `width` and `length` are declared as `private`, which means they can be accessed only by the class's member functions. The member functions, however, are declared as `public`, which means they can be called from statements outside the class. If code outside the class needs to store a width or a length in a `Rectangle` object, it must do so by calling the object's `setWidth` or `setLength` member functions. Likewise, if code outside the class needs to retrieve a width or length stored in a `Rectangle` object, it must do so with the object's `getWidth` or `getLength` member functions. These public functions provide an interface for code outside the class to use `Rectangle` objects.

NOTE: Even though the default access of a class is private, it's still a good idea to use the `private` key word to explicitly declare private members. This clearly documents the access specification of all the members of the class.

Using `const` with Member Functions

Notice the key word `const` appears in the declarations of the `getWidth`, `getLength`, and `getArea` member functions, as shown here:

```
double getWidth() const;
double getLength() const;
double getArea() const;
```

When the key word `const` appears after the parentheses in a member function declaration, it specifies that the function will not change any data stored in the calling object. If you inadvertently write code in the function that changes the calling object's data, the compiler will generate an error. As you will see momentarily, the `const` key word must also appear in the function header.

Placement of `public` and `private` Members

There is no rule requiring you to declare private members before public members. The `Rectangle` class could be declared as follows:

```
class Rectangle
{
    public:
        void setWidth(double);
        void setLength(double);
        double getWidth() const;
        double getLength() const;
        double getArea() const;
    private:
        double width;
        double length;
};
```

In addition, it is not required that all members of the same access specification be declared in the same place. Here is yet another declaration of the `Rectangle` class.

```
class Rectangle
{
    private:
        double width;
    public:
        void setWidth(double);
        void setLength(double);
        double getWidth() const;
        double getLength() const;
        double getArea() const;
    private:
        double length;
};
```

Although C++ gives you freedom in arranging class member declarations, you should adopt a consistent standard. Most programmers choose to group member declarations of the same access specification together.

> **NOTE:** Notice in our example the first character of the class name is written in uppercase. This is not required, but serves as a visual reminder that the class name is not a variable name.

Defining Member Functions

The `Rectangle` class declaration contains declarations or prototypes for five member functions: `setWidth`, `setLength`, `getWidth`, `getLength`, and `getArea`. The definitions of these functions are written outside the class declaration.

```
//***************************************************************
// setWidth assigns its argument to the private member width.  *
//***************************************************************

void Rectangle::setWidth(double w)
{
   width = w;
}

//*****************************************************************
// setLength assigns its argument to the private member length.  *
//*****************************************************************

void Rectangle::setLength(double len)
{
   length = len;
}

//************************************************************
// getWidth returns the value in the private member width.  *
//************************************************************

double Rectangle::getWidth() const
{
   return width;
}

//**************************************************************
// getLength returns the value in the private member length.  *
//**************************************************************

double Rectangle::getLength() const
{
   return length;
}
```

```
//**********************************************************
// getArea returns the product of width times length.  *
//**********************************************************

double Rectangle::getArea() const
{
   return width * length;
}
```

In each function definition, the following precedes the name of each function:

```
Rectangle::
```

The two colons are called the *scope resolution operator*. When `Rectangle::` appears before the name of a function in a function header, it identifies the function as a member of the `Rectangle` class.

Here is the general format of the function header of any member function defined outside the declaration of a class:

```
ReturnType ClassName::functionName(ParameterList)
```

In the general format, *`ReturnType`* is the function's return type. *`ClassName`* is the name of the class of which the function is a member. *`functionName`* is the name of the member function. *`ParameterList`* is an optional list of parameter variable declarations.

WARNING! Remember, the class name and scope resolution operator extends the name of the function. They must appear after the return type and immediately before the function name in the function header. The following would be incorrect:

```
Rectangle::double getArea() //Incorrect!
```

In addition, if you leave the class name and scope resolution operator out of a member function's header, the function will not become a member of the class.

```
double getArea() // Not a member of the Rectangle class!
```

Accessors and Mutators

As mentioned earlier, it is a common practice to make all of a class's member variables private, and to provide public member functions for accessing and changing them. This ensures that the object owning the member variables is in control of all changes being made to them. A member function that gets a value from a class's member variable but does not change it is known as an *accessor*. A member function that assigns a value to a member variable is known as a *mutator*. In the `Rectangle` class, the member functions `getLength` and `getWidth` are accessors, and the member functions `setLength` and `setWidth` are mutators.

Some programmers refer to mutators as *setter functions* because they set the value of an attribute, and accessors as *getter functions* because they get the value of an attribute.

Using const with Accessors

Notice the key word const appears in the headers of the getWidth, getLength, and getArea member functions, as shown here:

```
double Rectangle::getWidth() const
double Rectangle::getLength() const
double Rectangle::getArea() const
```

Recall that these functions were also declared in the class with the const key word. When you mark a member function as const, the const key word must appear in both the declaration and the function header.

In essence, when you mark a member function as const, you are telling the compiler that the calling object is a constant. The compiler will generate an error if you inadvertently write code in the function that changes the calling object's data. Because this decreases the chances of having bugs in your code, it is a good practice to mark all accessor functions as const.

The Importance of Data Hiding

As a beginning student, you might be wondering why you would want to hide the data that is inside the classes you create. As you learn to program, you will be the user of your own classes, so it might seem that you are putting forth a great effort to hide data from yourself. If you write software in industry, however, the classes that you create will be used as components in large software systems; programmers other than yourself will use your classes. By hiding a class's data and allowing it to be accessed through only the class's member functions, you can better ensure that the class will operate as you intended.

3 Defining an Instance of a Class

CONCEPT: Class objects must be defined after the class is declared.

VideoNote
Defining an Instance of a Class

Like structure variables, class objects are not created in memory until they are defined. This is because a class declaration by itself does not create an object, but is merely the description of an object. We can use it to create one or more objects, which are instances of the class.

Class objects are created with simple definition statements, just like variables. Here is the general format of a simple object definition statement:

```
ClassName objectName;
```

In the general format, *ClassName* is the name of a class, and *objectName* is the name we are giving the object.

For example, the following statement defines box as an object of the Rectangle class:

```
Rectangle box;
```

Defining a class object is called the *instantiation* of a class. In this statement, box is an *instance* of the Rectangle class.

Accessing an Object's Members

The box object we previously defined is an instance of the Rectangle class. Suppose we want to change the value in the box object's width variable. To do so, we must use the box object to call the setWidth member function, as shown here:

```
box.setWidth(12.7);
```

Just as you use the dot operator to access a structure's members, you use the dot operator to call a class's member functions. This statement uses the box object to call the setWidth member function, passing 12.7 as an argument. As a result, the box object's width variable will be set to 12.7. Here are other examples of statements that use the box object to call member functions:

```
box.setLength(4.8);         // Set box's length to 4.8.
x = box.getWidth();         // Assign box's width to x.
cout << box.getLength();    // Display box's length.
cout << box.getArea();      // Display box's area.
```

> **NOTE:** Notice inside the Rectangle class's member functions, the dot operator is not used to access any of the class's member variables. When an object is used to call a member function, the member function has direct access to that object's member variables.

A Class Demonstration Program

Program 1 is a complete program that demonstrates the Rectangle class.

Program 1

```
// This program demonstrates a simple class.
#include <iostream>
using namespace std;

// Rectangle class declaration.
class Rectangle
{
    private:
        double width;
        double length;
    public:
        void setWidth(double);
        void setLength(double);
        double getWidth() const;
        double getLength() const;
        double getArea() const;
};

//**************************************************
// setWidth assigns a value to the width member.  *
//**************************************************

void Rectangle::setWidth(double w)
```

```
{
    width = w;
}

//**************************************************
// setLength assigns a value to the length member. *
//**************************************************

void Rectangle::setLength(double len)
{
    length = len;
}

//**************************************************
// getWidth returns the value in the width member. *
//**************************************************

double Rectangle::getWidth() const
{
    return width;
}

//***************************************************
// getLength returns the value in the length member. *
//***************************************************

double Rectangle::getLength() const
{
    return length;
}

//*****************************************************
// getArea returns the product of width times length. *
//*****************************************************

double Rectangle::getArea() const
{
    return width * length;
}

//***************************************************
// Function main                                    *
//***************************************************

int main()
{
    Rectangle box;      // Define an instance of the Rectangle class
    double rectWidth;   // Local variable for width
    double rectLength;  // Local variable for length

    // Get the rectangle's width and length from the user.
    cout << "This program will calculate the area of a\n";
    cout << "rectangle. What is the width? ";
```

(program continues)

Program 1 *(continued)*

```
77        cin >> rectWidth;
78        cout << "What is the length? ";
79        cin >> rectLength;
80
81        // Store the width and length of the rectangle
82        // in the box object.
83        box.setWidth(rectWidth);
84        box.setLength(rectLength);
85
86        // Display the rectangle's data.
87        cout << "Here is the rectangle's data:\n";
88        cout << "Width: " << box.getWidth() << endl;
89        cout << "Length: " << box.getLength() << endl;
90        cout << "Area: " << box.getArea() << endl;
91        return 0;
92    }
```

Program Output with Example Input Shown in Bold

```
This program will calculate the area of a
rectangle. What is the width? 10 [Enter]
What is the length? 5 [Enter]
Here is the rectangle's data:
Width: 10
Length: 5
Area: 50
```

The `Rectangle` class declaration, along with the class's member functions, appears in lines 6 through 62. Inside the `main` function, in line 70, the following statement creates a `Rectangle` object named `box`:

```
Rectangle box;
```

The `box` object is illustrated in Figure 6. Notice the `width` and `length` member variables do not yet hold meaningful values. An object's member variables are not automatically initialized to 0. When an object's member variable is first created, it holds whatever random value happens to exist at the variable's memory location. We commonly refer to such a random value as "garbage."

Figure 6 State of the box object

The box object when first created

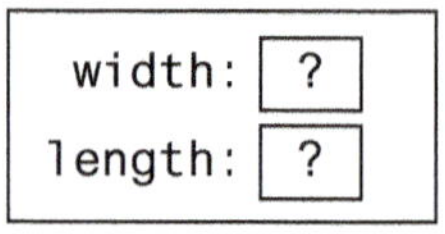

In lines 75 through 79, the program prompts the user to enter the width and length of a rectangle. The width that is entered is stored in the `rectWidth` variable, and the length that is entered is stored in the `rectLength` variable. In line 83 the following statement uses the box object to call the `setWidth` member function, passing the value of the `rectWidth` variable as an argument:

```
box.setWidth(rectWidth);
```

This sets box's `width` member variable to the value in `rectWidth`. Assuming `rectWidth` holds the value 10, Figure 7 shows the state of the box object after this statement executes.

Figure 7 State of the box object

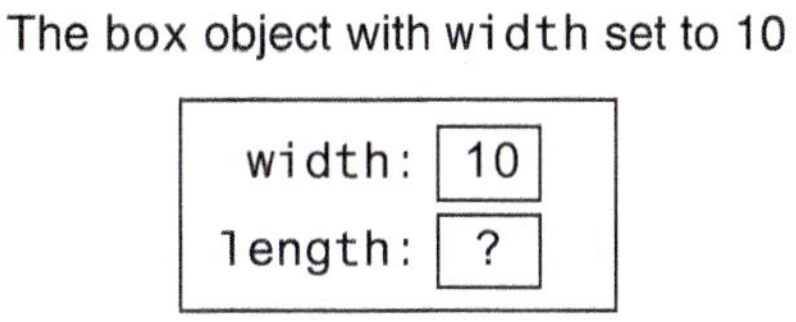

In line 84, the following statement uses the box object to call the `setLength` member function, passing the value of the `rectLength` variable as an argument:

```
box.setLength(rectLength);
```

This sets box's `length` member variable to the value in `rectLength`. Assuming `rectLength` holds the value 5, Figure 8 shows the state of the box object after this statement executes.

Figure 8 State of the box object

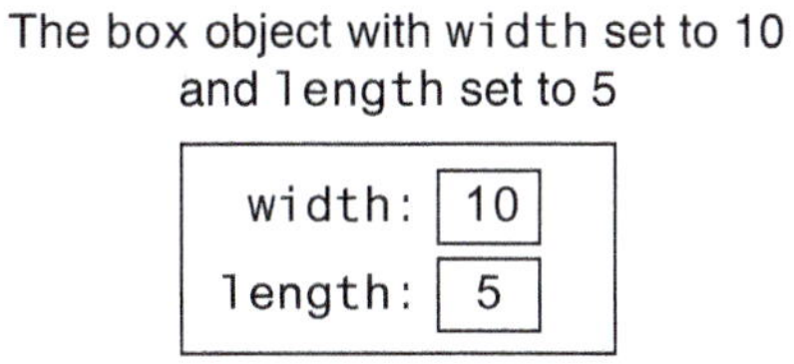

Lines 88, 89, and 90 use the `box` object to call the `getWidth`, `getLength`, and `getArea` member functions, displaying their return values on the screen.

> **NOTE:** Figures 6 through 8 show the state of the box object at various times during the execution of the program. An object's *state* is simply the data that is stored in the object's attributes at any given moment.

Program 1 creates only one `Rectangle` object. It is possible to create many instances of the same class, each with its own data. For example, Program 2 creates three `Rectangle` objects, named `kitchen`, `bedroom`, and `den`. Note lines 6 through 62 have been left out of the listing because they contain the `Rectangle` class declaration and the definitions for the class's member functions. These lines are identical to those same lines in Program 1.

Program 2

```
1   // This program creates three instances of the Rectangle class.
2   #include <iostream>
3   using namespace std;
4
5   // Rectangle class declaration.
```

Lines 6 through 62 have been left out.

```
63
64  //*****************************************************
65  // Function main                                      *
66  //*****************************************************
67
68  int main()
69  {
70     double number;          // To hold a number
71     double totalArea;       // The total area
72     Rectangle kitchen;      // To hold kitchen dimensions
73     Rectangle bedroom;      // To hold bedroom dimensions
74     Rectangle den;          // To hold den dimensions
75
76     // Get the kitchen dimensions.
77     cout << "What is the kitchen's length? ";
78     cin >> number;                          // Get the length
79     kitchen.setLength(number);              // Store in kitchen object
80     cout << "What is the kitchen's width? ";
81     cin >> number;                          // Get the width
82     kitchen.setWidth(number);               // Store in kitchen object
83
84     // Get the bedroom dimensions.
85     cout << "What is the bedroom's length? ";
86     cin >> number;                          // Get the length
87     bedroom.setLength(number);              // Store in bedroom object
88     cout << "What is the bedroom's width? ";
89     cin >> number;                          // Get the width
90     bedroom.setWidth(number);               // Store in bedroom object
91
92     // Get the den dimensions.
93     cout << "What is the den's length? ";
94     cin >> number;                          // Get the length
95     den.setLength(number);                  // Store in den object
96     cout << "What is the den's width? ";
97     cin >> number;                          // Get the width
98     den.setWidth(number);                   // Store in den object
99
100    // Calculate the total area of the three rooms.
101    totalArea = kitchen.getArea() + bedroom.getArea() +
102                den.getArea();
103
104    // Display the total area of the three rooms.
105    cout << "The total area of the three rooms is "
106         << totalArea << endl;
107
```

```
108        return 0;
109    }
```

Program Output with Example Input Shown in Bold

```
What is the kitchen's length? 10 [Enter]
What is the kitchen's width? 14 [Enter]
What is the bedroom's length? 15 [Enter]
What is the bedroom's width? 12 [Enter]
What is the den's length? 20 [Enter]
What is the den's width? 30 [Enter]
The total area of the three rooms is 920
```

In lines 72, 73, and 74, the following code defines three `Rectangle` variables. This creates three objects, each an instance of the `Rectangle` class:

```
Rectangle kitchen;    // To hold kitchen dimensions
Rectangle bedroom;    // To hold bedroom dimensions
Rectangle den;        // To hold den dimensions
```

In the example output, the user enters 10 and 14 as the length and width of the kitchen, 15 and 12 as the length and width of the bedroom, and 20 and 30 as the length and width of the den. Figure 9 shows the states of the objects after these values are stored in them.

Figure 9 State of the `kitchen`, `bedroom`, and `den` objects

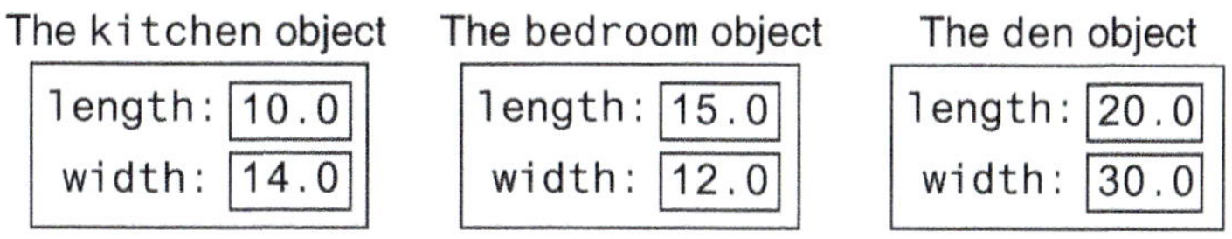

Notice from Figure 9 each instance of the `Rectangle` class has its own `length` and `width` variables. Every instance of a class has its own set of member variables that can hold their own values. The class's member functions can perform operations on specific instances of the class. For example, look at the following statement in line 79 of Program 2:

```
kitchen.setLength(number);
```

This statement calls the `setLength` member function, which stores a value in the `kitchen` object's `length` variable. Now look at the following statement in line 87:

```
bedroom.setLength(number);
```

This statement also calls the `setLength` member function, but this time it stores a value in the `bedroom` object's `length` variable. Likewise, the following statement in line 95 calls the `setLength` member function to store a value in the `den` object's `length` variable:

```
den.setLength(number);
```

The `setLength` member function stores a value in a specific instance of the `Rectangle` class. All of the other `Rectangle` class member functions work in a similar way. They access one or more member variables of a specific `Rectangle` object.

Avoiding Stale Data

In the `Rectangle` class, the `getLength` and `getWidth` member functions return the values stored in member variables, but the `getArea` member function returns the result of a calculation. You might be wondering why the area of the rectangle is not stored in a member variable, like the length and the width. The area is not stored in a member variable because it could potentially become stale. When the value of an item is dependent on other data and that item is not updated when the other data are changed, it is said that the item has become *stale*. If the area of the rectangle were stored in a member variable, the value of the member variable would become incorrect as soon as either the `length` or `width` member variables changed.

When designing a class, you should take care not to store in a member variable calculated data that could potentially become stale. Instead, provide a member function that returns the result of the calculation.

Pointers to Objects

You can also define pointers to class objects. For example, the following statement defines a pointer variable named `rectPtr`:

```
Rectangle *rectPtr = nullptr;
```

The `rectPtr` variable is not an object, but it can hold the address of a `Rectangle` object. The following code shows an example:

```
Rectangle myRectangle;          // A Rectangle object
Rectangle *rectPtr = nullptr;   // A Rectangle pointer
rectPtr = &myRectangle;         // rectPtr now points to myRectangle
```

The first statement creates a `Rectangle` object named `myRectangle`. The second statement creates a `Rectangle` pointer named `rectPtr`. The third statement stores the address of the `myRectangle` object in the `rectPtr` pointer. This is illustrated in Figure 10.

Figure 10 `rectPtr` points to the `myRectangle` object

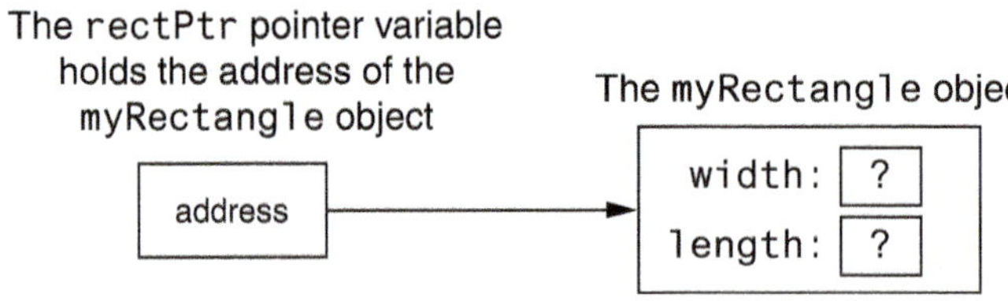

The `rectPtr` pointer can then be used to call member functions by using the `->` operator. The following statements show examples:

```
rectPtr->setWidth(12.5);
rectPtr->setLength(4.8);
```

The first statement calls the `setWidth` member function, passing 12.5 as an argument. Because `rectPtr` points to the `myRectangle` object, this will cause 12.5 to be stored in the `myRectangle` object's `width` variable. The second statement calls the `setLength` member function, passing 4.8 as an argument. This will cause 4.8 to be stored in the `myRectangle` object's `length` variable. Figure 11 shows the state of the `myRectangle` object after these statements have executed.

Figure 11 State of the `myRectangle` object

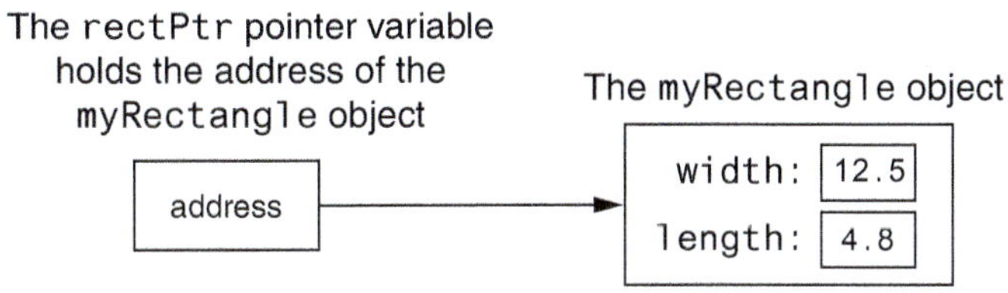

Class object pointers can be used to dynamically allocate objects. The following code shows an example:

```
1  // Define a Rectangle pointer.
2  Rectangle *rectPtr = nullptr;
3
4  // Dynamically allocate a Rectangle object.
5  rectPtr = new Rectangle;
6
7  // Store values in the object's width and length.
8  rectPtr->setWidth(10.0);
9  rectPtr->setLength(15.0);
10
11 // Delete the object from memory.
12 delete rectPtr;
13 rectPtr = nullptr;
```

Line 2 defines `rectPtr` as a `Rectangle` pointer. Line 5 uses the `new` operator to dynamically allocate a `Rectangle` object and assign its address to `rectPtr`. Lines 8 and 9 store values in the dynamically allocated object's `width` and `length` variables. Figure 12 shows the state of the dynamically allocated object after these statements have executed.

Figure 12 `rectPtr` points to a dynamically allocated `Rectangle` object

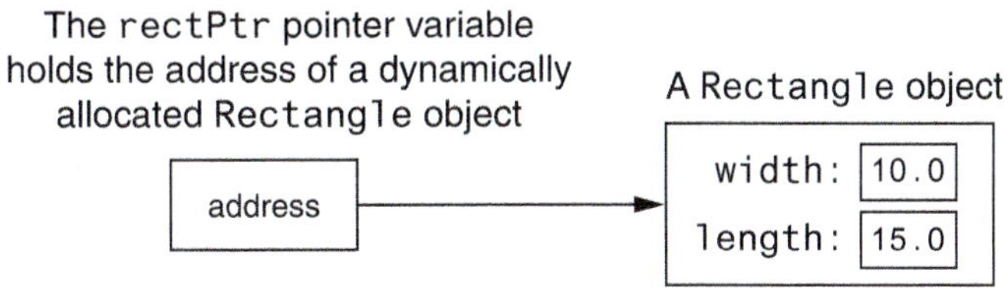

Line 12 deletes the object from memory, and line 13 stores the address 0 in `rectPtr`. This prevents code from inadvertently using the pointer to access the area of memory that has been freed. It also prevents errors from occurring if `delete` is accidentally called on the pointer again.

Program 3 is a modification of Program 2. In this program, `kitchen`, `bedroom`, and `den` are `Rectangle` pointers. They are used to dynamically allocate `Rectangle` objects. The output is the same as Program 2.

Program 3

```
1   // This program creates three instances of the Rectangle class.
2   #include <iostream>
3   using namespace std;
4
5   // Rectangle class declaration.
```

Lines 6 through 62 have been left out.

```
63
64  //*****************************************************
65  // Function main                                      *
66  //*****************************************************
67
68  int main()
69  {
70      double number;               // To hold a number
71      double totalArea;            // The total area
72      Rectangle *kitchen = nullptr; // To point to kitchen dimensions
73      Rectangle *bedroom = nullptr; // To point to bedroom dimensions
74      Rectangle *den = nullptr;    // To point to den dimensions
75
76      // Dynamically allocate the objects.
77      kitchen = new Rectangle;
78      bedroom = new Rectangle;
79      den = new Rectangle;
80
81      // Get the kitchen dimensions.
82      cout << "What is the kitchen's length? ";
83      cin >> number;                         // Get the length
84      kitchen->setLength(number);            // Store in kitchen object
85      cout << "What is the kitchen's width? ";
86      cin >> number;                         // Get the width
87      kitchen->setWidth(number);             // Store in kitchen object
88
89      // Get the bedroom dimensions.
90      cout << "What is the bedroom's length? ";
91      cin >> number;                         // Get the length
92      bedroom->setLength(number);            // Store in bedroom object
93      cout << "What is the bedroom's width? ";
94      cin >> number;                         // Get the width
95      bedroom->setWidth(number);             // Store in bedroom object
96
97      // Get the den dimensions.
98      cout << "What is the den's length? ";
99      cin >> number;                         // Get the length
100     den->setLength(number);                // Store in den object
101     cout << "What is the den's width? ";
102     cin >> number;                         // Get the width
103     den->setWidth(number);                 // Store in den object
104
105     // Calculate the total area of the three rooms.
```

```
    totalArea = kitchen->getArea() + bedroom->getArea() +
                den->getArea();

    // Display the total area of the three rooms.
    cout << "The total area of the three rooms is "
         << totalArea << endl;

    // Delete the objects from memory.
    delete kitchen;
    delete bedroom;
    delete den;
    kitchen = nullptr;    // Make kitchen a null pointer.
    bedroom = nullptr;    // Make bedroom a null pointer.
    den = nullptr;        // Make den a null pointer.

    return 0;
}
```

Using Smart Pointers to Allocate Objects

You can use a `unique_ptr` to dynamically allocate memory, and not worry about deleting the memory when you are finished using it. A `unique_ptr` automatically deletes a chunk of dynamically allocated memory when the memory is no longer being used. This helps to prevent memory leaks from occurring.

To use the `unique_ptr` data type, you must `#include` the `<memory>` header file with the following directive:

```
#include <memory>
```

Here is an example of the syntax for defining a `unique_ptr` that points to a dynamically allocated `Rectangle` object:

```
unique_ptr<Rectangle> rectanglePtr(new Rectangle);
```

This statement defines a `unique_ptr` named `rectanglePtr` that points to a dynamically allocated `Rectangle` object. Here are some details about the statement:

- The notation `<Rectangle>` that appears immediately after `unique_ptr` indicates that the pointer can point to a `Rectangle`.
- The name of the pointer is `rectanglePtr`.
- The expression `new Rectangle` that appears inside the parentheses allocates a chunk of memory to hold a `Rectangle`. The address of the chunk of memory will be assigned to the `rectanglePtr` pointer.

Once you have defined a `unique_ptr`, you can use it in the same way as a regular pointer. This is demonstrated in Program 4. This is a revised version of Program 3, modified to use `unique_ptr`s instead of regular pointers. The output is the same as Programs 2 and 3.

Program 4

```
1   // This program uses smart pointers to allocate three
2   // instances of the Rectangle class.
3   #include <iostream>
4   #include <memory>
5   using namespace std;
6
7   // Rectangle class declaration.
```

Lines 8 through 64 have been left out.

```
65
66  //*****************************************************
67  // Function main                                      *
68  //*****************************************************
69
70  int main()
71  {
72      double number;           // To hold a number
73      double totalArea;        // The total area
74
75      // Dynamically allocate the objects.
76      unique_ptr<Rectangle> kitchen(new Rectangle);
77      unique_ptr<Rectangle> bedroom(new Rectangle);
78      unique_ptr<Rectangle> den(new Rectangle);
79
80      // Get the kitchen dimensions.
81      cout << "What is the kitchen's length? ";
82      cin >> number;                        // Get the length
83      kitchen->setLength(number);           // Store in kitchen object
84      cout << "What is the kitchen's width? ";
85      cin >> number;                        // Get the width
86      kitchen->setWidth(number);            // Store in kitchen object
87
88      // Get the bedroom dimensions.
89      cout << "What is the bedroom's length? ";
90      cin >> number;                        // Get the length
91      bedroom->setLength(number);           // Store in bedroom object
92      cout << "What is the bedroom's width? ";
93      cin >> number;                        // Get the width
94      bedroom->setWidth(number);            // Store in bedroom object
95
96      // Get the den dimensions.
97      cout << "What is the den's length? ";
98      cin >> number;                        // Get the length
99      den->setLength(number);               // Store in den object
100     cout << "What is the den's width? ";
101     cin >> number;                        // Get the width
102     den->setWidth(number);                // Store in den object
103
104     // Calculate the total area of the three rooms.
105     totalArea = kitchen->getArea() + bedroom->getArea() +
106                 den->getArea();
```

```
107
108         // Display the total area of the three rooms.
109         cout << "The total area of the three rooms is "
110              << totalArea << endl;
111
112         return 0;
113     }
```

In line 4, we have a `#include` directive for the `<memory>` header file. Lines 76 through 78 define three `unique_ptrs`, named `kitchen`, `bedroom`, and `den`. Each of these points to a dynamically allocated `Rectangle`. Notice there are no `delete` statements at the end of the `main` function to free the dynamically allocated memory. It is unnecessary to delete the dynamically allocated `Rectangle` objects because the smart pointer will automatically delete them as the function comes to an end.

Checkpoint

1 True or False: You must declare all private members of a class before the public members.

2 Assume `RetailItem` is the name of a class, and the class has a `void` member function named `setPrice`, which accepts a `double` argument. Which of the following shows the correct use of the scope resolution operator in the member function definition?

A) `RetailItem::void setPrice(double p)`
B) `void RetailItem::setPrice(double p)`

3 An object's private member variables are accessed from outside the object by which of the following?

A) public member functions
B) any function
C) the dot operator
D) the scope resolution operator

4 Assume `RetailItem` is the name of a class, and the class has a `void` member function named `setPrice`, which accepts a `double` argument. If `soap` is an instance of the `RetailItem` class, which of the following statements properly uses the `soap` object to call the `setPrice` member function?

A) `RetailItem::setPrice(1.49);`
B) `soap::setPrice(1.49);`
C) `soap.setPrice(1.49);`
D) `soap:setPrice(1.49);`

5 Complete the following code skeleton to declare a class named `Date`. The class should contain variables and functions to store and retrieve a date in the form 4/2/2018.

```
class Date
{
    private:
    public:
}
```

4 Why Have Private Members?

CONCEPT: In object-oriented programming, an object should protect its important data by making it private and providing a public interface to access that data.

You might be questioning the rationale behind making the member variables in the `Rectangle` class private. You might also be questioning why member functions were defined for such simple tasks as setting variables and getting their contents. After all, if the member variables were declared as `public`, the member functions wouldn't be needed.

As mentioned earlier in this chapter, classes usually have variables and functions that are meant only to be used internally. They are not intended to be accessed by statements outside the class. This protects critical data from being accidentally modified or used in a way that might adversely affect the state of the object. When a member variable is declared as `private`, the only way for an application to store values in the variable is through a public member function. Likewise, the only way for an application to retrieve the contents of a private member variable is through a public member function. In essence, the public members become an interface to the object. They are the only members that may be accessed by any application that uses the object.

In the `Rectangle` class, the `width` and `length` member variables hold critical data. Therefore they are declared as `private`, and an interface is constructed with public member functions. If a program creates a `Rectangle` object, the program must use the `setWidth` and `getWidth` member functions to access the object's `width` member. To access the object's `length` member, the program must use the `setLength` and `getLength` member functions. This idea is illustrated in Figure 13.

Figure 13 Private member variables may be accessed only by member functions

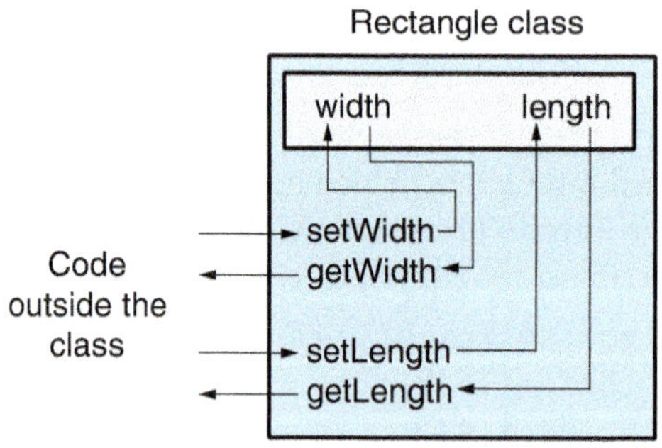

The public member functions can be written to filter out invalid data. For example, look at the following version of the `setWidth` member function:

```
void Rectangle::setWidth(double w)
{
   if (w >= 0)
      width = w;
```

```
        else
        {
            cout << "Invalid width\n";
            exit(EXIT_FAILURE);
        }
    }
```

Notice this version of the function doesn't just assign the parameter value to the `width` variable. It first tests the parameter to make sure it is 0 or greater. If a negative number was passed to the function, an error message is displayed, then the standard library function `exit` is called to abort the program. The `setLength` function could be written in a similar way:

```
    void Rectangle::setLength(double len)
    {
        if (len >= 0)
            length = len;
        else
        {
            cout << "Invalid length\n";
            exit(EXIT_FAILURE);
        }
    }
```

The point being made here is that mutator functions can do much more than simply store values in attributes. They can also validate those values to ensure that only acceptable data is stored in the object's attributes. Keep in mind, however, that calling the `exit` function, as we have done in these examples, is not the best way to deal with invalid data. In reality, you would not design a class to abort the entire program just because invalid data were passed to a mutator function.

5 Focus on Software Engineering: Separating Class Specification from Implementation

CONCEPT: Usually class declarations are stored in their own header files. Member function definitions are stored in their own .cpp files.

In the programs we've looked at so far, the class declaration, member function definitions, and application program are all stored in one file. A more conventional way of designing C++ programs is to store class declarations and member function definitions in their own separate files. Typically, program components are stored in the following fashion:

- Class declarations are stored in their own header files. A header file that contains a class declaration is called a *class specification* file. The name of the class specification file is usually the same as the name of the class, with a .h extension. For example, the `Rectangle` class would be declared in the file Rectangle.h.

- The member function definitions for a class are stored in a separate .cpp file called the *class implementation* file. The file usually has the same name as the class, with the .cpp extension. For example, the `Rectangle` class's member functions would be defined in the file Rectangle.cpp.
- Any program that uses the class should `#include` the class's header file. The class's .cpp file (which contains the member function definitions) should be compiled and linked with the `main` program. This process can be automated with a `project` or `make` utility. Integrated development environments such as Visual Studio also provide the means to create the multi-file projects.

Let's see how we could rewrite Program 1 using this design approach. First, the `Rectangle` class declaration would be stored in the following Rectangle.h file. (This file can be found in the Student Source Code Folder Chapter 13\Rectangle Version 1.)

Contents of `Rectangle.h` (Version 1)

```
1   // Specification file for the Rectangle class.
2   #ifndef RECTANGLE_H
3   #define RECTANGLE_H
4
5   // Rectangle class declaration.
6
7   class Rectangle
8   {
9       private:
10          double width;
11          double length;
12      public:
13          void setWidth(double);
14          void setLength(double);
15          double getWidth() const;
16          double getLength() const;
17          double getArea() const;
18  };
19
20  #endif
```

This is the specification file for the `Rectangle` class. It contains only the declaration of the `Rectangle` class. It does not contain any member function definitions. When we write other programs that use the `Rectangle` class, we can have an `#include` directive that includes this file. That way, we won't have to write the class declaration in every program that uses the `Rectangle` class.

This file also introduces two new preprocessor directives: `#ifndef` and `#endif`. The `#ifndef` directive that appears in line 2 is called an *include guard*. It prevents the header file from accidentally being included more than once. When your main program file has an `#include` directive for a header file, there is always the possibility that the header file will have an `#include` directive for a second header file. If your main program file also has an `#include` directive for the second header file, then the preprocessor will include the second header file twice. Unless an include guard has been written into the second header file, an error will occur because the compiler will process the declarations in the second header file twice. Let's see how an include guard works.

The word `ifndef` stands for "if not defined." It is used to determine whether a specific constant has not been defined with a `#define` directive. When the Rectangle.h file is being compiled, the `#ifndef` directive checks for the existence of a constant named `RECTANGLE_H`. If the constant has not been defined, it is immediately defined in line 3, and the rest of the file is included. If the constant has been defined, it means the file has already been included. In that case, everything between the `#ifndef` and `#endif` directives is skipped. This is illustrated in Figure 14.

Figure 14 How an include guard works

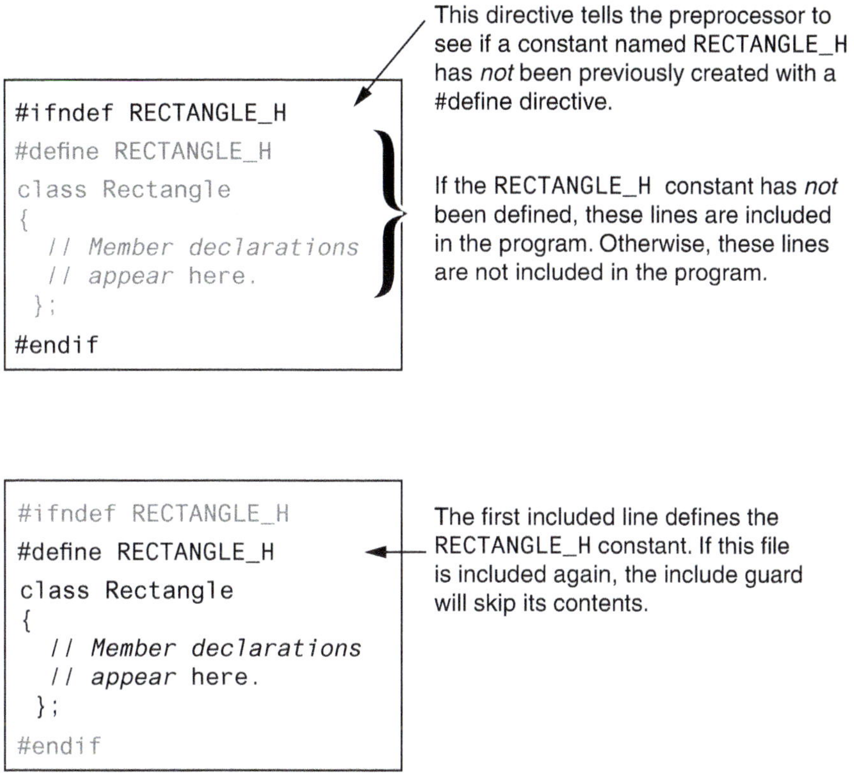

Next, we need an implementation file that contains the class's member function definitions. The implementation file for the `Rectangle` class is Rectangle.cpp. (This file can be found in the Student Source Code Folder Chapter 13\Rectangle Version 1.)

Contents of `Rectangle.cpp` (Version 1)

```
// Implementation file for the Rectangle class.
#include "Rectangle.h"   // Needed for the Rectangle class
#include <iostream>      // Needed for cout
#include <cstdlib>       // Needed for the exit function
using namespace std;

//**********************************************************
// setWidth sets the value of the member variable width.   *
//**********************************************************

```

```
void Rectangle::setWidth(double w)
{
    if (w >= 0)
        width = w;
    else
    {
        cout << "Invalid width\n";
        exit(EXIT_FAILURE);
    }
}

//**************************************************************
// setLength sets the value of the member variable length. *
//**************************************************************

void Rectangle::setLength(double len)
{
    if (len >= 0)
        length = len;
    else
    {
        cout << "Invalid length\n";
        exit(EXIT_FAILURE);
    }
}

//***************************************************************
// getWidth returns the value in the member variable width. *
//***************************************************************

double Rectangle::getWidth() const
{
    return width;
}

//*****************************************************************
// getLength returns the value in the member variable length. *
//*****************************************************************

double Rectangle::getLength() const
{
    return length;
}

//***************************************************************
// getArea returns the product of width times length.       *
//***************************************************************

double Rectangle::getArea() const
{
    return width * length;
}
```

Look at line 2, which has the following `#include` directive:

```
#include "Rectangle.h"
```

This directive includes the Rectangle.h file, which contains the `Rectangle` class declaration. Notice the name of the header file is enclosed in double-quote characters (" ") instead of angled brackets (< >). When you are including a C++ system header file, such as `iostream`, you enclose the name of the file in angled brackets. This indicates the file is located in the compiler's *include file directory*. The include file directory is the directory or folder where all of the standard C++ header files are located. When you are including a header file that you have written, such as a class specification file, you enclose the name of the file in double-quote marks. This indicates the file is located in the current project directory.

Any file that uses the `Rectangle` class must have an `#include` directive for the Rectangle.h file. We need to include Rectangle.h in the class specification file because the functions in this file belong to the `Rectangle` class. Before the compiler can process a function with `Rectangle::` in its name, it must have already processed the `Rectangle` class declaration.

Now that we have the `Rectangle` class stored in its own specification and implementation files, we can see how to use them in a program. Program 5 shows a modified version of Program 1. This version of the program does not contain the `Rectangle` class declaration, or the definitions of any of the class's member functions. Instead, it is designed to be compiled and linked with the class specification and implementation files. (This file can be found in the Student Source Code Folder Chapter 13\Rectangle Version 1.)

Program 5

```
// This program uses the Rectangle class, which is declared in
// the Rectangle.h file. The member Rectangle class's member
// functions are defined in the Rectangle.cpp file. This program
// should be compiled with those files in a project.
#include <iostream>
#include "Rectangle.h" // Needed for Rectangle class
using namespace std;

int main()
{
    Rectangle box;      // Define an instance of the Rectangle class
    double rectWidth;   // Local variable for width
    double rectLength; // Local variable for length

    // Get the rectangle's width and length from the user.
    cout << "This program will calculate the area of a\n";
    cout << "rectangle. What is the width? ";
    cin >> rectWidth;
    cout << "What is the length? ";
    cin >> rectLength;

```

(program continues)

Program 5 *(continued)*

```
22        // Store the width and length of the rectangle
23        // in the box object.
24        box.setWidth(rectWidth);
25        box.setLength(rectLength);
26
27        // Display the rectangle's data.
28        cout << "Here is the rectangle's data:\n";
29        cout << "Width: " << box.getWidth() << endl;
30        cout << "Length: " << box.getLength() << endl;
31        cout << "Area: " << box.getArea() << endl;
32        return 0;
33    }
```

Notice Program 5 has an `#include` directive for the Rectangle.h file in line 6. This causes the declaration for the `Rectangle` class to be included in the file. To create an executable program from this file, the following steps must be taken:

- The implementation file, Rectangle.cpp, must be compiled. Rectangle.cpp is not a complete program, so you cannot create an executable file from it alone. Instead, you compile Rectangle.cpp to an object file that contains the compiled code for the Rectangle class. This file would typically be named Rectangle.obj.
- The main program file, Pr13–4.cpp, must be compiled. This file is not a complete program either because it does not contain any of the implementation code for the `Rectangle` class. So, you compile this file to an object file such as Pr13–4.obj.
- The object files, Pr13–4.obj and Rectangle.obj, are linked together to create an executable file, which would be named something like Pr13–4.exe.

This process is illustrated in Figure 15.

The exact details on how these steps take place are different for each C++ development system. Fortunately, most systems perform all of these steps automatically for you. For example, in Microsoft Visual Studio you create a project, then you simply add all of the files to the project. When you compile the project, the steps are taken care of for you and an executable file is generated.

Separating a class into a specification file and an implementation file provides a great deal of flexibility. First, if you wish to give your class to another programmer, you don't have to share all of your source code with that programmer. You can give him or her the specification file and the compiled object file for the class's implementation. The other programmer simply inserts the necessary `#include` directive into his or her program, compiles it, and links it with your class's object file. This prevents the other programmer, who might not know all the details of your code, from making changes that will introduce bugs.

Separating a class into specification and implementation files also makes things easier when the class's member functions must be modified. It is only necessary to modify the implementation file and recompile it to a new object file. Programs that use the class don't have to be completely recompiled, just linked with the new object file.

Figure 15 Creating an executable file

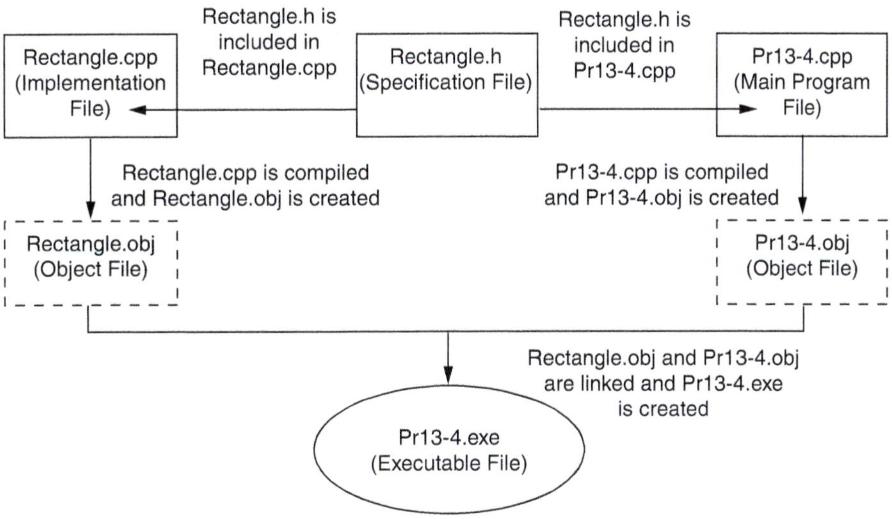

6 Inline Member Functions

CONCEPT: When the body of a member function is written inside a class declaration, it is declared inline.

When the body of a member function is small, it is usually more convenient to place the function's definition, instead of its prototype, in the class declaration. For example, in the `Rectangle` class the member functions `getWidth`, `getLength`, and `getArea` each have only one statement. The `Rectangle` class could be revised as shown in the following listing. (This file can be found in the Student Source Code Folder Chapter 13\Rectangle Version 2.)

Contents of `Rectangle.h` (Version 2)

```
// Specification file for the Rectangle class
// This version uses some inline member functions.
#ifndef RECTANGLE_H
#define RECTANGLE_H

class Rectangle
{
    private:
        double width;
        double length;
    public:
        void setWidth(double);
        void setLength(double);
```

```

        double getWidth() const
            { return width; }

        double getLength() const
            { return length; }

        double getArea() const
            { return width * length; }
};
#endif
```

When a member function is defined in the declaration of a class, it is called an *inline function.* Notice because the function definitions are part of the class, there is no need to use the scope resolution operator and class name in the function header.

Notice the `getWidth`, `getLength`, and `getArea` functions are declared inline, but the `setWidth` and `setLength` functions are not. They are still defined outside the class declaration. The following listing shows the implementation file for the revised `Rectangle` class. (This file can be found in the Student Source Code Folder Chapter 13\Rectangle Version 2.)

Contents of `Rectangle.cpp` (Version 2)

```
// Implementation file for the Rectangle class.
// In this version of the class, the getWidth, getLength,
// and getArea functions are written inline in Rectangle.h.
#include "Rectangle.h"   // Needed for the Rectangle class
#include <iostream>      // Needed for cout
#include <cstdlib>       // Needed for the exit function
using namespace std;

//************************************************************
// setWidth sets the value of the member variable width.    *
//************************************************************

void Rectangle::setWidth(double w)
{
    if (w >= 0)
       width = w;
    else
    {
       cout << "Invalid width\n";
       exit(EXIT_FAILURE);
    }
}

//************************************************************
// setLength sets the value of the member variable length.  *
//************************************************************

```

```
void Rectangle::setLength(double len)
{
    if (len >= 0)
       length = len;
    else
    {
       cout << "Invalid length\n";
       exit(EXIT_FAILURE);
    }
}
```

Inline Functions and Performance

A lot goes on "behind the scenes" each time a function is called. A number of special items, such as the function's return address in the program and the values of arguments, are stored in a section of memory called the *stack*. In addition, local variables are created and a location is reserved for the function's return value. All this overhead, which sets the stage for a function call, takes precious CPU time. Although the time needed is minuscule, it can add up if a function is called many times, as in a loop.

Inline functions are compiled differently than other functions. In the executable code, inline functions aren't "called" in the conventional sense. In a process known as *inline expansion*, the compiler replaces the call to an inline function with the code of the function itself. This means the overhead needed for a conventional function call isn't necessary for an inline function and can result in improved performance.[*] Because the inline function's code can appear multiple times in the executable program, however, the size of the program can increase.[†]

Checkpoint

6 Why would you declare a class's member variables `private`?

7 When a class's member variables are declared `private`, how does code outside the class store values in, or retrieve values from, the member variables?

8 What is a class specification file? What is a class implementation file?

9 What is the purpose of an include guard?

10 Assume the following class components exist in a program:

`BasePay` class declaration
`BasePay` member function definitions
`Overtime` class declaration
`Overtime` member function definitions
In what files would you store each of these components?

11 What is an inline member function?

---

[*] Because inline functions cause code to increase in size, they can decrease performance on systems that use paging.

[†] Writing a function inline is a request to the compiler. The compiler will ignore the request if inline expansion is not possible or practical.

7 Constructors

CONCEPT: A constructor is a member function that is automatically called when a class object is created.

A constructor is a member function that has the same name as the class. It is automatically called when the object is created in memory, or instantiated. It is helpful to think of constructors as initialization routines. They are very useful for initializing member variables or performing other setup operations.

To illustrate how constructors work, look at the following `Demo` class:

```
class Demo
{
public:
   Demo(); // Constructor
};

Demo::Demo()
{
   cout << "Welcome to the constructor!\n";
}
```

The class `Demo` only has one member: a function also named `Demo`. This function is the constructor. When an instance of this class is defined, the function `Demo` is automatically called. This is illustrated in Program 6.

Program 6

```
// This program demonstrates a constructor.
#include <iostream>
using namespace std;

// Demo class declaration.

class Demo
{
public:
     Demo();     // Constructor
};

Demo::Demo()
{
     cout << "Welcome to the constructor!\n";
}

//*****************************************
// Function main.                         *
//*****************************************

```

```
int main()
{
    Demo demoObject; // Define a Demo object;

    cout << "This program demonstrates an object\n";
    cout << "with a constructor.\n";
    return 0;
}
```

Program Output

```
Welcome to the constructor!
This program demonstrates an object
with a constructor.
```

Notice the constructor's function header looks different than that of a regular member function. There is no return type—not even `void`. This is because constructors are not executed by explicit function calls and cannot return a value. The function header of a constructor's external definition takes the following form:

```
ClassName::ClassName(ParameterList)
```

In the general format, *`ClassName`* is the name of the class, and *`ParameterList`* is an optional list of parameter variable declarations.

In Program 6, `demoObject`'s constructor executes automatically when the object is defined. Because the object is defined before the `cout` statements in function `main`, the constructor displays its message first. Suppose we had defined the `Demo` object between two `cout` statements, as shown here:

```
cout << "This is displayed before the object is created.\n";
Demo demoObject;    // Define a Demo object.
cout << "\nThis is displayed after the object is created.\n";
```

This code would produce the following output:

```
This is displayed before the object is created.
Welcome to the constructor!
This is displayed after the object is created.
```

This simple `Demo` example illustrates when a constructor executes. More importantly, you should understand why a class should have a constructor. A constructor's purpose is to initialize an object's attributes. Because the constructor executes as soon as the object is created, it can initialize the object's data members to valid values before those members are used by other code. It is a good practice to always write a constructor for every class.

For example, the `Rectangle` class we looked at earlier could benefit from having a constructor. A program could define a `Rectangle` object then use that object to call the `getArea` function before any values were stored in `width` and `length`. Because the `width` and `length` member variables are not initialized, the function would return garbage. The following code shows a better version of the `Rectangle` class, equipped with a constructor. The constructor initializes both `width` and `length` to 0.0. (These files can be found in the Student Source Code Folder Chapter 13\Rectangle Version 3.)

Contents of `Rectangle.h` (Version 3)

```
// Specification file for the Rectangle class
// This version has a constructor.
#ifndef RECTANGLE_H
#define RECTANGLE_H

class Rectangle
{
   private:
      double width;
      double length;
   public:
      Rectangle();                    // Constructor
      void setWidth(double);
      void setLength(double);

      double getWidth() const
         { return width; }

      double getLength() const
         { return length; }

      double getArea() const
         { return width * length; }
};
#endif
```

Contents of `Rectangle.cpp` (Version 3)

```
// Implementation file for the Rectangle class.
// This version has a constructor.
#include "Rectangle.h"   // Needed for the Rectangle class
#include <iostream>      // Needed for cout
#include <cstdlib>       // Needed for the exit function
using namespace std;

//***********************************************************
// The constructor initializes width and length to 0.0.     *
//***********************************************************

Rectangle::Rectangle()
{
    width = 0.0;
    length = 0.0;
}

//***********************************************************
// setWidth sets the value of the member variable width.    *
//***********************************************************

void Rectangle::setWidth(double w)
{
    if (w >= 0)
        width = w;
```

```
    else
    {
        cout << "Invalid width\n";
        exit(EXIT_FAILURE);
    }
}

//************************************************************
// setLength sets the value of the member variable length.  *
//************************************************************

void Rectangle::setLength(double len)
{
    if (len >= 0)
        length = len;
    else
    {
        cout << "Invalid length\n";
        exit(EXIT_FAILURE);
    }
}
```

Program 7 demonstrates this new version of the class. It creates a `Rectangle` object then displays the values returned by the `getWidth`, `getLength`, and `getArea` member functions. (This file can be found in the Student Source Code Folder Chapter 13\Rectangle Version 3.)

Program 7

```
// This program uses the Rectangle class's constructor.
#include <iostream>
#include "Rectangle.h" // Needed for Rectangle class
using namespace std;

int main()
{
    Rectangle box;     // Define an instance of the Rectangle class

    // Display the rectangle's data.
    cout << "Here is the rectangle's data:\n";
    cout << "Width: " << box.getWidth() << endl;
    cout << "Length: " << box.getLength() << endl;
    cout << "Area: " << box.getArea() << endl;
    return 0;
}
```

Program Output

```
Here is the rectangle's data:
Width: 0
Length: 0
Area: 0
```

Using Member Initialization Lists

The constructor in the previously shown `Rectangle` class uses assignment statements to store initial values in the `width` and `length` member variables, as shown here:

```
Rectangle::Rectangle()
{
   width = 0.0;
   length = 0.0;
}
```

You can use an alternative technique, known as a *member initialization list*, to initialize the members of a class. Here is an example of the `Rectangle` class's constructor, rewritten to use a member initialization list instead of assignment statements:

```
Rectangle::Rectangle() :
width(0.0), length(0.0)
{
}
```

In this version of the constructor, a colon appears at the end of the function header, followed by the member initialization list. The member initialization list shows each member variable's name, followed by an initial value enclosed in parentheses. The member variables are separated by commas in the list. This version of the constructor initializes the `width` and `length` member variables with the value 0.0.

Notice in this version of the constructor, the constructor's body is empty. Because the initialization of the member variables is handled by the initialization list, there is nothing to do in the body of the constructor.

Many programmers prefer to use member initialization lists instead of assignment statements inside of the body of the constructor because, in some situations, it allows the compiler to generate more efficient code.

NOTE: When a constructor has a member initialization list, the initializations take place before any statements in the body of the constructor execute.

In-Place Member Initialization

11

Prior to C++ 11, you could not initialize a member variable in its declaration statement. You had to use the class constructor to either assign initial values to the class's members or use a member initialization list in the constructor. In C++ 11, you can initialize a member variable in its declaration statement, just as you can with a regular variable. This is known as *in-place initialization*. Here is an example:

```
class Rectangle
{
private:
   double width = 0.0;
   double length = 0.0;
public:
     Public member functions appear here...
};
```

The Default Constructor

All of the examples we have looked at in this section demonstrate default constructors. A *default constructor* is a constructor that takes no arguments. Like regular functions, constructors may accept arguments, have default arguments, be declared inline, and be overloaded. We will see examples of these as we progress through the chapter.

If you write a class with no constructor whatsoever, when the class is compiled, C++ will automatically write a default constructor that does nothing. For example, the first version of the `Rectangle` class had no constructor; so, when the class was compiled, C++ generated the following constructor:

```
Rectangle::Rectangle()
{ }
```

Default Constructors and Dynamically Allocated Objects

Earlier we discussed how class objects may be dynamically allocated in memory. For example, assume the following pointer is defined in a program:

```
Rectangle *rectPtr = nullptr;
```

This statement defines `rectPtr` as a `Rectangle` pointer. It can hold the address of any `Rectangle` object. But because this statement does not actually create a `Rectangle` object, the constructor does not execute. Suppose we use the pointer in a statement that dynamically allocates a `Rectangle` object, as shown in the following code:

```
rectPtr = new Rectangle;
```

This statement creates a `Rectangle` object. When the `Rectangle` object is created by the new operator, its default constructor is automatically executed.

8 Passing Arguments to Constructors

CONCEPT: A constructor can have parameters and can accept arguments when an object is created.

Constructors may accept arguments in the same way as other functions. When a class has a constructor that accepts arguments, you can pass initialization values to the constructor when you create an object. For example, the following code shows yet another version of the `Rectangle` class. This version has a constructor that accepts arguments for the rectangle's width and length. (These files can be found in the Student Source Code Folder Chapter 13\Rectangle Version 4.)

Contents of `Rectangle.h` (Version 4)

```
// Specification file for the Rectangle class
// This version has a constructor.
#ifndef RECTANGLE_H
#define RECTANGLE_H

class Rectangle
```

```
{
    private:
        double width;
        double length;
    public:
        Rectangle(double, double);    // Constructor
        void setWidth(double);
        void setLength(double);

        double getWidth() const
            { return width; }

        double getLength() const
            { return length; }

        double getArea() const
            { return width * length; }
};
#endif
```

Contents of Rectangle.cpp (Version 4)

```
// Implementation file for the Rectangle class.
// This version has a constructor that accepts arguments.
#include "Rectangle.h"    // Needed for the Rectangle class
#include <iostream>       // Needed for cout
#include <cstdlib>        // Needed for the exit function
using namespace std;

//***********************************************************
// The constructor accepts arguments for width and length. *
//***********************************************************

Rectangle::Rectangle(double w, double len)
{
    width = w;
    length = len;
}

//***********************************************************
// setWidth sets the value of the member variable width.   *
//***********************************************************

void Rectangle::setWidth(double w)
{
    if (w >= 0)
        width = w;
    else
    {
        cout << "Invalid width\n";
        exit(EXIT_FAILURE);
    }
}
```

```
32
33  //***************************************************************
34  // setLength sets the value of the member variable length.  *
35  //***************************************************************
36
37  void Rectangle::setLength(double len)
38  {
39      if (len >= 0)
40          length = len;
41      else
42      {
43          cout << "Invalid length\n";
44          exit(EXIT_FAILURE);
45      }
46  }
```

The constructor, which appears in lines 12 through 16 of Rectangle.cpp, accepts two arguments, which are passed into the `w` and `len` parameters. The parameters are assigned to the `width` and `length` member variables. Because the constructor is automatically called when a `Rectangle` object is created, the arguments are passed to the constructor as part of the object definition. Here is an example:

```
Rectangle box(10.0, 12.0);
```

This statement defines `box` as an instance of the `Rectangle` class. The constructor is called with the value 10.0 passed into the `w` parameter and 12.0 passed into the `len` parameter. As a result, the object's `width` member variable will be assigned 10.0 and the `length` member variable will be assigned 12.0. This is illustrated in Figure 16.

Figure 16 Arguments passed to a constructor

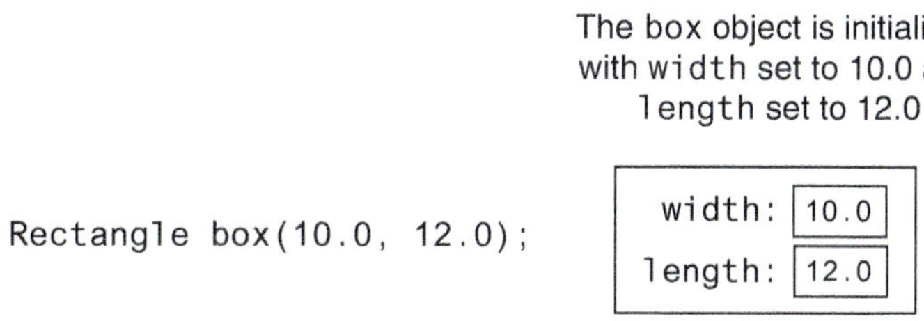

Program 8 demonstrates the class. (This file can be found in the Student Source Code Folder Chapter 13\Rectangle Version 4.)

Program 8

```
// This program calls the Rectangle class constructor.
#include <iostream>
#include <iomanip>
#include "Rectangle.h"
using namespace std;

```

(program continues)

Program 8 *(continued)*

```
7   int main()
8   {
9      double houseWidth,    // To hold the room width
10            houseLength;   // To hold the room length
11
12     // Get the width of the house.
13     cout << "In feet, how wide is your house? ";
14     cin >> houseWidth;
15
16     // Get the length of the house.
17     cout << "In feet, how long is your house? ";
18     cin >> houseLength;
19
20     // Create a Rectangle object.
21     Rectangle house(houseWidth, houseLength);
22
23     // Display the house's width, length, and area.
24     cout << setprecision(2) << fixed;
25     cout << "The house is " << house.getWidth()
26          << " feet wide.\n";
27     cout << "The house is " << house.getLength()
28          << " feet long.\n";
29     cout << "The house is " << house.getArea()
30          << " square feet in area.\n";
31     return 0;
32  }
```

Program Output with Example Input Shown in Bold

```
In feet, how wide is your house? 30 [Enter]
In feet, how long is your house? 60 [Enter]
The house is 30.00 feet wide.
The house is 60.00 feet long.
The house is 1800.00 square feet in area.
```

The statement in line 21 creates a `Rectangle` object, passing the values in `houseWidth` and `houseLength` as arguments.

The following code shows another example: the `Sale` class. This class might be used in a retail environment where sales transactions take place. An object of the `Sale` class represents the sale of an item. (This file can be found in the Student Source Code Folder Chapter 13\Sale Version 1.)

Contents of `Sale.h` (Version 1)

```
// Specification file for the Sale class.
#ifndef SALE_H
#define SALE_H

class Sale
```

```
6   {
7   private:
8      double itemCost;    // Cost of the item
9      double taxRate;     // Sales tax rate
10  public:
11     Sale(double cost, double rate)
12        { itemCost = cost;
13          taxRate = rate; }
14
15     double getItemCost() const
16        { return itemCost; }
17
18     double getTaxRate() const
19        { return taxRate; }
20
21     double getTax() const
22        { return (itemCost * taxRate); }
23
24     double getTotal() const
25        { return (itemCost + getTax()); }
26  };
27  #endif
```

The `itemCost` member variable, declared in line 8, holds the selling price of the item. The `taxRate` member variable, declared in line 9, holds the sales tax rate. The constructor appears in lines 11 and 13. Notice the constructor is written inline. It accepts two arguments, the item cost and the sales tax rate. These arguments are used to initialize the `itemCost` and `taxRate` member variables. The `getItemCost` member function, in lines 15 and 16, returns the value in `itemCost`, and the `getTaxRate` member function, in lines 18 and 19, returns the value in `taxRate`. The `getTax` member function, in lines 21 and 22, calculates and returns the amount of sales tax for the purchase. The `getTotal` member function, in lines 24 and 25, calculates and returns the total of the sale. The total is the item cost plus the sales tax. Program 9 demonstrates the class. (This file can be found in the Student Source Code Folder Chapter 13\Sale Version 1.)

Program 9

```
// This program demonstrates passing an argument to a constructor.
#include <iostream>
#include <iomanip>
#include "Sale.h"
using namespace std;

int main()
{
   const double TAX_RATE = 0.06;   // 6 percent sales tax rate
   double cost;                    // To hold the item cost

   // Get the cost of the item.
   cout << "Enter the cost of the item: ";
   cin >> cost;
```

(program continues)

Program 9 *(continued)*

```
15
16      // Create a Sale object for this transaction.
17      Sale itemSale(cost, TAX_RATE);
18
19      // Set numeric output formatting.
20      cout << fixed << showpoint << setprecision(2);
21
22      // Display the sales tax and total.
23      cout << "The amount of sales tax is $"
24           << itemSale.getTax() << endl;
25      cout << "The total of the sale is $";
26      cout << itemSale.getTotal() << endl;
27      return 0;
28  }
```

Program Output with Example Input Shown in Bold

```
Enter the cost of the item: 10.00 [Enter]
The amount of sales tax is $0.60
The total of the sale is $10.60
```

In the example run of the program, the user enters 10.00 as the cost of the item. This value is stored in the local variable `cost`. In line 17, the `itemSale` object is created. The values of the `cost` variable and the `TAX_RATE` constant are passed as arguments to the constructor. As a result, the object's `cost` member variable is initialized with the value 10.0, and the `rate` member variable is initialized with the value 0.06. This is illustrated in Figure 17.

Figure 17 Arguments passed to the constructor

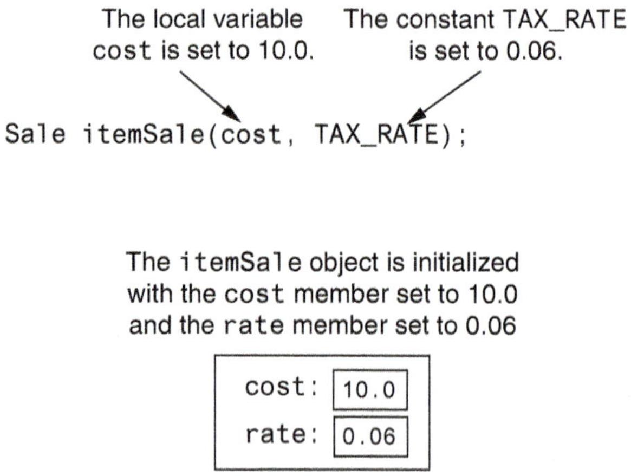

Using Default Arguments with Constructors

Like other functions, constructors may have default arguments. Default arguments are passed to parameters automatically if no argument is provided in the function call. The default value is listed in the parameter list of the function's declaration or the function header. The following code shows a modified version of the `Sale` class. This version's constructor uses a default argument for the tax rate. (This file can be found in the Student Source Code Folder Chapter 13\Sale Version 2.)

Contents of `Sale.h` (Version 2)

```
// This version of the Sale class uses a default argument
// in the constructor.
#ifndef SALE_H
#define SALE_H

class Sale
{
private:
   double itemCost;    // Cost of the item
   double taxRate;     // Sales tax rate
public:
   Sale(double cost, double rate = 0.05)
      { itemCost = cost;
        taxRate = rate; }

   double getItemCost() const
      { return itemCost; }

   double getTaxRate() const
      { return taxRate; }

   double getTax() const
      { return (itemCost * taxRate); }

   double getTotal() const
      { return (itemCost + getTax()); }
};
#endif
```

If an object of this `Sale` class is defined with only one argument (for the `cost` parameter) passed to the constructor, the default argument 0.05 will be provided for the `rate` parameter. This is demonstrated in Program 10. (This file can be found in the Student Source Code Folder Chapter 13\Sale Version 2.)

Program 10

```
// This program uses a constructor's default argument.
#include <iostream>
#include <iomanip>
#include "Sale.h"
using namespace std;

int main()
{
    double cost;   // To hold the item cost

```

(program continues)

Program 10 *(continued)*

```
    // Get the cost of the item.
    cout << "Enter the cost of the item: ";
    cin >> cost;

    // Create a Sale object for this transaction.
    // Specify the item cost, but use the default
    // tax rate of 5 percent.
    Sale itemSale(cost);

    // Set numeric output formatting.
    cout << fixed << showpoint << setprecision(2);

    // Display the sales tax and total.
    cout << "The amount of sales tax is $"
         << itemSale.getTax() << endl;
    cout << "The total of the sale is $";
    cout << itemSale.getTotal() << endl;
    return 0;
}
```

Program Output with Example Input Shown in Bold

```
Enter the cost of the item: 10.00 [Enter]
The amount of sales tax is $0.50
The total of the sale is $10.50
```

More about the Default Constructor

It was mentioned earlier that when a constructor doesn't accept arguments, it is known as the default constructor. If a constructor has default arguments for all its parameters, it can be called with no explicit arguments. It then becomes the default constructor. For example, suppose the constructor for the `Sale` class had been written as the following:

```
Sale(double cost = 0.0, double rate = 0.05)
   { itemCost = cost;
     taxRate = rate; }
```

This constructor has default arguments for each of its parameters. As a result, the constructor can be called with no arguments, as shown here:

```
Sale itemSale;
```

This statement defines a `Sale` object. No arguments were passed to the constructor, so the default arguments for both parameters are used. Because this constructor can be called with no arguments, it is the default constructor.

Classes with No Default Constructor

When all of a class's constructors require arguments, then the class does not have a default constructor. In such a case, you must pass the required arguments to the constructor when creating an object. Otherwise, a compiler error will result.

9 Destructors

CONCEPT: A destructor is a member function that is automatically called when an object is destroyed.

Destructors are member functions with the same name as the class, preceded by a tilde character (~). For example, the destructor for the `Rectangle` class would be named `~Rectangle`.

Destructors are automatically called when an object is destroyed. In the same way that constructors set things up when an object is created, destructors perform shutdown procedures when the object goes out of existence. For example, a common use of destructors is to free memory that was dynamically allocated by the class object.

Program 11 shows a simple class with a constructor and a destructor. It illustrates when, during the program's execution, each is called.

Program 11

```
// This program demonstrates a destructor.
#include <iostream>
using namespace std;

class Demo
{
public:
    Demo();       // Constructor
    ~Demo();      // Destructor
};

Demo::Demo()
{
    cout << "Welcome to the constructor!\n";
}

Demo::~Demo()
{
    cout << "The destructor is now running.\n";
}

//*********************************************
// Function main.                             *
//*********************************************

int main()
{
    Demo demoObject;  // Define a demo object;

    cout << "This program demonstrates an object\n";
    cout << "with a constructor and destructor.\n";
    return 0;
}
```

(program output continues)

Program 11 *(continued)*

Program Output

```
Welcome to the constructor!
This program demonstrates an object
with a constructor and destructor.
The destructor is now running.
```

The following code shows a more realistic example of a class with a destructor. The `ContactInfo` class holds the following data about a contact:

- The contact's name
- The contact's phone number

The constructor accepts arguments for both items. The name and phone number are passed as a pointer to a C-string. Rather than storing the name and phone number in a `char` array with a fixed size, the constructor gets the length of the C-string and dynamically allocates just enough memory to hold it. The destructor frees the allocated memory when the object is destroyed. (This file can be found in the Student Source Code Folder Chapter 13\ContactInfo Version 1.)

Contents of `ContactInfo.h` (Version 1)

```
// Specification file for the Contact class.
#ifndef CONTACTINFO_H
#define CONTACTINFO_H
#include <cstring>    // Needed for strlen and strcpy

// ContactInfo class declaration.
class ContactInfo
{
private:
    char *name;     // The name
    char *phone;    // The phone number
public:
    // Constructor
    ContactInfo(char *n, char *p)
    { // Allocate just enough memory for the name and phone number.
        name = new char[strlen(n) + 1];
        phone = new char[strlen(p) + 1];

        // Copy the name and phone number to the allocated memory.
        strcpy(name, n);
        strcpy(phone, p); }

    // Destructor
    ~ContactInfo()
    { delete [] name;
      delete [] phone; }

    const char *getName() const
    { return name; }

```

```
31      const char *getPhoneNumber() const
32      { return phone; }
33   };
34   #endif
```

Notice the return type of the `getName` and `getPhoneNumber` functions in lines 28 through 32 is `const char *`. This means each function returns a pointer to a constant `char`. This is a security measure. It prevents any code that calls the functions from changing the string that the pointer points to.

Program 12 demonstrates the class. (This file can be found in the Student Source Code Folder Chapter 13\ContactInfo Version 1.)

Program 12

```
// This program demonstrates a class with a destructor.
#include <iostream>
#include "ContactInfo.h"
using namespace std;

int main()
{
    // Define a ContactInfo object with the following data:
    // Name: Kristen Lee, Phone Number: 555-2021
    ContactInfo entry("Kristen Lee", "555-2021");

    // Display the object's data.
    cout << "Name: " << entry.getName() << endl;
    cout << "Phone Number: " << entry.getPhoneNumber() << endl;
    return 0;
}
```

Program Output

```
Name: Kristen Lee
Phone Number: 555-2021
```

In addition to the fact that destructors are automatically called when an object is destroyed, the following points should be mentioned:

- Like constructors, destructors have no return type.
- Destructors cannot accept arguments, so they never have a parameter list.

Destructors and Dynamically Allocated Class Objects

If a class object has been dynamically allocated by the `new` operator, its memory should be released when the object is no longer needed. For example, in the following code `objectPtr` is a pointer to a dynamically allocated `ContactInfo` class object:

```
// Define a ContactInfo pointer.
ContactInfo *objectPtr = nullptr;

// Dynamically create a ContactInfo object.
objectPtr = new ContactInfo("Kristen Lee", "555-2021");
```

The following statement shows the `delete` operator being used to destroy the dynamically created object:

```
delete objectPtr;
```

When the object pointed to by `objectPtr` is destroyed, its destructor is automatically called.

NOTE: If you have used a smart pointer such as `unique_ptr` (introduced in C++ 11) to allocate an object, the object will automatically be deleted, and its destructor will be called when the smart pointer goes out of scope. It is not necessary to use `delete` with a `unique_ptr`.

Checkpoint

12 Briefly describe the purpose of a constructor.

13 Briefly describe the purpose of a destructor.

14 A member function that is never declared with a return data type, but that may have arguments is which of the following?

A) The constructor
B) The destructor
C) Both the constructor and the destructor
D) Neither the constructor nor the destructor

15 A member function that is never declared with a return data type and can never have arguments is which of the following?

A) The constructor
B) The destructor
C) Both the constructor and the destructor
D) Neither the constructor nor the destructor

16 Destructor function names always start with _________.

A) A number
B) Tilde character (~)
C) A data type name
D) None of the above

17 A constructor that requires no arguments is called _________.

A) A default constructor
B) An overloaded constructor
C) A null constructor
D) None of the above

18 True or False: Constructors are never declared with a return data type.

19 True or False: Destructors are never declared with a return type.

20 True or False: Destructors may take any number of arguments.

10 Overloading Constructors

CONCEPT: **A class can have more than one constructor.**

When two or more functions share the same name, the function is said to be overloaded. Multiple functions with the same name may exist in a C++ program, as long as their parameter lists are different.

A class's member functions may be overloaded, including the constructor. One constructor might take an `int` argument, for example, while another constructor takes a `double`. There could even be a third constructor taking two integers. As long as each constructor takes a different list of parameters, the compiler can tell them apart. For example, the `string` class has several overloaded constructors. The following statement creates a `string` object with no arguments passed to the constructor:

```
string str;
```

This executes the `string` class's default constructor, which stores an empty string in the object. Another way to create a `string` object is to pass a string literal as an argument to the constructor, as shown here:

```
string str("Hello");
```

This executes an overloaded constructor, which stores the string "Hello" in the object.

Let's look at an example of how you can create overloaded constructors. The `InventoryItem` class holds the following data about an item that is stored in inventory:

- Item's description (a `string` object)
- Item's cost (a `double`)
- Number of units in inventory (an `int`)

The following code shows the class. To simplify the code, all the member functions are written inline. (This file can be found in the Student Source Code Folder Chapter 13\InventoryItem.)

Contents of `InventoryItem.h`

```
// This class has overloaded constructors.
#ifndef INVENTORYITEM_H
#define INVENTORYITEM_H
#include <string>
using namespace std;

class InventoryItem
{
private:
   string description;    // The item description
   double cost;           // The item cost
   int units;             // Number of units on hand
public:
   // Constructor #1 (default constructor)
   InventoryItem()
      { // Initialize description, cost, and units.
        description = "";
```

```
18          cost = 0.0;
19          units = 0; }
20
21     // Constructor #2
22     InventoryItem(string desc)
23        { // Assign the value to description.
24          description = desc;
25
26          // Initialize cost and units.
27          cost = 0.0;
28          units = 0; }
29
30     // Constructor #3
31     InventoryItem(string desc, double c, int u)
32        { // Assign values to description, cost, and units.
33          description = desc;
34          cost = c;
35          units = u; }
36
37     // Mutator functions
38     void setDescription(string d)
39        { description = d; }
40
41     void setCost(double c)
42        { cost = c; }
43
44     void setUnits(int u)
45        { units = u; }
46
47     // Accessor functions
48     string getDescription() const
49        { return description; }
50
51     double getCost() const
52        { return cost; }
53
54     int getUnits() const
55        { return units; }
56  };
57  #endif
```

The first constructor appears in lines 15 through 19. It takes no arguments, so it is the default constructor. It initializes the `description` variable to an empty string. The `cost` and `units` variables are initialized to 0.

The second constructor appears in lines 22 through 28. This constructor accepts only one argument, the item description. The `cost` and `units` variables are initialized to 0.

The third constructor appears in lines 31 through 35. This constructor accepts arguments for the description, cost, and units.

The mutator functions set values for `description`, `cost`, and `units`. Program 13 demonstrates the class. (This file can be found in the Student Source Code Folder Chapter 13\ InventoryItem.)

Program 13

```
// This program demonstrates a class with overloaded constructors.
#include <iostream>
#include <iomanip>
#include "InventoryItem.h"

int main()
{
   // Create an InventoryItem object with constructor #1.
   InventoryItem item1;
   item1.setDescription("Hammer");   // Set the description
   item1.setCost(6.95);              // Set the cost
   item1.setUnits(12);               // Set the units

   // Create an InventoryItem object with constructor #2.
   InventoryItem item2("Pliers");

   // Create an InventoryItem object with constructor #3.
   InventoryItem item3("Wrench", 8.75, 20);

   cout << "The following items are in inventory:\n";
   cout << setprecision(2) << fixed << showpoint;

   // Display the data for item 1.
   cout << "Description: " << item1.getDescription() << endl;
   cout << "Cost: $" << item1.getCost() << endl;
   cout << "Units on Hand: " << item1.getUnits() << endl << endl;

   // Display the data for item 2.
   cout << "Description: " << item2.getDescription() << endl;
   cout << "Cost: $" << item2.getCost() << endl;
   cout << "Units on Hand: " << item2.getUnits() << endl << endl;

   // Display the data for item 3.
   cout << "Description: " << item3.getDescription() << endl;
   cout << "Cost: $" << item3.getCost() << endl;
   cout << "Units on Hand: " << item3.getUnits() << endl;
   return 0;
}
```

Program Output

```
The following items are in inventory:
Description: Hammer
Cost: $6.95
Units on Hand: 12

Description: Pliers
Cost: $0.00
Units on Hand: 0

Description: Wrench
Cost: $8.75
Units on Hand: 20
```

11 Constructor Delegation

Often, a class will have multiple constructors that perform a similar set of steps, or some of the same steps. For example, look at the following `Contact` class:

```
class Contact
{
private:
    string name;
    string email;
    string phone;
public:
    // Constructor #1 (default)
    Contact()
    { name = "";
      email = "";
      phone = "";
    }

    // Constructor #2
    Contact(string n, string e, string p)
    { name = n;
      email = e;
      phone = p;
    }

    Other member functions follow...
};
```

In this class, both constructors perform a similar operation: They assign values to the `name`, `email`, and `phone` member variables. The default constructor assigns empty strings to the members, and the parameterized constructor assigns specified values to the members.

In C++ 11, it is possible for one constructor to call another constructor in the same class. This is known as *constructor delegation*. The following code shows how we can use constructor delegation in the `Contact` class:

```
class Contact
{
private:
    string name;
    string email;
    string phone;
public:
    // Constructor #1 (default)
    Contact() : Contact("", "", "")
    { }

    // Constructor #2
    Contact(string n, string e, string p)
    { name = n;
      email = e;
      phone = p;
    }

    Other member functions follow...
};
```

In this version of the class, the default constructor calls constructor #2. Notice that a colon appears at the end of the default constructor's header, followed by a call to constructor #2 with three empty strings listed inside the parentheses. Any time the `Contact` class's default constructor is called, it calls constructor #2, passing the empty strings as arguments. As a result, the empty strings are assigned to the object's `name`, `email`, and `phone` member variables.

Only One Default Constructor and One Destructor

When an object is defined without an argument list for its constructor, the compiler automatically calls the default constructor. For this reason, a class may have only one default constructor. If there were more than one constructor that could be called without an argument, the compiler would not know which one to call by default.

Remember, a constructor whose parameters all have a default argument is considered a default constructor. It would be an error to create a constructor that accepts no parameters along with another constructor that has default arguments for all its parameters. In such a case, the compiler would not be able to resolve which constructor to execute.

Classes may also only have one destructor. Because destructors take no arguments, the compiler has no way to distinguish different destructors.

Other Overloaded Member Functions

Member functions other than constructors can also be overloaded. This can be useful because sometimes you need several different ways to perform the same operation. For example, in the `InventoryItem` class we could have overloaded the `setCost` function as shown here:

```
void setCost(double c)
   { cost = c; }
void setCost(string c)
   { cost = stod(c); }
```

The first version of the function accepts a `double` argument and assigns it to `cost`. The second version of the function accepts a `string` object. This could be used where you have the cost of the item stored in a `string` object. The function calls the `stod` function to convert the string to a `double` and assigns its value to `cost`.

11 Private Member Functions

CONCEPT: A private member function may only be called from a function that is a member of the same class.

Sometimes a class will contain one or more member functions that are necessary for internal processing, but should not be called by code outside the class. For example, a class might have a member function that performs a calculation only when a value is stored in a particular member variable and should not be performed at any other time. That function should not be directly accessible by code outside the class because it might get called at the wrong time. In this case, the member function should be declared `private`. When a member function is declared `private`, it may only be called internally.

For example, consider the following version of the ContactInfo class. (This file can be found in the Student Source Code Folder Chapter 13\ContactInfo Version 2.)

Contents of ContactInfo.h (Version 2)

```
// Contact class specification file (version 2)
#ifndef CONTACTINFO_H
#define CONTACTINFO_H
#include <cstring>    // Needed for strlen and strcpy

// ContactInfo class declaration.
class ContactInfo
{
private:
    char *name;    // The contact's name
    char *phone;   // The contact's phone number

    // Private member function: initName
    // This function initializes the name attribute.
    void initName(char *n)
    { name = new char[strlen(n) + 1];
      strcpy(name, n); }

    // Private member function: initPhone
    // This function initializes the phone attribute.
    void initPhone(char *p)
    { phone = new char[strlen(p) + 1];
      strcpy(phone, p); }
public:
    // Constructor
    ContactInfo(char *n, char *p)
    { // Initialize the name attribute.
      initName(n);

      // Initialize the phone attribute.
      initPhone(n); }

    // Destructor
    ~ContactInfo()
    { delete [] name;
      delete [] phone; }

    const char *getName() const
    { return name; }

    const char *getPhoneNumber() const
    { return phone; }
};
#endif
```

In this version of the class, the logic in the constructor is modularized. It calls two private member functions: initName and initPhone. The initName function allocates memory for the name attribute and initializes it with the value pointed to by the n parameter. The initPhone function allocates memory for the phone attribute and initializes it with the value pointed to by the p parameter. These functions are private because they should be called only from the constructor. If they were ever called by code outside the class, they would change the values of the name and phone pointers without deallocating the memory that they currently point to.

12 Arrays of Objects

CONCEPT: You may define and work with arrays of class objects.

As with any other data type in C++, you can define arrays of class objects. An array of InventoryItem objects could be created to represent a business's inventory records. Here is an example of such a definition:

```
const int ARRAY_SIZE = 40;
InventoryItem inventory[ARRAY_SIZE];
```

This statement defines an array of 40 InventoryItem objects. The name of the array is inventory, and the default constructor is called for each object in the array.

If you wish to define an array of objects and call a constructor that requires arguments, you must specify the arguments for each object individually in an initializer list. Here is an example:

```
InventoryItem inventory[] = {"Hammer", "Wrench", "Pliers"};
```

The compiler treats each item in the initializer list as an argument for an array element's constructor. Recall that the second constructor in the InventoryItem class declaration takes the item description as an argument. So, this statement defines an array of three objects and calls that constructor for each object. The constructor for inventory[0] is called with "Hammer" as its argument, the constructor for inventory[1] is called with "Wrench" as its argument, and the constructor for inventory[2] is called with "Pliers" as its argument.

> **WARNING!** If the class does not have a default constructor you must provide an initializer for each object in the array.

If a constructor requires more than one argument, the initializer must take the form of a function call. For example, look at the following definition statement:

```
InventoryItem inventory[] = { InventoryItem("Hammer", 6.95, 12),
                              InventoryItem("Wrench", 8.75, 20),
                              InventoryItem("Pliers", 3.75, 10) };
```

This statement calls the third constructor in the InventoryItem class declaration for each object in the inventory array.

It isn't necessary to call the same constructor for each object in an array. For example, look at the following statement:

```
InventoryItem inventory[] = { "Hammer",
                              InventoryItem("Wrench", 8.75, 20),
                              "Pliers" };
```

This statement calls the second constructor for `inventory[0]` and `inventory[2]`, and calls the third constructor for `inventory[1]`.

If you do not provide an initializer for all of the objects in an array, the default constructor will be called for each object that does not have an initializer. For example, the following statement defines an array of three objects, but only provides initializers for the first two. The default constructor is called for the third object.

```
const int SIZE = 3;
InventoryItem inventory [SIZE] = { "Hammer",
                                   InventoryItem("Wrench", 8.75, 20) };
```

In summary, if you use an initializer list for class object arrays, there are three things to remember:

- If there is no default constructor you must furnish an initializer for each object in the array.
- If there are fewer initializers in the list than objects in the array, the default constructor will be called for all the remaining objects.
- If a constructor requires more than one argument, the initializer takes the form of a constructor function call.

Accessing Members of Objects in an Array

Objects in an array are accessed with subscripts, just like any other data type in an array. For example, to call the `setUnits` member function of `inventory[2]`, the following statement could be used:

```
inventory[2].setUnits(30);
```

This statement sets the `units` variable of `inventory[2]` to the value 30. Program 14 shows an array of `InventoryItem` objects being used in a complete program. (This file is stored in the Student Source Code Folder `Chapter 13\InventoryItem`.)

Program 14

```
// This program demonstrates an array of class objects.
#include <iostream>
#include <iomanip>
#include "InventoryItem.h"
using namespace std;

int main()
{
   const int NUM_ITEMS = 5;
   InventoryItem inventory[NUM_ITEMS] = {
                  InventoryItem("Hammer", 6.95, 12),
                  InventoryItem("Wrench", 8.75, 20),
                  InventoryItem("Pliers", 3.75, 10),
                  InventoryItem("Ratchet", 7.95, 14),
                  InventoryItem("Screwdriver", 2.50, 22) };

```

```
    cout << setw(14) <<"Inventory Item"
         << setw(8) << "Cost" << setw(8)
         << setw(16) << "Units on Hand\n";
    cout << "-------------------------------------\n";

    for (int i = 0; i < NUM_ITEMS; i++)
    {
       cout << setw(14) << inventory[i].getDescription();
       cout << setw(8) << inventory[i].getCost();
       cout << setw(7) << inventory[i].getUnits() << endl;
    }

    return 0;
}
```

Program Output

```
Inventory Item   Cost  Units on Hand
-------------------------------------
        Hammer   6.95        12
        Wrench   8.75        20
        Pliers   3.75        10
       Ratchet   7.95        14
   Screwdriver    2.5        22
```

Checkpoint

21 What will the following program display on the screen?

```
#include <iostream>
using namespace std;

class Tank
{
private:
   int gallons;
public:
   Tank()
      { gallons = 50; }
   Tank(int gal)
      { gallons = gal; }
   int getGallons()
      { return gallons; }
};

int main()
{
   Tank storage[3] = { 10, 20 };
   for (int index = 0; index < 3; index++)
      cout << storage[index].getGallons() << endl;
   return 0;
}
```

22 What will the following program display on the screen?

```
#include <iostream>
using namespace std;

class Package
{
private:
   int value;
public:
   Package()
      { value = 7; cout << value << endl; }
   Package(int v)
      { value = v; cout << value << endl; }
   ~Package()
      { cout << value << endl; }
};

int main()
{
   Package obj1(4);
   Package obj2;
   Package obj3(2);
   return 0;
}
```

23 In your answer for Checkpoint 22, indicate for each line of output whether the line is displayed by constructor #1, constructor #2, or the destructor.

24 Why would a member function be declared private?

25 Define an array of three `InventoryItem` objects.

26 Complete the following program so it defines an array of `Yard` objects. The program should use a loop to ask the user for the length and width of each `Yard`.

```
#include <iostream>
using namespace std;
class Yard
{
private:
   int length, width;
public:
   Yard()
      { length = 0; width = 0; }
   setLength(int len)
      { length = len; }
   setWidth(int w)
      { width = w; }
};

int main()
{
   // Finish this program
}
```

13 Focus on Problem Solving and Program Design: An OOP Case Study

You are a programmer for the Home Software Company. You have been assigned to develop a class that models the basic workings of a bank account. The class should perform the following tasks:

- Save the account balance.
- Save the number of transactions performed on the account.
- Allow deposits to be made to the account.
- Allow withdrawals to be taken from the account.
- Calculate interest for the period.
- Report the current account balance at any time.
- Report the current number of transactions at any time.

Private Member Variables

Table 4 lists the private member variables needed by the class.

Table 4 Private Member Variables

Variable	Description
`balance`	A `double` that holds the current account balance.
`interestRate`	A `double` that holds the interest rate for the period.
`interest`	A `double` that holds the interest earned for the current period.
`transactions`	An integer that holds the current number of transactions.

Public Member Functions

Table 5 lists the public member functions needed by the class.

Table 5 Public Member Functions

Function	Description
Constructor	Takes arguments to be initially stored in the `balance` and `interestRate` members. The default value for the balance is zero, and the default value for the interest rate is 0.045.
`setInterestRate`	Takes a `double` argument, which is stored in the `interestRate` member.
`makeDeposit`	Takes a `double` argument, which is the amount of the deposit. This argument is added to `balance`.
`withdraw`	Takes a `double` argument, which is the amount of the withdrawal. This value is subtracted from the balance, unless the withdrawal amount is greater than the balance. If this happens, the function reports an error.

(continued)

Table 5 *(continued)*

Function	Description
`calcInterest`	Takes no arguments. This function calculates the amount of interest for the current period, stores this value in the `interest` member, then adds it to the `balance` member.
`getInterestRate`	Returns the current interest rate (stored in the `interestRate` member).
`getBalance`	Returns the current balance (stored in the `balance` member).
`getInterest`	Returns the interest earned for the current period (stored in the `interest` member).
`getTransactions`	Returns the number of transactions for the current period (stored in the `transactions` member).

The Class Declaration

The following listing shows the class declaration:

Contents of `Account.h`

```
// Specification file for the Account class.
#ifndef ACCOUNT_H
#define ACCOUNT_H

class Account
{
private:
   double balance;          // Account balance
   double interestRate;     // Interest rate for the period
   double interest;         // Interest earned for the period
   int transactions;        // Number of transactions
public:
   Account(double iRate = 0.045, double bal = 0)
      { balance = bal;
        interestRate = iRate;
        interest = 0;
        transactions = 0; }

   void setInterestRate(double iRate)
      { interestRate = iRate; }

   void makeDeposit(double amount)
      { balance += amount; transactions++; }

   void withdraw(double amount); // Defined in Account.cpp

   void calcInterest()
      { interest = balance * interestRate; balance += interest; }

   double getInterestRate() const
      { return interestRate; }

```

```
      double getBalance() const
         { return balance; }

      double getInterest() const
         { return interest; }

      int getTransactions() const
         { return transactions; }
   };
   #endif
```

The withdraw Member Function

The only member function not written inline in the class declaration is withdraw. The purpose of that function is to subtract the amount of a withdrawal from the balance member. If the amount to be withdrawn is greater than the current balance, however, no withdrawal is made. The function returns true if the withdrawal is made, or false if there is not enough in the account.

Contents of Account.cpp

```
// Implementation file for the Account class.
#include "Account.h"

bool Account::withdraw(double amount)
{
   if (balance < amount)
      return false; // Not enough in the account
   else
   {
      balance -= amount;
      transactions++;
      return true;
   }
}
```

The Class's Interface

The balance, interestRate, interest, and transactions member variables are private, so they are hidden from the world outside the class. The reason is that a programmer with direct access to these variables might unknowingly commit any of the following errors:

- A deposit or withdrawal might be made without the transactions member being incremented.
- A withdrawal might be made for more than is in the account. This will cause the balance member to have a negative value.
- The interest rate might be calculated and the balance member adjusted, but the amount of interest might not get recorded in the interest member.
- The wrong interest rate might be used.

Because of the potential for these errors, the class contains public member functions that ensure the proper steps are taken when the account is manipulated.

Implementing the Class

Program 15 shows an implementation of the Account class. It presents a menu for displaying a savings account's balance, number of transactions, and interest earned. It also allows the user to deposit an amount into the account, make a withdrawal from the account, and calculate the interest earned for the current period.

Program 15

```
// This program demonstrates the Account class.
#include <iostream>
#include <cctype>
#include <iomanip>
#include "Account.h"
using namespace std;

// Function prototypes
void displayMenu();
void makeDeposit(Account &);
void withdraw(Account &);

int main()
{
    Account savings;    // Savings account object
    char choice;        // Menu selection

    // Set numeric output formatting.
    cout << fixed << showpoint << setprecision(2);

    do
    {
        // Display the menu and get a valid selection.
        displayMenu();
        cin >> choice;
        while (toupper(choice) < 'A' || toupper(choice) > 'G')
        {
            cout << "Please make a choice in the range "
                 << "of A through G:";
            cin >> choice;
        }

        // Process the user's menu selection.
        switch(choice)
        {
        case 'a':
        case 'A': cout << "The current balance is $";
                  cout << savings.getBalance() << endl;
                  break;
        case 'b':
        case 'B': cout << "There have been ";
                  cout << savings.getTransactions()
                       << " transactions.\n";
```

```
                  break;
        case 'c':
        case 'C': cout << "Interest earned for this period: $";
                  cout << savings.getInterest() << endl;
                  break;
        case 'd':
        case 'D': makeDeposit(savings);
                  break;
        case 'e':
        case 'E': withdraw(savings);
                  break;
        case 'f':
        case 'F': savings.calcInterest();
                  cout << "Interest added.\n";
        }
    } while (toupper(choice) != 'G');

    return 0;
}

//****************************************************
// Definition of function displayMenu. This function *
// displays the user's menu on the screen.           *
//****************************************************

void displayMenu()
{
    cout << "\n               MENU\n";
    cout << "--------------------------------------\n";
    cout << "A) Display the account balance\n";
    cout << "B) Display the number of transactions\n";
    cout << "C) Display interest earned for this period\n";
    cout << "D) Make a deposit\n";
    cout << "E) Make a withdrawal\n";
    cout << "F) Add interest for this period\n";
    cout << "G) Exit the program\n\n";
    cout << "Enter your choice: ";
}

//************************************************************
// Definition of function makeDeposit. This function accepts *
// a reference to an Account object. The user is prompted for *
// the dollar amount of the deposit, and the makeDeposit      *
// member of the Account object is then called.               *
//************************************************************

void makeDeposit(Account &acnt)
{
    double dollars;

    cout << "Enter the amount of the deposit: ";
    cin >> dollars;
```

(program continues)

Program 15 *(continued)*

```
    cin.ignore();
    acnt.makeDeposit(dollars);
}

//****************************************************************
// Definition of function withdraw. This function accepts      *
// a reference to an Account object. The user is prompted for *
// the dollar amount of the withdrawal, and the withdraw       *
// member of the Account object is then called.                *
//****************************************************************

void withdraw(Account &acnt)
{
    double dollars;

    cout << "Enter the amount of the withdrawal: ";
    cin >> dollars;
    cin.ignore();
    if (!acnt.withdraw(dollars))
        cout << "ERROR: Withdrawal amount too large.\n\n";
}
```

Program Output with Example Input Shown in Bold

```
                    MENU
-----------------------------------------
A) Display the account balance
B) Display the number of transactions
C) Display interest earned for this period
D) Make a deposit
E) Make a withdrawal
F) Add interest for this period
G) Exit the program

Enter your choice: d [Enter]
Enter the amount of the deposit: 500 [Enter]
                    MENU
-----------------------------------------
A) Display the account balance
B) Display the number of transactions
C) Display interest earned for this period
D) Make a deposit
E) Make a withdrawal
F) Add interest for this period
G) Exit the program

Enter your choice: a [Enter]
The current balance is $500.00
```

```
                 MENU
-------------------------------------------
A) Display the account balance
B) Display the number of transactions
C) Display interest earned for this period
D) Make a deposit
E) Make a withdrawal
F) Add interest for this period
G) Exit the program

Enter your choice: e [Enter]
Enter the amount of the withdrawal: 700 [Enter]
ERROR: Withdrawal amount too large.
                 MENU
-------------------------------------------
A) Display the account balance
B) Display the number of transactions
C) Display interest earned for this period
D) Make a deposit
E) Make a withdrawal
F) Add interest for this period
G) Exit the program

Enter your choice: e [Enter]
Enter the amount of the withdrawal: 200 [Enter]
                 MENU
-------------------------------------------
A) Display the account balance
B) Display the number of transactions
C) Display interest earned for this period
D) Make a deposit
E) Make a withdrawal
F) Add interest for this period
G) Exit the program

Enter your choice: f [Enter]
Interest added.
               MENU
-----------------------------------------
A) Display the account balance
B) Display the number of transactions
C) Display interest earned for this period
D) Make a deposit
E) Make a withdrawal
F) Add interest for this period
G) Exit the program

Enter your choice: a [Enter]
The current balance is $313.50
```

(program output continues)

Program 15 *(continued)*

```
                 MENU
-----------------------------------------
A) Display the account balance
B) Display the number of transactions
C) Display interest earned for this period
D) Make a deposit
E) Make a withdrawal
F) Add interest for this period
G) Exit the program
Enter your choice: g [Enter]
```

14 Focus on Object-Oriented Programming: Simulating Dice with Objects

Dice traditionally have six sides, representing the values 1 to 6. Some games, however, use specialized dice that have a different number of sides. For example, the fantasy role-playing game *Dungeons and Dragons*® uses dice with four, six, eight, ten, twelve, and twenty sides.

Suppose you are writing a program that needs to roll simulated dice with various numbers of sides. A simple approach would be to write a `Die` class with a constructor that accepts the number of sides as an argument. The class would also have appropriate methods for rolling the die and getting the die's value. An example of such a class follows. (These files can be found in the Student Source Code Folder Chapter 13\Dice.)

Contents of `Die.h`

```
// Specification file for the Die class
#ifndef DIE_H
#define DIE_H

class Die
{
private:
     int sides;    // Number of sides
     int value;    // The die's value

public:
     Die(int = 6);      // Constructor
     void roll();       // Rolls the die
     int getSides();    // Returns the number of sides
     int getValue();    // Returns the die's value
};
#endif
```

Contents of `Die.cpp`

```
// Implememtation file for the Die class
#include <cstdlib> // For rand and srand
#include <ctime>   // For the time function
```

```
#include "Die.h"
using namespace std;

//*********************************************************
// The constructor accepts an argument for the number   *
// of sides for the die, and performs a roll.           *
//*********************************************************
Die::Die(int numSides)
{
    // Get the system time.
    unsigned seed = time(0);

    // Seed the random number generator.
    srand(seed);

    // Set the number of sides.
    sides = numSides;

    // Perform an initial roll.
    roll();
}

//*********************************************************
// The roll member function simulates the rolling of    *
// the die.                                             *
//*********************************************************
void Die::roll()
{
  // Constant for the minimum die value
  const int MIN_VALUE = 1; // Minimum die value

  // Get a random value for the die.
  value = (rand() % (sides - MIN_VALUE + 1)) + MIN_VALUE;
}

//*********************************************************
// The getSides member function returns the number of   *
// for this die.                                        *
//*********************************************************
int Die::getSides()
{
  return sides;
}

//**********************************************************
// The getValue member function returns the die's value.*
//**********************************************************
int Die::getValue()
{
  return value;
}
```

Here is a synopsis of the class members:

`sides` Declared in line 8 of Die.h. This is an `int` member variable that will hold the number of sides for the die.

`value` Declared in line 9 of Die.h. This is an `int` member variable that will hold the die's value once it has been rolled.

Constructor The constructor (lines 11 through 24 in Die.cpp) has a parameter for the number of sides. Notice in the constructor's prototype (line 12 in Die.h) that the parameter's default value is 6. When the constructor executes, line 14 gets the system time and line 17 uses that value to seed the random number generator. Line 20 assigns the constructor's parameter to the `sides` member variable, and line 23 calls the `roll` member function, which simulates the rolling of the die.

`roll` The `roll` member function (lines 30 through 37 in Die.cpp) simulates the rolling of the die. The `MIN_VALUE` constant, defined in line 33, is the minimum value for the die. Line 36 generates a random number within the appropriate range for this particular die and assigns it to the `value` member variable.

`getSides` The `getSides` member function (lines 43 through 46) returns the `sides` member variable.

`getValue` The `getValue` member function (lines 51 through 54) returns the `value` member variable.

The code in Program 16 demonstrates the class. It creates two instances of the `Die` class: one with six sides, and the other with twelve sides. It then simulates five rolls of the dice.

Program 16

```
// This program simulates the rolling of dice.
#include <iostream>
#include "Die.h"
using namespace std;

int main()
{
    const int DIE1_SIDES = 6;    // Number of sides for die #1
    const int DIE2_SIDES = 12;   // Number of sides for die #2
    const int MAX_ROLLS = 5;     // Number of times to roll

    // Create two instances of the Die class.
    Die die1(DIE1_SIDES);
    Die die2(DIE2_SIDES);

    // Display the initial state of the dice.
    cout << "This simulates the rolling of a "
         << die1.getSides() << " sided die and a "
         << die2.getSides() << " sided die.\n";

```

```
21        cout << "Initial value of the dice:\n";
22        cout << die1.getValue() << " "
23             << die2.getValue() << endl;
24
25        // Roll the dice five times.
26        cout << "Rolling the dice " << MAX_ROLLS
27             << " times.\n";
28        for (int count = 0; count < MAX_ROLLS; count++)
29        {
30            // Roll the dice.
31            die1.roll();
32            die2.roll();
33
34            // Display the values of the dice.
35            cout << die1.getValue() << " "
36                 << die2.getValue() << endl;
37        }
38        return 0;
39    }
```

Program Output

```
This simulates the rolling of a 6 sided die and a 12 sided die.
Initial value of the dice:
1 7
Rolling the dice 5 times.
6 2
3 5
4 2
5 11
4 7
```

Let's take a closer look at the program:

Lines 8 to 10: These statements declare three constants. `DIE1_SIDES` is the number of sides for the first die (6), `DIE2_SIDES` is the number of sides for the second die (12), and `MAX_ROLLS` is the number of times to roll the die (5).

Lines 13 to 14: These statements create two instances of the `Die` class. Notice `DIE1_SIDES`, which is 6, is passed to the constructor in line 13, and `DIE2_SIDES`, which is 12, is passed to the constructor in line 14. As a result, `die1` will reference a `Die` object with six sides, and `die2` will reference a `Die` object with twelve sides.

Lines 22 to 23: This statement displays the initial value of both `Die` objects. (Recall that the `Die` class constructor performs an initial roll of the die.)

Lines 28 to 37: This `for` loop iterates five times. Each time the loop iterates, line 31 calls the `die1` object's `roll` method, and line 32 calls the `die2` object's `roll` method. Lines 35 and 36 display the values of both dice.

15 Focus on Object-Oriented Design: The Unified Modeling Language (UML)

CONCEPT: The Unified Modeling Language provides a standard method for graphically depicting an object-oriented system.

When designing a class, it is often helpful to draw a UML diagram. *UML* stands for *Unified Modeling Language*. The UML provides a set of standard diagrams for graphically depicting object-oriented systems. Figure 18 shows the general layout of a UML diagram for a class. Notice the diagram is a box that is divided into three sections. The top section is where you write the name of the class. The middle section holds a list of the class's member variables. The bottom section holds a list of the class's member functions.

Figure 18 General layout of a UML diagram

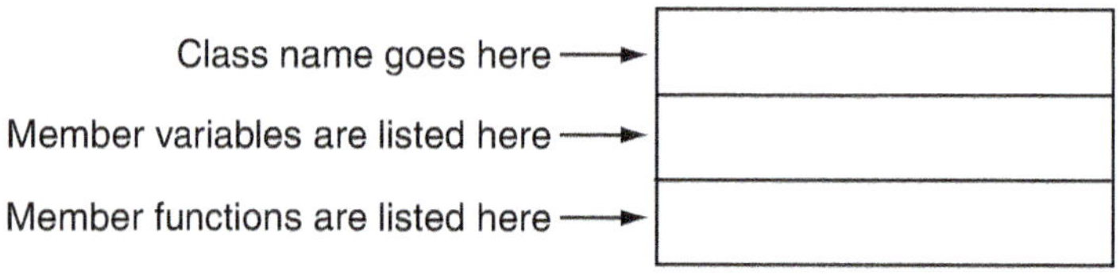

Earlier in this chapter, you studied a `Rectangle` class that could be used in a program that works with rectangles. The first version of the `Rectangle` class that you studied had the following member variables:

- `width`
- `length`

The class also had the following member functions:

- `setWidth`
- `setLength`
- `getWidth`
- `getLength`
- `getArea`

From this information alone we can construct a simple UML diagram for the class, as shown in Figure 19.

Figure 19 `Rectangle` class

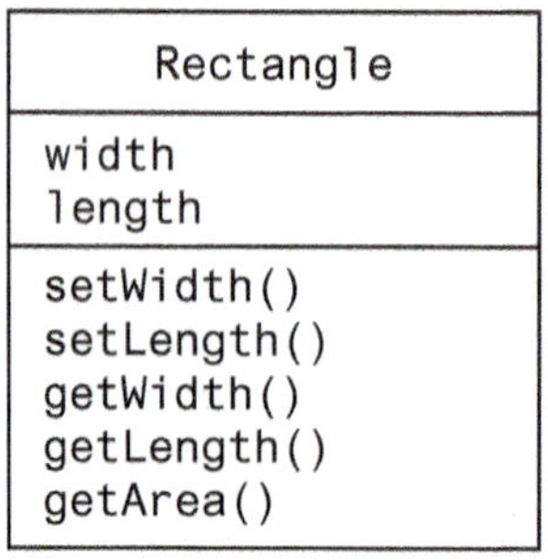

The UML diagram in Figure 19 tells us the name of the class, the names of the member variables, and the names of the member functions. The UML diagram in Figure 19 does not convey many of the class details, however, such as access specification, member variable data types, parameter data types, and function return types. The UML provides optional notation for these types of details.

Showing Access Specification in UML Diagrams

The UML diagram in Figure 19 lists all of the members of the `Rectangle` class, but does not indicate which members are private and which are public. In a UML diagram you may optionally place a – character before a member name to indicate that it is private, or a + character to indicate that it is public. Figure 20 shows the UML diagram modified to include this notation.

Figure 20 `Rectangle` class with access specification

```
Rectangle
-------------
- width
- length
-------------
+ setWidth()
+ setLength()
+ getWidth()
+ getLength()
+ getArea()
```

Data Type and Parameter Notation in UML Diagrams

The Unified Modeling Language also provides notation that you may use to indicate the data types of member variables, member functions, and parameters. To indicate the data type of a member variable, place a colon followed by the name of the data type after the name of the variable. For example, the `width` variable in the `Rectangle` class is a `double`. It could be listed as follows in the UML diagram:

```
- width : double
```

NOTE: In UML notation the variable name is listed first, then the data type. This is the opposite of C++ syntax, which requires the data type to appear first.

The return type of a member function can be listed in the same manner: After the function's name, place a colon followed by the return type. The `Rectangle` class's `getLength` function returns a `double`, so it could be listed as follows in the UML diagram:

```
+ getLength() : double
```

Parameter variables and their data types may be listed inside a member function's parentheses. For example, the `Rectangle` class's `setLength` function has a `double` parameter named `len`, so it could be listed as follows in the UML diagram:

```
+ setLength(len : double) : void
```

Figure 21 shows a UML diagram for the `Rectangle` class with parameter and data type notation.

Figure 21 `Rectangle` class with access specification and return types

```
Rectangle
-----------------------------------
- width : double
- length : double
-----------------------------------
+ setWidth(w : double) : void
+ setLength(len : double) : void
+ getWidth() : double
+ getLength() : double
+ getArea() : double
```

Showing Constructors and Destructors in a UML Diagram

There is more than one accepted way of showing a class constructor in a UML diagram. In this chapter, we will show a constructor just as any other function, except we will list no return type. For example, Figure 22 shows a UML diagram for the `InventoryItem` class we looked at previously in this chapter.

Figure 22 `InventoryItem` class

```
InventoryItem
-----------------------------------
- description : string
- cost : double
- units : int
-----------------------------------
+ InventoryItem() :
+ InventoryItem(desc : string) :
+ InventoryItem(desc : string,
        c : double, u : int) :
+ setDescription(d : string) : void
+ setCost(c : double) : void
+ setUnits(u : int) : void
+ getDescription() : string
+ getCost() : double
+ getUnits() : int
```

16 Focus on Object-Oriented Design: Finding the Classes and Their Responsibilities

CONCEPT: One of the first steps in creating an object-oriented application is determining the classes that are necessary and their responsibilities within the application.

So far, you have learned the basics of writing a class, creating an object from the class, and using the object to perform operations. This knowledge is necessary to create an object-oriented application, but it is not the first step in designing the application. The first step is to analyze the problem you are trying to solve and determine the classes you will need. In this section, we will discuss a simple technique for finding the classes in a problem and determining their responsibilities.

Finding the Classes

When developing an object-oriented application, one of your first tasks is to identify the classes you will need to create. Typically, your goal is to identify the different types of real-world objects that are present in the problem, then create classes for those types of objects within your application.

Over the years, software professionals have developed numerous techniques for finding the classes in a given problem. One simple and popular technique involves the following steps:

1. Get a written description of the problem domain.
2. Identify all the nouns (including pronouns and noun phrases) in the description. Each of these is a potential class.
3. Refine the list to include only the classes that are relevant to the problem.

Let's take a closer look at each of these steps.

Write a Description of the Problem Domain

The *problem domain* is the set of real-world objects, parties, and major events related to the problem. If you adequately understand the nature of the problem you are trying to solve, you can write a description of the problem domain yourself. If you do not thoroughly understand the nature of the problem, you should have an expert write the description for you.

For example, suppose we are programming an application that the manager of Joe's Automotive Shop will use to print service quotes for customers. Here is a description that an expert, perhaps Joe himself, might have written:

Joe's Automotive Shop services foreign cars, and specializes in servicing cars made by Mercedes, Porsche, and BMW. When a customer brings a car to the shop, the manager gets the customer's name, address, and telephone number. The manager then determines the make, model, and year of the car and gives the customer a service quote. The service quote shows the estimated parts charges, estimated labor charges, sales tax, and total estimated charges.

The problem domain description should include any of the following:

- Physical objects such as vehicles, machines, or products
- Any role played by a person, such as manager, employee, customer, teacher, student, and so on.
- The results of a business event, such as a customer order, or in this case, a service quote
- Recordkeeping items, such as customer histories and payroll records

Identify All of the Nouns

The next step is to identify all of the nouns and noun phrases. (If the description contains pronouns, include them as well.) Here's another look at the previous problem domain description. This time, the nouns and noun phrases appear in bold.

Joe's Automotive Shop services **foreign cars**, and specializes in servicing **cars** made by **Mercedes**, **Porsche**, and **BMW**. When a **customer** brings a **car** to the **shop**, the **manager** gets the **customer's name**, **address**, and **telephone number**. The **manager** then determines the **make**, **model**, and **year** of the **car**, and gives the **customer** a **service quote**. The **service quote** shows the **estimated parts charges**, **estimated labor charges**, **sales tax**, and **total estimated charges**.

Notice some of the nouns are repeated. The following list shows all of the nouns without duplicating any of them:

address
BMW
car
cars
customer
estimated labor charges
estimated parts charges
foreign cars
Joe's Automotive Shop
make
manager
Mercedes
model
name
Porsche
sales tax
service quote
shop
telephone number
total estimated charges
year

Refine the List of Nouns

The nouns that appear in the problem description are merely candidates to become classes. It might not be necessary to make classes for them all. The next step is to refine the list to include only the classes that are necessary to solve the particular problem at hand. We will look at the common reasons that a noun can be eliminated from the list of potential classes.

1. **Some of the nouns really mean the same thing.**

In this example, the following sets of nouns refer to the same thing:

- **cars** and **foreign cars**
  These both refer to the general concept of a car.
- **Joe's Automotive Shop** and **shop**
  Both of these refer to the company "Joe's Automotive Shop."

We can settle on a single class for each of these. In this example we will arbitrarily eliminate **foreign cars** from the list, and use the word **cars**. Likewise, we will eliminate **Joe's Automotive Shop** from the list and use the word **shop**. The updated list of potential classes is:

address
BMW
car
cars
customer
estimated labor charges
estimated parts charges
~~foreign cars~~
~~Joe's Automotive Shop~~
make
manager
Mercedes
model
name
Porsche
sales tax
service quote
shop
telephone number
total estimated charges
year

Because **cars** and **foreign cars** mean the same thing in this problem, we have eliminated **foreign cars**. Also, because **Joe's Automotive Shop** and **shop** mean the same thing, we have eliminated **Joe's Automotive Shop**.

2. **Some nouns might represent items we do not need to be concerned with in order to solve the problem.**

A quick review of the problem description reminds us of what our application should do: print a service quote. In this example, we can eliminate two unnecessary classes from the list:

- We can cross **shop** off the list because our application only needs to be concerned with individual service quotes. It doesn't need to work with or determine any company-wide information. If the problem description asked us to keep a total of all the service quotes, then it would make sense to have a class for the shop.
- We will not need a class for the **manager** because the problem statement does not direct us to process any information about the manager. If there were multiple shop managers, and the problem description had asked us to record which manager generated each service quote, then it would make sense to have a class for the manager.

The updated list of potential classes at this point is:

address
BMW
car
cars
customer
estimated labor charges
estimated parts charges
~~foreign cars~~
~~Joe's Automotive Shop~~
make
~~manager~~
Mercedes
model
name
Porsche
sales tax
service quote
~~shop~~
telephone number
total estimated charges
year

Our problem description does not direct us to process any information about the **shop**, or any information about the **manager**, so we have eliminated those from the list.

3. Some of the nouns might represent objects, not classes.

We can eliminate **Mercedes, Porsche,** and **BMW** as classes because, in this example, they all represent specific cars and can be considered instances of a **cars** class. Also, we can eliminate the word **car** from the list. In the description, it refers to a specific car brought to the shop by a customer. Therefore, it would also represent an instance of a **cars** class. At this point the updated list of potential classes is:

address
~~BMW~~
~~car~~
cars
customer
estimated labor charges
estimated parts charges
~~foreign cars~~
~~Joe's Automotive Shop~~
~~manager~~
make
~~Mercedes~~
model
name
~~Porsche~~
sales tax
service quote
~~shop~~
telephone number
total estimated charges
year

We have eliminated **Mercedes, Porsche, BMW,** and **car** because they are all instances of a **cars** class. That means these nouns identify objects, not classes.

> **NOTE:** Some object-oriented designers take note of whether a noun is plural or singular. Sometimes a plural noun will indicate a class, and a singular noun will indicate an object.

4. **Some of the nouns might represent simple values that can be stored in a variable, and do not require a class.**

Remember, a class contains attributes and member functions. Attributes are related items that are stored within an object of the class, and define the object's state. Member functions are actions or behaviors that may be performed by an object of the class. If a noun represents a type of item that would not have any identifiable attributes or member functions, then it can probably be eliminated from the list. To help determine whether a noun represents an item that would have attributes and member functions, ask the following questions about it:

- Would you use a group of related values to represent the item's state?
- Are there any obvious actions to be performed by the item?

If the answers to both of these questions are no, then the noun probably represents a value that can be stored in a simple variable. If we apply this test to each of the nouns that remain in our list, we can conclude that the following are probably not classes: **address, estimated labor charges, estimated parts charges, make, model, name, sales tax, telephone number, total estimated charges**, and **year**. These are all simple string or numeric values that can be stored in variables. Here is the updated list of potential classes:

~~address~~
~~BMW~~
~~car~~
cars
customer
~~estimated labor charges~~
~~estimated parts charges~~
~~foreign cars~~
~~Joe's Automotive Shop~~
~~make~~
~~manager~~
~~Mercedes~~
~~model~~
~~name~~
~~Porsche~~
~~sales tax~~
~~service quote~~
~~shop~~
~~telephone number~~
~~total estimated charges~~
~~year~~
service quote

We have eliminated **address, estimated labor charges, estimated parts charges, make, model, name, sales tax, telephone number, total estimated charges,** and **year** as classes because they represent simple values that can be stored in variables.

As you can see from the list, we have eliminated everything except **cars, customer,** and **service quote**. This means that in our application, we will need classes to represent cars, customers, and service quotes. Ultimately, we will write a `Car` class, a `Customer` class, and a `ServiceQuote` class.

Identifying a Class's Responsibilities

Once the classes have been identified, the next task is to identify each class's responsibilities. A class's *responsibilities* are

- the things that the class is responsible for knowing.
- the actions that the class is responsible for doing.

When you have identified the things that a class is responsible for knowing, then you have identified the class's attributes. Likewise, when you have identified the actions that a class is responsible for doing, you have identified its member functions.

It is often helpful to ask the questions "In the context of this problem, what must the class know? What must the class do?" The first place to look for the answers is in the description of the problem domain. Many of the things a class must know and do will be mentioned. Some class responsibilities, however, might not be directly mentioned in the problem domain, so brainstorming is often required. Let's apply this methodology to the classes we previously identified from our problem domain.

The `Customer` class

In the context of our problem domain, what must the `Customer` class know? The description directly mentions the following items, which are all attributes of a customer:

- the customer's name
- the customer's address
- the customer's telephone number

These are all values that can be represented as strings and stored in the class's member variables. The `Customer` class can potentially know many other things. One mistake that can be made at this point is to identify too many things that an object is responsible for knowing. In some applications, a `Customer` class might know the customer's e-mail address. This particular problem domain does not mention that the customer's e-mail address is used for any purpose, so we should not include it as a responsibility.

Now let's identify the class's member functions. In the context of our problem domain, what must the `Customer` class do? The only obvious actions are to

- create an object of the `Customer` class.
- set and get the customer's name.
- set and get the customer's address.
- set and get the customer's telephone number.

From this list, we can see that the `Customer` class will have a constructor, as well as accessor and mutator functions for each of its attributes. Figure 23 shows a UML diagram for the `Customer` class.

The `Car` Class

In the context of our problem domain, what must an object of the `Car` class know? The following items are all attributes of a car and are mentioned in the problem domain:

- the car's make
- the car's model
- the car's year

Figure 23 UML diagram for the Customer class

```
Customer
--------------------------------
- name : String
- address : String
- phone : String
--------------------------------
+ Customer() :
+ setName(n : String) : void
+ setAddress(a : String) : void
+ setPhone(p : String) : void
+ getName() : String
+ getAddress() : String
+ getPhone() : String
```

Now let's identify the class's member functions. In the context of our problem domain, what must the Car class do? Once again, the only obvious actions are the standard set of member functions that we will find in most classes (constructors, accessors, and mutators). Specifically, the actions are:

- create an object of the Car class
- set and get the car's make
- set and get the car's model
- set and get the car's year

Figure 24 shows a UML diagram for the Car class at this point.

Figure 24 UML diagram for the Car class

```
Car
--------------------------------
- make : string
- model : string
- year : int
--------------------------------
+ Car() :
+ setMake(m : string) : void
+ setModel(m : string) : void
+ setYear(y : int) : void
+ getMake() : string
+ getModel() : string
+ getYear() : int
```

The ServiceQuote Class

In the context of our problem domain, what must an object of the ServiceQuote class know? The problem domain mentions the following items:

- the estimated parts charges
- the estimated labor charges
- the sales tax
- the total estimated charges

Careful thought and a little brainstorming will reveal that two of these items are the results of calculations: sales tax, and total estimated charges. These items are dependent on the values of the estimated parts and labor charges. In order to avoid the risk of holding stale data, we will not store these values in member variables. Rather, we will provide member functions that calculate these values and return them. The other member functions we will need for this class are a constructor and the accessors and mutators for the estimated parts charges and estimated labor charges attributes. Figure 25 shows a UML diagram for the `ServiceQuote` class.

Figure 25 UML diagram for the `ServiceQuote` class

```
ServiceQuote
-----------------------------------
- partsCharges : double
- laborCharges : double
-----------------------------------
+ ServiceQuote() :
+ setPartsCharges(c : double) :
    void
+ setLaborCharges(c : double) :
    void
+ getPartsCharges() : double
+ getLaborCharges() : double
+ getSalesTax() : double
+ getTotalCharges() : double
```

This Is Only the Beginning

You should look at the process that we have discussed in this section as merely a starting point. It's important to realize that designing an object-oriented application is an iterative process. It may take you several attempts to identify all of the classes that you will need and determine all of their responsibilities. As the design process unfolds, you will gain a deeper understanding of the problem, and consequently you will see ways to improve the design.

Checkpoint

27 What is a problem domain?

28 When designing an object-oriented application, who should write a description of the problem domain?

29 How do you identify the potential classes in a problem domain description?

30 What are a class's responsibilities?

31 What two questions should you ask to determine a class's responsibilities?

32 Will all of a class's actions always be directly mentioned in the problem domain description?

33 Look at the following description of a problem domain:

A doctor sees patients in her practice. When a patient comes to the practice, the doctor performs one or more procedures on the patient. Each procedure that the doctor performs has a description and a standard fee. As the patient leaves the practice, he or she receives a statement from the office manager. The statement shows the patient's name and address, as well as the procedures that were performed, and the total charge for the procedures.

Assume you are writing an application to generate a statement that can be printed and given to the patient.

A) Identify all of the potential classes in this problem domain.
B) Refine the list to include only the necessary class or classes for this problem.
C) Identify the responsibilities of the class or classes that you identified in step B.

Review Questions and Exercises

Short Answer

1. What is the difference between a class and an instance of the class?
2. What is the difference between the following `Person` structure and `Person` class?

```
struct Person
{
   string name;
   int age;
};

class Person
{
   string name;
   int age;
};
```

3. What is the default access specification of class members?
4. Look at the following function header for a member function:

   `void Circle::getRadius()`

   What is the name of the function?

   Of, what class is the function a member?
5. A contractor uses a blueprint to build a set of identical houses. Are classes analogous to the blueprint or the houses?
6. What is a mutator function? What is an accessor function?
7. Is it a good idea to make member variables private? Why or why not?
8. Can you think of a good reason to avoid writing statements in a class member function that use `cout` or `cin`?
9. Under what circumstances should a member function be private?
10. What is a constructor? What is a destructor?
11. What is a default constructor? Is it possible to have more than one default constructor?
12. Is it possible to have more than one constructor? Is it possible to have more than one destructor?
13. If a class object is dynamically allocated in memory, does its constructor execute? If so, when?

14. When defining an array of class objects, how do you pass arguments to the constructor for each object in the array?
15. What are a class's responsibilities?
16. How do you identify the classes in a problem domain description?

Fill-in-the-Blank

17. The two common programming methods in practice today are ________ and ________.
18. ________ programming is centered around functions or procedures.
19. ________ programming is centered around objects.
20. ________ is an object's ability to contain and manipulate its own data.
21. In C++, the ________ is the construct primarily used to create objects.
22. A class is very similar to a(n) ________.
23. A(n) ________ is a key word inside a class declaration that establishes a member's accessibility.
24. The default access specification of class members is ________.
25. The default access specification of a `struct` in C++ is ________.
26. Defining a class object is often called the ________ of a class.
27. Members of a class object may be accessed through a pointer to the object by using the ________ operator.
28. If you were writing the declaration of a class named `Canine`, what would you name the file it was stored in? ________
29. If you were writing the external definitions of the `Canine` class's member functions, you would save them in a file named ________.
30. When a member function's body is written inside a class declaration, the function is ________.
31. A(n) ________ is automatically called when an object is created.
32. A(n) ________ is a member function with the same name as the class.
33. ________ are useful for performing initialization or setup routines in a class object.
34. Constructors cannot have a(n) ________ type.
35. A(n) ________ constructor is one that requires no arguments.
36. A(n) ________ is a member function that is automatically called when an object is destroyed.
37. A destructor has the same name as the class, but is preceded by a(n) ________ character.
38. Like constructors, destructors cannot have a(n) ________ type.
39. A constructor whose arguments all have default values is a(n) ________ constructor.
40. A class may have more than one constructor, as long as each has a different ________.
41. A class may only have one default ________ and one ________.
42. A(n) ________ may be used to pass arguments to the constructors of elements in an object array.

Algorithm Workbench

43. Write a class declaration named `Circle` with a private member variable named `radius`. Write set and get functions to access the `radius` variable, and a function named `getArea` that returns the area of the circle. The area is calculated as

    `3.14159 * radius * radius`

44. Add a default constructor to the `Circle` class in Question 43. The constructor should initialize the `radius` member to 0.
45. Add an overloaded constructor to the `Circle` class in Question 44. The constructor should accept an argument and assign its value to the `radius` member variable.
46. Write a statement that defines an array of five objects of the `Circle` class in Question 45. Let the default constructor execute for each element of the array.
47. Write a statement that defines an array of five objects of the `Circle` class in Question 45. Pass the following arguments to the elements' constructor: 12, 7, 9, 14, and 8.
48. Write a `for` loop that displays the radius and area of the circles represented by the array you defined in Question 47.
49. If the items on the following list appeared in a problem domain description, which would be potential classes?

Animal	Medication	Nurse
Inoculate	Operate	Advertise
Doctor	Invoice	Measure
Patient	Client	Customer

50. Look at the following description of a problem domain:

    The bank offers the following types of accounts to its customers: savings accounts, checking accounts, and money market accounts. Customers are allowed to deposit money into an account (thereby increasing its balance), withdraw money from an account (thereby decreasing its balance), and earn interest on the account. Each account has an interest rate.

    Assume you are writing an application that will calculate the amount of interest earned for a bank account.

    A) Identify the potential classes in this problem domain.
    B) Refine the list to include only the necessary class or classes for this problem.
    C) Identify the responsibilities of the class or classes.

True or False

51. T F Private members must be declared before public members.
52. T F Class members are private by default.
53. T F Members of a `struct` are private by default.
54. T F Classes and structures in C++ are very similar.
55. T F All private members of a class must be declared together.
56. T F All public members of a class must be declared together.
57. T F It is legal to define a pointer to a class object.
58. T F You can use the `new` operator to dynamically allocate an instance of a class.

59. T F A private member function may be called from a statement outside the class, as long as the statement is in the same program as the class declaration.
60. T F Constructors do not have to have the same name as the class.
61. T F Constructors may not have a return type.
62. T F Constructors cannot take arguments.
63. T F Destructors cannot take arguments.
64. T F Destructors may return a value.
65. T F Constructors may have default arguments.
66. T F Member functions may be overloaded.
67. T F Constructors may not be overloaded.
68. T F A class may not have a constructor with no parameter list, and a constructor whose arguments all have default values.
69. T F A class may only have one destructor.
70. T F When an array of objects is defined, the constructor is only called for the first element.
71. T F To find the classes needed for an object-oriented application, you identify all of the verbs in a description of the problem domain.
72. T F A class's responsibilities are the things the class is responsible for knowing, and actions the class must perform.

Find the Errors

Each of the following class declarations or programs contain errors. Find as many as possible.

73.
```
class Circle:
{
private
   double centerX;
   double centerY;
   double radius;
public
   setCenter(double, double);
   setRadius(double);
}
```

74.
```
#include <iostream>
using namespace std;

Class Moon;
{
Private;
   double earthWeight;
   double moonWeight;
Public;
   moonWeight(double ew);
      { earthWeight = ew; moonWeight = earthWeight / 6; }
   double getMoonWeight();
      { return moonWeight; }
}
```

```
int main()
{
   double earth;
   cout >> "What is your weight? ";
   cin << earth;
   Moon lunar(earth);
   cout << "On the moon you would weigh "
        <<lunar.getMoonWeight() << endl;
   return 0;
}
```

75.
```
#include <iostream>
using namespace std;

class DumbBell;
{
   int weight;
public:
   void setWeight(int);
};
void setWeight(int w)
{
   weight = w;
}
int main()
{
   DumbBell bar;

   DumbBell(200);
   cout << "The weight is " << bar.weight << endl;
   return 0;
}
```

76.
```
class Change
{
public:
   int pennies;
   int nickels;
   int dimes;
   int quarters;
   Change()
      { pennies = nickels = dimes = quarters = 0; }
   Change(int p = 100, int n = 50, d = 50, q = 25);
};

void Change::Change(int p, int n, d, q)
{
   pennies = p;
   nickels = n;
   dimes = d;
   quarters = q;
}
```

Programming Challenges

1. Date

Design a class called `Date`. The class should store a date in three integers: `month`, `day`, and `year`. There should be member functions to print the date in the following forms:

12/25/2018
December 25, 2018
25 December 2018

Demonstrate the class by writing a complete program implementing it.

Input Validation: Do not accept values for the day greater than 31 or less than 1. Do not accept values for the month greater than 12 or less than 1.

2. `Employee` Class

VideoNote
Solving the `Employee` Class Problem

Write a class named `Employee` that has the following member variables:

- **`name`**—a string that holds the employee's name
- **`idNumber`**—a n `int` variable that holds the employee's ID number
- **`department`**—a string that holds the name of the department where the employee works
- **`position`**—a string that holds the employee's job title

The class should have the following constructors:

- A constructor that accepts the following values as arguments and assigns them to the appropriate member variables: employee's name, employee's ID number, department, and position.
- A constructor that accepts the following values as arguments and assigns them to the appropriate member variables: employee's name and ID number. The `department` and `position` fields should be assigned an empty string (`""`).
- A default constructor that assigns empty strings (`""`) to the `name`, `department`, and `position` member variables, and 0 to the `idNumber` member variable.

Write appropriate mutator functions that store values in these member variables and accessor functions that return the values in these member variables. Once you have written the class, write a separate program that creates three `Employee` objects to hold the following data:

Name	ID Number	Department	Position
Susan Meyers	47899	Accounting	Vice President
Mark Jones	39119	IT	Programmer
Joy Rogers	81774	Manufacturing	Engineer

The program should store this data in the three objects and then display the data for each employee on the screen.

3. `Car` Class

Write a class named `Car` that has the following member variables:

- **`yearModel`**—an `int` that holds the car's year model
- **`make`**—a string that holds the make of the car
- **`speed`**—an `int` that holds the car's current speed

In addition, the class should have the following constructor and other member functions:

- **Constructor**—The constructor should accept the car's year model and make as arguments. These values should be assigned to the object's `yearModel` and `make` member variables. The constructor should also assign 0 to the `speed` member variables.
- **Accessor**—appropriate accessor functions to get the values stored in an object's `yearModel`, `make`, and `speed` member variables
- **`accelerate`**—The `accelerate` function should add 5 to the `speed` member variable each time it is called.
- **`brake`**—The `brake` function should subtract 5 from the `speed` member variable each time it is called.

Demonstrate the class in a program that creates a `Car` object, then calls the `accelerate` function five times. After each call to the `accelerate` function, get the current speed of the car and display it. Then, call the `brake` function five times. After each call to the `brake` function, get the current speed of the car and display it.

4. **Patient Charges**

Write a class named `Patient` that has member variables for the following data:

- First name, middle name, last name
- Address, city, state, and ZIP code
- Phone number
- Name and phone number of emergency contact

The `Patient` class should have a constructor that accepts an argument for each member variable. The `Patient` class should also have accessor and mutator functions for each member variable.

Next, write a class named `Procedure` that represents a medical procedure that has been performed on a patient. The `Procedure` class should have member variables for the following data:

- Name of the procedure
- Date of the procedure
- Name of the practitioner who performed the procedure
- Charges for the procedure

The `Procedure` class should have a constructor that accepts an argument for each member variable. The `Procedure` class should also have accessor and mutator functions for each member variable.

Next, write a program that creates an instance of the `Patient` class, initialized with sample data. Then, create three instances of the `Procedure` class, initialized with the following data:

Procedure #1:	**Procedure #2:**	**Procedure #3:**
Procedure name: Physical Exam	Procedure name: X-ray	Procedure name: Blood test
Date: Today's date	Date: Today's date	Date: Today's date
Practitioner: Dr. Irvine	Practitioner: Dr. Jamison	Practitioner: Dr. Smith
Charge: 250.00	Charge: 500.00	Charge: 200.00

The program should display the patient's information, information about all three of the procedures, and the total charges of the three procedures.

5. `RetailItem` Class

Write a class named `RetailItem` that holds data about an item in a retail store. The class should have the following member variables:

- `description`—a string that holds a brief description of the item
- `unitsOnHand`—an `int` that holds the number of units currently in inventory
- `price`—a `double` that holds the item's retail price

Write a constructor that accepts arguments for each member variable, appropriate mutator functions that store values in these member variables, and accessor functions that return the values in these member variables. Once you have written the class, write a separate program that creates three `RetailItem` objects and stores the following data in them:

	Description	Units On Hand	Price
Item #1	Jacket	12	59.95
Item #2	Designer Jeans	40	34.95
Item #3	Shirt	20	24.95

6. Inventory Class

Design an `Inventory` class that can hold information and calculate data for items in a retail store's inventory. The class should have the following *private* member variables:

Variable Name	Description
`itemNumber`	An `int` that holds the item's item number.
`quantity`	An `int` for holding the quantity of the items on hand.
`cost`	A `double` for holding the wholesale per-unit cost of the item
`totalCost`	A `double` for holding the total inventory cost of the item (calculated as `quantity` times `cost`).

The class should have the following *public* member functions:

Member Function	Description
Default Constructor	Sets all the member variables to 0.
Constructor #2	Accepts an item's number, cost, and quantity as arguments. The function should copy these values to the appropriate member variables and then call the `setTotalCost` function.
`setItemNumber`	Accepts an integer argument that is copied to the `itemNumber` member variable.
`setQuantity`	Accepts an integer argument that is copied to the `quantity` member variable.
`setCost`	Accepts a `double` argument that is copied to the `cost` member variable.
`setTotalCost`	Calculates the total inventory cost for the item (`quantity` times `cost`) and stores the result in `totalCost`.
`getItemNumber`	Returns the value in `itemNumber`.
`getQuantity`	Returns the value in `quantity`.
`getCost`	Returns the value in `cost`.
`getTotalCost`	Returns the value in `totalCost`.

Demonstrate the class in a driver program.

Input Validation: Do not accept negative values for item number, quantity, or cost.

7. **`TestScores` Class**

   Design a `TestScores` class that has member variables to hold three test scores. The class should have a constructor, accessor, and mutator functions for the test score fields and a member function that returns the average of the test scores. Demonstrate the class by writing a separate program that creates an instance of the class. The program should ask the user to enter three test scores, which are stored in the `TestScores` object. Then the program should display the average of the scores, as reported by the `TestScores` object.

8. **`Circle` Class**

   Write a `Circle` class that has the following member variables:

   - **`radius`**—a `double`
   - **`pi`**—a `double` initialized with the value 3.14159

   The class should have the following member functions:

   - **Default Constructor**—a default constructor that sets `radius` to 0.0
   - **Constructor**—accepts the radius of the circle as an argument
   - **`setRadius`**—a mutator function for the radius variable
   - **`getRadius`**—an accessor function for the radius variable
   - **`getArea`**—returns the area of the circle, which is calculated as

     `area = pi * radius * radius`
   - **`getDiameter`**—returns the diameter of the circle, which is calculated as

     `diameter = radius * 2`
   - **`getCircumference`**—returns the circumference of the circle, which is calculated as

     `circumference = 2 * pi * radius`

   Write a program that demonstrates the `Circle` class by asking the user for the circle's radius, creating a `Circle` object, then reporting the circle's area, diameter, and circumference.

9. **Population**

   In a population, the birth rate and death rate are calculated as follows:

   Birth Rate = Number of Births ÷ Population
   Death Rate = Number of Deaths ÷ Population

   For example, in a population of 100,000 that has 8,000 births and 6,000 deaths per year, the birth rate and death rate are:

   Birth Rate = 8,000 ÷ 100,000 = 0.08
   Death Rate = 6,000 ÷ 100,000 = 0.06

   Design a `Population` class that stores a population, number of births, and number of deaths for a period of time. Member functions should return the birth rate and death rate. Implement the class in a program.

   Input Validation: Do not accept population figures less than 1, or birth or death numbers less than 0.

10. Number Array Class

Design a class that has an array of floating-point numbers. The constructor should accept an integer argument and dynamically allocate the array to hold that many numbers. The destructor should free the memory held by the array. In addition, there should be member functions to perform the following operations:

- Store a number in any element of the array
- Retrieve a number from any element of the array
- Return the highest value stored in the array
- Return the lowest value stored in the array
- Return the average of all the numbers stored in the array

Demonstrate the class in a program.

11. `Payroll` Class

Design a `PayRoll` class that has data members for an employee's hourly pay rate, number of hours worked, and total pay for the week. Write a program with an array of seven `PayRoll` objects. The program should ask the user for the number of hours each employee has worked, and will then display the amount of gross pay each has earned.

Input Validation: Do not accept values greater than 60 for the number of hours worked.

12. Coin Toss Simulator

Write a class named `Coin`. The `Coin` class should have the following member variable:

- A `string` named `sideUp`. The `sideUp` member variable will hold either "heads" or "tails" indicating the side of the coin that is facing up.

The `Coin` class should have the following member functions:

- A default constructor that randomly determines the side of the coin that is facing up ("heads" or "tails") and initializes the `sideUp` member variable accordingly.
- A `void` member function named `toss` that simulates the tossing of the coin. When the `toss` member function is called, it randomly determines the side of the coin that is facing up ("heads" or "tails") and sets the `sideUp` member variable accordingly.
- A member function named `getSideUp` that returns the value of the `sideUp` member variable.

Write a program that demonstrates the `Coin` class. The program should create an instance of the class and display the side that is initially facing up. Then, use a loop to toss the coin 20 times. Each time the coin is tossed, display the side that is facing up. The program should keep count of the number of times heads is facing up and the number of times tails is facing up, and display those values after the loop finishes.

13. Tossing Coins for a Dollar

For this assignment, you will create a game program using the `Coin` class from Programming Challenge 12 (Coin Toss Simulator). The program should have three instances of the `Coin` class: one representing a quarter, one representing a dime, and one representing a nickel.

When the game begins, your starting balance is $0. During each round of the game, the program will toss the simulated coins. When a coin is tossed, the value of the coin is added to your balance if it lands heads-up. For example, if the quarter lands heads-up,

25 cents is added to your balance. Nothing is added to your balance for coins that land tails-up. The game is over when your balance reaches \$1 or more. If your balance is exactly \$1, you win the game. You lose if your balance exceeds \$1.

14. Fishing Game Simulation

For this assignment, you will write a program that simulates a fishing game. In this game, a six-sided die is rolled to determine what the user has caught. Each possible item is worth a certain number of fishing points. The points will not be displayed until the user has finished fishing, then a message is displayed congratulating the user depending on the number of fishing points gained.

Here are some suggestions for the game's design:

- Each round of the game is performed as an iteration of a loop that repeats as long as the player wants to fish for more items.
- At the beginning of each round, the program will ask the user whether he or she wants to continue fishing.
- The program simulates the rolling of a six-sided die (use the `Die` class that was demonstrated in this chapter).
- Each item that can be caught is represented by a number generated from the die. For example, 1 for "a huge fish," 2 for "an old shoe," 3 for "a little fish," and so on.
- Each item the user catches is worth a different amount of points.
- The loop keeps a running total of the user's fishing points.
- After the loop has finished, the total number of fishing points is displayed, along with a message that varies depending on the number of points earned.

15. Mortgage Payment

Design a class that will determine the monthly payment on a home mortgage. The monthly payment with interest compounded monthly can be calculated as follows:

$$\text{Payment} = \frac{\text{Loan} \times \frac{\text{Rate}}{12} \times \text{Term}}{\text{Term} - 1}$$

where

$$\text{Term} = \left(1 + \frac{\text{Rate}}{12}\right)^{12 \times \text{Years}}$$

Payment = the monthly payment
Loan = the dollar amount of the loan
Rate = the annual interest rate
Years = the number of years of the loan

The class should have member functions for setting the loan amount, interest rate, and number of years of the loan. It should also have member functions for returning the monthly payment amount and the total amount paid to the bank at the end of the loan period. Implement the class in a complete program.

Input Validation: Do not accept negative numbers for any of the loan values.

16. Freezing and Boiling Points

The following table lists the freezing and boiling points of several substances.

Substance	Freezing Point	Boiling Point
Ethyl alcohol	–173	172
Oxygen	–362	–306
Water	32	212

Design a class that stores a temperature in a `temperature` member variable and has the appropriate accessor and mutator functions. In addition to appropriate constructors, the class should have the following member functions:

- `isEthylFreezing`—This function should return the `bool` value `true` if the temperature stored in the `temperature` field is at or below the freezing point of ethyl alcohol. Otherwise, the function should return `false`.
- `isEthylBoiling`—This function should return the `bool` value `true` if the temperature stored in the `temperature` field is at or above the boiling point of ethyl alcohol. Otherwise, the function should return `false`.
- `isOxygenFreezing`—This function should return the `bool` value `true` if the temperature stored in the `temperature` field is at or below the freezing point of oxygen. Otherwise, the function should return `false`.
- `isOxygenBoiling`—This function should return the `bool` value `true` if the temperature stored in the `temperature` field is at or above the boiling point of oxygen. Otherwise, the function should return `false`.
- `isWaterFreezing`—This function should return the `bool` value `true` if the temperature stored in the `temperature` field is at or below the freezing point of water. Otherwise, the function should return `false`.
- `isWaterBoiling`—This function should return the `bool` value `true` if the temperature stored in the `temperature` field is at or above the boiling point of water. Otherwise, the function should return `false`.

Write a program that demonstrates the class. The program should ask the user to enter a temperature, then display a list of the substances that will freeze at that temperature, and those that will boil at that temperature. For example, if the temperature is –20 the class should report that water will freeze and oxygen will boil at that temperature.

17. Cash Register

Design a `CashRegister` class that can be used with the `InventoryItem` class discussed in this chapter. The `CashRegister` class should perform the following:

1. Ask the user for the item and quantity being purchased.
2. Get the item's cost from the `InventoryItem` object.
3. Add a 30 percent profit to the cost to get the item's unit price.
4. Multiply the unit price times the quantity being purchased to get the purchase subtotal.
5. Compute a 6 percent sales tax on the subtotal to get the purchase total.
6. Display the purchase subtotal, tax, and total on the screen.
7. Subtract the quantity being purchased from the `onHand` variable of the `InventoryItem` class object.

Implement both classes in a complete program. Feel free to modify the `InventoryItem` class in any way necessary.

Input Validation: Do not accept a negative value for the quantity of items being purchased.

18. A Game of 21

For this assignment, you will write a program that lets the user play against the computer in a variation of the popular blackjack card game. In this variation of the game, two six-sided dice are used instead of cards. The dice are rolled, and the player tries to beat the computer's hidden total without going over 21.

Here are some suggestions for the game's design:

- Each round of the game is performed as an iteration of a loop that repeats as long as the player agrees to roll the dice, and the player's total does not exceed 21.
- At the beginning of each round, the program will ask the users whether they want to roll the dice to accumulate points.
- During each round, the program simulates the rolling of two six-sided dice. It rolls the dice first for the computer, then it asks the user if he or she wants to roll. (Use the `Die` class demonstrated in this chapter to simulate the dice).
- The loop keeps a running total of both the computer and the user's points.
- The computer's total should remain hidden until the loop has finished.
- After the loop has finished, the computer's total is revealed, and the player with the most points without going over 21 wins.

19. Trivia Game

In this programming challenge, you will create a simple trivia game for two players. The program will work like this:

- Starting with player 1, each player gets a turn at answering five trivia questions. (There are a total of 10 questions.) When a question is displayed, four possible answers are also displayed. Only one of the answers is correct, and if the player selects the correct answer, he or she earns a point.
- After answers have been selected for all of the questions, the program displays the number of points earned by each player and declares the player with the highest number of points the winner.

In this program, you will design a `Question` class to hold the data for a trivia question. The `Question` class should have member variables for the following data:

- A trivia question
- Possible answer #1
- Possible answer #2
- Possible answer #3
- Possible answer #4
- The number of the correct answer (1, 2, 3, or 4)

The `Question` class should have appropriate constructor(s), accessor, and mutator functions.

The program should create an array of 10 `Question` objects, one for each trivia question. Make up your own trivia questions on the subject or subjects of your choice for the objects.

Group Project

20. Patient Fees

1. This program should be designed and written by a team of students. Here are some suggestions:
   - One or more students may work on a single class.
   - The requirements of the program should be analyzed so that each student is given about the same workload.
   - The parameters and return types of each function and class member function should be decided in advance.
   - The program will be best implemented as a multi-file program.
2. You are to write a program that computes a patient's bill for a hospital stay. The different components of the program are

   The `PatientAccount` class
   The `Surgery` class
   The `Pharmacy` class
   The `main` program

   - The `PatientAccount` class will keep a total of the patient's charges. It will also keep track of the number of days spent in the hospital. The group must decide on the hospital's daily rate.
   - The `Surgery` class will have stored within it the charges for at least five types of surgery. It can update the charges variable of the `PatientAccount` class.
   - The `Pharmacy` class will have stored within it the price of at least five types of medication. It can update the charges variable of the `PatientAccount` class.
   - The student who designs the main program will design a menu that allows the user to enter a type of surgery and a type of medication, and check the patient out of the hospital. When the patient checks out, the total charges should be displayed.

Answers to Checkpoints

1 False

2 B

3 A

4 C

5
```
class Date
{
private:
     int month;
     int day;
     int year;

public:
     // Mutators
     void setMonth(int m)
        { month = m; }
     void setDay(int d)
        { day = d; }
     void setYear(int y)
        { year = y; }
     // Accessors
     int getMonth() const
         { return month; }
     int getDay() const
         { return day; }
     int getYear() const
         { return year; }
};
```

6 To prevent code outside the class from directly accessing the member variable. This protects the variables from being accidentally modified or used in a way that might adversely affect the state of the object.

7 Through public member functions

8 A class specification file is a header file (with a name that ends in `.h`) that contains a class declaration. A class implementation file is a `.cpp` file that contains a class's member function definitions.

9 To prevent the contents of a header file from being included more than once in a program

10 The `BasePay` class declaration would reside in `basepay.h`.

The `BasePay` member function definitions would reside in `basepay.cpp`.

The `Overtime` class declaration would reside in `overtime.h`.

The `Overtime` member function declarations would reside in `overtime.cpp`.

11 A member function whose body is coded in the class declaration.

12 A constructor is automatically called when the class object is created. It is useful for initializing member variables, or performing set-up operations.

13 A destructor is automatically called before a class object is destroyed. It is useful for performing housekeeping operations, such as freeing memory that was allocated by the class object's member functions.

14 A

15 B

16 B

17 A

18 True

19 True

20 False

21 10
20
50

22 4
7
2
2
7
4

23 4 (This line is displayed by constructor #2.)
7 (This line is displayed by constructor #1.)
2 (This line is displayed by constructor #2.)
2 (This line is displayed by the destructor.)
7 (This line is displayed by the destructor.)
4 (This line is displayed by the destructor.)

24 Some member functions are meant for internal processing, and should be called only from other member functions of the same class. Such member functions may have adverse effects if they are called at the wrong time. For example, a function might initialize member variables, or destroy a member variable's contents. To prevent a member function from being called at the wrong time, it can be made private. Then, it can only be called from another member function, which can determine if it is appropriate to call the private function.

25
```
const int SIZE = 3;
InventoryItem items[SIZE];
```

26
```
#include <iostream>
using namespace std;

class Yard
{
private:
      int length, width;
public:
      Yard()
         { length = 0; width = 0; }
      setLength(int len)
         { length = len; }
      setWidth(int w)
         { width = w; }
};

int main()
{
      Yard lawns[10];
      cout << "Enter the length and width of "
           << "each yard.\n";
      for (int count = 0; count < 10; count++)
      {
         int input;
         cout << "Yard " << (count + 1) << ":\n";
         cout << "Length: ";
         cin >> Input;
         lawns[count].setLength(input);
         cout << "width: ";
         cin >> input;
         lawns[count].setWidth(input);
      }
  return 0;
}
```

27 The problem domain is the set of real-world objects, parties, and major events related to a problem.

28 Someone who has an adequate understanding of the problem. If you adequately understand the nature of the problem you are trying to solve, you can write a description of the problem domain yourself. If you do not thoroughly understand the nature of the problem, you should have an expert write the description for you.

29 Identify all the nouns (including pronouns and noun phrases) in the problem domain description. Each of these is a potential class. Then, refine the list to include only the classes that are relevant to the problem.

30 A class's responsibilities are the things that the class is responsible for knowing and the actions that the class is responsible for doing.

31 It is often helpful to ask the questions "In the context of this problem, what must the class know? What must the class do?"

32 No. Often responsibilities are discovered through brainstorming.

33 A) We begin by identifying the nouns: doctor, patients, practice, patient, procedure, description, fee, statement, office manager, name, address, and total charge. After eliminating duplicates, objects, and primitive variables, the list of potential classes is: *Doctor*, *Practice*, *Patient*, *Procedure*, *Statement*, and *Office manager*.

B) The necessary classes for this problem are: *Patient*, *Procedure*, and *Statement*.

C) The *Patient* class knows the patient's name and address.

The *Procedure* class knows the procedure description and fee.

The *Statement* class knows each procedure that was performed.

The *Statement* class can calculate the total charges.

Answers to Odd Numbered Review Questions

1. A class describes a data type. An instance of a class is an object of the data type that exists in memory.
3. `private`
5. A class is analogous to the blueprint.
7. Yes it is. This protects the variables from being directly manipulated by code outside the class, and prevents them from receiving invalid data.
9. When the function is necessary for internal processing, but not useful to the program outside the class. In some cases, a class may contain member functions that initialize member variables or destroy their contents. Those functions should not be accessible by an external part of the program because they may be called at the wrong time.
11. A default constructor is a constructor that is called without any arguments. It is not possible to have more than one default constructor.
13. Yes, the constructor executes when the object is created.
15. A class's responsibilities are the things that the class is responsible for knowing and the actions that the class is responsible for doing.
17. procedural programming, object-oriented programming
19. object-oriented
21. `class`
23. access specifier
25. `public`
27. `->`

29. `canine.cpp`

31. constructor

33. constructors

35. default

37. ~

39. default

41. constructor, destructor

43.
```
class Circle
{
private:
    double radius;
public:
    void setRadius(double r)
       { radius = r; }
    double getRadius()
       { return radius; }
    double getArea()
       { return 3.14159 * radius * radius; }
};
```

45.
```
class Circle
{
private:
    double radius;
public:
    Circle()
        { radius = 0.0; }
    Circle(double r)
        { radius = r; }
    void setRadius(double r)
        { radius = r; }
    double getRadius()
        { return radius; }
    double getArea()
        { return 3.14159 * radius * radius; }
};
```

47. `Circle collection[5] = {12, 7, 9, 14, 8 };`

49.

Animal	Medication	Nurse
Doctor	Invoice	Customer
Patient	Client	

51. False

53. False

55. False
57. True
59. False
61. True
63. True
65. True
67. False
69. True
71. False
73. There should not be a colon after the word `Circle`.
    Colons should appear after the words `private` and `public`.
    A semicolon should appear after the closing brace.
75. The semicolon should not appear after the word `DumbBell`.
    The function header for `setWeight` should appear as:

    ```
    void DumbBell::setWeight(int w)
    ```

    The line that reads:

    ```
    DumbBell(200);
    ```

    should read:

    ```
    bar.setWeight(200);
    ```

    `bar.weight` cannot be accessed outside of the class because no access specifier appeared before it in the class, making the variable private to the class by default. This means the `cout` statement will not work.

Index